Flying Men and Metal Birds

Bryan N McCook

Bryan N McCook 2

Book Layout © 2019 BookDesignTemplates.com

Cover Design by Green Light Design

Flying Men and Metal Birds
ISBN: 978-0-6452722-3-9
ISBN: 978-0-6452722-4-6 eBook

This book is dedicated to my Dad, William A McCook, (Bill) Sergeant, Wellington Regiment 1st NZEF, wounded at Gallipoli 1915, (1892-1964), my mother, Minnie, nee Silberbach, (1888 –1987), my only brother Jack, Sergeant, Wellington Regiment 2nd NZEF, wounded and a prisoner of war, Stalag V111B, Stalag 383 Germany, 1941-1945, (1917–1989) and all other members of my family.

Special Thanks

Special thanks to my wife Betty, my children, Kathryn, Dianne, Roger, Jack, Scott and grandson Craig who have all experienced the highs and lows of having a pilot for a husband, father and grandfather.

Cover photo. Bryan N McCook at 21 years of age, Christchurch NZ 1948. Promotional image used for joining the RNZAF.

FOREWORD

This book is the account of some of the life-long experiences of air pilot Bryan McCook. Bryan has flown not only in many parts of the South Pacific including Australia, Fiji and Papua New Guinea but also the Caribbean, the Americas, Africa, Europe and South East Asia, while piloting an extraordinary variety of aircraft, ranging from some of the early bi-planes, to landplanes and flying-boats of all descriptions, military and civil. Bryan flew more than 40 aircraft types in a flying career stretching over 50 years, during which time he accumulated the incredible total of 28,000 flying hours. No doubt in all that time there were many other air adventures of his too that are not included here.

The privilege of knowing Bryan was mine during his sojourn in the then Territory of New Guinea and Territory of Papua & New Guinea. During my long period there as a Patrol Officer, District Officer and District Commissioner with the Department of Territories, there were times when certain tribal emergencies called for a charter flight being made into some of the most isolated parts of the Morobe District and the Highlands. Those areas always included a host of cloud-bedecked towering mountains with hog-backed ridges on their slopes. Many of my flights were made with Bryan acting as pilot.

An urgent flight from Lae to the patrol post at Wantoat in the Finisterre Mountains, with its tiny airstrip that ended at the foot of a very high mountain, will always be remembered. That harsh, mountainous, country was well known to me having walked over much of it while leading government patrols. Communications with the Wantoat Patrol Post were always difficult. Several days had been lost while waiting for the weather to clear.

The clouds at the time were pressing down well below the top of the ranges in the broader Markham Valley accompanied by a fine incessant drizzle. Visibility was so restricted that not for a moment did I think that it would be possible to fly through the narrow valley leading to the patrol post to complete my task. But we did. Without the slightest hesitation Bryan flew the Cessna low beneath the cloud, to wind our way along the valley, flying as one would drive an automobile through a twisting mountain pass, leaving me with an uncanny feeling that was something like ' what on earth am I doing here?'

On another occasion we were on a flight from Marawaka, an isolated patrol post situated in a narrow valley in the central mountains of the big island, notoriously subject to sudden weather changes that could close the valley to aircraft for days at a time. Of necessity the strip had been laid on a steep slope, aircraft must land uphill and take off downhill. After taking off that day monsoonal weather caught us which forced Bryan to climb up through cloud to the Cessna's ceiling. The mountains there go way up too. Just as the Garuda birds of SE Asia are coastal lovers and are seldom found in high mountainous terrain, so were airline aircraft seldom seen in the more remote parts of the hinterland of the Territory. That was one of the times when I had really been afraid of flying in a light aircraft in PNG, the graveyard of so many good pilots down the years.

Thankfully we made it. Bryan admitted that the flight had been a tight squeeze for the Cessna, his local knowledge had given him space to climb to top the cloud and 'hang on the prop' while heading for a more cloud free area. Years later I flew with him again, that time in the big G111 (one eleven) Grumman Albatross amphibian, from Seletar airport in Singapore via the Riau islands to a water-based, island depot in the South China Sea, that was another memorable experience.

Papua New Guinea has a cruel, unforgiving environment for the airman and owes a great deal to pilots like Bryan. Three pages of his manuscript are devoted to a list of pilots who died in crashes in the mountainous areas of that country, although I know that there are a great many more not listed. There were, and still are, few good roads in PNG. When McCook was flying there, the only means of transport into most parts of the hinterland of the Territory was the light aircraft. The scene in those parts is much the same today, although the gradual arrival of better roads in the interior of the country has seen some of the more treacherous airstrips closed. Technical advances in aircraft and engines too, have somewhat improved the lot of the mountain pilot.

Bryan was born in a farming community on the southern slopes of Mount Taranaki, New Zealand and learned to fly in the Royal New Zealand Air Force, serving with No 5 Catalina Squadron at Laucala Bay, Suva, Fiji. When the Catalinas retired he converted to the Sunderland Mk V four-engine flying-boat. He also writes a story of a hair-raising account of a near-fatal crash in an Australian De Havilland Drover in the interior of Viti Levu, Fiji's largest island.

His descriptions of aerial search operations in PNG are frequently harrowing, in particular the search for the well-loved flying priest, Father Joseph Walachy SVD. Bryan provides also an amusing account of a flight from the 'Friendly Islands' after re-possessing a leased Piper Aztec that he had succeeded in snatching from under the close eye of the lessee, after which he was not only confronted by a fuel crisis en route with a limited amount of fuel in the tanks, but also with one of Australia's worst tropical cyclones, on his flight around the Coral Sea and the east coast of Queensland to Sydney.

McCook formed his own air company, Macair Charters, based at first in the Eastern Highlands PNG, which became very successful. He writes with calm authority of his long flight across USA and the Pacific delivering his company's first aircraft to Goroka, a Beechcraft Baron formerly owned by the Hughes Tool Company, another offshoot of the famous aviator, film maker and 'Spruce Goose' designer Mr Howard Hughes.

Tied to a single company governed by a Board of Directors comprised of coffee planters, ex senior public servants, accountants and pharmacists, each with their own agenda and who never saw eye to eye with him or each other, he became frustrated, restless and so moved on.

His Caribbean, South China Sea and African adventures on lakes and seas in Grumman amphibians and a lone Catalina as described here, makes delightful reading too.

Bryan was one of the most experienced pilots of flying boats and amphibians and his love of water birds comes through strongly, particularly in the truly amazing flight across the North and South Atlantic in a fifty-year old Catalina. The diversion to Aberdeen, Scotland, from the North Sea when an engine failed and the owner of the Catalina Mr Pierre Jaunet had leaned out the 'tower' window into the slipstream to successfully open an under-wing fuel-tank drain-plug to dump fuel to help save the day. That makes stirring reading, also of the Sir Charles Kingsford-Smith (Smithy) and Sir Patrick Gordon Taylor (Pee Gee) kind, in 'Southern Cross' over the Tasman Sea.

After a spell with Air Niugini flying Douglas DC3's and Fokker F27's on domestic services and with a yearning for flying boats again, Bryan left PNG for the United States Virgin Islands where he was to await a Sandringham operation to open up that would utilise the former Ansett Airlines 'boats' that had plied the route Sydney-Lord Howe Island. At first came a training period when he flew Grumman Goose and Mallard amphibians for Antilles Air Boats, a renowned company headed by one of America's great pilots, Captain Charles Blair, husband of the famous Hollywood movie star Maureen O'Hara, who became President of AAB after 'Charlie's' tragic demise. That tragedy brought about the 'grounding' of the Sandringham project for AAB, when Bryan joined up with Englishman Edward Hulton, the new owner of one of the machines, an ex Royal New Zealand Air Force (NZ4108), ex Ansett Airlines Sunderland Mk V, that is here jocularly called a 'Sunderingham'.

This book is strongly recommended, McCook writes very well. He handles words with imagination and precision. This is a work that should find a place on the shelves of all lovers of aeroplanes and flying, Papua New Guinea especially and also those in the many other countries and places mentioned.

James Sinclair OBE
Alexandra Headlands
Queensland Australia

PNG Patrol Officer 1948, District Officer 1959
District Commissioner 1969-1974
Department of Territories

CONTENTS

FROM THE AUTHOR

This book is not, nor meant to be an autobiography or a work of fiction. The principal episodes in the several stories are authentic and taken from my own experience as recorded in flying log- books and diaries. I flew over, into or out of the countries described and knew many of the characters depicted, my aim being not to spoil a good story by including too many boring statistics or dull and dreary facts which can be taken from Type or company Operations Manuals. There are many of us who do not seem to understand that in any war there can be heroes on both sides.

A desire to fly comes in many forms. In the main those who like flying - fly. Those who fear long distances from home or want the security of a nearby airport with aero club facilities - teach. Flyers are men of many dimensions, the explorer, the hero, the ace, the mouth, the stubborn, the reserve bidder, the egotist, the conformist and non-conformist, the ambitious, the space ace, the manipulator, the company man and some like me, who no matter where he's at, dreams of a better place to be.

The ingredients for the narrative of parts of my life as an aircraft pilot have been gathered in many parts of the world. Any particular one of the several events described here would make a book in itself that might not be such an acceptable product as the one I have endeavoured to produce, which is supported by many excellent pictures.

Only a few of the many adventures occurring in my life in the air are described here. Many a reader will no doubt say, in relation to some of the events, that no mention was made of 'this or that' day, person or incident. I can only say sorry, space, decency, memory, sometimes protocol, does not permit. Much endeavour has gone into humanising the work. A highly professional industry has been included in easy to read form without me becoming phlegmatic or venomous. Surprisingly, no doubt to some, there is a lot of venom in and about civil and military aviation, jealousy, even spite around pilots, administrators, mechanics, engineers and aeroplanes in general. As stated before, any one of those incidents taken from memory would be a book in itself and would be of interest only to those concerned.

This narrative may arouse memories, nostalgic or otherwise, in those who have been involved with some of the countries mentioned and the impact the 'airplane' and pilots made on that particular culture, Papua New Guinea especially when administered by the post-war Australian Department of Territories through the United Nations. But for the 'airplanes' and the pilots, mission, military and civil who flew them that land might still be deep in the Dark Ages, along with parts of Africa and the Americas.

All countries have their own special air heroes who mostly remain unknown outside their own borders. My thanks go to James Sinclair and his 'Wings of Gold' for recording PNG's aviation facts of those early times so painstakingly. In some episodes, names have been either changed or simply not used, to protect privacy and eradicate some of the venom I speak of.

During the writing of the worldwide Catalina episodes, by my being so familiar with PBY's and Papua New Guinea my thoughts always went to the early days of the Pacific war and the RAAF Catalina squadrons. Night bombing and rescue missions were planned regularly from northern Queensland to New Britain, flights of more than 20 hours airborne, deep into the heart of enemy occupied territory. The Catalinas were, in the main, crewed by young men approaching, or in, their early twenties, the missions designed to confuse a fanatical foe as to the size of the tactical air-fleet in nearby Australia. A dozen or so out-dated Catalina flying-boats were the only aircraft available that were able to reach occupied New Britain and return non-stop to their bases in Northern Queensland. The enemy's Intelligence was left wondering just how many strategic bombers were hidden away in Australia to harass them, following their terrorised, piratical, unannounced and unwanted occupation of the northern parts of the Territory of New Guinea.

In modern 'press-button' warfare it is doubtful whether the courage, tenacity and devotion to duty such as displayed by the RAAF Catalina crews, will ever be repeated. Some of those men are still with us, but not many. As with them, 'the 'ol Cat-boat', 'Pee Bee Why' or 'Pee-Boat', as used by several allied Air Forces and Navies around the 'Free World' of the times, will always have a place in my heart too.

By my being quite mad about flying-boats, as this story begins with stories of Catalinas, so it ends with my own special 'Owed to the Catalina', to wax poetic, 'crost the Indian, China and Coral Sea, the open sea, the blue, the fresh, and ever free'.

The main object of this book though is not necessarily historical either, but more to bring to notice the human side of non-airline aircraft operations in undeveloped, out of the way parts of the world. Or maybe an insight into what might have been the early working life of a good many pilots who command the 'Jumbo' jet airliners of today, ex 'crop-dusters', shark-watch pilots, Christian Mission pilots, cattle musterers, charter pilots, aerial surveyors, ice-pack patrollers, fish spotters, outback and off-shore oil-rig suppliers, Flying Doctor, Nurse, Priest and Pastor, fire-fighters, parachuting, glider towing, aerobatic, Sky Writers, 'War Birds', pilots have to start their desired career somewhere.

Those specialist branches of aviation about which little is written about, also have their many heroes. On thinking back to the present day flying scene however, to have been more 'politically correct', a better title for this book might well have been 'Flying Persons & Metal Birds' or even 'Flying Birds with Metal Wings and Wedding Rings', where 'bird' is meant to convey a much softer, warmer meaning than metal can.

As with all pilots who have grown old in the game and have been left with the trace of a niggle urging them to 'fly on regardless', I know that 'when everything's a kilter and time seems out of phase, stop and think that before too long, they'll be 'the good old days' to look back on! At least that's how it is with me.

Bryan

FROM BRYAN'S CHILDREN

This entire manuscript has been written by our Dad, air pilot Bryan McCook. These are his words and his memories of incredible flying adventures carefully recorded in diaries and four well-worn log books. His flying career began in New Zealand in 1948 and took him (and then us) across the world from the rugged beauty of New Zealand to the warmth of Fiji, the vast landscapes of Australia and Papua New Guinea, the distant shores of St Croix USVI, Puerto Rico, Singapore and SE Asia. His wings carved a path through history, adventure and home.

He flew an incredible array of aircraft types including the Tiger Moth, Harvard, Avro Cadet, Catalina, Sunderland, de Havilland Dragon Rapide and Drover, Fox Moth DH83, the Grumman Goose, Mallard and Albatross, as well as Cessnas, the Beech Baron and Queen Air, Twin Otters, Dorniers and Dakota DC3's to name a few but above all his true passion lay in amphibious aircraft.

Our father's flying adventures were nothing short of extraordinary – some exhilarating, others heart-stopping. Over 50 years in the air and more than 28,000 flying hours, he navigated the skies with skill and determination. But behind every takeoff and landing, every daring flight, stood our mother Betty – his steadfast companion. Together they moved from country to country, building a life of adventure while raising five children along the way.

This is our Dad's story – one of skyward dreams and boundless adventures. Flying wasn't just what he did, it was who he was – he was born to fly.

Kathryn, Dianne, Roger, Jack and Scott

GLOSSARY OF SOME TERMS

AAB. Antilles Air Boats
DO. District Officer
DC. Depth charge
DC. District Commissioner
DCA. Dept of Civil Aviation
DUNNY. A non flush outdoor lavatory
GG. Governor-General
GNB. Good News Bible
HM. Her Majesty (s)
ILS. Instr.Landing System
MT. Motor Transport
NZEF. NZ Expeditionary Force
NIUGINI. Pidgin for New Guinea
NZNAC. NZ National Airways Corp
OC. Officer Commanding
PNG. Papua New Guinea
POW. Prisoner of War
QANTAS. Australia's major airline
SBD. Dauntless dive-bomber
STD. Subscriber Trunk Dialling
SVD. Society of the Divine Word
TBF. Torpedo – Bomber - Fighter
TEAL. Tasman Empire Airways Ltd
'tower'. Catalina flight engineer station
TOWER. Airport control Centre building
WAAF. Womens Auxiliary Air Force
WPM. Words per minute

FLYING MEN & METAL BIRDS

'God made us plain and simple but we have made ourselves very complicated'

(Ecclesiastes: 7.29 GNB)

Sixty five years afterwards, the third of September 1939 is the day most vividly retained in my memory and has never been forgotten. The dawn came with a thump on the wall of my bedroom with Dad calling in a throaty voice. "Run down to the gate Bryan and fetch the newspaper in before it gets too wet. The paper car has just gone past, hurry up."

The 'Hawera Star' was our paper in those days, delivered from Hawera 18 miles away about dawn, it could soak up the rain and become wet and soggy if allowed to lie for too long where it landed. Rubbing sleep from my eyes, through my bedroom window I could see the steady drizzle falling from a dark, heavy overcast. Outside, a chilly west wind coming via the Southern Ocean and Tasman Sea could be expected, bringing with it the rain from Cape Taranaki. Throwing off the warm eiderdown that my mother had made from innumerable squares of various coloured woollen materials that was so warm and snug, I sprang out of bed.

My first thoughts were not on any war, but on my approaching birthday and whether or not I might receive the long promised 'BB gun' as a gift, if I 'was a good boy'. The days were being counted, in just 22 the days of infancy would be over, teen age would begin, manhood at last. The age of responsibility my parents had placed on me, for ownership of the Daisy air rifle would be the most important step in my life. A quick response to Dad's bidding without a moan, groan, or even a hint of reticence or resentment coming from me, I knew would help to achieve my greatest dream, long trousers and a sports coat would come a close second.

Barefooted and in flannel pyjamas, I scampered from the front veranda to the gate, to find the news paper, hand rolled then bent in half, in its usual place, a hollow in Dad's neatly trimmed, much admired, macrocarpa hedge. The deliverer always chucked the paper from his moving car, seldom missing his target but always making small tears in the paper, that were not seen until it was unfolded. Back inside the house, the paper was tossed on to Dad's bed while I made for the bathroom that was off the kitchen porch, passing mother on the way, who was busy at the wood-fired stove, heating water and making the breakfast porridge.

"We're at war again Min. " Dad, who must always be first to read the paper, yelled a few minutes later, loud enough for all those in the house to hear. "Hitler's invaded Poland, England's declared war on Germany, turn the wireless on Bryan, I'm getting up, there's bound to be a special broadcast at seven o'clock."

'Bryan' (my Irish grandmother's family name) was the one who always got those chores on cold, wet mornings, there were plenty of them.

A war with Germany again, how could it be? My heart was racing as the oval shaped Phillips receiver in the kitchen was switched on, which when rain was about, only received 2YA Wellington through an ear-shattering crackle and scratch. In night attire, with ears cupped towards the set, all the family listened to Neville Chamberlain's declaration of war on Germany, relayed from the BBC by the announcer. Our mother cried, Dad was very quiet except for muttering under his breath,

"Now now Min, don't cry for God's sake." Along with me, Lorna and Doris looked to be stunned too.

The news had spread quickly. At school that morning, the coming war was all that was talked about by other students after Mr John Dash the school Principal, had made the official announcement. Like me, most other pupils had fathers or uncles who had served in France or Gallipoli during the Great War, there were many who had lost relatives in the 'war to end wars'. Every town in the province had a war memorial of some kind on which the names of those from the district who had served were engraved. To see Dad's name on the memorial rotunda in the town square at Manaia in the Taranaki Province had made me proud. Although we were young, we were also bold. We'd been brought up on stories of war and played them out in some of our games. From the many stories told, we thought we knew what war was all about. Once in my hands the BB gun would play a more important role in some of those games.

Even in those early days we boys began to choose our preferred Service should the war last that long. The Army sought volunteers aged twenty-one and over. The Navy and the Merchant Navy drew most interest from my friends for their early enlistment age of sixteen years with parental consent, little was known about the Air Force. It seemed that airmen were bred only from privileged stock of some sort, to be able to fly an aeroplane about the skies, shoot an enemy 'plane down, or throw bombs out on to the trenches in France as in World War 1. Dad said that there'd not be any 'cow-farm boys' from around our district 'brainy' enough to fly a 'plane, which was a job for English public school boys.

New Zealand's then Governor-General, Sir Arthur Newell, sometimes known as Cyril, a high-ranking Royal Air Force officer, was the first G-G from a British 'junior service' background ever to be appointed. Sir Arthur dressed not in a drab khaki uniform but one of blue with gold epaulettes and shiny brass buttons. He brightened up the governor-generals high office and brought with him a new dimension to the New Zealand Armed Forces, some said 'a breath of fresh air', although not everyone would agree. Sir Arthur fell out of step with the Army, when at the Basin Reserve at Wellington he addressed the First Echelon of the 2 NZEF, before they embarked to sail off to an undisclosed destination, that was a big event at the time. His speech to the huge assembly which began with " Men of the Army, boys of the Navy, gentlemen of the Air Force" was not that well received by the former two services or their offspring and gave our own 'boys in blue' an extra burden of mockery to carry for many years. In all probability that's where I first got the impression that Air Force men came only from privileged stock. Ahead of his time was our Governor-General with his political correctness.

Six or seven days after the declaration, my brother Jack rode in on his Harley-Davidson motorbike, circa nineteen twenty something, from the road-survey camp where he worked as a surveyor's assistant, with the news that he had been 'called up'. Jack was then a weekend warrior with the Territorial army. My mother wept openly again when she heard him announce his intentions, because of Dad she hated war, the thought of her eldest, most dear son, going off to another was too much for her.

My father, badly wounded at Gallipoli in hand to hand fighting with rifle and bayonet, had been paying the price ever since. At that time he was laid up with his annual bout of pleurisy that the cold, wet weather always brought on. Three of his brothers had also served the Empire in France or 'Palestine', all were wounded and returned home. Two of my uncles died from war effects when I was very young, I knew only my Dad's youngest brother James, to me Uncle Jim.

In those days there were no counselling or other services to help rehabilitate those young men who had witnessed the slaughter of their comrades by bullet, shell-blast, shrapnel, bayonet or gas, or seen the heaps of mangled fly-blown corpses, or parts of corpses, lying in muddy shell-holes, or in the 'no-man's land' of stinking hot sandy places, or heard the screams and pleas of the dying whether friend or foe.

During my young life Dad never spoke much of his Gallipoli experience. Our mother cautioned all her four children to not ask their father too many questions about his war. Were boys brought into the world just for 'fodder for the guns' is how she angrily expressed Jack's early enlistment? Jack was the oldest of the family and ten years older than me, we didn't see a lot of each other during my early childhood. He attended a live-in agricultural training school 'Flock House' before working on various dairy farms, that I'm sure he must have hated, before joining up with the road surveying group and able to buy the Harley-Davidson. On hearing that he was destined for the Army and foreign parts of the world I hero-worshipped him.

Months later Jack had been called up and railed along with hundreds of other young men to Trentham Military Camp near Wellington. After several months of serious training he was to sail with the Second Echelon of 2 NZEF, to England most likely was the rumour going around.

An injury during a game of the national sport of rugby however, caused him to be switched to the Third Echelon, that departed a month or two later. By not being as tough as I thought I was, I couldn't say goodbye and sobbed my heart out in the bathroom the morning he left home for the special army train at Eltham station, on completion of his second 'final leave'. 'Final' was the word that caused the involuntary sobbing in me that couldn't be stopped. Second Echelon went to England, the Third, with my brother, to Egypt.

Cousins and friends were all joining up for one force or another, the Army, Navy, or contrary to Dad's prophetic statements, the Air Force or Fleet Air arm, while women were moving in to take over men's jobs, on the land, in government departments and private enterprise. Cousin Alistair Macleod had been accepted by the Royal Navy to train for the Fleet Air Arm, becoming for me another hero to worship. A year after war started, people were looking askance at anyone

who seemed old enough to be serving but were not in a military uniform. I felt that there were those who were even looking at me with
sinister intent! Others not much older than me, had found an envelope
with a white feather enclosed, in their mail.

Dad said not to worry, the war would be over before I could be
called up and there was not the slightest chance that he would give his
consent to a 'voluntary or runaway call up' before I reached the age of
twenty-one, he'd see to that. He claimed that the war wouldn't last
that long, both his statements were passionately endorsed by my
mother.

In 1941, following a period spent training then warring with the
Italians in Egypt and after the campaign in Greece, Jack was reported
'missing in action'. That was a terrible time, for both our parents and
us siblings that I will never forget. Months later, the Postmaster personally delivered a telegram declaring that Jack was known to be
wounded also and captured by the Germans in Greece. Again many
months passed before we received his first letter from a hospital at
Stalag V111B, wherever that was. After so many painful months of
waiting and hoping, Jack was alive, that was all that mattered to us.
Mother insisted we go to St. Marks on Sunday and give our thanks to
God for the sparing of his life. My sister Lorna began work in our
small town's Post Office, a job that in those days was strictly for 'men
only'.

Leaving Home

I was accepted for duty with the Post and Telegraph Department as
message-boy delivering telegrams, Telephone Exchange assistant,
brass polisher, flag raiser and mail sorter. Following much negotiation
bordering on argument between the Postmaster and my parents, I was
literally 'shunted off' to Auckland by steam train where after a course
in Morse telegraphy at Three Lamps, Ponsonby, I graduated as a
'clicketty clicker', a Telegraphist.

Months later, after graduating from the Telegraph School at twenty-five words per minute, both send and receive, came a transfer to the Telegraph Office at the General Post Office, Wellington, commonly known by its' many communication enlightened 'serfs' as the Gee Pee Oh Tee Oh. Dad commented that in just a few months his youngest son had travelled much further through the country than he. Since his Gallipoli trauma never again would he travel anywhere that was out of sight of our beloved, usually snow capped extinct volcano of a mountain, known by the Maori people as Taranaki but then called Mount Egmont for some obscure reason.

With 'Pearl Harbour' and the entry of Japan into South East Asia and the Pacific, the war was much closer to home, New Zealand was on a real war-footing, no longer was the terror and strife on the other side of the world. The arrival of thousands of American Marines and other troops almost turned the North Island into another American State, Wellington and Auckland into Los Angeles or San Francisco. Many of our citizens took illicit trips to those cities just to 'see the Yanks' at work (or play). Passes were required for train or bus travel.

The work at the 'Tee Oh' was extremely stressful and grossly underpaid, the days and nights long and hard, but one couldn't complain, 'there's a war on you know, the Japs are getting close, an enemy 'plane has already flown over Wellington at night'. Life had changed dramatically, to us everything then depended on the outcome of the war in the Pacific.

A sense of shame came over some parts of the country through the hostility shown to many of the Americans who were in the main very young men experiencing their first time 'away from home'. One incident, fighting between US servicemen and young hoodlums in 1942 became known as the 'Battle of Wellington' with some of our soldiers and sailors on leave from the Middle East or the Pacific also taking part, mainly those who had lost wives or sweethearts over to the 'Yanks'. Several fatalities resulted from the clash.

In time I qualified on the most modern telegraphic technology of the day, the Creed perforated tape machine and the not so modern Murray multiplex. A typing speed of 66 words per minute on the Creed was required to keep the tape rolling through the perforator from a perfect vertical loop, 44 wpm on the Murray! On both machines one didn't 'send' a telegram but 'cut' it, or 'receive' one but 'paste' it. Duties were allotted as to whether you would be 'cutting' or 'pasting' on the particular circuit. No sooner had you 'cut' one heap of the public's telegrams on the tape, than a supervisor would dump another pile in your 'send' tray, usually with a warning too: "Get a move on McCook the tape's catching you up, 'Crump' next door can build a loop twice as large as you, big enough to leave it running while he goes to the lavatory, get a move on, there's a war on you know! "

'Well you're old enough you stodgy old 'so and so', why don't you go to it then and leave me alone' were my secret, rebellious thoughts at some of those times. Given or Christian names weren't used in the Public Service in those days.

With the typing learned on a Creed course behind me, when working a town with only a Morse telegraph circuit, instead of writing by hand I could then type the telegrams on to the requisite forms while receiving by ear on the sounder, that was quite an achievement at the time.

While working at the 'Tee Oh', as a very patriotic young man from a very patriotic family, I joined the Air Training Corps. After attending only a few night parades, sitting in a Harvard cockpit mock-up with my spittle spraying the instrument panel, or watching training films, I knew I must fly.

One of the highlights of my time at the Tee Oh came after an operation at Wellington hospital for peritonitis, when a transfer to Stratford, Taranaki came so as to be near home while recuperating. At Stratford I took over as telegraphist for a few weeks before returning to the grind of the Tee Oh again.

Into the Blue 1944

The year was 1944, the war was turning our way, running down as it were, but not to those in the firing line in Pacific jungles or the plains, forests and cities of Europe of course.

At 17 years of age I was too young for aircrew selection and training without parental consent, which was not forthcoming. I settled for Signals and at the age of 17 years and five months I was inducted into the RNZAF at Harewood, near Christchurch, as an Aircraftman 2nd Class, the bottom rung of the steep Air Force ladder. The overnight trip on the ferry Wellington/Lyttelton was my first trip across Cook Strait and visit to South Island.

After initial weapons and disciplinary training, as to how to shoot accurately with the Le Enfield .303 rifle or Sten 'subbie', bayonet a sack filled with straw, hurl a grenade without being tempted not to go to ground and crane your neck over the parapet to watch it explode, how, when and where to address and salute officers, without grazing your hand on wall or fence and never capless or whilst sitting down, came postings to several wartime stations. Some members of that intake won postings to the Aerodrome Defence Unit, ADU, much to my envy.

Gradually I worked my way up to the warmer climes of North Island, first at Levin, then Te Awamutu, the Signals Office at Whenuapai Air Station near Auckland and finally Northern Group Headquarters at Mount Eden, Auckland.

As the war had progressed the only telegraph line solely in RNZAF hands was between Whenuapai Air Station and Waipapakauri, an isolated airfield in the far north of North Island.

Communications with Waipapakauri were by Morse key and telegraph sounder. There seemed to be no-one else who could master the sounder, except the bloke at the other end of course, the line was my own with not a lot to do. I was probably the most privileged Leading Aircraftsman in the Air Force by that time, having a six-man hut to myself, with a good mess nearby (excuse the pun) and no compulsory parades to attend because of the shift work. Bathing and laundry facilities were at Camp X, only a short walk from the Signals Office.

Whenever a senior officer or NCO was snooping about on trouble bent, I would make myself look busy by keeping up the 'clickety click' on the key knowing (or hoping), that he wouldn't have a clue as to what I was doing. In the main, I was left much to my own devices, my immediate supervisor an overworked NCO who was always busy with the wireless side of things or more secret code affairs, gradually my job was being taken over by the wireless.

The landline suffered many a breakdown, sometimes for days, leaving me free to visit other parts of the busy wartime station. Thinking I'd pull a fast one on Dad by my being then 'in uniform', applications for a re-muster to aircrew were filed in plenty, without success.

On any free time I made for the hangars in the hope of being offered a ride on an air-test in a Dakota (C47), Airspeed Oxford or Dominie (DH89), with much more success. A promised ride in a Ventura (PV1) bomber was rejected at the last minute when the pilot chose a pretty, cute WAAF MT driver oozing with intoxicating 'parfum' instead, which was a little unfair.

" Next test flight I do son, you can come with me, that is if you're around and that pretty piece of fluff isn't. Test flights can be called for at very short notice."

What a thrill it was to be in the air in a Dakota chatting to an officer-pilot as man-to-man as old friends would, (man to boy in my case), peering at the ground through the drift-sight, while imagining it was a bomb-sight and the Dakota a Lancaster on a bombing mission over Europe. The flying men there, were most understanding, willingly taking me up on local test flights without asking too many questions, for the hangar area was out of bounds to the likes of me. Even the WAAF's working on the metal monsters in the hangar gave me withering looks and a feeling of inferiority.

I was wise enough not to become over familiar with any of the pilots by always giving them salutes befitting a Governor-General, without bashing my hand on any part of the metal bird, before asking their permission to ride along and after the flight was over too. The flying men were much less snobbish than ground crew technical, or administration officers. My thoughts when I climbed aboard a C47 for the first time were. " What a giant of a 'plane, one of the world's biggest, surely they'll never get bigger than this, what must a Lancaster, a Sunderland, Flying Fortress or a Liberator be like? "

On several occasions, after I was tagged as the 'kid who is mad on flying', when on a leave pass I 'hitched a ride' on the inter-station communication 'plane, usually an Airspeed Oxford, to the airfield nearest to my home-town, to be picked up a day or two later and returned to Whenuapai. Those who saw me climbing out of the Oxford at Bell Block airfield must have wondered how a mere LAC arrived and departed by air as would a Prince. From Bell Block to home meant a hitch hike of forty miles. Dad took some convincing that he was hearing the truth when told of my flight by courtesy of the Air Force although it seemed at last his approval had been won by him showing me a bit more respect by my becoming the first in our family to take to the air. On one of these visits home I met Jack Carlisle who had been at the Kaponga Post Office during my time there. Jack was on leave before sailing off to be the lone coast-watcher on Pitcairn Island and looked very smart in his Army uniform. He certainly had a formidable task ahead of him

At the X Camp mess at Whenuapai I ran across, another home town boy, older than me, who was pilot of one of the many 'side-saddle' C47 Dakotas that plied the route Whenuapai to Torokina, Bougainville, in the Solomons, on supply and personnel exchange missions. The RNZAF had a huge commitment on Bougainville with several squadrons of both bombers and fighters, Venturas, Hudsons, Kittyhawks and Corsairs. Jim assured me of a ride in the cockpit of his 'plane, on a flight that would proceed via Norfolk Island, Espiritu

Santos, Guadalcanal to Torokina, I'd be away about six days if time off could somehow be arranged. Jim recounted some hair-raising tales of war on the Japan dominated island that stirred me up as he made his offer for the ride, which was scheduled for departure within 48 hours. Even in the new millennium there has not been a lot written about the fierce fighting, on sea, land and in the air, on and around Bougainville in World War Two. Veterans of the campaigns in Europe received a much higher proportion of the accolades in the media of the time, those airmen who served in the active Pacific areas were somehow degraded to become known as 'the coconut bombers'.

All that was required to pass the Loadmaster's check when boarding the 'Dak,' were the 'New Zealand' flashes to be sewn on the shoulder of my khaki drills. The flashes were zealously guarded by anyone entitled to wear them. To be caught with them on shirt or jacket without an entitlement to do so, would mean a court-martial, to board the 'plane without them would be tricky, boarding at Torokina for return even more tricky, nigh on impossible. Reluctantly, I told Jim the following day that the risk couldn't be taken. To this day I very much regret giving up the offer without a try like a coward. Thank you Jim, sorry to disappoint, although in doing so you were probably saved from facing a court-martial too!

Still being under nineteen years of age when the A-bombs came down and hostilities ceased, my discharge was compulsory and came through within two weeks. With a gratuity of thirty pounds in my pocket plus the appropriate rail-travel passes, my instructions were to attend the Telegraph Office in Wellington pronto, after a week's leave at home and not spend the gratuity before I got there!

I loved the time spent in the Air Force and thought it most unfair that I was discharged so rapidly. My service record was 'clean' with no black spots, (having not taken the ride to Torokina). Before leaving I was advised that I might stand a chance of joining up with the post-war Air Force the world situation being what it was with Korea, to keep the applications going.

Working conditions at the 'Tee Oh' were worse than ever, as soon as I could I resigned to take on an apprenticeship with a manufacturing jeweller known to a cousin of mine Nevis Silberbach, a jeweller himself and a wartime air-gunner in an SBD squadron in the Pacific.

For the first time in my short life I had money to spend and spent most of it on flying at the Wellington Aero Club, when that club re-opened post-war. As a jeweller's apprentice, I moved through the making of plain gold wedding rings to those with a white-gold top, or platinum topped with gold, always getting closer to being considered skilled enough and entrusted to work with with filigree and diamond engagement rings. The trade however, did not have my whole heart,

I yearned for the weekends (or week-days) and the rush of air past my ears produced by the Tiger Moth's propellor. By assisting with re-fuelling of the Club's machines, swinging props or giving wing-tip assistance on windy days, I might earn a half-hour's dual with the Club Instructor, Lieutenant Ken Young RN, in addition to what flight time I was already buying.

Re-entry as Aircrew man

RNZAF 1948

In that way almost two years slipped by before I was again inducted into the RNZAF at Wigram, Christchurch, that time as a Cadet Pilot with a civil 'A licence' and a previous history with the Air Training Corps. Though somewhat put out, my employers, Gilbert & Morris, Manufacturing Jewellers, had allowed me to sever my apprenticeship.

Ted Arundel, who later became my brother-in-law, was also flying training at the Club at Wellington through the Air Training Corps. He joined the first post-war pilot's course with me. Ted, who was then apprenticed in the motor trade, hit the headlines in the newspapers when he applied for permission to terminate his apprenticeship in favour of an Air Force career, a move that was strongly opposed by his employers, a major car firm in Wellington.

Ted eventually won his case and made good of the change, spending all his hard-fought-for aviation career as a permanent officer with the force, rising to the rank of Wing Commander, serving in Malaya as a jet fighter pilot too. For a period Ted led the RNZAF Aerobatic Team that was acclaimed to be one of the world's best, using piston-engine North American Harvard aircraft. He was awarded and justly deserved, the Air Force Cross for services in flying training.

Some of the ground subjects were tough for me, the flying stages the easiest. Those precious 'wings' were awarded and pinned on my puffed out chest, eighteen months later, by Air Commodore Cyrus Kay (lots of awards, military and civil) and of 1934 England/Australia Air Race fame, at a dignified 'passing-out' ceremony at Wigram, again excuse the pun.

Most of the Instructors at the Flying Training School had seen action in Europe or the Pacific. To me they were heroes who had a big influence on all of us. One particular Instructor I was privileged to learn from, was Flight Lieutenant Laurie Edwards, a man from Taranaki also, who had been flying the first British aircraft to be shot down by the Germans in WW2.

On the first day of declared hostilities Laurie was flying an antiquated Anson aircraft on a reconnaissance mission over the North Sea from a base in Scotland. Picked up from the sea by the Dornier flying-boat that had 'come alongside' to give his Anson a broadside as in the times of the Spanish Armada, he had the dubious honour of becoming their first 'British' POW. In those days New Zealanders were recognised as British subjects. The days of chivalry however, were then not over, after spending some time in a German castle as prisoner, Laurie was returned home on the condition that he took no further active part in the war.

As a permanent officer, having been a top-line player himself pre-war, in addition to instructing, Laurie coached the station's rugby team. On his advice I gave the game up after receiving a broken nose during play, an injury that could end an Air Force pilot's career. There were other 'heroes' too who influenced my life for the better, Ernie Gartrell particularly, Al Parlane, Lloyd Burch, Ken Sawyer, Jack Scott, the list goes on.

The 'Wings' course took me through the De Havilland Tiger Moth, the North American Harvard and the twin-engine Airspeed Oxford.

The then young Ted Arundel asked me if I would partner his sister Betty at our up and coming 'Wings Ball' in Christchurch, which I did. We were married six months later and remain happily married, although there have been some trials in more than fifty-six years together in some of the world's most colourful places. Following 'wings' came multi-engine and instrument training and in April 1950 a posting to No. 5 Catalina Squadron at Laucala Bay, Fiji. After a short honeymoon I flew to Suva as passenger on a RNZAF 'side saddle' C47 Dakota, leaving Betty to follow by TEAL flying-boat service when approvals were granted for her to join me.

With my posting came a warning that there would not be a lot of flying for me at Laucala Bay at that time, except maybe in the right-hand seat as 'second Joe', due to several boats and crews being sent to the RAF at Hong Kong to participate in the Korean conflict leaving the squadron bereft of flying-boat instructors. That was disappointing, for I was hungering to fly the famous old boat and join the foray in SE Asia too.

The reverse however, was the case. I had 'fallen on my floats' as the saying goes around flying boats. The squadron at Laucala Bay was undermanned. From the first day after arrival I was in the air almost daily, learning from a competent Instructor the local flying procedures, the art of long-range water-based flying and some of the tricks the cumbersome boat could play on learners like me, water loops and porpoising included. Wonder of wonders, I took to handling a flying-boat as a duck takes to water, instead of the flyingboat taking to me.

Having never been out of my home country before and fresh out of a tough training course, to me life on the tropical flying-boat station was idyllic. Situated on the eastern side of the peninsula that formed Suva's harbour, Laucala Bay was enclosed by a coral reef on which there were a number of small islands that were used not only for mooring, anchoring and water taxi-ing practice, but also for recreation, for sleep-overs, barbeques and rather naughty Sunday picnics as well.

With Suva being the centre of government for the British colony and the residence of His Excellency the Governor, the social life for us was along more 'pukka' British lines, or so we thought.

Close co-operation existed between the squadron and the Fiji Military Forces whose senior officers were either British or New Zealand nationals. The Fiji Battalion had built up a formidable reputation in the jungles of Bougainville against Japan forces during WW2 and by that time, had been moved into the conflict in Malaya, where with the Ghurkas, they added to their already fearsome reputation as jungle fighter. The story of the enemy soldier, who after hearing the 'swish' of the Fijian's hand-held, razor-sharp bayonet cum kris, during a skirmish in Bougainville's jungle, hissed. " Ha ha you missed. " Only to be told. " No I didn't, try shaking your head. " Could really be true!

On the northern side, the muddy Rewa river delta poked several fingers of low-lying islands into 'the bay' well away from the stone pile breakwater, beaching ramp and hangars. The expansive alighting area was not normally muddied in any way from the river, almost always retaining its' brilliant, sparkling, whites and blues, except when typhoons or hurricanes were about to batter the island, dumping vast loads of water about. The station's Marine Section patrolled 'the Bay' constantly, on the lookout for any debris that could harm a flying boat when taking off or alighting.

In the strong sou' east trade winds at periods of high tides, 'the Bay' could test the skill of any pilot with it's roughness, while in calmer weather, particularly at night, the surface might more resemble a mirror. At maximum weights under those conditions, the Catalina needed a very long take-off run, which at times was assisted only by the curvature of the earth.

The city of Suva was only a mile or two away over the peninsula. Laughing Fijians, big and strong, comprised most of the civilian staff in the several messes on the station, Airmen's, Sergeants and Officers, engineering shops, the main hangar and the marine section. Always a happy lot, the Fijians were very good at their work, the envy of many an Australian or American flyingboat's crew visiting the station.

We were particularly proud of our Fijian ramp crew, the speed at which a Catalina could be attached to the header buoy to have the beaching gear fitted and be hauled from the water with the flight crew still aboard, was nothing short of remarkable.

In a few short flying hours under the expert tuition of the Squadron's Flight Commander, Flight Lieutenant Bruce Oliver, I had 'soloed' on the Catalina and was building up crew experience to make me a useful member of 5 Squadron.

Our 'Cats' were fully armed. While we qualified in and practiced bombing, high and low, glide and dive, long range patrolling, laying the colored POBRYG markers used in submarine hunting, (Purple, Orange, Blue, Red, Yellow, Green), depth charging, strafing, the Squadron's main role was Search and Rescue for the international air services that were springing up over the Pacific. A radius of 750 miles from Laucala Bay had been declared as New Zealand's area of responsibility, with US Navy 'Black Cats' also providing over-lapping Search and Rescue coverage from Pago Pago on Tutuila, US Eastern Samoa. I was learning that the Pacific and the world was a very big place.

The Squadron also provided transportation between island groups, for the British Colonial Administration and the Western Pacific High Commission. There were frequent calls for our services to search for missing canoes or fishing boats and assist those merchant ships un-lucky enough to run aground on one of the many reefs that abounded the island groups of the south-west Pacific.

PEARLS FROM PENRHYN

I'd been attached to the squadron for only six weeks and was on Dumbo Duty Crew, when a call came from Rarotonga via Wellington. A doctor, midwife and anaesthetist from the Colonial War Memorial hospital at Suva, would be flown to Penrhyn Island in the far north of the Cook Islands group, where a woman was having a difficult childbirth and in danger of losing her life.

From Laucala Bay the direct distance to Penrhyn was 2300 nautical miles (3350 km). A round trip without re-fuelling was impossible. The availability of fuel stocks meant that the flight would have to be done in three stages. Pilot III Charlie Grey was assigned as Captain with myself as Second Pilot. There were six other crew including two navigators.

On the first day, with so much planning and preparation to be done before departing, there was only enough time to fly to Satapuala, the flying-boat alighting area for Apia, the capital of Western Samoa on Upolu Island. Charlie made the alighting, pointing out to me that a high tide, coupled with a cross-wind and swell, could make alighting in Satapuala difficult, a situation that he then faced. The alighting at Satapaula on the return flight would be mine if conditions were favourable, he explained.

The night was spent at the locally famous, 'Aggie Grey's' hotel. For the first time, we were able to meet our medical passengers informally, Dr Doran (Surgeon), Sister O'Keefe (Midwife) and anaesthetist

Tom Uluilakemba, all of the Colonial War Memorial Hospital in Suva.

The road from the Satapuala alighting area to Apia wound along the coast passing through a number of beautifully kept, eye catching, Samoan villages, with neatly trimmed grass, bright flower gardens, clean, thatched houses, smiling people. The twenty-mile ride on a gravel road, except for the dust, was a tourist and first-timer's delight.

The experience of being driven on the right hand side of the road in a large American car was mine, which was scary. Being an ex-German colony and to be consistent with American Eastern Samoa and the European way, Western Samoa had kept to the right hand rule for road traffic. The driver, with a foot hard down on the accelerator, relied on consistent horn blowing to clear the road for him, as a South American General might make a dash away from the 'Front'. The sheer arrogance must have driven the villagers mad, although they seemed not too disturbed and waved happily at all vehicles passing through.

Samoa had been a German colony until the Great War. The German influence could still be seen in the cleanliness and tidiness of the Polynesian inhabitants and the extensive green carpet of coconut plantations rising up the slopes of the jungle-draped mountains of Upolu Island. The remains of a German and American warship lost during a hurricane in 1898 graced the coral at Apia's harbour entrance. The captain of a British 'man o' war' in the harbour at the same time was able to take his ship out to sea, the bounder and so escaped a shipwreck.

From the first moment, I thought that Samoa, the adopted home of Robert Louis Stevenson, must be one of the most beautiful places on earth. The climb to his gravesite on a mountaintop behind his beautiful home 'Vailima', at that time the residence of the New Zealand High Commissioner, is a sweaty one, but not too difficult if care is taken. The inscription on Robert Stevenson's grave reads :

'Under a wide and starry sky,
Dig a grave and let me lie,
Glad did I live and gladly die,
And I lay me down with a will'.

Tusitala 'Teller of Tales' RLS.

During later visits to Samoa, with others I trekked to Robert Louis's gravesite several times. The second day saw us in the Cook Islands, alighting in the blue transparent waters of Aitutaki's lagoon, after a seven-hour flight from Samoa. Aitutaki was the closest point to Penrhyn with a stock of aviation fuel. Our Catalina would need to make a round trip from Penrhyn before refuelling. Doctor Doran, Sister O'Keefe, Tom Uluilakemba and Charlie were whisked away by launch to the island's main centre for the night, the village of Arutanga, where Doctor Doran would get an update on the woman's condition as to whether or not she was still alive. From there Charlie would also arrange a weather forecast for the next day.

That was the place of my first attempt as a pilot in charge of an 'anchor-watch' on board a Catalina. A skeleton crew sometimes slept aboard as a precaution should the Cat need to be taxied out of trouble during the night after breaking free from a mooring during a savage storm, or spring a leak, or drag the anchor.

John Harrington, an American who had fallen in love with the Pacific, the Cook's and a Cook Island girl in particular, during his wartime experience, had set himself up in a trading business at Arutanga that included a fuel agency. Under his directions, in a well-practised manoeuvre, a large flat-bottomed punt loaded with more than twenty drums of high-octane fuel, was towed alongside our 'Cat boat'. Before one could say Captain Cook or Jack Robinson his Cook

Island crew began heaving on the pumps, fuel was gurgling into the tanks. Shortly before dark the job was finished, the dockets signed by our Scots engineer, Eng.1 Jock (what else?) Macleod, the barge's towboat 'chug-chugging' across the lagoon to a berth somewhere near Arutanga.

The night was spent at anchor in flat calm water, off a picture post-card tropical islet. Those of the crew who could be spared thought they would sleep ashore on the white, sandy beach, but a plague of mosquitoes soon drove them back to the mosquito free haven of their airboat at anchor. While some dived into the lagoon off the wingtip for a warm water swim our crew man in charge of victualling, Eng IV Ed Brown, bought some papaya, (paw paw), banana and coconuts from the islanders who paddled their dugout canoes around the Catalina, while strumming home-built ukuleles and singing both some mournful or lively island tunes. The moon was coming up before they left, paddling at their very best 'into the west', the sounds of their harmonious voices drifting back to us through the warm night air. The whole scene, the stillness, the palm clad island, the water gently lapping on to the sand, the flying-boat at rest, was so peaceful and incredibly moving to one like me who had never experienced the real tropical islands before.

The distance Aitutaki-Penrhyn was some 600 nautical miles, Penrhyn being a few small, low islets on a ring of coral reef surrounding a wide lagoon. There were no radio aids on the island that could be received by our Direction Finder, navigation would have to be by instinct, air plot, drift-sight and sun-line, a real challenge for our young navigators. At that stage I was beginning to learn that tropical weather could change quite rapidly. The low-lying island could easily be missed in conditions of poor visibility, caused by rainstorms or even sun-glare. There was also a chance that the co-ordinates of the island on an out-dated chart were incorrect, that was not an uncommon occurrence found to be the case with several other islands in Polynesia, their original surveys dating back to the early 19th century.

In WW2 in the Pacific the misaligned islands had been the cause of many an aircraft ditching. An error of a mile or two compounded with navigational error, could mean missing Penhryn altogether. I was made aware then, that although Catalinas might be slow, the environment that they often faced could be just as hazardous for the crew as that of the more slick, faster vessels of the air.

Heavy with fuel we were out of the lagoon at Aitutaki at eight next morning, after a long 'sluice' in glassy water down the 'runway' before lifting off, the Flight Engineer on the intercom warning of rising cylinder-head temperatures as we fought to get unstuck. The lane through the coral heads was marked with red buoys and was easy to see.

Airborne and climbing, with breeze in the cockpit cooling us off, cylinder head temps declining we flew at first in clear sunny weather, with an estimated time of flight of five hours. An hour later, a high overcast was forming, shutting out the sun. The navigator for the day, Nav 3 Peter Evans pleaded for exacting courses to be steered, accurate, steady airspeed maintained, while he worked hard on plotting while using the drift-sight to maintain an accurate track. Regularly, he passed a scrap of paper up to the cockpit on which was scribbled a very small change in the 'compass course to steer', never more than a degree or two, that kept me on my toes. Charlie's night ashore at the island's centre had left him slightly bedraggled and 'queasy', he was by that time taking a nap, to prepare himself for the arrival at Penrhyn.

As our Cat bored on northwards the wind gradually decreased, until the sea was flat calm, making things difficult for the navigator with the drift-sight. Then we began to run into light rainstorms with low scattered cumulus causing a confusing world of shadow and variable breezes occasionally riffling the surface. Visibility was reduced to about 8 kilometres. At that time Peter announced our groundspeed to be 112 knots, Penrhyn should be sighted on ETA as expected.

He lived in the hope that the sun would re-appear, when an accurate shot would be taken with the sextant that would result in a 'sun-line' being drawn on his chart. Clear sight of the sun would be required for at least four minutes. Unfortunately, the sun chose to remain hidden for longer periods than that. Should the atoll be missed altogether for one reason or another, a 'square search' had been planned on. Time for searching would be limited to one hour, should Penrhyn fail to be found, a return to Aitutaki would have to be made to arrive there before dark, as the lagoon, flush with bombolas, wasn't equipped in any way to handle night arrivals. Everything depended on sighting the tiny atoll within that time frame. I found out then, that the Pacific could be a very lonely place.

I'm certain that a flight through the Cook Islands could not be made without the pilot giving at least some thought to Captain Cook and HM ship Endeavour. At that time I was wondering whether the famous sea-captain ever envisaged an aircraft, 180 years on, doing Aitutaki - Penrhyn return in one day, a journey that could have taken him weeks, after being becalmed while waiting for favourable breezes.

The rainstorms, although quite some distance away, made for the wind to be eccentric, varying in force and direction. The drift (wind angle), had to be guessed from the cockpit, a skill both Charlie and Peter claimed to have acquired as they sniffed the air as would a tracker-dog. .

After four and a half hour's in the air, all crew were alerted to keep a good lookout for the reef at Penrhyn, both pilots, the engineer from the tower, other crew from each blister.

The cloud shadows then confused any view of the surface. At times the sea would be flat calm as a lake would be on a still, frosty morning, then suddenly it would be ruffled by a resurgence of the wind. The effect made it appear that reefs and low-lying islands were numerous. After only a few minutes flying, the scene on the blue of the water would change once again. Resolutely we held onto our course, ignoring the temptation to 'go chasing shadows', a tense time for all of us, my guess was that all other hearts aboard were thumping as hard as mine was.

Five minutes before ETA and still with no sight of Penrhyn, both Charlie and Peter were showing concern, while my eyes darted from side to side taking in an area from the bow to the starboard wingtip. What made me turn my head around a little further I'll never know but there, five kilometres or so to the right, behind the wingtip, a line of surf could be seen. The intercom had been busy with calls from other crew members about possible sightings that turned out to be shadow mixed with haze, but this I knew was the real thing when the darker profile of a small low-lying island broke the straight white line that was the surf.

" There's a low-lying island out there for sure Captain. Maybe seven or eight kilometres away, can't tell exactly " came my call across the cockpit to Charlie.

By my being a 'new boy on the block, 'a junior on the job', Charlie was reluctant to swing the Cat around to take a look himself for fear of incurring the wrath of the navigator who by then had his face deep into the radar tube. Charlie had to be convinced to leave his seat to take a peek out my window. Only just in time did he spot the islet, in another few seconds it might not have been visible to the naked eye. Our radar hadn't picked the lagoon up either, probably because of little swell and surf that day and the dryness of the lagoon's vegetation, we had almost flown past Penrhyn, into the never-never!

After unplugging the auto-pilot, Charlie took over and brought us around in a descending turn. Eight minutes later, breathing sighs of relief, we were over the atoll's wide lagoon, searching for the main island where the Resident Agent, the Medical Assistant, police, pastor or priest and the wireless operator, would be located. The flight time had been five hours and ten minutes.

The reef around the lagoon was roughly circular in shape and about twelve miles wide. The few small islands on the rim, with only one or two exceptions, were on the western side of the lagoon, the name really should have been 'Penrhyn Lagoon' or 'Penrhyn Landspits'. The highest point of land on any of the islands on a spring-tide would not be more than about two meters leaving little to provide the radar with a return on the dry, windless day that it was.

By the layout of the thatched houses amongst the Pacific palms, the number of canoes and signs of human activity, it was easy to guess which island was awaiting the arrival of the medical party.

We circled low, to judge where best to put down only to find that two to three hundred meters out from the shore, the water off the main island on the lagoon side was studded with large bombolas or dead reef, that from on high looked to be less than a meter below the surface. From the air, the anchoring scene didn't look any good at all, a horrifying sight in fact. Further out, the water surrounding the bombolas looked to be very deep, far too deep for our anchor chain. The prevailing wind would set our tail to the shoreline leaving no room for swinging should there be a wind change, the anchor drag, or the cable break. Anchoring close to the island's headquarters we agreed was a 'no-no'.

Charlie and I thrashed the choices out for a few minutes as we circled, before deciding to take a look at an island on the eastern side of the lagoon. On course across the expansive lagoon over the bluest of blue water, we buzzed low over the brown coloured, woven flax sails of speeding outriggers sporting playfully far from shore on the spar-kling water about the many bombolas in the centre of the lagoon. Peter got down to checking the position of some of the more promi-nent coral outcrops on an old map, for future reference. Adding to or taking away from the old maps was always a duty, coral had a nasty habit of growing inexorably while changing its pattern that could be a trap for marine pilots or navigators years on.

At the eastern islet we found the perfect setting for our PBY, a small, uninhabited strip of sand sprouting a few palms with a white sandy beach. Anchored close offshore, bow to the beach, our Cat would lie in clear, relatively shallow water, with a sandy bottom, still with lots of room to swing if needed.

Charlie brought her around for a perfect touchdown on the tail of the front step and taxied quite close to the beach before signalling 'stop engines'. The anchor went out into two metres of the clearest of water. In less then a minute she drifted back and came up firm on the cable. First things first, then we were faced with getting the medical party and their equipment across 12 miles of Pacific lagoon to their patient.

An hour later, the first canoe was seen coming in, flying the out-rigger two feet above the water. The two island men aboard knew not a word of English or 'how she should be spoke'. Then my turn had come up for a spot of terra firma, I'd not touched land since leaving Samoa. By hand signals and very bad English it was decided that they would take me over to the main island where I would ask for the Resi-dent Agent's motor-yacht to come over for the doctor. By that time two more outriggers had arrived who offered to take the rest of the party across, but Doctor Doran opted for a more sedate crossing of the lagoon aboard the yacht when it came.

The outrigger's 'skipper' showed me where to sit on the narrow hull, that decreased the freeboard to about six inches and then we were off on the trip of a lifetime. The canoe flew the outrigger all the way across, crossing over the crown of many bombolas at high speed, where the depth was judged to be only about a metre. The entire trip was thrilling in every way. The two men handled their canoe with its triangular woven flax sail, at a fast and steady speed with a skill that would be the envy of many a world-class yachtsman!

Forty-five minutes after leaving the Catalina I was talking to Mr Dalliston, the Resident Agent, (we never did get on to first names) who had anticipated the problem and was making ready to leave with his yacht. He seemed a little uptight about us not alighting at the island's headquarters, being anxious about the woman's condition which was understandable. Before the RA set out for the Catalina I was shown his grass house where I would be accommodated for the night. Sail assisted, at six to seven knots the trip would take him about two hours each way, the sun would be setting before Dr Doran reached the patient. By then three days had elapsed since the call for help had been received.

On the return trip from the Catalina with the medical party aboard, the yacht's engine failed, the remainder of the crossing was completed under sail only. The doctor and his assistants arrived at the main island after dark and went straight to work at an improvised surgery.

Walking to the radio house cum dwelling, with its thatched roof and walls of plaited flax of some kind, I met the wireless operator, a Cook Islander by the name of Tere Snowball (pronounced Terry). Tere seemed very shy as he spoke of how relieved and grateful he was to see the Catalina come over, he'd almost convinced himself that help from the air wasn't possible. The patient was a relative of his, the last few days had kept him busy on the radio and looking after the woman as best he could. Small boats from Raratonga came to Penhryn infrequently, without the radio it could mean a wait of a month or more for help, or setting out for Aitutaki with the woman on the RA's yacht. Both he and the Resident Agent possessed only minimal medical knowledge, life at Penrhyn was certainly precarious.

That night was spent at the Resident Agent's house where his cook provided me with a good meal of pan-fried, freshly caught fish, the staple diet of the islanders, washed down with coconut milk. The house possessed a kerosene refrigerator that could produce ice. Apart from the RA's personal stock, there were no other alcoholic beverages on the island. I saw the RA only a couple of times that night, he kept watch at the surgery during the operation.

A remarkable thing I discovered was that Penrhyn almost always suffered from a shortage of fresh water. One would hardly believe that an atoll so far out in the equatorial Pacific could ever be short of water? But as the RA explained, rainstorms by the dozens missed the island altogether, a rain shower where water was most needed was a rare occurrence.

Early next morning I met Dr Doran strolling along the beach for an appointment with some islanders who were taking the opportunity to visit the physician while he was on the island. The operation, that had taken a good part of the night, had been successful, both the woman and baby were doing well. All the Penrhyn islanders had shared in the drama and to many, the Catalina's arrival with a doctor was an answer to prayer. With mother and child then safe, they were all smiles.

" Had it been a European woman she would have died two days ago." Dr Doran prophesied in the clipped tones of a British Doctor. " These island women are certainly very tough and strong, but one more day and I think she would have succumbed." I was overjoyed, No. 5 Squadron had notched up another successful mercy mission.

While Doctor Doran was taking his clinic I joined a group at the beach in the hope of obtaining a pearl or two, or three even, from my 'skipper' of the outrigger the day before. I had discovered that pearls were a big part of the island's economy, the daily or weekly haul was zealously guarded and accounted for by the RA, I wasn't sure whether anyone would, or could, enter into a private sale with me. Several of the islanders had pearls with them but were reluctant to sell. Finally, with the RA's permission, I was offered some that were quite small and which cost me all the Fiji currency I had with me, the larger ones were just not available for sale.

I said goodbye to all who were gathered on the beach and took another fast ride across the lagoon on the outrigger with my two newfound friends, the pearls safely stowed in a shirt pocket. The crossing of the lagoon gave me time to think what best to do with them. Set into a ring they would make an ideal gift for Betty I decided, as we sluiced along fast, the outrigger sometimes skipping in a long slow bounce off the water. One of my jeweller friends could do the design I decided, sometime, somehow.

The fresh breeze of the afternoon of the day before had stilled overnight, nevertheless in an hour and with a very wet bottom, I was being greeted at the anchored Catalina, that was perfectly mirrored floating in the stillest of water on the lee side of the islet, while surf pounded the rocky shoreline on the opposite side.

Charlie and the crew had spent a trouble-free night on and around their Cat boat, having fared better than me, with a cooked meal mixed with lots of beer, swimming and no grumpy RA grizzling about what could have been if only we'd alighted nearer to 'his' island. By their being out of view of the RA, some of the crew members had been able to trade with the visiting islanders, tinned meat plus a tin-opener for pearls, that if not better, were equally as good as mine.

The islet where the Cat lay at anchor was entirely free of mosquitoes. Our Scots engineer Jock Macleod, was suffering from sunburn from the previous day's sporting on the beach, or taking a ride in one of the many outriggers that sailed across for a sight of the flying-boat, the first to visit the lagoon. Charlie was getting nervous and anxious to leave.

We discussed starting up and taxying into the lagoon to save some time and meet the RA's motor-yacht, whose engine had been fixed, at some point midway. We decided to wait though, for the yacht had a tall mast that might cause damage to wing or tail-plane in coming alongside to transfer the passengers. The yacht with the medical party arrived just before midday, the RA, although anxious to come alongside the port blister, was ushered to anchor a hundred metres to port.

The passengers were transferred by small dinghy that needed to make two trips. With that over, we were left with just enough time for the five-hour run down to Aitutaki before dark.

At that time the bowman called out that the ship's anchor, the stainless steel Northill special to the Catalina, that was stowed in a compartment in the bow and accessible from the sponson, was so firmly lodged in the coral that it couldn't be weighed on its winch, even with the added assistance of some other crew-members. He suggested that the anchor might be broken loose after a good pull on the cable was made using either one of the engines. That method was often used and could place a big strain on the bollard and must be done with caution to avoid damage to the aircraft. After trying unsuccessfully a couple of times, with the aircraft rotating around the anchor wedged in coral on the seabed, Charlie gave up. Possible damage to our bollard, the distance to shore, the yacht standing by, the canoes in close proximity, didn't allow for a safe turn if the anchor should come free or the cable snap while the Cat was facing the wrong direction. The engineer was ordered to stop the engine, the bowman to cut the cable.

At last freed of the anchor, the Cat, sailed out into the lagoon on a light breeze in reverse until there was room enough to start engines again, having lost not only the ship's anchor but a good deal of precious time also. We taxied into the lagoon for take off, all eyes on the lookout for any of the deadly bombolas in the lagoon, that is when we weren't watching the clock ticking on. Somehow though, through no fault of our own, we avoided all the underwater obstacles in our path during the extended take-off run.

Before setting course, we paid a visit to the main island across the lagoon and gave a good 'buzz' along the beach and over the trees, with all the population it seemed waving madly at us from the beachfront.

And so it was goodbye to Penrhyn, a happy, laughing place despite the isolation in the vastness of the Pacific. We all hoped that our Officer Commanding, Squadron Leader Hutton, wouldn't be too cross about the loss of the anchor. Eventually it could be recovered by some of the island's pearl divers and be returned to the Squadron, or put to good use on the island was our hope. If by the present time it hasn't been recovered, but is discovered in ages to come, it might serve as a clue for some archaeologist, as to the whereabouts of the ancient, lost civilisation with the knowledge to cast a perfect, incorruptible, stainless steel anchor.

At Aitutaki that night, a party was turned on for us at the Agent's residence, to celebrate the success of the mission as he had received word that every few hours that the Penrhyn woman's condition was improving.

Charlie and some others of the crew took up the Agent's invitation and again it was my duty for the 'anchor watch'. Next morning, those who attended were still wearing hibiscus flowers behind their ears and Doctor Doran had gained a reputation as an accomplished hula dancer! When males wear a flower behind an ear at party time in Polynesia, I've never really learnt which ear means what.

After re-fuelling, next came Samoa for another night at 'Aggie Grey's' and then it was home to Laucala Bay, proud Officer Commanding and our dear wives and kids, feeling pretty good for ourselves. Total flying time for the mission was 36 hours.

I wasn't to know then, that Charlie along with six other squadron air personnel, would be killed at Satapuala a few months later. Taking off for the Tokelau Islands, fully laden on glassy water that hid a light swell, with a pilot under instruction at the controls, the aircraft had become unstable, 'porpoised', then dived into the water with force enough to strike the bottom through three fathoms of sea. The flight to Penrhyn had been for me a remarkable learning experience that when I hear, see, or get near to any sort of a flying boat stay with me until this day. I flew into and out of the alighting area at Satapuala without incident many times after Charlie's crew perished there, always watchful and using great care. With the coming of regular services on the Coral Route to Tahiti, the facilities that included a marked water-way, a jetty, suitable marine craft and experienced marine personnel on hand made things a lot easier.

Two months after the 'flight to Penrhyn', my promotion to 'Junior Captain' came through. That allowed me to captain emergency 'dumbo calls' within the Fiji Group and other flights that began and ended at Laucala Bay, such as training and long-range navigation exercises.

One of the most hazardous alighting areas was at Makogai Island, a leper colony, (hansenide these days), between Viti Levu and Vanua Levu where there was a fairly frequent exchange of medicos, approved visitors and government officials. The alighting area was very exposed, rough seas accompanied by strong offshore winds were the norm at Makogai. We would tie up to a huge, steel ship's buoy and pray that the wind wouldn't change during our stay. In rough conditions the bowman sometimes found the buoy hard to grab with the grapple-hook, whilst remaining securely strapped to the bow of the Catalina. To release the safety harness for a better reach, could mean a dip in the ocean as sometimes happened, with the bowman having to be hauled aboard before he was swept past the blister and out to sea. The pilot's main worry was in preventing the propellers striking the tall steel buoy while getting close enough for the bowman to get the strop with his boathook with the bow rising and falling on the waves.

The take-off towards the island at Makogai too, was always a thrill, with a wingtip close to the water while making a turn immediately on becoming airborne, to avoid the low cliffs.

There were no inter-island air services operating in Fiji, alighting areas were devised as we went. Mercy missions and searches for missing boats were in great demand, particularly after the many 'blows' that wracked the Fiji group every 'hurricane season', officially declared as the period through November to March. Those calls containing a task gauged to be beyond my level of experience could be supervised by a more senior pilot.

During the period as a Junior Captain under supervision supported by the crew I was able to locate and assist several overseas merchant ships in minor distress, having grounded on one of the group's many coral reefs, been blown off course, or lost their way for some other reason. Searches for boats large and small, happened frequently.

In February 1951 a search for the missing yacht 'Argo' off the East Cape of New Zealand, while I was under supervision by Flight Lieutenant Doug Clarke, was unsuccessful - the yacht has never been found.

The beginning of the night trip to Auckland through tropical thunderstorms, to position for the search for 'Argo' will always be remembered, as too will the return flight from the search area to Hobsonville, there were times when I thought the wings would surely part company as we were forced to fly through turbulent cloud with our Cat at 17,000 feet!

In flying hours I had by then 'amassed' more than 500, wow!

Four months after arriving at the Laucala Bay I was commissioned as a Pilot Officer, a promotion that took me to New Zealand for a two month Officer's Course, that among many other important lessons, taught me how to RETURN salutes for a change and behave in the Officer's Mess as a 'gentleman of the Air Force' should. (Sir Cyril Newell, the then Governor-General of New Zealand made that blunder, not me). This is not griping, the course taught me a lot and was very good for me. Eight months after arrival at Laucala Bay I was confirmed as a full-blown captain, at a time when there were many foreign submarine 'scares' requiring long patrols, with naval exercises also going on. Flying hours were mounting, with me nearing the first thousand of my final twenty-eight plus.

THE DEPTH CHARGE AFFAIR

During a Commonwealth air and sea exercise in the Hauraki Gulf east of Auckland, one of the four depth charges being carried on the underwing racks of my Catalina failed to release. Out over the Gulf, while keeping in close touch with the air gunner who was responsible for the armaments settings carried, I went through all the procedures that might free the depth charge, yawing roughly, diving, pulling or pushing positive and negative 'g', but the DC didn't budge and could be seen as being slightly misaligned on it's rack as if a latch was jammed. The Flight Commander at Hobsonville, Flight Lieutenant Bob Weston was alerted. Orders came from him to return to base via the Auckland harbour route where shipping was in process of being warned of my predicament.

On the way in to Hobsonville in the upper reaches of the Auckland harbour my mind was full of what might happen should the DC accidentally let go its hold on the rack during flight. The two-fifty pounder's pressure fuse had been set to go off at a depth of 100 feet which would cause a big eruption in the water and might cause a panic in the city itself, even if it didn't land close to one of the smaller vessels that plied the harbour, or kill or injure someone. Following instructions, with bated breath as with all the crew, I flew a line directly up the middle of the busy harbour, breathing a sigh of relief when we passed the Devonport naval base or one of the north shore hillside suburbs.

Another particular concern was the possibility of the DC being released of its own accord on touch down, when it would bounce off the water, taking part of the wing with it before flying through the starboard blister. The end result could only be a major disaster. That was not a pleasant thought. A soft, gentle alighting was required at the lowest speed possible. We would then anchor, or drift if conditions allowed, while the armaments section checked the DC over from a barge under the wing.

Approaching Hobsonville, the stiff, easterly wind was seen to be creating whitecaps, ruling out the straight-in downwind approach that had been planned on to avoid flying over any land. At that point the alighting area in the upper reach of the harbour was quite narrow. A 'one-eighty' turn was called for to allow for an alighting into the wind. In order to do so I swung the 'Cat' out to the right over some harbour-side farmland, then brought her back in a moderate left turn to line up for the alighting area over the narrow waters of the upper harbour, where the control launch could be seen in position.

When over land, the gusty air waffled the Cat about with some unexpected turbulence. The wings had only just been levelled for the final approach when 'Spud' Narbey the gunner called frantically from the blister. "Blister to Captain, the DC's gone, it fell off as we were turning around, yeh, it's gone alright, I lost sight of it before it hit the ground."

Hit the ground? That caused some worry. There was little I could do except carry on with alighting, while our wireless 'op' let the base know of the most recent development. Once on the water I step-taxied on return to a mooring abreast the slipway where the bowman with his boat hook grabbed the eye of the floating strop expertly and slipped it over the ship's bollard. Leaving the crew to secure the mooring, the gunner and I went to meet the OC, who was waiting for us at the jetty. Soon a group of armaments 'experts' and other helpers gathered and in three cars we set off for the DC's alleged 'drop site'. The Auckland Police had been notified and would meet with us there. So far there had not been any reports of explosions or other complaints from residents of the area that could be linked to a falling DC, although some local radio stations were already broadcasting warnings of the incident. Although the DC would have met with the ground about four to five kilometres away across the neck of harbour from Hobsonville, we were faced with a 50-kilometre drive to round the harbour reaches to get to the Greenhithe area.

Once in the general area, we formed into lines and directed by 'Spud', began searching the dairy farmers paddocks one by one for signs of our DC. The rather nervous gunner then swore that he recognized a nearby farmhouse as the one close to where he'd last seen the DC tumbling down. The owner of that property met us at the fence bordering his house.

" I guess you're looking for the cowling or whatever it was that fell from a Catalina a while ago, I was at the rear boundary of my place, it seemed to come down pretty close to the house, I've had a good look around but there's not a sign of it anywhere."

The Armament Officer's voice was most anxious as he replied. " It wasn't a cowling you saw, but a two-fifty pound depth charge! Parallax error, maybe it was further away than where you thought, in which case the search will continue in that direction? "

" Well I'll be blowed, a two-fifty DC you say, I can assure you it's not anywhere around here. How the hell could that happen. An accident I suppose? Was it armed? You might as well know I was once in the Air Force myself." The farmer's tones were by then becoming sarcastic.

"Well yes, but for a hundred feet of water, if it had hit anything hard and burst it might have exploded, at least that hasn't happened, let's know if you see anything suspicious" the Armament Officer said quietly, a worried look on his face. "Here's our 'phone number, ask for the Duty Officer."

For the remainder of the afternoon the search went on, with the residents of adjoining properties joining in, until the darkness of a moonless night crept over the area. Police remained at the scene making further inquiries, while we headed back to Hobsonville for supper.

At nine o'clock or thereabouts the 'phone rang in the officer's mess. The call came from the man who'd witnessed the 'cowling' fall from the aircraft. Only minutes before, he explained in a frightened voice, he had gone to his 'dunny' beside a pumpkin patch five metres from the back door of the house. In the dark he'd nearly fallen into a small, freshly dug crater that shouldn't have been there! In his mind anyway, there was no doubt, the missing DC had been found!

We were rushed back to Greenhithe at high speed, arriving at the house to find the owner in a sorry state of nerves, threatening to sue the Air Force for its last nut, bolt, prop, parachute and flying officer. Apparently he lived as a bachelor for there were no other persons about.

From the back door of his house, a two metre concrete block cracked in parts, separated the house from a small vegetable garden. Past a couple of rows of potatoes, a small patch of pumpkins bordered his backyard 'dunny'. Right there, by the light of several flashlights, a large, recently made crater four to five feet deep could be seen. There was no sign of the DC for the earth had fallen in and buried it. Another five metres and the two-fifty pound missile in free fall would have gone through the house!

Using shovels, the armaments men widened the hole so as to scoop out the earth and expose the metal casing, all seemed to be cock-sure that there wouldn't be an explosion! As I stood watching, I was wishing that I'd paid more attention during armaments lectures. The property owner kept grumbling about the damage to his vegies, for a good deal of his very tidy garden had been dug up or trampled over in the process.

A portable hoist and winch then arrived. In less than two hours the offending armament was appropriately stowed aboard a truck and on its way to Hobsonville Flying-Boat Station under police escort. The following day I had the privilege of dropping the same DC from a Catalina in the seas of Hauraki Gulf, 250 metres astern HM Submarine Telemachus, that went off with a big thump and splash in the normal fashion of DC's.

SEARCH FOR 'VILA STAR'

Our base at Laucala Bay, Suva, Fiji, received requests for assistance from all parts of the Pacific. Nothing was too hard, no-where too far. 24 hours a day, 7 days a week crews were on standby for a quick getaway on a 'Dumbo' mission. Bonus points for 5 Squadron were always earned, whatever the task might be.

One such mission began early on a sultry morning when the 'dumbo' sirens blasted out the call-up signal. As Duty Crew we assembled in the Briefing Room in the bayside hangar adjoining the beaching ramp. Flight Lieutenant Bert Dwerryhouse ('Merrymouse' to his equals) gave us 'the gen'. A small islands vessel, the 'Vila Star', with an islands crew of about fifteen was five days overdue at Port Vila, New Hebrides, on a voyage from Sydney.

An hour later, with Pilot 3 Grant Miller as 2nd Pilot in the right-hand seat, I had Catalina NZ 4056 in a curving take-off around the end of Laucala Bay's rock-pile breakwater, floats retracting to the wing-tips, at the start of a five-hour journey to the search area. On a bomb rack under the left wing a 'storp' filled with rescue gear sat snug with its sharp nose looking exactly like a torpedo. Probable or exact search areas to the west of the New Hebrides would be radioed to the aircraft later as Operations received more follow-up information.

Aboard 4056, the radios were in the capable hands of Master Signaller 'Nobby' Clark. He lived in a world of sound, dials and electrical leads, at a small table in a corner of the navigation compartment and also stood a watch on the APS3 radar, at the head of the navigation table across the catwalk, the direction finder in the ceiling above.

At briefing we'd learnt that radio signals from Vila Star were likely to be mutilated, patchy and hard to copy. It was thought that Vila Star's engine had broken down, resulting in the batteries going sour. Shortage of water, with undisclosed navigation difficulties, added to their woes. Heavy seas and continuous rain, in league with a tropical depression that the area was noted for, were also being experienced, to render the vessel's estimated position even more doubtful.

With more than 600 miles to go before any searching could begin, the navigators began preparing the search patterns on the information available at that time. A wide, 'creeping line ahead' search along the ship's expected inbound course to Port Vila, was decided on. Having been unable to sight the sun for several days, obviously 'Vila Star's' navigator hadn't a clue as to exactly where the ship was.

Our two navigators, Nav 3 Peter Evans and Nav 3 Harry (Shorty) Butterworth, were forced to use some guesswork in setting up a searching procedure to fit the circumstances. In the cockpit Grant Miller and I shared shifts at flying, steering courses provided by the navigator while working up a fuel conservation scheme with the engineers, Eng 3 Alan Treadgold, who was in the engineer's 'tower' and Eng 3 Ed Brown.

On his perch in the centre section, Alan was committed to 'his' engines and the aircraft, to whatever action I might need to take with changes to the power settings. Ed would share watches with him and in addition act as 'galley custodian' in charge of the auxiliary power unit, electric stove, food and drink rations. Gunner 3 Eric Leech busied himself with a check-over of the armaments selector panel, to ensure that if and when required, the 'storp' would leave the under-wing rack on the jab of the release button on my control wheel. Once in the search area and equipped with binoculars, Eric would take up station in the port blister.

My responsibility was to plan where we would go if before night-fall the ship hadn't been found, or the afternoon weather made searching impossible. There were no night facilities for 'boats' any-where in the New Hebrides, we were advised that fuel on an appropriate barge was available only at Luganville, Espiritu Santo.

One of the advantages a Catalina possessed over certain other air-craft, was that time was usually available to work things out with a crew acting together as a 'think tank'. If required, we worked things out as we went.

After a couple of hours while we forged on towards the New Heb-rides, I could sit back and relax knowing that we had the most important points covered. With about 15 hours of fuel aboard at that time, we flew on at 6000 feet in clear weather, eating up the miles at 105 'rate of knots'.

Catalinas were 'worked up' in much the same way as a small naval ship or submarine, with crew constantly on watch from their allotted stations, all in contact with each other on an excellent intercommuni-cation system that required disciplined procedures for best results, not just a chat line as in the movies.

When nearing the New Hebrides group five hours later, the weath-er deteriorated rather rapidly. To search successfully for small targets at sea, the Catalina was flown in visual contact with the ground or wa-ter. The navigator was advised that we'd be descending to 1000 feet ASL (above sea level), who then guided us safely past Tanna one of the New Hebrides many perpetually smoking volcanic islands, to start into the search pattern west of the group. At that point the wind on the surface was beginning to kick up masses of white-caps, with low cloud and light rain beginning to develop, one didn't need a sixth sense to know that a wet afternoon lay ahead.

After the first two hours, with so little worthwhile information about Vila Star's position being available, my instincts told me that our search was going to be either lucky or lengthy. With visibility re-duced to 3 kilometres it was going to take a week of Sundays to adequately cover the area, but the 'ground-work' had to be laid. The radar was operating perfectly, returning a good picture of an extremely turbulent sea for that part of the world.

Those on watch in the 'blisters' were all using powerful binoculars to scan the sea on either side of our 'boat'. The engineer in the 'tower' (the pylon supporting the parasol wing above the fuselage) enjoyed the very best of viewing through each side window of his den as also the pilots from the cockpit. Ours was a top-line crew who all took great pride in their respective roles, nothing would escape nine pairs of eagle eyes.

With the power closed off to 55 per cent of maximum, we chugged back and forth across the search pattern for hours, sometimes homing in on a radar target only to find a heap of flotsam and jetsam, driftwood and other rubbish, rising and falling on the sea.

At 1630 hours, with nothing sighted except the tossing sea and the warning of an even more darkening sky, 4056 swung on to a course for Luganville, Espiritu Santos, where an alighting was made in the protected bay at nightfall under a heavy overcast, after spending ten hours and fifty minutes in the air.

A regulation Catalina mooring cancelled the requirement for a skeleton crew to remain aboard throughout the night. After tidying up and making her fast we were taken to a grass-roofed, island style, French administered hotel, on the beach 5-6 kilometres along the coast. Alas, no 'Folies-Berge`re' or topless Polynesian grass-skirted dancing girls, came those frivolous 'complaints' from some of the crew.

Early next morning the crew worked hard in the warm air to pump the contents of 14-15 drums of high-octane fuel into 4056's tanks from a barge tethered alongside. Nobby waited patiently for the APU (auxiliary power unit) to be started before he could have the radios on so as to update with Laucala Bay on Vila Star's probable position. Sparks emanating from electrical connections mixing with the fumes of high octane fuel were not recommended.

The time was 0930 before fuelling was finished and we were sluicing into an extended take-off across the choppy, weather protected water of the bay and turning again for the search area.

On the radio 'Nobby' was receiving the day's briefings, which included the revised co-ordinates of Vila Star's probable position. Again he guessed those to be somewhat mutilated in transmission and not completely reliable.

A wide area of search around the position had already been planned by Laucala Bay Operations and with all haste we made for the start point that was much further west than where we'd finished the afternoon before. We were instructed that on finding Vila Star, or at the end of day, we were to return to Port Vila where fuel on a properly equipped barge was reported to have become available.

The actual search began in weather conditions that were much worse than on the previous day with strong, gusty, north to northeast winds on the surface and continuous rain falling through a low murk at 500 feet. With visibility so reduced, for hours the radar was the most reliable set of eyes we had at our disposal. Due to the late start and the more distant commencing point, the day's program was uncompleted before we had to leave the area for Port Vila, where we alighted in the harbour after flying a total of 8.5 hours for the day, that were not all spent on the search.

Avoiding the reef that had caused problems for 4047 and disaster for the Qantas Sandringham, was foremost in my mind as I taxied up cautiously to the mooring. The re-fuelling barge was ready and waiting to come alongside. An hour after arrival the tanks were again topped to capacity. The mooring was sound in every way and would be visible from the Port Vila Hotel where we were to be accommodated. Again we were relieved at not having to leave an 'anchor-watch' aboard, all crew could sleep ashore, we were living rich.

The hotel had only just been reached when the owner of 'Vila Star', an Auckland businessman, suddenly appeared. He was a prickly customer with a slightly arrogant air about him, who seemed to think his ship should have been found on the first sweep on the first day! His opinion was that we must have been searching in the wrong place or in the wrong way. The most alarming thing though, was that his version of the delay to the ship's arrival at Port Vila differed widely from the briefing we'd received at Laucala Bay. It was hard to know who to believe as according to our information at that time, Vila Star was a week overdue. He felt certain his precious ship was holed up on one of the islands of the group with the crew 'playing about' with women as happened with the 'Bounty' at Pitcairn Island more than a century before, insisting that we should search there instead of the outer seas. Of course there was no way that I could or would take search instructions from him as he seemed to think I would.

Although I was slightly confused I was very pleased when an hour later he took his leave looking a little 'narked' at the outcome of our meeting. 'Shorty' and Peter, the two proud navigators, who both had short fuses when it came to a disagreement, were ready to give him a really fast serve. Fortunately I was able to come up with some 'words of wisdom' befitting a 23 year old junior officer and was able to con-strain them in time.

Just after the crack of dawn next morning, in blustery conditions we made a mixed downwind/crosswind take-off out of the harbour to the open sea. Ten minutes after becoming airborne, Laucala Bay passed us some revised information on the ship's most probable posi-tion. Again that was further west of where we'd searched previously. With Port Vila then being closer to the chosen area than Luganville, at least an hour of daylight had been saved for searching. Two hours passed before we were in position to commence the adjusted square search as decided on by operations at 'the Bay'. In rain, heavy at times, we searched through the morning and into the afternoon, again relying only on the radar for eyes.

'Shorty' had only just passed me the final course of the search pattern to be steered before we turned for 'home', when Peter's excited voice came through on the intercom.

"Radar to Captain, target twenty degrees right of the bow, eight kilometers, steer zero one eight compass, by the shape it's a small ship alright."

" Good on you Pete, bless your heart, you never miss." were my thoughts, as I motioned Grant to look after things in the cockpit, slipped down from my seat then stooped through the bulkhead door to stand at the navigating table. Peter's face came out of the long black tube as he motioned me to take a look.

The view at the end of the tube was amazing, with the cursor sweeping back and forth across the screen, each sweep left behind for a second or two, the exact profile of Vila Star as sketched for us at briefing three days before! Scrambling back to my seat to stare through the windshield, the ship still could not be seen through the rain, until we were within a kilometre. At 300 feet I bored on towards the white-painted vessel, then seen to be heaving up and down on a turbulent sea, the bow throwing up lashings of slop over the forward deck, to mix with the rain as she dipped into each trough. Vila Star was taking a battering. The crew were elated at their find after all the hard, sometimes boring work, that had been put into finding her over three days.

As we flashed over her bow, it was only too clear that our sudden arrival out of the murk had taken those on board completely by surprise, as startled faces on the bridge gaped up at us through the spray lashed windows. The APS3 radar was forward-looking, thirty degrees either side of the bow. In the poor visibility, not wishing to lose her again, we flew straight out for over a kilometre before making a 'tear-drop' reversal, waiting for the navigator to pick her up on radar again. Closer in to the ever-tossing vessel, the Cat was leaned into a tight left circle from where we could keep her in sight visually.

With the amount of foam that was flying around her, it was hard to decide whether she was making way under power or was simply heaved to, stopped dead in the water, facing into the lumpy seas. After a few circles using the naked eye or staring through binoculars, the majority of the crew ruled that she was moving very slowly under power. Although no one had been able to read the ship's name on the bow, our briefing material was enough to tell us that Vila Star had at last been found and only just in time by the look of the weather and the time of the day.

After several circles had been made, an Aldis lamp blinked Morse code from the bridge, WATER, FOOD, MED, ENG, at least that's what those who could read Morse jointly made of the letters. With the ship rising and falling high and steep and with us circling low around him, the sender was probably having difficulty keeping balance while aiming the lamp. We all believed that the 'storp' contained the items requested. The Navigator, along with all of us, was getting 'itchy' about a possible arrival after dark and in conditions of poor visibility at Port Vila's harbour.

Swinging into position from circling, an approach was made on to the ship from astern. There was no time available for a dummy run, at 100 feet on the radio altimeter, as the ship disappeared below the nose turret a jab of the button on my control wheel released the 'storp', flying straight for a few seconds before laying over into a steep left turn again. Eric reported from the blister that he'd seen the parachute snagged on a stay of the mast, the 'storp' was dangling on the shrouds over the starboard side, looking to be perfectly intact. Retrieving the heavy 'storp' tho' he reckoned, could be dangerous for the crew with the tossing about that Vila Star was receiving from the extremely rough seas.

Since the first sighting the whole process had taken more than half an hour. There was no time left for further appraisal of the success or not of the drop, or even a playful 'buzz' of the vessel to cheer the crew up, precious minutes were slipping by. All I could do was 'waggle' the wings whilst flying on the course for Port Vila, hoping that would be taken as an invitation for the ship to 'follow me'. In less than half a minute the blister reported that Vila Star had disappeared behind us, smothered in the gray, misty murk of a late, wet afternoon.

Although he'd tried many times 'Nobby' had not been able to contact the lost ship by radio on the advised frequencies. Laucala Bay had been informed of our sighting. There at base, they couldn't be anything other than very pleased with the success of the search.

For a while the intercom buzzed with excitement. Looking forward into the grey, sodden weather, I hunched down apprehensively, letting the light-hearted banter go past me until gradually it petered out. My gut was getting itself into a knot, decisions had to be made. Not willing to climb up to top the cloud lest there be difficulty in getting underneath again over the New Hebrides group, the task before me then was to plod on into the weather and reach a safe harbour before darkness set in.

Our homing run to Port Vila started in from a DR (deduced reckoning) position, that could be miles in error after changing course dozen of times during the day, without a reliable bearing or sun-line in support.

After signalling the engineer for seventy-five per cent power on 'his'engines' to hurry us along, the navigator came up with an estimate for arrival at Port Vila that was very close to last light. The clouds were thickening, a blue-black curtain of heavy rain hung before us, the sea barely visible from 100 feet at times. Except for the navigator preferring to remain in sight of the surface to better gauge the wind velocity, a climb to a more comfortable altitude would have been preferred.

Aboard a Catalina, co-ordination between pilot and navigator could not be quick enough to bring an aircraft safely through the conditions we were flying in. Flying from the right seat Grant too was looking nervous. I was about to use my powers of command and climb up through the cloud and rain when 'Nobby' came through on the intercom.

" Radio to Captain, a signal from operations Laucala Bay. The wind at Port Vila is 90 km per hour at present, expected to increase, visibility in the harbour zero, on no account alight there, you are to proceed to Ile Nou, Noumea, New Caledonia, forthwith. Arrangements for your arrival will come later, after the British Consulate has been contacted."

The signal was public news on the ship's intercom, all crew were propelled into action. My call went across the cockpit to Grant while pointing to the navigator's last course correction, clipped to the yoke.

" Stay on that course until the navigator feeds us with some revised calculations. We'll have to climb soon. "

The navigator of a Catalina had a very hard job with head down over his table, plotting and calculating, particularly in rough flying conditions. It would take a few minutes for the navigator to switch us on to a course for Ile Nou. An arrival after dark at Port Vila had been getting me quite worried, some of the responsibility had then been taken from me, for that at least I was relieved and grateful.

At the navigating table, Peter and 'Shorty' were sorting through the ship's charts to find a topographical map of New Caledonia.

On intercom 'Shorty' gave me a time to alter course and a rough estimate for Ile Nou that was almost three hours away! Obviously that wasn't my day. A bit like jumping from the frying pan into the fire, two hours down the track and in the dark, instead of Port Vila's rather difficult harbour, there would be an extended, oblique crossing of an extremely mountainous island to contend with before reaching Noumea and Ile Nou.

New Caledonia stood high and formidable across the south-east winds, where almost daily, storm clouds built up to levels three times that of a Catalina's rated altitude. Following that, an alighting would need to be made in a darkened harbour without a standard flare-path and where a clutter of ships of all classes and nations would be anchored. I hunched further down into my seat, vowing not to leave it again until my metal water-bird was safely tethered on a seaplane mooring at Ile Nou.

Three minutes later, still embedded in thick cloud and rain, we swung through almost fifty degrees on a turn towards the safety of our new destination. The air in the stuffy, damp conditions of the several compartments was tense as thoughts of the tasks ahead gradually filtered into weary brains.

Through a perished seal in the sliding hatch above me, water began to run into my flying suit and trickle down my back. More responsibility was then with the navigators, with the pilots flying very accurately the courses they supplied. In solid cloud with rain hammering on to the airframe, without sight of sea or sun, we climbed to 7000 feet in the hope that we could break clear for a while before it was dark. Hanging alone in cloud-filled space, 4056 waded into the miles, buffeting and rolling until a darker than normal cloud brought the day to a sudden end and it was night.

With the darkness came the news that a topographical map of New Caledonia hadn't been found, the navigator was unsure of the several major heights of the big island. By the sound of his voice I knew that he was about to be taken up with a bout of airsickness. No wonder, after more than 11 hours with head down, eyes glued to the plotting chart or peering into the radar tube, while the aircraft rolled, pitched and yawed about all three axes. How our navigators could draw such straight lines and print so neatly under such conditions had always baffled me. He'd hardly finished before 'climb power' was called for as we 'headed for the heights', anything over 7,000 feet. The more than two hours that followed were amongst the worst of my Catalina flying memories for a very long time.

With no responses coming from the navigators I sensed that they were in disagreement with each other or 'non compis mentis' with'mal de mer'. Being completely absorbed with flying the aircraft, all I could do was hold fast to the last given magnetic course and wait for more directions from the navigator. Without the help of the auto-pilot both pilots would soon be exhausted from the effort required on the controls. As a mariner might adjust his sails properly so that even contrary, adverse winds, would help him reach his goal, so 4056 was trimmed to meet with heavy weather conditions. On the intercom 'Nobby' was directed to tune the direction finder to the Tontouta non-directional beacon, or any other station he could find on New Caledonia, to obtain a bearing. 'Nobby' advised that Magenta, the domestic airport that was much closer to Noumea than Tontouta International, so far as he knew or could find, was not equipped with a beacon of any sort.

My heart dropped a gear or two when shortly after that he added that nothing could be heard on Tontouta's beacon frequency either, it was as if the beacon was either out of action or simply turned off for the night, but he'd continue to search. A single broadcast radio station only could be heard, but only weakly and then was sometimes completely obliterated by static. We were on our own.

Two hours after leaving Vila Star, by the sudden increase in severe turbulence and the spasmodic display of lightning I sensed we had driven into the heavy clouds expected to be over 'Nouvelle Caledonie', but that was only a guess.

In the darkened cockpit, with the fluorescent instrument lighting turned up, Grant and I sat without talking, glare screens over the windshield, absorbing the black of the night, rolling with the movement of the aircraft, both control wheels assisting the auto-pilot with corrective inputs as without a break the bow jabbed into solid, turbulent cloud.

Out of range of any known radio station and with the stars obliterated, there was nothing to navigate on! All contact with the world and the heavens too had been lost! The thoughts of mountain peaks being close below us, or worse still, directly ahead and higher, were always there. Any time the turbulence decided to take us upwards, the bird was given a free rein. If similar conditions existed over the southern parts of New Caledonia we were going to be in a serious plight.

'Nobby' began a series of exchanges with base, who in turn, strove to get some answers from the French officials, although at that hour most were expected to be well into their 'evening aperitifs', no responses had been received. We needed weather reports, an assessment of some kind of the terrain we were about to cross, non directional beacons to be turned on, radio station frequencies and locations, a flare path of sorts in the harbour at Ile Nou. All that took time, a lot of time, while loaded to the ears with apprehension, we ploughed on through the dirtiest of weather, that was obviously the outskirts of the build up to a tropical cyclone that we'd been battling all day.

The ETA for overhead Noumea came and went, without any sign of a light below or a comforting signal from the beacon at Tontouta airport, that although many miles from the harbour city could have been used to guide us to seawards of the mountainous island. Through a gap in the clouds, lights of some kind on the surface would tell us we were in contact with the real world again. All hands then turned to the job of spotting any lights down through the clouds, while our Cat forged on, rocking, skidding, even trembling and shaking. Much lighter by then, the frame was better able to withstand the shocks of swirling air, the radar returning so much hash from the rain clouds, coastlines, mountains or hills that could not be defined.

Voices on the intercom became more strident with tension. Any attempt to maintain a steady altitude would be suicidal in the vicious up and down-drafts, 4056 was left to ride out the turbulence. If the air wanted to take her up we let her go, without any major corrections on our part. Fortunately she showed more of a tendency to ride up than down, only if she wanted to go below 7,000 feet did we make a correction with the elevator and that ever so gently.

As each minute passed without anything being sighted, more and more responsibility for decision making fell on my shoulders, there was little anyone else could do except hold on, look and keep looking.

A feeling of desperation crept over me that had to be dealt with, knowing that under the circumstances we could have missed New Caledonia altogether and be flying a course to the 'sea of nowhere'.

Ten minutes after ETA and still without any knowledge of the safety heights, in desperation I was about to try to descend to get below cloud, that wasn't going to be easy in the rising air, when a call came from the observer in the port blister, an excited voice trying hard to be casual.

"Lights behind us skipper, lots of 'em, looks like we've passed smack bang over Noumea, the lights are behind us."

In time with that we lurched from the clouds, the air turning smooth as silk, my hands flew to the throttles to draw them back, the engines died to a quieter tone, while Grant released the glare shields as we started on the way down on a course at first to seaward, then in wide descending circles. For only a minute or two we ran through bumpy air and a cloud or two not of the vicious kind, before I was able to keep the city's lights constantly in view as we came around in each circle. The cloud we'd passed through over the island stood out against the lightning and was now hanging like an umbrella over the city, but without the rain falling underneath. The relief felt was overwhelming, like passing into a new beginning of life itself.

Arrival over Noumea was nothing short of a miracle thanks to the navigators' thirteen and a-half hours of unbelievably accurate DR (deduced reckoning). Whoops of delight rang through the cabin and over the intercom as all the crew released their pent up emotions.

Then came the time to alight in the harbour, seen by me as black as ink blobs around and between the glowing of deck lighting reflected on the water from ships at their moorings in the roadstead. That many large and small islands adjoined the harbour and coastal area of Noumea was well known, some between four and five hundred feet in height with a fairly narrow entrance to the harbour itself. The flying-boat alighting area was off the island of Ile Nou, a wider expanse of water.

Below 2000 feet and in the clear the floats came down with a 'whirrr' as Grant ran through the alighting checklist with each crew station. With intense concentration on my part and in a wide sweep, 4056 was positioned for an approach from seaward into the harbour, towards the city lights.

To assist in locating a suitable path down and on to the blackest of water, I drew back the sliding window beside me, a blast of air whipped at my face. With my left hand shielding both eyes from the sudden warm wind, I was able to pick out the silhouette of the nickel works before swinging my wide-winged metal bird around on to a low, final approach. As a type, the Catalina was not equipped with flaps, that made for flat approaches..

That was an incredibly tense period, getting low enough without running smack bang into some part of an offshore island hidden in the dense blobs of blackness, or the tall smokestacks of the nickel works that were remembered to be on a point adjacent to the harbour entrance. Sometimes guided by Eric in the blister or Alan in the tower or me with my head out the storm window, the Cat was weaved from right to left until some of the shipping became silhouetted against the lights of the city that put me on the north side of the wartime alighting area, on an almost direct path to the city lights.

At 100 feet on the radio altimeter the rate of descent was reduced to 75 feet per minute that meant taking power off and raising the bow a little, as I aimed for a black hole between two ships that Grant reckoned would lead to the seaplane mooring, if one existed, all the time hoping that there were no unlighted pleasure or fishing craft of the smaller variety between the two. From the lights around the harbour town, there was then some sort of an horizon to work with as we slid down to the water.

Down lower, by the silhouettes and reflections, the water was seen to be fairly smooth if not glassy. That was a most welcome, pleasant surprise. The landing lights would not be required. Relentlessly I held on to a steady rate of descent while checking and re-checking the radio altimeter, all the time feeling that I was living in a different world. Touchdown was slow to come as 'surface effect' held our keel above the water. She just wouldn't carve through the last foot or two of air, but floated along and along, while I waited for the familiar 'hissing' sound when the heel of the planing step sliced into the water. The 'critical point' had been passed, where any attempt to abort towards the city would be suicidal.

4056 was well into the harbour itself when the 'hissing' and the slight deceleration told me that we'd met with the water. Slowly, smoothly, the throttles were drawn off while holding her steady on the elevator, until the bow was thrown up in a last heave and she came off the step with a forward flop.

With the motors ticking over quietly, both blister drogues streamed and holding, we passed alongside a large ocean going ship, evidently attracting little attention from any of her night-watch crew. In seconds the bowman crawled between the pilot seats and under the yoke, opened the bow hatch and after a sweep or two, picked out the mooring with the hand-held spotlight. Without any wind to cause weathercocking and the sea anchors holding, taxiing without blasts of power for steering was easy enough. Closer in both engines were 'blipped' down to minimum revs with the magneto master switch, as we crept up slowly to the mooring. That was another tense moment - not knowing whether or not there was swinging room ahead of the buoy should the bowman fail to pick up the strop to the mooring.

Wonder of wonders the buoy couldn't have been better, exactly what was wanted, perfect for a Catalina. With the aid of the spotlight, a strop, a very old one showing green slime on its floats, was picked out streaming directly towards us, a small launch with weak navigation lights hovered behind the mooring. How much a pilot relies on a good bowman, he picked up the floating strop with the first jab of his boat-hook, slipped the eye over our bollard and with a 'thumbs up' signalled that the mooring had been made. I flipped the 'stop engines' lamp to the engineer who shut off the mixtures, with only a few more rotations the engines wound to a stop. Only a slight tug could be felt as she came up on the strop.

The sudden silence almost hurt the ears and set up a ringing in them that would last for hours. After thirteen and a half anxious hours in the air 4056 was safely down and tethered at Noumea, her pilot acting calm but feeling stretched, worn out almost. While some of the crew bustled about on the bow securing the mooring, others slipped out of their flying suits and began to don the approved shore garb, keen for Noumea's sociable nightlife.

With the fresh night air coming in through the hatch above me, I slumped in my seat, sucking in air, stretching my legs, relaxing tired muscles, letting the tension drain from me, not caring whether or not my flying garb was presentable. I remained there until Peter tugged at my sleeve, his breath reeking of a recent spew.

"The British Consul gentleman wants to see you " he mumbled, " he's waiting for you to board the launch, he'll take us to the Hotel du Pacifique, it's the best in town he says, everyone else is getting aboard, the mooring's okay, no need for an anchor-watch the engineers say, I s'pose you'll agree to that, we've had a pretty tough three days in the beast haven't we? " The smell of spew came up again as I stared down at him.

"You can say that again, are you alright, didn't hear much from you, or should I say, anything, in the last hour aloft. Up front here Grant and I were completely taken up with keeping the right way up, it gets lonely not hearing any directions, was it a fluke that got us over Noumea almost on time, or your better than average skills. Whatever happened to that topographical of Nouvelle Caledonie? " I hissed.

"Yeah, both I think, I was really crook you know, really crook, couldn't move a muscle, didn't even care if I never moved again either, we left the selection of the maps to the senior navigator at Lauthala Bay, there was no time to check through them before leaving, who would have thought we'd end up here anyway and need it, can't think of everything can we? "

"You're supposed to. "

I boarded the launch in flying suit and carrying my kit, to be greeted by the Consul who was full of apologies for his inability to conjure up some worthwhile ground support. " I would never have dreamt that you could bring a flying-boat into this place without lights of any kind, I can't imagine how you did that " he queried.

I was tired, relieved like everyone else, just glad to be safe and couldn't be bothered answering questions.

"It's quite easy really sir. " I replied, not caring whether he would be offended by my sarcastic, un-diplomatic tones. " It's all done with mirrors, and the knot in your guts, but thanks a lot for your personal, most timely assistance, how did you find a Catalina buoy at this time of night? "

He shook off the rude, amateurish remarks, before explaining most apologetically, that he had not been able to contact any of the French officials in the time available to him, he was most relieved to see the lights of the Catalina glide overhead then out to sea, even more relieved to see it approach the mooring that was a relic of the war, since then maintained by harbour authorities, only for use by governmental small boats. (or the occasional visit of a flying boat). Judging by the slime, the floating strop had been afloat for a very long time.

A few hours passed before I came to realize that without the Consul's help things might have ended differently, tragically even, Catalina dramas didn't all occur in the air!

At Du Pacifique, the crew in a drinking mood began practising their schoolboy French on the barmen. Words like 'garsonns', 'm'sewers' , 'cart veeno', lots of 'erns' and 'ders' floated around the bar. I stayed with them until the subject of the lack of assistance from the French air authorities came up and things began to turn shall we say, ugly, with the hotel staff. Half clothed I dropped on to the bed in my very small, hot room, with wooden shutters for a window that opened above the street. Sleep came before I hit the covers.

At our Fiji station more than a week later, we heard that Vila Star had limped into Port Vila several days after being sighted. The 'storp' had provided them with everything needed, even a battery that helped to bring their radio on line, for which they were most grateful.

The squadron's Catalinas underwent major overhaul at the Tasman Empire Airways flying-boat facility at Mechanics Bay, city-side in the Auckland Harbour. Months later I was assigned to deliver one of our metal birds there for heavy maintenance and return with another to Lauthala Bay. On a visit to the nearby Auckland wharves, lo and behold, there was our old friend Vila Star in all her glory, floating straight as a die alongside the wharf. We never did hear where the vessel was, or what she was doing during the seven or more days overdue, we'd been told that those who would know had been tight-lipped and un-co-operative when it came to the accounting.

That happened a long time ago. A total of 38 flying hours were spent on the search, the aircraft and crew seriously endangered, it would be nice to know what it was all about from someone who really knew.

'BLOODY TARAWA'

1952

Not all flights were filled with drama as of the Vila Star search. The one I liked most was to be assigned a Western Pacific High Commission excursion to Tarawa in the Gilbert & Ellice Islands, which are now known as Tuvalu and Kiribati. Each travel flight was announced well in advance, leaving time for proper and decent preparation. All the crews of 5 Squadron looked forward to a flight to the Gilberts and Tarawa particularly. To one of our pilots, Flight Lieutenant at the time Jack Wilson, Tarawa will always have a special meaning. After alighting and coming up to where his Cat would anchor for the two-day stay, Jack found himself without water brakes and any form of communication with the blister, due to a fault in the intercom system. Both drogues were required to be streamed and soon, to slow the aircraft. Unable to attract attention by blasts of the horn Jack opened the sliding hatch above him and stood in his seat. Looking aft along the hull he caught sight of the crewman in the port blister and gave him a hand signal that meant "Stream the drogues and pronto."

Alas, the closeness of the propellers above and behind him had temporarily been forgotten, there were horrible smacking sounds as a blade of the left prop took all the fingers of his left hand off, down to the knuckles, together with half his thumb and splattered them off into the water.

Jack had been shot down in an A20 Boston over Belgium in WW2 after a bombing raid on Lille surviving the crash landing. He had been incarcerated in a prison camp in Poland until war's end. Nothing would stop Jack and after the wartime crash landing to him the Catalina incident was child's play. After being bandaged by a medic on Tarawa and treated for shock, an extra day's rest was all that was needed before he was ready to undertake the return flight to Laucala Bay. Thereafter he was known as 'Knuckles' Jack and finished his Air Force career flying a desk as a Group Captain.

In November, 1943, Betio island, a strip of sand covered in palms on a triangular shaped coral reef, had earned the title 'Bloody Tarawa' for the horrific battle fought there when 15,000 United States Marines landed to re-take the atoll from the Japanese whose garrison of 4800 had constructed in-depth fortifications on the reef, bomb-proof bunkers and tunnels behind the beach, with 8 inch calibre artillery in support, British guns that had been captured in Singapore. Post-war, most military critics agree that with the increasing dominance of the Allies over air and sea, the landing should never have been undertaken, Tarawa could have been left to rot in isolation. But who knows the truth, hindsight being what it is?

The 2nd Division US Marine Corps had trained at Paekakariki, near Wellington New Zealand, for the assault, suffering heavy casualties in the bitter, short-lived battle. I had been in Wellington when the casualty lists went up on the notice board outside their headquarters, a hotel in Willis Street. Thousands of very young marines, 17-20 years of age, some well known to New Zealand families and friends, had been killed, thousands of others wounded. Some of the marines had married during their short stay in New Zealand, hundreds had met their sweethearts, promising to return when war was won to take them over to the 'land of the free'. Wellington was in a state of shock, the war having been drawn a lot closer. With the exception of seventeen wounded soldiers and a handful of Korean labourers the entire Japanese garrison had been wiped out, many of them by the newly introduced weapon of war the flame-thrower.

Post-war the Western Pacific High Commission had returned to the Gilberts to set up civil government on Bairiki, an island separated from Betio by less than a few hundred meters of shallow water that could be waded at low tide.

Our flights were arranged to provide medical assistance to the islands, or transfer personnel and/or equipment of the Commission. The carnage of war was very visible on parts of Betio where the battle took place, the palms not having been re-planted, the bunkers showing signs of the flame-throwers, cannon still lying askew in the sands as a result of the heavy US bombardment prior to the marine's landing. The airstrip built by the Japanese, now a waste of rubble and sand was pocked with shell and bomb craters. Fragments of human remains were still being unearthed from the sandy soil without too much digging to be done, if one felt that way inclined. The bones so unearthed it seemed were Japanese in origin. The US casualties left Betio in mortician ships to be buried in the huge US National Military Cemetery at Tuowaina (Hill of Sacrifice), Honolulu, known as the Punchbowl cemetery. Skeletons of landing craft and barbed wire pickets lay rusting along the reefs on the lagoon side, where the misguided US landings took place.

For me, no visit to the Gilberts was complete without further exploration of Betio and to the monument marking the spot where the westerners serving there in various civil government capacities at the time of the Japan occupation, were brutally slain. Before Pearl Harbour, with me a junior at high school, a more senior student had left to train in radio with the Navy and had been sent to Tarawa as wireless-operator and coast-watcher. He had been able to radio a warning that a Landing Force had been sighted approaching Betio, which was the last message ever received from the atoll. Mr John Dash, the school's highly respected School Principal, announced the uncertainty of his fate at a morning assembly some weeks later. Almost every boy 'joined up' with the school Army Cadets following the tragedy.

More than two years later, following the US victory, it was learned that he, along with six other civilians, had been executed by the sword of a Japanese officer, at the spot where the monument stands. Except for the First Lady's hanging pot-plants imported per our Catalina, flowers were very hard to find on Betio. In place of a wreath, I bowed my head and murmured a quiet prayer on each visit to the memorial. .

The First Lady, wife of the British Resident Commissioner, would hold a reception at The Residence on the evening of the Catalina's arrival that was always quite a formal affair, dress uniforms or black ties for the British, neatly pressed khaki drills with long trousers for the RNZAF commissioned aircrew. Those who had forgotten, or neglected to bring their long 'daks' along, simply stayed home in the quarters provided, with a kerosene refrigerator well stocked with beer so recently provided by the Catalina.

On arrival, one of the duties of the Captain was to submit the names of those attending the dinner, together with their decorations or awards if any, to the 'aide de camp', who wore the dress uniform of the colonial administration, shiny black shoes, white pith helmet topped with a spike, high-necked red jacket with shiny brass buttons and belt buckles, black trousers with a red stripe. The ADC took his job most seriously, it was as if he had just stepped out of, or was about to step into, a Gilbert & Sullivan play. The sight of him so dressed under a hot sun on a Pacific atoll was incongruous, causing some merriment amongst the Catalina's crew, out of earshot that is.

The Residence, the Buckingham Palace of the Gilberts, a masterpiece of a grass house with a high gabled roof, had to be seen to be believed. So magnificent, The Residence had been built by the Gilbertese as a work of art, a thank-you for the return of the British 'to rule over us'. The Residence was entered only after having first signed the Visitor's Book on a small table in the porch.

Slowly and to the stirring sounds of a bugle, the Union Jack was lowered from the flagpole at the front of The Residence. The guests, including the women in their elegant evening gowns, all stood to attention in the still, warm air of a setting sun during the ceremony, which was somehow very moving. Drinks were then served under a large, open-sided, grass garden house on the sand that stood for a lawn, accompanied by the rumble and grumble of the surf breaking on to the seaward reef no more than 200 meters away 'on the other side of the island' and with everyone 'putting on the dog' in aristocratic British tones.

Life at Tarawa was in the balance when it came to a three-metre high tidal wave, or a blue-black coloured waterspout that the Pacific is noted for. Can you imagine the scene, the highest point of land on Bairiki being not more than a meter and a half above sea level, the colourful dress of the governors on an island where most of the locals wore only 'holey' shorts or grass skirts? The island's sandy soil grew little except Pacific palms.

From Suva, when space was available in the Catalina, we brought with us rich, black garden soil in small drums, for the First Lady's hanging pot plants.

Even in such an out of way place the British did things with the pomp, ceremony, and a dignity befitting Buckingham Palace. The stalks of the tall palms replaced fences or hedges to divide one property from another. To the islanders watching from a distance, who'd not seen any other part of the world, I always thought that the gathering of decked out Caucasians, chatting, laughing, jesting or clinking their glasses together, might be taken as some sort of a military or religious ceremony and must have appeared quite comical.

The dining table scene could have been taken from Singapore's Raffles or London's Claridges, with the starched, damask tablecloths and 'nanner dipkins', Harrod's silverware, crystal glassware and table service to match. How the First Lady at Tarawa managed to serve those delicious culinary delights, or how the staff of 'The Residence' had been trained to European perfection, I'll never know. The dining table was a place where colonial boys needed to watch their manners to prove they were not 'dragged up'.

Fish was always on the menu, 'poisson cru' or disguised in a dozen other ways. On a sand-spit, 1500 miles out into the Pacific we marvelled at the class and refinement shown by the British 'raj', in keeping up appearances always to their Gilbertese subjects.

On the morning of departure, I would take the Catalina out over the lagoon in a wide swing to position for a low buzz of Betio and Bairiki, before beginning the 12-hour haul over the equator on return to Suva, on course only after sighting the tragic monument in the palm trees, the First Lady in a short sleeved cotton frock and Commissioner in his white shirt and tie, waving from the sand at the front of their grass castle.

"Farewell not so bloody Tarawa", were my thoughts on my final flight from there. " You're in good hands again."

BACKWARDS INTO THE FUTURE

A night trip from Lautoka, on the western side of Viti Levu Island, Fiji, to Auckland New Zealand with a patient who was restricted to 1500 feet altitude, which necessitated a flight through two bad weather zones, brought me to the end of my Fiji posting. Had it not been for the radar operating perfectly and the skill of the airborne operator, the last sector of the flight, in rain and inky blackness between or around numerous off shore islands, might well have ended in disaster.

My tour at Laucala Bay with 5 Squadron ended with a posting to No 6 Squadron at Hobsonville, for Sunderland ferry duties. The 'Hobby' flying-boat base was situated in the upper reaches of the Auckland harbour. The big four-engine Sunderland flying boats built during the war were being acquired by the RNZAF to replace their Catalinas. Refurbished at Short Brothers & Harland's factory at Belfast, Northern Ireland the big boats would be flown to Fiji by RNZAF crews, a scheme that was scheduled to begin after my taking two weeks leave in New Zealand followed by an uncertain period of type briefing training with 6 Squadron at Hobsonville. Rumours of the Squadron re-equipping with the big 'flying porcupines', the name given them by Goering's Luftwaffe, had been circulating for some time, now they were true, soon I would be on my way to the Emerald Isle.

The prospect of visiting Ireland and the flying of the Sunderland was quite thrilling. My grandfather John had come from Londonderry to Australia in 1865 (fare paying not transported), thence on to farm in New Zealand about the time the Maori Wars were winding up in Taranaki. My hopes at the time were that during the training phase on the Sunderland at Belfast, there would be opportunity enough to contact those distant relatives that little was known about, also a visit to pay my respects at my great-grandparent's gravesite and the farm 'Edenbann' near Garvagh in County Derry.

There comes a time in everyone's life, when a major decision has to be made, a decision that if made wrongly might change the course of one's life. Mine came to me about that time. At first we must unlearn before we can relearn. We never know what any major decision we make might lead us to.

My posting to the Sunderland ferry unit had been premature, there was really no need for me to have left the squadron in Fiji at that time, the Sunderlands' date of delivery to the RNZAF had been deferred by several months. During the first week of my leave I was recalled to Hobsonville and seconded to Tasman Empire Airways Limited (TEAL) if I agreed. My training on the Mark IV Solent flying-boat would not only be beneficial to TEAL during a pilot shortage crisis with new rules about pilot duty times about to be enforced, but as well would serve me in good stead later for command of the Air Force Sunderland. How could I refuse such an opportunity?

Four only Solent Mark IV's had been built and TEAL, one of the last big flying boat operators in the world, had acquired all four. They were a superlative 'boat' for the period, with power and accommodations to match the competition in the post-war years, but fell short in not being pressurized. Flights with passengers were restricted to below 10,000 feet altitude, where turbulent clouds abounded, particularly over the Tasman Sea, that were upsetting to passengers and crew alike. In competition, the new Douglas and Lockheed airliners then being designed were pressurized, allowing smoother, faster flights above the weather at or above 20,000 feet.

After initial training as a Second Officer on the Solent with TEAL, I was assigned to the 'Coral Route', Auckland, Suva, Western Samoa, Cook Islands, Tahiti and return, while occasionally doing a day or night run across the Tasman Sea between Auckland, Sydney and Wellington.

Following the experience with military rigged Catalinas, the Solent to me was the epitome of airborne luxury. On stepping out on to the pontoon at Lauthala Bay, Suva, my old stomping ground, after a 6 hour trip from Auckland, my uniform looked as if it had just been returned from the dry-cleaners.

Except for Tahiti, the 'Coral Route' was familiar to me but the change from military to civil scheduled passenger flying, was more difficult than expected, mostly from the psychological perspective in flying second row back from the controls and the Captain on one occasion pointing out that my shoes, with a smooth toe instead of a cap, did not meet with TEAL's strict summer dress regulations! I loved the shoes that had cost me more than a week's salary and was more than a little put out.

Gone too were the Air Force days with all the crew at about the same level of experience, still learning from one another, where the camaraderie of the Service continued on station or in the respective messes long after the 'boat' had reached the mooring or been tugged up the slipway. An Air Force 'General Duties' officer also had station duties in abundance to perform, Duty Officer, parades and other such likes, which did not include any flying.

The senior pilots of TEAL were mostly of pre-war Imperial Airways, or wartime RAF or RNZAF origins, the flight deck the equivalent of the bridge of HM Battleship with a distinct feeling of superior class between captain and 'the rest'. I soon learned though, that being experts in the art of pressure pattern flying, what they didn't know about the navigating of heavy class flying boats wasn't worth knowing. In addition to the pilots, the Solent was crewed by a Navigator, Radio Officer, Flight Engineer plus a Purser cum Steward and a Hostess, that is today a 'politically incorrect' term for a female cabin attendant, hostesses evidently having been relegated to being rather naughty girls who 'worked' in dance-halls or night-clubs.

The 'Coral Service' departed Auckland on Sundays and returned the following Saturday after spending two nights each at Papeete, Apia and Suva. The airline was clinical in all ways and ran like well-oiled clockwork. On returning to Mechanics Bay the crew all went their own way and weren't seen by each other again, sometimes for weeks, depending on how the service rosters went. For only a short time, the trip through the islands brought crew members closer together, the 'Coral Route' with the Solents was the only regular air service operating to Tahiti for a number of years.

Having just returned from Fiji, with no time allotted for settling in locally with my wife and family of two, accommodation within a reasonable distance from the base and at a reasonable price was hard to find. There was a lot of study to be done for a license type rating, new International Civil Aviation Organisation regulations had arrived with revised up-to-date civil flying practices to contend with. The only thing that kept me focused at that difficult time was the possibility of a recall from the Air Force Reserve to the Sunderland Ferry Unit, that would eventually mean a posting to Laucala Bay and 5 Squadron again, only then would I be in my real comfort zone.

During that period many overnight stays were made at Suva. During one of those, Fred Ladd the senior pilot of the foundling airline Fiji Airways, approached me at the Grand Pacific Hotel, with the offer of an appointment. Fred was a well-known personality, an icon you might say, ex-RNZAF Grumman TBF (torpedo – bomber- fighter) pilot in the Pacific theatre, who since war's end had flown Rapides for NZ National Airways Corporation in the south of the South Island of New Zealand. There Fred had gained quite a reputation for a type of youthful exuberance, friendly frolicking, with his 'Dominie' aircraft (DH89) that led to everlasting hero worship from those who had never before witnessed the National Airways Corporation 'calling in for breakfast' after landing in a paddock at a hill-country sheep station.

Coupled with his piloting skills, Fred was also a public relations man who exuded a personality ahead of it's time, jovial, convivial, with a smile or a humorous quip or rhyme for anyone he met, 'hello Bryan how's the flyin' or 'good morning stop yawning' sort of stuff, it was hard for him to be serious about anything except his own image, even flying, and it was thought, just the man to kick-start a small new airline in the Fiji Islands. A fitness fanatic, Fred always went up stairs or steps two at a time to prove his fitness, regardless of where or what he was at, or who might be watching or accompanying him. He could walk for quite some distance on his hands too and was reported as having entered the Grand Pacific's lobby in that manner on some important social occasion.

He was a good deal older than the average WW2 veteran pilot, having somehow wangled his way into the wartime Air Force when approaching thirty years of age. He was an accomplished swimmer and diving from high river bridges was another of his larks. Fred had many loyal followers. It could be said that he was the life-blood of the fledgling airline.

Owned by the famous Harold Gatty, navigator of round the world 'Post and Gatty' fame in the Lockheed Vega 'Winnie Mae', Fiji Airways had been granted license to operate domestic air services within the Fiji group. Fiji Air was in the process of taking over the New Zealand National Airways Corporation's 'Sunderingham' services (a cross bred Sunderland and Sandringham), and extending it's network to other major centres on the northern islands of the group, where sites for airstrips were then being surveyed for the ubiquitous De Havilland Rapide aircraft, that would be operated. When Fred first spoke to me, those flying boat services were in process of being withdrawn.

My interest was aroused when he intimated that in the future, Harold Gatty intended to re-introduce flying-boat services to adjoining island groups that were as yet without air communications of any sort. The whole idea appealed to me, the pioneering, the independence that went with it, but not to Betty my wife, a woman's intuition I suppose.

Between us we tossed the idea around for some months before accepting. That meant a transfer to the RNZAF Reserve of Officers, which would require Sunderland conversion and refresher training at Laucala Bay by me, for three weeks each year, for four years unless recalled to permanent service in the meantime. That was a pleasant surprise, ties with the Air Force weren't completely severed, but it was soon obvious that a major decision had been made that would affect the remainder of my life.

Fiji Airways had started from scratch with two de Havilland Rapides (DH89A) imported from Britain, to operate from a PSP (Pierced Steel Planking) or Marston matting runway, in the sugar cane-fields on the Rewa river delta at Nausori, 13 miles from Suva. The International airport at Nandi, on the western side of the island, up to that time had been accessed from Suva only by a twisting, turning gravel road, about a five-hour fairly rough ride in a motor vehicle. An air service was certainly needed. Nausori's steel matting was covered in six inches of the muck of floodwater from the Rewa after any of the teeming rains the east side of the island often experienced. Since the end of hostilities drainage ditches blocked with silt and rotting cane fronds had not been attended to. A small servicing hangar adjoined the barracks hut, a leftover of WW2 that served as a passenger terminal and airport offices.

The period spent flying the Rapide and later the de Havilland Australia Drover for Fiji Airways, was another part of my life I shall never forget. On my arrival the only services operating were across Viti Levu the largest island in the group, between Suva (Nausori) on the east, the international airport at Nandi on the west and Lautoka (Drasa) the CSR's 'sugar mill town' on the west side. The west of the island was referred to as the 'dry side' and the east as the 'wet side' because of their startling differences in rainfall, the on-going effect of the southeast 'trade winds' that prevailed throughout the 'hundred island' group.

A new airfield at Lambasa on Vanua Levu, the second largest island of the group north of Viti Levu, had replaced the flying boat service of NZNAC.

Prior to Fiji Air's arrival, departing or arriving international passengers had been faced with the long dusty drive on the gravel coastal road on the south coast of Viti Levu or.for those travelling from or to Lambasa, a day-night journey by sea around the tip of Vanua Levu. With Hunt's Travel in support as booking agents, although running on a shoestring, Fred had all services humming, morning and afternoon flights to Nandi, a daily to Lambasa with always room for a late 'special' if required as was the norm. All services were well patronized, particularly by the Indian residents of the northern islands who were good businessmen but not good sailors. I had not been told that I would replace an ex-New Guinea, Australian pilot, who was close to a nervous breakdown, which set me thinking, I couldn't feel good about that. The weather, the pressure of keeping to the tight schedules, the state of the runway at Nausori, the shoddy maintenance carried out on the aircraft, the long days spent without radio over restless seas specked with wild rain-storms, an ever increasing number of flying hours, but mainly the low pay, the cost of living and the difficulty in finding decent accommodation for his wife and son had turned him into a mental wreck, he wanted out. Too fond of the bottle was how it was told to me, an explanation I never accepted. On the few occasions I flew with him before he departed, his flying was of the very highest standard.

I was learning and found out later, that Fred never chose to employ a pilot with more flying experience in total flying hours than his own, the ex New Guinea man with thousands of hours was doomed from the start.

Since the inauguration of Fiji Air, several pilots had been hired but soon resigned I discovered, the job (pay) not being up to their expectations in providing their families with three meals a day and a roof over their head. In the earliest days with Fiji Air, many of the finer points of employment, (such as asking a question or two before signing up) went over my head too so taken up with the 'glamour' of being a civil aviator in an international community as I was.

Two weeks after arrival, route familiarization and license endorsements were completed, I was keen and ready to face the tropical elements alone in a single pilot, twin-engine bi-plane, authorized to carry seven passengers, but without any radio or navigation aids.

The Rapide was lovely to fly, I loved every minute, but through it being short on power with two Gypsy Queen normally aspirated engines, was virtually a single engine machine. Lose power in one engine while fully laden and you're on the way down! Fortunately, the engines were very reliable.

Fred put out the flying rosters, mostly sharing all scheduled hours between us. The roster meant that we would each spend two nights of each week on an overnight at Nandi airport. In the days before expense accounts, naïve as I was, the accommodation and mealing expenses at the Mocambo Hotel were my personal responsibility not Fiji Air's, which put a further strain on my small income. That was about the time when a proper contract was called for from Mr Gatty as to salaries and refundable expenses. Fred had a private income from a New Zealand source. There was a lot of learning in that for me, how wrong choices lead to regret but it's never too late to make a right choice.

Thereafter, flight hours of between 100-120 hours per pilot per month were flown, counted from wheels off to wheels on, not chock to chock. Fiji Air saved both engine and airframe servicing and pilot hours by that method. Being new to civil aviation the method of logging flight times was accepted without question. The only night facilities were at Nandi and the Rapide was not equipped for instrument flying in any case. The hours flown and the small number of pilots on strength meant that there were few days off for pilots.

I found it rather galling to fly the Rapide over the Laucala Bay flying boat base sometimes twice a day to see the mighty Sunderlands tethered or moving about on the water and realize what a great chance had been missed, that amounted to impatience on my part for not waiting for the ferrying from Belfast to commence. I knew then that a big mistake had been made that I would have to be content with. For three weeks a year only, would I spend with the big metal 'water birds' and not fifty-two as desired. My bed had been made ready, I then had to lie on it.

In the wet, tropical, humid climate, the woodwork and fabric of the Rapides began to deteriorate. The engineers were constantly making major replacements of the Canadian spruce that had been used in construction and then had to be ordered in quantity and sea-freighted to Fiji via the UK.

All seasons around Nausori were wet ones. In the official 'wetter yet season', Nausori airport more resembled a wetlands lake, on landing or take-off, muddy water flew into all those parts of the machine covered by cowlings, spats or laced up fabric, including the wing spars, where it could do most damage in the high-humidity climate, by rotting the fabric and soaking the wood. I used to joke that flying-boat experience should be an essential requirement for pilot recruits, where the joy of water flying could be experienced in a Rapide's 'splashdown' on a water-logged runway.

When parked the Rapide was quite tail down and water that had entered the cockpit during flight, drained out via the floorboards to the tail section to leave a large puddle underneath adjacent to the boarding steps, that could be seen by the passengers when it dripped out on to a dry, sun-burnt tarmac such as at Nandi airport. To the experienced world traveller, transferring from a Boeing Stratocruiser to a prehistoric fabric covered biplane, the puddle was often mistaken for a fuel leak. Invariably an explanation of the phenomenon was requested, accompanied by much finger dipping into the puddle and sniffing of fingers! Once airborne and away though, the passengers all seemed to enjoy the flight in a Rapide, particularly when able to view the reef on the south coast at such close quarters. Fred insisted that all flights with passengers must fly at 1000 feet altitude via the reef on the south coast.

With an aircraft grounded for repairs of any kind, the other flew all services, the engineers (sometimes singular) might be grumpy at having to work overtime to 'keep 'em flying', engines flew over their due overhaul time while awaiting spares. In the weather preceding a 'big blow' pilots sometimes flew all day soaked to the skin by the rain that drove into the fragile glasshouse of a cockpit.

One 'boffin' of an engineer modified the pitot (airspeed) system with an extra long tube poking out about four feet from the nose. Sir Geoffrey's famous Rapide looked more like the up and coming de Havilland Comet! At taxi-ing speed the indicator could read over 50 miles per hour, at cruising settings, between zero and 20 miles per hour, one was never sure of the accuracy of the instrument! Who needs an airspeed indicator in a Rapide anyway? The modification was declared to be a failure. Having left his mark, the 'boffin' voyaged off to join the public service on the aviation side 'somewhere in Africa'. There were some real characters about the aviation scene in those days.

The wet weather at Nausori also played havoc with the engines' ignition system, causing rough running, pops and bangs. Magnetos or plugs sometimes needing cleaning or some other adjustment between flights, in view of nervous travellers set on seeing the engines' innards.

To improve the Rapides' performance, the newer acquisitions from Britain came fitted with de Havilland electric variable pitch propellers. The wind-driven generator as on the Rapide however, could not cope with such modern technology, in not being able to keep the battery sufficiently charged after the starters had been used frequently or the new-fangled radios draining the battery throughout a solid flying day. Both Fred and I had experienced propellers that were reluctant to change pitch at that most critical time after taking off, caused by a flat battery. Both props had stayed FINE, with the pilot not feeling at all fine with engines over-speeding and thoughts of a prop flying off. We recommended that the props be changed back to fixed-pitch, the difference in performance being scarcely noticeable. The recommendations made were accepted and dealt with by Mr Gatty, everything was fine, (in the sense of well-being, not the blade angle of those props).

Fred had an amazing escape when he crashed in a Rapide at Lambasa. Immediately after take-off the left engine gave a severe vibration, the spinner on that propeller somehow came off hitting the cabin just behind him, narrowly missing but severely scaring the six passengers.

Fred thought he'd been hit with a missile from Japan's 'Dead-eye Dick's' famous gun at Rabaul, that he'd had a tangle or two with during WW2. He picked out a cane-field in fallow straight ahead and attempted to land. After only a very short bumpy run, across the furrows unfortunately, both wheels ran into a drainage ditch simultaneously, the Rapide flipped on to its back and burst into flames. Somehow, he never knew how, although inverted in the cockpit he was able to extricate himself and with the help of one of his passengers pulled the others out through the door at the rear. Many times since I've tried to imagine that scene, the Rapide on its back with petrol induced flames licking at the highly inflammable fabric, the passengers suspended by their seat-belts upside down, the only door, now where would that be? It was a miracle to me just how anybody escaped. Ten minutes later, there was little left of the aircraft except the burnt out engines and a tangled mass of tubular frames. An old Fijian man on his first air trip to Savu Savu and who had been told on boarding that his would be a very short trip, was unperturbed by all the excitement and while still suspended inverted in his chair called to Fred.

"Are we at Savu Savu now turanga?(chief)."

The old man thought that he'd arrived for a warm welcome at Savu Savu! The rumour that went around, that Fred had walked away from the fire on his hands was not true!

The first radio message received of the crash from Jaganath the airfield attendant at his vantage point on the airfield, had given little hope for any survivors. I arrived on the scene less than an hour later, to find the passengers all in the pink of condition, thanks to Fred's excellent post trauma handling and his irrepressible good humor. All were soon bundled into my aircraft to continue with their flight to Suva via Savu Savu. To the best of my knowledge no official inquiry was ever held into the accident.

Harold wasn't seen a lot during that time, often being away from Suva on more important business. Fiji Air was in trouble until the third Rapide that had been ordered, arrived only just in time to avoid a complete shut-down of services

Out of the blue one day, Fred announced that Harold had not been wasting his time as was supposed, but had bought three de Havilland Australia Drovers from Qantas in New Guinea. Two would arrive in crates within a month, assembly and testing would have a priority to occupy as short a time as possible. At last we were equipping with a metal bird more suited to the climate, pilots and ground crew alike sparked up, rejoiced might be a better word, to meet the challenge.

Two additional pilots were hired to meet the expected expansion of Fiji Airways. Don Williams and Morrie Morrissey were both ex-RNZAF fighter boys with good records in and about the Solomon's air battles during WW2. Don, who had exited his wounded Kittyhawk by parachute over Segi, New Georgia, would arrive first, followed by the F4U Corsair man Morrie later.

The Drover was an immediate success with both passenger and pilot, the three Gypsy Major engines producing more power overall than the two Gypsy Queens of the Rapide, which meant for the tri-motor type, a positive performance with a failed engine. Sadly though, the

Drover came with a doubtful history in New Guinea, with three crashes reported, two of which were attributed to the shedding of a propeller blade during flight, the other to extremely poor weather while attempting to land at a coastal airport where it was thought the machine had accidentally been driven into the sea.

The general opinion in New Guinea had been that the Drover was unsuited to airline highland operations. The electric variable pitch propellers, similar to the ones that were used briefly on the Rapide, had been replaced with fixed pitch, the reduced performance judged not to be a problem for Fiji where there were no highlands operations to contend with. Fiji Air's routes in the main were over water, the airfields close to sea level. The tri-motor Drover was good-looking with much more passenger appeal too, a delight to fly and performed well in the lower atmosphere.

The descriptions written here of some of the weather in Fiji is not meant to be all-inclusive, there were many glorious days of rich, sunny weather, when flying 'crost ocean and reef'' was a pure delight for the pilot, when his tubular steel, fabric covered but otherwise metal bird was navigated scenically for the enjoyment of the passengers.

In spite of the mainly well-concealed internal problems, Fiji Air was growing rapidly, each day becoming more popular. The booking agents, Iris and Harvey of Hunt's Travel, were doing a fine job with their tour business taking on a new look. The engineering branch was stocking up with personnel more familiar with metal birds. Working with wood, fabric and glue, was fast becoming a dying art attracting with some difficulty, only the semi-retired older man for a last fling at his trade. The turn around time of a Rapide after undergoing a major overhaul was days if not weeks longer than that of a Drover on similar major maintenance.

The 'new' Fiji Airways soon turned me into a workaholic with a pick up in the dark of early morning, returning to Suva on the last service bus each night between 6.30 - 7pm, again in the dark, several days a week, there were times when for days on end my wife and two young children were rarely seen in daylight, the expected married bliss in tropical Fiji as a civil pilot, just wasn't happening.

Month after month Fred and I flew very long hours until the new pilots were checked to the line. Once away from Nausori on a trip via the regional airfields in use, we became public relations chiefs, booking agent, mechanic, radio technician, purser, refueler and counsellor, the days were long and tiring, often filled with some kind of a drama.

We had rented a house, a very old house, on a point of the harbour north of the city. Without a car, Betty had to cadge a ride with neighbours or take a local bus, a converted truck, around the harbour to shop at BP's, Carpenters or Morris Hedstrom's stores, leaving our two children in the care of a Fijian 'marama' maid-servant. Having bought a kerosene 'fridge' for eighty pounds from the proceeds of my Air Force gratuity, we lived from hand to mouth for weeks while playing 'catch up' with the finances but never quite succeeding.

On landing back at Nausori one afternoon with still another flight to do before dark, the airport office manager Ellen Scott arrived at the aircraft to inform me that an earthquake and tidal wave had struck at Suva, lines were down, communications with the city had been lost. Altogether the situation sounded rather grim. The afternoon flight to Nandi had been cancelled through Suva's anticipated isolation for hours, or maybe days. Ellen had a bus standing by to take me into Suva plus anyone else who needed to go, warning us that we might have to walk part of the way if the road into town was closed to traffic either through damage or congested with the city's multi racial population fleeing the harbour area.

As we boarded the bus I asked the driver Muna Ali, to put his foot down, a habit of his that usually needed little encouragement. Muna lived at Nausori, he showed some reluctance to start out for Suva under the circumstances and needed coaxing until assured he could return home as soon as we were delivered to the depot in the city centre.

Ellen had been right, we all had to leave the bus where the road had cracked open a foot or two wide, on the harbour side of Tamavua. Naturally enough Muna refused to go an inch further. Police on the scene reported that it would be hours before repairs to the road would allow traffic to pass.

From there I walked or trotted down the remainder of the hill then along the harbour-side road, all the time taking in the large cracks in the roads, footpaths and the more open unimproved areas. The 'quake had certainly changed the face of Suva. An ominous silence seemed to hang over the normally busy wharf area. Nearer to the harbour, moderately sized fish wriggled their last wriggle, high and dry across the road, 100 meters inland from the then placid water. Debris from an upturned sea was strewn everywhere, the wave had struck at low tide, bringing with it long forgotten ancient litter from the seabed outside the reef.

Follow up tremors were still being felt, panicky people of all makes and sizes, races and religions, were making for the heights above the town, concern for my family grew, as wet with sweat I sloshed on, my shoes filled with dirty sea-water, my trousers spattered with wet sand and mud. With each step I took, I became more convinced that our rented home so close to the harbour, would have been swept away. Dreaded thoughts clouded my brain when the last bridge before home was seen to be pushed upstream of the creek as if by a giant hand, leaving more than a meter of space between road and bridge on each bank, its railings draped with seaweed and other muck. Somehow, by using the same railing I managed to clamber across. Blessed relief, from there I could see the house, standing on the knoll exactly as when last seen that morning. Breathless from running I arrived at the front gate calling loudly.

"Hello, it's me, are you alright in there, is everything alright? "

With no response coming to my repeated calls, I charged up the rickety steps two at a time to find the door open, swinging on its hinges. From there lots of litter could be seen scattered around the rear of the house, parts of the grass that stood for a lawn were flattened. My stomach felt as if it was in a knot, anguish, remorse and concern clouded my mind. What kind of a mess had I then got my family into, living in such a dump of a house I asked myself?

The scene inside wasn't good, with the family nowhere in sight, crockery strewn on the floor, glassware too, what little furniture we possessed had moved about, the 'fridge had slithered along the wall from its usual place. Somehow our 'much-loved' white goods possession had stayed the right way up in the 'big shake', had it been tilted in any way the raw flame might have ignited the kerosene to cause a fire.

It was then that I could see that the grass on the flat area at the back of the house nearest the sea, had been flattened by the swirl of water, first one way then the other it, leaving litter in its wake. Coupled with the level of the knoll above the water, the house, having been mounted on piles more than a meter high above the ground, had not felt the full force of the wave and was unharmed although anyone near or underneath at the time, would have been in danger of being swept away, especially a toddler or a baby or both having a romp on a blanket on the grass, as was sometimes the case at our place. My heart pounded even more.

There was no sign of any of my family or the marama and in a panic I clambered down the littered face of the knoll to begin a search, out to where the sea was than lapping quietly on an incoming tide. Near the water's edge were several lumps in the sand that caused my heart to flutter, but a closer look told me that sand-packed litter had built up over the protrusions of coral rocks in the sand. That was the most harrowing time, for all the while my loud hailing was echoing along the deserted beachfront without result as if I was the only person left on earth. People were obviously keeping well away from harbour-side.

Soon the owner of my house who lived in a fairly new home on the adjoining property at a level closer to the sea, heard my loud calling and yelled out that she thought my family were safe and well, at a home further along on the high side of the road. The relief was enormous, my knees almost buckled. As often happened I had feared the worst.

My landlord's new house had not fared at all well, being lower and closer to the sea, the wave had caused severe damage so the place would need extensive repair and could not be lived in. I thought then that she rather regretted building the new house and putting her old home up for rent.

Betty with Kathryn (3) and Dianne (1) somehow learned of my arrival and returned soon after. The two girls I'm sure didn't realize the danger that they'd been in, to this day both have no recollection of the incident.

From the back-yard with both girls close at hand, Betty had been quick to see the huge wave smashing on to the outer reef, roughly a mile away across the harbour and with the help of the 'marama', had gathered the girls up and fled, just as the tidal surge crossed the harbour and crashed around the knoll, in all a terrifying experience. The low tide at the time of the tectonic 'quake, had undoubtedly saved Suva's harbour side from a major calamity, and my family too.

Betty was still in a state of shock that was highly magnified when she saw the kitchen, the girl's bedroom with its twisted floorboards and our bedroom with now a mobile dressing table and oddments of clothing strewn about the floors.

The city, harbour lights and all, was blacked out that night with a power shutdown. The house cleaning up was done by candlelight. We thanked God for our deliverance, and the designers of the kerosene 'fridge too, which apart from a tiny dent or two was again operating at full chill, able to scoff at the power outage.

A week or so later the landlady indicated that she would be moving back into her old home while the new was repaired, we would be moving again, a place well away from the sea would be the best and only choice for us we both agreed. A number of deaths were reported from the tidal wave, mostly Fijian fishermen in small canoes on or outside the reef. Marine officials all agreed that the very low tide at the time had saved Suva from becoming a second Atlantis!

Following the 'quake, things in Fiji Air went from one crisis to another. A call on a day off one Saturday had me scampering for the airport clad in 'bula' shirt and shorts, with my foot hard down on the accelerator of our recently acquired Austin A30, at a recklessness and speed matching that of our Indian driver who drove the crew to work at the airport in Harold's car. The pilots all agreed that the regular, early morning dash to work by road was the most dangerous part of the day!

Aeradio had received a Mayday call from Fred about fifteen minutes before he was due to land at Nausori from Lambasa. He reported that all three engines had failed on the Drover. He was ditching in the Koro Sea with seven passengers aboard, somewhere near Levuka on Ovalau Island, about 60 kilometres north-east of Nausori.

At Nausori airport, the engineers had a Rapide ready and waiting. Rescue stores were aboard and both engines were ticking over. Two volunteers stood by to act as 'chuckers out'. They were given a quick briefing on how to hold the door open against the slipstream, whilst pushing each package down and out, without the drop man following them! If after Fred's 'plane was found, an air drop was required the aircraft would need to be flown at low speed to make the 'cracking' of the door easier. The Rapide simply wasn't built for delivering goods from the air, but that was all we had, improvisation became the order of the day.

By that time almost an hour had elapsed since Fred's distress call had been received. With a sideways shuffle between the seats along the aisle I scrambled into the 'one pilot only' cockpit, buckled the seatbelt and waved the chocks away. In less than a minute the Rapide was airborne over the acres of brilliant green sugarcane, leaning into a turn towards Ovalau, on a cruise-climb to five hundred feet. The weather was perfect with a light southeast wind and only a trace of fair weather clouds on the horizon.

With the taps wide open and assistance from the wind, the Rapide seemed to sense the urgency of our rescue mission, probably flying faster than ever before in all of it's more than 25 years, while I began to retrace the reciprocal of Fred's estimated track into Nausori. In only a few minutes we were crossing the coast near Bau Island, sacred home of the Fijian chieftains and heading out over the open sea, with Ovalau Island already in sight close on the horizon.

Six or seven minutes passed when from the surface of the sea, a brief flash of light directly ahead caught my eye, that might have been the reflection from a mirror, or the sun glinting on metal. I was sure that it was the Drover, remarkably, by the way it looked from a distance, it was still afloat?

My two observers were warned to get ready, one at the door, prepared to jettison the packages down through the gap left with the door cracked open, the other midway down the cabin to relay signals to the dropper and generally assist him without getting too close to each other. Two persons at the rear of the cabin with the forward seats unoccupied could leave me with a 'tail heavy' out of balance situation.

Closer in I was able to see a small boat near to the Drover, but not until the Rapide was overhead the site was the coral head seen on which the 'Pride of Fiji Air' stood. Fred had pulled off an emergency landing on an isolated 'bombora' half the size of a football field! The reef looked to be rough and crusty around the edges, the Drover right way up in flying attitude as if it had been carefully placed there as a monument of some kind, with the sea already lapping over wings and engines. As seen from above the Drover appeared to be intact in every way after having undergone a miraculous forced-landing cum ditching or whatever else it might be called. The small boat was crowded, Fred's whites, safari jacket and long trousers, stood out from the khaki shorts and shirts of the others on the boat. The water glistening like diamonds on his jacket told me that he'd had a ducking.

I leaned the Rapide into a tight turn over the rather dismal scene. Fred waved both arms, a signal that conveyed to me all on board were well and accounted for. The boat began to move from the reef across the open water towards Levuka about 15 kilometres away. A closer inspection on the next run, indicated that no-one had been killed or seriously injured for all the occupants were on their feet waving, as if on a holiday excursion.

Beckoning my two observers to move themselves forward again, I passed the details to Nausori on the radio as I turned on to a homeward bound course, while reflecting on the plight of our precious Drover. Who would know, the incoming tide might be enough to float her off the reef into deeper water to be lost forever? Immersion in salt water alone would spell the end of her flying days even if she was salvaged was my assumption, while on return, Fred would have some explaining to do. A simultaneous three-engine failure, if that's what it was, could only be attributed to a lack of fuel, contaminated fuel, a major fuel blockage or mismanagement of the fuel system. We would only know when we heard more details from the pilot. The forecast for Fiji Air that day was " Some difficult days are on the horizon."

The next full tide completely submerged the aircraft while it clung to the reef. After being recovered and returned by barge to Nausori by way of the Rewa River delta, it never flew again, nor were any spare parts available for use on any other machine due to them being immersed in salt water for so long, in short that Drover was a complete loss.

Naturally Fred was mortified, since being in Fiji he had become a national icon, extremely popular with all races and classes. An investigation of a sorts and his own admission, brought about the conclusion that he had somehow mishandled the fuel system. Harold called for his resignation and Fred complied shortly afterwards. It fell upon me to fly him and his wife Mabel to Savu Savu, Lambasa and Taveuni, airports both he and I had put on the map with air service, and where at each place he was accorded a dignified though sometimes tearful farewell from his many supporters and friends. There was a feeling in the air that Fiji Airways would never be the same again, which turned out to be true.

It would also be true to say that Fred, or Freddie as he was better known, had been the life and breath of Fiji Airways since it's inception. It wasn't long before he was reported as having started up a very successful seaplane charter business out of Mechanic's Bay, Auckland using Grumman Widgeon amphibians, where again he was quickly becoming a living legend amongst the off-shore islands of Auckland.

Those who were left had to get on with the job, less one aircraft, for several months, until a replacement machine arrived. The maintenance men too had to revise their schedules. The high number of hours being flown with three aircraft instead of four meant that certain inspections came around more frequently. Night maintenance was introduced, that wasn't at all popular with the engineering branch as the open-sided hangar at night was subjected to a plague of vicious mosquitoes.

For reasons best known to himself, Harold appointed me to the position of Chief Pilot, supposedly with an eye to the future because of the experience with multi-engine flying-boats that I would bring with me to Fiji Airways. I was at least ten years younger than Fred and the youngest pilot then on strength. The older, war-experienced pilots but with single engine time only before joining the company, began to see me as the 'fly in the ointment' who might have been the reason for them being by-passed by Harold for the promotion. Not long after, the pilots became even more discontented, not only with the salary structure, but also by having a young boss, who in their opinion was somewhat immature, which probably was true.

When discussing with Harold what might be the result of Fred's 'prang' in the Drover as regards bad publicity, he told me that his feeling was: 'There is no such thing as bad publicity, at this stage of our development any publicity at all is good publicity, it doesn't matter

what they say about you so long as they pronounce your name correctly and spell it correctly.'

Harold was proved right in that anyway, for the bookings on all
routes increased dramatically after Fred's miraculous 'ditch landing'
made the front page of the 'Fiji Times' in very descriptive terms.

The Chief Pilot position didn't carry with it an increase in salary,
or an appropriate office. My first task in that capacity was to write an
Operations Manual using the office at Harold's residence at Tamavua,
assisted by his secretary-typist when she was available. Harold's varied business interests took up most of her office time and left little
time for her to work on the manual with me.

Since starting up, Fiji Airways had not used any form of a manual,
the bible of any respectable airline, which was mandatory under the
Colonial Air Navigation Orders. With Fred then gone from the scene
and my flying of the air routes most days from dawn to dusk, time for
the compilation of the 'ops' manual was available only in the morning
or evening on broken days, before or after flying duties. More often
than not and definitely not after normal working hours, the typist was
not available at a time that suited me when space had been created for
work on the manual. The pressure for it to be approved at first by the
government's aviation regulatory office continued to be applied relentlessly.

While Fred had done a great job at the outset in getting the services
going to the airfields already provided I felt that more could be done
for the smaller, more isolated island communities or market gardeners
without transport of any kind, except maybe by canoe down river or
across an open sea in small boats. The only airfield on the big island
of Vanua Levu was at Labasa. Taveuni's Matei airfield was at the extreme eastern end of that rugged island. Both places had few roads.
The intention was to write my dreams into the manual.

While accumulating massive flying hours, writing a complicated
document without any technical support that would take Fiji Air back
into the future, a plan for the enlargement of the network with both

flying boats and specialist single and multi-engine aircraft was also taken on. Oh the dreams of a flying-boat man, oh the agony of not seeing them realized. I simply didn't know anything about the world of commerce or the economics associated with operating an airline, being naive enough to believe that passenger fares were all that was needed to fund the operation. Harold reprimanded me for some of my efforts along those lines in relation to air-freighting produce that he said, had embarrassed both him and the government.

All that I had dreamed of and planned on has happened today, with regional and international air services alive and well all over the Pacific. Sad to say I was ahead of my time, without any worthwhile standing in the political and financial world.

Long after the appointment as Chief Pilot was made I heard a story of an Englishman who was offered a promotion to a newly created position in his company. He could either take a salary increase or be approved for the company's rather 'snazzy' business card with the new title above his name, whatever that was. He decided on taking the business card! When I heard that I drew a parallel and knew that I had fallen for an old trick by those wiser to the world. . Spectacular times came and went, each one placing additional loads on our small airline.

On HM Yacht 'Britannia' the recently crowned Queen Elizabeth 2 with Prince Philip paid a Royal Visit. I flew 8 hours each day over their four day visit, fully occupied in flying a shuttle service to and from Lambasa bringing official participants across the Koro Sea in to the ceremonies at Suva, plus wherever else passenger demand had to be met. The venue for most of the ceremonies was Albert Park, the scene of Sir Charles Kingsford-Smith's spectacular and historic landing after 36 hours of flight from Hawaii on his first Pacific flight in 1928. The rest of the time was my own!

I saw little or nothing of the ceremonies relying on descriptions of the events from returning passengers, or later from Fred who had charge of the pilot rosters and had witnessed several! Owing to the manner of construction the entry door on the Rapide took more energy from the pilot during passenger loading than the Drover with a wider, less obstructed door. Assisting the station agent to 'sort' passengers through the cramped door was a priority, while keeping their shoes from piercing the doped Irish linen fabric was a work of art. Bare-footed passengers were rare but most welcome. Aeroplanes were something new to many of our passengers who may not have seen an aircraft before and were making their first flight, heaviest to the for-ward seats, lightest to the rear. Luggage was stowed where it did most good for the centre of gravity. 'Buckling up" the passengers 10-12 times a day while chanting and demonstrating life-vest drills, also took up precious time and energy.

A close watch needed to be kept on any re-fuelling at out-stations where four- gallon 'jerry' cans were used. Preventing any water going into the tanks during rainstorms (or any other reason) while getting soaked as well was another trial pilots faced every day somewhere 'around the traps'. On hot days there was always the risk of fire from smoking, spillage, or both. Writing up the flight times and other op-erational information, with the ink running on paper soggy from sweat or rain, while time ticked by with still more jobs to be done, meant that always the pilot was having to race the clock.

The first of what became an annual event, the 'Miss Hibiscus' fes-tival, drew huge crowds to the city from outlying islands, additional intra-island flights were on demand too. I can't remember Hunt's Travel ever turning any special flights away, due to an expected epi-demic of pilot fatigue. Crossing Viti Levu from Nandi to Nausori after dark and in poor weather, to complete the day and to be in position for the next day's start was not uncommon.

The Fiji Visitors' Bureau too was gearing up for the expected ex-plosion in tourism from North America. The 'yachties' had also found 'an island paradise'. Suva was becoming host to many ocean class races that were becoming popular worldwide. Fiji style hotels beside the sea with separate 'bures' for accommodation in Pacific Palm island settings, sprang up along the south coast road to Nandi and on adjacent islands, drawing lots of Americans to Fiji.

Hollywood movies with well-known stars were being made at several locations around the group. Fiji had been a popular haven with the US Navy and Air Forces during WW2, now as a debutante, the colony was coming out.

With Pan Am, Canadian Pacific and BCPA (British Commonwealth Pacific Airlines) bringing in hosts of purportedly rich North Americans, Fiji was all go, while I was flying my heart out on the poverty level in support and not keeping up with the situation on the home front, where Betty and our three children were desperate to see husband and father sometime, somewhere, in daytime.

Two Rapides in very bad shape, were taken out of the air for major re-construction, pending a decision on their future use with Fiji Air. The woodworkers, known as 'chippies', were supervised by an expert in restoring the wood and fabric components, Australian Licensed Engineer Charlie Ogilvie, who although he was an expert artisan with wood and glue, had missed his vocation, he should have been a singer, an entertainer or a 'tusi tala' (teller of tales, mostly dirty ones). Charlie brought a lot of much needed humour into Fiji Airways. A single Rapide was then the only part wooden aircraft in the fleet. The sudden arrival of another metal bird, a replacement for the Drover lost on 'Freddie's Reef', soon made things a lot easier for pilots and engineers alike.

Suitable accommodations with a reasonable rental and in a respectable location were still hard to find in Suva. That particular problem had plagued me ever since arriving in the Colony as a civilian. Not once had Fiji Airways offered any assistance in locating suitable accommodation for my family. Harold via Fred had turned down two of my applications for a form of subsidized relief. Following the tidal wave we had managed to 'house sit' a few places, resulting in us having to move several times. The uncertainty of proper housing, the hurricane that almost wiped Suva out, the earthquake and tidal wave, the enervating climate, our respective workloads, had got to Betty who wanted to return home to New Zealand. The next few months without her and the children was a time that's hard to write about, nothing short of ghastly and rated as some of the worst days of my life.

DROVER DOWN

Get better, not bitter, for out of the shadows a new figure emerges.

Numb all over, blind-eyed, not conscious of my body, a terrible struggle went on within me to arrest the nausea emanating from the whirling sensations in my head. For a long, long time, with the sun's rays jabbing at my face until it hurt, my head wobbled around until my eyes were forced open and began to focus. How was it possible that my body was lying on the soft, leafy floor of what seemed to be a dense forest? About ten meters away, a pile of crumpled metal and shredded fabric dangled from broken trees. Was the brightly painted logo vaguely familiar, incongruous as it was in the all-over green of the jungle?

Whether seconds, minutes or hours went by will never be known, but slowly things began to fall into place. Flat on my back, head still spinning, blinking repeatedly to clear the blur in my eyes the scene began to untangle. Through a spotty haze the gaping hole of jagged metal, forward of what was recognized as the aircraft's cockpit windshield, where the centre engine had once been, drew my eyes like a magnet! Somehow the engine had been ripped from the airframe and thrown to one side. With the propeller still attached, the engine then lay in the wet undergrowth beside the cockpit frame, a nook very familiar to me. The sight was confusing and very hard to comprehend with those spinning sensations still going on in my head. Just what had brought me to that place and why was a mystery.

Tall, jungle-green trees, thick with foliage and with vines like manila ropes twisted about their branches, towered over me. Sunlight filtered through gaps in the forest overhead, glinting on the wreckage. My body was numb with fear and dread, without feeling of any kind. Somewhere underneath the twisted airframe, a branch splintered and creaked under the weight of a displaced engine or some other part of the metal bird. Through a permanently fixed open mouth, air was sucked into my lungs, which caused vomiting by the intake of petrol fumes and the rotten smell that came with it. Cast like a beetle on its back, spread-eagled, stunned and gasping for breath, without pain of any kind, my world had suddenly become a closed space of shrouded leafy green jungle.

Panic seized my very being when more understanding flooded in. Was someone trapped in what was left of the 'plane? Taking a deep breath while cursing the fumes, slowly my mind began to function enough to induce my body to turn or sit up, anything that would take my eyes away from the Drover's shredded tail-plane hanging dismally in branches supported by the shattered trunk of a tree.

Tears flooded my eyes before they were closed seeking the oblivion of sleep and peace, instead of the horrible, unbelievable picture of the smashed Drover draping in several parts from Viti Levu's rainforest greenery. As if magnetized my eyes were drawn to the wreckage again for more understanding. A propellor blade poked up through the leaves beside the main body of the Drover. As I went to put my hands over my eyes, to shut out the frightful scene and bring me back to reality, only one hand answered the call, giving me the feeling that my left arm was missing.

Slowly, more feeling began to creep back into my limbs bringing pain with it. When next my eyes were opened, whether minutes or hours later, never to be known, my expectation was that the scene would have changed in a way similar to the passage of a most terrible nightmare.

The sun had moved from over the gap in the trees, leaving the small clearing in shadow. The air was still and ominously quiet, the ripple of running water somewhere down the slope of impenetrable jungle, the only sound. As I struggled to my feet sharp jabs of pain shot through me, my hair was matted with blood from a wound across my scalp. My jaw felt gashed and lop-sided as if out of joint. Now the difficulty I'd experienced in turning my body over came to light. My left arm hung useless, out of control in every way. That hand was caked with mud mixed with dried blood from a wound that had slashed the palm down to the bones, leaving the little finger dangling by a piece of blood-soaked skin, the other fingers not much more.

A bleeding nose, a mouth full of leaf, mud and twigs, ribs that began to pain like the devil with my every move, were amongst other injuries that could be felt if not seen. I thrust my way through prickly undergrowth towards the wreckage. Only then did I see that my right shoe along with the sock was missing, while the left shoe had been split open along the laces.

Sharp brambles ripped and tore through my muddied trousers, scratching the skin.

In a daze and using only one hand I stuffed some mail bags that had been flung loose, under a wing or a part of what had once been the airframe. Some went back into the cabin through a broken window, scoring my arm and drawing blood in the process. My thoughts were still those of unbelief in reality, the stowing of the mailbags an automatic reaction that was all a dream from which I'd soon awaken. My watch, my wedding ring, had been torn off my wrist and finger. Only by the position of the sun could the time be guessed as about midday.

Gradually it began to sink in that I was not dreaming, but instead was actually involved in a real-life drama. The Drover had crashed on the highest point of land in the centre of Viti Levu, Fiji's largest island and home of the colony's capital city, Suva.

The last I remembered before impacting with the jungle was the sudden increase in turbulence, the wooded ridge ahead under the aircraft's front engine, the walls of the bush-clad gorge pressing in from each side. I had been trapped, unable to turn away with the speed falling off and not enough airspace beneath the aircraft's belly for flight over the ridge, the last real obstacle before the downhill run to the destination, Nandi airport.

From the time the climb was started from above Viti Levu's most isolated village, smack in the centre of the rugged island, the Drover felt to be sluggish. Only lightly loaded it just wouldn't climb at a normal rate, although there was no evidence to show for that, the three throttle levers were full forward, the rev. counters exactly where they should be.

As the under-belly collided with a treetop higher than the rest, I shouted to God for help, a cry that came from the depths of my soul and is still well remembered. The aircraft seemed to rise a little in a soft, gentle bounce, before nosing down sharply on the right wing and plunging into the thick bush at the peak of the rise. A sickening deceleration could be felt on my wide, heavy-duty webbing seat belt, as inertia threw me forward and upwards. The rest was a curtain of blackness, a whirlwind of confusion.

Whimpering and weeping as the full realization of my plight hit me, spitting out blood, earth, twigs and leaves from my half-opened mouth, I knew that if I was not found soon I could die in the bush, or even be cannibalized. I knew that Reverent Baker, a Methodist missionary and several of his assistants had been devoured by the inhabitants of the area in 1860 which was not a comforting thought.

Flight training over the years had taught me how to react in crash situations. Survivors should remain near the wreckage after a crash into jungle where they would be easier to spot from the air, to wait until help arrived. Looking up to the gap in the tree-tops I could see that only a massive fluke would see the Drover wreckage spotted from the air, help therefore, might be days or weeks away, by which time I could easily be reduced to pig-meal, those charging, bunting and ripping animals were amongst my biggest concerns .The enticing ripple of the stream down in the gully was enough to spur me on. Lots of blood had been lost. I was suffering from a severe thirst with my tongue now feeling like fur, I needed water.

A mud spattered yellow packet, which contained a life-vest that was part of the aircraft's normal safety equipment, had been thrown out in the crash and lay on top of a crumpled wing. Unconsciously, I was going through the actions taken after a ditching in the sea as I worked the vest on over the remnants of my shirt. The effort put into donning the life-vest although bringing on terrible pain in the hand and arm was well rewarded later on.

Choosing a spot where the sun would be at my back, after getting settled I began to slide on my buttocks, feet first down the steep slope to the creek, skidding from tree to tree through undergrowth that pulled, tore and ripped. That wasn't so easy, my left arm hung limp, while giving out dreadful pain with every bump, my body bruised and sore all over. There were times when a missed handhold would cause a sideways roll that could only be arrested by grabbing at a vine with my good arm, or locking an ankle or leg onto a sapling or tree. The effects of the battering received in total in the crash then set in as each meter gained was an agonizing experience.

Just how long that painful slide to the creek lasted was anyone's guess, as the jungle thickened, leaving me with the feeling that I'd made a mistake in departing the wreckage with it's warm sunlight and telescopic view of the sky. When, through a tangle of vines and ferns, I first saw the water trickling under rotting, moss covered tree trunks and over shiny black rocks, darkness was setting in, the scene gloomy and dismal. An ever mounting weakness in my right arm forced me to release my hold on the sapling that was being used as an anchor, the last few feet over the steep bank to the water were made in a sideways tumble and roll, while I groaned with the pain in every part of my body and legs, but much worse through my damaged hand and arm. No matter when or how I moved, the arm always took the worst of the jarring. For ages I sat in the chilly water, in a blurry daze, drinking and washing myself by flipping water up in a cupped right hand and whimpering like a wounded dog.

That night my mind was in a torment, ears pricked for the sounds of wild pigs through the tinkle of running water, many hair-raising stories had been told about their devilish resistance to any human invasion of their territory. My eyes constantly searched the ghostly black shapes of jungle for any furtive movement, while my mind began the search for all I needed to know about gangrene or septicaemia.

With the steady brightening of the sky in the morning, I had the good sense somehow to check the direction of the flow of the creek, for I knew that I must move east not west. I regretted having left the wreckage but to return now would be impossible in my weakening condition.

With the rising sun then at my face whenever it could be seen through the heavy overcast of foliage, I began to stagger down the creek, picking my way around boulders and fallen trees. I moved only a few meters at a time between spasms of intense pain, with all parts of my body being scraped and lashed by a never-ending array of prickly vines or branches.

There were periods when the creek rushed with force through narrow vertical walls, which meant a climb up a cliff-face or around the cataract, to join with the rush of water again further downstream. A waterfall with a drop of 20 meters or more, proved to be the worst, necessitating a crawl-climb for what seemed to be more than an hour, to intercept the creek again while gaining only fifty meters eastward as the crow flies. There the creek began to turn more into a river (I shall call that a 'creever'), wider and with a swift flow that sometimes swept me off my feet.

Through the thick blanket of forest above, the sounds of aircraft engines could be heard occasionally but there was no way to signal or reveal myself in any way. The 'creever' was my lifeline, my only hope. I grew weaker and moved more slowly. Real fears of being caught in a flash flood while in the narrower parts of the gorge began to plague my mind.

The area was sparsely populated, if any village could be found it would be on a river. There was no way of knowing just how any villager I met on the way would treat me. The inhabitants of the central area of the island had a reputation for being quite wild and primitive. Ninety years had passed since the Baker affair. By all reports the villagers of central Viti Levu had not made much progress since those days, there were no roads, the colonial style development of the day had left them isolated with little contact with the outside world.

Hopes of finding a village egged me on, step by step, metre by metre. All day I went on in this way. After tripping and falling over, which happened frequently, only a brief rest was taken before struggling to my feet as best I could, then pushing on again. The clear mountain water was doing wonders for the cooling and sanitizing of my bleeding feet. Rapids with only a short drop to deeper, smoother water, warned me to pull the toggles and inflate the life-vest, before climbing on to the large boulders along the riverbank. There the vest saved me from more bruising or even certain drowning, when a slip followed by a fall, carried me downstream in a rocky, bumpy ride to deeper water at a bend in the river. The upper body protection provided by the vest allowed me to gain the shallows with little bruising from the rocks. To feel gravel under my feet again was a great relief. The unexpected all-over dip in the rushing mountain water temporarily refreshed and cleansed me.

Gasping for breath, pained all over, I lay in the sun on a gravelly beach, marvelling at the open space, thinking that was the only time I might have been seen from the air since the crash. The air was very still and without sign, sight or sound of any search aircraft. I forced myself on to my feet and staggered downstream again, before having to make a river crossing to avoid high vertical cliffs cut away by floodwaters. Twenty meters along the opposite side of the river saw me completely enclosed in the forest again.

Late that afternoon, in a narrower part of the 'creever' where the rainforest turned into a dark, shadowy tunnel, a black shape, a human shape, stood ankle-deep in the stream about five meters downstream of me, blending with the shadows, motionless and silent, partly hidden by vines or overhanging branches. Numbed with fright my skin crawled as we both stood our ground, alert and watching, with me fully expecting to hear the rustle of a black-palm spear hurtling towards me.

As my eyes adjusted to the changing light, the apparition was seen to be a Fijian bushman with a muscled body supporting a tangled crop of frizzy hair. He wore only dirty, tattered, what would once have been, khaki-coloured shorts held up by a thin strip of supple vine. At his shoulder he gripped a long wooden spear, the sharp tip pointing my way. He seemed as frightened of me as I of him and made no move. We stood that way for a long time, with me hardly daring to breathe as with his eyes he took me in.

The effort of standing unsupported in any way was beyond any strength I could muster. Before I collapsed I was able to mutter through swollen lips in a throaty saliva filled voice the common greeting in Fijian.

" Bula, bula vinaka. " then running out of my limited Fijian vocabulary. " Help me, please help me, I need your help."

The shape made no move as I made to stumble the few metres of river separating us. As I put my good arm around his neck to take some of the weight off my body he remained as still as a statue.

Quite unexpectedly, without uttering a sound and with his whole frame quite rigid, he turned us both around by propelling me with his hip. My arm locked us together as we set off in slow motion downstream again, one step at a time and still without a word being spoken.

We'd only gone a few meters when all the strength in my legs failed. Putting one foot in front of the other became too difficult for me. Somehow he caught on and began to take my full weight. My hand and arm felt red hot, sharp pain racked through me every step we took. Later I was told that he was scared stiff when we first met, believing me to be one of his ancestors returning from the spirit world.

At dusk while taking a rest on the river's bank, my rescuer signalled that I should stay where I lay while he went for help. At least that's what I made of the gesticulations he made with his hands and the mumbled sounds coming from somewhere behind his lips. As for running away, that would not in any way be possible considering the state I was in, all I wanted was to sleep, or die. After he'd gone I turned over on to my belly and lay with my mouth only inches from the water and drank by splashing water over my face and into my mouth. Sleep came only in microseconds.

With my head pounding and my good arm lying in water barely a couple of inches deep, my face on the gravel, every time I closed my eyes a whirlwind of fears and doubts flooded in. What if a flash flood suddenly swept down the narrow gorge and the current swept me away? Would the Fijian ever be seen again? My family, what would they know about all this, what would they be thinking? If a pig or pigs came to the water what would I do? Oh dear God, what is going to happen to me?

Not long after he'd gone when I must have dozed off, I opened my eyes to find that day had turned to night. I could sense rather than see my rescuer standing near with two other men. Their voices seemed to come to me from down a long, dark tube.

With a Fijian man supporting me on each side, we set off downstream again. They must have known every stone, branch or tree along that part of the river. We seemed to move more rapidly than before, with me as deadweight, my feet and ankles dragging through the rockstrewn water. While moving on a narrow path alongside the stream we met up with more village people. The air was filled with their whoops, shrieks, 'oohs' and 'aahs' as they each studied me from close quarters, some even running their gnarled hands over my legs and arms. The thought struck me that they were sizing up the condition and quality of the meat on my bones, which was not a pleasant thought. Every few minutes my two supports were swapped over, good speed was made, although some of the handling of my injured parts when the men changed over, made me grit my teeth.

Suddenly we seemed to be in the centre of a small village a cluster of six or so grass huts beside a wide bend in the river. There was no way of knowing the time of night. Everyone, including children, milled about talking excitedly all at once, while some of the older poked me with their fingers. It was clear that by my dishevelled state and mode of arrival, I was an object of considerable interest to them, as man or spirit who would know?

My carriers helped me into a hut filled with the inevitable village smells of unwashed body, smoke and cooking, where gratefully I slumped on to the flax mat covering the earth floor. An old, grey-haired Fijian, assumed to be chief of the village organized some women to bring food, big hunks of boiled dalo, to be washed down with river water. Although it was my second complete day without food of any kind, there was no way that I could eat, which seemed to worry those who watched studying my every move.

Speaking softly, one of the women made a shy, nervous attempt to clean up my left hand. Her slightest touch brought on more severe pain, which forced me to pull my hand away. By signs I indicated that I would like to be left alone, to sleep and recover from the day's ordeal.

At regular intervals from then on, the chief entered the hut to take a look at me. With my jaw and mouth being so swollen, coupled with the chief's scant knowledge of English, conversing with him was difficult between my own grunts and groans. In the village outside the hut, all was quiet, although I sensed that ears everywhere would be pricked, everyone seemed to be talking in whispers. The shock of receiving a white man, bare-footed, bleeding and in tattered clothing, stumbling along a river-bed in their wild territory, was too much for their superstitious minds, they must have thought that some kind of a ghost had come to haunt them over the Baker affair!

By what I could fathom from their brand of English and the waving of their arms, the man who I'd first met had been tracking a pig, to kill for the village larder. The sounds made by me thrashing along the creek, had been close enough for him to expect the customary ferocious charge the breed of pig was noted for when hunted and cornered, using not only their considerable weight to butt but also their long, sharp tusks, to rip and tear. He was ready and willing to hurl his spear, when fear at the sighting of a ghostly scarecrow of a white man had frozen him to the spot. As I approached to plead for his support he thought his time was up, his hands and legs turned to jelly, he was tongue tied, he couldn't raise a yell. Only when I touched him did he know that I was real.

Late that night the chief helped me to sit up. By signs and a mud map that he drew on the floor, I learned that the same man had gone down river to break the news of my arrival. The chief's voice shook with emotion, as if he didn't quite know what to do about me, or the situation. As for me, I rolled on to my back again to remain motionless, insects buzzed about my face, my heart pounded like a jackhammer, while thunder and lightning began to shatter the night. Sleep was impossible with the pain of my wounds ripping through me. The chances of the grass hut going up in flames if hit by the jagged lightning, was never far from my thoughts either.

With the calming of the storm at dawn the village came to life, roosters crowed, dogs yapped, grunts could be heard from the partly domesticated pigs that roamed through the village. Steamy hot dalo was again offered. I was depressed, without appetite, shaking a 'no' with my head and pointing to my lips, which needed wetting. That time the chief held half a coconut shell up to my lips. I managed to sip a little kava from the bowl, but most ran down a gash in the side of my cheek, over my chin and on to the mats. Clapping could be heard outside the hut, as word spread that the friendly ghost had at last consumed a portion of the country's traditional beverage, the peacemaker, the 'fixit' of all intra-tribal wars or quarrels. All was then going to be well.

The day wore on with me losing count of time and with all the villagers, men, women and children entering at some time or other for another look at the strange mangled white man. By now it was obvious that they had worked out that the stranger in their midst had come from a 'plane out of the sky, that he was real.

Late in the afternoon an aircraft was heard approaching. The villagers waved, jumped and ran about wildly and 'willy-nilly', near the water's edge, frantic with excitement. I pleaded with the chief to take me outside to a clearing by the river and set me in the middle of a circle formed by the villagers. There was no doubt that he was feeling the urge to see the 'plane himself, for he was slow to act, leaving me in fear that the aircraft would be gone before I could reach the riverside.

Only just in time did I arrive there as the last flyable Rapide of Fiji Airways was seen to be roaring low up the river. I motioned with my arm for everybody to gather around me then move back to leave me more prominent in the middle of the circle formed. Over the village the Rapide laid over into a tight left circle. When the pilot 'waggled' the wings I knew that he'd spotted me and could guess by the manoeuver, so well executed in a tight valley, that the pilot was Morrie Morrissey, the ex Corsair pilot.

An hour later, a RNZAF Sunderland flying-boat from Laucala Bay was overhead and dropping food and medical supplies by parachute. For the villagers that must have been their greatest time, from the chief down all were mad with excitement as they recovered the 'chutes from trees, or rocks in the river.

Very late that night there was great excitement outside the hut again. At first somebody could be heard speaking English mixed with Fijian. With a hurricane lantern glowing in his hand, a European man, tall and lean, was framed in the doorway and proceeded to squat on the ground beside me. He told me that he was Arthur Phillips, a farmer settler from a long way down river, who had been summoned by the Fijian I'd first met up with. Arthur had already heard on the radio that a 'plane was missing in the area since the morning of New Year's Eve.

He spoke quietly, with the accent of a 'kai viti' (a European born in Fiji), it was easy to see that although he was very shy he was full of purpose as he spoke to the chief in Fijian on the best, and fastest way to get me to a doctor hospital and civilisation.

After appraising my wounds he offered to clean them up and put my arm in a sling with the bandages dropped from the Sunderland. Arthur claimed that he'd bandaged up many a Fijian following them being gored by wild pigs, he knew how to go about it. Using the anti-septics delivered in the airdrop mixed with boiled water from an old pot, he started into giving me a preliminary wash, while I gritted my teeth as best I could in an attempt to ease the frightful pain.

The wounds by then were three days old and under the existing conditions the chances of them becoming gangrenous were very real. As I lay back to rest after that ordeal, feeling a little more comfortable, Arthur left the hut to organize a bush stretcher he'd asked to be made. His intention was to move me out that night.

It wasn't long before the stretcher arrived outside the 'bure'. Long saplings were the carry poles, flax stretched between them served as base for the blankets that were air dropped, with a single blanket rolled up tight for a pillow. Arthur helped me on to the stretcher and made me comfortable.

Without a word four big muscular village men hoisted me high on their shoulders as Arthur led off to blaze the route to be followed. Six or eight other men followed to assist with the carrying in shifts as required.

Even though I was still very dazed, it was amazing to see the inherent bush skills of the porters. In what was for me, pitch-black darkness, the stretcher was taken around sharp, steep corners of a jungle track on the bank above a swift torrent of a river without a falter, the Fijians were as sure-footed as mountain goats. My head was sometimes lower than my feet as they fought their way up or down a steep slope by digging their toes into the muddy soil or raising the stretcher high with their arms, one step at a time, without a slip or a fumble where the slightest slip by any one man could see me being tipped off into the always roaring river somewhere 'down there' in the darkness.

The Fijians had superb night vision, Arthur too. Branches or vines often scraped across my face as I slithered and slipped across the mattress while we moved on at a cracking pace judging by the numerous changes in motion that were made.

Daylight found us resting beside a river that was in full flood following heavy rains in the uplands. There, to avoid the washed-out portions of track, the stretcher was taken along the shallows or through the bush beside the river. In daylight I could see that the pace, thought to be fast, was actually the effect of the carriers 'short-stepping' around tight corners or up and down steep slopes. Progress was in fact quite slow. Hour after hour they laboured, the carriers exchanging while on the move. Increasing pain in my arm forced me to cry out whenever the poles got twisted when being maneuvered around hairpin bends. I knew that Arthur, who was always near at those times, was getting worried.

By the ever mystical 'jungle telegraph', word of my rescue had spread to other small villages down river. Dozens of helpers now joined the line, all willing and eager for a turn on the poles. About the middle of the day, at a bend in the river, we met with a very long and narrow Police boat, purpose built to negotiate rapids. An officer of the

Fiji Police with a broad 'national' smile from ear to ear, then took charge.

At first he subjected me to a close inspection both physical and verbal. Although I tried, returning that smile wasn't possible with a dislocated jaw and me choosing the time to break out into a nauseous sweat, plus excruciating pain in my arm. After conferring with Arthur, he told the men to place me in the boat that was being manhandled into position for a run downstream.

While the village men steadied the craft in the rapids, the blankets were transferred to the boat. After lying down and being made comfortable a waterproof cape was thrown over me. Arthur, the policeman and his crew then joined me in the narrow hull. After much bumping and grinding the flat bottom cleared the rapids then we were afloat and heading downstream under paddle power at a good speed with the current. Before long, heavy rain drenched us all, the paddlers baling as the boat began to fill.

With night and a black wall of rain beginning to roll across the outlying forest, we pulled in to a riverside village. The pelting rain cooled and refreshed me by washing off some of the caked blood and somehow eased the pain. The headman of the village provided a hut for the police, Arthur and me. We were all by then beginning to feel the chill, following the drenching we'd received. Life in the tropics is like that, a shiver often follows a good drenching.

My rescuers all huddled around a fire, drying out, while I lay on a mat in the glow and warmth, listening to the coughing that was going on through the smoke-filled hut. Food was provided generously, but again I couldn't eat. The others filled themselves with boiled dalo and drank kava, while someone strummed a ukulele. I wished for the journey to be over, to hear news of my family who for all I knew might already be preparing a memorial service for me.

Next morning the cataracts were left behind. In bright sunshine we came to the confluence and the wide expanse of the Rewa River with its lazier flow and brown, muddy looking surface. With the slower current the men on the paddles had to work much harder to get the long, narrow hull going at the same speed as before as the grassy banks slid by. Sweat poured from each man, who always had a broad smile on hand when they caught my eye.

In the middle of the day we drew in to the left bank, a few kilometres upstream from the river bridge at Nausori, where an ambulance was waiting on the road beside the river. The blankets with me inside were hoisted off the boat and up the bank as if I was a feather. After looking me over and asking a few questions, a doctor who by the tones, was British, gave me a small injection of morphine, or so he said. So magical was the instant relief from pain that came with that shot. In a minute or two I was floating in a painless, drowsy state of mind, the first respite from severe pain I'd had in five or six days. I had no idea just how many days had passed since the take-off was made from the airport there.

As the ambulance started its run to the Colonial War Memorial hospital in Suva, no chance was offered for me to convey my thanks to those sturdy men, for the mighty job they'd done carrying the stretcher through thick jungle and across swift flowing rivers. My thanks would have to be sent to them later.

The side and after effects of the accident remained with me for a very long time, particular portions will no doubt stay with me forever. Many years passed before I could say to myself "Moses is dead, finish with the mourning and get on with life". I had climbed to the top of the ladder only to find that it was leaning on the wrong building.

My hand remained in plaster for weeks while maggots cleaned the wound out, when the small finger known as 'Little' was amputated. Tendons in two of the remaining fingers had been severed and couldn't be rejoined. Fifty-five years on my hand more resembles a claw, ugly and partly useless, a nasty reminder always of the accident. Slivers of jungle timber deeply embedded in my jaw and mouth were removed surgically, while others surfaced naturally as months went by, some when shaving the beard off. A misplaced bone in my left shoulder was left to fix itself, but never has.

I am left pondering on just how, without Divine assistance, I could have been catapulted from the cockpit of the Drover, through the tree-tops at 130 km/ph, onto ground covered in stumps and tree roots, while receiving only the injuries described here. Taking the route from the pilot's seat to where I woke up, directly in front of the wreck, at the very least I should have been dismembered or decapitated. Shoes and socks ripped off without serious damage to my feet or legs. A broken leg or legs might have seen me stranded at the wreckage that along with me might not have been found for a very long time. Some claimed that I had been flung from the cockpit via the emergency escape hatch in the roof of the passenger cabin, my heavy-duty-webbing seat belt sliced in two as if by an extremely sharp hatchet. To me, the location of the escape hatch rules that out.

To this day my belief is that God answered my plea for help and placed, not threw me, on the spot where I became conscious, there can be no other explanation. He now has my full trust. There will be many who would say that the spiritual awakening that was mine would assure my future life being trouble free and just one big smooth ride, that the accident had started a sort of healing within me, which is partly true. There were however, more challenges ahead that needed many years to be fully understood. It certainly provided others with material to shoot me down, quite frankly there are many things that are always private, one's story is not necessarily cathartic, the telling of it as a safety valve is really over-rated.

Nearing the end of the first week of my convalescence, Mr Gatty, who had been in England on a trip when the accident occurred, arrived at the hospital and requested he pay me a visit. Dr Shaw asked me for my consent to the meeting.

"You don't have to say yes, you are my patient. I'm in charge here." the good doctor said, obviously knowing the situation, lots of rumours were flying around. " He can come back some other time if you're not up to it today, just say the word."

A meeting with Harold had to come sometime although it wasn't really welcomed whilst cast in bed and partially sedated. Not able to speak with my jaw bound up, my ribs wrapped in sticking plaster, my arm heavy with plaster of Paris, all I could do was blink my eyes and nod my head in acquiescence, the blinking mainly to blot up the tears that were already forming in my eyes. "Does that mean you will see him? "

After another blink and a nod or two, Dr Shaw left the veranda and spoke to someone at the door. Guess who? Without asking any questions immediately Harold began to accuse me of taking the opportunity when with mail only aboard and without passengers, of flying low through a gorge while operating a geiger counter, in search of uranium thus having run into the trees while my attention to flight was diverted! He came out with that in a very amateurish way, his face flushed as if he'd had a tipple or two before arrival, to summon up some Dutch courage.

Harold acted as investigator, judge and jury leaving me without opportunity to deny the accusation. I'm fairly sure he never asked me how I was feeling, which you can understand wasn't really good for my morale at the time. Bandaged as it was for repairs, my jaw wouldn't move to allow me to speak, but it must have dropped a bit further of its own accord when I heard that!

"As from that day you're fired, my solicitors will send you the pay due to you at the time." Those were his last words as he turned on his heel and left the verandah ward without offering me any chance for an explanation or more importantly, any sort of an apology or denial. The word 'fired' was new to me. That expression was heard only in American movies in our part of the world. The usual word was 'sacked' which is not so cruel. One thinks of a 'sack race' that only restricts movement of the legs and one is not incinerated at the finish line. No doubt though, I knew what Harold meant.

I try not to write with venom having found it best to try to get a look at the person who acts in such a way, his thoughts, what made him what he is, what he believes, the reasons for man's exploitation of man? I know now most honestly, just how hard, even dangerous, the flying work had been for such little reward from the famous Mr. Harold Gatty in the setting up of Fiji Airways. Harold through his RAFT BOOK was known as a man of nature but was he aware of the vulnerability of humanity? Whether he was atheist or agnostic I'm not certain but he had spoken. Alas for the rarity of Christian charity. He was well known as a navigator of some excellence. As he peeped through his bubble sextant at the heavens did he not know who named the stars, millions of them and there is never one missing? 'God hung the stars in the sky, the Dipper, Orion, Pleiades and the stars of the south' (Job 9.9 GNB) 'He knows how many there are and calls each one by name'. (Isaiah 40.26 GNB)

The woodpecker sat in the Cardinal's chair, Bishop, Abbott and mistress too were there'.

An inquiry into the accident was held three weeks after my rescue and a week after discharge from the hospital. The forecast for the outcome was heavily in favour of the Fiji colonial government of that time. Now it's known that the period from accident to inquiry was far too short, although the time set had been agreed to through my being anxious to rejoin my family as soon as the inquiry was over. There had been no opportunity for me to re-vitalize my Full-Alert memory bank. Since leaving the hospital, still with bandages about face, body and limbs, accommodation had been provided by friends Ewen and Pattie Evison, on the flying-boat base at Laucala Bay, where Ewen (Shorty) was senior Air Traffic Controller.

Looking back, as compared to the present day the inquiry was a travesty of justice. My lawyer is best described as an absolute dud. Any agreement made by me to the date set would have been overridden by a more competent legal counsel, with a request for postponement of the proceedings on the grounds that more time for my recovery should be allowed until my mind was clear as to the events leading up to the crash. What can only be described as a corrosive examination became my lot, with much personal character assassination thrown in. In those days the colony had to be the biggest rumour mongered place in the world.

Never were the so-called expert witnesses statements questioned; the meteorologist who swore that it was not possible for any wave turbulence to have affected the crash site area that morning and the 'expert' who'd never heard of the effect carburettor icing had on aircraft engine performance. The composition of the Board of Inquiry and their secretaries as to whether any participant had a conflict of interest in the proceedings, or undue bias as some had was never queried. An astute lawyer genuinely doing his best for his client today would have such an inquiry shut down and new members appointed.

The company had operated for years without an operations manual. Since my appointment as Chief Pilot the manual had been well advanced but was not presented in any shape or form at the hearing. No mention was made of the excessive hours I'd flown in the months preceding the accident, caused by Fred's departure from the scene, or the duty and travel times involved to achieve the hours. The 'shonky' (loose, careless) way engine, airframe and pilot hours were recorded by the colony's approved air carrier were never 'discovered' either or brought to the notice of the Chairman.

As the inquiry moved on, in every way Fiji Airways were seen to be favoured, with me as the scapegoat. Even early in the piece it was obvious that the struggling little airline owned by the famous Harold Gatty of Wiley Post, Winnie Mae,' around the world fame, was receiving preferential treatment owing to him being a member of the Legislative Council of Fiji. No mention was made of the poor salaries and living conditions offered by the company that was subsidized by the colonial government, factors which badly influence piloting performance, while the 'Boss' lived in luxury seeming not to care two hoots about his very loyal staffers. This placed enormous stress on all expatriates and their families, particularly pilots. Human, organizational and management influences behind a Fiji Airways piloting job were never brought out into the open, the airline breezed through with a clean bill of health.

Long after the inquiry was over, it was learned that the technical member of the crash investigation team, an Air Force officer, never laid eyes on the wreckage, because of, he claimed, 'excessive bush-travel fatigue', he just couldn't make the stiff climb to the wreck-site. The responsibility for reporting on the technical standard of the Drover had been taken over 'in the field' by the chairman of the inquiry, who to the best of my knowledge was not a qualified civil aeronautical engineer. The technical report although null and void, was therefore 'cooked up', read out and accepted as damning evidence without any rebuttal, queries or cross-examination coming from my attorney. To add insult to injury, seventy-five pounds was deducted from the little over one hundred due to me as severance pay, for the services my attorney had rendered after having been appointed to the task by the Fiji government.

Low in self-esteem, humiliated, not much good at denial, I sat through the two-day hearing in a trance-like state although putting on a brave face, seemingly light-hearted but feeling more like a 'shag on a rock', with everyone blazing away at me with double-barrel shotguns. My chest and ribs were wrapped tight in sticking plaster, my hand and arm with a load of maggots inside the cast was heavy in a sling, my jaw held in place with a bandage. Blamed for pilot error, I left Fiji very low in spirit and self-esteem, although determined to fly again, prepared to forget about the unfair treatment received and get on with starting a new life somewhere, somehow. Hush, say not a word, 'revenge is Mine says the Lord', became my philosophy.

The final straw that only came to my knowledge months later, was that during the inquiry a fellow pilot who'd been employed by me in his first civil flying job, (but not named in this description of the event) volunteered to fly a Drover on an engine-out test at 4000 feet, that was roughly the level of the crash-site, to prove that the machine could maintain that height fully laden on only two engines. His report stated that the Drover could do so quite easily, which meant that the de Havilland approved performance figures as per the type's manual were incorrect. That really hurt, not only me but several other well-informed aviation heads also. Fortunately, New Zealand's Civil Aviation Department who were handling some civil aviation matters in Fiji at the time, ruled out the possibility of the vindictive, so-called flight-test being anywhere near plausible, flight performance tests had not been called for and were not done that way. Unfortunately, their opinions came too late and never went before the inquiry.

And what is friendship but a name, a charm that lulls to sleep. Yea mine own familiar friend, in whom I trusted which did eat of my bread, hath lifted up his heel against me. Ps. 41.9

Full recovery from the wounds took a long time with the vision of the crashed Drover only gradually fading from memory. There was one thing though that wouldn't go away. The short glimpse I'd had, while still dazed and confused after the crash, of the tip of one blade of a propeller standing up straight through the undergrowth, apparently undamaged. There were some, including the chairman of the inquiry, who claimed rather vindictively, that I would never fly again, that sounded like 'if he had his way', which goes to show just how wrong some judgments can be.

About eighteen months after the accident, Mr Harold Gatty suffered a cerebral haemorrhage while on a visit to the Nausori airport and was pronounced dead soon after the ambulance arrived to convey him to the Colonial War Memorial Hospital in Suva. The ownership of Fiji Air was almost taken over by Pan American Airways of USA for Harold had some high-level connections with Pan Am's Pacific Division prior to and during WW2 and had earned a lot of respect for his wartime efforts in Australia, New Zealand and New Guinea too. However the proposed 'take-over' was thwarted when Mrs Fenna Gatty was advised and urged to keep Fiji Air in British Commonwealth hands with the co-operation of Qantas the Australian international airline.

Almost two years after the accident I returned to Fiji and along with a friend, a young Air Force officer who wanted a taste of adventure, we made a four-day journey up to the Drover's wreck-site by riverboat and on foot. From inquiries made before we set out, we assumed that the wreckage had probably not been tampered with, due to the inaccessibility of the site in such a mountainous rain-forest region. Heavy tools and some mechanical knowledge would be required to remove major parts such as engines, propellers or landing gear, tools that were not available to Fijian inland villagers, there would be a good chance that the prop under question would still be there in the tangle of jungle shrubbery. An undamaged, or not too much damaged prop, could mean that the engine to which it had been attached was not under power on impact and that my statement about a slow rate of climb due to a suspected loss of engine power, coupled with severe mountain turbulence, had been true. At the Nausavere village my previous acquaintance with those who took part in my rescue was renewed. For the second time the villagers were taken completely by surprise at seeing me, healthy, hot and in tidy clothes. The pig hunter I first met in the 'creever', had left the village to seek his fortune in other parts. The chief was either absent on a hunting trip or had passed on, what exactly could not be established due to language difficulties. Two men, who claimed they knew the location of the Drover but had not been part of the rescue in any way, were hired to show us the way although their attitude towards the task seemed to be somewhat un-co-operative.

The route from the village was tough and it seemed to me didn't exactly retrace the flow of the 'creever' that I had followed down, shortcuts known only to the men were taken. A hard, hot climb through dense bush from the creek, took us to the summit where the Drover lay. Sweating from every pore, fighting for gulps of air, in memory my journey down the mountainside was re-lived, it was hard to believe that the creek had been reached by sliding down that slope, bare-footed and with a hand and arm out of commission, a dislocated jaw, battered, bruised and with cracked ribs.

When the men indicated that we were at the site there was not much to be seen except the thick, dark forest and dense prickly under-growth, with scarcely a gap overhead to the sky. The jungle had certainly sprouted up and taken over, leaving not even a twig to be recognized. For some time it was hard to believe that we were at the right place. Through vines and heavy foliage I gaped about in and out of the shadows, in the expectation of seeing things much as last seen two years before. The view of the site was disappointing, there was precious little left, the wreckage had certainly been picked over and completely stripped by someone with 'know-how'.

A thorough search by the two of us brought to light only several pieces of metal tubing, that could have been part of the engine mounts and several strips of unpainted aluminium that were embedded in the fork of a tree well above ground level. In the interval the tree had grown around the metal that made it immoveable, not that we were interested in its salvage. Another strip of aluminium, bent and bat-tered, jammed under a fallen tree trunk, was thought to be part of a wingtip or horizontal stabilizer. Of props or engines, nuts, screws or bolts there wasn't a trace.

Questioning the men got us nowhere, both seemed reluctant to talk. It was clear to see that the wreckage had been pirated, or more correct-ly, completely uplifted from the site, certainly by someone who knew what they were doing. I had no idea how the heavy bits and pieces could have been removed from such a site without an army to help. It was hard to imagine the villagers collecting materials that apart from natural curiosity were of no use to them. Of things metal they knew nothing, it was most unlikely that by this time Fiji Air, the government or any other body, had provided funds for the Drover's complete sal-vage.

There would be nothing to prevent the village from purloining parts from a wrecked 'plane, after a period of time, that in itself that would not be a felony. An undamaged metal propeller however, would be a valuable prize for anyone, as a memento or even a re-cycled use-able part. My friend Josh was also disappointed at not being able to gain a control wheel, flight instrument or identification plate for his air museum. In less than an hour, gloomy with disappointment we began to retrace our steps for 'a long way home'.

En route, a careful scan around the village brought only a passenger chair from the Drover to light, with most of it's stuffing gone and leaning awkwardly against the wall of a hut, nothing else, although of course we couldn't inspect the interior of every bure.

Back in Suva, inquiries were made among those who might have had an interest in aircraft salvage, but to no avail, the subject of that particular Drover was a closed shop. Whoever it was who had removed the wreckage had certainly covered their tracks, whether officially or unofficially was not certain.

Fiji Airways had replaced their Drovers with the more sophisticated four-engine De Havilland Heron. New staff had been employed in the engineering section, who claimed to know nothing of the Drover and who had obviously been instructed to have nothing to do with me. If certain parts were stored away, then they were well hidden.

My search was getting nowhere, costs were rising, I gave up knowing that the prop in question was by then most probably in the guise of a wall-clock gracing a wall of a billiards room, golf club, aero club or palatial residence, 'somewhere in New Zealand or Australia' The owner might, or might not, be aware of the propellers interesting history.

I had been resentful, full of rage, when first returning to Fiji to review the wreckage. The disappearance of the prop in question plagued me for months, until I realized that further pursuit of an answer was beyond my means, physically and financially. The best thing to do was to forgive, forget (the hardest of all) and get back to making a better life with what skills I had.

For a short period I tried to establish an air charter company in the Fijis, utilizing a crop-duster Tiger, Fox Moth and Piper Cub for flight training and a leased Cessna 180 float-amphibian. I soon learned that four different types in a fleet of four, all under differing funding arrangements, was not the way to make profits or establish good relationships. It wasn't long before I realized that another big mistake had been made.

At the time Mr Gatty lodged an objection with the Air Transport Authority to my company's application for an operating license. The Air Transport Authority's chairman was lawyer, Maurice Scott DFC, son of a prominent Suva barrister, who had been a RAF fighter pilot during WW2. He was a close friend of Mr Gatty. When Harold arrived for the hearing in the government buildings on Albert Park, which was the first time I'd seen him since his visit to the hospital, we both sat without speaking at opposite ends of a row of chairs in an ante room while waiting for the call from the committee.

The air service license eventually granted to the company was discriminatory, a long time in coming through and proved to be economically unworkable. The Authority's decision reeked somewhat of spite and vindictiveness. Passengers or freights were not to be uplifted within a thirty-mile radius of any Government or international airport. Air Viti was left without any reasonable operating area! The cards were stacked against us. Along with me, Fiji just wasn't ready for an operation of that kind. It was then that I learned that if there is anyone in government who wants to disprove you, they will not be beaten.

During the period of waiting for Air Viti to be cleared for operations which was several months I was standing beside the Fox Moth on the Matei airfield about thirty meters or so from a Fiji Air Heron that was starting engines to continue with the regular service from the island. On the attempt to start the number three engine, a long flame was seen to come from the exhaust. The propeller was kept turning, the engine failed to start. A Fijian attendant was on hand with a fire extinguisher but seemed uncertain as to what to do as the prop kept going and the flames got longer, by then licking at the fabric-covered flaps on the inner trailing edge of the Heron's right wing. The situation was extremely dangerous as an explosion could be expected at any moment.

The pilot had by that time removed his finger from the starter-button, the propeller had stopped although the flames persisted. I could not bear to stand by watching idly any longer, so ran over to the burning aircraft. With the appropriate gesture the pilot was signalled to shut off the fuel and hit the starter button again, a drill that I knew would draw the flames through to starve the fire of fuel, or as some might say 'blow them away'. By that time the flaps were well alight. There was nothing else for me to do but again signal the pilot, by drawing a hand across my throat, to shut all engines down, while I grabbed the extinguisher and attacked the flames from the trailing edge of the wing. Fortunately the fire-fighting equipment was in good order, the flames were damped just as the extinguisher was used up and after all the passengers had been evacuated, leaving the Heron with a very charred, useless flap and parts of the starboard wing showing signs of heat stress.

On that one, I felt that I had allegedly 'lost' a Drover for Fiji Air but 'saved' a Heron, my debt had been paid although a receipt was never received or anything more heard about the incident. The pilot admitted later, but not to me, that during the emergency he had failed to shut the fuel off when at first the flames appeared, a drill he should have known well, to starve the fire of fuel while using the starter. Fires on starting that type of engine were not uncommon and the drill for quelling the flames well known. The Heron remained at Matei for a long time undergoing repairs.

On the day of the Drover crash, God had answered my prayer for help. I had made some real commitments to Him that I had problems fulfilling but I was determined to go on, the learning curve had finished it's plunge and had started to rise.

While in deep despair over my apparent failure and immediate future, suddenly out of the blue a letter came from Australia inviting me with my family to move to Victoria. For a two-year period I would base in Victoria with a mission-oriented, aerial agriculture firm. On completion of my contract I would be considered for selection to serve in New Guinea as a full-time mission flyer. Although I wasn't so interested in the aerial agricultural aspects of the offer, the chance of seeing wild, untamed New Guinea some day really appealed to me. Many stories had been told of exploration in a land of dark, secret jungles, three-mile high mountains capped with snow, smoking volcanoes, rugged bush-clad coastlines with reef-protected, crocodile infested bays and river estuaries, tribes of wild, savage, feathered warrior bushmen, countless dialects and languages flavoured with stories of daring flying men in a land where roads were few. New Guinea, I felt, was the place for me, although I still had much to learn about the wiles of governments and the politics of aviation.

TO VICTORIA, AUSTRALIA

A sad goodbye was said to Fiji before we travelled by air to New Zealand at first, for a short visit with family and friends. Then it was on to Victoria aboard a Qantas 'Connie", arriving at Essendon, Melbourne, around eleven o'clock at night. The Manager and Field Manager of the company respectively, Colin Le Couteur and Doug Hunt met us there, jovially and cordially. As a family we were made to feel welcome and at home. Col broke the news that we would be taken that night to our temporary accommodation in the 'woop woops' about a 2-hour drive from the airport.

"Oh you won't be there very long, only until something else is found for you" he told us, while watching our faces for signs of any disappointment. "It's a nice big caravan, on a sheep farm, parked near the owners house, the Mountjoys. Real nice people, they can't wait to meet you in the morning. I'll guarantee you'll like it there. Doug and I will take you, it's late, we'd better be going".

My heart dropped a beat or two, it was unbelievable to think that we were in Australia and bound for a caravan, but before I could talk to Betty privately we were in the parking lot splitting passengers and luggage between Col's car and Doug's utility, then heading along the road for a town with the unlikely sounding name of 'J'long'.

Betty and the kids travelled with Col while I went with Doug in the 'ute', a new name for me for that type of vehicle. Not knowing what to expect, I felt that Betty would be horrified at the thought of having to live in a caravan with four children, her nerves were already stretched taut after the events of the previous year, any more stress could break her apart altogether.

Two hours later we neared Maude, which was a district not a town, I was told. At the top of a rise the headlights picked out a deserted looking farmhouse.

"That's Mountjoy's late father's old place. "Doug said to me. "Your caravan is close to his new modern house on the next driveway. Ah here we are, your home for a while, isn't that a beauty? "

We drew up beside a shiny new 34 footer, a converted semi-trailer, fully electric and with welcoming lights shining bright. When Betty joined us her face showed just how happy she was with the impeccably kept interior of the giant of a caravan that was in fact a mobile home. The fridge was stocked, the stove shiny clean, the double bed was made up with the sheets turned back as with four single beds that could be stowed in the walls. The toilet and shower, squabs, cushions, chairs and tables were all in as new condition. To us the van was luxurious. The kids came to life and were all very happy, exploring from end to end, choosing their beds. Col faced a return to Melbourne on leaving, after we'd taken it all in and showed our appreciation. Before he left I was told that my services were required most urgently. Doug, who lived in Geelong would pick me up in the 'ute' at eight o'clock for Moorabbin airport at Frankston where I would start in to a license exam.

We retired knowing that our state of living was going to improve. We were going to love our life in Australia and the people of the great land. Even the early morning air oozed a warm, caring, friendly welcome.

LET US SPRAY

The caravan was our home for several weeks while I became licensed and settled in to a heavy aerial spraying season. After finishing a job I could fly home to Mountjoy's property, land the Tiger amongst the sheep in an adjoining paddock, walk through a gate to the van to be greeted by my wife and kids. Or conversely, take off from the paddock with the dawn, to make off for the property calling for spraying services, herding the same bleating sheep from the take-off path by blasts of the engine or slipstream. Unlike the white sheep common to New Zealand these were grey coloured.

The mode of navigating over the sunburnt countryside to a property some distance away was by IFR (I follow roads), not Instrument Flight Rules. It took only a few days for the sheep to learn to stay near the fence lines during the 'plane's arrival and departure, the 'ozzie' sheep were not so dumb. Following the farmer's directions to the letter as to how to find his property and the loader-driver with the truck could be very confusing. A landing alongside a road or farmhouse or a low run over a road sign was sometimes necessary to gain more expert advice as to his exact location.

As a family we made good friends with the Mountjoys, who to this day remain amongst the most considerate, kind and generous people we've ever known and who made our introduction to country Australia such a wonderful experience. Shopping trips to Geelong for Betty were organised in my absence, the pantry was always well stocked. When the Mountjoys' needed the caravan for a beach holiday with their family, we moved into their new home as caretakers of the entire property, sheep, dogs and house cow and with unrestricted use of a new FJ Holden and farm 'ute'.

In a few short weeks Fiji was almost forgotten, things were looking so much better, Col and Doug's aerial spraying marketing skills were returning very good results.

For Victoria at that time, the aerial application method of pest and weed control had not really taken on, the man on the land needed a lot of convincing as to the probable outcome when applied to his crops, however a full season's work was close to being booked up.

My second major accident occurred at Cressy, Victoria, soon after arriving to work with Aerial Missions, as the company was named. AM was also a training ground for would-be mission pilots in New Guinea, operating DH82 (Tiger Moth), Avro 643 (Avro Cadet) and Cessna 180 aircraft. I began with the Tiger, which was considered to be a good spray vehicle for the smaller jobs.

After finishing a spraying job late one afternoon, my loader-driver drove me to another property nearby to inspect a linseed crop that was first on the list for the following morning. Crop spraying is best done in flat calm conditions in the cool of the morning or evening, to prevent evaporation of the liquids during the heat of day, or some of the lethal spray drifting on the wind to poison an adjoining neighbour's vegetable crop, where it would not be welcomed.

One late afternoon the farmer showed me the paddock where I'd land and where the chemicals on the truck would be mixed and pumped into the 'hopper' that had taken the place of the Tiger's forward seat.

The 'Moth' (DH82) had been designed in the '30's as an initial flying trainer, to carry instructor and pupil in tandem in open cockpits in the fuselage. The Instructor sat in the forward cockpit, the pupil in the rear, communicating with each other through a 'Gosport' mouthpiece that fed through tubes to the pilots' helmets. When flying the Tiger solo, the pilot used the rear cockpit for optimum balance. Post-war, the Tiger was approved for agricultural purposes by the fitting of a hopper in the forward cockpit authorised to carry 225 kgs (500 lbs) of super phosphate or liquids. When filled with the requisite material the Tiger was then carrying the equivalent in weight of two and a half well-built Instructors and was a much different aircraft to fly than the trainer version!

The dimensions of the crop of linseed would allow the job to be completed with one load of pesticide mix (50 gallons) at the recommended rate of application. The loader-driver suggested that there was no need for him to bring the truck over to the farmer's property for such a small job instead he would load the Tiger at our temporary base about 30 kilometres away. At dawn I would fly directly to the paddock (with the spray already mixed in the hopper) ready to start work. The farmer readily agreed, for he would be saved a lot of trouble. His cows would not be disturbed by a 'plane landing or the arrival of the truck, the pests destroying his linseed would be exterminated before he was awake.

As we talked over some of the ramifications of spraying by air, which was foreign to him, I took a look over the paddock from the nearest fence. From there a tall power-pole near some trees at the opposite end of the paddock was spotted. Rather than drive around for a closer look, that meant opening and closing three farm gates twice, I accepted his word on the exact route the wires took from the pole in relation to the paddock when with a stick he scribed a 'mud map' in the dust at our feet.

The crop was rectangular in shape and otherwise free of obstructions. 'Crop dusters' often face the hazards of some farm equipment being left parked in the crop and are dangerous to a low-flying 'plane. Long handled shovels, scarecrows and the like, or shorter poles carrying farm telephone lines from 'headquarters' to cow-shed or shearing shed, were some of the hazards a pilot might need to know about. Rather than take someone's word that the paddock is ready for spraying, the pilot should check for himself. Aerial spraying was new to many farmers at the time, they didn't understand that the 'croppie' must fly very low to achieve the best results.

In my case, with the crop being relatively small, it would be quite easy to spray the paddock without using human markers standing in the crop and pacing out a swathe distance for each run by waving a rag tied to a pole. Marking a crop by that method could be a scary job with always the chance of getting sconed by some part of the 'plane, or being splattered with, or inhaling, highly toxic spray.

Before leaving, I told the farmer that the Tiger would start on his crop before 5 am, each run paralleling the greatest length of fence-line nearest his house and would occupy a total of less than 30 minutes. When finished with the one load, I would go on to other jobs that were lined up for me in the district. Doug would follow up by road for the payment cheque.

4.45 am next day, saw me on the way to the client's property in the silver coloured 'Tiger' Uniform Yankee Kilo, with 50 gallons of pesticide in the hopper, flying low enough to sight a fox or two loping off to the day's lair, or scattering sheep in the paddocks lining the road. In the first week of summer the Western District was already beaten to a sunburnt brown, interspersed with brilliant green squares of cropping.

I picked my target out and manoeuvred for the first run, which was to be over a spot marked with a white rag tied to the fence. The air was hot for the time of day, the 'Tiger' felt heavy as with throttle wide open I flashed over the first mark, while shoving the control lever forward to release the brake of the wind-driven pump, the wheels of the Tiger almost brushing the crop. The tip of the left lower main-plane was then below and about two metres in from the side fence. As I flattened for the spraying run, the 'Tiger' began to rock as the pesticide surged back and forth in the hopper. Surging always occurred on the first few spraying runs until the level of fluid in the hopper dropped as the spray was used up.

With the far fence coming up fast, the pump was flipped off as I eased the Tiger up out of the crop at the beginning of a sharp, left-banked climbing turn which continued for a few seconds until at about 50 feet (18 metres) altitude the Tiger was rolled over hard to the right while I twisted my head around to get a sight of the fence as it came into view again. Not much spray had been used up in the one run the 'plane was acting very heavy which was normal. 'Tear-drop' is the modern term used for that type of reverse turn.

The morning air was so very still. As the paddock came in sight I could see the wide band of discharged pesticide, settling down on to the crop, which gave me a perfect guide for the next run. The nose was pushed down and aimed for the fence as we swept in for the second swathe. The right wingtip was then running along where the first band of the delicate, lacelike spray ended.

A reverse turn in a fixed wing aircraft when aerial spraying, is a form of art with time economy playing a big part. To watch a good 'croppie' at work in his fixed wing air machine is like watching the performance of an accomplished circus trapeze artist. The manoeuvres require perfect rhythm, intense concentration, emotions of a concert pianist, the co-ordination and timing of a maestro.

The pilot's adrenalin pumps as the 'plane skims across the fence and levels off close down on the crop, closely following any natural undulations in the paddock as would a tractor.

From the corner of my eye, the nozzles below the trailing edges of both lower wings could be seen emitting in the slipstream behind the aircraft a swirling white cloud of spray along the wingspan.

A pilot in a bi-'plane with an open cockpit, wind buffeting and whistling over a leather helmet or 'bone-dome', is taken back to the early days of aviation, it's thrilling, it's fun and something akin to Baron von Richtofen and the World War 1 air battles, not to mention the daring exploits of Bert Hinkler, Kingsford-Smith or the US Mail pilots. For the period of the spraying the pilot becomes an integral part of his fabric covered though otherwise 'metal bird'. That's how it was with me that day. The thrill coming from being able to throw the tiny bi-plane about in perfectly calm air, at lunacy levels so close to the ground is exhilarating.

In seconds it's time to 'turn about' for the next spraying run in the opposite direction, which will be further into the paddock. First, ease up over the fence while banked to the right followed by a switch to a left climbing turn until the crop comes into view and down on to the crop again, tail high, leaving a 'vapour- trail' 'a la' Battle of Britain, in the opposite direction. This is all done by feel, there's scarcely time or opportunity to check on airspeed with a quick look down in the cockpit. A pilot must be extra careful with the first few runs and not use the controls too harshly with the aircraft heavy as it is.

The nasty smell of the poisonous pesticide in the hopper, whipped back by the slipstream now gets to my nose, the small protective mask dangling around my neck that should have been in place has been forgotten. Too bad, the rhythm cannot be interrupted, both my hands are fully occupied, the right on the control stick, the left split between throttle, pump lever and the 'cheese-cutter' of an elevator trim. All the time the 140 horsepower Gypsy Major engine is locked on full throttle, running without a falter although due to the warm air not turning out much more than 120 hp.

High temperatures play havoc with the older, normally aspirated engines. That is one of the main reasons for such early starts to the work.

With the four-strand fence at the end of the paddock coming in fast the spray-pump lever is slammed off only meters before a steady back pressure on the stick lifts the Tiger up over the fence. The level of the fluid in the hopper has not dropped that much, my metal bird still feels heavy. A cautious left bank is made while gaining height followed by a more positive roll to the right until it seems we're standing on a wingtip. My head on its 'rubber neck 'twists to look over the shoulder to judge the next swathe across the crop. With the paddock in sight again the nose goes down towards the fence-line, to build up that precious speed.

Suddenly, as if a giant hand had plucked it from the air, the 'Tiger' is thrown about as might a child discard an unwanted toy. Through the propeller the fence span around faster than any real spin I'd ever been in. The force slammed me to one side of the cockpit, tore the control stick from my hand and my feet from the rudder pedals. My 'Tiger' is completely out of control, my mind a whirlwind of confusion. Has a stall occurred? Was the turn too tight were my thoughts as the fence spins around again while rushing towards me at the rate of knots?

Near to vertical now the Tiger's nose with its whirling propeller, slams into the green of the crop. Whether I'm right way up or left way down I'm not certain as my head jerks forward and smashes on to the frame and my forehead takes the full force of the collision. The leather padding over the curved woodwork had not been replaced after the last inspection for some reason.

Following a loud 'crruuunch' the engine stops dead, the propeller flies into splinters. Clods of earth fly in all directions, the wing becomes a crumpled heap of twisted wires, bent woodwork, metal struts and torn to tatters fabric. With me suspended in the shoulder harness, stunned by the impact as the Tiger shows just how well it can stand upright on its' nose of its own accord and with the engine embedded deep into the softer soil below the lush-green of a healthy crop, the next few seconds seemed like hours.

Blood from the wound across the forehead ran from under my 'bone dome', streamed into my eyes and began to drip down on to the inward side of the shattered windshield. Both my eyes were blinded and stinging, the wreckage seen as through a haze. Wincing from pains all over and suspended upside down, my gloved hands sought the seat-harness locking-pin that would be about level with my navel, which was hard to find and harder still to release with the harness now carrying all my weight. When it did come free, without the shoulder straps then in support, I fell forward on to the metal windshield bracing which left me with my eyes staring at the fuel tank from very close quarters, too close. The smell of fuel dripping from the tank through an over-strained fuel-line and mixing with fumes from the pesticide spilling from the hopper, began to choke me to cause the involuntary retching of my belly. Panic seized me as with my arms and headfirst I managed to lever myself from the cockpit and fall into the crumpled mass of the lower left main-plane now a grotesque heap of ripped fabric, twisted flying and landing wires, splintered wooden ribs and spars.

Hauling myself to my knees somehow I shoved my way through that jungle, fully expecting the 'Tiger' to erupt in flames at any second should the fuel become ignited by a spark of some kind. The heavily doped fabric on its own was fuel enough for a fierce fire. In only a few short minutes, or even seconds, the 'plane with me trapped inside like a monkey in a cage, could be reduced to ashes.

There were no witnesses around who could tell me just how long it took to evacuate 'ol UYK'. It must have been only twenty seconds later that the stupefied pilot of the wrecked aircraft was clear and standing knee-deep in the as yet, untreated crop of linseed. My 'bone-dome' had taken a heavy knock but seemed to be fully intact, although blood was still oozing out from under the rubberised sealing. A decision was made then to leave the 'bone dome' on, for all I knew it could be holding my brains in. Stinking of pesticide I began to stagger off in the direction of the farm house, climbed the barbed-wire fence somehow and cleared the crop. Thankfully the expected explosion never came, the early morning air remained still and quiet.

When about 30-metres from the house, the farmer's wife, clad in a dressing gown, came running towards me grabbed an arm and helped me up the steps to the house. That lady must have been shocked by meeting up with such a bloody apparition on her doorstep so early in the morning. Motioning me to lie on a couch and remove the 'bone dome' she began to bathe my head wound, washed the blood from around my eyes and ordered 'hubby' to 'phone for an ambulance.

Just what had happened to induce the mad spin and sudden plunge to earth couldn't be fathomed. A failed wing spar, a flying wire breaking or becoming loose under strain, a stall, those were but some of the possibilities that went through my mind.

The answer to that came when Farmer McNaughton returned from a visit to the linseed paddock, in a grim frame of mind by the look on his face. My 'Tiger' he claimed, had hooked a wing on the power-line and pulled the line from two poles without it breaking. Power to both his milking-shed and house was disrupted, although part of his linseed crop being ruined seemed to be his main gripe.

How my 'Tiger' could have collided with the high-tension wire baffled me. Care had been taken on each turn over the wire to watch through the corner of my eye for the post near the trees and not dive on to the crop until it was safely past. The wire itself had never been visible. My 'sorries' were still being mumbled to the angry farmer when the ambulance arrived to take me to the hospital at Colac, forty or fifty kilometres from the farm.

The ugly gash on my forehead ran from eyebrow to eyebrow and required 20 or more stitches. There was no doubt that my two days old, or young, 'bone dome', that had replaced the antiquated leather helmet previously worn in the 'Tiger', had saved me from more severe head injuries or possibly death itself.

Before 7 am and after an injection of a sedative of some kind, the medicos had attended to me and placed me in a nice clean bed. What would Betty's reaction be when she heard of the accident, she was so happy in the van at Maude. How long am I going to be laid up, how will Col and Doug cope without the 'Tiger' were most of my thoughts before the sedative took over.

Days later, after statements had been taken, with the investigator we were able to piece together what had actually happened. The high-tension wire between the two posts, known as a 'single-phase', had a span of more than the width of the paddock. At certain angles and conditions of light, from the air the line would not have been visible.

The wire however did not run exactly parallel to the paddock's bottom fence but angled closer to the side that was first to be sprayed. The post I used as marker was approximately 75-metres back from the fence, the other post, completely hidden behind trees, brought the wire to within about 25-meters of the fence-line. How the line had been missed on the first pass was hard to understand, except for the early pull-up initiated through the 'Tiger' being at it's heaviest. On that occasion I must have missed the wire only by inches.

Had time been taken to open and close three gates twice and the angle of the line in relation to the fence been more closely inspected, instead of assuming that it ran parallel, the accident I'm sure would not have happened.

Both Col and Doug were quick to visit me at the hospital.

"Get well soon we need you. " was the cry. "There's plenty of spraying yet to be done, we know you won't be doing that again. Tiger's are easily fixed, don't worry, the McNaughton job was finished with another Tiger. "

That was such a relief 'firing' or 'sacking' was never mentioned. I really did learn from that. Never again was a crop sprayed without me first taking a very close look around the boundaries, gates or no gates to open and close. Although in later times I flew under many a wire, beside or over them, never again did I fly through them, which was the lot of many a good 'croppie' at the time.

When after a time the pain an accident causes wears off, there is often a humorous side to be seen. At home some time after, an explanation was given to my long-suffering wife within earshot of some of the children as to how a pilot must act quickly to undo the harness, scramble from the cockpit and crawl through the debris to safety, before a fire started. In fun, to amuse the children, I did an imitation of just how that was done by diving off a sofa on to the floor while flailing my arms and lags about vigorously.

When flying the open-seat Tiger or Cadet in the cold Victorian weather, I wore leather, fleecy-lined flying-boots of WW2 vintage, which were cleaned and generally well looked after by Betty or myself. Betty was giving the boots a touch-up one-day when son Jack, then almost four years of age, came out in delightful baby talk.

"Are those Dad's 'quickly boots' Mum? "

Unwittingly he had created a family joke, a small thing perhaps, thereafter the boots became known as my 'quickly boots'. Forty years later the boots were presented to Jack for use on his 'Harley'. He keeps them in good order to this day 'en France', not so very far from the country where they were manufactured originally. The early model bone dome, that I'm sure had saved my life, was kept in possession for many years until finally meeting it's Waterloo in a warehouse fire while being stored prior to shipment from Port Moresby PNG.

AERIAL TOP-DRESSING

(Superphosphate is not sprayed but 'sowed' or 'spread')

The name of the game is 'aerial top-dressing', the 'spreading' of granulated pellets of super-phosphate from the air for rejuvenating pasture growth, usually on hill country carrying, cattle or sheep. The tactics employed are somewhat different to those used in spraying liquids. Some of the differences are:

When sowing 'super', the aircraft can be flown at up to100 feet above terrain for the best spread;

'super' is discharged from the aircraft when the pilot pulls the lever that opens the doors at the bottom of the hopper, the slipstream, altitude and sometimes the wind, being enough to spread the quantity required per acre on to the pasture. The 'super' leaves the aircraft's hopper in a few seconds. Application rates differ from place to place and can be adjusted by the settings of the doors of the hopper. One big advantage the aircraft has over other types of spreaders is that super can be applied to hilly, broken or stony country that could be out of the reach of horse-drawn or motorised spreaders. The aircraft therefore, needs to be re-loaded frequently.

(c) with care being taken as to wind drift and aircraft operating limitations, 'spreading' super can continue in conditions of moderate winds.

(d) a great deal of expert co-ordination must exist between pilot and driver of the loading tractor.

The super-phosphate is dumped in a heap at the head of the airstrip from where the 'plane will start its take-off run. Small farms around Victoria might spread ten tons annually, bigger landholdings between 100-300 tons, or even more.

With a Cessna 180 I was once left to spread 800 tons, a complete trainload, over a huge Victorian property with lots of stone fences, while flying from the several strips on the property. That amounted to at least 1600 flights for the Cessna. After battling on for several days, rain showers began to interfere with loading and flying, the Cessna was unserviceable. With more rain forecast for the area the property owner was getting anxious at the thought of having many tons of super being turned into rock-like cement when summer came. Col sought the aid of another operator to share the work. With all the paddocks becoming boggy with the rains, the final 50-tons was finished using an Avro Cadet, flying off a public gravel road about 18 feet in width, with the take-off having to be made across a railway line that was sometimes active.

The tractor driver was forced to carry each load from the heap of super through a very soft, boggy paddock to a wooden platform at the roadside loading point. There was no room on the road for the Cadet to turn around. Each landing was made towards the tractor to park most accurately for re-loading. The tractor on its platform of planks over the bog was limited in manoeuvre. After being loaded the take off must be straight ahead across the railway line. That was life in the super-spreading lane in those early days, job completed satisfactorily but not on time.

With the grab on a crane-like arm, the tractor scoops the super up from a heap and weighs it to the agreed amount for the aircraft type and/or conditions. From his cockpit the pilot, opens the lid of the hopper as the tractor moves towards the aircraft at an angle behind the wing and guides the canvas sleeve of the grab into the mouth of the hopper to allow the 'super' to be dumped inside. The driver must take great care not to damage any part of the aircraft in the process. The aircraft must always park accurately in the same position for each loading and with engine running, propeller spinning. The moment the tractor backs off and is clear, the aircraft commences the take off run, to spread the 'super' methodically over a nearby paddock as per instructions.

3-5 minutes later, the super having been expended, the aircraft lands towards the tractor to position for another load. The driver needs to be ready and waiting to dump another load in. It takes only a few loads before a practiced pilot and tractor-driver, begin working to an appropriate rhythm. Short breaks are made for re-fuelling or equipment checks.

Early morning starts are the norm, with work continuing until the heap of super is dispersed as required, or as sometimes happens, a mechanical fault or unsuitable weather curtails the operation. A very real rhythm of movement needs to exist between pilots and drivers when more than one aircraft eats into the one heap of super.

One very hot Victorian day I was flying a 'Ceres' aircraft, a conversion of the famous Wirraway, to spread 50-tons of 'super' on hill-country farmland at Bungleboori, near Mangalore in Victoria, using the ground equipment and driver of a sister aerial agricultural company with whom I'd not worked with before. The modified Wirraway in some ways resembled the AT6, SNJ, North American Harvard. My machine was the very first 'Wirra' to be converted.

Having flown both types I can say that in performance there is not much resemblance between the two, the Harvard being much more lively in control response than the Ceres, which was more of a 'dray' or 'bag of nails' with it's one ton load of 'super' in a hopper in front of the pilot. The cockpit is roomy, the visibility good, the pilot sat on, rather than in, the Ceres which was one of the largest single engine 'super spreaders' of the time. The Ceres also sported a more powerful engine than the Harvard. I'm sure a Harvard wouldn't respond happily to a one ton load of super in the fuselage in front of the pilot.

I flew to the farm at Bungleboori, Victoria early in the morning, recognizing the strip from the air by the tractor-loader parked near a whitish-coloured heap of 'super'. Col as operations manager had established and advised me accordingly, that there were no power lines at all in the operating area which was all hill-country. The fifty tons would take about four hours to spread, for he had been warned of a longer than normal carrying distance from the only strip available to the chosen paddocks. .

Before starting, the tractor driver had agreed on the weight to be uplifted on each trip from the 500 meters airstrip, which was of marginal length for a fully loaded 'Ceres'. The strip's surface was mildly rough and sloped down from the heap at about 5%, which was somewhat encouraging, ending above a deep, rocky, scrub-infested gully.

My 'sour grapes' feeling must have been noticed when it was learned that parts of the area to be treated were up to 4 kilometres distant, my bonus was paid for tons spread, not flight time.

To sound out the Cere's performance on that strip initially, a load of 900 kilograms was agreed to between us. At that time we were calculating loads by 'bags', one bag being 90 kilograms. The metric system of weights had not then been introduced. Twelve 'bags' would be a full load for a Ceres under ideal conditions on an 800-metre level strip, with appropriate temperature and wind conditions prevailing. Therefore it was decided that with the assistance offered by the slope, there would be the equivalent of 10 'bags' in the hopper not 12 to get the feel of things.

With the load decided on we got down to starting the work, two men, a tractor, a Ceres that the driver was not familiar with and a 50-ton heap of super. With the briefing over I climbed up into the cockpit, tightened the harness, snugged the 'bone dome' on firmly, wriggled into a comfortable position, checked the brakes were holding, before going into the start procedure.

The big radial engine, a Pratt & Whitney 1340, coughed into life, dust from the heap was stirred up and began to fly in a great white cloud behind the aircraft. Under my bone-dome only a quiet world of my own existed when the lid of the hopper was raised as the tractor charged me from the heap for the first time. With the stick provided, the delivery end of the sleeve was poked into the opened hopper when the 'Ceres' shuddered and 'squatted' as suddenly the weight of 10 bags of super was delivered into her inner parts in one foul swoop. With the tractor retreating I wound the engine up to full power, re-leased the brakes and roared off down the sloping paddock, henceforth called a 'strip'.

The first round trip took more than ten minutes, for the correct boundary had to be found and a decision made on the best way to go about the spreading runs. Farmers took exception to the fertilising of their neighbour's property. Is that any wonder? The first spreading run went along the fence-line furthest from the heap of super, subsequent loads would then see the trips getting shorter as the spreading drew closer.

While things were quiet before we started, together we'd arranged appropriate hand signals. With the engine running and 'super' dust flying in the slipstream I would be encased in a world of my own, conversing with the tractor driver would not be possible.

To begin, ten 'bags' was the yardstick. One finger up from me meant that the driver could load the Ceres with 11 bags' for the fol-lowing trip. The finger pointed down meant the load must be reduced to 'nine bags', or eight if I signalled two fingers down. Loads of less than 9 bags though would make the job uneconomical from my com-pany's point of view, mine too, with too little tonnage sown for the airtime taken. As previously stated extended distances for delivery were not welcome. The job of quoting was left to the operations man-ager, who would aim for a certain profit price per ton.

The first dozen take-offs with 10 bags aboard gradually got tighter, with the fence at the top of the gully getting closer and closer each time and the Ceres tail becoming harder to lift in the distance available. Three-point take offs in most tail-wheel aircraft are not good for the health! Airborne over the gully, the Ceres was taking time to reach a safe manoeuvre speed. Overall the machine felt sluggish, which was put down to a very hot morning, or too much load for the local conditions. The engine instruments seemed to read correctly, a quick magneto check showed the drop on one set of plugs to be close to the maximum allowable, but were within acceptable limits. The sluggishness was put down to a sharp increase in temperature and the increase in wind speed which was following me down the hill.

Returning to the loading point after the 18th flight and a very 'dicey' take-off, I gave the driver the 'one down' signal, which meant he would load the equivalent of nine 'bags' into the hopper. Carrying that amount for such a long distance, would mean that the sowing thereof would not only be uneconomical, but the original estimate of four hours for completion of the job would now be six or more. I could see that the job was not suited to my big metal bird like all the others I flew and was beginning to love. Sowing the 50-tons was going to take longer than planned. For a time, operations might have to be suspended until the wind abated, which could mean an overnight stay in the area, or at the very best, if conditions improved during the afternoon, working on until last light to complete the job. The tractor crew would also be inconvenienced by having to delay other work awaiting them..

The decreased load went in with the usual thump and characteristic squat as the gear took up resistance to the sudden weight. From the corner of my eye I saw the tractor moving away with its arm high, as I 'poured on the horses' to the big radial with it's three bladed propeller. That was a little too much for the brakes, we began to creep forward, for a second a slight 'gurgle' to the engine was detected. Another glance at the instruments confirmed the engine to be operating at peak. The brakes were released, the eager to go Ceres ploughed off down the slope, as per tradition, leaving the heap of super enveloped in a huge cloud of whitish dust. On previous take-offs I had been able to lift the tail-wheel about two-thirds of the way down the strip. Now at that point it was firmly on the ground, with the Ceres tail not showing any inclination at all to come up with the stick hard forward, while the fence above the gully rushed in.

At that time everything happened in microseconds. I knew that we'd never make the air without losing some weight from the hopper, all the weight, every single pellet. With my left hand I jerked the toggle that opened the dump doors, shoved hard on the stick and pushed the throttle 'through the gate' too as she tried to launch herself into the air over the gully at a critical angle. The rusty wire fence flicked by underneath, how the wheels and left wing tip missed it I'll never know. For a second, only a second, I thought she was going to fly as we sank into the gully, with the super just beginning to dump from the hopper.

There was air beneath although the Ceres was fully stalled, under full power. The left wing flicked down as the big metal bird started to roll with the wing almost vertical or so it seemed. Instinctively I kicked on the right rudder while holding the stick hard forward. All to no avail, the left wing contacted the ground, the aircraft slewed, collapsing the gear like matchwood until sliding down the rock strewn slope on her belly in a cloud of white 'super' dust and with the hollow, 'scrunching' sounds of tortured metal.

The big propeller chopped into the rock-strewn soil, sparks flew as the metal blades were shattered, clods of earth were tossed high, up and over, while the engine was torn from its' mountings to bounce ahead of the airframe down the slope, with me sitting as upright as one would when watching television from an easy chair.

At a time like that the mind is frozen, things seem to happen in slow motion. With me secure in the engineless airframe with the big hopper up front taking all the shock, my metal bird came to a sudden stop. The engine with a twisted propeller still attached, also ceased it's cavorting further down the gully.

In a daze I watched the flames flickering around the circle of cyl-inders and propeller blades as the grass ignited, then spread quickly with flames licking hungrily at the scrub creating a perfect setting for a scrub-fire. Easy to see was the effect of the wind taking the fire up the opposite side of the gully, for the time being I was safe.

Numbed by the shock, watching the fire spread, I released the shoulder harness before clambering out on to the top of the left wing that was then flat to the ground. As if in a dream, for some reason or old habit, the lid to the hopper was raised to allow me a look inside. Surprisingly, there was still a large amount of super there that set me thinking.

The Ceres looked to be a complete wreck minus the engine and propeller. The landing gear had been torn from its mounts and was now somewhere underneath the dented airframe. The left wing was bent and twisted and was trailing several ripped panels of the alumini-um skin. Keeping an eye on the fire across the gully, I staggered clear of the wreckage to await the driver's arrival.

The aircraft had come to rest down the gully below the level of the airstrip. To be able to sight the loader at the heap of super meant a climb of 30 meters or so up a medium slope, a climb that I didn't feel up to making, my thoughts being that the sight of smoke in the gully would be enough to bring the driver to the scene in a hurry. The smoke from the scrub fire was by then rising to a considerable height and should have been well within view of anyone at the top end of the strip. Part of the loader-driver's job was to monitor the position of the machine throughout the take-off and all other times if possible. My man was expected to arrive within a few minutes. Ten minutes that seemed like ten hours went by before he, with the property owner and a jackaroo, began to skid and slide down to me through the trail of super. I couldn't help but say that they'd taken a long time to arrive. Their delay was passed off by the driver as his being occupied talking to the two men. All their heads were down studying a map showing some revised boundaries for the spreading that would be passed to me on my next arrival, neither of them had noticed anything amiss until the smoke was seen rising from the gully.

A 'croppie's' life can be hard. He can trust only himself, all the time. In the ten minutes when the progress of the 'plane was not being followed by the driver, I would have re-loaded at the heap and taken to the air again! Being somewhat disappointed at his explanation I pressed on with some questions as to just how many 'bags' had been loaded on before the abortive take-off. Mention was also made that although the toggle to the dump doors had been activated, the hopper remained well filled. His answer was evasive and interrupted by the property owner yelling for helpers to stem the fire.

Rightly so, the fire took precedence over everything else, I grabbed a dampened sack, thrown down from a truck, to begin batting at the small patches of burning grass now closing in on the wreck. Workers from neighbouring properties then began to arrive and in an hour the fire was well under control while for me shock was setting in.

I left the scene wondering just what had really happened to prolong that take-off. By the thin trail of super over the lip of the airstrip it was obvious that the 'dump' doors had not been fully open. Had they been, the load would have dumped in only a second or two, the Ceres would have flown away as if rocket propelled and climbing after a quick turn down the gully, or had the driver inadvertently given the Ceres an overload for the prevailing conditions? Had the 'dump' failed in some way? Was the engine delivering full available power? An answer to all of those questions niggled at me for a long time. The good news was that the 'Ceres' could and would be, rebuilt.

The top-dressing season was in full swing. The following week I was at it again in the Western District that time in the delightful Avro Cadet (A643) bi-plane. In 'super' spreading the Avro needed to do four trips to the Ceres one. My personal record for one day's work in the Avro was 155 landings for 40 tons spread in 8.5 hours flying, an average of about 18 landings per hour over the period.

About forty Avro Cadets were built for the RAAF prior to WW2 and were considered to be a grade above the 'Tiger' Moth as an initial trainer. That comparison was decidedly true. Upper and lower mainplane ailerons, wheel-brakes, tail-wheel and a nice soft, spring-hydraulic undercarriage for bump-free paddock landings were but some of the superior features of Cadets over Tigers. The seven-cylinder Genet Major radial engine delivered 150 horsepower. All those features made the Cadet a delight to fly making much more smooth aerobatics possible. The rapid rate of roll more resembled that of a Spitfire. Even at the end of a long day's spreading, the temptation to make a roll, a loop or an 'ozzle-twizzle' over the loader, or the property owner's grey-stone mansion as a signal that the job was completed was hard to resist.

More specialist 'super spreaders' were by now coming on to the market along with better and safer airstrips. Power-lines that created another hazard to crop-dusters were beginning to be marked with red coloured balls on their wires. Loading equipment was being updated, courses for pilots in spraying and top-dressing were becoming available.

My life had been spared 3 times in 3 separate miracles, accidents in which I could easily have been killed, it could be said that plenty of warnings had been given me. In the interim I'd done some Bible reading, listened to 'The Word' from ministers, teachers, priests and preachers, my view on life was quite different to that of a few short years before. I was being changed, coming to terms with my mistakes, errors, sins if you like, while not blaming anyone but myself.

My good guardian angel was telling me that I'd been living too close to the wind of fortune. A step of faith was needed. My vision to serve in New Guinea as a mission pilot was reinforced when I knew that Betty had undergone a similar change and would support any decisions made in me taking up a post there.

At the end of a 'super' season and before spraying started again, I accepted a request for an appropriately qualified pilot for a mission in the Territory of New Guinea. Col was handling Aerial Missions on his own, Doug having departed for Irian Jaya to serve with Summer Institute of Linguistics, some weeks before me.

We left many good friends behind in Victoria, counting our time there as some of the happiest days of our lives. After a few weeks in that lovely caravan, we had moved to Wurrook South, Rokewood and then to Belmont, Geelong.

For certain jobs an appropriate aircraft might be chartered from another operator, quite often, my 'crop duster' machine of the day could be a Cessna 180, a Tiger, Avro Cadet, Ceres, EP9 or Fletcher. At Geelong the 'planes were quartered on the Geelong Common a stretch of open land on the banks of the Barwon River, only a short walk and a climb over a barbed wire fence to our house in Francis Street. On finishing a job late one Saturday afternoon the Fletcher was left parked on the Common.

An inquisitive youth on the loose at the Common was able to slide the hood open, take the pilot's seat in the cockpit and fiddle with the controls. Somehow the engine fired into life with the throttle set fully open. Having been shut down for only a short time the engine started with a roar, the tie-down pickets were pulled out, the aircraft jumped forward. He was able to leap from the cockpit and tumble off the wing on to the ground. The tricycle undercarriage of the Fletcher probably saved him from serious injury by allowing the tailplane to pass over him and prevent any damage as the 'plane gathered speed. In a slight left curve and pilotless the machine took a short run across the undulations in the Common before crashing into the Barwon river with a mighty splash to sink almost directly under the traffic bridge! On hearing the noise I ran to the Common in time to see the tail disappearing below the surface of the river and not knowing whether or not someone had been in the cockpit at the time. Soon the bridge was lined with spectators none of whom had sighted 'who dun it' or where he was.

That kid must have spent a few frightened hours before deciding to confess to his 'misdemeanour' and save the police a lot of trouble, which he did late that evening. No charges were ever laid. I've often wondered if he ever became a pilot, he must have had leanings that way. Aircraft engines are not so easy to start, except for the throttle setting though, the twelve-year old youngster had somehow found out how to make it look easy! The Fletcher was salvaged and put into service again before too long, the Barwon's fresh, clean water having done little damage in the way of corrosion.

Well remembered are the many other humorous incidents that occurred during my time in the Western District country of Victoria pioneering a new agricultural industry. Some of the directions from country clients early in the morning for the best route to their property are amongst some of the best.

"Follow the road out from the town for about twenty miles till you come to three forks, take the middle one, follow that for about ten miles, you can't miss it, we're well back from the road, long driveway with gums on the far side, you can't miss it, a dam on the other side with two gums on one end, that's the end farthest from the house, you can't miss it. There's usually a 'Chevvy' truck parked beside the shed, sometimes a car if it's not in the shed if me son's gone to town. When I hear y' comin' I'll be behind the shed waving a rag just to make sure you don't miss it."

Those sorts of directions were among some of the best, or worst depending on how they're viewed. Well I could 'miss it' and frequently did, when I would land in a paddock and seek directions from a shepherd or the driver of a Fordson tractor ploughing or whatever, which sometimes turned out to be just as obscure.

Here's another. The time is 2 pm on a very hot day in the Western District of Victoria. I'm lying in the shade under the wing of the Avro when the owner of the property drives across the paddock in a dusty, mud-spattered Rolls, yes a Rolls and with two Border Collies in the back seat admiring the view. After letting the dogs out for a romp he begins.

"I've been watchin', you haven't finished, only half of the paddock's been done "

The dogs start circling me and the other thing on the wheel of the Avro, sniffing snuffling and licking until I'm forced to stand up in the hot sun.

"It's too hot Mr Farmer, there's too much wind, we're going to wait until it cools down and the wind drops before finishing off, you know, evaporation, drift and all that, don't worry the job will be finished before dark."

He's a very amiable fellow. After doing a walk around with him, admiring the Rolls while keeping a wary eye on the two Collies at our heels, he joins me under the wing and listens while I tell him all I know about aerial spraying before asking him a few questions, the talk was that he was very rich.

"This property has been yours for many years I suppose Mr Farmer? "

"Yeh I was born here, me grandfather started it well back, when he died me father took it on, then me, this is the first time we've had sprayin' done by a 'plane."

"I suppose your son will follow in your footsteps and carry it on?"

"No, I've got no son. Only one daughter and she don't like bein' 'ere"

Now that is sad, what does she do?"

"She's a typewriter down in Melbourne!"

MISSION TO NEW GUINEA

Operating from Madang, on the north coast of the world's second biggest island, 'Lutmis' Aviation served more than 30 isolated mission stations situated in jungle covered hills, mountain valleys or on volcanic islands. Two Cessna aircraft and a Piper Super Cub were operated. Three pilots, including two who were also rated as maintenance engineers, comprised the mission's aviation staff.

Madang itself was a gentle, picturesque, tropical harbour town, with shady, tree-lined roads and avenues, together with many offshore islets and inlets close by along the coast with clear, blue water lapping gently onto sandy beaches. Although it was unbelievably hot for us having left Victoria only the day before, if there ever was a Paradise on earth it would be Madang. At least those were my first impressions when the town was first seen from the air as we circled to land on the day of arrival. Flown by Captain John Simler the Douglas C47 had met our DC6 and brought us over those formidable Owen Stanley and Bismarck mountains from Port Moresby making one stop at the highlands port of Goroka.

Our modern bungalow in an open compound on a rise across a neck of the harbour from the town, provided us with a magnificent view of the harbour and other offshore islands. Mission children went to school by a diesel-powered clinker-built dinghy, piloted by Kikintau a happy, smiling New Guinean. When they heard of this our children were thrilled at the prospect. En route the 'school-boat' passed by the battered, rusting hulks of several Japanese vessels bombed and beached during WW2. Everywhere there was evidence of the air, sea and land battles of war in marked contrast to the present day peace of Madang's harbour. There were no connecting roads from Madang to other commercial centres or to the hinterlands. The town was served by sea and air only.

Flying from Madang to Lae via Shaggy Ridge, the Ramu and Markham valleys, up to 30 WW2 aircraft wrecks could be counted lying on hillsides in clearings or in tall kunai grass, unfortunately all of them 'ours' and none of 'theirs'. Dr Braun the Chief Physician at the Lutheran Mission Hospital at Yagaum, along with Mrs Braun, became prisoners of the Japanese after the occupation of Madang. Dr Braun told me that one rainy day whilst he was tied to a tree in the town centre, the Japanese garrison were rejoicing, for more than thirty US aircraft returning from a raid on Hollandia in Dutch New Guinea had been forced to land along the Madang coast. Some suffered combat damage, others were out of fuel or unable to find their way to their bases in the Markham and Ramu valleys through poor weather. The ship, which was taking Dr. and Mrs Braun from Madang to Wewak was attacked by American planes. Both managed to escape injury and remained prisoners until war's end.

Almost a year passed before the results of the investigation into the Ceres accident reached me, when I received an unexpected visit from the aircraft's former owner. He had always thought and had spread the word that I had 'goofed' the take-off in some way. He wanted to apologise and set things straight which was very decent of him, not that I knew about that or had ever harboured any grudges myself.

Before I came to fly the Ceres, another pilot of his had complained of the engine dropping power at times. When his complaint had not been resolved that pilot had refused to fly the machine and had resigned. The owner admitted that he had disregarded the complaint for reasons of his own, mainly commercial and had not told me of the problem. He had his engineers run the engine on several occasions without any fault being found. He had come a long way to set matters right between us. For him to tell me must have been hard for him and made me feel a lot better, for the real reason for the cause of the accident was now coming to light.

Long after the accident and on receipt of a report from the previous pilot, the engine had been taken to the Government Aircraft Factory at Fishermen's Bend for testing. Full credit must go to the engine experts, who found that at the time of impact the valves in two of the cylinders were sticking, the engine was not delivering full power.

The departmental accident investigators too had done a wonderful job. The 'dump' doors on the hopper were found to be not fully open as the Ceres impacted which was probably due to a large clod of earth and grass blocking the doors from inside! The tractor had probably picked up the clod accidentally during a previous loading when the forks of the shovel dug the clod from the ground which was scooped up and deposited in the hopper. Due to impact damage to the doors this theory could not be fully proved. A sigh of relief came from me when that part of the report was revealed. To know about the hopper was pleasing for I'd often wondered whether the poor grip of my injured left hand might have contributed to the doors not opening fully when the toggle was activated.

Thirdly, by observer's reports on drifting dust and a flapping windsock, the wind was estimated to have increased to 12-15 mph since the start of the operation, an appreciable amount directly down the airstrip making for an undesirable tailwind take-off with the aircraft already overloaded for the distance available. Had the strip been one third longer, the Ceres might have been able to leave the ground while dumping the super from the hopper and return to the strip with me breathing hard.

Fourthly, the 'super' remaining in the hopper and along the 'dumping trail' had been estimated as far as was possible. The result was inconclusive as to the actual amount, although there was certainly a good load remaining when the two were combined.

The hand signals arranged between driver and pilot that day and whether one of us made a mistake in making or receiving the hand signal remains unsolved. The accuracy of the tractor's weighing system used, 'bags' to kilograms to pounds, also came into question.

As happens mostly in air accident investigation the cause is seldom attributed to a single factor. Human errors and oversights can compound the initial indications of a malfunction or error of some kind. For my part I should have been more aware of the source of the 'gurgle' I felt through the frame when the magnetos were checked before take-off. The hand signals should have been better arranged, particularly as we had not worked together before. From the beginning, my being aware that the airstrip was marginal for the operation of my big 'metal bird' should have been enough for me to speak up and lay out a better 'game plan'.

My wife was beginning to think that she could soon be a widow with four children on her hands. Our respective families too were questioning my choice of a vocation. Many times we went over the question as to whether flying should be given up for a safer job. That was the frame of mind I was in when we first moved to New Guinea to work with 'Lutmis' Aviation.

THE GREEN MACHINE – DORNIER 27

Church and Sunday school projects in Germany had contributed to the purchase of a Dornier 27 for 'the Mission' in faraway New Guinea. As from 1914, ex German New Guinea had been administered as a Mandated Territory by the Australian Department of Territories, through at first the League of Nations until after WW2 and the birth of the United Nations. Post WW2 the Territory became 'The Territory of Papua and New Guinea.' Name changes, when will our leaders in high places learn to resist the temptation to change the place names of a budding new country or nation? The German period was well remembered, many German interests were retained, particularly the work of Christian Fundamental, Evangelistic and Catholic missions.

The Do27 is a single-engine high-wing monoplane with a capacity for a pilot and five average-weight passengers with luggage. The mission's gift was fitted with a more powerful engine than fitted in the standard factory-built models. Soon after being put into service the Dornier received the title 'the Super Do27' from its two pilots, for the aircraft had outstanding performance.

With a GSO 480, super-charged, flat-six Lycoming engine of 340 hp and fixed leading edge slats, the Super Do27 handled problematical airstrips at high elevations with ease and without loss of any payload. But for the title sounding sacrilegious, the Super Do27 might well be named 'The Homesick Angel' for its fast rate of climb.

Soon after beginning its work from Madang, the Dornier' became very popular, especially with the missionaries on the more isolated stations with marginal airstrips. Much bigger payloads could then be flown in, with little or no restriction on outward-bound loads. The shorter airstrips, previously available only to the Piper Cub, could then be used with the bigger aircraft carrying a maximum load, which was four to five times greater than that of the Cub.

Although slower than a Cessna and more expensive to operate, that was offset by the Dornier's short take-off and rapid climb ability, a huge advantage in New Guinea's tough, hot and high, bush-flying conditions. Missionaries then had the means to contact those tribes without knowledge of the Gospel or what went on in the outside world of the 20th century. The flying of the Dornier was shared between the chief of the aviation department Ray Jaensch and myself on an alternate day basis. We both enjoyed the change from the Cessnas. With a full load aboard we soon became accustomed to leave even the most marginal airstrip behind with height to spare.

At that time the mission sold the smaller Cessna 170 to Mr Joh Bjelke-Petersen (later Sir Joh), Premier of Queensland, for private use. Sir Joh was a keen flyer. The Piper Super-Cub was retained for Dornier back-up and flown always by Tom Johnson of the State of Washington, USA, an expert in the field of short, boggy, one-way airstrips ringed by tall trees of the rain-forest. Many tribes-people owe their lives to Tom and the Cub that willingly provided sustenance, spiritual and medical aid without hesitation. For reasons best known to him, Tom was not keen in any way to fly the 'flash-looking' Dornier as mechanical and Super Cub duties kept him fully and gainfully employed.

The mission at Boana, in the mountains near Lae, had been established in German times. Prior to WW2 the work there was in the hands of missionary The Reverend Gustav Bergmann with wife Anna in support. During the war, their entire family had been interned in Australia along with all other German nationals. Gustav had pledged his life to serve the Lord in New Guinea and Boana particularly. When war was over he returned to Boana with its bullet-holed house and re-started his ministry. Post war he and his family became citizens of Australia.

Besides being a most devoted missionary of the practical type and highly respected by the local people, Gustav was also an avid, green-fingered gardener and one not afraid to take on anything that might be thought to be 'different', new, or 'too modern' for the area. Under his guidance the mission land grew many varieties of vegetables, which were flown to the markets in Lae, the proceeds going to the local church. Post-war, coffee was planted and soon became Boana's major export commodity. Without a connecting road through to Lae from the mission the only means of transport to the shipping port was by air.

Being so close to Lae, Gustav used Laurie Crowley of Crowley Airways, a local aircraft charter operator for most of the station's marketing needs. Gustav and Laurie were very good friends of many years standing. After the Dornier's arrival and settling in period tho', his German pride came to the fore and he began to request that the mission 'plane be used for some of the station's needs, mission and commercial.

At one time, with inclement weather restricting aircraft move-ments, the coffee storage shed at Boana was full to the roof with sacks of coffee beans. Gustav requested that during breaks in the weather the coffee be moved to Lae speedily in time for shipping. The Dornier was called in to compete with the operator's Piper Aztec in order to have all the coffee in Lae by the afternoon.

In the Green Machine from Madang, about eight in the morning I landed on Boana's undulating and sideways sloping grass strip set on an island-like plateau at the confluence of two rivers, to find the Crowley's twin-engine Aztec having already completed one trip and loading up for the second. It was easy to see that Laurie was after the major share of the work. The coffee-growers and the mission staff were all helping with the loading, carrying bags from the shed to be loaded aboard the Aztec. Wet grass prevented the sacks being placed on the ground, each man waited with the bag on his shoulder until it could be passed to a man on the wing for stowage in the cabin. The passenger seats had been removed to allow room for the bulky sacks.

The job for the loaders was a sweaty one and quite difficult. The Aztec had been designed for self-perambulating passengers, not such awkward cargo. However, the loading crew were very familiar with the over-wing loading job. In only a few minutes the Aztec was loaded and the two engines were started up. Without hesitation the line of Morobe men, each with a bag of coffee beans on his shoulder changed direction for the Dornier.

With mud flying from it's wheels the Aztec roared past the parking bay with Laurie giving me a ' see y' later' wave with two fingers only as he went by. I knew Laurie, I knew a race was on.

Boana mission was situated in a mountain valley at an elevation of 2800 feet, a valley that led directly south-east to Lae. After leaving the strip on take-off, further climbing wasn't necessary with Lae as a destination. A quick turn to the left was all that was required to be on course for the busy seaside airport, a 'downhill run' all the way. I watched as the twin flopped off the end of the strip and in to a descending left turn down the valley with the landing gear sliding up into the nacelles.

The 'Morobe men' who were loading had not laid eyes on a Dornier before. A few minutes were spent on showing them the best method of stowing the sacks aboard. The door on each side of the passenger cabin, cargo hold in that case, could be latched up under the wing and would be left open for the whole period, which rather surprised them. They were quick to understand and seemed eager to get on with the job on learning that the Dornier was 'their plane'.

Loading the coffee bags was quite easy for the smaller hill-men, with the sill to the cabin being at a most convenient height for their smaller than normal frames. One at a time they flipped a bag into the cabin from their shoulder with ease, for the two men inside the cabin to stack in a more orderly fashion. When the pre-arranged twelve bags, a maximum load, were stacked neatly aboard and secured under the net, I climbed to the cockpit with its push-up, wrap-around windshield and started up.

While swinging the Dornier around to face the take-off direction and doing all the radio things, 'vital actions' checks were completed, the throttle eased up smoothly to pour on the three hundred and forty horses of power that was always available from the supercharged engine. Less than halfway along the soggy strip the Dornier leapt into the air. With the route to Lae being all 'downhill' further climbing wasn't necessary. I drew the power off to cruise mode over the end of the strip to start into the descent at better than normal cruising speed. On the radio, Laurie could be heard receiving a landing clearance at Lae.

After landing at Lae, the Dornier was parked in front of the Crowley hangar close by the wreck of the 'Tengyu Maru' whose rusting bow rose from the reef off the end of the runway. The Aztec was moving away from the heap of coffee bags already delivered, at the start of a return flight to Boana.

The loading staff at Crowley's knew nothing of the Dornier. The engine was shut down while a demonstration was given to the two men as to how the doors were to remain latched open to the underside of the wing and the quickest way to hurl the bags from the cabin on to the tarmac so that the aircraft could depart promptly. The apron at that time was perfectly dry. That was the only time the Dornier was shut down that morning.

The flying time to Boana for the Dornier was only ten minutes and for the Aztec about eight or nine. There was little in the way of air traffic, the air was calm. Full of co-operation, the tower operator cleared me for an intersection take-off on the runway nearest to the heading for Boana. Two minutes after I became airborne, Laurie was heard reporting his arrival at Boana. I knew that the Dornier had gained a little and also knew that Laurie would be doing his damnedest to stop me closing another inch.

All morning the battle between us went on, with the Dornier gradually closing the gap by quicker turn-rounds while at the same time carrying more load than Laurie. The Aztec needed to shut down both engines for loading, the Dornier's engine could be kept running. Sensing that a race was on, the loaders trotted from the shed with a bag perched upright on a shoulder, as if their life depended on getting it into the Dornier before the world ended.

At Lae where the seaside airport was close to the centre of town, after each take-off and before landing, both aircraft would pass over a neatly laid out suburb and a tree-dotted, well-patronised, bright-green golf course in a beautiful setting of leafy green trees. The upturned faces of the spectators in backyards and on the golf course fairways, could be seen gaping up at the two machines coming and going regularly, with the green Dornier creeping closer to the yellow twin each time.

The control tower operators at Lae had been quick to accept the challenge by keeping other air traffic flowing smoothly without hindrance and coming up with some perfect separations for each aircraft during approach and departure. At an airport where everybody knew everybody no complaints came from the 'big boys' in their big metal birds nor was any dreaded Form 225 action called for as could often happen.

News had somehow spread of the 'race' and the cargo the 'planes were carrying. On each inbound trip I was asked for the 'bee oh bee' (bags on board) in place of the usual 'pee oh bee' (persons on board). We learned later, that in true Aussie fashion bets were being offered and taken as to which aircraft would be first next time in and which would shift the most coffee by the end of the day.

After almost three hours of 'follow me catch up' a break was needed for re-fuelling. Laurie was first to pull in to his company's bowser, which was also available for the Dornier. Because of the Aztec's fuel tanks being in the low wing, refuelling was easy and speedy.

Unable to unload due to lack of staff, I watched from the Dornier as the New Guinea national on the hand pump, worked like a slave in the pits at a Grand Prix to get the fuel in, while Laurie hustled about with the hose, replaced the tank caps, checked the fuel drains, in the shortest possible time. There was a chance then to get ahead of the Aztec that was thwarted by the unloading crew not being available to unload the Dornier. Laurie was airborne just as the last 'bag o' beans' on the Dornier hit the tarmac with re-fuelling still to be done.

A folding ladder was used to drag the hose up on to the high wing, while the attendant pumped away urgently under my directions. His pumping action was not quite as vigorous as before. It looked to me that he might have his money on his boss's Aztec.

Because of the ease of loading and unloading the Dornier a minute or two could be gained on the faster machine if I used my 'nouse'. On the next flight my aim was to be first at the loading site at Boana, but only by a narrow margin so that Laurie would have to stop engines, park and wait while the Dornier was being loaded, which was similar to an athlete leading in a long distance race, taking a rest and losing his rhythm.

Using those tactics, the Green Machine gained the lead and the Aztec had been lapped. By 2 pm the shed was completely cleaned out, with not a coffee bean in sight. Gustav was very happy to know the area's coffee harvest was safely on the way to the factory. Whether Laurie was so happy is not certain for the Dornier had appreciably eroded his charter company's business!

The 'coffee job' had been finished just in time. An hour after the last bag was under covers in the hangar, the town and airport was 'socked in' as violent rainstorms swept in from the stormy Huon Gulf. Lae could be rated as one of the wettest towns on earth.

In the hills at Boana, by that time fierce winds with low clouds would be sweeping up the river from the Gulf to envelop the airstrip, the mission, the river valley and the rain forest in driving rain to make flying impossible.

After a sandwich, a 'cuppa', a good laugh and a wait for the weather to clear up enough for take-off, I scudded off to Kaiapit in the upper Markham valley, to do some 'real' mission work by taking 'sick and injured' to the mission's hospital at Yagaum near Madang.

Twenty kilometres into the Markham River valley from Lae the weather began to clear until the Dornier flew in the broad, green valley under a clear sky and hot sun. That's how it's always been at Lae and there's not a lot that can be done about it. The day had been an exciting one for me, the closest thing to aerial-top-dressing encountered since being in New Guinea, where pilot and ground crew must focus on the job and work in perfect rhythm as the Morobe men had done.

The Dornier had proved its worth. The green machine was then flying 85 hours a month, supplying mountain stations, medical evacuation and offering full co-operation with the various branches of the Administration, to or from those otherwise inaccessible areas.

There were many other very successful days for 'Lutmis' Aviation. The mission's annual conference held at the historic mining town of Wau kept all the 'planes busy from daylight to dark moving missionaries from their raw, isolated stations, to the secluded, cool, highland valley that in the 1920's and '30's was home to one of the largest and most successful gold-mines in the world, that in 1942 became one of Japans most desired possessions..

In a unique operation never dreamed of before, huge dredges weighing thousands of tons were flown from Lae into the valley piece by piece and re-assembled near their 'ponds' to gouge out their own lake from which to dredge the valley. The work went on, eight dredges in all, until the Japanese invasion early in 1942 when the Wau 'aerodrome' was the scene of a bitter engagement between Australian and Japanese ground forces. The Bulolo valley only a short distance away also suffered air-raids that not only destroyed some dredges but several of the highly prized Junkers G31 tri-motor aircraft as well that had made the dredging of the valleys possible. New Guinean labourers by the hundreds were to be employed in the various mining activities as little-known Wau became a leader in the Air Age.

Wau had been chosen by the mission as venue for the annual conference, because of the equable climate at 3,500 feet elevation, a unique hillside airfield and adequate accommodation facilities. With the conference over, the missionaries were returned to their outposts in the mountains, the valleys, coastal plains or offshore islands, while there was always a casualty or two to be taken to doctor or hospital at Lae or Madang during the period.

On another important project, the mission's three aircraft were used to fly materials and builders in to Tarabo a Lutheran mission private airstrip and the closest to Okapa in the Eastern Highlands. When completed the hospital would be the main collecting centre for the care and treatment of the victims of the dreaded Kuru disease, commonly known as 'laughing death'. The thought-to-be, incurable sickness mostly affected the 'meris' of a fierce pygmy tribe known as the Kukukuku. (see picture). The dedicated doctors in the project took many years to study and research the cause which was eventually found to be connected to the funerary rites of the Kukukuku where women and children consumed the brains and offal of the deceased during the tribe's sacrificial feasts.

From the port at Madang, the building materials for the hospital were flown first to Goroka by DC3 aircraft. From there, items that could be broken down to fit into the mission aircraft went onto Tarabo which lay in a swampy depression at 6000 feet elevation to the east of Mount Michael (12,303 ft).

After unloading some timber cuts and roofing iron for the hospital one day, I was bent on doing another trip. There was no sign of the clouds that often covered the hills surrounding the strip in the afternoon that would close the depression for the rest of the day. My plan for another trip was thwarted when the engine of the Dornier refused to start. Frustrated after trying every known method and fearing that too many attempts might flatten the battery, I walked up to the missionary's house to use his radio to advise the chief, Ray Jaensch in Madang, of the problem.

Returning to the aircraft 30 minutes later a perfect start was my reward for patience. A careful run-up proved the engine to be faultless. My feelings were one of a fool at the time, for the delay prevented another trip being made, leaving others to think that the Dornier's pilot had either 'boobed' or suffered an attack of 'finger trouble'.

Later with Ray we came to the conclusion that the carburettor had been flooded, the trip to the radio had allowed time for the fuel to drain. We left things that way.

The airstrip at Monono in the Chimbu area of the Eastern Highlands was one of the shortest in the mission's field of operations. The numbers are easy to remember, 600 feet in length at 6000 feet elevation, with a slope of 6%, all the sixes. Reverend Bob Heuter with wife Ruth, were the missionaries at Monono. They had eight children, all girls except for one boy who was the youngest.

Bob, a US citizen, had spent most of his life in New Guinea his father having been an ordained missionary there prior to WW2. Ever since I had joined the mission, a sound friendship had grown between his family and mine. We'd spent holidays in Monono's guesthouse much to everyone's delight and a wonderful experience for our children.

Bob had succeeded in the building of his airstrip where few others would have tried, by 'bulldozing' a hill that bounded the rear of the house. The task had called for a bulldozer or two but instead was completed by hundreds of tribesmen of the area using only shovels, spades and sacks. The mission provided the equipment, the tribesmen the feet for packing the soil firm. The end result was truly amazing.

On our flights through that area while the strip was under construction, we always gave Bob and the workers a 'buzz' to encourage them in the gruelling work. We marvelled at the rate of progress, until months after work started the time came for the 'grand opening'.

The mission property nestled in very rugged country, on the slopes and in the shadow of Mount Elimbari (8957 ft), that was a long, sharp sandstone escarpment, what others might describe as a fault-line, running down from Mount Wilhelm (15,387 ft) the tallest mountain in the then Territory. The north side of Elimbari had slopes to the summit that could be climbed fairly easily, the south side however was a different picture, a spectacular 1,000 foot vertical wall of sandstone, two or three kilometres in length. At the time I write of, Elimbari was undiscovered as a site for ab-sailing enthusiasts as it is today. Monono lay near to the base of those gigantic cliffs.

When completed, the strip ran up from a cutting 10 metres or so above the mission house, to end at an almost vertical wall of cutaway hill. While waiting for the grass to grow, Bob had a parking area excavated that was flat, as a precaution against a 'plane tumbling on to the roof of the house should it be unable to stop when taxying downhill on a greasy surface that would follow any rain.

The Chimbu was a densely populated area, the opening of a new strip, whether mission or administration owned, was always a big affair. Thousands of colourful warriors, Birds of Paradise plumes waving from flower be-decked headdresses could be seen lining each side of the new runway, as we came round on a short final approach for the first landing.

Ray brought the Dornier in under power, skimming over the house and on to the muddy strip for a perfect 'three-pointer'. As the 'plane raced past them on its uphill landing roll, the mob surged across the strip to follow it up the hill. Ray had to gun the engine and swing around without stopping to taxi downhill to the parking bay. With the engine running and the brakes hard on we waited until the tribesmen cum spectators were made to understand that standing in front of the whirling prop blades was dangerous. Somehow they were convinced to make a clearway and FOLLOW the aircraft down to the parking bay, or even better, to toddle off to the sides of the strip.

With that done, amid much shouting, yodelling and whooping, the cargo was unloaded with the Dornier ringed by hundreds of tribesmen, meris and 'pikininis' alike, watching our every move with eyes as big as saucers.

In the next hour we each made 3 landings to get familiar with the strip, and to help the tribes-people understand how a 'balus' was supposed to be treated. Only a miracle saved several of them from being mangled by the prop when they got too close for comfort while waggling their long spears about recklessly.

As was the custom, tribal elders and fight leaders made lengthy, repetitive speeches as the afternoon rain began to fall. Bob prayed in the local language for the future success of the strip and the 'balus', in service to 'Anutu', the mission, medical aid evacuation and the local community. A 'sing sing' started and went on despite the rain, until late afternoon, when everyone began to troop back to their hilltop villages, singing and whooping at the top of their voices, in the guttural, yodelling style common to the highlands.

With the strip officially open, Monono began to flourish as many trips in from the Lutmis Supply House at Madang were made to raise the level of the various stocks used by a Christian mission. Prior to the strip being built Bob would get his supplies through Kundiawa, a hard day's work for him with a Land Rover, over almost impossible tracks and terrain that included the fording of several rivers subject to flash-flooding. He was well known and liked by the people of the area, having trekked on foot thousands of kilometres across the area visiting the many villages, some of whose residents spoke a different language to those of a village in sight across a deep river gorge or on the next hilltop. Very soon Monono was being supplied directly from Madang on a regular basis. With the expansion of the mission, Bob's children growing up and Ruth needing some relief from her manifold duties came the need for a qualified schoolteacher.

Brooding storm clouds covered a good part of the highlands inland from the Bismarck Range the afternoon the Green Machine with me as pilot came in to Monono with a load of cargo and Miss Querengesser of Canada as passenger beside me. Unfortunately for her, the weather that day precluded any sightseeing or worthwhile photography being done.

Flying low over the mountainous terrain with grey, wet clouds pressing down heavily over all parts of the landscape, the only way to get to Monono by air was to approach from the Asaro gorge to the south-eastern end of Mount Elimbari and along the southern side of the sullen, menacing wall of the escarpment. Several waterfalls were seen to be in full flow as I brought the green machine around and along the base of Elimbari. With the long summit of the escarpment hidden in thick fog, from the Dornier the falls appeared as separate massive stalactites streaming from the cloud. The base of the escarpment provided me with an excellent tracking aid to Monono.

First a turn to the left away from the escarpment, then a long, wide, right hand swing brought the mission house into sight through a rent in the low hanging clouds while rain spattered the windshield. In restricted visibility, from a kilometre away I dragged the Dornier in at low speed, hanging as it were, on the propeller. Closer in it looked like the landing would have to be abandoned, until the roof of the house came into view again to become the best of approach aids. My mind was then set firmly on making the landing.

Mud flew up from the Dornier's big wheels to smack the rear fuselage and empennage as we 'sploshed' on to the greasy strip and ran uphill to a stop. My breath came fast, my heart pounded, while the lady passenger seemed quite unconcerned about the low approach in the rain as she took in the many half naked village people huddled together on each side of the strip staring at the 'balus' (metal bird). So low was the cloud that in the final stages I had been forced to use all the power available and make a very flat approach to the strip border-ing on what could be called a 'climbing approach' which can be a very dangerous manoeuvre.

This was the teacher's first visit to the highlands, so different from the coastal station where she'd taught previously. The Heuter family and four other men, suitably rigged against the rain, were on hand at the parking bay to greet the new teacher. As she climbed down from the cockpit a great sigh could be heard before a shrill chatter came from the watching meris who were then seeing an unmarried white woman for the first time. Through the drizzle Ruth and family whisked her away to the shelter of the house.

It was then I learned that Bob and two other men were to be dropped off at Goroka on the return flight. Two others would go on with me to Madang. The four had just completed a building job at the mission. They all helped to unload the cargo and place luggage aboard, when we all clambered into the aircraft, more to escape the rain than anything else, chatting while waiting for the clouds to lift enough to permit a safe take-off being made. Bob sat with me in the cockpit, the others in the passenger cabin behind a separating bulk-head, where they could be heard but not seen. Bob had accepted the role of 'public address system', having been asked to relay any special instructions to the passengers through the bulkhead.

Bob had been listening on the mission radio network the day the engine of the Dornier had been reluctant to start at Tarabo. Being me-chanically minded, he was curious and wanted to know more about that incident. As we talked, the thought occurred to me that we were then in a similar situation at 6000 feet elevation, with the engine hav-ing been stopped for almost twenty minutes while unloading went on. Should the same thing happen again with a flooded carburettor, I re-solved not to attempt a start at that point to give the fuel enough time to drain itself out. Passengers can become nervous when engines fail to start at the touch of a button. The weather at the time was another good reason for delaying the take-off.

Twenty minutes later the 'Green Machine' had started perfectly and the normal engine run-up completed. Madang Radio had acknowledged my 'Madang this is Alpha Mike Keebec, taxying Monono for Goroka, six POB' (persons on board). The cloud base had lifted a little and light rain had taken over from the drizzle.

When lined up at the top of the strip, through breaks in the heavy cloud and the rain, I could see out to the Mai River. Following that river north would take us to the Dalou Pass (8000 feet), a popular point of entry by air to the Goroka valley although subject to the proliferation of soggy, wet clouds. Should the Dalou be clouded in I would switch to the Watabung Gap or the Asaro Gorge a few miles to the south.

By all reports, Goroka at the time was experiencing rain showers across the valley. With the departure plan firmly in my head, I stood on the brakes and began to 'open the tap' while giving Bob a quick glance and a 'thumbs up'. I could see that he was excited at the prospect of zipping over the family home, hidden from view from where we sat, below the level of the airstrip.

Well before the engine peaked at full power, the brakes couldn't hold the aircraft from sliding on the slippery surface. The brakes were released quickly while the throttle was shoved full forward. The thrill of those short take-offs in the Dornier will always be with me. In less than half the length of the strip, we were in the air, levelling out so as not to rush up into the clouds. That often happened in New Guinea, much to the vexation of the performance chart 'boffins', who from their cosy offices in Port Moresby or Melbourne, frequently complained of the illegality of some New Guinea flying operations and operators. Monono was one of those 'aerodromes' where a positive rate of climb after take-off was not called for or even necessary, the nearest 'obstacle' being several kilometres away and well below the level flight path of an aircraft leaving the strip.

The 'downhill' run to the Mai at descent speed was over with the flight visibility improving all the way. Approaching the river a right turn was made in order to follow the river 18 kilometres up to the Dalou Pass while climbing as high as the heavy, 'drizzle-dropping' clouds would allow. The summits of the Dalou Pass, the Watabung and most of the Kaw Kaw range that separated the Mai from the Asaro valley were hidden in cloud.

While deciding on a change of course that would take us down the range to a lower spot where we could slip across the ranges into the broader reaches of the Asaro valley, suddenly the engine began to splutter and surge. At first I couldn't believe my ears, the 'green machine' couldn't do that to me! My eyes darted over the instrument panel in search of an answer, as the engine fired up, ran smoothly then chopped and spluttered again. The problem smelt of fuel starvation although the gauges of the tanks selected were showing as ample for the short flight planned. That it could be water in the fuel also crossed my mind. As a precaution I switched to the fullest tank, rammed the throttle lever forward, moved the mixture control to full rich and flipped the booster pump on. Nothing changed, the engine continued to splutter and surge.

In drizzle and low down in a narrow, twisting river valley with steep, rocky slopes on each side and with the mountains smothered in 8/8ths cloud above 7000 feet and with a sputtering engine, the Dornier was in an unenviable predicament, with little chance of a successful forced landing being made within gliding distance. The nearest landing strip was Monono, minutes away around the corner of the western end of Mount Elimbari and our only hope. Instinctively I turned in that direction with the engine surging and the altitude slipping away at a steady rate.

Over Chuave patrol post, 8 kilometres from Monono we were down to 6500 feet which was about the elevation of the strip. Ground clearance was less than 500 feet. To reach Monono in a glide from there was impossible. The one and only reach of the Mai that could be called straight was a cauldron of frothy waters devoid of any suitable sandy beaches, or even a stretch of smooth water between rapids that could be used for an emergency landing. The river was running very swift from the recent rains. It was there that I grabbed the mike and put out a 'Mayday' (distress) call, my first ever.

With the Dornier now over the rock-strewn hillocks of limestone pressure ridges at the foot of Mount Elimbari, the engine was of no further use, all I could do was choose a hill within gliding distance and glide in for an uphill touchdown.

Regular practice of simulated forced landings had left me confident of being able to touch down exactly on the chosen spot without using the engine. As an Instructor too, I had put many students through their paces in the art. To practice engineless landings on to a familiar aerodrome or paddock is one thing, a real-life test of one's ability to make it down safely to the spot chosen, is quite another. In a practice 'forcy' from 2000 feet altitude or more above the surface, the engine is throttled back to idle and the aircraft trimmed to a glide. There's plenty of time to circle, or glide to the chosen final approach area, losing height while judging the touchdown point, which was usually a familiar mark on a familiar paddock or runway.

Jammed as the Dornier was at low altitude between low clouds and mountainous terrain, without a flat piece of terra firma anywhere in sight, time was not on my side. A forced landing was inevitable. Bob was signalled to tighten up his harness to the maximum and get on with what he did best as a Pastor, pray, while I trimmed the machine for the glide. The engine was surging intermittently each burst shorter than the one before. I took a left turn to aim at what was thought to be a small native garden in a leafy grove on the upslope of a grassy hillock judged to be in gliding distance. On the slope above the grove were several round shaped grass huts, the style common to the area. I yelled to Bob to warn the passengers to tighten their seat belts and brace themselves for a rough landing.

Descent without the engine going in the Dornier was more of a dive than a glide. Pushing the nose down even further for the extra speed needed for a flare up what was estimated as a 20% slope, my whole focus was on the spot seen to be a banana grove below the round houses. My mouth was dry, my heart pounding as the grove rushed in with me easing back on the control stick in an attempt to skim up the slope and pancake on to those leafy, soft-looking banana trees. I still couldn't believe all that was happening and harboured the feeling that when I awoke the horrible nightmare would be over.

Countless pre-landing emergency procedures flashed through my mind as the magneto switches the throttle and mixture levers were shut off, the control stick fully back on my belly. Low down, with tufts of grass brushing the wheels and with the speed washing off as the Dornier began the flare uphill, the grove was then seen as a bad choice, extra large rocks now showed up around the trunks and under the wide leaves of the trees. Too late then for a mind change, the steep glide had taken us exactly to where expected, but it could be the wrong choice.

Bob had hardly uttered the first line of 'Our Father' before the Dornier's long, heavy, under-gear bashed through the leafy foliage with the horrible sounds of metal 'scrunching ' and thumping, it was the 'Ceres' all over again. Then came the jabs of pain as the sudden stop threw me forward with my shoulder harness taking the strain and cutting into my shoulders. There is a saying that it is not the speed that kills but the sudden stop. My feet flew from the pedals to flip both my legs under the control panel with tremendous force.

The 'Green Machine' came to such a quick halt except for Bob's voice going on in prayers my emotions told me that I must have 'bought the farm', an Air Force term for sudden death. The Dornier, renowned for it's short landing ability had made the shortest ever, by landing on to large rocks hidden beneath the leafy banana trees to stop after a landing run of only 20 feet if 'landing run' it could be called.

Then came the silence, complete and utter, so quiet that I felt I must be dead. Seconds elapsed before Bob's voice was heard. " We're all okay, we're all okay. Praise the Lord."

It's good to have a Minister beside you at such a time were my first thoughts as my very being returned and I gazed about at the crumpled engine cowling, the bent propeller, while coming to realize that the mission's highly prized, green Dornier, with it's super-strong landing-gear torn out from it's extra-heavy fittings, was lying flat on it's belly, a wreck. The thick wings too with their fancy leading-edge slats had shared a lot of the impact and were bent and broken. What could be seen from where I huddled in a shocked state was for me a sickening sight.

Motioning Bob to get out on his side I released the harness and swung my door up. There was no feeling in my legs as I tried to pull them out from under the panel, while Bob scrambled around to open the 'swing-up' doors to the passenger cabin and let the occupants out. Mixed with the yodelling cries from the villagers at the nearby huts, came the excited voices of the passengers as they counted their limbs and after a few 'hallelujahs', came to realize there were no broken bones or other injuries to report.

Bob arrived beside me and helped to get my legs disentangled from the rudder pedals under the instrument panel. The mode of dress for flying in the hot climate was shorts and shirt, with black shoes and knee-high white socks on the legs and feet. I groaned as my legs came free and I looked down on to red, blood-soaked, socks and shoes. Slipping the socks down revealed both shins grazed raw to the bone but unbroken so far as we could see. Bob told me to wait while he found the medical kit to bandage me up before I climbed out.

Whooping and wailing in true highlands fashion, tribes-people by the dozen were gathering around the grove but thanks to Bob's fluency in the local language and his loud voice they were keeping their distance. Standing clear of the aircraft on the up hill side, we both stared towards Monono station. Looking up through the drizzle, the house and airstrip could be seen peeping out from under the low-lying clouds, so near and yet so far.

Twenty-five minutes from when the Mayday call had gone out, a Territory Airlines Cessna, piloted by Peter Hurst suddenly and somehow appeared from a break in the clouds and began circling, an example of New Guinea's highly efficient civil aviation Search and Rescue organization operating at full steam.

We all gathered together near the wreck and signalled the Cessna's pilot that all were up and able to walk. After a few more circles he headed away through the mists when we began to make plans. Bob's expert knowledge of the local dialect, the district and the people paid off handsomely. After closing the doors and securing the Dornier as best we could, he gave instructions that no one was to go near the 'balus' until rescuers or investigators arrived at the scene, receiving assurances from their headman that it would be so. With each man carrying his own swag and helped by the tribesmen, we began the climb uphill to intercept the nearest part of the track to the mission, where it wound under the vertical escarpment of Mount Elimbari.

My clothes were wringing wet from the persistent drizzle, not to mention sweat, my legs were becoming very painful. Muscled, feather-bedecked warriors, smelling of a smoky upbringing, supported me on each side. They both looked fierce but were always gentle, always careful, sucking in their lips in sympathy when after taking only a few steps the excruciating pain in my legs caused me to wince or groan.

So slow was my progress on the climb, we must have taken an hour to intercept the track that led to Monono, when we caught sight of a yellow Volkswagen Beetle coming slowly up the hill from Chuave patrol post in what could only be, low gear. From higher ground Bob called saying that the vehicle belonged to Joe Nitsche the Agricultural Officer (Didiman) for the area. .

Big Joe, a long-time, well-known admin officer, had done exceedingly well in getting his beloved Beetle that far along the track for the first time in such wet weather. After a conference beside the tiny mud-spattered car, Bob decided that he and the others would walk the several kilometres by track up to Monono. He feared that by then, Ruth would have heard on the mission radio network that the Dornier had come down, she would be getting anxious. Joe was asked to take me to Chuave in his Beetle where there was an expatriate government Medical Assistant who could attend to my legs and so that was settled.

With help from Bob, the passengers and some of the warriors Joe managed to turn his car around, although not without some difficulty, while I sat watching on the verges of the track with my legs stretched flat to the ground. At times the vehicle had to be lifted on one end or the other until it faced down the track in the direction desired. Bob and the others helped me in to be supported by the rear passenger seat with my legs stretched out on to the front passenger seat. Accompanied always by the never-ending yelling and wailing of the watching clansmen, there we said goodbye.

My eyes were closed for most of the hair-raising drive down to Chuave. Joe was fully occupied in keeping his vehicle from wandering sideways off the slippery track that served as a road, there was little opportunity given for any sort of social banter. He had witnessed the Dornier in trouble over the patrol post. Using his initiative he'd set out to where he thought the 'plane might have come down.

The Beetle rattled into the government settlement at Chuave just before nightfall. Having been lost temporarily, my faith in the safety of flying above all other means of transport, was now restored.

Thoughts of home and family at Madang and what would the mission be saying about the loss of their aircraft were constantly on my mind as the Medical Assistant cleansed and re-bandaged my legs using generous applications of iodine, that made me 'yelp' with the sting. When he'd finished I lay under a blanket in Joe's well-kept, homely cottage, while my clothes dried on a rack in front of a roaring fire.

At suppertime he announced that I would be taken to the Goroka Hospital that night by a mission vehicle that would arrive at about 9 pm which would mean a tortuous climb up through the Dalou Pass for the driver. It was surprising to hear that the difficult and dangerous route would be tackled in darkness and in wet weather to boot! An alternative to my evacuation would be a drive to Kundiawa in the morning to be uplifted by air. My guess was that a night drive over the Pass, where landslides often blocked the primitive 'road' for days, would be amongst the first ever attempted.

The Land Rover arrived three hours later and soon Myra Radke, a senior and very professional nurse herself, had me bundled up in blankets and placed on some kind of a mattress on the floor of the Land Rover behind the driver's seat. Knowing full well that the road would be rough and bumpy she gave me a sedative that a few minutes later took effect, my eyelids began to droop just as Joe and I set out.

Not a lot can be remembered about that ride, always the drizzle, bumps, bumps and more bumps, thick fog at times, wipers 'clacking' back and forth on the flat windscreen, squeezing past fallen rocks, forever twisting and turning as we upped and downed the desolate-looking Pass, the only light, the Rover's very weak headlights. I couldn't help wondering what would happen if we went over the side on one of the dozens of sharp curves, or if the Rover decided to give mechanical trouble of some kind.

Immersed in his own thoughts, Joe spun the wheel, worked the clutch and shifted the gear lever continually, while in a daze, I watched from behind like a zombie, but a very admiring one.

In the early hours we reached the grass-roofed hospital at Goroka, where I was handed over to another very professional nurse. There was only time for a quick goodbye and thanks to Joe before he sped off into the night, or more precisely early morning. No doubt in a few short hours Myra would be facing a queue of injured or sick patients of her own at the mission clinic, her night adventure forgotten. Missionaries seldom get into the record books, nor do they aspire to.

Although I was flying a couple of weeks later with my legs bandaged the injuries took a long time to heal. Due to the slow, natural repairing of the circulation in the wounded areas, the pain sometimes was excruciating. The young American doctor at Yagaum Lutheran Hospital near Madang, Dr Erwin Heist, had warned me of that and he was right on the button. Regardless of where I was, or what I was doing, the spasms only ended when I sat down with my legs extended flat to the ground. Weeks went by before I could stay upright for long periods. In flying an aircraft however the legs gave me very little trouble.

To those aircraft operations manuals that include a section on forced landings for fixed-gear single-engine aircraft, in terrain where the landing-gear could be ripped off by a rough surface and the aircraft skid along on its' belly, another paragraph or two could be added. That is a pilot should remember to take his feet off the rudder pedals before the gear is carried away. The cables from the pedals to the rudder in most single-engine craft, run under the floor, which when buckling during a crash may force the pedals to jerk with great force to one side or the other, strong enough to break a leg or ankle or graze the shins, as in my case.

The Dornier was replaced by another similar model a short time later that soon became known as the 'Red Machine'. Before it went into service with the mission, Ray, a very sound, skilled engineer, went over the engine with a fine toothcomb, but couldn't find any fault that might have caused the failure in the 'Green Machine'. The new Dornier was cleared to carry on with the mission's air services. Things began to settle down into a routine operation again.

At Monono a couple of months later with the 'Green Machine' almost forgotten, the starting problem again surfaced. Not wishing to flatten the battery, I decided to try again only after the fuel in the carburettor had been given enough time to drain. While walking past the nose of the aircraft on the way to the house, 'gurgling' sounds were heard coming from inside the engine. On raising the cowling, the transparent fuel filter bowl was seen to have fuel bubbling away merrily inside, as a kettle of water would boil on a hot element. Ray in Madang was radioed for some re-assurance. He suggested I cool my heels for twenty minutes or so before taking another look. If the bubbling in the filter bowl had ceased by then, he suggested I try starting up again. I did that and sure enough the engine started first time and ran sweetly.

During the delay, down at the house Ruth Heuter collapsed suddenly and had become quite ill. Bob asked me to take her to the mission hospital at Madang.

The morning was cloud free and sunny, Ruth sat in the cockpit beside me, as she preferred to see where she was going she explained. After a faultless engine run-up we took to the air 'like a homesick angel' in typical Dornier style.

The return to Madang called for a stop to be made at Saidor on the north coast of mainland New Guinea, to uplift some native patients and their 'watch men' for the hospital. The route took us through the Bena Gap to the Ramu valley, then over a corner of the formidable Finisterre Mountains to Saidor. Several of the mountain peaks on track were close to 12,000 feet, to round them with sufficient ground clearance at 10,000 feet I tracked 3-5 miles to the left of the direct route.

As we began to cross the ranges, in a spectacular way the view to the north of the great island opened out on to the sea, glorious in the sunshine, a sparkling blue with Astrolabe Bay and the northern coastline outlined by crisp white bands of coral reef. On many days of the year the track we were following would be covered in clouds.

"You've struck it lucky with the view today Ruth, there's not many days when you can see that far, the clouds see to that."

Those words yelled across the cockpit were meant to cheer her up. From more than 100 kilometres, the islands of Kar Kar and Bagabag, both Lutmis stations, could be seen clearly. Ruth perked up and began to take more of an interest in the topography. The black, scoria laden peaks of the Finisterres towering above us on the right side looked grim and sullen as always. We both stared ahead, taking in the magical scene of sea, islands and mountains before us. From altitude, whether sunny or not, New Guinea could always come up with a breathtaking view of mountain or sea, like no other place on earth. The tall mountains of the big island, the valleys, the coasts, the reefs, plantations, rivers and wetlands were a photographers' delight, one must try hard not to come up with a good picture.

In only a minute or two a descent to the coast could begin were my thoughts as the scenic wonderland before me unfolded, a descent that would need to be gentle so as not to cause Ruth any discomfort for she looked to be pale, with dark rings under her eyes as I passed some advice to her. "We're starting to descend Ruth, if your ears give you trouble let me know and keep swallowing."

She hardly had time to nod when suddenly the engine gave a cough, spluttered and died. Ground clearance at the time over the shoulder of the mountain was about one thousand feet.

My eyes flew to the instruments, my right hand to the engine controls. The tank selectors were seen to be selected correctly, the gauges reading half full, there was swags of fuel. Before there was any time to move anything the engine started as if nothing had happened then began sputtering again. My heart was in my mouth, first Bob then his wife, what was going on? A glance in Ruth's direction told me that she didn't look too worried, probably thinking that we always shut the engine off when letting down and that she had been pre-warned.

Fearing that the engine might cut fully, a drill for a landing in some of the most formidable mountains in the country flashed into my mind. The only place for an engineless landing that I could see, was a steep slope of scoria-strewn mountainside to the right of the aircraft that could be made in a gentle turn, there was nothing else available that could be taken in and diagnosed in a second's glance. Any approach to that area would have to be steep and very, very fast to allow for a flare up such a steep slope. The area chosen was guessed at being about 8,000 feet elevation, my heart pounded, in my view a landing there would see the aircraft completely wrecked, along with the occupants.

The right wing was on the way down for a turn towards the chosen site when miraculously and without any help from me, the engine fired up again and ran evenly, purring like a kitten and continuing to do so all the way to Saidor! There a wide, orbiting slow descent was made over the coastal airstrip to be on the safe side should the engine decide to sputter again.

On the ground at Saidor the walking patients and their 'watchmen' were loaded on with the engine still running, to avoid any hitch to the re-start. En route to Madang, instead of cutting across Astrolabe Bay the coastline route was the safest way to go. Every foot of the way the instruments were scanned for any danger signs.

"I'll get the twitch if the engine ever splutters like that again for no reason" I announced to Ray when advising him of the incident.

He assured me that by hook or by crook he would find the reason for the falter and fix it, with the co-operation of engineers of the Department of Civil Aviation. The machine would be grounded until the mystery was solved and a remedy found. By that time Ruth would have been at the mission hospital, completely unaware of the drama she'd been involved in.

First things first, the fuel system was checked for water contamination without finding anything amiss. To prevent the over-heating of the fuel in the filter, the bowl was moved from the engine bay to behind the firewall, where it should have been in the first place. That move it was hoped, would prevent any air bubbles forming in the bowl from the heat of the engine after shut down, to be drawn through to the carburettor and cause air locking, making starting difficult particularly at high elevations. The Dornier's engine was cowled very close, European winter style, without a vent of any kind to allow the hot air to escape. Other possible causes of a stammer in the fuel supply to the engine were closely investigated. Lines from the fuel tanks

that ran through the wing, at one point crossed over a rib in an inverted U. The vents for the fuel tanks were very small, pin-sized holes in
the tank filler- caps, that could easily be blocked by grit, dirt, or even
the lint from a polishing cloth. Thanks to Ray and Tom the mission's
aircraft were very well maintained.

For almost a month Ray and the DCA engineer worked to find any
fault that would cause the engine to hesitate in any way. Any suggested changes to the design required professional engineering drawings
to be drawn up and referred to the manufacturer before any modifica-
tions could be approved. Finally, all was done to everyone's
satisfaction and the 'Red Machine' took to the air to give faultless service to the mission again.

My family all loved Madang, but in no way enjoyed the hot, sunny,
sticky, sweaty days or thunderous, lightning-lit nights. There was no
doubt that the heat was affecting Betty's health, while almost every
day my flights took me to where I was able to suck the cool, sweet
mountain air into my lungs. Annual vacations were spent at a guesthouse at either Monono, or Banz in the Wahgi valley. In only a week
of holidaying inland and a mile above the sea, it was plain to see that
the change in Betty brought on by the highlands climate, was very
real. Approaching the completion of my original agreement with the
mission we began to consider some alternatives to the hot life that was
ours. We'd arrived at Madang with a family of four, which had by
then increased to five. By a big margin Betty's workload had increased, something had to be done. With employment offered in the
highlands and with more than a few regrets, we decided to accept that
offer and move to where the climate boasted to be amongst the best in
the world.

After leaving the mission Ray and I would sometimes meet
'around the traps', he always spoke well of the 'mods' done to the
Dornier and the co-operative spirit shown by the Department's engineering branch. Tragically, Ray was killed in the 'Red Machine' about
18 months later, when the engine failed shortly after take-off from a

mountain airstrip. There lies another story, which is recorded here in "Tragic events at Tauta". Ray was one of the most experienced pilots in New Guinea at the time of his death. After serving in the RAAF in Europe he'd been called to the mission immediately after WW2. There he undertook the studies to become a Licensed Aircraft Maintenance Engineer along with the practical skills required and was then able to accept full responsibility for the 'Lutmis' Aviation Department. The time spent at Madang under Ray's expert guidance is for me counted as the greatest of privileges.

TERRITORY AIRLINES

GOROKA PNG 1963 - LATER TALAIR.

The day arrived for our departure from Madang, a sad day in many ways for all the family had loved the time spent there. Somehow I felt myself to be a traitor leaving a group of loyal Christians behind and going off to what was a well-paid job at the time, relatively speaking of course. At the airport farewell, none of our well wishers showed any sign of resentment to our leaving. Without me there to fly the Dornier, Ray would be hard-pressed to handle both the administration, mechanical and flying side on his own. I couldn't help but feel a real heel.

Our transport to Goroka was a 'side-saddle' C47 chartered by the mission to move building materials, with passengers seated each side of a stack of pre-cut timbers, galvanised piping, cement bags which were all secured by nets. The flight was a memorable event, for the children particularly. With eyes sparkling they all gaped through the windows at the mountains passing so close to the wing tips as we slipped past Mt Helwig and into the broad, grassy reaches of the Asaro Valley. Was it my imagination I wondered, that the children were already benefiting from the draught of mountain air coming in through an inch-wide crack in the cargo door, surely their cheeks were glowing? For their sakes alone we'd made the right choice.

Territory Airlines of Goroka was a very progressive company with a backlog of air charter work always waiting for the six or so aircraft operating from Goroka in the Eastern Highlands, Mount Hagen in the Western Highlands and Mendi in the Southern Highlands.

Dennis Buchanan, Managing Director and owner, known by all as 'Junior' in those days, could best be described as a young, self-willed, brash, tough, abrasive person to some, from the 'school of hard knocks', who ran his company from a stack of coffee bags in a corner of Goroka's large hangar and who wouldn't take no for an answer. Dennis tho' was not at all skilled in the art of diplomacy, caring not a twit if he trod on people's toes, particularly the regulating boffins and the 'big airline boys'.

The strength of his beloved company, Territory Airlines, lay in the support of an Administration that was eager and willing to get slow-moving, primitive New Guinea on to the world map after almost 100 years of tedious progress under several different colonial and military systems of government.

Base as Territory Airlines was in the highlands, well distanced from the seat of government, councils and departments, in a country without connecting roads between the main centres the company operated with a fairly free hand. Until, or unless that is, the major airlines' rights were allegedly infringed by a 'charters only' company making a flight over one of 'their' regular public transport routes. The hammer fell then, no matter how nonsensical the so-called 'breaches of regulations' were.

The regulations imported from mainland Australia ruled that charter flights by other than those licensed were not permitted over airline routes except once in 28 days, without specific approval. The rules were fine in Australia and were meant to protect the rights of the regular carriers, but it must be remembered that Australian capital cities had two airports at their disposal when the regulation came into being, one for the regular carrier, the other for the general aviation industry that included non-scheduled air services, training and charter. The scheduled airlines operated between the main airports, leaving the secondary airports available for use by the general aviation field. Thus a charter flight from Bankstown airport at Sydney to Archerfield at

Brisbane would not be an infringement of the Regulations for the airline route was from Mascot to Eaglefarm. A charter flight over such a route would cost the hire ten to twenty times more than a one-way air ticket. The cost alone would be a sufficient deterrent to the hiring of a 'plane except in some extreme emergency.

Without exception, all the main towns in New Guinea were blessed with only one airport but not blessed by a road. Applying the same rules as in Australia meant the closure of a good part of the Territory to charter flights. Imagine telling a New Guinea Districts Commissioner, or an accident victim, that there may be a delay of up to 28 days before a charter flight from Goroka to Mount Hagen or Port Moresby could be arranged, or from Madang or Goroka to Lae and many other places. Imagine trying to balance the books commercially! The straight-line air distance between the two major highland centres, Goroka and Mount Hagen, was 120 kilometres there were no connecting roads. The rule certainly placed the airlines under a huge protective umbrella for objections could be raised to any so called 'illegal charters' at will, the airline had the assurance of winning the argument every time.

After arriving at Goroka to take up my appointment as Chief pilot, Air Navigation Regulation 197 (2) gave Dennis and I all sorts of trouble. Pilots could be held responsible for any such breaches of air laws, a pilot's licence could be suspended or revoked, while there were no particular penalties laid down for Managing Directors like Dennis. Today those sorts of regulations would not get past their first reading.

Pleas to authorities over the stupidity of it all fell on deaf ears, the airlines must be protected at all costs from those who 'pirated' prospective regular airline customers was always the reply.

Several of the regular airline routes were serviced only once or twice per week in some cases, with time schedules emanating from the 'bean counters or managers' of statistics' at Papuan Port Moresby, not the New Guinea highlands. The regular airlines' schedules did not always suit a charterer's business interests either, or the Administration's by any means.

Regardless of the rules, the demand for speedy, safe, un-scheduled air transportation between several highland and coastal centres built up steadily. Single engine aircraft for middle of the market passenger movements were now becoming unpopular for safety reasons that are obvious.

After quite a spat between a major airline and Territory Airlines where I was the pilot of an alleged infringement, Dennis and I were summoned to Melbourne to confront the Director-General himself to answer a complaint where Territory Airlines had undertaken a charter over highlands air routes, requested by the airline that had 'dobbed us in'. The meeting was designed to make us tremble in our shoes but there were some red faces around the DG's office when the truth came out! It was a case of 'let not the right hand know what the left hand doeth' on the part of the airline concerned. For the first time we were clear winners.

On another occasion we were ordered to withdraw all aircraft, staff and other assets from Mendi while Ansett Mandated Airlines moved into that base with their light aircraft. A public outcry over the decision saw TAL moving back to Mendi a month later that left the 'MAL boys' grinding their teeth.

With all that in mind and with a push from me, Dennis lodged an application to import a twin-engine Beechcraft Baron in support of the fleet of six Cessna 185 machines to fill the gap between the administration's mixed cargo-passenger single-engine requirements and VIP executive transport.

Approval for the importation and operation of the Baron didn't come easily. The total number of passenger seats available over TAL's whole fleet of single engine Cessna's was around 35 at the time. The Department was reluctant to grant us another five seats through the purchase of a Baron, as that was considered to be too much of a threat to the airlines. That sort of decision-making is hard to believe these days, as it was to us at the time. In support of the high level policy of airline protection and to rub salt into the wound, the regulators claimed that the Baron was unsuited (unsafe, was how that was phrased) for New Guinea operations. That drew an angry response from Beech Aircraft in Wichita USA! Some are left wondering just who told Beech of the matter.

After some months of BWB negotiations (battling with bureaucrats) in Port Moresby and another trip for Dennis and I to Melbourne to confront the Director-General of Civil Aviation again however, the day was won. The cost to the Department for that rather pitiful licensing exercise must have equalled the price of the Baron!

At that time TAL was finding it hard to cope with the amount of charter work being offered. New airstrips were coming available, the southern and western highlands districts were opening up to precious metals exploration and mining, the coffee and tea industries were also growing rapidly

The flying times of all TAL pilots were always on the maximum allowable. Dennis, who in his mind was 'chief of all company departments' including engineering and operations, without my knowledge wrote a memo to pilots that promised a bonus for every hour flown over the maximum allowable of 900!

That was a foolish thing to do, had the memo been written by me, my licence would have been suspended or revoked. One must have an appropriate licence to fly an aircraft but a non-pilot owner of several metal birds only needs a sign, a telephone and perhaps a secretary, if one could be found, without any business experience or qualifications. Never hire anyone with more knowledge of the subject than yours seemed to be the yardstick at TAL. The memo fell into the hands of DCA. Dennis called them the Department of Continual Aggravation. He was instructed to withdraw the offer to pilots without receiving even a pat on the wrist. The incident further delayed our application for a twin engine ship though, on the grounds that the memo proved we were irresponsible operators of metal air machines!

With approval almost through, the Beech agents at Sydney flew a Baron to New Guinea for our evaluation. As observer I flew in that aircraft with the Beech pilot to show him through the highlands, when I was able to report to Dennis that so far as could be seen, a Baron with only a few minor changes, would fit the bill for TAL. A large deposit was paid, the order for one aircraft was confirmed, the whole process up to that time having taken several months.

A couple of months later I flew to Sydney for training on the new type. A US ferry organization would bring 'our' Baron out from the Beech factory at Wichita, Kansas, USA. My training would be done on the agent's demonstration model at Bankstown Sydney after which the newly registered VH-GKA would be flown by me to it's first ever permanent home in New Guinea. Even at that stage I knew that our decision to include a Baron in the fleet had been a right one, although GKA would be the first of its type in the country. The training included an evening trip to Melbourne and a daylight flight to Coonabarabran to demonstrate the Baron at the opening of the new airport through which it came with flying colours.

Per capita, the Territory was home to more crack 'aviation buffs' than any other country in the world. There were many 'experts' there at the time who were already circulating rumours that the machine wasn't suitable for New Guinea's short, soft strips some of which were subject to 'subterranean erosion' as one senior departmental officer put it, whatever that meant, or that it was too fast, the nose-wheel too small, the list of its' supposed failings went on. We were up before bureaucracy at it's worst. Some were saying that it wouldn't be long before the Baron was written off in some way, someone would be killed and TAL would be faced with ruin. Proving those 'prophets of doom' wrong almost became an obsession with me.

November 5, 1963. Very early on a lovely, clear, sun-filled morning, training completed and with Dennis and Bobby Gibbes aboard, we set off from Bankstown, Sydney for New Guinea with plans to be in Goroka by nightfall. For Bobby, a Western Desert fighter pilot ace of WW2, the flight in the Baron was a first for him. During the first hour of the flight to the first refuel stop at Rockhampton, he could not believe the result of the true airspeed computation he'd made, when the cruise speed was shown to be190 knots (220 mph). He remarked that the P40 (Kittyhawk) in which he'd fought with distinction wasn't that much faster with its Rolls Royce Packard engine throttled down in cruising mode. At the time I thought it inappropriate to agree to his request for a comparison between the two types in the diving or inverted mode, I knew that he was itching to roll or loop the Baron en route!

After re-fuelling at Rocky, we planned to fly on to Cairns for outward customs clearance. Daru, an island off the coast of Papua and the administrative centre of the Western District of the Territory, would come next for PNG inward customs before going on to Goroka.

As the day wore on I sensed that all of New Guinea aviation would be checking on our progress. Dennis and Bobby were keen to make it a 'one dayer', Bobby to attend to his plantation and hotel business while Dennis was desirous of getting to his bank in Port Moresby before his cheque for the Baron that had been left with the agents, was presented. Up to that time it was the biggest cheque in monetary terms he'd ever endorsed. He left us at Daru as chirpy as a bird, so as he could catch a flight from there direct to Port Moresby the following day.

STD (subscriber trunk dialling), international dialling, telegraphic transfers, e-mails etc were not then invented for Papua New Guinea, a feature that would probably preserve Dennis's financial reputation. Three days after arrival, when several airmail services from Australia to the Territory must have come and gone and the Baron hadn't been seized, we knew that Dennis had made Port Moresby and the bank in time. Since leaving us at Daru nothing had been heard of him.

The customs officers at Daru caused us some delay by not being at the airport when we arrived. With formalities completed and minus Dennis I left there with just enough time to reach Goroka before dark and with enough fuel to fly on to Madang should the Asaro valley be closed with cloud or rain as was often the habit in the late afternoon.

Fortunately the weather over New Guinea's central mountains was favourable for the time of day. We set down on Goroka's sloped runway three minutes before the airfield closed for the night to be met by hordes of TAL staff, well-wishers and no doubt a few curious 'unbelievers' and unwell-wishers from the Ansett terminal that was next to ours.

The Baron had behaved perfectly, exactly as written in the Beech aircraft Flight Handbook. Flying time from Bankstown for the 'three nautical miles a minute machine', Bankstown, Rockhampton, Cairns, Daru, Goroka, was ten hours and forty minutes. TAL's pride was then at stake, the company's most expensive acquisition to date must be put to work, to prove that Dennis was right and the doubters wrong.

Soon after it's arrival and with Dennis returned to base the new aircraft was kept busy. Requests started to come in for back-up charters for the airlines, that caused a chuckle, after 'their fully owned' passengers destined for the southern flight to Australia from Port Moresby had been off-loaded or stranded in the highlands due to weather or mechanical breakdown. In the first full month of highland operations GKA was chartered on 25 days and flew 76 revenue hours. Dennis walked tall and stood proud, beaming, grinning like a Cheshire cat, his good humour although sometimes coarse or crude, spilling over to friend and foe alike. For payment in those situations the practice used was for the airline to pass the tickets over to us, when we would return them with an invoice to cover the total amount of the tickets. Some of Denis's smiles disappeared however, when 90 days later the airline concerned refused to pay up on the grounds that we were not the holders of an airline licence, plus the arrangement had not been approved by their accountant before the passengers embarked, null and void insurances, etcetera etcetera! The replies that Dennis gave to those rather haughty letters cannot be printed here, eventually he won, but some of the profit had been eroded.

With a machine that could be called a competitor to the Piaggios operated by one airline, the work pattern area gradually grew wider as the Baron became better known. Our vision for the aircraft as a spic and span VIP carrier for senior administration or diplomatic officers also changed when it became obvious that we had acquired a 'go anywhere with any thing' machine. With the Cessna 185 fleet fully stretched in operations from Mount Hagen and Mendi, the engineering branch was always working overtime on repairs to them following ground loops, long landings and short stops with or without an overturn, or sideways drifts after cross-wind landings.

When paying a courtesy call with Dennis on Father Joe Walachy SVD, the flying priest at Madang, so that he could admire the latest in small twin engine metal bird technology produced in his country, 'The Land of the Free and the Home of the Brave', talk got around as to whether a US 50 gallon drum of diesel or kerosene could fit into the Baron through its rear door. The door was an Australian inspired modification to that originally designed for the type. We both thought the drum would be too large for the short but wide, lower half doorway. Dennis, who was always willing to assist the various missions, helped me to remove the seats and experiment with an empty drum as to whether or not it would fit through the door.

With some assistance from the mission's labour and Father Joe himself, a full drum of diesel was lifted onto the sill lying flat, only to find that it was a tight squeeze and wouldn't go in because of the raised ribs of the drum fouling the lintel. Not being too shook on the whole idea, I was breathing a sigh of relief until Father Joe arrived with an axe and with a heavy wallop or two with the blunt end, flattened a part of each rib on the drum, while I stood well clear seemingly intent on other business. Phew, the expected explosion

from leaked diesel and the resulting flames that could be expected after the heavy battering it received from the axe didn't eventuate!

With some shoving from all of us, the drum passed through the
door and into the cabin where it was made to stand upright again on
the brand new carpet and shiny new Douglas floor-tracks. Treated in
the same manner two more drums followed, when Dennis, in the role
then of 'Marketing Manager', with Father Joe, went into the rusty-
roofed hangar to arrange a contract for the carriage of the mission's
fuel stocks on a monthly basis from Madang, not only to Bundi, but
several other river stations also served by the mission that were of a
soft, muddy and sticky reputation!

On hearing that, I could have wept, that was the last thing needed
for my new toy. Visions of flying VIP's or tourists about to some of
the more exotic parts in New Guinea, while clad in a crisp, clean
white shirt, bright gold bars, navy blue trousers, shiny black shoes,
were forgotten the moment I knew that those three drums, one diesel,
one kerosene and one petrol, weren't going to come out until they
were unloaded at Bundi.

As if by magic Father Joe turned up with a favourable weather and
strip report from the mission station, favourable meaning that from the
mountain airstrip, through the drizzle, the observer could see down to
the Ramu Valley. Those types of reports had to be taken with a grain
of salt. Dennis was nowhere to be seen. In thirty minutes the flight
plan had been filed and I was speeding on my way, tho' feeling rather
miffed at the outcome of our 'courtesy call' and wondering how Father Joe managed to have the drums on hand so conveniently, not to
mention the weather report? In short I smelt a rat. With my limited
experience on the Baron, a trial run to Bundi with less of a load would
have been preferred.

The airstrip at Bundi (substitute 'oo' for the U), situated at 4000
feet elevation in the ranges leading up to Mount Wilhelm, was a 'one
way 'strip boasting a heavy rainfall and could get very slippery, having claimed a number of single engine aircraft over the years. With

their wheels locked hard while skidding sideways in the mud, or having landed successfully but long and fast, attempted to stop short, only to run out of distance and come to grief. That meant tumbling down from the top end of the landing strip into a deep gorge or buckling the landing gear in a violent swerve. Low clouds frequently covered the area, blocking the one-way approach. En route, I couldn't help thinking what a 'hey-day' our critics would have if the shiny new Baron ended up the same way.

Those grim thoughts served to put me on my mettle, as in a light drizzle I brought the Baron down on to the sodden grass 'mudway', speed well back, flaps fully out, powered up, hanging on the propellers. My aim was to make good use of the first fifty meters of the strip that ran uphill, chop the power, then hold the nose-wheel up until it fell of its own accord on to the rutted, slushy mud, to get the very best of aerodynamic braking, all the while ignoring the temptation to use the brakes. The use of brakes might only lock the wheels, bringing about little in the way of deceleration. My toes were on the pedals, not the brakes, as the Baron was flared to make contact with the short up-slope.

Mud could be heard splattering the underparts and empennage, as the main wheels contacted terra firma if the surface could be called that, not 'terribly firm' would be a better description. More 'whacks' under the fuselage were heard as the nose-wheel came down gently on the wet surface. With the Baron slowing of it's own accord I could breathe again. So soon after arrival in the Territory from the production line at Wichita Kansas, the immaculate, slick-looking 'Golf-Kilo-Alpha' (GKA) had been mud-spattered at Bundi of all places and loaded with dangerous cargo to boot, with fifty meters to spare before the strip ended in a sudden drop into a tree-lined gorge.

Unloading the drums presented another problem. A couple of mission workers came to my aid with a plank or two. With much grunting and the bawling of advice from me, the drums were removed without causing any more damage to the sill, which had already been scratched and dented slightly during loading at Madang.

On the flight up to Goroka later that afternoon, Dennis and I had a good laugh, Dennis louder than me, about our first plans for the modern twin and how its future role had then been changed. From that time, the VIP aspects of operation that had prompted the purchase of the Baron were set aside, the aircraft was unbelievably popular, bookings just rolled in, taking it to all corners of the highlands and the Territory with all sorts of clients and all sorts of cargo. Dennis and TAL had indeed hit the jackpot.

The accidents that had plagued me were things of the past and forgotten, as I threw myself into the training and administration of TAL's ever-growing field of operations.

Shortage of qualified pilots was always a problem with three volatile bases to be staffed and more work being offered than could be coped with, without bending the regulations even more. Aeroplanes that had been bent at inaccessible places, were fixed where they'd ended up or flown back to base for further fixing, our ground engineers sometimes worked magic under incredibly difficult situations. Young pilots soon learned how to take off, land and taxi without a tail-wheel. TAL's hard-worked pilots always ran close to the limitations set, some grumbled if they didn't achieve maximum allowable figures each month, week or day.

Not enough of my time was spent in the office and I longed for the day when some breathing space would allow me to catch up on the paper work. Through all this the Baron performed magnificently, in a class of its own. There was no doubt that the acquisition of a twin was a huge success and more than a thorn in the side of our rivals.

BELLY DOWN – WHEELS UP

A Beechcraft Baron charter booked for the Administration at Goroka was delayed one foggy morning. The clients had requested a departure at 8am, that was the very worst time of day for ground fog often saw the airport closed until after 9am. Four government departmental officers were to be taken to Mount Hagen and Mendi in the western and southern highlands respectively. Alan Ross, Department of Forests, Norrie Ford, Department of Education, Bill McMahon, Department of Education, a valuer-cadet of Department of Lands whose name has been misplaced and Alec Tryhorn a coffee dealer, who was to be dropped off at Banz in the Wahgi valley. All were to be brought back to Goroka later in the day.

By the time the fog lifted enough for a take-off to be made, we were running about half an hour late. However, once out of the Goroka valley and into the Wahgi, the weather was perfect. A clear blue sky framed the mighty Bismarck and Kubor mountains on either side of the valley, which were the tallest in the Territory. The Baron's excellent viewing windows gave the passenger's plenty to see as we scudded down New Guinea's most spectacular valley, densely populated by the proud, feather be-decked indigenous inhabitants. The great rift between the mountains was also home to New Guinea's most productive coffee area. The six-place cabin was alive with chatter as everyone took in the magnificent mountain scenery floating past on either side.

Twenty minutes after leaving Goroka we were banking in for land-ing at Banz on the north side of the river that split the valley's plain. Alec, the coffee dealer, was seated in the front passenger seat beside me to allow him to disembark without the engines having to be stopped. His only luggage was a business satchel that was probably full of 'greenbacks' for the buying of native coffee. All those aboard were frequent flyers, using aeroplanes in the Territory as one would a 'number six' bus 'down south'.

Without applying the brakes on the upslope the Baron was allowed to roll to a stop with engines running near a corrugated iron shed that served as the airport agent's terminal and office. In no time Alec had swung the door open, climbed out on to the walkway on the wing and with a wave, jumped off on to the ground, being careful not to put any weight on the flaps as he went, his trousers flapping and his hair get-ting blasted by the slipstream. A passenger in the middle seat was then asked to move to the front seat. When he'd done so and fastened his lap-strap, I locked the door, a job I always did myself, while I swung the Baron around to line up for a take-off down the slope and out into the valley.

With all appropriate radio calls and take-off checks completed and everybody secure, I pushed the throttles up, or 'opened the taps' as some say and buzzed off down the recently mown grass runway. The strip was of more than ample length for the Baron. Airborne and climbing a 'snick' of the gear switch set off the whirring of the elec-tric motor as the wheels retracted while I watched the green light change to red, retracted the flaps and commenced to turn for the next destination which was to be Mount Hagen, a flight of only 5-6 minutes. Time spent on the ground at Banz had been less than two minutes. My next radio call went to the control tower at Mount Hagen who was quick to advise that his airport was closed due to fog which would take some time to clear.

" What are your intentions? " he asked.

After advising him of the details, a change to the flight plan was radioed to Madang and course set for Mendi in the Southern Highlands, with always a plan in mind to drop the Mount Hagen passengers off afterwards when the fog dispersed.

Our track to Mendi then took us over the airport and town of Mount Hagen and through the basin between Mount Ialibu (11,368 ft) and Mount Giluwe (14,327 ft), a flight of 25 minutes only in my blue-coloured metal 'speedbird' on such a beautiful clear morning. The route through the Ialibu basin was another spectacular one and full of interest for the passengers. All eyes were glued to the windows again as we proceeded through the basin until we flew over the airstrip at Mendi to go into a pre-landing circuit pattern.

The single runway at Mendi, situated at 5500 feet elevation, favoured the southern side of the narrow valley and was uncontrolled so far as air traffic services went with a one-way only landing approach to the north. From overhead the windsock near the threshold of the southern boundary was seen to be fully extended horizontally by the catabolic surface wind expected at that time of morning. With the wind on my tail that meant a high speed touchdown. To allow more distance for the landing roll without going too heavily on the brakes, I would aim to have the wheels meet with the runway as near to the threshold as possible. Landing long and stopping short on the brakes as some pilots chose, was not on the agenda.

While on a right hand downwind for landing, the flight plan was cancelled with Madang, a 'no other traffic' acknowledgment received when turning for final approach. From lower down, the wind was seen to be very strong with the windsock flicking its tail angrily in the gusts. I rather dreaded the fast touchdowns that Mendi offered at that time of day, for flakes of gravel or small stones flying up from the wheels chipped away at the factory paint job on the under belly and empennage.

Suddenly the speakers in the ceiling crackled into life.

"Golf Kilo Alpha this is Madang, if you haven't landed at Mendi DO NOT land, we have an urgent message for you, I say again do NOT land at Mendi."

As my Baron was now down to about 300 feet over the hilly terrain and lined up with the runway, there was nothing left for me to do but acknowledge the call, pour on the power, retract the gear and flaps, climb to a safe height, then find out what was going on. As I circled back over the field again, over the radio I learned that an aircraft wheel had been found on the Banz airstrip, could, or did the wheel belong to Golf Kilo Alpha?

Seated in the cockpit, I had no real way of knowing. At a safe height and at the appropriate speed I operated the gear switch, heard the motor 'whirr' and watched the green light come on. That done I reported that so far as the gear extend and retract was concerned all was well but as for the wheels, there was no way of knowing from inside the aircraft whether or not a wheel was missing from one leg. With all the radio talk able to be heard by the passengers they were looking askance at me and were in need of an explanation. No doubt they were getting anxious over the aborted landing and the other more unusual manoeuvres over the airport.

A locally operated Cessna of Ansett Mandated Airlines flown by Neil Keag, a friend of mine, was brought into the picture. While still circling I was able to make radio contact with him and watch his Cessna take off and climb up. The Baron was flown straight and level and slow with the gear extended, while Neil flew alongside and under, for a closer look. My heart gave a bit of a flutter when he reported that the wheel was missing from the left leg of the gear!

This would mean that any landing would have to be made either on the belly or on one main gear wheel, one stub axle and the nose-wheel, which could result in a dangerous ground loop as the axle bit into the gravel. If I ever had to do that somewhere, it wouldn't be at Mendi with a 15-20-knot wind chasing me up the runway, which also ruled out the belly idea.

The situation called for a command decision. There was only one thing to do, return to Goroka. The main runway there was under repair at the time, with the original bitumen-gravel surface being graded off down to the clay for re-surfacing and would be next to perfect for a landing on the belly. For the period of re-construction, all aircraft were using a gravel runway that ran parallel to the main. Both runways had a slope of about 5%. I asked myself, 'what could be better for a belly job than wide, smooth, flat dirt running uphill'? A fire truck appropriately equipped and with a trained crew was always on standby for the regular air services during daylight hours.

At about that time I came to realize how lucky it was that we had not flown into Mount Hagen direct from Banz, a flight of only a few minutes, when the wheel would not have been discovered in time to prevent me from landing on Hagen's sealed runway on a stub axle! That was the first miracle in a day of miracles.

After advising Madang of my intentions we bade farewell to Mendi and set course for Goroka, about a forty-minute more nervous ride that time, with little chatter coming from the passengers when I told them that they might soon be making local aviation history!

The flight gave me time to think over the problem, work out a scheme for landing and brief the passengers on how to evacuate the aircraft quickly and smoothly through the one and only main door or the push-out side windows if necessary. That was to be my first belly landing although I had brought many a flying boat down on its hull (belly), to both rough and smooth water.

As there was nothing written in the emergency section of the Baron's flight manual or TAL's approved operations manual about landing on the belly, I decided that my experience with the smooth water technique as for a flying boat would be quite useful. Provided the surface was smooth enough to slide over, there wasn't a lot of difference I found out later.

Goroka airport staff were well prepared, a fire tender could be seen getting into position, when forty minutes later we arrived over the airport from the Kaw Kaw Gap. I was advised that a section of the dirt runway would be lightly treated with some water, just enough to lay the dust, making for a smoother slide on the delicate belly. The runway surface at the selected touchdown point was the red clay common to the area without any layers of stones or gravel underneath, again a next to perfect situation.

During almost an hour of circling, while awaiting things to be ready on the ground, allowing some regular air traffic to arrive and depart and burning off some fuel, I carried out a stalling check to confirm an approach speed with only five degrees of flap out. While the passengers all seemed to enjoy the sudden drop experience, nevertheless by that time they all looked to be a little up tight.

Some heavy gear had been stowed in the locker behind the rear seats, with a long, heavy crowbar flat along one wall. Being unsure of exactly what to expect in the way of deceleration or swing, when loose articles might fly about the cabin, the rear seat passenger was briefed on how to dispose of the gear. With the rear cargo door cracked open against the slipstream and with the tip of the crowbar poked out, he was briefed to watch for my signal as we came up over the runway at 100 feet when he would shove the crowbar out and down. On subsequent runs he disposed of the remainder of the gear in the same manner. The crew waiting on the ground were to clear all the gear away before we landed. With a lot of practice bombing under my belt using missiles long, large, short and small I had the confidence to be able to land them right on target. All the gear dropped that day was recovered intact except the crowbar, which has never been found. The bar must have pierced the surface at high velocity and gone deep towards the centre of the earth to record the only loss of any piece of equipment for the incident.

I've been a praying man for a long time and so offered a prayer as we made the final approach to the landing pad, aiming for the white stripe across the runway provided by the fire-crew, while keeping the machine flat for the touchdown to prevent any serious damage to the flaps.

Holding off above the runway with the touchdown marker coming in fast, back came the throttles, off went the magnetos, fuel cocks and mixture levers. The Baron's smooth and shiny belly hit firmly and stayed there, sliding straight as a die for what would be about 80 metres. That time I remembered to take my feet off the pedals as the feeling in the controls was wiped out. A cheer went up from in the cabin as we came to a stop.

As rehearsed in the air, I leaned over and unlatched the door. Evacuation was swift and well ordered. The front seat passenger pushed the door forward, latched it open then slipped out on to the wing, followed closely by the others from the rear seats, while I came out last. We all moved away from the then helpless looking metal bird, as the fire-crew began to run hoses out from the tender although there was not a hint of a fire anywhere, which was rather an anti-climax to a rather trying morning.

Both propellers had contacted the ground as we slid along and were bent near the tips. Apart from that GKA looked to have been little damaged. In hindsight, had I known more about belly landings the props could have been spared any damage at all by positioning the blades to the horizontal with the starter in the seconds before touch-down.

The passengers all thanked me for a safe arrival, particularly Norrie Ford who was a highly rated golfer. A leading professional, Norman Von Nida, was to play that day on the Goroka course, part of which extended across the town's main and on to the aerodrome. Norrie had cursed his luck at having to be away at Mendi on governmental duties, thus not able to watch the great golf champion in action. From where we stood near the Baron we could see the crowd gathered around the first tee, watching not Von Nida about to drive off but the drama being enacted right in front of their eyes on the runway! Mumbling more thanks, with a wave of his hand Norrie sloped off to join them, having been delivered rather dramatically by air to his beloved sport!

Later that day TAL's chief engineer 'Poppa' Raasch had GKA raised on jacks, the gear extended and a fresh wheel fitted before she was moved to the hangar. There were a few red faces in the engineering division when it was discovered that on an inspection late the day before, the wheel bearing must have been over-tightened somehow, allowing the wheel to spin off the axle over the main retaining nut.

Later, from Peter Harbeck the agent at Banz, I heard the story of the finding of the wheel. An indigene labourer cutting grass along the bottom end of the airstrip had watched the Baron take off and heard a rustle in the grass nearby. He found the wheel and decided he'd better take it up to Peter, a walk of almost half a mile. Another miracle was in the making.

As 'finder's keepers', the man could have souvenired the wheel and taken it to his village, or put it aside until he'd finished work, or simply forgotten about it as being of no concern to him. By that time the aircraft would have been end up on Mendi's airstrip, with some of the occupants being either killed or injured.

For weeks past, Peter's radio had been misbehaving causing him much frustration from the lack of communication for orders and instructions with the Ansett/MAL's office in Madang, the DC3 services to Banz being the main line of communication 'tween coast and highlands. Peter had called many times over the days without any responses coming his way. Fiddling with the set proved fruitless. Believing the wheel had come off the aircraft he'd heard but not seen, as its movement didn't concern him, he called Madang to report the find and received an answer to his first call! At that time I would probably have been near Mendi and about to cancel the flight plan.

The airline office immediately notified the Madang control tower, who notified the Radio Section smartly, who in turn called me only just in time. Ah, it was good to be in New Guinea where people use their brains!

Considering that the assigned air-radio frequencies were some-times choked with traffic and the message was relayed three times, only a miracle got that warning out in time. Had it been delayed for any one of those reasons, GKA would have landed at Mendi down-wind on a stub axle at close to 100 miles per hour, which might have brought an end to GKA and the complement of civil servants in a wreck or fire following a ground loop or flip-over, who knows.

The most dangerous time would be when we were on close final approach at Mendi, green undercarriage warning light shining bright-ly, completely unaware that one leg was not 'dangling the Dunlop'.

The belly landing closed the chapter of my serious accidents. The next thirty years of solid flying in many parts of the world, under all sorts of conditions saw me faced with several serious emergencies. By that time I had gathered much more experience and was a much better pilot, by knowing most of the situations that could trap the over-confident or unwary flying man and his metal bird.

A week later GKA was flown to Archerfield, Brisbane, for a major check over, which was completed with flying colours and without any serious stresses or strains being found. She was missed a lot while tak-ing a rest from her labours, with our critics having a real 'hey-day' to the tune of 'I toldya so'. On returning, there was plenty for her to do and Dennis, being extremely satisfied with the economics of his high-ly prized twin, was considering the purchase of another.

The man who 'goofed' with the wheel bearing was beside himself with remorse, which was eased only when we shook hands in a 'for-give and forget' unofficial private ceremony in an office off the hangar. The same aircraft went on to serve the company for years, logging thousands of flights in one of the most difficult flying coun-tries in the world. Dennis as always, took the setback in his stride with the company expanding as twin engine 'metal birds' became very popular.

A new, shall we call it Territory regulation was announced and came into being. Fuel drums would no longer be carried in anything other than a twin-engine aircraft, a decision which would leave many places with a Category D airstrip and no connecting road, without fuel supplies, particularly governmental patrol posts and river stations. Many of the Territory's airstrips were classified as Category D and available to single engine aircraft only.

The Cessna 336 fitted with bigger wheels was the only twin that could fit into the specifications set by the Department of Civil Aviation for Cat D operations. To comply with the regulation Dennis ordered three of the centre-line thrust machines from Rex Aviation in Sydney, in so doing bagging some of the first of the type into Australia, thus gaining a 'lead by a nose' on Ansett's light aircraft division, our biggest competitor. TAL's 'push-pulls' were in operation before Ansett gained a delivery slot.

In 'pidgin talk' the 336 became known as a 'pullim ikam, pushim igo balus', or in more perfect Queen's English 'as she should be spoke', simply a 'push-pull'.

While ferrying a 'push-pull' to Goroka from Sydney with Dennis aboard, we were over the Torres Strait readying to switch over to New Guinea frequencies when an exchange of radio messages between Madang and Port Moresby were intercepted. An eavesdropper can only hear bad news. As we listened we heard that Baron GKA was in trouble at our old friend Bundi of all places. We both pricked our ears up to the speaker to learn further that TAL's pride and joy had up-ended there with a broken nose-wheel strut and very bent props. From what we could gather from the indirect radio discussions, the Baron remained standing tail high on the strip, the pilot unhurt.

Dennis was ropeable, while I was mystified, for the pilot in command of GKA had not been endorsed for flights into Bundi with the Baron until gaining more experience on the type. One of the first TAL pilots to qualify on the Baron, Peter the Pilot was going to be in trouble when Dennis arrived on the scene the next day. The good news that we also intercepted was that Chief Engineer Paul Raasch (Poppa), was already on the way to Bundi and had things under control. Without having to ask any questions on an already busy frequency, magically, although several hundreds of miles away from the scene, we had all the answers.

It took a few days for Dennis to simmer down. I was flown to Bundi to ferry the Baron to Goroka. 'Poppa' had made a temporary fix of the nose gear, the props and skin dents. Peter the Pilot had decided that his future lay with helicopters and had departed for Australia.

Return to Goroka through the Asaloka Gap was made without incident with the gear fixed down. After further work by the engineers in the hangar, the Baron went off to Brisbane again for a complete check of all her under hangings. After the delivery to Archerfield I carried on to Sydney to pick up another 'push-pull' for ferry to Goroka. By that time, without a doubt I was getting to know the east coast of Australia north of Brisbane, better than Captain Cook.

THE LAIAGAM LESSON

The loss of a propeller counter-weight from Beech Baron GKA on take-off at Laiagam, a patrol post at 7000 feet elevation in New Guinea's Western Highlands, gave me another 'close call'. From early morning, packaged provisions were being shuttled in the Baron to the post from Mt Hagen, back-loading with male recruits for the Highlands Labour Scheme.

Laiagam's gravel-packed coronous runway sloped down to the southeast. Regardless of the wind, take-off was always made down the slope. With the airstrip located in a narrow valley surrounded by rugged hills, coupled with high elevation, the aircraft's maximum allowable weight for take-off was severely reduced. For the return flights to Mt. Hagen that day, precious little fuel was being carried and five light-weight passengers only, without luggage, instead of six heavy-weights with heaps.

Having completed five return flights by the mid-afternoon, it came as a surprise to hear from the District Officer Dennis Faithful, that the supply of recruits had 'dried up' or in more explicit terms had deserted, which was a fairly common habit. The return flight therefore would be the last for the day and a solo one for me. Obviously my good guardian angel was staying close, keeping an eye on things.

With secondary mountains rising sharply ahead and on each side of the recommended departure flight path, a positive rate of climb after take-off at Laiagam was essential for any type of aircraft in order to avoid the terrain. A straight course into rising terrain must be steered until altitude enough was available for a turn to be made to clear the valley. To pilots, Laiagam was known as a 'pretty tight place' and no place for learners.

The usual afternoon katabatic breeze was on the tail, when GKA was lined up to take-off down slope for the sixth time that day. When over the local hospital after becoming airborne, with the wheels swinging up, suddenly there was a loud 'bang', small bits and pieces flew past the right window, the aircraft yawed crazily, the right engine's tachometer gyrated madly. My left foot was called into action to lay on hard and keep her going along the desired track between contours in the terrain, with the right propeller acting as a useless, whirling disc of drag. An attempt to feather the prop failed. My first thoughts were that an eagle had hit the propellor, the big birds were often seen soaring over the valley.

Forward of the aircraft the ground rose towards the crest that would be impossible to reach except with two engines running harmoniously. To the right, the valley slopes were closing in, with that wing almost scraping the hilltops. My whole being prayed as a Mayday (distress) call was transmitted, my feeling was that the end was near for me, or the start, whichever way you look at it.

The following wind played a big part in my survival. The air following the Baron must also rise over the terrain directly ahead and turn into a welcome updraft that would be a glider pilot's delight, gaining altitude through inertia in the rising air.

Most air training manuals stipulate that following an engine failure after take-off, a pilot should not attempt to turn back to the field he's just left but try to bring off the best possible landing in the direction of flight in gliding distance making small deviations as necessary to avoid obstacles, preferably into wind and using flaps intelligently. Most aircraft need at least 300-400 feet of ground clearance to complete an engineless 'one-eighty' in the glide mode. Any attempt to do so at or below that can end in disaster and often does. The drill taught by most flying schools for single engine aircraft is for the pilot to select a spot somewhere in modest angle of the nose and head in there for an emergency landing.

Some of those rules came to taunt me as I started to turn back to the strip, to all intents and purposes I was flying a single engine type by being well above the density altitude for best single engine performance with a failed engine and a prop that wouldn't feather. The thought of our beautiful Baron lying aflame in a crumpled heap on a New Guinea hillside was more than I could bear! Had there been passengers aboard to further restrict the climb angle, a different decision might have been made. My thanks to those 'deserters'.

The valley to the left offered more clearance than the other side and was chosen as my only hope. Disregarding all the rules and while I still had some lift going for me, I laid her over into a left turn that could be described as steep for the conditions. With the good engine on full available power, a rate of descent showing up on the altimeter and the speed washing off to a minimum the Baron entered a turn into the going engine, which in the early days of aviation was considered suicidal. The longer I held to the turn, the more the aircraft 'juddered' the better came the ground clearance, allowing the nose to go down and gather some lost airspeed, until Laiagam's strip began to show up.

After dodging a grassy hillock or two, the turn was completed at an angle to the strip that required some adjustment by a turn in the opposite direction. Low down and lightly banked we skimmed over the hospital directly into the breeze, with the flaps coming out and the gear light changing to green. The main wheels met with the runway 100 metres or so up the slope, we slowed without the use of brakes. Much to my relief GKA was safely down.

On remembering that the last radio call made was an automatic 'Mayday' I grabbed the mike again and called Madang several times, without an answer, the HF radio seemed to be dead.

The Baron had only been gone for two or three minutes before I taxied back into the parking bay again. The HF radio aerial was trailing along the ground, the pilot breathing hard. There was no sign of

Dennis the DO or anyone else, my watch read ten minutes past four. After letting my heart catch up, I walked to his residence to let him know of the 'Mayday' situation before he took the cap off his first 'stubby' for the day. He was more than surprised to see me and promised to let Madang know by government radio, that I was safe and would be remaining overnight. Being an aircraft owner with considerable flying experience he was quite shocked when later he saw the prop and it's battered spinner. He confirmed that I'd had another close shave and should take a ticket in Tatts.

He ordered his police to search around the hospital area for any fragments of the spinner and counter-weight. We were both back at his house when the searchers arrived to report that nothing had been found, which was not surprising from what I saw of the fragmentation and the short search made of the area by those who probably weren't quite sure what to look for!

There were several important factors that came to my aid that day, the first one being that the aircraft without passengers or cargo and with little fuel, was very light at the time of take-off. (I never was able to thank the Labour Scheme recruits for their desertion that day!) With the take-off being made downwind and down slope, the air from that direction coupled with the density altitude at Laiagam meant a longer take off roll with which I'd become quite familiar, Laiagam was always a tight squeeze. That same air that the Baron was in however, was forced to rise over the terrain in the flight path, providing me with a better climb rate that could be expected with a head-wind or no wind at all. That the fragments flying about hadn't damaged any vital part of the aircraft other than the spinner and aerial was another redeeming feature. Without the counter-weight, the prop could not be feathered, the engine had gone into an 'overspeed' by a big margin and was going to need a thorough check over.

In my opinion, no other light twin of the time would have been able to complete that turn under the same conditions. Thank you Mrs Olive Beech and your Beech engineers for your wonderful, sturdy, speedy little Baron, that will go down in history as one of the better general aviation metal birds to see service in New Guinea.

GRAVEYARD OF FLYING MEN AND METAL BIRDS

New Guinea's inhospitable weather coupled with mountainous terrain claimed the lives of many capable pilots many of whom were known to me personally, or through their relatives and friends, by the nature of the work we shared. Some of the accidents were similar to mine. My hope had been that my first crash would be my last. Unfortunately that hope was cancelled out during the time I was engaged in agricultural flying, 'crop-dusting' so-called.

The pilots and passengers killed in PNG's light 'plane air disasters that not much is heard about and not mentioned here, attributed to either inclement weather, mountainous terrain or pilot error, would fill the biggest of a modern day jumbo jet airliner.

During the 1960's New Guinea was on a 'boomer'. For the day, the Territory's administration operated on a generous budget supplied by the taxpayers of Australia. The aim was to contact every tribe in the Territory and bring to them roads, good health practices, medical aid, law and order, education, the workings of sound government and commercial business, to allow them to handle their own affairs, that was then a hazy, uncertain date sometime in the future.

With possibly more than 100 years to overtake what could be called normal progress, theirs was a race against time. The Territory of New Guinea under Australian administration covered a huge area and was in parts extremely mountainous. Outside the major towns and cities, there were few roads. No common language bonded the population that consisted mainly of primitive tribes-people, existing on what was grown or reared on their own lands. Many of the clans were war-like, one to the other.

From early in the nineteenth century, the islands that made up the Territory had been ruled by three great powers, Germany, Britain and Australia. The ex-German territory was administered by Australia under the League of Nations from 1914. Japan as an invader took over much of the Territory from 1942. Australia regained control for the second time under the re-organised United Nations when the Second World War was over. The western half of the island of New Guinea now known as Irian Jaya, was administered from Batavia by the Dutch as a part of the Dutch East Indies, with, in those years, little impact on the Territory.

The frequent but spectacular changes in ownership had left little time for development of the interior of the massive island of New Guinea and the other larger islands, New Britain, New Ireland, New Hanover, Bougainville and others that comprised the Mandated Terrritory.

World War 2 brought about a more diverse use of the aeroplane other than military and helped to uncover the large populations that existed in parts of the hinterlands. While huge air bases had been constructed during war, these were sometimes in areas not always suitable or convenient for retention as commercial centres in peacetime. By and large though, New Guinea had some resources left over from the war that made for a positive start to post-war domestic aviation, both airline and general.

Small airstrips, their locations more suited to peace were constructed on open plains, in bush-clad valleys, on islands and steep mountainsides where more recently discovered populations were known to exist. The women of New Guinea usually worked in the mountain gardens, which could be at levels of 10,000 feet elevation, in rain forest areas, on wide, open plains, or in low-lying wetlands nearer the sea adjoining the many large rivers. Pulp was made from the sago palms in those areas. Funding and supply of the equipment necessary for the building of an airstrip was provided by the administration, while the labour force, known as the 'rice-power', was recruited from the local indigenous population.

Christian missions, catholic, evangelical and others, operated their own air services to their private airfields in the highlands or on the riverbanks of the country's largest rivers, the Fly, Sepik and Ramu. The word 'airfield' is a misnomer for they were mostly 'strips', cut through rainforest, bush, hillocks, muddy river-banks or alongside deep, steep gorges, anywhere that gave access to the populace of an area as a whole.

During that time a new word 'development' was coined and hung on everyone's lips as overseas cargo ships unloaded at Madang on the north coast where their cargoes were transhipped by air to the highland valley ports of Goroka, Minj, Banz or Mount Hagen. Rice, all manner of canned food, general provisions, corrugated iron, steel piping, power cables, cement, glass louvres, timber, fertiliser, seedlings, live animals, small vehicles and always the tinned fish and 'bulimakau' (meat), by the hundreds of tons. Nothing was too hard for the fifteen or so DC3's that operated daily from Madang on a highlands shuttle service. In later times those were joined by four nose-loaded Bristol Freighters, with a cargo capacity almost twice that of the DC3.

Whatever the item was it went by air, plantation labour, mail, petrol, oil, kerosene, cash or kina shells. Madang soon became one of the world's biggest air cargo ports in terms of the movement of cargo that in more developed countries would be shifted by canal, river, rail or road.

At the time, on-carriage from the highland ports to the smaller posts and centres came into the hands of several licensed air charter operators who had graduated from the fabric covered pre-war biplanes, to the ubiquitous, single engine, all-metal Cessna, aircraft much more suited to the tropical climate. The missions also operated private air services in a big way to their many mission stations scattered through all parts of the Territory.

The largest highland charter operation in that field was owned by Dennis Buchanan, (later Sir Dennis), of Territory Airlines at Goroka in the Eastern Highlands. As a very young man Dennis had come to the Territory to serve with Gibbes Sepik Airways as a cargo superintendent. After gaining experience, he had branched out to take over the ownership of Territory Airlines and had been most successful in co-operating with the administration. To all and sundry he was known as 'Junior'.

In the company of Father Joe of the Catholic Mission (SVD), Dennis had walked into the Lutmis hangar at Madang one day with a job offer for me, having heard that my contract with the mission was almost over, which was the first time we'd met. To work and live in a highlands climate was most appealing after the sweaty heat of Madang. After some time and at his request, I became the Chief Pilot of his company, a position subject to the approval of the Department of Civil Aviation.

After opening Territory Airlines up with the De Havilland DH84 Dragon, Dennis had moved on to the Cessna 170 and Dornier 27. With charter work building up fast, through Rex Aviation the Australian Cessna dealers he had added five new Cessna 185's to his fleet, that were at that time the pride and joy of Australasian general aviation. Each passing year saw lots more of the type introduced to New Guinea, with not only Territory Airlines, but several other companies too. Operations not quite as vigorous went on all over the Territory, out of Lae to ports on the Huon Peninsula, the Wau, Bulolo and Garaina valleys, while Wewak served as the hub for air services in the Sepik area. Rabaul, Kavieng and Buka were bases for New Britain, New Ireland and Bougainville with charter operators licensed in each area. An administration backed Highland Labour Scheme utilised DC-3's to transport highlands men for work on coastal and island copra and cocoa plantations as indentured labour.

Pilots for all types of aircraft were always in big demand and short supply. With the airlines of Australia growing fast, Air Force retirees were virtually assured of a job under one of the big umbrellas, Qantas, Trans Australia Airlines and the up and coming Ansett Airlines.

Aerial crop-spraying, dusting and top-dressing was getting under way in Australia too in a fairly big way, absorbing many young would-be commercial pilots. During the sixties there were just not enough pilots to go around the flourishing New Guinea aviation industry.

Once trained in New Guinea and having survived two years or so there, a 20-25 year old pilot was almost guaranteed a highly paid (for the times) Australian airline job, which almost all preferred to the hard, more dangerous slog in New Guinea for less reward. There were many who left their New Guinea jobs just as they were becoming fully productive, when the operator would have to start all over again with a 'new boy on the block' if one could be found. The increase in flying hours brought about an increase in fatal air accidents. No company or mission was spared.

With the Administration always clamouring for service, a lot of pressure came on a Chief Pilot to approve his company's pilots to fly over certain routes before they were completely ready to go it alone. This is not meant to imply that regulations had to be broken, a lot depended on the pilot under training and his ability to be able to meet the standard required, having completed all the tests and checks as laid down.

"He's completed all that's required plus more and is eager to go on his own. I'm still not completely sure that he's up to the job just yet, he flies like a young aero club instructor with a head full of rules, no 'dash' to him at all " was often the dilemma faced by a Chief Pilot, with a Traffic Manager or Managing Director calling for the completion of urgent and profitable work that should have been done the day before yesterday. That was a difficult sort of situation for a Chief Pilot, who could be under a lot of pressure with keen young pilots itching to be out on their own. Although fully trained in the eyes of the law they were about to face one of the most difficult flying countries in the world with limited experience.

For the work in the highlands with the ever-present mountain formidability, a pilot needed experience, particularly in the handling of the ever-changing weather patterns, seasonal and diurnal. Many of the mountain airstrips were either poorly or dangerously located from a pilot's point of view.

For pilots new to such conditions, the strips were tricky, with high elevations, varying gradients and a greasy or rough surface which if not handled properly could lead to an accident, minor or major. Some strips were on slopes that varied from 5% to 15% or an undulating mixture of both and could be approached from only one direction, leaving the pilot with nowhere to go except into a hill or narrow canyon should the approach be aborted. An area that allowed for a missed landing 'go around' was not available in some cases. An uphill landing and a downhill take-off, regardless of wind or visibility was necessary on many of those landing grounds. Those who hired aircraft as part of their livelihood could be adversely affected too by an airfield's location or dimension with the possibility of severe payload restriction applying to landing, take-off, or both.

The official performance charts for take-off, climb out and landing of the aircraft type, although well meant by the provider, were not wholly reliable when high elevations, coupled with steep or varying slopes, meant that the chart might have to be interpolated guardedly, a procedure that was frowned on and not permitted by the regulatory authorities. That sort of view never altered the elevation of the particular airfield, nor was the owner ever threatened with the strip's closure and again the Chief Pilot must carry the burden.

Thus a Catch 22 situation developed. Companies licensed for the vital work soon found that conforming strictly to the regulations was an impossibility that could only lead to the grounding of all their fleet for one reason or another. In the event of an accident occurring at one of those places, the Chief Pilot of the organization involved was left to bear the responsibility. Managers, Managing Directors, Traffic Managers or Finance Managers never put their hands up where responsibility was concerned, 'passing the buck' was relatively easy. That unfair system went on for years, with the administration on one side urging that the work be done and the Department of Civil Aviation on the other side, unable or unwilling, to provide the legal means of doing so, the 'escape route' of course being the Chief Pilot of the operator in question, as meat in a sandwich.

To a young man fresh from training in a developed country, the flying in New Guinea in total presented a huge challenge. Most employers required a minimum of one thousand hours of flying-in-command on the aircraft type operated, or similar type, before any appointment was made. A series of rigorous checks by company approved check pilots, on general aircraft handling, route and airstrip familiarisation would follow any initial training in the Territory. Notwithstanding, with the big increase in flying, came a big increase in accidents, a high proportion of them fatal to the pilots concerned.

The cause of any accident could often be put down to inclement weather, an aberration of some kind on the part of the pilot, or a mechanical fault. But the root cause I believe was the standard of training the young pilots had received before arriving in the Territory. Competent aircraft handling was the most important ingredient a prospective pilot needed to fly confidently and survive in New Guinea. In my view, not all, but some would-be New Guinea pilots were psychologically and mentally unsuited to the conditions and better suited to 'flying the clocks' in the heavy aircraft airline role, although there were many of course who graduated with honours in both systems.

The central mountains of mainland New Guinea presented a formidable barrier to the type of aircraft used at the time. Except for the Andes of South America, the spine of mainland New Guinea is the largest cordillera in the world. Closer to the equator the Inter-Tropic

Zone with its monsoonal surges can attract unstable weather conditions, the worst of thunder, lightning and heavy rain that has to be seen to be believed.

A very high proportion of New Guinea's population live in the valleys of the mountain country, known as the highlands, where the soil is fertile and the climate equable. Fog in the morning, thunder, lightning and rain mixed with low cloud in the afternoon, is a normal condition for most parts. For expatriates, the climate in the several highlands areas is idyllic, mosquito-free warm days featuring cool to cold nights with medium to low humidity.

The saying goes that there are old pilots and bold pilots, but no old-bold pilots. I would venture to say that saying is true when applied to New Guinea. The mountains close to some airports in the highlands can lay claim to a large number of air accidents involving pilots' loss of life. Viewed from that angle, most highland airports have earned a bad reputation with the number of pilots killed while approaching or departing their airport that reads more like a war casualty list.

Because of its slope, Goroka in the Eastern Highlands, the then home base of Territory Airlines, has always been a 'one-way' airport, with landings made up-slope, take-offs down-slope. The two parallel runways are generous in length and blessed with a good surface. There's plenty of room in the valley to climb after take-off too. The town and airport sits on the eastern side of the valley at an elevation of 5000 feet, in the shadow of Mount Otto (11,634 ft), a major peak in the Bismarck chain of mountains.

The summit of Mt. Otto is only 5 kilometres from the airfield. The mountain can throw up heavy rain-clouds at any time but particularly in the afternoon, which produces a thick fog over the valley floor in the early morning. All landing approaches are made from the open valley on the south and west so as to remain clear of Mount Otto's slopes.

In the days written about here, aircraft exited or entered the valley via one of several passes called 'gaps' in the parlance of New Guinea aviation. The Bena, 'Dirty Water' and Arona to the east of the field, the North Goroka and Asaloka to the north, the Dalou, Watabung, Kaw Kaw and Asaro South to the west and south-west. Both valley and mountain are dotted with crash sites, where pilots young and old, experienced and inexperienced, have lost their lives.

Here, with the deepest respect, the names of some of those pilots who died in mountainous terrain, mountain passes or near to highland valley airfields are recorded as a sincere remembrance.

Doug Tapsall, (AUS). Qantas Airways. DH84 aircraft. Collided with terrain on the eastern upper slopes of Mount Kerigomna, outside the Dalou Pass.

Father Harry McGee, (USA). Divine Word.Mission. Dornier 27 aircraft. Collided with an escarpment that stands apart from Mount Otto, 2 kilometres from Goroka's airfield.

Harry Hartwig, (AUS). Lutheran Mission. Auster aircraft. Collided with terrain on the south side of the Asaloka Gap in cloudy weather.

Jack Gray, (AUS). Territory Airlines. (Part owner). DH82 aircraft. Collided with terrain in the Arona Gap on a private flight to Lae.

Garth Stockell, (AUS). Territory Airlines. Cessna 206 aircraft. Clipped a ridge after passing through the Dalou Pass.

Father Joe Walachy, (USA). Divine Word Mission..Cessna 206 aircraft. Collided with terrain on the northern side of the Asaloka Gap.

John Gaffney, (AUS) Territory Airlines. Cessna 205 aircraft. Collided with terrain at the Bena Gap on a flight Madang - Nambaiufa.

Laurie Wright, (AUS) Territory Airlines. Cessna 205 aircraft. Collided with terrain at the Bena Gap on a flight Madang - Nambaiufa

Geoff Vendvill, (AUS). Territory Airlines. Cessna 206 aircraft. Landing into the sun at Omkolai airstrip, collided with embankment of parking bay at speed.

Ian Oliver, (NZ), Territory Airlines. Beechcraft Baron aircraft. Stalled after take-off on Goroka's runway 17 left. Root cause never discovered. Six other Bank Officer fatalities.

Laurie Shields, (AUS). Seventh-Day-Adventist Mission. Cessna 207 aircraft. Crashed short of Goroka's runway 35 left, after attempting to return to land following an engine malfunction after take-off.

Robert Gray. (PNG). Talair. Cessna 206 aircraft. Collided with high terrain en route to Marawaka after leaving Goroka.

Dennis McKillop. (NZ). Trans-Australia Airlines. DHC6 Twin Otter aircraft. Struck terrain near Raipinka during low approach to Kainantu in bad weather.

Ray Jaensch. (AUS). 'Lutmis' Air Services. DO27 aircraft. Attempting a forced landing in a river-bed near Tauta in the Surinam valley after engine failure on take-off.

G. Maungano (AUS) Ansett/MAL. Cessna 170. Crashed en-route to Simbai from the Ramu Valley. Had arrived in PNG and been married only weeks before.

G. Cabrero. (USA). Talair. Embraer Bandereinte aircraft. Struck terrain when circling to cross ranges near the Watabung Gap en route Goroka.

Tom Peninsa. (PNG). Goroka Air Services. DHC6 Twin Otter aircraft Struck eastern slope of Mt Otto 5 km from Goroka airfield during attempt to land through low clouds.

Ian Leslie. (AUS). Lesair. Cessna 185 aircraft. Crashed while attempting to land at a newly opened airstrip near junction of Asaro and Wahgi rivers.

Mount Hagen, Western Highlands Area

The same could be said for Mount Hagen at the northern end of the Wahgi valley, Mount Giluwe and the nearby Kubor mountains. Then there is Mendi on the southern side of Mt Giluwe and Lae, gateway to the Huon Gulf and Markham Valley.

George Wicks. (UK). Territory Airlines. Cessna 185 aircraft.
Attempting a return to Mt Hagen field after having taken off with a double load of corrugated iron.

Maurice Aldridge. (NZ). Ansett Mandated Airlines. Cessna 336 aircraft. Collided with terrain 3 km south of Kagamuga airfield, shortly after take-off.

Brian Badger. (AUS). Trans Australia Airlines. DHC3 Otter aircraft.
Rimus Zuydam. (AUS). Trans Australia Airlines. DHC3 Otter aircraft.
Collided with an escarpment 8 kilometres west of Mt Hagen airfield on climb-out after take off.

Peter Arnold. (AUS). Ansett Mandated Airlines. Short Skyvan aircraft. Collided high on northern slope of Mount Giluwe after leaving Minj for Mendi.

Tony Kosowski, (AUS). Macair Charters. Cessna185 aircraft. Crashed near the Tomba Pass after leaving Mt.Hagen.

Gavin Dennis, Qantas Cadet (AUS) Territory Airlines. Cessna 206 aircraft. Collided with an escarpment near the East gap while attempting to exit the Porgera valley.

Father Henry Hoff. (USA). Macair Charters. Cessna 185 aircraft. Crashed approximately 5 km west of the Kimil Gap, on a flight Mt Hagen - Tabibuga.

Malcolm Hawkes. (AUS). Talair. Beechcraft Baron aircraft. Crashed at the Tomba Pass after leaving Mount Hagen.

Alex Ignatieff. (AUS). Hawker De Havilland test pilot. Beechcraft Musketeer aircraft. Crashed after take-off from Kagamuga, Mt. Hagen, believed to have been overloaded for the prevailing weather conditions and choice of runway.

Doug Hunt. (NZ). Summer Institute of Linguistics. Piper Aztec aircraft. Crashed in flames while making an emergency landing approach to the then unused Nadzab airport, after a wing failure, having glided the Aztec from 6,000 feet with an engine on fire. (Doug had met my family at Essendon, Melbourne on the night we first arrived in Victoria).

Robert John Smith. (AUS) Macair. Cessna 206 aircraft.
Robert Bruce Smith.(AUS) Macair. Cessna 206 aircraft.
Crashed in high country near Mount Sarawaket after taking off from Pindiu, Huon Peninsula at the beginning of a return flight to Lae.

Jim Miller. (AUS). Mendi Air services. DHC6 Twin Otter aircraft. Struck Clancy's Knob on approach to Mendi airport in marginal weather.

If that's not enough there are many others not listed here who also lost their lives, attributed to the difficult flying conditions in New Guinea. During my several periods of flying in that great land many company name changes took place preceding the nation's bid for independence that included Territory Airlines (TAL) becoming Talair, Macair Charters becoming Melanesian Airline Company Pty. Ltd, but nevertheless, because of the mouthful, always preferring to be called Macair.

Hereby also remembered is an ex Air Force associate turned priest, Father Larry Zampese (NZ), who was killed in mountains near Yangoru, Wewak area, while piloting a Dornier 27 of Divine Word Airways (Catholic Mission), after serving only a short term as a mission pilot in New Guinea and Father Doug McCraw, (AUS), of Anglican Mission, who after many years of mountain flying in New Guinea, both mission and commercial, was tragically killed in a highlands motor accident while transferring his car and personal effects by road on posting from Mt Hagen to Lae for a senior position with Talair. After war service with the RAAF, Doug who was also a qualified flight instructor had accumulated thousands of hours, mission and commercial in PNG. He was a special soul, a man for all seasons and all people, with always a genuine smile for anybody and everyone, a man of intelligence and compassion. Father Doug practiced commercial flying as a means to an end, to earn a living without becoming a financial burden on his church and to give him freedom of movement to minister the Gospel as opportunities arose outside his parish.

Infirmioribus, succurendo, fortior
(we grow strong in service to the weak)

The hazards flying men faced in New Guinea were not always in the air. A young New Zealander, Peter Slater, who even in the early days of his introduction to New Guinea and its' unusual flying conditions, was showing great potential as a future airline pilot. Peter lost his life while taking a shower in the TAL quarters at Mendi after a hard flying day. His death was put down to him having inhaled a mixture of steam and gas from a leak in the shower's gas fuelled water-heater although that was never proved to my complete satisfaction.

Peter was on the way up in his chosen profession, apart from that he really deserved a more professional, thorough investigation into his death, which was not forthcoming. Peter was and is sadly missed by his friends formerly in New Guinea with him at the time and his loving relatives in New Zealand. May he, along with all the others mentioned here, rest in peace.

SEARCH AND FIND

Within twenty minutes of an aircraft being reported overdue at a compulsory position reporting point or destination, anywhere in the Territory, the Search and Rescue Organization would mount an air search. I took part in many of those searches, some close to home, some further afield. The searches were sometimes short-lived, while others lasted for days.

Always remembering my own escape from death in Fiji I went out on a search with a heavy heart for I knew even then that the pilot would probably be dead. The Drover scene always seemed to re-surface to haunt me at those times. Scanning the terrain from above I knew exactly what to look for. If a choice came my way and the suspected crash site was not far away, a Cessna 185 would be my choice as the search vehicle. With its' high wing, the visibility from the 185 was excellent and matched by its top-line performance. Many of my searches in jungle areas were successful for I flew low, sometimes very low, 200 feet or less over the terrain. The 185 is easy to manoeuvre and most suited to the task. My opinion was that many of the other participating aircraft and pilots, in searches of that kind were quite unsuited to the task, misguided, or simply taking the opportunity to gain experience in searching forest areas from the air.

Search briefings in New Guinea usually called for the searching aircraft to fly at a minimum of 1000 feet over their allotted area. To me that was far too high. An area of jungle 'combed' by an aircraft flying at 1000 feet over the terrain is not an area 'properly combed'.

One only has to fly over an airport at 1000 feet and observe the light 'planes parked on a sealed tarmac with their wings and tail attached, to know just how small they appear to be. Add the cover of the rainforest, the colour of the terrain, sun glare, poor light or drizzle, a dismembered aircraft and there's not too much left to be seen. For success in sighting aircraft wreckage from a fixed wing aircraft in forested regions, one must fly quite low and at a speed appropriate to the terrain and flight conditions.

Observers were always ready and willing to take part in a search. I preferred to work with a maximum of three persons on board a C185, certainly not 'all seats filled'. Any more than two observers aboard and the cabin was too congested, sometimes with those who went along just for the ride and weren't too sure what they were looking for, causing distractions for the ones that did. Some might get airsick too from the tight manoeuvres that were sometimes called for.

My experience on sea searches in Catalinas and Sunderlands had shown that almost always the target, whether on sea or land, was first seen by one of the pilots in the cockpit, or a pilot being used as a searcher in some other part of the aircraft. The same rule applied I believe to land searches in New Guinea. The pilot was the one most likely to be the first to sight the target whatever it was. Credit must go to the Imperial Japan Navy in World War 2 where trained eyes were found to be as good as, or even better than radar. In those grim days it was believed that all Japanese wore spectacles with thick lenses, obviously that was not the case.

On becoming airborne to join in a search, one must know what to look for, what was likely to be found and where. A burnt out or a crushed, twisted airframe, smoke, part of a wing here, an aileron there, a tailplane dangling from a tree or cliff face, apparently intact. No sign of life.

In the event that a pilot might have transmitted a 'Mayday' call after a mechanical malfunction of some sort, a reasonably intact aircraft could be found with the pilot most probably still alive.

In the short twilight that comes before a beautiful evening in the tropics, I was over the wet-lands to the north-west of Port Moresby in a Beechcraft Baron, on a long and lazy approach to Jackson's Airport. Moresby Control suddenly advised that a Mayday call had just been received from an aircraft quite close to and below my position and who was attempting a forced landing through engine failure. That was the quickest search I was ever involved in. Immediately, I dropped the right wing of my Baron for a look at the ground in the direction indicated by Control. Through the gloom of 4000 feet altitude a Cessna was sighted below, apparently gliding in for a landing in the tall kunai grass that covered the area. Dropping off height rapidly while circling, I watched the 'plane reach the ground, come to a stop the right way up and the four occupants clamber out and begin waving. It was easy to see that no one had been hurt.

A quick dash over the 50 kilometres or so to Jackson's followed with a return to the site in semi-darkness with helpers aboard to drop some overnight comforts to the party at the aircraft. With the job done I could only hope that mosquito repellent had been included with the 'comforts'. As explained before, if a pilot is at the controls and well knows the drill, during an emergency forced landing the chances for survival are very good.

The end result of the landing described here would have been quite different if the emergency had occurred over mountainous terrain covered in rainforest, nevertheless the chances of survival are still good when contact is made with ground or forest with the pilot still in control of the aircraft.

In the days before the advent of the helicopter to New Guinea, a call on the radio of a positive sighting would see a well-equipped ground party on the way to the scene within a few hours, the party usually under the control of a young Patrol Officer of the Department of Territories. In mountainous or rain-forest areas, their journey could take anything from a day to a week. After locating the wreckage, many hours could be spent by the search aircraft in guiding and supplying the ground party from the air.

When engaged in search activities I often wondered whether the pilot concerned, having survived the crash, would 'walk away' in much the same way as I had been able to in Fiji, where stumble would be a better word. Sadly, that seldom happened in my sphere of operations, the ground party nearly always reporting that on their arrival at the site the pilot was found dead in or near the wreckage.

Why I had been spared to fly again I was never sure of, but nevertheless the privilege awarded me was greatly appreciated. I acted tough, but fatal accidents involving pilots always had a deep effect on me. From the air, a newly crashed aircraft is a horrid sight, each one I saw, I prayed would be the last.

Over the years, the accident toll in the Territory mounted and men, some of them boys full of zest for the flying life, were cut off in their prime, some over-confident, some under-confident. Others were mature men, laymen or priests, with long seasons of flying in New Guinea behind them.

There are always exceptions to the rule. One 'walk away' I knew of was Stan Read, an American of Lutheran Mission, who 'walked away' from a Cessna 206 crash at 7000 feet on the summit of the Bena Gap near Goroka, much to the relief of his wife Betty and their young family. Ian Leslie of Talair was another who had a miraculous escape at the Bena Gap when the Cessna 402 of Talair he was testing slid into the rainforest (Ian's words) atop the Gap between 7-8000 feet ASL.

Waiting for news after a 'plane goes missing and a search starts, is an anxious time for those relatives, friends or co-workers of the pilot and others involved. At those times the various missions' personnel were the ones who really showed the true spirit of their faith by their cool and calm demeanour at such emotional, uncertain and critical times. Naturally there were always a few tears about, but never did I see any panic or hear any recriminations, while everything in the way of practical and spiritual aid was offered to relatives, friends and searchers alike.

June 28, 1965. Very early one lousy, cloudy morning, in a Beech Baron laden to the gunnels with freshly killed beef, I was in a circling climb on the Ramu side of the Bena Gap looking for a 'hole' in the cloud, big enough to dart through into the Goroka valley. There was a lot of cloud about on the mountains although the Ramu valley was completely clear. One morning every week we'd fly into Dumpu cattle station which was owned and pioneered by Bruce and Barbara Jephcott. The awaiting 1200lbs load of beef, now wrapped in cheesecloth, had been slaughtered the night before. The cool of the morning, the climb to 10,000 feet and the highlands destination, served for refrigeration. Loading the Baron occupied about half an hour when I soared off the ex wartime strip and climbing hard, turned for the Bena Gap.

There were few aircraft about at that hour of the morning, all was quiet on the radio waves until Madang Radio called to advise me that a Cessna 206 was unreported on arrival at Kegl Sugl, a Catholic mission station at 8000 feet on the eastern slopes of Mount Wilhelm (14,783 ft). That mountain, the tallest in the Territory of New Guinea, was about 50 kilometres from where I was making my circling climb. Madang requested that I overfly the mission station at Kegl Sugl and report whether or not the Cessna was on the airstrip. Early morning radio blackouts were common. 'Safe landing' reports from pilots were sometimes lost in the ether.

There was nothing unusual about the request, so I levelled the wings and scudded off up the Ramu Valley towards Mt Wilhelm and the Bundi Gap. Heavily laden as the Baron was, coupled with the rising storm clouds, it took some time to climb over 15,000 feet and fly across the Bismarck range, to where for only a few seconds, it was possible to sight the mission station through the clouds and report that there was no sign of the Cessna on the strip.

The pilot, Father Joe Walachy, an American priest of Divine Word Mission, had been flying from Madang since the end of World War 2. He was well known to me. Father Joe had probably made more trips into that area from Madang than any man living. Had he not been able to get through the weather, which was quite bad, he would have returned to Madang or diverted to another landing place, there to await a clearing of the weather before attempting another try for Kegl Sugl. By the state of the weather on the mountains, I could see that he would have returned to Madang if that had been the case.

Through an exchange of radio calls it was learned that the last progress report received from him stated that he was climbing above 10,000 feet outside the Bundi Gap and expected to arrive at Kegl Sugl ten minutes later. More than thirty minutes had elapsed since that report. A full-scale search was called up for the icon of a flying priest and his brand new Cessna 206, for it was now obvious that Father Joe was in serious trouble.

The weather on the Wahgi Valley side of the Bismarcks was clear. The task allotted me by the Searchmaster that I knew would be fruitless and a sheer waste of time, was to comb the heights of the rugged shoulders of Mount Wilhelm above 12,000 feet. In clear weather I droned up and down the granite walls of the mountain for as long as my fuel reserves allowed, before a return to Goroka was necessary for me to unload the meat and refuel to maximum capacity.

Returning to the area after unloading and recruiting three observers it was to find that a number of other aircraft had by then joined the search, including DC-3's of the regular airlines. It seemed to me that the DC-3 was not the best choice of equipment for the darting or diving that might be required through cloud breaks over high mountains covered in tropical rainforest and with other aircraft doing likewise. There were moments when I feared that the searchers might very well end up being the searched for.

The high country above 9000 feet from Mt Wilhelm south to Mt Otto was allotted to me with the Baron. Grey, black, rain-sodden clouds rose to 25,000 feet and more, right along the range, again my time was being wasted. The aircraft assigned the lower altitudes weren't making any progress either, mainly circling in the Ramu valley, miles away from the ranges where Father Joe's 206 was thought to be. Occasionally one would attempt to probe in closer, only to be turned back by the wall of 'stuffed' cloud, the radio waves clogged by a cacophony of useless pilot 'cackle' about the location of one aircraft to another most of the time. No real searching was done. We all kept going, but most of that day was a waste of time for all the aircraft concerned, a rather useless effort that ended with little or no improvement in weather conditions.

The next day started out to be the same with my being first on the scene having left Goroka at the crack of dawn, or, I must admit slightly before. At dawn the north side of the Bismarcks were seen to be pushing up huge rain clouds. That lasted for a good part of the morning, completely obscuring the most likely target areas. The afternoon saw the clouds lifting, but not enough to allow anyone a good view of the wooded ridges in the Bundi Gap area close to Kegl Sugl where it was thought Father Joe's aircraft might be found.

By that time the Baron was beginning to show it's true worth as a search 'plane. She was fast, light and easy to handle, the power developed by the two engines allowed for tight turns and quick climbs. From the cockpit the low wing presented no real problem with visibility. With a trickle of flap out the Baron handled nicely at slower speeds too.

The short tropical twilight was creeping across the hills as I left the search area that evening, in a fast dive through gaps in the cloud cover to the north of Goroka valley. Without a doubt the following morning would see a marked improvement in the weather. All other aircraft involved returned to Madang on the coast. With the oncoming of darkness and as if by magic the mountains were beginning to throw off their blankets of soggy cloud that had shrouded them for days.

That night, I was briefed by 'phone at the Goroka Control Tower by the Searchmaster from his headquarters at Port Moresby. My request for a lower altitude search pattern the following day was granted. There were now about ten to fifteen aircraft taking part in the search, should the weather be good, the search area was going to be even more crowded.

First light again saw the Baron with three observers aboard, scudding across the Bundi Gap that was partly under early morning mountain range shadow although the sky and the ranges were both cloudless. Over the Bundi Gap I began to take the Baron into a gradual descent from 9000 feet, down and along the range towards Mount Otto with the forested ridges of the range just off the right wingtip and the observers gaping out of the windows on the starboard side. My guess was that Father Joe's Cessna would be on the northern side of the range, as the southern side in that area was mostly densely populated and only wooded in patches. Had he come to grief on that side, in two days he would already have been found.

Closing rapidly on the shoulders of Otto at the finish of the run, the Baron was swung to the left away from the ranges on a turn that would retrace the flight path up towards Mt. Wilhelm again. That put the ranges on the pilot's side allowing me to tuck in even closer to the face of the many sheer cliffs that were full-flood waterfalls from the previous days' heavy rains, a photographer's delight.

On the third run down the range at varying altitudes and just skimming over the trees, up from the rain soaked forest came a sharp glint of light that could only come from something metallic as a small hand-held mirror might be used in signalling. The sudden flash of light came from a cliff face quite close to and below the Asaloka Gap, twenty kilometres or more from Kegl Sugl. Adrenalin pumped through my veins plus a surge of relief, the Baron was part of me as I laid her over into a tight left turn, holding her there until we had gone around 270 degrees or so to point directly at the sharp V of the narrow gap between the mountains that formed the Asaloka Gap. The sun-flash from metal that had first been seen would be just to the right of the V and slightly below.

With the cliffs coming in rapidly, both throttle levers were pushed full forward. A light back pressure on the column was enough to aim the nose of the Baron at the small slit in the mountains. Committed now as to the direction of flight, there was no room on either side to turn away from the narrow gap while seeking to re-sight the spot where some part of a 'metal bird' hung suspended precariously on a bush above a 'reddy-brown' landslide. For only a split second a fragment of shiny metal could be seen impinged on the reddish colour of the almost vertical landslip, which by the looks was freshly made. Then it was gone as the ridges on each side closed in forcing the Baron to fly straight through. In only a few seconds we burst out into the north of the Goroka valley, my comfort zone.

To give the observers a chance to confirm the find, another snappy, steeply banked turn was made to return through the 'gap' again, low and not too fast, while from the left windows they craned their necks at the spot indicated as we zipped across that time. I was sure that what had been seen was a part of Father Joe's Cessna, confirmation was needed from at least one of the observers.

The sun's rays were then shut out by Mt. Otto, no more was there the glinting of metal to home in on. Several more passes were made from either side of the Gap that increased my familiarity with the terrain while getting me closer to the almost vertical face each time. Every pass necessitated a very low flight through the 'gap', the wing-tips almost brushing the forest to get a closer look down at the vertical face that had first been seen and to give everyone a chance to sight the wreckage. By that time one fellow was looking rather seedy from the positive or negative 'g' from the sharp turning, descending and climbing, but sticking bravely to his job. He indicated to me that he'd spotted the wreckage, which was estimated to be lying at about 7,000 feet elevation.

Now with the aircrew more familiar with the location of the wreckage, on each successive run other parts of the Cessna could be seen embedded in the cliff-face. The sight was sickening, a wreck that left little hope of anyone surviving the terrible impact. There could be no doubt that Father Joe's life on earth had ended about the time I left Dumpu in the Ramu Valley with the load of beef a couple of days before. A shudder ran through me as I realised that grim fact.

Only then was our find reported to the Searchmaster at Madang, who requested we fly there to give him full details on the location of the wreckage. The observers clapped when they were told that we would be going to Madang for a spot of breakfast without 'greasies'. All three looked to be very relieved to end the continual tight turning banking and zooming when we were flying level only for seconds at a time.

During the day the wreckage was inspected by many of the officials engaged in some way in the search. All were amazed at how difficult it was from the air to see what had once been the Cessna. Without the sun glinting onto that detached aileron, or whatever it was that was first seen, Father Joe might never have been found.

Days passed before the ground party led by Patrol Officer Richard Giddings reached the scene after struggling through, up and over the Asaloka Gap and reported from the crash site on what remained of the mission Cessna. Only a few aircraft and human body parts were recovered, the Cessna had collided with the cliff face at very high speed. The climb down to the wreckage on the north side of the range had been extremely difficult and also very dangerous for the rescue party. From the air, the almost vertical route to the wreckage certainly looked to be impassable except perhaps for a trained mountaineer cum bushman. Richard and his party of New Guinea highlands men made it there in three days to come up with a report that the two known occupants of the Cessna were considered dead. By the quite small fragments found at the site it was obvious that the impact had caused a landslide, which had taken most of the wreckage further down the almost vertical cliff-face and was irretrievable.

Viewing the ground party from the air after their most dangerous climb and descent to the wreckage turned my thoughts again to the Drover and the 'technical expert' who failed to make the distance through fatigue but who nevertheless filed a report on that machine's state of serviceability?

The search party found few remains of Father Joe or his passenger, a fellow priest. Father Joe was very well known, loved and respected for his ministry as priest, mission pilot and mechanic. For years he had lived a Spartan's life in an open-air hangar beside the runway at Madang supplying the many Catholic mission stations in the interior. Over many years, almost all his flights would have included a crossing of the mighty Bismarck Mountains in a well-known, well-maintained Cessna 180. A hush seemed to fall over the harbour-town as the news spread of his tragic demise.

The weather had not 'caused' the accident as some would say but had certainly contributed to it. That was the case also in other air tragedies where I was involved.

For years Father Joe had amassed hundreds of hours between Madang and the highlands in the mission's Cessna SVD (Sierra Victor Delta), a smaller, tail-wheel product than the 'tricycle' he was flying at the time of the accident.

The 206 in which he crashed was relatively new to him, larger, heavier and fitted with a tricycle undercarriage. There were other differences between the two types, the most important in my opinion being the arrangement of the fuel tanks selector lever in the floor between the two pilot seats.

With the 'one eighty's' tank selector centred forward, both tanks were ON. In the 206 the fuel was OFF when the fuel tank selector was centred forward. Changing from one tank to the other on the 206 meant that the selector must go through OFF. It could be that Father Joe had always flown his 'one-eighty' with both tanks selected, which was a fairly common practice for pilots of that type. During the climb near the Bundi gap with his mind fully occupied while searching for a way through storm clouds and rain, if he had any reason to change tanks the fuel might have mistakenly been shut off during the switch-over. Old habits die hard. Could it be that Father Joe was taken by surprise when the engine cut while he was fully taken up in trying to avoid clouds over the high terrain, which led to him losing control of the aircraft? Could it be that he flew into the highlands on one tank and came home on the other? This is all conjecture of course for the parts that would support this theory were never found.

With the search over, for me it was a return to the daily grind of flying through the mountains with a lot of catch up charters to do which left me wondering when the next air catastrophe would see me flying searches again. New Guinea had a nasty habit of grouping crashes in cycles of three.

Father Joe and other mission pilots who had lost their lives in New Guinea up to that time, have been remembered with a memorial stone on the airport at Madang. On the peak is a bronze replica of Father Joe's much cared-for Cessna 180 in a banked attitude.

Every time I see the memorial I am reminded of Ray Jaensch, chief pilot of Lutheran Air Services, who like Father Joe, had been flying from Madang for years. Both men were near neighbours and friends in 'friendly competition' one could say, on mission air routes.

Ray's life was lost I believe, because of an amateurish, bureaucratic 'bungle'.

TRAGIC EVENTS AT TAUTA

My first task on the morning of that fateful day was to fly an Aero-dromes Inspector of the Department of Civil Aviation from Goroka to Nondugl, an airstrip in the Wahgi Valley and the collecting point for the Bird of Paradise and many other New Guinea wildlife specimens for Sydney's Taronga Park Zoo. Following heavy rains the airstrip could become soggy and too soft for the DC3's that periodically brought in supplies and building materials for the station and took away the wildlife specimens. An A class report on the strip was mandatory before the strip could be used by the heavier aircraft. The Inspector had requested a Cessna 185 be made available for the job, with me as pilot. The aircraft would wait for him to complete his inspection before returning to Goroka.

After landing at Nondugl and before I shut the Cessna down, quite unexpectedly Madang Radio came on the air and asked me to zip over to Tauta in the Finisterre mountains (the end of the earth) and report on the whereabouts of Dornier 27, Echo, X-ray, Alpha. My heart skipped a beat or two, for the call-sign was that of the Dornier that had replaced the one that had been wrecked in a forced landing near Mount Elimbari. Nothing had been heard of the aircraft since a 'taxiing for Madang' report from the pilot had been acknowledged. An 'uncertainty phase' was in process with Search and Rescue.

The 'Lutmis' Dornier or 'Red Machine', was well known to me of course, having logged several hundred hours in both the 'Green and Red Machines' during my time with the mission. Since my departure

Ray Jaensch had been the only pilot available to fly the Dornier. The purpose of his flight I learned later as the day went on was to assist the District Commissioner at Madang open a recently prepared airstrip at Tauta, at the head–waters of the Surinam River on the northern side of the Ramu Valley.

On his being advised of the change of plans and my immediate departure from Nondugl, the aerodromes inspector wasn't too pleased until he was assured that I would return for him later in the morning, emergency duties done.

Through my being uncertain as to the location of Tauta I flew fly over Dumpu cattle station, in order to locate the Surinam valley that ran down from the Finisterres to the Ramu valley. From there the narrow, jungle enclosed river was followed upstream until it petered out on a steep slope of forest covered mountain. The flight had taken forty minutes. .

As I looked down on the mostly bare earth of the new landing strip my first impressions of Tauta weren't good. The wheel marks of the Dornier stood out as railway lines on the man-made gash in the forest. As I circled, the notorious 'Shaggy Ridge', scene of a bitter battle between Australian and Japan forces during WW2 could be seen standing up prominently a few miles to the west. There were no other signs of the Dornier, although by the marks on the muddy surface it was plain to see where the aircraft had landed, parked and where the wheels had left the ground on take-off, as per usual for the Dornier, only a very short distance from the start of its run.

The newly completed strip was still without grass and had a steep slope down to the tree-lined river valley. Without wasting any time I swung the 185 into a tight circuit for an uphill landing. Dozens of the local bush people mobbed the 'plane as the Cessna spun around, at the top of the incline to park at right angles to the slope. They were all very excited, there was no way of telling whether men, meris and 'pikininis' were either scared out of their wits or enjoying the 'big fella wind' created by the propeller.

The newly completed strip although heavy and soggy was judged to be useable. The Dornier should not have experienced any problems with the surface. There was no way a heavy roller could be brought in to such an isolated area and dragged up and down such a steep slope manually. More packing of the surface under those circumstances would no doubt be done in days to come by the tribesmen's bare feet during a special 'sing-sing dance time'. That was the story behind many a strip in New Guinea. In all ways without the use of any heavy equipment, another remarkable job had been done at Tauta.

Fearing that the propeller could easily kill or decapitate any of the half-naked bush people, I switched the engine off and held my breath until the prop came to a stop. The Cessna was only the second aircraft those people had seen at close range and quite different to their first. Completely unaware of the danger, they were taking scary 'death wishes' with the spinning metal blades.

As I slithered from my seat and on to the ground the whole tribe was yelling and pointing down the strip into the valley below. I soon learned that not long after the Dornier had lifted off the strip, the engine faltered. The 'plane descended suddenly, never to rise again. At times smoke had been seen coming from the river. All of the talk came from all of the people, all of the time, in excited, rapid-fire pidgin or 'talk place' with the volume at maximum, accompanied by much sign language with their hands, chin or eyebrows.

At first glance the ground features down the valley looked formidable, with thick rainforest all the way down to a winding, very narrow, boulder-strewn mountain stream that could be rated as a waterfall about to happen. There was nothing else to do but climb in, start up and take-off for a look down the narrow valley. The villagers seemed uncertain as to which way to move as they scampered away from the spinning blades in all directions as the Cessna began to swing around to face down the strip.

Without any climbing to do after take off I coasted off the strip in descent mode below the treetops lining the valley. In less than half a minute, a curl of smoke was seen coming from the wreckage of the Dornier, which was lying amongst huge boulders in the stream. Somehow the 'red machine' had been missed on my flight up that same narrow valley, when my eyes were fixed on sighting the new airstrip before a sharp turn away from a sheer wall of forested mountain would be needed. Flying downstream now, allowed me to push the nose down and zoom over the wreckage at tree height. Four persons were seen on the rocks in the river with two of them waving frantically.

Once over and past, the Cessna was climbed at a fast rate until with height enough to make a turn without clouting the bush each side of the stream and return to the wreck with altitude enough for an orbit.

Doctor Laurence Malcolm, District Medical Officer Madang, was easily recognised for he was well known to me. He seemed to be unhurt as he attended to another person stretched out on a rock, 20 meters or so downstream of what was now a tangled mass of burnt out metal.

The survivors were given a low buzz and a wing waggle as I radioed Madang with the details before setting off for Goroka, adding that a 'storepedo' (a cylindrical container in the shape of a torpedo) often used in those sorts of emergencies, be made ready to load on to the Cessna on arrival.

After landing at Goroka thirty minutes later, the right-hand side passenger door was removed, together with the rear bench seat. With re-fuelling over the 'storepedo' was loaded into the cabin along with Max Parker a fellow pilot as handler, who well knew how to launch it out of the Cessna when we arrived over the crash scene.

Half an hour later we were 'playing bombers' over the wreck, coming in low and slow with some flap down for a downstream drop of the 'torp'. On my signal, Max bundled the 'storp' out on a static line, while I pushed the power on and climbed down the narrow valley again, gaining height until a reverse turn could be made. On flying over the wreck, the parachute could be seen draped over a boulder very close to the wreckage. For the first time that day I felt assured, knowing that Doctor Malcolm had some of the tools of his trade to work with.

On taking stock of the crash scene from on high, the straight line distance to Tauta was gauged to be a little over a kilometre. No doubt it would be a tortuous uphill climb for the survivors, over boulders and through thick bush, but not impossible by any means if assisted by the local men of the village. For all I knew there could be a track somewhere underneath the densely thick foliage. Slick as the mountain men were in the bush with their razor-sharp machetes, stretchers were easily made from saplings and vines if anyone needed to be carried and things were certainly heading that way. With all that in mind it was thought best for me to land back at Tauta and get a ground party organised to go down to the crash-site and assist the survivors.

After reporting my intentions to Madang I received what was to me the greatest shock of my life as a terse message, under the signature of the Director of Operations, Department of Civil Aviation, Port Moresby, was passed onto me. Tauta strip was not to be used again under any circumstances. Further, my landing there of the morning was considered to be a breach of Air Navigation Regulations for the strip had not been approved at the time. That would have to be dealt with by the filing of an Incident Report Form 225, on my return to Goroka! Yah-yah, frightening stuff!

For a while I gave some thought to the faking of a radio failure while I landed and got things organised with the villagers. But the Madang operator was persistent in an appeal for me to confirm receipt and acceptance of the instructions. My duties, he informed me in tones imperial, were to remain in the vicinity of the Dornier while reporting the situation each hour and half hour, when a 'chopper' would come to the rescue!

Even recounting the story distresses me. The Dornier was circled for hours that day, with me knowing quite well that things down in the river weren't good at all and time was running out for the injured. Each hour the story was the same. The 'chopper' was 'on the way', but a specific time of arrival could not be given. There were then two persons wrapped in blankets stretched out on the rocks with Doctor Malcolm and others faithfully in attendance.

A message telling the doctor of the expected arrival of the chopper, was written on a slip of paper, weighted with a bolt on a short length of rag then dropped from the cockpit's small push-out window. On the next low pass, from near the wreck site Dr Malcolm signalled receipt of the note with a 'thumbs up', that meant to me that all was understood and under control.

Fortunately, the weather further upriver towards those towering Finisterre mountains remained fine and looked to be stable enough. Such a narrow, steep gorge, would be prone to sudden flash flooding following a downpour in higher country upstream from which there would be no escape for the survivors.

Three hours slipped by without a sign of the 'chopper'. Every hour and half hour an 'ops-normal' report was sent to Madang, whatever 'normal' meant under those circumstances. The circle I flew, each time took me quite close to the Tauta airstrip. Villagers could be seen making their way down into the riverbed. The sight of them made me wonder what they might be thinking after all the hard work they'd put in over months and probably years getting the strip prepared for the grand occasion.

Chopping down huge trees, splitting and removing them, levelling, filling would all have to be done without machinery of any kind, the only tools being axes, saws, shovels and bare feet for packing the soil. The sight of them using their 'nouse' gave me more hope in the success of the rescue.

As requested, again I flew to Goroka to uplift a drum of avgas for the chopper when he arrived at Dumpu cattle station and to give a full report on the state of the Tauta airstrip. Once at Goroka I reported through the air control system that in my opinion the Tauta airstrip was quite suitable for operations under the weather conditions existing and that I was prepared to uplift the survivors from the airstrip and fly them to Madang. The answer was the same, 'Tauta is closed to all operations', the 'chopper', will uplift all survivors and transfer them to the DC3 at Dumpu.

After a hurried refuel, a drum of avgas was loaded into the Cessna and the door replaced. I returned to the wreck-site via the Bena Gap and Dumpu. For some reason the old enemy, an afternoon build up of rain cloud along the Bismarcks and the Bena Gap was nowhere in sight, the weather remained abnormally clear and stable with the mountain tops and the cattle station only a few miles from Tauta, all basking in bright sunshine. To me though, a very dark cloud of another kind was hovering near.

For hours I circled, frustrated and angry, while watching the two pitiful figures stretched out on the rocks, with the doctor and the others ministering to them. By that time extreme anxiety for the wellbeing of those seriously injured had taken me over, my stomach sick with frustration. There was still no sign of the 'chopper', nor could a precise estimate for its arrival be given.

A DC-3 of Ansett Mandated Airlines was heard giving out a landing report at Dumpu when 'time out' was taken for a briefing there. Tom Deegan, a New Guinea airline veteran was in command of the DC3 with Rob Hopkins as First Officer and a Medical Assistant to attend to the survivors. Now taking the major role in the rescue the DC-3 would remain at Dumpu to transport the survivors to Madang when the 'chopper' brought them in! Tom was interested in the location of the wreckage but could not be enticed into flying his DC3 to take a look, although he was assured that it was perfectly safe for his bigger charge over the site at 4000 feet with all surrounding heights clearly visible. Again I returned to take up my circling watch over the wreck in a more than angry state of mind.

At about the same time a pilot with a North American accent was heard on the radio. At long last the 'chopper' was somewhere near, at least in 'very high frequency' radio range. He reported that he was having weather problems leaving the highlands for the Ramu Valley and Dumpu. His estimate was given, or guessed more likely, as four o'clock. My heart sank even further. The Dornier had already been down for seven hours and there was still some time to go before the 'chopper' could be on the scene.

On the many low runs made down the Surinam valley I'd been looking for a suitable 'chopper' pad within reasonable distance of the Dornier without any real success. That information had been passed to Madang several times. There were no sandy beaches or clearings within 'coo-ee' of the wreck. Big trees spread their branches out over the huge boulders that ran bank to bank, leaving nothing that I could see, exposed and flat enough for the 'copter to put down on. I began to hate myself for not landing in defiance of the order and get the 'Tau-tuans' started on a ground rescue. Had that been done at the beginning the entire party might have reached Tauta by this time. The inland bush-men, 'the fuzzy wuzzy angels', became supermen when it came down to such Herculean tasks. From Tauta, the survivors could be flown directly to Madang in the Cessna, a flight of about twenty-five minutes in favourable weather.

Looking down on the scene in the river a sneaky feeling came over me that a tragedy of some kind was in the making. How would a man, in far-away Port Moresby, know whether the Tauta strip was safe or not and also without seeing for himself or questioning me. He had already been told that Tauta was suitable and safe for the Cessna. The accident with the Dornier was not related in any way to the state of the strip. Whether or not it would be possible to land the 'chopper in the narrow, boulder strewn mountain creek still had to be decided.

The 'chopper's' progress was followed anxiously on the radio as he entered the Ramu valley, thirty kilometres away. Finally the 'whirly bird' landed beside the drum of fuel that had been placed conveniently to allow for a speedy turnaround. The time was now four-thirty. It was mortifying for me to learn that the pilot had only been in New Guinea a week or two and hadn't been to that part of the country before. He had been on a sortie from a surveyor's camp to faraway Mount Karimui when notified of the crash, about an hour after I had been called in at Nondugl. He knew little or nothing of what was going on!

With no one to brief him on the best route to follow to Dumpu and poorly equipped with maps and after returning the surveyors to their camp, he chose a route that had at least doubled the distance. His 'whirly-bird' cruised at only 65-70 knots. It was easy to see that he was tired and nervous as I told him of the urgency of the situation in the Surinam valley.

There was no time for idle chatter. The Dornier's location was pointed out on the map that had been lent to him, my outstretched arm showed him the route to follow across the Ramu valley plains to the entrance of the Surinam. He didn't seem to be too sure of himself, for that I couldn't blame him being new to the country. In a way I felt a bit sorry for him, but his attitude also angered me, for it was getting late and he wasn't acting as if he was in any sort of a hurry. I watched from the Cessna as the time ticked on until finally he got the rotors turning.

The 'chopper' lifted up and with the characteristic 'rattle and pop' sounds 'of the type chattered off across the flat, open plains of the Ramu. The summits of the ever towering mountains of the Finisterres, purple in colour now with the sun going down, were hidden under huge, billowing, dirty-looking cloud build-ups. After the 'whirly' had gone I followed in the 185, passing the slower mover to take over the lead where the river poured out into the valley. There I climbed some, to allow for the orbiting over the crashed Dornier that would be mine, while the 'copter' flew lower, following the river.

Communications had been established between us on a VHF (very high frequency) emergency channel, although it was obvious to me that the chopper wouldn't be able to set down close to the wreckage. While watching from above, I traced his movement as he began a hunt for a landing place first upstream and then down-stream. My spirits were very low during that period of uncertainty, at the thought of him not being able to find a suitable place and the day wasted from a rescue point of view. The whole scene was a nightmare. I really couldn't believe what was happening.

Finally a pad was found that didn't look to me to be ideal. A flurry of leaves and other foliage flying from the tips of the rotor blades as they cut through some of the branches overhanging the river told me that he had made a dangerous decision with night coming on. My respect for helicopter pilots, which hadn't been high, grew rapidly, particularly for the one down below.

The 'chopper' was by then however, a long way downstream of the wreckage. The rotors free-wheeled to a stop, the engine was off, he was safe, but how a lift-off could be made in such a confined space was anyone's guess.

A long time passed before a number of local men were seen hopping from rock to rock towards the 'chopper', path-finding for a group carrying a blanket between them with what could be Ray wrapped inside. The stream was almost all in dark shadow as the sun took a dip behind the mountains.

Ten precious minutes elapsed before the Tauta villagers with the blanket and Dr Malcolm reached the parked chopper. The black wall of night would soon roll down over the valley and darkness alone would then prevent a safe take-off being made. Why the others were still at the wreck some two hundred meters upstream I couldn't understand.

Watching that 'chopper' rise from the dark valley was an experience never to be forgotten. The young pilot may not have known his way around New Guinea but he certainly knew his way around his helicopter. Tauta men with their machetes were seen hacking away at branches that would interfere with the rotor blades during the 'whirly bird's' lift-off. Then came a delay while a mob of local men milled about the 'bubble' of the 'chopper'. The pilot radioed that they were having serious trouble. Ray would have to be shifted from the pannier where he was lying to inside the bubble. Due to the very restricted area, only one person could be lifted and he would have to be seated inside the 'bubble' beside the pilot to compensate for the most critical balance of the 'whirly-bird'.

While the Cessna circled above, it's pilot fretting with frustration, time raced on without a sign of the 'chopper' starting up. Six o'clock came before the rotors began to rotate, thick foliage under the trees on the river banks began to flatten and fly as the blades speeded up for the lift-off.

From above, the whole manoeuvre looked to be very dangerous, the gap between the trees was so narrow. I hated to watch, but couldn't take my eyes away for a second. Then the canopy of the riverside jungle began to quiver in the downwash as the 'copter came up in a vertical lift-off, a manoeuvre fraught with danger even in the open.

I held my breath until some forward movement of the bubble with its skeletal rear frame could be seen. Judging by the foliage being whipped about, he was still below the level of the branches. That reminded me of a horrible dream I once had, flying an aircraft down a busy street, trapped under tram or power lines unable to rise, with a busy intersection coming up, before I woke with a start and very happy to be in familiar surroundings.

Slowly the frantic waving of the foliage died down with the 'copter then moving steadily down the darkening valley. I breathed a sigh of relief while skimming down the river to speed out on to the plains and Dumpu to be on hand when the chopper arrived.

Tom and Rob of the DC3, after spending a boring afternoon were eager to go but not so eager to get some engine starting out of the way before the chopper arrived. The sun had gone down, the short twilight had set in, a race was then on to beat the failing light. They were encouraged to save precious minutes by starting the engines, ready for a quick departure when the 'copter arrived. Being airline men that suggestion from a general aviation man wasn't received with any great enthusiasm, nor was there any sign of the engines being started up.

Minutes later the chopper put down beside the DC-3, I could see Ray in the transparent 'bubble' beside the pilot, head and shoulders slumped as if he was supported only by the seat harness, his colour an ashen grey, he was unconscious. As I lifted him out to carry him to the DC-3, I could see that both his legs were broken. He was very cold and life-less, it seemed to me that there was only a rasp of breath at times to show that he was still alive.

The Medical Assistant and I laid him on a stretcher on the sloping floor of the DC-3 while a couple of retaining straps anchored to the floor were passed over his body. Too many minutes later, Tom took the 'three' away along Dumpu's dusty, grass strip and turned low for Madang, disappearing quickly into the gloom of approaching night. I knew that I'd never see my good friend again.

When they'd gone, I turned to the 'chopper's' pilot who was sitting on the pannier on the guide rails of his machine, his head bowed low to his knees. A fierce anger swept over me like a tide, as cruel, harsh words formed on my tongue, words that were meant to hurt. I yelled about how his lateness might be the cause of Ray's death, about how I'd spent most of the day circling in a tight valley uselessly, waiting for him to arrive, about how were the other four survivors going to be uplifted out of the river now that darkness had overtaken their rescue?

My outburst I'm sure was the result of the many stresses and strains of the day, frustrations too, the words should never have been uttered. I was merely letting off steam. After it was over I deeply regretted what had been said and quickly apologised for I could see that he was hurt badly.

A peace was called for, there was nothing more we could do that night. We both stayed at Dumpu homestead with Bruce and Barbara Jephcott, who had taken a great deal of interest in the day's events, all the occupants of the Dornier were well known to them.

Over an excellent dinner we pilots got to know each other better, when the Canadian recounted his day's many trials. With the 'chopper', he was in a precarious situation on the summit of Mount Karimui (8428 ft) over in 'old Papua', waiting for some surveyors to complete their work, when he received the 'rescue' call. Those men had to be shuttled back to their camp before he could set out for Dumpu. A necessary task that occupied more than a couple of valuable hours. Didn't the 'Chief of Operations' know, understand or realize, that those men must not be left on the top of Mount Karimui for the night I wondered? The rest I knew.

Again I apologised profusely. He finished by saying that he would not re-enter the Surinam valley again, ever, under any circumstances. The landing and take-off there had been a really close shave for him, he would not take the same risk again come hell or high water. Before sleep came and without telling him of my plans, my mind was made up.

In darkness next morning, Bruce drove me over to the airstrip. Preflight checks, fuel dips and drains on the 185 were completed rancher style under the flickering light of a hurricane lamp. Madang Radio didn't come on watch until six am. Without making a radio call, I taxied out in radio listening mode only. In the warm air, the flat six Continental engine of the Cessna was already warm enough to accept full throttle and didn't have too long to wait. Throttle wide open I tore off for the Surinam and Tauta like a Spitfire pilot in the Battle of Britain. To the southeast, over the broad plains of the Ramu, the sky was just beginning to light up for a new day.

As the sun's rays first hit the upper slopes of the Finisterres, in intense radio silence except for occasional static, I brought the Cessna in for a 'three-pointer' on Tauta's 'notorious' airstrip. There'd been no rain overnight, that was a miracle in itself, the surface was firmer than on the day previous.

There weren't any villagers about, most were solid sleepers in their windowless, darkened huts. It would take more than an aircraft arriving to wake them at that hour of the morning. As I switched off, much to my surprise Dr. Laurence Malcolm, Vin Smith, District Officer at Madang and Patrol Officer Tony Cooke, three of the Dornier's passengers, appeared from a nearby bush house. Their faces all showed signs of the stress suffered, during and after the crash. All were scratched, mud-spattered and grubby, but not seriously hurt. As openers they all praised Ray for the landing he'd made on the huge boulders in the river.

District Commissioner Kaad was nowhere to be seen, he'd been seated beside Ray in the cockpit and was lying in the hut seriously hurt. On hearing this I'm sure that my shins began to sting, having previously been scraped to the bone in the Dornier's forced-landing near Chuave. All were very pleased to see me as could be imagined.

Guided and assisted by village men, they had reached Tauta in the early hours, after trekking up from the crash site in darkness, commencing shortly after the 'chopper' had departed with Ray. They had watched the 'chopper' take off and decided that was not going to be for them, even if the pilot did come back, better the overnight trek through the bush to Tauta!

DC Kaad, who was suffering a spinal injury was carried over to the aircraft on a bush stretcher. Dr Malcolm considered the District Commissioner's injuries to be very serious which told me that Ray with DC Kaad should have been evacuated by Cessna from the airstrip in the afternoon of the day before. The promise of a helicopter for their uplift and the ban on the airstrip was a wrong and costly decision on the part of the authorities.

DC Kaad was obviously in some intense pain. When told of the banning of the Tauta strip by a bureaucrat in Port Moresby, all three were ropeable. That didn't make me feel good for the look in their eyes told me that I should have gone in regardless of the consequences. Can you understand what I've written about Chief Pilot responsibilities, you're damned if you do and you're damned if you don't.

Laurence was beside himself with rage, DC Kaad too, about the contents of the 'storepedo', which contained only blankets, bandages and dressings. Sedatives, opiates, syringes or antiseptics were not included. Both men were spitting sparks about the omission and swore to lodge their complaints immediately on arrival at Madang!

On the way to the aircraft they were warned that they were about to join what would be an illegal flight and could turn it down if they wanted to as no one except Bruce and Barbara Jephcott knew that the Cessna was again in the rescue plan. As expected, they couldn't make for the 'plane quick enough.

For safety's sake on the untried airstrip, it was agreed that the load should be split for take-off. Fred Kaad would go first and needed to be stretched out with gentle handling. He was laid on some blankets on the floor with Dr. Malcolm squatting beside him. District Officer Vin and Patrol Officer Cooke were asked to remain behind for a second trip.

Lined up with the strip, checks done and ready to go, I wondered just how the two men with me would feel about their second attempt to fly away from Tauta, I could see that they were nervous at the prospect as they questioned me about whether the 185 would lift off the heavy turf with two passengers aboard. They weren't kept waiting for an answer as I powered up on the brakes until the locked wheels couldn't hold us any more and we began to slide. With the brakes released we began to roar off down the slippery slope.

Once airborne and with lots of room to spare not a lot of altitude was required. I raised the flaps throttled down and pointed the nose of the 185 down into the Surinam only to find the narrow valley hidden in fog. At that early hour the wreck of the Dornier could not be seen, it lay somewhere below a thick white blanket that ran down the river. After clawing for height down the valley we made a right turn to fly over the 'Shaggy Ridge' area to Bogadjim in Astrolabe Bay and on to Madang, in perfect morning weather, cloudless and still, the fearsome mountains etched against a deep blue sky.

Thirty miles out and in line of sight, I supplied and no doubt surprised Madang Tower with the details of my flight plan and passengers, all survivors of the Dornier had then been accounted for, the time was 6.30 am.

At the mission hangar, from where the Dornier had last departed, we were told that Ray's wife Betty had met the DC3 the night before only to learn that Ray had died aboard just minutes before landing. That was a sombre moment for everybody, particularly Laurence and I, for Ray was a close friend, a brother you might say to both of us.

After seeing DC Kaad into his hospital transport, Laurence, who was very upset at the news, irate would be a better word, said he would go to see Ray's family, before going on to the hospital to attend DC Kaad. He was heard to say that had he received some pain-killers with the air-drop, he might have been able to relieve Ray's suffering, if not prolong his life, not forgetting DC Kaad also during those long hours in the river with only a boulder for a mattress.

Although suffering serious internal injuries, broken legs and severe shock, much to Laurence's dismay Ray was made to be strapped in the sitting position for the short but dangerous flight in the helicopter to Dumpu. That posture alone would have been a contributing factor in his death under the circumstances.

There was work to be done, the 185 was urgently required at Goroka. After seeing the survivors off, I filed a plan for Tauta, that by then I was informed, was approved for any further landings at my discretion, I could manage my own affairs! That was great news, proving that if you don't stand for something, you fall for everything. Vin and Tony were back home in Madang before eight-thirty. Next it was a return to the highlands for me, the company urgently required the aircraft to uplift an irate Aerodromes Inspector from Nondugl, where this story began!

As I taxied into the parking bay at Nondugl, the Inspector's style of walk across the grass to the aircraft told me that I was in for a 'bollicking' over his enforced overnight stay. I started in with my explanation first, while he was climbing in and buckling up. By the time he was seated beside me and in his harness he had cooled down. Rather sulkily at first, he listened while I continued to explain my predicament. By the time we arrived at Goroka, he had heard my story, our previously good relationship had been restored.

On the short walk to the terminal he even admitted his night had been quite enjoyable in the care of the manager of the Bird of Paradise sanctuary, a quarantine collecting point for the Taronga Park Zoo. Those beautiful birds and their protection then meant much more to him, outclassing by far the metal bird in which he had just flown, he remarked with a scornful smile as he trudged off down the tarmac towards his office in the Tower.

Later that day I summed up the previous day's search/rescue flying as 7 hours 48 minutes that would be invoiced to Search and Rescue only at cost. Those times in my log-book are purely for historical purposes, seeing them always brings back bad memories and always that modern proverb as quoted before too, 'if you don't stand for something you fall for everything'.

A few days passed before all the facts could be co-related for completion of the Form 225 (Incident Report) that DCA required. Doctor Malcolm, DC Kaad and the others were to file their own independently through their separate departments.

Rumours had spread about the lack of common sense shown by the Department during the crisis. Ray and his family were long-time residents of Madang, well known, liked and loved by New Guineans and expatriates alike. Ray had been responsible for the establishment of many of the airstrips that were then in operational use in the district, having worked in close co-operation with the Administration for years. With the word 'negligence' looming on the horizon, for the Search and Rescue organization and the co-ordinators in Port Moresby, the problem wasn't going to go away.

The operations chief who had denied access to Tauta by a fixed wing, had been acting for the permanent chief of operations of the same name, who was on leave, his replacement had little knowledge of the country! At first that was hard for me to swallow. With his attachment to the Territory over he had returned to Western Australia I was told. With communications from the highlands being what they were, a chance to speak to him never arose and I was left with the same name switch sounding like a 'believe it or not Ripley story'. Many years passed before it was discovered that the 'Ripley' explanation, two operations chiefs of the same name, was in fact true.

The Form 225 that was completed contained some criticism of the disastrous event, the use of the helicopter, the pilot's lack of familiarity with New Guinea that caused long delays, the lack of sedatives, opiates, syringes and antiseptics in the 'storepedo' that had been picked up at Goroka. A family man's life had been lost, a senior Administration officer was on the way to being a paraplegic, some person must be made responsible for the mess-up.

From that time my previous good relationship with the appropriate DCA officers began to founder. Criticism of the Department in any way could not be tolerated. There were times when I felt that certain officers deliberately harassed me in any way they could. 'Nit-picking' is what that game is called. Their agenda seemed to be to make things hard for me as a Chief Pilot. But I had a lot to be thankful for, believing that my attitude to the whole affair would be my best friend and not my worst enemy. Through all that I was on my own while Dennis 'sat on the fence' without putting in a word on my behalf.

As time wore on many of those officers, but not all, were transferred within New Guinea or returned to Australia, gradually the heat wore off while accidents still happened and my services were often required. I can say with a certain amount of 'pride', that's a word I don't really like, that during my term as Chief Pilot and when hands on in office, not one company pilot was ever lost in a flying accident.

Ray, a close friend of mine had died after an aircraft accident, his first after war service in Europe with the RAAF, while with several near misses to my credit I still flew about the mountains of New Guinea each day. I must have been doing something right, so I 'stuck to my guns' as the saying goes, while under a lot of pressure as to pilot acceptance and training.

With pressure mounting as the country pushed on towards independence, we began to recruit pilots from New Zealand's aerial agriculture industry, Australasian or Royal Navy Aviation. Those pilots could handle aeroplanes and that's what was wanted, the kinky little up or down airstrips meant nothing to them. Many of those pilots went on to serve out their careers in New Guinea as jet endorsed airline pilots, to the best of my knowledge accident free. One of those, Malcolm Douglas had walked away from a forced landing in a TAL Cessna 185 in the jungle between Madang and the Ramu Valley after a fire in the engine bay, which proved the theory about the better chances of survival when an aircraft in distress crashes while still under control. Like me, some of the others might have met with accidents before coming to New Guinea, there were not too many who had been agriculture flying for a year or two without having had a major mishap. Knowing this didn't prevent them being hired although there are some differences in the two styles of flying, 'crop-dusting' or charter.

In 'ag' flying for instance, take off commences with a big overload but whatever the material it doesn't have to be carried far and can always be jettisoned quickly in an emergency. Landings are made with an empty hopper on a strip you soon become well acquainted with.

Charter flying in mountainous New Guinea is different. The take-off is made with a maximum load from an airfield at high elevation that must be carried for a considerable distance over high mountainous terrain, seas, plains or crocodile infested wetlands, without a chance to dump the load in any emergency, whether passengers or cargo. Most landings are made with a comparatively heavy aircraft on a marginal airstrip that might be badly sited and not known so well, often hated.

The heavy loads carried also restrict the aircraft's altitude performance. Avoiding 'stuffed clouds' means flights above 12,000 feet, where the light 'plane really struggles, or a circuitous route, more befitting the 'plane's performance might need to be followed.

Having flown in many parts of the world, I can say that for a charter pilot with minimal hours, New Guinea is one of the most difficult to conquer. There is something about that country, so different from any other.

Bryan with first Instructor Ken Young. Wellington NZ 1947

RNZAF Flight Training School, Christchurch NZ 1948

Taxiing RNZAF Catalina NZ4043 1951, Fiji

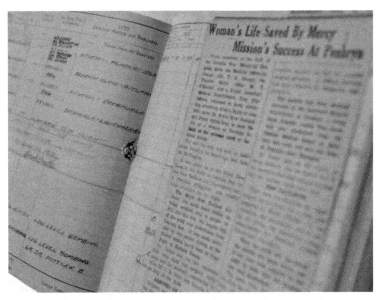

Log book entry for Pearls from Penhryn 1950

Fiji Airways de Havilland Drover and Rapide 1954

Bryan crop dusting with VH-PRT Avro Cadet, Victoria 1959

Avro Cadet spraying job Nth Victoria 1959

Spraying with Aerial Missions Cessna 180 Victoria 1959

Loading the Aerial Missions Tiger Moth, Victoria 1958

Lutmis Dornier DO27 VH- AMQ and Kuku Kuku tribesmen,
Wonenara PNG 1961

Tom Johnson and Ray Jaensch with Dornier DO27, Madang PNG
1961

Dornier DO27 VH-AMQ crash site near Monono, PNG 1962

Bryan with TAL's first Beech Baron VH-GKA in Goroka after ferrying from Bankstown, NSW 1963

On arrival with TAL's first Twin Otter after ferrying from California
USA to Goroka PNG May 1972

With Chief Minister Michael Somare (later Sir Michael Somare,
PNG's first Prime Minister) on a flight to New Britain 1972

TAL's first Twin Otter VH-GKR loading Kaukau runners to the
southern highlands for drought assistance

TAL's Beech Baron VH-GKA belly landing Goroka PNG July 21
1964

Over Canton Island, solo over the Pacific ferrying Macair's first
Beech Baron from Miami USA to Goroka PNG April 1967

Macair Beech Baron fleet, Goroka PNG 1968

Bryan with Macair's VH-MKC at Omkolai PNG 1968

Milne Bay Air Grumman Goose

Bryan wih Antilles G21 Grumman Goose, St Croix USVI 1979

Landing G111 Grumman Albatross PK-PAM at Matak, Indonesia

Z-CAT on the tarmac at Malawi. East Africa Tours 1992

Z-CAT at anchor on Lake Tanganyika, East Africa Tours 1992

Windscreen clean for Z-CAT before another flight 1992

Flying Z-CAT over France during the Atlantic Odyssey 1993

MACAIR AND THE BEECHCRAFT BARON

Of all the light twin-engine aircraft on the market in the nineteen sixties, the Beech Baron was favoured as being the best suited to New Guinea operations. During the period when Macair was in the process of formation my Board was persuaded to support the application for a charter licence from Goroka, Lae and Mount Hagen, utilising Beech Baron twin-engine aircraft only. That decision was a major leap for New Guinea highland operators at the time.

For years the two regular airline carriers had been 'hand fed', sharing the air routes in the country using an Australian air licensing system that was discriminatory when applied to the Territory. Lawfully protected policies and practices stifled competition from the general aviation field, regardless of the fact that charter operators were already severely restricted by aircraft type and the operating areas allotted them.

Charter companies were restricted to operations in quite small areas and used only single-engine aircraft. Approval for Macair's proposed operations was strongly contested by airline and general aviation companies alike and was a long time in being approved. After waiting six months for operating approval, calling for and being called to numerous meetings and discussions, it was decided to purchase a suitable machine direct from the USA for our initial inquiries confirmed that there would be considerable savings in doing so. The Macair Board, 'my Board', which consisted mainly of retired government officials, 'nouveau rich' coffee planters, trade-store owners and other businessmen including one pharmacist, somewhat reluctantly gave their approval for me to proceed to the USA, purchase a suitable aircraft at the best price then fly it over to New Guinea to commence operations.

Two weeks later I was aboard an Air New Zealand DC8 out of Sydney for California via Auckland and Honolulu. My association with the Beechcraft Baron had started when four years earlier as Chief Pilot of Territory Airlines I had flown the first Baron to the Territory. Since then that aircraft type had more than proved itself in all the skies over New Guinea. Territory Airlines now had several Barons in operation and were planning on stepping up to a larger twin engine type.

At Los Angeles I was met by Betty Miller and her husband Chuck, the owners of Santa Monica Flyer's at Santa Monica Airport, where Chuck was a Federal Aviation Agency designee and Betty the Senior Instructor. Shortly before my arrival Betty had been awarded the Harmon Trophy for a solo flight across the Pacific to Australia, becoming the first woman to do so. Her award had been received alongside that of Colonel John Glenn the first astronaut.

Betty and Chuck were wonderful, dedicated, friendly people, who up to that time were known by me only through an exchange of correspondence. They were not expected to meet me, my plans were to use those hotels convenient to the areas of my search. After our first meeting in the arrival hall at LA's International Airport they invited me to be their house guest while going 'shopping for an airplane'. Looking back I don't know how I could have managed without their help. Their offer gave me a wonderful start to my quest for Santa Monica Flyers was home to some well-known aviation personalities, Hollywood stars and other notables. Later and with a good laugh, they admitted that they hadn't quite known what to expect, after all a man from New Guinea arriving on a not so well known Air New Zealand flight could be wearing a bark G-string and a bone through the septum of his nose! They weren't quite sure how such a situation could be handled diplomatically.

After the long and tedious flight, the first thing for me was a good long sleep. That was readily forthcoming in their well-appointed Santa Monica home, which left me feeling somewhat self-conscious about our modest cottage in highlands New Guinea as much as that was loved by all the family. While Chuck and Betty went about their work at the nearby airport I slept away the day in comfort.

Los Angeles is also home to more than twenty busy airports, each with several aircraft sales organisations or their representatives in attendance. My thinking needed to be adjusted for it seemed to be that everyone in America must fly, buy or sell aeroplanes. The word is soon spread, anyone and everyone on the lookout for a purchase gets plenty of offers on all sorts of 'airplanes'. During the next few days visits were made to several of those places that ended in disappointment for the very popular type I was after had not yet reached the Californian second-hand market in competitive numbers. Of all the Barons presented none were available at the price expected.

On a call to my Betty in New Guinea I learnt that a letter from Bellomy-Lawson Aviation in Miami, Florida had arrived after my departure. "Charles Lawson sounds nice, she said. He feels sure that Bellomy-Lawson could meet our needs, call him as soon as possible". After conferring with Chuck and a check on the time difference a call went to Charles in Miami

Two or three days later National Airlines flew me on a fabulous trip across those wonderful States in beautifully clear weather. With the help of my trusty computer the prize for 'time over the Alamo' was won, with me leaving the flight at Miami with a bottle of 'champers' stashed in my flight bag. That night I met Charles at my hotel downtown. He too confided in me that he hadn't quite known what to expect of a man from New Guinea. His appearance and quiet manner of speaking was that of a gentleman, Chuck had warned me not to be too trusting of 'airplane' sales people in Florida. For the time being anyway, I felt myself to be in good hands.

The following day Charles took me to his ramp, hangar and offices at the Miami International Airport to show me a beautifully maintained Baron with three blade props and only 300 hours since new on the clock. With nary a scratch or a chip on the factory paint scheme that was white with a green stripe, it was as if the Baron had been built specially to suit Macair. Even on my first walk around the machine in the sales lot I knew she was the one for us.

"This is very nice, what price do you have on it." I asked, fully expecting to hear some prohibitive sum.

"Mr Hughes was asking where you were from and what your plans were for the airplane. I told his chief adviser that you were from New Guinea. He remembers Amelia's (Amelia Earhart) last flight from there and how well she was looked after. He says that you can have it for $58,000, if that's not too much. The Hughes Tool Company has run out of use for it, they need a bigger airplane. Incidentally this is the smallest 'plane we've ever handled, I usually deal with heavy piston or jet sales, like the Curtis C46 Douglas DC6 and BAC One Eleven you see over there. I don't have much of an idea on this one. The price would apply to you only." Charles replied.

It was thrilling to know that we were dealing with the great Howard Hughes, who was by now a recluse in Los Angeles. The slipstream of a falling feather would have knocked me over, little me 'hob nobbing' with the world's greats of aviation, who'd have thought?

Back in Charles' office the deal was agreed to, test flying of the machine would not be possible until he caught sight of the funds. With a certain amount of enthusiasm, for the offer was less than half of what was expected, I telexed the Board at Goroka with a full description of the Baron and a request for funds ASAP, (an acronym for 'as soon as possible' in case they didn't know). Charles had specifically requested that the funds be sent by any means other than 'Letter of Credit', information that was passed on to the Board in my telex.

The 'democracy' at Goroka wasn't in a hurry and gave all Board members, when each man was available, a say in how, when and where the payment would be sent that culminated in me waiting three weeks for the Letter of Credit to arrive. After waiting a week without any funds arriving Charles offered accommodation at his house at Miami Springs, a stone's throw from the airport. Bellomy-Lawson almost ran out of patience with us too as offers came in from others willing to pay more for the Baron.

On April 8, 1967 with the 'Letter of Credit' at last safe and sound in Bellomy-Lawson's care, an acceptance flight was called up by the brokers.

Miami International Airport handled about 3000 movements a day, mostly jet or piston engine heavy aircraft. The test flight was commenced with some misgivings on my part believing that Air Traffic Control might not be too happy about a 'puddle jumper interfering with their flow of heavy traffic, or some tough airline pilot giving me a taste of some US 'air rage'. In the right hand seat Charles, an experienced pilot himself, did some of the interpreting. However, nothing could have been easier. Except for the continual jabber on the tower frequencies being used and the interpretation thereof, in thirty-five minutes November Two Four One Whisky had successfully completed five take-offs and landings and had been returned to the hangar for a maintenance update, a feat that in those days would have made some Australasian air traffic control centre hide their face in shame. No complaints from other aircraft, no near misses, no bawling out from the controllers, no sense of being 'that irresponsible idiot in the 'lightie'.

Six mechanics charged in with the relevant equipment as my new toy went up on hydraulic jacks. Up and down went the gear, in and out went the flaps, off came the prop spinners, out came the old oil, in went the new. Two hours later, looking as bright as new, N241W was returned to the ramp, paperwork perfect. After re-fuelling all tanks to the brim Charles presented me with the keys, N241W was ready to set out on the long journey to her new home via the contiguous United States and the Pacific Ocean.

Feeling a little jumpy in a foreign environment with a completely different view of aviation, the first day saw me making the first leg to New Orleans, Mississippi, to land at Lakeside Airport, which at the time was a busy place too. It was early. After speaking to a pilot in the terminal about my desire for a quiet night in the country, for I was tired of 'get up and go' big cities, turnpike traffic and fast talking aircraft salesmen, Charles excluded, a decision was made to fly on to Texas for a night stop where the pilot reckoned there was a town with bat-wing doors, wooden sidewalks, horses and dusty streets. To my disappointment, I learned later that horses, carriages and gigs had been out of fashion there for more than fifty years, having been replaced by brightly coloured, engine driven utilities.

Following re-fuelling I departed Lakeside in clear weather on a trouble-free flight over plains and cultivation as far as the eye could see, reaching Junction, Texas at sundown. The airfield too lay in a vast plain of desert tussock and scrub, there was no-one around, all the buildings including the Flight Service Station with its telephone appeared to be closed. Before landing, I had spotted the small town a few miles down a long straight road from the airfield. If the bat-wing doors and dusty streets were to be seen it would mean hitch hiking or simply walking down that long straight road.

The night covers and control locks of the aircraft were almost all in place when a 'Dodge' station wagon marked Sheriff arrived on the scene followed by a cloud of dust. Immediately a six foot two inch replica of John Wayne, complete with gun-belt, revolver, white broad brimmed hat and high-heel boots, emerged from the driver's seat. After giving me a verbal as to my activities and hearing my story, he offered to drive me to a good motel and show me around his town. That night he was never far away from me. To the many townsfolk who seemed interested in the new arrival he always introduced me with:

"This here guy is a 'horstralian' whose flyin' a cute li'l baby all the way to Noo Guinea over the Percific, how 'bout that? "

The saloon cum restaurant was equipped with fly-screened batwing doors and air-conditioning. Garish neon signs blinked the various wares on offer from behind the bar. In a well-practiced act he gave me a demonstration of a quick draw of his revolver that was so lightning fast that I couldn't believe it was done without hidden springs or magnets of some kind or the use of a replica plastic six-shooter.

We had plenty of fun that evening, most of the town seemed interested in New Guinea. One fellow came forward to tell me that he had been with the US Navy at Milne Bay 'Noo Guinea' during WW2. The motel was at the rear of the saloon, I raced to my room and came back with a topographical map of the Milne Bay area and presented it to him, drawing a round of applause from the patrons. Following that I was able to shoot a line or two about life amongst cannibal tribesmen that also drew 'oohs' and 'aahs' from the assembly. On retiring for the night I felt the most relaxed since arriving in the USA, the long, anxious wait for the funds with all the uncertainties had particularly taken its toll. Sleep came as soon as my head touched the pillow.

Soon after dawn the following morning, the Sheriff drove me to the airport. The Flight Service agent was ready with fuel and open for business as usual. As the Sheriff and I shook hands I again thanked him for the courtesy rides.

"Could I offer you something, a few bucks maybe for some of your expenses without even a hint of bribery or corruption? " I asked.

He laughed and smiled. "Sorry no, just doin' m' dooty seein' you outa town."

Morning fog clung low to the desert as N241W streaked off Junction's sealed runway and turned to the west for Buckeye in Arizona.

Four hours later, over the Buckeye VOR (visual omni range) I was shaken to the core after being hit by one of the biggest shocks of my life. The Jeppesen Radio Navigation Chart had been misread. There was no airfield in sight or reference to any on the flight charts! Fuel remaining was down to twenty minutes. The immense countryside around me had suddenly turned menacing, hostile almost, I had fallen into a trap for young players, the Buckeye VOR was a continental en route aid only, a waypoint and not an aerodrome approach aid. Visions of a forced landing and a broken aircraft floated before me as the Board in Goroka called an emergency meeting plus the reports required by the FAA (Federal Aviation Agency), the shame of it all. Almost in a panic I called the nearest Flight Service Station and asked for a bearing on any airport within a radius of twenty-five miles, fully expecting to be told what a silly ass I was.

As I circled the VOR aerial tower, impatiently I'm ashamed to say, I was given a few helpful suggestions, all without even a hint of sarcasm in the tones. The Flight Service operator suggested I try to contact a Piper Cub that was on a training flight 'somewhere in the area' to request the use of his landing pad, or if I headed my Baron on 'zero two zero' for twenty miles I would see an airfield where ex WW2 aircraft were parked in their hundreds alongside the runway, awaiting disposal. It was not known whether or not that airfield carried any fuel stocks but it was worth a try.

As the Cub couldn't be contacted or seen, the aircraft wrecking yard was chosen, N241W was swung smartly on to 'zero two zero' with my fuel reserves now something under twenty minutes.

With the runway in sight and no time available for a survey I approached from a low, tight left base to land on a long sealed runway pot-holed in patches and between row upon row of junked, engineless airplanes. Some were standing on bare wheels, some leaning on a wingtip, nose or tail. All looked to be well pillaged. The Baron was slipped into a vacant site between a scrapped Mitchell (B25) and what appeared to be the remains of a Flying Fortress (B17). After switching off I sat motionless to settle my heart-beat a little before climbing out into the hot sun for a leg stretch. Only a few minutes passed before the 'caretaker' arrived in an antiquated, door-less truck that was itself due for disposal. A rifle could be seen in the crook of an arm as he leaned out and bellowed.

"Whatcha' up to man, this is private prupperty? "

When he learned that I was off to the other side of the world in the neatest 'plane he'd seen in years, my accent plus my frightened look must have allayed his fears. The shiny as-new Baron must have ended up parked in 'slum alley' for he offered to drive me around the lot to see some of the better preserved ex war machines two and three rows away from the runway, but as much as I would have liked to accept his invitation, there was no time for that.

With us both standing on the roof of the cab of his truck, he pointed to a faraway clump of trees that he claimed hid a crop duster's field and suggested I should go there for fuel as he didn't have any that was less than fifteen years old! His truck had run for years on the dregs extracted from the wrecks. A quick gauging of the distance by eye and appraisal of the fuel gauges told me I could make it if run-ups and taxying were dispensed with. We both pushed N241W on to the runway to face the right direction. Both engines started like magic, in only a few minutes I was skimming over the wires at the crop-duster's strip readying to set down on his short, dirt runway.

The 'croppie' was away on a job, his wife being short of cash, readily sold me a load of fuel which would allow me to reach Santa Monica LA and my friends Chuck and Betty. At this point I'm amazed at the friendliness of people in country US, including the caretaker of the wrecked 'planes with his rifle. The feeling was that of living in a dream world, completely at ease with US aviation 'off the beaten tracks' of the major air routes.

Crossing the Sierra Nevadas in perfect weather and over the immense sprawl of Los Angeles, N241W was on final as number 8, journeying in to Santa Monica's active runway via Fox Film Studios behind a Ford Tri-Motor, with instructions to clear at the first taxiway on the left. Understanding the continual jabber coming from the tower and sorting out the instructions meant for me was by now a little easier. I'm almost, but not quite, a local, only my accent gives me away. Gone are the crypt, formal, radio procedures used back home, here the radio is used like a telephone, at last I've caught on and have begun to sound my Rrr's and sharpen up my A's from 'ois'.

It's five o'clock in the afternoon. At Santa Monica Flyers Chuck is waiting with the 250-gallon ferry tank and Douglas tie-downs, ready to install the tank in the cabin. I've hardly said 'hello' before the customised red leather seats start to come out. By seven o'clock the tank is securely in position, the seats stacked neatly out of sight in the nose locker and cabin. Chuck works long hours like most Americans. It's been a long two days since leaving Miami with plenty of fond memories to dwell on. An inspection by the FAA of the ferry fuel system has been arranged for the following day. Hopefully all will be approved after a two-hour flight test of the installation. The thought of the long flight I'd made to the US in a comfortable high speed jet airliner now gives me butterflies in the stomach when comparing that to the Baron's quarter of the speed.

On the way home in Chuck's auto, he tells me that he's very impressed with N241W and that I've done a good job, the Baron is easily the best of the type that he has seen, the price unbelievable. I'm able to sit back while we roll along the wide palm-fringed avenues, to watch the orderly traffic slip past at moderate speed and with few lane changes and the neat street signs with their highly flavoured Spanish names.

For homework after supper Chuck has prepared a route briefing. Together with Betty we'll go over that, there'll be lots for me to learn from their personal experiences for both the Millers have made several trips out to Honolulu and beyond, some in smaller 'planes than the Baron.

In some ways I'm content, but even as I sleep I'm aware of the ocean of all oceans waiting tirelessly in its vastness, forever rolling and waiting. Let's hope the Board is more than pleased when they receive the telex telling them that at last I'm ready for the big jump and home with their aircraft.

Following Chuck's advice at the briefing and after the FAA inspection was finished the Baron was ferried to San Francisco from where the flying distance to Honolulu was 120 miles less than from LA. Saying farewell to those people who had been so generous, kind and helpful was difficult for me. After paying for the tank installation, in the days before hugs, I said it all in a handshake and a promise to keep them informed of progress and to meet again before too long.

The two-hour flight along the Barbary Coast alone in the sturdy Baron that was beginning to be a part of me was very relaxing. Time was of no importance that day as I took in some really astounding scenery, rugged, vertical cliffs and coastlines, pink roofed villas perched precariously around white, foamy, surf-filled bays and inlets, coastal highways winding through forests of tall 'Christmas-tree like' conifers. Inland the sun glinted on the snow-capped Sierra Nevadas. To me the whole scene unfolding before my eyes was unreal, magical.

For the first time since being in the USA I felt the harmony that can exist between man and machine when flying in familiar places. The steady rhythm of the harmonised engines of the recently acquired metal speed-bird that would soon be setting out to where lay the mightiest of seas, empty, enormous and sullen was music to the ears. The hill city of San Francisco then came into view, the Golden Gate Bridge, Alcatraz, Oakland Bridge, as N241W zoomed over the harbour on the way in to land at San Francisco's International Airport amongst a gaggle of other aircraft large and small that darted in every direction in obedience to the rapid-fire instructions of the air-traffic controllers.

Although the dense radio traffic sounds heard around large US city airports was becoming increasingly familiar, I flew with my ears pricked. Somehow a call meant for me was missed which left me being told politely that I must speed up, close on the 'plane I was following, or leave the long line of landing aircraft pronto. The standard phraseology used at home would not work at those busy US airports, where there is no time for anything other than plain, hard talk on air control matters.

At Butler Aviation all tanks including the ferry tank were filled. Part of the tank was shaped to occupy the space beside me normally taken up by the passenger seat. Because of the small space between the ceiling and the filler cap, a special nozzle was needed that was not on the truck. The ferry tank had only been partly filled for the test run at Santa Monica. With the tank completely filled N241W would be more than 450 kilos (1000 lbs) over the maximum allowable weight, a situation that was approved by the FAA for ferrying long distances over water. With typical American know-how in the land of everything mechanical, a smaller than usual type of nozzle for the hose was soon found, fuel began to flow. My metal bird now squatted much lower on the landing gear than before with her tail very close to the tarmac, her nose strut fully extended with the nose-wheel just brushing the surface.

With all the wing tanks topped to capacity, oil levels in each engine checked she was locked for the night. After paying ramp and fuel charges, I was about to take a taxi to the nearby airport motel that Chuck had recommended, when it was remembered that the high-frequency radio (HF) that had been installed in Miami, had never been tested. I clambered into the cockpit past the ferry tank again and on batteries alone gave a number of calls to Airinc the provider, on several different frequencies. A faulty radio at that point could mean a considerable delay to the flight, taking into account that some fuel would have to be de-canted during any radio repairs. I was mortified as Airinc was called again and again without reply. Next thing to do was to start both engines to bring the batteries up to 'full steam' with the alternators. After several attempts again there was no response from Airinc. Dejectedly, cursing myself for not making a test of the equipment days before, I walked to the terminal and told the Butler manager my troubles.

"You better 'phone Airinc and find out if you're getting through " was his suggestion. With that he gave me the number and handed me the receiver.

"Yessir we heard all your calls sir, your transmission was good, you came through loud and clear." The Airinc operator announced.

With that I nearly exploded. "But you never answered me, I heard nothing, not a sound, what's going on? "

"You don't seem to have an account with us sir, we only respond to account holders unless there's a genuine emergency, such as a Mayday or Pan call."

So that was it. High frequency service was not free as in the Australasian area so without further ado my company name and address and a few other minor particulars was passed to him and I became an authorised user of Airinc's Pacific network from henceforth guaranteed to receive a reply to all my calls.

The service was used all the way across the Pacific and as it turned out, was well worth the money. I'll never forget the sinking feeling experienced when I tried the HF without result that late afternoon at San Francisco, which quite spoilt my day.

The taxi ride to the motel allowed time for me to recover. The plan was to take off for Honolulu at 3am the following morning to ensure that a thirteen-hour crossing would end with still plenty of daylight in hand. A long trouble-free sleep was needed.

When taxying to the take off point next morning, having already received the relevant clearances, only then did I remember that the sandwiches and thermos I'd ordered from the motel had been forgotten. It was going to be a hungry, thirsty day, but at that point with the butterflies stirring in my stomach I couldn't have cared less.

Part of my pre-take-off obligation was to advise the Control that N241W was operating considerably over maximum allowable gross weight. Nearing the take-off point the required information was passed to the Tower.

"You goin' to Honolulu in that, right, sure you got 'enuf' gas? OK, the runway's all yours sir, you're cleared for take-off, have a good day sir, call departures at the Gate." (Golden Gate Bridge).

A quick prayer was offered as I pushed the throttles up to maximum power while holding her on the brakes. Both engines ran as smooth as silk. Under the extra load I half expected her to waddle along slowly at first, but when the brakes were released she jumped away like a sprinter out of the starting blocks! I'd made thousands of take-offs in Barons, many at high elevations, that one felt exactly the same. With barely a third of the huge runway used she was up and away, heading for the bright lights of the hilly city so beautiful in the quietness of early morning, climbing like a' homesick angel'.

In the event of an engine failure occurring during the lift-off, gear retract was left off the checklist until a glide to the runway would no longer be possible. On flicking the gear switch up when the runway disappeared from sight beneath the nose, the electric motor gave a solid 'whirr' as a gentle thump and a red light on the panel told me the gear was safely housed for the next 12 hours or more.

It is said that San Francisco never sleeps. My eyes feasted on the scene of lights and neon signs until, as I turned out over the Golden Gate, a wall of blackness took over as the sky and the Pacific merged as one. In seconds I was flying 'on the clocks' on track to the Farallon Islands beacon, from where a great circle route over Ocean Station November and on to Honolulu would be taken up.

Owing to the increase in gross weight by the excess fuel being carried the flight had been planned at 4000 feet (1200 metres) for a few hours, to burn off some of the weight, but on reaching 4000 feet N241W was still ascending at 800 feet a minute. My request for a higher level was answered with a clearance to cruise at 8000 feet that allowed a climb through a stratified cloud layer to the clear sky above. So good was the Baron's performance with an overload that the ferry tank, which wasn't fitted with gauges, came under suspicion as having been partly drained by some thief overnight. In order to thump the side of the tank while pressing an ear on the metal to feel and hear whether the tank was full or not, required the ability of a circus acrobat. The doubtful result of that manoeuvre helped to relieve my feelings but was no real test.

On reaching the assigned altitude the time was noted in the log. A switch over to the ferry tank was made at the same time while trying to keep N241W exactly on the heading for Ocean November's base position without the help of an auto pilot. The Ocean Station did not heave to in a fixed position but journeyed up or down the meridian for a considerable distance, always transmitting on a non-directional beacon the code letter of each particular sector A, B, C, or D. Thanks to Chuck that information was recorded in my notes, his expert advice was well remembered.

"If you don't sight the Ocean Station, don't start searching and wasting fuel, 'git' on to Honolulu, don't waste time, his beacon is low powered and can sometimes be faulty and misleading."

When daylight came with the sun beginning to rise, I found myself skating along on top of a layer of cloud that stretched forever and ever in all directions. That gave me the first impression of speed I'd had since leaving the lights of San Francisco.

Before long, dollars were being spent with Airinc on the first position and weather report of the day. Somewhere, not seen below the cloud layer, the Pacific, like Father Thames, would 'just keep rollin' along'.

Ocean Station November, in reality a US Coastguard cutter, held station on the 140th meridian, approximately 900 miles (1,680 km) from San Francisco, more than 200 miles short of the halfway point 'Frisco, Honolulu'. As the hours went by a real sense of loneliness crept into my bones. Except for the voices on the radio the feeling was that the Baron, with me, had planet Earth to itself. The layer cloud was persistent in intensity, only occasionally allowing me time for a quick look at the sea through a small gap in the white blanket of cover.

Someone with not too much knowledge of airplanes or the Pacific, had once told me that an alternative method of navigation to Honolulu from contiguous USA in a small 'plane, was to follow the vapour trails of passenger jets high in the sky above. Lots of trails could be seen, although not all seemed to be going my way. Whoever it was who had suggested that couldn't have heard of Australia, Tahiti, Japan, the Philippines, Vietnam, Indonesia, Hong Kong, Taipei, or understood that not all jet traffic to Honolulu left from San Francisco either. Thank goodness his advice wasn't taken seriously.

A weather zone had been forecast about the 135th meridian with little effect on the Hawaiian Islands expected. Every hour Airinc's bill was added to with a position report or a weather analysis at the altitude being flown. Each half-hour was spent listening out for a minute or two on the international distress frequency free of charge. A surprising amount of idle chatter between airline aircraft could be heard on that channel. So high did the big jets fly that seldom would their high frequency (HF) radios be needed the 'line of sight' VHF radios alone provided ample coverage on many ocean routes.

Fiddling with my VHF by flipping from one frequency to another, I managed to intercept a conversation from an Air New Zealand DC8. When that call finished I broke in. The ANZ Captain was an old acquaintance from the Air Force who was slightly mollified when he discovered who and where the mystery voice was coming from!

We both enjoyed the mid-Pacific chat, he in his 'cool' DC8 moving along at more than seven miles a minute, with a harem of pretty flight attendants serving morning tea, me in a tiny Baron at three miles a minute thousands of feet below, without even a sandwich or a glass of water. By our co-ordinates and according to him, we were about 300 miles apart and moving in opposite directions. The radio encounter was a great boost to my morale and when our chat closed off, that lonely feeling set in again.

Six hours slipped by without a sign of the cloud clearing below. Up-dating the log, passing position reports, checking and manipulating the ferry fuel system which meant re-filling the right outer auxiliary fuel tank periodically from the cabin ferry tank, kept me busy. The ferry fuel system that Chuck had installed at Santa Monica was excellent, for the auxiliary tank was equipped with a fuel gauge. At a glance I could see whether or not fuel was transferring from the cabin tank. Suppose that didn't happen? Well then I had almost four hours of fuel remaining in the wing tanks that would allow time for me to alert the US Coastguard of my predicament. That service had an enviable reputation for plucking downed airmen from the sea. Each time fuel was transferred it was a great relief to watch the gauge erect itself to the 'F' for Full position again. The time would be noted in the log, the hours ticked by. A position report came next followed by another ferry tank fuel transfer, all was going like well-oiled clockwork.

The time came to tune the only direction finder the Baron possessed and listen for Ocean Station November's code letters - dah dah dah - dah dit - followed by the letter of the sector the Ocean Station was in at the time and hope for a positive reaction on the needle. At times like that there is a tendency for a pilot to get nervous, impatient even. I worked at keeping cool for more than thirty minutes before the faint letters - dah dah dah - dah dit - dit dah - were heard. 'Whoopee' the letter A tacked on the end told me that Ocean Station November was in his base sector closest to the Great Circle track I was following. Ten to fifteen minutes later the needle showed him to be five degrees to the right of my metal bird's nose. As for the distance, there was no means of telling, I could only guess at about fifty miles. All I could do then was to keep on flying towards him.

Ten minutes later I couldn't resist the temptation to let-down through the clouds only to receive a severe shock. At five thousand feet it seemed that all of the Pacific Ocean was in full view, millions of acres of deep blue rolling sea void of ship, sail, cutter, or even a whale on the blow, the scene was actually frightening. Only then did I realize the immenseness of the great ocean and the insignificance of flying-man Bryan and his metal air machine.

With the code letters getting louder by the minute we bored on towards where the cutter should be in the great wastes of sea while I began calling on the radio. After three or four calls the Ocean Station responded although there was not a sign of any vessel on the surface in the direction the needle indicated. I had expected to see something about the size of a destroyer broadside on, but the Great Ocean kept its secret hidden until the flying man and his metal bird were less than five miles away.

The Ocean Station in fact was quite a small vessel and looked to be much more lonely than I felt. The ship's radioman encouraged me to come down for a closer look. The invitation for a frolic was accepted with a couple of tight circles around the unexpectedly vulnerable looking vessel before climbing above cloud again to join with the sun and re-set course for Honolulu. The Captain passed his compliments and thanked me generously for taking the time to give the crew a close up. Theirs was a lonely monotonous job for many high flying aircraft were talked to but few were ever seen. During the circling I had been able to take in the immensity of the ocean with a tiny boat rolling about on a confused, rumpled sea that came relentlessly from nowhere and headed for nowhere, to me the scene was somehow quite breathtaking and has never been forgotten. The climb to altitude was continued with me in a despondent frame of mind knowing that the flight was less than half completed and me wondering how Chuck would feel about the time wasting diversion made contrary to his advice.

As cloud enveloped the Baron again, the sea disappeared, cockpit duties took over and the terrible, lonely, empty feeling within me began to subside as practicality took over. Airinc was always there for me to talk to I told myself, having then gained more experience in handling their informal style of radio procedure.

Sighting Ocean November seemed to have shortened the long flight. The feeling was similar to starting all over again after having been refreshed by damping the forehead with a wet towel. In my previous experience many hours had been spent out of sight of land, sea, moon or stars, but always in an aircraft with crew or passengers, never alone as I was then. Once again came the feeling that I was the only person conscious on the planet.

Having now gone about fifty miles from Ocean Station November I radioed a last goodbye several times without receiving any acknowledgment, as if I was transmitting blind, which was mystifying. The silence was put down to their being busy with more important duties on a different frequency. The air-to-sea frequency allotted seemed dead as we flew on towards brooding storm clouds.

An hour later, cloud and rain smothered the Baron while moderate turbulence began to shake her frame. Glimpses of the wind-lashed ocean alive with froth were few and far between as we plunged further into the stormy weather zone. Eight, nine, ten hours of total time passed without let up in the gloomy-looking, all surrounding weather. The engines continued to drone on steadily and hypnotically, my eyes began to droop with fatigue. Lots of concentration was summoned up, from where I don't know, in order to stay awake. San Francisco, Santa Monica, Buckeye, Junction, New Orleans, Miami were by now only pleasant memories in bright sunshine far behind my metal bird.

There was always Airinc to attend to with a position report, the tank switching to take care of, the air plot to keep up to date, every line I drew now was slightly crooked or smudged. The most heartening sight at that time was to see the Automatic Direction Finder needle fixed firmly on to a Hawaiian commercial broadcasting station, although it's exact location was unknown and the announcers were not giving out any hints.

The fuel in the ferry tank had all been used up, N241W's engines were by then running on the aircraft's inbuilt system with approximately four hours fuel remaining and slightly more than two hours to go to Honolulu by estimate. Again I was ahead of my 'airplane', fears of ramming into one of the Hawaiian Islands began to eat at me as we flew on with almost nothing in the way of visibility, all the time passing in and out of dark, wet cloud.

At the estimate for Hawaii's Air Defence Zone (ADZ) I grabbed the mike to call Honolulu Approach only to find that the VHF radio was dead, as it probably had been since leaving Ocean November hours before. The Baron was equipped with only one VHF short range set. On approach to Honolulu's extremely busy civil/military airport several frequency changes could be expected. My heart sank. Fatigue forgotten, I sat up and took notice, while deciding what I should do, beginning by taking the set from it's housing, inspecting it for signs of water contamination then shoving it firmly in place again before attempting to transmit, only to be greeted again by a stony silence.

Using Airinc more than 2000 miles away in California as my communicator seemed ludicrous but I had no choice. The final two hours of the flight were dreadful, frustrating, infuriating at times using such a top-heavy system and having to wait minutes for an answer to my requests. Airinc would need to relay my message to Honolulu Radio who in turn would contact the Control Centre for further instructions and pass the answer back to Airinc for return to me. The relaying all took time with time running out as I flew on towards a heavy traffic area. If ever there was a period when I 'lost my cool' it was then.

While looking down for a second or two through a small gap in the cloud a US Navy DC4 was spotted about 1000 feet below slipping at right angles across my flight path. Immediately that information was passed on to Airinc. Five minutes later Airinc advised that I had been seen by the DC4 and at that time N241W was 150 miles from Honolulu on a correct course and cleared to proceed. Blessed relief!

Ten minutes after that Airinc advised that Honolulu Control had N241W on radar, to steer 200 degrees for two minutes, about 40 degrees off course, before returning to heading, for positive identification. To know that we were then on a radar screen at Honolulu Tower was a great relief, confidence building, something like feeling that nothing could go wrong, go wrong, go wrong!

About 100 miles out, a US Coastguard C130 (Hercules) was alongside to shepherd me on a 'follow me' approach to the huge islands airport, not such a simple exercise without rapid communication between us. The clouds were low with drizzle coming through the overcast.

The Coastguard's big metal bird weaved through in expert fashion always leaving me room to keep him in sight without plunging into cloud or flying through his slipstream (wake). Needless to say my eyes were riveted to the big aircraft. A glance at my instruments told me that we were descending as we both went down twisting and turning, the speedy little Baron to the left of him and slightly behind. I could see that we were still over water. To slot me into the landing traffic the Herc was bringing me around in a wide 'zig-zag' arc, gently and smoothly, no doubt under Radar Control himself, my altimeter hovering on 1000 feet with cloud smoking over the wing at times.

"What's your fuel state sir?" Airinc asked from more than 2200 miles away.

"One hour thirty minutes." went the reply.

"Your gear should be down and locked now sir, confirm? At 500 feet the Charlie One Thirty will break right, away from you, and climb. The landing runway will be directly ahead. You are clear to land. Clear promptly by the first taxiway, you got following traffic. Proceed to HATS ramp (Hawaiian Air Tour Service). Good afternoon sir. Have a nice stay in Hawaii. "

With that he'd gone, I was left with only a quick look at the city while N241W was steered to the longest and widest runway I'd ever laid eyes on, scarcely moving a degree from the heading left me by the C130.

The Baron's almost new tyres 'eeked' on the runway, exactly thirteen hours after leaving San Francisco, some time having been lost in the escorted, non-standard approach to the airfield.

On clearing the runway, automatically and without thinking, I selected and called Ground Control on the finicky VHF radio. To my pleasurable shock he replied immediately. Suddenly the 'phones were alive with requests and instructions to other aircraft as the radio came alive again and operated perfectly, seemingly having fixed itself after giving me the biggest headache I'd had in a long time.

Approaching the designated ramp I unlatched the door to admit fresh air and blow away some of my sweat. On arrival I knew that there would be some explaining to do, a lot of effort on the part of controllers and Coastguard airmen had gone into my safe arrival under marginal weather conditions.

After switching off and unbuckling I sat in the seat for several minutes, letting the strains and stresses ooze from me before I clambered past the tank and out into the warm air. Several minutes after my feet had reached terra-firma a utility vehicle with a female driver arrived to collect the landing fees, obviously my name wasn't 'Smithy' or Amelia.

Being a domestic flight there were no Customs or Immigration formalities to contend with. I made my way to Hans Mueller's office, the owner of Hawaiian Air Tour Service. Six or more of his de Havilland Heron aircraft were parked on the ramp, which confirmed that the weather hadn't been suitable for island air touring. Hans instructed his radioman to pull the VHF set out and put it on test to see whether a fault could be found, intermittent failures are sometimes hard to trace.

I checked into an hotel a block or two from the beach at Waikiki, taking in the holiday atmosphere that is Hawaii, never out of the sound of guitars strumming the melodious 'aloha' tunes the guitar is noted for. Eighteen hours after 'get-up' with a 13 hour flight in between I tumbled into bed.

The following day was spent preparing for the next stage, each engine of the Baron needed very little oil to be added, and I was carrying four one quart cans. Finding a fuel company who would fuel the ferry tank though became my biggest concern as several of the tankers contacted were prohibited from fuelling any other than the factory in-built tanks on any aircraft. It was hours before a call to the head office of Mobil in faraway New York gave approval and fuel gurgled into the ferry tank. Again the sun was on the way down before that job was finished. My rest day hadn't quite turned out that way. The radio was re-installed, the technician having found no fault with it.

At 5 am the following day I lifted off the long superbly lit runway, bound for Canton Island a flight of 1900 miles without the comfort of an Ocean Station down the track. N241W was running like a charm.

The flight had been going for an hour with the engines at normal cruise before the sun came up to reveal a cloudless sky. When the Canton non-directional beacon was tuned, the needle of the Baron's T12C direction finder immediately steadied on the nose, with the identification signal coming in as clear as a bell. That was so hard to believe that I turned the finder off. When two hours later I tuned the frequency again, the result was the same, unless the finder packed up, finding Canton was going to be easy.

During the planning of the flight the leg to Canton had been viewed as the hardest. In the Phoenix Group and sometimes known as Enderbury, Canton was reported to be an uninhabited low-lying atoll 9 miles by 4, a few small islands on the rim of a longish shaped lagoon that was itself surrounded by a 'fence' of coral reef jointly administered by the United Kingdom and the USA. Canton boasted an airstrip of generous proportions. In the days of large piston-engine airliners it was used as a re-fuelling depot between Fiji and Hawaii. Prior to WW2 the big Boeing and Sikorsky flying boats (Clippers), had used the lagoon for the same purpose.

Except for the weekly supply flights to the NASA station on Canton, there was little in the way of air traffic that could be relied on for any assistance should an unexpected emergency arise. That part of the vast Pacific was a lonely place in daytime so far as air traffic was concerned.

Canton's high powered beacon had by then dispelled some of my fears. Relaxing a little more I went about attending to the navigation and fuel flows, hoping all the time that the beacon wouldn't be turned off for some reason before the atoll was sighted or the tiny T12C give up the ghost.

Then came the time when the ferry tank was drained. Running solely on the aircraft's system from that time would see N241W safely on the ground at Canton with two and a half hours fuel remaining.

An hour before arrival Canton had been contacted by VHF radio, while I was on the edge of the seat trying to sight the atoll. There were many dark, conflicting cloud and water shadows on the ocean resembling low-lying islands that tempted a straying off course to investigate. I began to wonder if Amelia might have been tempted in the same way in her early morning search for the island in 1937, quite some determined concentration was needed to trust the direction finder.

There was nothing to be seen outside the aircraft as we drove on, except the deep blue ocean blending with the lighter blue of a clear sky. The surf pounding on the island's reef was the first giveaway sign of its existence in the vast wastes of sea. In a few minutes the brown strips of a treeless island and the lighter strip of sealed runway could be seen glinting in the afternoon sun, my heart was in my mouth. Since leaving Honolulu in perfect weather, there'd not been a sign of any aircraft, ship, yacht or other human kind of trail. I felt like whooping with joy. Without buildings of any kind, the huge airstrip was all ours as a circuit was made of the lagoon while taking a look at the NASA camp on an adjoining islet some distance away. The radioman advised that a mobile fuel tanker was on the way. After discovering that fuel was so cheap and in plenteous supply, I decided to fill up again, although the next leg to Nandi in Fiji was little more than a six-hour run.

"Only two-fifty gallons? " the tanker's driver queried. "Our birds spill more than that on gassing up."

The extremely efficient US Navy crew had N241W fuelled in less than fifteen minutes and accommodation had been offered for the night. Americans don't do things by halves, I had a bungalow to my-self, transportation provided to and from the mess-hall and return to the 'plane the next morning. Except for the supply DC4 no other air-craft had used Canton in months. For security reasons a restriction had been placed on itinerant aircraft arrivals. For some unknown reason my application for a whistle stop at Canton had been accepted when it was inferred that after re-fuelling the Baron would leave Canton for Fiji. However, it seemed that the arrival of such a 'plane was some-thing of a novelty, I was treated like a King (or President in that case). All the personnel were close-lipped about what was going on there and I was wise enough not to ask too many questions.

At mealtime the officer-in-charge sought me out to ask if a mem-ber of his staff could go along with me to Fiji. The man had urgent compassionate reasons for returning to Hawaii. From Nandi he could take an airline flight to Honolulu the following evening. What could I say but OK. I certainly owed them a favour. If the man accepted the very cramped seating arrangement with a metal tank for a backrest, I would agree to him coming along.

Next morning after seeing his travelling situation he OK'd the pro-posal. He'd been provided with ample stocks of lunches, hot and cold drinks in quantity enough for a feast. With this came an offer of a gal-lon or two of ice cream that had to be ruled out due to the Baron not having a refrigerator! The thought of cruising at 8,000 feet over the equatorial Pacific with a plate of ice cream on my lap brought out a chuckle or two.

Getting my very willing passenger seated took some time with a lot of squeezing to be done. There was only one door, how he would evacuate in the event of a ditching had to be discussed, practised and accepted that wasn't so easy, but he was agreeable and I must say, most capable of executing the tricky entry to the cabin.

At 7am Canton time the following morning the camp was subjected to a low buzz from the very pretty green striped Baron before we turned out over the lagoon and set course for Nandi. By then the equator had been crossed and we were flying into a more familiar area of the Pacific, even the air 'down under' smelt of home. Skies were clear, the ocean ruffled only by light breezes.

With a little more than an hour to go to Nandi and the tension gone, I have to admit that my 'no breakfast' rule on eating aboard was broken as I tucked into some delicious slices of turkey with hot black coffee from my passenger's plentiful supply! The Canton homer beacon clung to the tail of the dial for the whole of the 1200-mile journey, bringing us into the Fiji group of islands between the eastern tip of Vanua Levu and Yasawa Islands, exactly where we should be. Early in the afternoon, six hours and thirty minutes after leaving Canton the tyres squealed on Nandi's runway, so well known to me and full of memories of arrivals and departures in weather light and dark, fair and foul. There were customs and immigration formalities to contend with that all went smoothly.

An hour after arrival I'd bid farewell to my brave American friend after the pains in his back had been taken care of after which I checked into one of the airport's tropical style hotels that Fiji is noted for. At the pool were several crew members of the TEAL (Tasman Empire Airways Ltd) DC6 aircraft from Auckland that was parked at the terminal for an overnight stay.

With the sun going down as we lazed and sported around the pool, my thoughts turned to the following day and the final leg of the flight to Lae in New Guinea. After a customs check there, if time was available I would fly on to Goroka in the Eastern Highlands, home, family and friends and the starting up of Macair. The flight to Lae would occupy almost twelve hours plus thirty-five minutes to Goroka. There were no night facilities at Goroka or Lae, official closure of all airports in New Guinea other than Port Moresby was 6.30 pm local time. Excitement ruled the night, allowing me little sleep.

Before the crack of dawn, with little fuss or bother from officialdom and while my TEAL friends would be asleep, N241W soared off Nandi's runway and turned to the west on climb to 8000 feet to join a track that would pass between the New Hebrides and Solomon Islands.

In less than an hour the weather began to change, the fine, lazy, clear weather experienced ever since leaving Hawaii had suddenly taken on a sour look as we began to rattle and roll through medium sized rain clouds. Some of those could be dodged but not all. As at other times I began to get ahead of the aircraft and imagined mountainous New Guinea waiting for me, hiding in or under some of the worst tropical thunderstorms imaginable.

Shortly after clearing the Solomons area radio contact with Port Moresby was established on the high frequency radio that was the only New Guinea frequency available on the twelve-channel set that had served me so well. The set had been swapped at Miami for a transponder that would be of no use in New Guinea but pretty well mandatory in USA.

After flying for ten and a half hours parts of the north coast of New Guinea came in sight as we headed into the Huon Gulf while keeping a sharp lookout for the weather around Lae that at times could be unpredictable and subject to change without notice.

When fifty miles out from Lae it was time to use the short-range (VHF) radio again which would be the first time that equipment had been required since signing off with Nandi Tower early that morning. Alas, nothing was heard, the radio was again dead. After a number of calls on the VHF without the desired result, a return to the HF was necessary to gain permission to complete the arrival using HF only. While that was not a particularly popular arrangement with the Control Tower man, for messages both ways had to be relayed via the radio room, we somehow managed. At thirty miles the instructions were for me to circle to allow other traffic with the appropriate communications equipment, to arrive or depart in sequence. As we circled the minutes ticked by, I could see that time was running out for an onward flight to Goroka. Finally instructions were received that cleared me for a straight-in approach from the sea.

There was no sign of a hero's welcome awaiting us. The airport was quiet, no doubt getting ready to close down for the night. My only admirer, Martin Skeates a Trans Australia Airlines pilot resident in Lae and an ex Air Force colleague, was waiting with his camera and reeled off a few shots. Fortunately, Customs officers were on hand and anxious to clear the aircraft quickly and get away to either home or one of Lae's numerous clubs, the latter probably being the most popular choice. It was surprising to see Frank Ekas there too, a company director, who asked for a ride to Goroka. He was told, albeit jokingly, that he could come along if he dropped on his knees and apologised for the long delay in transmitting the funds to Miami for the purchase of N241W. I'd been away for five weeks when the job could have been done in two! The 'on your knees' bit was dispensed with, he was helped into the back-breaker of a 'seat' previously used by the American from Canton.

Climbing in again past the ferry tank, I started engines and prayed for a miracle. If the VHF radio didn't respond to my professional touch, I knew that a take-off clearance would not be forthcoming from the Tower. New Guinea's air regulators were party to very strict regulations regarding aircraft radio equipment. I shoved hard on the set in its housing, pulled it out a little and shoved it in hard again, a procedure I'd followed without result on several occasions en route. That time the practice worked, the tower answered my call loud and clear.

The hands on my watch told me that Goroka's airport would close in forty minutes, the flight would take thirty-five. The Tower must have sensed the urgency in the air and was most co-operative. With fuel a-plenty I was cleared to the runway and for take-off, all in the one sentence. Minutes later we were climbing fast up the Markham Valley, pointing in the direction of the Kassam Pass, where the still as yet primitive road left the valley and zig-zagged it's way up the steep slope into the highlands.

The mountains were throwing up plenty of cloud but nothing one couldn't 'zip' or 'zap' around, over or under.

Soon the open plain of the valley gave way to hill, mountain and rain forest. At the Pass the clouds lowered, I let N241W slide underneath and flew low between earth and cloud along the smaller valleys that ran like spider's legs on both sides of the Pass where the terrain was well over 5000 feet above sea level. Kainantu, a few miles further inland from the Pass was the only town of any size along the route, I zipped over the airstrip there at about 500 feet above terrain and flushed with excitement poked the nose of my American beauty towards her new home up the narrow valley that led to the broader Asaro with Goroka in the north-western corner at the foot of Mount Otto. So elated, at times the feelings within me were those of dreaming, with the country I knew and loved so well speeding past below, the upturned faces of the village warriors on hilltops or on the rocks in swift-flowing mountain streams, with the string of their black-palm bows stretched to the limit. They wouldn't know that the 'balus' they were aiming their arrows at had come from the other side of the world. Their world ended at the next range of hills or across the gorge where the river raced as frothy white water.

"Goroka Tower hi ya, this is Novemberr Two Fourr One Whisky, Beech Baron, white with green stripe, from Miami Florida, y'hoonited States, entering the valley twenty miles to the south-east, estimate yours at two seven, request an overfly pass, (sharp a, as in ass) before landing? "

There was a bit of a hush after that, for a while I thought the radio had failed again or the Tower operator who was known to me, had fallen off his chair in a rage over the brazen misuse of correct radio procedure.

A familiar voice with clipped but rounded tones then came back, a well-known voice, a 'Fudgie' sort of voice that brought a smile to my lips.

"November Two Four One Whisky, what a fake accent. We heard you were in South America. This is Goroka Tower. Overfly approved, there's no traffic, you are clear to land runway three five left with two minutes to go before we close and send you back to Lae. Congratulations and happy landings."

It was nice to be home. My continental and great ocean flight was nearly over. Running the power up on both engines I set her into a fast descent and aimed at the landing strip. The town I loved so much could then be seen clustered about the sloping runway. Years seemed to have passed since I'd left that beautiful fertile valley, with the mixed races of peoples and cultures, tall gums, conifers too, flowers, blooms and the well-kept coffee plantation bordering the runway. All was peaceful in those days, the town and valley was a happy place.

The Baron streaked up the runway at maximum pace and 'dot feet' (less than fifteen) towards the town and airport buildings, then with the post-war planted but mighty tall gums at the top end of the runway coming in fast, pulled up steep in a left wing-over, holding tight to the runway over the western part of the town and without levelling the wings intercepted a very short final approach.

The uphill runway always acted as an effective brake. After touchdown N241W was left to coast along to the curving taxiway that led to the parking ramp and the crowd that could be seen waiting at the hangar. For weeks I'd been dreaming about that moment. The time was exactly 6.30 pm. Then came Fudgie's voice again through the 'phones.

"I thought I approved an' overfly' not an under-fly. Good night, sleep tight, tight meaning well. "

For fear of taping more unapproved, un-airmanlike radio language that might end up in the DCA Director of Operation's office in Port Moresby, I finished the 'Flight from Miami' with a tentative and polite. "Goodnight to you too sirrr."

Before I could emerge from my fuel tank trapped warren, a big crowd of 'believers' were crossing the tarmac led by Betty and Scott the youngest of our five and Jack the air enthusiast. I've often wondered whether his desire for a flying career began that late afternoon in the New Guinea highlands when Dad came in from the world's biggest sea.

Our two girls Kathryn and Dianne and Roger our eldest boy, were in Australia at school and so missed the fun. I missed them very much at that time too. With Betty was Warren Knight our bank manager, who had served in the Royal Australian Air Force in WW2 and who had showed particular interest in local aviation and Macair. It was not so dramatic as to say I could see signs of relief on his face but it was something like that. His looks were certainly approving as he cast his eyes over N241W. No doubt during my absence with all the rumours flying about, he must have had doubts as to his bank's underwriting of the Macair project. Betty had been left with all the worrying to do during my absence, with rumours being circulated that I had taken the 'plane to South America accompanied by a Spanish senorita! In such a small place, the same concerns must have filtered through to Warren too.

A small reception was held on the tarmac in front of the hangar near the 'plane, while everybody viewed the town's newest metal bird. Questions, questions, an hour passed and it was dark before the car was loaded and final course set for home around the western side of the airport.

That night the drizzle and fog clamped down as was normal, the house warm and snug, the home-cooked meal absolutely delicious, bringing about the return of my New Guinea taste buds. The drizzle was so gentle that it couldn't be heard on the roof. Ah, home, sweet, sweet home again.

Several times on the way whether over land or sea, when things had gone wrong, I swore I'd never do the same thing again. Lying secure in my own bed I was flooded with memories of the journey while trying to concentrate on thinking only of the good ones. Some day with the experience then under my belt and given the opportunity, I knew that I would take on the mighty Pacific again in all its sullen beauty.

What I shall call a sequel to this story arrived by post some three weeks after my return, in the form of an invoice from Airinc, San Francisco for $US300.00 for three hundred high frequency calls at $1.00 per call! For the assistance, the reassurance that came from that company in those tense times, that bill was cheap at twice the price, although our accountant didn't think so. However he sat in an immoveable office for most of the day, gazing across the valley at those magnificent, green, forest-clad mountains that have yet to feel the bite of a pile in the soil as a radio mast or power pylon goes up. He was hard to convince that the price paid for the Baron, plus the costs of ferrying to New Guinea were less than half that could be expected for a Baron purchased from an Australasian dealer.

Another 'sequel' should be mentioned also. After being registered in New Guinea N241W became VH-MKA (Victor Hotel-Mike Kilo Alpha). In the first few months of operations the VHF radio failed several times and was the subject of many a complaint from the air authority, who at one point threatened to ground the aircraft and I feel sure would have loved to be able to carry out their threat.

Two separate approved radio repair facilities were approached to deal with the problem. Both returned the set to service without having found any fault with the equipment.

Finally MKA was taken to the Summer Institute of Linguistics facility at Aiyura, Eastern Highlands, who were equipped with a test harness applicable to that type of set. In less than ten minutes the fault was found, a wire on the board had split slantwise, only making occasional contact. Problem solved, no more complaints, the saga of the faulty radio ended. Such is the life of a flying man.

FLIGHT FROM 'THE FRIENDLIES

'Wanda-ring' Around the Coral Sea 1974

Port Moresby's Jackson's Airport sizzled in the blast of midday tropical heat as I came down the steps from the Fokker Friendship on to the burning hot tarmac. In seconds my shirt was saturated with sweat and beginning to cling to my skin.

"Go straight to departures." the attendant at the foot of the steps snapped. "Your flight's about to leave, have your documents ready."

Foggy weather in the highlands, that was par for the course, had delayed my flight, leaving me with only minutes to join the flight to Australia. I scuttled through departure formalities, rushed to the inter-national departure lounge to find the hall emptied out, the only movement there being three rows of ceiling fans whirling away use-lessly in the girders overhead, as they had for as long as could be remembered, without a breath of air ever reaching the floor. Two cleaners were tidying up the trash on and between the rows of chairs, eyeing me as if their 'sit-down nothing' time had been interrupted.

The dispatch supervisor ushered me through the littered, untidy hall to the gate, throwing his voice over his shoulder as he went.

"You better hurry mate (not that I was, I'd heard funny stories about 'mates), the Captain's getting cranky, schedule keeping, the jet age you know, go straight to the forward steps now and hurry. "

Flight bag in hand I scampered along the tin-roofed walkway and across the black tarmac to the steps of the red-tailed Boeing 727. The pavement felt hot enough to fry an egg on. Ground crew waited at the head of the stairs, readying to close the door. With the usual fixed smile, a pretty flight attendant dolled up to the nines and looking incongruous in the tropical heat, grabbed my boarding pass and led me to my seat. The entire passenger complement was already seated. A sea of stony-faced accusers who resembled judges in a court, stared at me, sizing me up as if to say.

"So this is the joker whose keeping us waiting, he can't be that important? "

My travelling companion-to-be was obviously annoyed by having to vacate the window seat as I stowed my bag in the overhead locker and squeezed past his knees when he changed seats.

I've never been sure why so many air travellers prefer a seat by a window. There's usually nothing to see except the top of a broad expanse of metal wing and the chances in an emergency of the escape route to the aisle being jammed by panicky passengers. My thoughts always went to the possibility of being sucked out should a window get cracked for some reason. Then there's the inconvenience to others in vacating a window seat over two or three sets of knees with your rear in someone's face. I always like to be buckled up when seated there. However, that's what my boarding-pass read, that's where the flight attendant had indicated, so that's where I sat. My seat mate, the term is used loosely again, took on a sulky look as the cabin door thumped shut and the engines began their whining hum. Several flight attendants scuttled about slamming overhead lockers, preparing for the safety procedures demonstration.

"Sorry to keep y' waiting." I puffed apologetically while cinching the lap-strap." My flight from the highlands was late, I just made it."

'We've got connections to make too you know." he chirped, Aussie ventriloquist style, scarcely moving his lips.

The jet began to roll as the cabin attendants finished the safety spiel, discarded the demo vests and shook their hair back into place. It was time to relax.

A pleasant surprise awaited me when a quick look out of the window revealed that my seat was well forward of the wing, providing a good view across the airport to the mountains of WW2 Kokoda Track fame. A brilliant sun glared down on the towering, tumbling masses of rain-cloud that were already piling up on to the jagged peaks of the Owen Stanley's.

The aircraft began to move into a sharp turn, the old terminal began to slide by the wingtip when I caught sight of a small tractor with a single luggage trolley attached parked inside the security fence, the driver making semaphore-like gestures with his arms, to nobody in particular. I assumed that he was making some sort of a signal to the pilot. Somewhat startled I sat up for a better look.

The only object on the trolley was a black suitcase, smothered in touristy travel stickers. To my dismay the suitcase was recognised as my very own. Nicknamed Samson, the popular brand of 'port' always went along with me on my travels. The flamboyant stickers had been applied to allow for easy recognition when on baggage trolleys or carousels at busy airports. Like all air travellers of the time I had assumed that my checked luggage would be taken care of by the airline, not a thought had been given as to its whereabouts during the rushed transfer of flights.

The scene outside, in very hot sunshine, caught at my heart-strings as Samson stood on the trolley looking lost and lonely, menaced by an arm-waving stranger, while his owner slid by encased in a glossy, pressurised aluminium tube, powerless to assist. The Flight Attendants were by then ensuring that the passengers' seat belts were fastened.

Unbuckling, I stood as much as I could, to lean on the seat in front and call the nearest attendant across the shirtfront of my fellow traveller.

"Miss, please, my suitcase, it's back there on a trolley, it hasn't been loaded on, ask the Captain to return for it please? I'm off to America tomorrow out of Sydney, I must have it."

While seeming to ignore my plea I received from her only a withering look plus a severe reprimand.

"Ever heard of safety regulations? You must be seated while the aircraft is in motion on the ground, the fasten seat-belt light is on can't you see? Now sit down."

Feeling more like a truant schoolboy than a paying passenger a temper of a bad kind rose within me.

"But I can't leave my suitcase behind." I spluttered. "It's not my fault, ask the Captain to return for it will you, pleeease? "

A not so pretty frown now creased her brow.

"Alright then, give me your boarding pass. I'll refer to my senior about it."

Somehow the thought came to me that I was about to fight a lost cause. The jet was about to backtrack down the runway and the girl seemed to be in no hurry to move forward with my boarding pass while attending to another passenger who was in some sort of a quandary about a lap strap. My neighbour seemed to be amused. He spoke cynically, the trace of a smile parting his lips.

"You gotta' fat chance of 'im turnin' roun' now mate. Look atcha watch, he's already behoin' toim, that little bitch won't tell him neither. "

As we jetted down the runway then rotated towards the heavens I could only say "I guess you're right." which seemed to put a rather smug little smile on his face.

We must have been at thirty thousand feet plus when the attendant passed a verbal to me from the Captain who advised me to consult with the company's airport manager at Sydney on arrival. How original! No regrets, no explanations and no apologies. I readied an answer to him but on second thoughts decided against a delivery, instead making my feelings known by refusing the lunch offered.

In no mood for eating for the remainder of the four-hour plus flight that included a short stop at Brisbane I sulked, tilted my chair back, closed my eyes and dozed. Some time went into amusing myself with thoughts of a sign that would be designed to hang around my neck on a string, next time I travelled with that airline, 'THIS PASSENGER SULKING OVER LOST LUGGAGE – DO NOT FEED – DO NOT DISTURB' or something to that effect.

There were times when through the corner of my eye my fellow traveller's midriff was seen to be shaking. As if wrapped in his own thoughts, he was chuckling to himself.

Sydney's early evening weather was chilly as I waited for the company's airport manager to deal with the problem. He seemed to be somewhat prickly as he strove to shift the blame.

"According to the telex we received, your luggage was labelled incorrectly, your fault or ours?"

My hackles rose as I pointed to the copy of my ticket with the butt of a luggage check attached that read in large black letters, SYD.

"Yours without a doubt, I was ticketed to Sydney, you claim to run interconnecting services up there don't you? I didn't sight my port after it was checked in, I'm off to USA on PanAm tomorrow afternoon, no use in going without any gear."

For the first time he looked a little uneasy.

"Do you live in Sydney?" he asked. "If that's the case, we will get your bag out to you after our next service on Thursday. Sorry"

"No I don't live in Sydney, my flight bag here is all the luggage I have with me, no clothes, no personal gear whatever, no toiletries, nothing. That means four days waiting and a week late in the US, I'm not going on without my suitcase." Then I decided to throw a bomb into the works for good measure.

"There'll be hell to pay when my agents hear of this." I hissed.

That did the trick. He simmered down to inquire politely. "What are you going to the States for? "

"That's no business of yours." I replied, trying to sound arrogant and rude. "But if you must know, I'm booked to ferry an aircraft from the US to Manila starting next Thursday. Apart from everything else there's a lot of paper-work in my port pertaining to the flight that I'll need."

"Oh so you're one of those mad ferry pilots, well I do take my hat off to you, I apologize for our slip-up if that's what it was, the only thing I can do for you right here and now is to advance you some funds. In your case all I'm allowed at this stage is one night's accommodation plus expenses for clothing, toiletries et-cetera, your suitcase can be picked up at our freight depot on Thursday after 8 p.m."

"It's a major calamity as far as I'm concerned." I mumbled, then on second thoughts added. "How much are you offering? "

"We'll get you an hotel in the city, one we have an agreement with, that's on us, for which you'll get a company Purchase Order for one night's accommodation plus dinner and breakfast. In addition I'll give you one hundred dollars for expenses, it's getting late, you'd better get in touch with me tomorrow, late morning say, to see if anything's changed."

"That's generous of you." I called sarcastically as he disappeared into an office behind the counter.

Ten minutes later, with only my flight bag for company but a hundred bucks and a Purchase Order better off, I was one of six persons in a mini-bus on my way to the city.

The hotel in King's Cross wasn't anything like the Ritz. Three stars flashed in the neon sign above the entrance. Once in my room a call was lodged to my agent in Miami, through the hotel operator. Five minutes later the 'phone tinkled. As per usual Charlie was ruthless, in the way of American big business. With the receiver a foot from my ear he could be heard ranting on about my unexpected delay.

"G'dammit the deal was for you to be here Wednesday to depart for Manila Thursday night, the necessary clearances have all been filed, right, we're not going to change that, right, the clients in Manila have been guaranteed delivery on time, the ship's ready to go, there can't be a delay, sorry about your bag, or portmanteau, or whatever you call 'em there down-under in Awstralia. The program can't be postponed for three days or more so I'll replace you, I can git another guy to do that one in the interval, a guy whose been itchin' for it anyway, it was good of you to let me know, I'll put a hold on your tickets. So long for now."

My lucrative moonlighting job, while on leave from the hard slog of mountain flying in New Guinea had come to a sudden end. Long after hanging up, I was sitting on the edge of the bed cursing the cause of my hard luck, a certain airline Captain who wouldn't wait a minute or two for a single suitcase to be loaded on, that is if he ever got my message. There was nothing else to do but to call Pan Am and cancel my booking.

Early next morning, in the hope of finding a friend to have a long lunch with while I poured out my sorrows, I started 'phoning around. Not much luck came my way with any of the numbers called. My last call went to Danny de Berto a business friend, known as either Deedee or Dee to those who knew him well. Dee worked in aircraft sales for an up-market, successful aviation business at a secondary airport on the outskirts of Sydney. While we talked I thought he must be preoccupied with other matters, for he didn't acknowledge much as I poured out the sob story of the missing suitcase and the ferry job that went with it. Before my story of woe finished he interrupted, his voice coming to life.

"Hey, can you come out here, there's something you might be interested in, oh, I'm sorry about your luggage, tough luck. "

"What've you got on your mind this time? " I replied cautiously. " Remember that job I did for you, the one to Musswellbrook with Dennis and Della that got me back after dark with an airport blacked out and permanently closed for repairs that you must have known about, you didn't give me the whole story, no more of that I hope."

"That happened quite by accident, anyway it's water under the bridge now. No nothing like that, I don't want to talk about it on the 'phone, around here there are too many extensions, it's too easy for anyone to listen in, come on out."

"It's a long way to go out there without knowing what it's all about, a few clues before I spend the money would be handy? " I winged, hoping that he'd recognise the big hint.

"Look I'll pay for the taxi. You say you've got your flight bag with you, bring it, check out of that mouldy hotel too, hurry you've nothing to lose, see you soon then. "With that he'd hung up.

Shortly after nine o'clock I was out on Macleay Street signalling taxis while dodging the spray from street cleaning trucks. City cabbies prefer inner-city jobs and are known to be very independent. Only after several refusals was a driver found who would undertake the drive without the surety of a fare back to the city. For almost an hour he droned on about the hard life of a Sydney cabby.

Dee's office was in one of several large galvanized iron hangars, standing in a row along the airports apron with their rears to the roadway. Leftovers of the war, all the buildings were kept in a good state of repair, painted in assorted colours and adorned with neat, conservative signs on their walls and entryways.

True to his word, Dee met me in the parking lot beside his hangar and squared the cabby off, adding a small tip for the driver after hearing how co-operative he'd been.

"We'll take the staff entrance if you don't mind, follow me." he said as he led me along a concrete path set between trim, well groomed shrubs and flower-beds, to the rear of the hangar. We climbed an open stairway on the back wall to enter a neat and tidy staff kitchen. From there a short passageway led to his office.

Through an all glass wall I looked down on to the expansive floor of the hangar, with sunlight streaming in through fully opened sliding doors at the front. Three clean-looking twin-engine 'planes, one on jacks plus several single engine types were there, being worked on by several mechanics.

I started in jokingly. "You sure can keep a close eye on your workers from here."

"And them on me too, it's rather like a two-edged sword. " Dee replied, after motioning me to a chair and getting right down to business.

"What I'm going to ask of you must remain shall we say, confidential between us, whether you decide to do it or not that is, can you promise me that? "

"I guess so, we've had dealings before remember? I can keep my mouth shut. There's nothing illegal of course? Tell me everything this time. I'm a big boy, can take care of myself."

Dee assented with a nod of his head. "Pull that curtain across, so you won't be seen from the floor, there's some nosey parkers around here, it might have been better if we'd met in town, but I couldn't leave here today, you might soon know the reason why." As I flipped the curtain over he started right in.

"About a year ago we leased an Aztec to a bloke in the Friendly Islands. You know where they are I imagine? "

"Yeh, sure do, I flew there a number of times in Air Force days."

"Somehow he secured an operating license from the government there. There have been no leasing payments for quite some time and it's known that he's doing plenty of business and receives a subsidy. We've gone easy on him because at the beginning he ordered a Baron from us to replace the Aztec that was really only a stand-in to get him started. The Baron's already been imported and is down there on the jacks getting ready to go, tho' I'm not sure where now, unfortunately. After it arrived here everything's come to a grinding halt, we've learned that there are two Norman Islanders being prepared in Singapore, destined evidently for the 'Friendlies' operation. I'm led to believe he has no intention of completing the deal with the Baron, which means we're to be left holding the baby. "

"Surely you can put the screws on him through the legal people, yes?"

"No. That won't work, no good at all, we've tried that, a Bill of Sale wasn't filed, only a loose contract, sort of gentleman's agreement pending arrival of the Baron here, something that would kick-start their flying program. Not only would a legal challenge cost an arm and a leg but it would take months to settle, our machine could rot away by that time, we've got a sale lined up for it too. Letters are the only way and there hasn't been a reply to any of them up till now, there'd be high court costs because of the various jurisdictions, we'd be broke before it was half over and still wouldn't have the aircraft. The boss and the Board want everything straightened out and pronto." he moaned. " Before things deteriorate any more."

"Well what do you want of me." I said evenly, although guessing what he was leading up to.

"There's no sense in beating about the bush." he replied. " I'd like you to go to the 'Friendlies', grab the Aztec and fly it back here, simple as that. But it won't be easy, it could be their only source of revenue at present, they may not want to part with it so soon. Besides he's got friends and no doubt some enemies within the government there too who may not want to lose sight of the aircraft. Once you make up your mind as to whether you'll help with this one or not, I'll tell you some more."

"What happens if the whole thing is cleared up while I'm en route to grab it?"

You can fly back to Sydney and collect a few days pay."

My reply to that was a long time in coming. I'd flown all over the South Pacific in flying boats and was at a loose end, seeing some of my old haunts again somehow appealed to me. The failure of the US arrangement had left me with nothing to do.

"OK I'll go." I replied while trying to act nonchalant.. " I'll need a good briefing, also a plan to work to, details, details, fuel carnets, working capital, maps, charts, mine don't cover that area and last but not least, tickets, can you come up with some of that. When will all this start and how much am I offered, if I accept? "

Dee looked at me long and hard. When he spoke I nearly fell off the chair, the man was so well prepared.

"There's only one service a fortnight to the 'Friendlies' that leaves tomorrow morning from Suva. There's a flight from Sydney to Nandi this afternoon with a connecting flight to Suva. If you agree you will need to fly out on that one, I don't want any more delays. While the ball is in our court I want this finished with, there's just enough time for you to make that flight, I've had an agent arrange ticketing for you at the International airport. I gave them your personal details, is that okay with you? "

Things were moving a bit too fast for me. "Easy now. How much will you pay me for this? Task completed satisfactorily of course and may I ask what you would have done if I hadn't turned up so unexpectedly? "

"Kept prayin' " he said lightly, a sickly grin on his face.

It was easy to see that Dee had started into planning after first talking to me on the 'phone that morning. He'd certainly done his homework and came straight out with contract conditions without a falter.

"You'll get tickets, an advance in cash and traveller's cheques for three grand. Much the same as in New Guinea plastic money isn't used much in those parts. All receipts are to be returned to me here of course." He paused before continuing, leaned back in his chair to pat his belly as if congratulating himself. " There'll be a whole grand in cash for you on completion, fuel carnets, appropriate documents regarding ownership of the aircraft for customs, police et-cetera. You'll be safe with those if there's a dispute."

I cut in. "Make those return tickets in case something goes wrong, mechanical or otherwise. You never know, in some places you must show your return ticket before they let you in, he might cough up if he knows what you're up to."

"We're quite familiar with international ticketing. No, it's all over so far as I'm concerned, no more promises, I'm fed up to the ears, I want our 'plane back. He's not to know what we're up to, that's part of your job, that's what you'll get paid for. "

The next two hours were spent in frantic activity. We drove to a nearby shopping complex, to a bank first to draw the traveller's cheques, then a clothes store where he purchased a week's 'out of suitcase' travel clothing items for me and a soft bag to carry the things in.

On our return to the airport we really got down to going over details of the trip and some of the hazards that could be expected. The main risk seemed to be that some hostility could come my way if our intentions to re-possess the aircraft became known. While the Friendly Islands were so-named appropriately by Captain James Cook and had lived up to their reputation in present days, a friendly reception under the circumstances would not necessarily be mine.

"Get possession without anyone knowing what you're up to, we don't want to start a war of words, try not to get mixed up with anyone you know. You'll have all the necessary papers. The aircraft belongs to us and you're appropriately licensed and authorised to fly our possession. That amounts to nine points of the law you know. "

Dee made that pronouncement several times to ease my mind and drive home the legality of ownership.

"OK I think I understand, snatch and go stuff eh, say keys, a fuel dipstick and an Owner's Manual for an Aztec might come in handy. I have a licence chop for the Aztec but haven't flown one for some time, could you come up with those for me to study on the way over? " He dropped his eyes and rubbed his forehead.

"Keys no, by mistake they all went with the aircraft, I believe there's a manual here that you can have. I'll see if I can get a dipstick from down below when no-one is looking. Word travels quickly, there's bound to be someone who'll twig if I ask for an Aztec dipstick, damn funny way to run a business isn't it? "

Following that we went over the plans together for an hour or more. He couldn't answer a lot of my questions. A big problem was an extra fuel tank for the longest sector from Noumea to Brisbane should the weather turn sour. When things got too hard he'd say "On that one, just use your initiative." He must have said that a dozen times.

Two hours before departure time at the international airport, that was at least an hour's drive from Dee's airport, I called out to him from the taxi.

"Better make it fifteen hundred, five hundred for using my initiative. This job could be harder than it looks. I'll see y' next week all being well, and please call New Guinea and let Betty know what's happened, I've not had a chance today. She's expecting me to leave for the USA on Pan Am this afternoon."

Whether or not he'd taken me seriously was hard to discern as he waved goodbye, Dee had asked the taxi driver to make a speedy trip with me. The tyres squealed as he swerved out of the parking lot.

The public 'phones in the departure hall were all in use and time was short, leaving little chance for me to call Dee to tell him I'd made the flight and remind him about a call to Betty in New Guinea.

With me comfortably seated at a window and buckled up, on the dot of three o'clock the loading gate finger slid away as the jumbo was pushed back at the start of the flight to Nandi, Fiji's International airport.

As we soared into a cloudless sky and I looked down on the sparkling blue Tasman Sea, the sight of the ocean triggered thoughts about the flight back to Australia and whether the Aztec was equipped with an inflatable life raft. In all our discussions no mention had ever been made of a dinghy for the over-water return flight. The oversight on my part was inexcusable, my only hope then lay in the Aztec already having the appropriate safety equipment, if not, borrowing a floatable was on the cards. Some time was spent on the flight in browsing through the Aztec manual while dreaming up possible alternatives for a life raft.

Late that night while ensconced aboard a modern Hawker Siddeley turboprop for the short flight across Viti Levu from Nandi to Suva, it was hard for me to realise that twenty-five years before, the airline I was now travelling on had only just got away to a 'shaky, shoe-string start'.

Things were very much different in those early days. Flying had been a 'seat of the pants' affair, nothing in the way of ground aids and not too many meaningful facilities apart from the very loyal ground staff at each airfield we used. Tubular framed, fabric covered biplanes with normally aspirated low powered engines. The wings and some wooden sections of the frames were held together with glue and sus-ceptible to 'tropical erosion', a modern term for wood rot. After a rough flight a pilot might be heard to say. "I'm telling you, through all that turbulence, I'm so glad the termites in the spars held hands."

The flight on the Hawker Siddeley began to bring back memories of some of the most vicious tropical storms I'd ever encountered. The Fiji Islands lie in what is sometimes called a hurricane belt. November to March each year saw several 'blows' of varying proportions tearing through parts of the island group, leaving behind a trail of destruction. Thousands of coconut palms destroyed, villages wiped out, canoes and boats with their occupants missing, some never to be heard of again. I'd searched for many of those, with and without success.

Well remembered too was the hurricane of '52 that virtually did wipe Suva out. There were four Catalinas on the base at the time two of which were cast immobile in the hangar, not able to be flown while undergoing major maintenance. As the wind increased it was known that the eye of the storm would pass close to the capital and the base, the flyable Cats were ordered out crewed by those without accompa-nying wife or family in Fiji. All married aircrew with their families were to remain on base. With the wind at 80 knots or more from the southeast across the bay and rain pelting down slantwise, in order to avoid taxying in huge waves the departing aircraft, fully laden with fuel, were forced to make spectacular take-offs directly from the ramp towards and over the breakwater at the start of their flights to New Zealand (Hobsonville) and Australia. (Rathmines). After seeing them away I raced on foot along the walking route to our town-house cum flat at Suva Point, not far from the hangar, to warn Betty to get our baby girl Kathryn ready, that we must leave for shelter at the Officer's Mess, transport for us was already on the way. In driving rain and with the rising wind lashing at everything in its path the visibility was now reduced to zero with the tearing rain forcing the eyes to squint. En route to the flat the hurricane hit in all its fury, by the time I reached the steps to the front door the thought of any further journeys outside were discarded as being too dangerous. The black flag, the final warning or 'batten down the hatches', had been hoisted at the meteorological office that was almost in our back yard. Common sense told me that the transport to the Mess could not be expected as promised. We were on our own.

Somehow in that tiny wooden flat, for five hours the three of us weathered 150 knots of hurricane split in opposite directions. Thanks to the builders and the strapping on the roof and beams the building held together, although there were times when we thought it would be forced to yield to the pressure and we were doomed. Looking out from a shuttered window as the 'calm' of the eye of the storm passed over, a dog was spotted flipping over and over in the wind while being chased by a 50-gallon oil drum down the road. That so-called 'calm' was not really so calm, although there was little rain and the visibility lifted for the short period as the 'eye' crossed the base.

Late that day, with the tempest over, the once neat camp was seen to be demolished, the hangar having lost part of its roof. All that re-mained of some of the barracks and administration areas were the concrete slabs on which the buildings once stood. Documents, tally cards, clothing stores items, even a set of dentures were later returned from as far away as Mbenga Island 50 kilometres away. Reinforced concrete power poles lay twisted across the roads with huge trees for company, vehicles had been overturned or hurled into most unusual places the harbour included. The alighting area of 'the Bay' was littered with floating debris and was unusable for two days. Relief aircraft from New Zealand were forced to use the airfield at Nausori until our two Cats could return. Commercial flying boat services by Qantas and TEAL were also curtailed.

Our six months old baby Kathryn, had slept through the worst, although moved between rooms from time to time, to avoid a drenching from the rain being forced in through small gaps in the timbers not seen by the eye. I would never forget the lead up to, or the aftermath of that hurricane although there were many other more localised storms to contend with as time went on.

Well remembered too was the relief felt when the more frail passenger 'plane built for peace not war, popped out of a big black thundercloud to find things still in one piece and the right way up. There were flights over very angry seas, under a blue/black mass of swirling cloud, in pouring rain at 'dot' feet, using only the surf pounding on a familiar section of coral reef as a guide to navigation. The only directional aid in the aircraft of the time was an antiquated magnetic compass, swivelled by hand and primitive flight instruments that were also being doused with rain. The pilot's clothing became soggy from rain penetrating perished windscreen seals and the cockpit's side windows. Water, surprisingly cold, would run down into the trouser cuffs and shoes to form puddles, or exit the cockpit through holes in the five-ply wooden floor then into the belly's laced up fabric cover. The smell of vomit from the cabin would reek the cockpit, in time with the cries of nervous passengers as the Rapide dropped, bumped, skidded and wallowed, was it any wonder we flew with a lot of our thoughts mulling over the long-term effect of water on wood? Serious attempts were made to maintain flight schedules while the airline began to increase its network, as more airstrips were cut through jungle or coconut plantation at some of the larger outer islands.

Thanks to the pilots who flew long, hard hours almost every day through weather thick and thin and the maintenance men who kept the 'planes flying, the little airline gradually gained some respect from the public. The satisfaction of a safely completed flight and a job well done, seemed to make up for the lousy one hundred pounds per month a pilot received from the owners. Modest living accommodation in the British Colony's capital cost as much as seventy 'quid' a month.

Of course there were many days when one felt so privileged to be aloft in that part of the world, the cockpit flooded with warm rays from the sun, cloudless skies, the ever-changing colours in the deep lagoons which no artist could ever hope to emulate. The mixing of creamy white surf with the deep blue of the ocean as waves from an ocean swell crashed in a regular pattern on to the rings of multi-coloured coral that encircled every island, large or small. Brilliant green, palm-smothered islets, sat like jewels in the centre with isolated, inviting, virgin white beaches where few white men had yet trod. There were times when I thought that the indescribable beauty of the scenes below must be the closest thing to the Garden of Eden.

With the flight half over, the Hawker Siddeley was estimated to be over the centre of the big island close to where I'd met my Waterloo twenty years before. My mind turned to the small village, nestled alongside the river somewhere in the blackness below. Half a dozen grass huts (bures) set on a bend of a swift flowing, always rumbling river, that wound its way through rugged mountains lush with rain forest. The memories of the days and nights I'd spent there, hazy of mind, bruised and battered in a pit of despair, shoeless, shirtless, my left hand almost severed, my jaw hanging loose, my face cut in several places raced through my mind while the Hawker Siddeley purred along effortlessly through the night.

I would always be grateful for the kindness and gentleness of the villagers, who with few appropriate resources tried to treat my wounds. I also remembered the not so kind villager who furtively riffled through my wallet and pockets in the middle of the night, while I lay helpless, racked with pain, on a mat on the dirt floor of the hut, feigning sleep. I badly wanted to be out of there and lived only in the hope of gaining enough strength for another painful trek downstream to civilization, family and friends. .

Pinning my nose on the window, I peered down into the black mass of night, seeing nothing. In the darkness below, the villagers in their rain-sodden, smoke-filled grass bures, would hear the turbo-prop whine overhead. By that time no doubt, through their village being located under the direct route from Suva to Nandi, the sound of aircraft flying overhead at night would be a regular occurrence.

As if in answer to my thoughts, the fasten seat-belt light flashed on, the red light at the wingtip glowed against the heavy cloud we'd entered. Bumping, yawing, rocking and rolling went on for a minute or two before we burst out under a starlit sky again. The props changed tone as the pilot commenced a steady descent to Suva's domestic airport. Situated on the left bank of the Rewa river near the town of Nausori, the airport was a legacy of the Pacific war when PSP (Pierced Steel Planking) sometimes known as Marston or Marsden matting, was laid on the overburden of flood silt. A squadron of USAF P39 Aircobras soon arrived to guard the island from an expected attack from Japan forces.

Post-war, the airfield had fallen into neglect until our little airline started up. Tall sugar cane, ten feet high, had been planted right up to the edges of the runways to feed the Colonial Sugar Refining Company's mill in the town. Little worthwhile maintenance had been done since, the hastily designed drainage network became blocked with silt and the rubbish from the harvesting of hundreds of acres of cane.

In the years I'd flown from there, it was not unusual to find that with the Rewa river in flood, six inches of water, mud and slush concealed the matting. In fact as time went on, even in the driest of weather the matting remained unseen under the grass and silt. Under wet conditions wheel brakes were useless. On take-off or landing, with water and mud flying from wheels, spats and empennage, our 'planes would slither and slide as if skating on ice. Pilots could hold to the matting runway only by using the engines and props asymmetrically with the slipstream to hold the tail down. During abnormally wet times, many a likely catastrophe was averted only by the generous length of the runways and the skill of the pilot. During and after rain the runways could be a moving 'sea of brown cane-toads' with their hopping and leaping type of frolicking. Better to enjoy a frolic in the wet than become a victim of a mongoose, thousands of which inhabited the cane but were seldom seen in the open.

With all that in mind I held my breath as the landing gear of the Hawker Siddeley jerked into place and the pilot started into a direct approach, breathing freely again only after passing over the scattered lights of Nausori town and hearing the squeal of tyres on a bitumen surface.

Although the flight had been short, so many memories pleasant and unpleasant, had been stirred up, it was hard for me to believe that Nausori was the same airport that I had known.

On the outward-bound part of my journey to the 'Friendlies' I had been advised to remain incognito. Close ties existed between the new Pacific nations with their modern air and communication services and I was known to many of the aircrew working in those parts. In full agreement Dee had gone along with my style of keeping a low profile, forward ticketing, hotel or transport reservations were made using my given name as a substitute for my surname.

The airport to city complementary bus dropped me off at one of the cheaper hotels on Suva's main thoroughfare one block from the harbour's waterfront. Before reaching the hotel that I'd selected en route to the city, the driver pointed out to me the regional airline offices where I would check in the following day, only a few minutes walk from the hotel, while there'd always be the usual glut of taxis to choose from as well.

After jabbing the buzzer on the reception counter, I waited for the sleepy-eyed clerk to write some details into a grubby register. When finished he handed me a key while pointing to the stairs. Passport details were not asked for. Registration was made under the name of J Bryan of Sydney, Australia. Dee had also telexed my ongoing flight reservation using that name. At the airline check-in where a passport would be required, if asked, I could argue that a mix-up with my given name must have occurred. Such a late change to the passenger manifest would probably not be sent on to the 'Friendlies', at least that was our hope, in most Pacific islands places incoming passenger lists were public knowledge.

I'd seldom been in any part of the world without running into someone I'd known, or who knew someone else who knew someone else etcetera. The aviation world is fully charged at all times. If one wants to spread a rumour, weave a yarn, reveal the truth behind the headlines, just tell an aircrew man, so the saying goes. Word gets around the Pacific faster than a satellite around the earth.

In my first-floor room, the sole window opened on to a bare concrete wall a metre away. The smell of copra from store-sheds near the wharves wafted in on a night breeze. The room was not too enticing. The day had been long and exciting and to avoid any chance meetings I decided to turn in, retiring to the sounds of a string band playing a fast beat at a 'tra la la' somewhere down the street, or in the bowels of the hotel.

Late the following morning, after a short but surprisingly bumpy flight I was looking down on a beautiful reef-locked harbour as the BAC One Eleven zipped over the Friendlies King's palace, on a wide sweep into the tiny kingdom's international airport.

With gaudy pennants and flags swirling from tall masts and surrounded by dozens of canoes and small boats, an ocean passenger liner lay at anchor 'twixt reef and shore' inside a turquoise lagoon. Before the BAC swung on to final approach to the airport, ten kilometres inland, I was able to catch a glimpse of a long sealed runway, laid to the southeast, set among acres of Pacific palms. A one–storey terminal, sun glinting from a white roof, stood on one side of a neat square of bitumen, with a narrow taxiway leading to the runway, while a tall, white control tower looking every bit a coastal lighthouse, dominated both the palms and airport complex. The road from the capital could be seen, dirty white in colour, winding its way through grassy plains and palms to end at the tower by way of the terminal.

My heart sank somewhat on realising that there was no sign of the Aztec anywhere in the parking area. Dee had told me that his aircraft met every international arrival to convey passengers to outlying islands. At other times it was used for charters, mostly on government business. Any of those situations might cause the aircraft to be absent from its base for days at a time. My hope had been that my arrival would not clash with any of those times. Dee had no knowledge of those sorts of movements. For me to hang about awaiting the 'plane's return from such a sortie would make it difficult to keep my intentions a secret, my cover which would be that of an innocent tourist, would be blown. Completion of the unsavoury task would best be over and done with in the shortest possible time. The absence of the 'plane from it's base gave me something to think about as the BAC's flaps and landing gear bumped and whirred into position for landing.

The pilot planted the One Eleven firmly on the threshold. With little fuss, we glided into the square of bitumen that was the parking area, to stop with only a slight jerk opposite a gap in the wire security fence where a sign read 'ARRIVALS'. Long before we came to a stop, most of the passengers had grabbed their belongings from the overhead lockers. Their faces were wreathed in smiles as they pushed and shoved each other to squeeze into the already long queue in the aisle for the door. Not wishing to be conspicuous by being last out I followed suit, exuding goodwill with a wide smile while forcing my way into the line using my flight bag, elbows and hips for some not so subtle leverage. .

The usual blast of hot air common to the tropics greeted me at the door. Outside all was Polynesian informality. A burning sun bore down relentlessly, immediately sweat began to stain my shirt. The air was filled with the oily smell of coconuts. Official greeters rushed forward with sweet-smelling leis of hibiscus flowers to adorn the necks of arriving friends or relatives. Ukuleles strummed, while outside the fence a mixed voice choir began the 'Friendlies' song of welcome as only Polynesians could. Soon there were more greeters than passengers jammed in the entryway of the open-air building. Laughter, hugs, cuddles, tears, back slapping, solemn hand shaking, even a nose rub or two, it was all there.

With no sign of the baggage being unloaded and everyone milling around it was going to be some time before customs and immigration checks were made. To the locals time meant nothing. No one took any notice when I moved away from the welcoming groups to take in the scene that was brilliant in colour and very happy in sound.

The BAC's cargo doors opened, piece by piece baggage began to fill several hand-drawn trolleys. Stacked high, the trolleys were then wheeled to the baggage collection section that was a long table-like platform at the front of the terminal. Voices rose as the more impatient passengers pointed and called for personal service from the handlers.

With so little air traffic to be handled, surely the elaborate tower was a financial extravagance were my thoughts when the tall, glass-capped sentinel of white cement came into view. While wondering about the reasons for such a large structure in the faraway 'Friendlies', much to my relief the Aztec was spotted scudding across the palms beyond the runway before banking in for landing.

With both engines ticking over quietly it taxied to a grassed area ahead of the parked BAC One-Eleven, before stopping alongside a wire cage that housed a number of fuel drums, hoses and other such-like fuelling equipment. My heart missed a beat or two now as for the first time I was faced with just how 'gassing up' would be done for the Aztec's flight to Sydney. That very necessary item hadn't been talked about in the rush before leaving. In the scramble to depart the means whereby fuel could be obtained covertly at a place where everybody knew everybody, had been overlooked. Most major airports have mobile tankers or bowsers that are available for all approved operators, fuelling is relatively easy. In the 'Friendlies' it appeared, things were different. Fuel for the local operator was under their own control. The fuel problem would have to be worked out somehow. Had that thought crossed my mind before departure from Sydney the flight might never have been accepted, using my initiative was going to be put to the test.

Even from a distance the Aztec showed evidence of almost twelve months hard usage while being maintained in the open in hot, humid and wet tropical weather. The white and blue trim paint scheme showed signs of fading, engine cowls were streaked with oil and a flat oleo strut gave the low-wing monoplane a lopsided appearance as it pivoted on the inner wheel before parking.

As one, both engines wound down to a stop, the door on the right side above the wing was flung open. Two huge islander men dressed in the traditional 'Friendlies' sulu (kilt-like skirt) spotless white shirt, obviously in a hurry, began to climb out to sidle down the walkway to the step inboard and behind the trailing edge of the wing. Both made heavy going of it while the small 'plane wobbled and shook. Judging by their size, guessed as more than 170 Kilos, the two together with an average weight pilot, would constitute a maximum load for the tired looking Aztec. The 'plane's tail almost contacted the ground as each man used the rear step. When both were off the wing and on the ground, of its' own accord the partly flat oleo sprang back into place. With what could be taken as a sigh of relief the wings became level again. A heavily built pilot, with an agility born of long familiarity with the 'plane, followed the two giants down the wing and on to the ground. After exchanging a few words to an attendant, the three hurried past the parked airliner to the terminal without so much as a glance in my direction.

Keeping out of sight from those in the open-sided building as much as possible, with my Yashica on a strap around my neck I sauntered along the fence and across the sizzling hot tarmac forward of the BAC One Eleven. There was no sign of a security official, as common to all of Polynesia the airport was run quite casually, it was not uncommon for tourists to have the freedom after arriving to wander on to the operating area to photograph their metal bird from close up.

Where the bitumen ended about 25 metres from the BAC's nose, my camera came into play focusing on the Aztec, where a big Polynesian attendant in white overalls was dragging luggage from a side-opening locker at the rear of the cabin. For the benefit of anyone who might be watching the shots were faked, the main reason being that my Yashica was out of film. My intention had been to purchase film in Sydney as my journey progressed, supplies of the appropriate rolls of celluloid in the highlands of New Guinea were sometimes unavailable, or well over their 'use-by' date. Moving closer to the smaller 'plane where the attendant seemed friendly enough the time seemed ripe for a 'friendly' call.

"What is your name, is it alright to take a picture of your 'plane, you too, if you want to be in it?"

He dropped the basket he was holding as one would a hot potato, straightened the collar on his overalls and stood straight as the statue of a King, one arm resting on the wing. The camera was brought into action only as a pointer, my voice deliberately disinterested when next I spoke while squizzing through the lens.

"OK that's good, move just a little further over that way, what's your name again, more yet, that's enough, good one, where has the 'plane come from just now? "

"My name Wesley, he comes from up island, can I have one picture? "

We shook hands. "Of course Wesley, this is not a Polaroid camera though, first the film must be developed, I'll get one for you and bring it when next I come to the airport, are you going to put fuel in the 'plane now?"

"Cannot, all benzene for 'plane is finished, tanker has not yet come from Suva, one week more yet."

"Do you mean to say there is no benzene for your 'plane anywhere here? " I questioned, my voice rather mournful, using the 'pidgin' term for petrol or avgas while trying not to sound too interested in the kingdom's affairs.

The big man shrugged his shoulders and cast his eyes down.

"Big 'plane has fuel, small 'plane not, ship that brings benzene goes to Suva, there's some trouble there, no benzene here yet, ship must go on slip." With that came the need for me to dig deeper.

"So your 'plane cannot fly at all until the ship comes with the benzene. Is that right? "

Wesley seemed to have had enough of my questions. He walked around the wing tip and began to open the small locker in the nose.

"Pilot say he 'nuf benzene for one trip tomorrow, that's all. Now I must take these bags over to big 'plane." He mumbled. The interview was over.

"Well goodbye then. If it turns out I'll get a picture for you." I muttered, my voice loaded with despondency.

As I strolled back to the terminal my mind was full of dark thoughts at the prospect of an enforced stay in the islands with certain folk who might not be so very friendly after all.

With arrival formalities completed and luggage in hand at the front of the terminal taxis were at a premium. A small, rusty Japanese model was shared with two oversized islanders whose string baskets occupied most of the rear seat and floor, that forced me to sit with my knees under my chin with other baskets serving as arm rests. Both my companions seemed on good terms with the driver and took little notice of me. Avoiding eye contact with them, all my concentration went on the scenery. With the setback over the absence of fuel playing on my mind and being submerged in gloomy thought, social banter had no place in my mood as the taxi left the airport and joined the road to town.

White dust from the coral-sand roadway swirled in through open windows and holes in the floor, threatening to choke me. At a pace much too fast for the conditions we wound our way past dozens of farm carts drawn by skinny, depressed looking ponies. Most were loaded, overloaded would be a better description, with coconuts and other produce, while some carried live animals, pigs and fowls as well as passengers young and old.

The driver had his mind set on his decrepit taxi owning the road. Without letting up on the accelerator, cracked exhaust blaring like a Harley, he tore along, honking the horn incessantly. Panic-stricken horses, their carts loaded with squawking fowls and squealing pigs, made for the nearest side of the road while the taxi swept past without a falter. Several times I found myself ducking my head below the back of the front seat in anticipation of the crash which never came.

On the outskirts of town where the dusty, coronous road became tar-sealed, the two islanders disembarked, laughing by that time, giving the driver a slap on the back or a knowing nod of the head as they went. With the baskets gone, the rest of the journey was comparatively comfortable, save for odd particles of dust or grit flying up through holes in the floor from the wheels. For the first time, the driver turned his attention to me.

"Hotel have big party tonight, Friendly Islands welcome for tourist, many will come from ship, dancing, singing, you will enjoy, all tourist from ship go there."

He turned into the white gravel, palm-fringed driveway of the Royal Sunrise, stopping at the foot of a broad flight of steps leading to the entrance. Polynesian carvings by the dozen adorned the walls and floor on each side of the doors. As I dusted myself off, a uniformed porter in the traditional sulu and military-style high-collar white jacket, retrieved my dusty bags from the trunk. The fare was to be the equivalent of thirty Australian dollars I discovered, which was twice the amount announced on the BAC flight. The local 'sting' was about to raise its head. An inkling of an idea was forming in my mind, a friendly relationship with a taxi driver that I could lean on for cheating in those foreign parts, might well work in my favour.

"I have no local currency yet." I told him noting that he was finding it difficult to look me in the eye. "You wait while I get money changed, what's your name? "

"Me Toutai." he replied, pointing to the name on the door of his taxi. "I stay in car outside, across road there."

At the counter, the Polynesian female receptionist large in size and with a real friendly smile, held up a copy of an aircraft passenger manifest which was the booking list, running a finger down the list of names. An upside down quick glance told me my name wasn't on that list, which had been sent from Suva the night before my departure.

"I don't see your name on our list for room booking, you came in Toutais taxi. Our bus should bring you from airport, they not tell you, the bus-driver should have called you. The airline people are always making mistakes like that. "

I drew a deep breath. " No one called me that I know of, that's a pity, yes there must have been a mistake, I'm sure a booking was made for me through the airline a week ago, they forgot to tell you eh, I hope no harm's been done, you have a room for me? "

I waited as she pondered over the complexity of the issue while running a pencil through her long black hair. Then came the official verdict.

"We don't accept casual people without a booking" she piped. "That is government rule. Now the airline people make mistake, I will give you a room. You have passport that is kept here, how many nights will you be staying for? " That was something of a surprise. The thought of being separated from my passport didn't go over well with me.

"I will be in the islands for up to seven days. Sometimes I will not be staying in your hotel." I explained as she wrote down some details in a register. "Fishing trips, boating, diving, sightseeing, that sort of thing, visits to other islands even."

As she turned to the row of pigeon holes behind her, she talked over her shoulder.

"Minimum booking here is two nights, here is your room key, our porter will show you where to go."

"My passport, may I have it please, I might need it." I pleaded.

She smiled sweetly. "Here we must keep your passport in your room mailbox. Police might check, government rule, it will be safe, police will not ask for it unless you very naughty boy. When you leave hotel, you return key, pay account, we give you passport."

Rather helplessly, I watched as without showing any interest whatever in the passports personal details she slid it into the recess above the number of my room.

After cashing a traveller's cheque to local currency I walked out to Toutai's taxi. His eyes gleamed with avarice when he spotted the fifty in my hand. "I have no change but you not worry, I stay here always, everyone knows Toutai, I bring you change Mr Bryan when I get from tourist tonight, I not cheat you."

So audacious was that coming from a man who had already stung me, I could have laughed. In a childishly simple way Toutai was after a 'double banger'. Still turning over a muddled plan in my head, instinct told me that he could be used later in some way a good relationship was highly desirable. I thought it better to trust him and not complain about his friends' free' ride on my account although I couldn't remember giving him my name. He must have spotted the tag on my flight bag where, thanks to wear and tear, my surname had been partly obliterated. Toutai was smarter than he looked.

"Since you operate from around here through the night" I murmured. "I'll collect my change sometime then, if that's OK with you "

In my room, feeling a bit dejected over the turn of events I stripped down to my skivvies and lay on the bed, air-con at maximum full blast and not quite coping. That the kingdom could run out of aviation fuel had never entered my head, nor Dee's obviously. I was in a jam and knew it. The difficulty of getting fuelled with avgas had never been considered in the hurried planning. Time and time again I ran over some of the options at my disposal although there weren't a lot. The safe arrival of the island 'tanker' would only fix part of the problem. There was still the matter of acquisition.

When filled, the 50-US-gallon drums in which avgas was transported in those parts, weighed more than 150 kilos, a hand pump would also be required.

My guess was that the stocks of fuel would be held by a government agency somewhere, for use only by the local air service and would not be for sale. Any inquiry by me over fuel would fall into the suspicious category.

Transporting the heavy drums to the airport for such a covert operation would be impossible even given the availability of a driver with a suitable vehicle. Too many of the tiny kingdom's citizens would learn of the plan for the aircraft. To conscript a local person into helping was ruled out as being too risky, Dee hadn't been able to name anyone who might be an ally. I was on my own in what could be called a hostile environment where my intentions might be seen by some as being criminal. I was then driven by the thought that I had to act quickly or be stranded there for weeks.

The afternoon slipped away as scheme after scheme was turned over in my mind as I strolled through the island town, lost amongst the hordes of tourists purchasing film or 'gawking' at the King's Palace.

Hot and tired I returned to the hotel, drew the blinds until only a chink of light came in through the louvers, upped the air-con, undressed to skivvies and flopped on to the bed again. Outside, the light was fading, the deeper than expected 'doze' was accompanied by the hypnotic whirring sound of the ageing air-con.

When I awoke, eerie flashes of lightning lit the sky to the north-west. Thunder rumbled, black clouds hanging over the town shortened the tropical twilight even more. The air was hot and humid as the sounds of a thunderstorm drew nearer.

Feeling heavy after one of those quick, deep sleeps I showered for ten minutes letting lukewarm water stream over my body. When patting myself dry with a towel, a possible solution suddenly hit me, a simple one, missed before for some reason.

Clearing the room's writing table of all the clutter of hotel and tourist information, with my computer, charts, parallel rules and dividers, I went over the flight plan again, paying particular attention to the first compulsory over water hop to Nandi airport, on the west side of the island of Viti Levu in the Fiji group.

On completion, I knew that the key to any successful flyaway lay in just how much fuel remained in the tanks of the Aztec as it stood at the airport. I'd learned from Wesley that the pilot was planning a trip the following day. There must be fuel enough aboard for such a trip. Just how much was the question I needed an answer to.

Several of the inter-island destinations used by the operator were less than a hundred miles from the capital. However, by my estimation the most likely destination for the 'plane would be a well-known cluster of islands to the north, a distance of about 150 miles. A computer wasn't required to tell me that the total distance of a return trip still fell far short of a single leg to Nandi. Somehow I had to know just how much fuel remained in the Aztec's tanks before morning, but how?

I'd not eaten much since leaving Sydney, my stomach was grumbling as I paced the room pondering on the problem until it was time for a meal.

In the dining room, the head-waiter showed me to an afterthought of a table, set in a corner recess bordered with leafy pot plants.

"Sorry sir." he apologized while setting a chair for me. "You can sit here. Tonight many tourist will come from ship, all other tables reserved already. Soon there will be singing, dancing, you will enjoy."

Actually I couldn't have asked for anything better. I was in no mood for small talk which would come with the sharing of a table with a stranger. Being partly hidden behind the shrubbery suited me fine. My delicious prawn and avocado cocktail was only half disposed of when a mixed bag of diners trooped to a table marked 'RE-SERVED', a couple of yards around the corner, that left only part of their table visible through the shrubs.

Anyone who has visited Polynesia will know how easy it is to recognize a tourist in those parts. To the islanders, a tourist's mode of dress can be either comical or offensive. In many ways Polynesians are much more modest than westerners. The ladies getting seated at the table wore shorts that were far too brief for their chubby limbs, while their red, sunburnt shoulders were girded with leis of sweet smelling hibiscus. Hotel dress rules were relaxed on tourist ship nights. Locally made straw hats, only recently acquired by the look, dangled from sunburnt hands or were hung about the waist with the chin cord. That night, sunglasses parked on reddish foreheads were the fashion. The men in the party all wore khaki 'Bombay Bloomers' with loose fitting aloha shirts, the requisite sunglasses also draped on cords around their necks. Knee-length socks sprang from African half boots and disappeared into the cuffs of the 'bloomers'.

The only exception to the style 'a la mode' was their guide or host. He ushered everyone to their seats amid giggles, a stumble or two and jovial, frivolous sounding chatter. A big man, he wore dark coloured slacks topped with a short-sleeved white shirt with military style pockets and shoulder tabs, the uniform shirt of a pilot the world over. All the party looked and acted as if they were well in their cups. Before he took his seat at the head of the table with his back to me, he was recognized as the pilot of the Aztec who was entertaining clients, friends, relatives or visitors from the ship.

With my head down and my ears pricked I concentrated on the cocktail, never even glancing in their direction. It wasn't long before voices became raised, corks popped and glasses clinked. I listened intently. Rewards soon came.

"Sorry, I won't be able to see you off tomorrow." I heard him say. "I've got to fly darn it, you'll be out to sea before I return but I might be able to give your ship a buzz on the way in. You know what? The blasted island's run out of avgas, that is aircraft fuel, when I get back from my trip in the morning, that'll be the finish until the so-called tanker gets here from Suva. I'll get a few days off to go fishing, how's that for organization, can you imagine, like the pub with no beer, we're the air service without a 'plane. "

Sitting there behind the foliage my mind was made up. The band was strumming a fast beat. When the pilot escorted one of his lady friends to the dance floor for their own variation of the hula, I chose the moment to make my exit. With the room key in my pocket I went straight to my room without stopping at reception.

The hands on the bedside clock showed three a.m. when fully dressed I peeped out from the door of my room feeling more than a little guilty over the upcoming nocturnal adventure. Finding the dimly lit corridor deserted a few cautious steps took me to the head of the stairs leading to the lobby. Looking down from the half-pace, I could see a fat night watchman sprawled out on a couch behind the counter. Intentionally or not, he presented a formidable obstacle to the successful retrieval of my passport from the row of pigeon holes above his fat belly. Otherwise, the lobby was also deserted.

A minute passed while I chewed things over as I took in the scene. I needed to work out a way to substitute the envelope that held my room key and the estimated amount of cash required for payment of my bill, for my passport from the pigeon hole.

To sound out whether or not the guard was in a deep sleep, I shuffled across the deserted lobby with my soft-soled shoes making little sound. My two small bags were deposited silently, close to the heavy, grotesquely carved main doorframes while I turned and listened. Hotel security snored on without interruption. Bending low, I crept across the floor to the low security door at the end of the counter. My heart pounded when within six feet of the sleeping giant, the half-door was seen to be held shut by a bolt on the inside, which meant leaning over the door to jiggle the bolt free without making any noise that might disturb the sleeper. That wasn't so easy, the fitting was tight. Up and down went the handle of the bolt while I tried various pressures to free the door without the sound of metal on metal shattering the air.

The bolt needed jiggling a number of times before coming free. More cautiously then, the short door was pushed open as I edged my way into the inner sanctum. Snuffling softly, the night guard slept on. Lingering in the stuffy air was the smell of recently unwashed body and stale beer, as I reached to draw the passport out from its receptacle. With the passport came a guest message-slip that fluttered to the floor beside the couch. Now was not the time for any reading of the note. After sliding the envelope into the pigeonhole, I scooped the bit of paper up and shoved it into a shirt pocket. Without even a squeak, I retreated slowly across the shiny floor of the lobby towards the doors breathing a little easier, only to find that another obstacle to a successful exit had presented itself. The main doors were secured from the inside by a large flat chrome bar that was hinged at one end. Obviously, the guard's duties included protecting the office while maintaining a 'dog-watch' on the door for any latecomers. Should anyone requiring entry arrive then my game would be up as they would create enough noise to wake the sleeper. Shading my eyes from reflections, with my nose pressed to a glass panel on the door I took a quick look outside. Luck was with me, the immediate driveway and the porch were deserted.

From outside, there was no way to secure the door again, but that was the least of my worries. The bar was extremely tight in its supports. While with one eye on the counter and the other constantly scanning the porch, some muscle was also needed to free the bar.

Sweat began to drip off me as I wrestled with it, until rattling and creaking, suddenly the bar came free with a 'crack' as loud as a rifle shot. I pulled the door open just enough to let me through with my two light bags. In seconds I was outside and never looking back, crossing the driveway in search of Toutai's cab.

Heavy clouds hid the moon. A gentle breeze rustled the tall palms lining the driveway. Only the rumble of distant thunder and the crunch of my feet on the gravel broke the silence. The air smelt of rain. Eerie light coming from faraway flashes of lightning lit the path as I scuttled past sweet-scented frangipani bushes on a patch of the hotel's lawn.

Toutai's now more familiar vehicle was found on the grass verge across from the hotel. Out to the world he lay sprawled across the rear seat with one leg hanging out an open door on the left side. I was again greeted with the smell of sweat and stale beer as I leaned in, while shaking his leg.

"Toutai wake up, I've come for the money you owe me, wake up."

Muttering incoherently while rubbing his eyes slowly he began to stir. My two bags were kept from his view as he eased himself out. When he was standing and getting his eyes focused, I tossed the bags on to the rear seat while climbing into the front passenger seat. We were through the darkened town, on to the gravel section of the road before he was fully functional. Adding bribery to corruption I explained briefly that he could keep the change of the trip from the airport and I'd give him more for such an early morning ride. That seemed to cheer him up.

"But sir, what time is now, early morning yet, 'plane not go now, why you go there? " he muttered.

"I've just remembered that I left some of my fishing tackle there. I must have it before morning, you will wait while I look then bring me back? " I replied somewhat deceitfully.

"Government building will be closed, locked, we not allowed in there night time when airport is closed, I get into much trouble."

My tones then were pleading, whining, coaxing.

"I put the gear down beside the building while I was taking photo. It will be easy to find."

Toutai could be heard grumbling to himself as he continued to speed along the lonely, deserted road. Occasionally the weak headlights picked out a skinny, pitiful looking dog slinking along the verges on a night prowl. After a few minutes, flakes of rain begin to mix with the thick dust on the windscreen.

"The wipers don't go." Toutai said by way of explanation as he stopped to wipe the grime away with a bare hand before getting behind the wheel again.

The airport was shrouded in darkness, not a light showed as we swung in through the main entrance.

"Keep going Toutai, stop up there beside the Tower." I called.

The car's lights picked up the Aztec, standing forlornly where last seen. Purposely I made no remark, as if the 'plane was of no interest to me whatsoever.

Before Toutai could come up with any questions I clambered out, grabbed my bags from the back seat and reached for my wallet. Even in the poor light I could see his eyes glitter when he spotted the two notes I pressed into his sweaty palm.

"Turn your lights off before your battery goes flat. You wait here while I go and look."

My best commanding voice was used that time, my intentions being a dip of the Aztec's tanks before firming up on a plan.

"But this not place you say Mister Bryan." I heard him stammer, his head stuck out of the door window as I cut around the corner of the tower and out of sight.

Moving in an arc and keeping the building between us allowed the Aztec to be approached from the opposite side. My trousers were soon soaked to the knees from the long, wet grass. Stealthily, I climbed on to the wing and tried the door. A sigh of relief welled up when a half-turn of the handle brought the door open. My small flashlight soon helped me to find the master switch and flip it on to check the fuel gauges. Two gauges served four tanks. No pilot with any sense believes gauges to be infallible. All they told me was that the tanks would have to be dipped for any degree of accuracy.

Airmen are creatures of tradition, the 'plane's fuel dipstick was found easily and exactly where expected, in a pocket on the wall next to a pilot's left knee. That saved a search for the one in my flight bag that Dee had given me. A light rain had started to fall, increasing the already poor light, which slowed the task of dipping the tanks, reading the dipstick and checking the oil levels in each engine. .

I was about to finish with the second engine when Toutai's taxi was heard starting up, followed by a long blast from the horn as he began to turn around. Before the lights reached me I dived under the wing. The lights lit up the Aztec only for a second or two without any hesitation. After a gravel-raising skidding turn and the rattle of flying stones resounding in the air, Toutai's taxi was last seen by it's one faltering tail light, speeding off past the terminal and out to the road.

Watching that one and only tail light recede, I somehow knew he wouldn't be coming back. Either he had woken up to the fact that I was up to something he didn't quite understand or he was scared of officialdom. Having been well paid in advance he'd decided to retire from the game prematurely. Later, if accused of leaving me stranded, he could and would no doubt, plead a misunderstanding as to his waiting. However, my biggest worry now was that he might have gone to raise the alarm about a mad European by the name of Mister Bryan on the loose at the airport.

Everyone knows, or is related to everyone in the 'Friendlies'. If Toutai was about to make a report it would take thirty or forty minutes for the local gendarmerie to arrive. Unless I was mistaken, knowing a little of Pacific Islanders' nocturnal habits, some considerable time would be required for Toutai to arouse and assemble anyone willing enough to accept his story then journey to the airport at such an un-godly hour.

Throwing caution to the winds, with nervous hands I fumbled for the interior switches that were needed to throw some light on the route chart to allow me to calculate as to whether the fuel remaining in the tanks would make a flight to Nandi in Fiji possible.

Rain pattered down on to the metal fuselage as the storm approached. With the door closed, the air inside was thick and oppressive. Globules of sweat dripped from my brow on to the chart as I worked, sometimes having to hold the chart or computer close up to the light for reading. The four tanks had dipped to a total of 65 gallons. Much to my disappointment the calculations in no way favoured a flight to Nandi.

Taking into account that some of the fuel, probably five gallons, would be unusable, the Aztec would run out of fuel half an hours flying time from Nandi assuming that a direct track and normal cruising speed could be maintained. Inwardly I gave myself the privilege of a re-think, on its own the fuel problem could see me trapped on the island for a week if not more.

Clambering out into the rain, I used my flashlight to pick out a short pole on the ground alongside the wire compound. In the hope that some of the drums inside the heavy wire netting might hold some left-over fuel, the pole was poked through gaps in the wire and jabbed at any drum in range. My brainwave was not rewarded, only a hollow sounding 'ding' was heard each time the pole made contact with a drum. Several of the drums were seen to be tilted over, with their caps parked on top, a sure sign they were empty and were being aired of fumes prior to them being returned to the fuel agents.

The certainty of failure to seize the aircraft, due to the non-availability of fuel was then uppermost in my mind. Several other 'brain-waves' mocked me too. Maybe in the poor light the dipstick had not been read correctly? With the coming of daylight, still more than two hours away, a more accurate reading might change the scene to make a flight to Nandi possible. On the other hand, daylight would bring with it airport workers, passengers and possibly the pilot himself, as intelligence so far gathered hadn't included the expected departure time of the Aztec's morning flight.

While thinking things over with my flashlight getting weaker by the minute, the aircraft was given a once-over with the covers coming off and her skin checked for any dents or damage. When large droplets began to drum Pacific tunes on the hollow aluminium wings and cabin, seeking the shelter of the cabin I shuffled up the wing again.

While I ducked down to gain the piloting seat. the cockpit was lighted by distant sheet lightning that turned a black night an eerie light blue. In only a few seconds the light faded leaving only two daubs of white light, low down on the horizon. My heart thumped as I stared. Without a doubt the two lights were the headlights of a car on the airport road, not much more than a mile away. In a flash my mind was made up. Settling down into my comfort zone behind the control wheel and without thought I went into a check of the control surfaces by moving the wheel, the column and the rudder through their full range, a check that only took a few seconds.

Before the car or whatever it was would have travelled three hundred meters, I had hit the master switch, buckled up, selected the fuel cocks to the fullest tanks, set throttles, mixture levers, prop controls and magnetos for the start. A further three hundred meters for the car saw me with my fingers feeling for the starter rocker switch as I peered out into the now rain-soaked night through the tiny bad weather window. Twisting the switch to the left, six, eight, ten rotations of the prop were counted without even a hint of a start. My gut was in a knot. What drove me on from there remains a mystery as at that time an intention to leave had not entered my head, at least not until dawn after having made some more precise calculations.

Every type of aero engine has its own particular starting technique to be followed. Suddenly I remembered that in my haste the fuel booster pump had been forgotten. Slowly, deliberately, with every fibre in my body telling me to hurry, I took a deep breath.

Starting engines on almost any aircraft fitted with carburettors is an exercise that must be learnt. Starts can be finicky, with only a very thin line between success and failure, the main problem being too little or too much fuel being fed through the carburettor to the engine. One has to be careful not to over prime. Fouling a start with too much fuel can cause a fire, or the carburettor can become 'flooded'. In the latter case, a wait of several minutes to give time for the fuel to drain out might be necessary before attempting another start. Many an allied airman in WW2 missed an opportunity to escape through not being able to start the engine of an enemy aircraft he hoped to purloin.

A pilot who flies the same aircraft constantly such as a private owner, soon gets to know his engine's idiosyncrasies. For someone unfamiliar with a particular aircraft starting can sometimes be embarrassing, there's always the chance of flattening the battery. Lady Luck plays a big part.

As the lights drew closer, a search began again for the booster pump switches and the starter rocker switch. Seconds were lost as my hand fumbled across the darkened panel. I was rewarded with a loud bang as the engine fired up after only a few rather weak rotations.

The engine was set to run at a fast idle speed while I worked on getting the right one going. My worry then was that the battery might give up. Using the flashlight I checked the ammeter under the right hand instrument panel. The good news was that the battery was alive and charging from the generator, the applicable engine instruments 'born again'.

By that time the headlights were at the last straight stretch of roadway before the main entrance, less than half a minute away. The right engine was again different from the left, preferring a lot of fuel. My hand twisted the switch to the right harder and harder as if a heavy pressure was the only way to get those cylinders firing. With my right hand I flipped the booster pump on and off, jiggled the mixture lever, while counting a heart-stopping twenty blades before the engine fired into life.

A glance over my shoulder saw the lights of the car passing the terminal, only 70 meters from the Aztec, its lights, much stronger than those of Toutai's taxi already had the Aztec targeted. The vehicle's speedy arrival on the darkened airport at such an early hour had something to do with me, which was obvious. Toutai would not have had time to return from the town after notifying a hotel official or the police. The vehicle certainly wasn't his taxi. Whoever it was, I wasn't willing to wait to find out, I knew what had to be done.

The cockpit was then filled with light as the car came to a stop on the bitumen, aimed obliquely at the aircraft, by its shape a similar make as Toutai's. The guess was that he had parked in front of the well-worn path used by the aircraft to taxi from the grass, as a precaution against the aircraft gaining the sealed tarmac should it decide to move out. A shadowy figure blocked the light as someone ran towards the aircraft.

There was something sinister about his movement that triggered me into action. The next few minutes were a blur of confusion. Releasing the pedal brakes, I thrust the throttle levers forward. Both engines backfired as the 'plane leapt ahead to chop a path through the long grass with the props. Of its own accord the control wheel began to wriggle, thumping as it hit the stops as 'that someone' grabbed an aileron and worked it up and down. With the aircraft now rolling my control wheel was slamming up and down in a positive, firm action without any help from me.

The ailerons, the hinged section on the outboard trailing edge of an aircraft wing, are connected to the pilot's control wheel by cables. Moving the control wheel moves the aileron, or conversely, moving the aileron up or down moves the control wheel or 'stick' on some aircraft, although they're not meant to be used that way. Although not in the rulebook, that method is sometimes used to attract the pilot's attention when the aircraft is stationary on the ground with engines running. The conclusion I came to was that whoever was waggling the aileron must know about aeroplanes and their controls, certainly not Toutai and probably not the police or any other local official.

Unable now to roll on to the bitumen with the car blocking the way, I motored forward, with both props slashing at the long grass. At that time there was no way of telling what speed the old bird was making as we bumped and slashed along, lighted only by the car's headlights. Realizing that couldn't go on forever I booted on the right brake, gunned the left engine and swung towards where the bitumen should be, while I searched frantically for the landing light switch.

The control wheel gave it's last flutter, whoever it was who had signalled via the control surfaces had either fallen, slipped, or been forced to give up by having to slog through the long wet grass against the blast of wet air coming from the props. Simultaneously an angry shout was heard above the noise of the engines, followed by a loud thump and thrashing sounds, as some sort of a missile bounced across the wing and on to the engine nacelle, to be splattered into fragments that hit the windshield and cockpit canopy as watery mud. Little wonder the thrower was angry, rain lashed by the slipstream was then pelting down, he would be drenched.

After more fumbling, the landing light came on, my eyes searched for the narrow strip of taxiway that led to the runway. With the landing light now supported by the car's headlights the right prop could be seen whirling away tho' having suffered some damage to the tips of each blade. From that moment I knew I wasn't going to stop, although I had no real plan for continuing. Whoever had thrown the missile meant business, dirty business.

Apart from a peculiar whistling sound that only a tuned ear could detect, no vibrations or other ill effects could be felt. Because of the suddenness of the missile's arrival and the angry voice heard a decision was made that to stop and negotiate wasn't on the agenda. Acrimonies, courts, fast-talking lawyers and officials were not for me.

Unsure as to whether the route being followed might hide a drainage ditch or something worse, a zig-zag course was started in an effort to move the lights across a wider arc. The rain bucketed down now making the taxiway hard to find until I fluked a sighting of it and eased off on the power. A heavy thump at the sharp end told me that the nose-wheel had mounted the raised edge of the taxiway, bringing to an end the sound of the props slashing the grass, magically the ride became smoother, but with the whistle from the damaged prop now more pronounced.

Taxying on the seal with virtually no forward visibility became the next problem. Slowing down a notch or two, my eyes began searching for the runway's centre-line that would lead me to the broader 'piano keys' at either threshold. Alarm bells rang. Not for a second did I dare to look away from taxying so as to remain on the shiny black surface. The car's lights then told me that it was beginning to follow. For the first time I was scared.

The taxiway melded with the runway about halfway down its length. Once there back tracking one way or the other would have to be made to gain distance for a take-off. Should the car reach that point ahead of me it could easily block entry to the runway. From the cockpit, with the darkness not offering a reference as to rate of movement plus a confusion of lighting on a runway glossy with rain, the speed was misjudged badly. Dragging both throttles back my feet jabbed at the brakes on realizing that the runway centre-line was nowhere to be seen. The Aztec came to a skidding halt, possibly cock-eyed across the runway. More than anything on the dark surface, a sight of the broken white line lying under more than an inch of water was number one priority, that meant me being brutal with brakes and throttle with the Aztec slewing to the right. The move was partly thwarted by the lights from the car blinding me even more. The reflections from the oily looking, rain soaked bitumen and the intermittent glare from flashes of lightning made the search even harder.

My eyes stung from the mixture of water and sweat running down my face. There'd been no opportunity to get radios on line or connect my headset. For a period far too long I was uncertain as to whether the Aztec was facing across the runway or down its length. My hands were full using the flashlight to read the magnetic compass.

The vehicle's headlights were now bright enough to give me a better look at the runway. Through the tearing rain I saw enough to allow me to align the aircraft parallel to the prominent white cone markers on the grass verge, a few meters out from the bitumen.

Coming along the taxiway to join the runway as it was, the chase vehicle could head me off like a stockman rounding up cattle, in seconds either 'plane or car would need to alter direction or collide and I was determined that it wasn't going to be me.

Keeping the cone markers in view through the rain while guessing the distance from them to the runway was my main objective as I slammed the throttle levers forward.

With little warm-up time both engines coughed, spluttered and almost died out until the levers were pulled back and jiggled a couple of times before being advanced again more slowly. Magneto checks, props and instruments and a dozen other pre-take-off semi-vital actions were forgotten as I strove to outpace my pursuer. Props surged, acceleration faltered momentarily then regained itself again as the props bit the air. The two 'searchlights' were now perilously close inboard and not far behind the trailing edge of the right wing.

Steering by the cone markers alone shifted when a quick glance at the directional gyro told me that the aircraft was headed roughly in the right direction. The sudden surge pressed me back into the seat. The car began to drift back, unable to keep pace probably because of the limited visibility caused by the slipstream blasting water on to his windscreen.

Next the lights were seen to be moving more to one side, as if the driver was attempting to get clear of the slipstream, draw level with the wingtip and force me off the runway. If that was the intention, it was a mistake that cost him the race, for the side he chose took his vehicle close to the edge of the bitumen and into the rough, not only had he run out of space but he'd lost traction or control on the greasy soil adjoining the bitumen. With my hands and feet fully occupied in the battle to keep to the bitumen and making adjustments to throttles, props or trims, the car's antics were no longer a worry, it was time to say goodbye. As if aware of my needs, both engines roared evenly under full power, the whistle from the right prop no more a worry.

The familiar sounds, the feel of approaching flight, engines humming, the firming up of flight controls, air rustling over the cabin, brought with them a heady sort of elation for me. The adrenalin flow, the hype that comes from being in a dangerous situation tingled in my every nerve, the tiny aircraft was now running with me. For the first time I felt that I was in charge, with the Aztec also eager for the run into the air.

Oblivious to the ugly scene being left behind I was balanced on a knife-edge of anticipation. Shutting out all other thoughts, my mind was set only to the challenges of take-off along half of an unlighted runway with my tail to a strong cross-wind, in darkness and rain that reduced visibility to the distance between two cone markers.

The two Lycoming engines held maximum power without a stutter. As a jockey in the Melbourne Cup might I hunched forward into the take-off. The needle on the right engine's rev counter waved regularly and evenly over a range of less than 25 revs a minute, which would mean that the prop was slightly out of balance. Nothing could be heard above the roar of the engines and the ripping, drumming sounds of heavy rain on the frame.

In such wet conditions the chase vehicle could not match the acceleration of my propeller driven craft, the race was mine as the glare from his lights faded as the car began to fall back. In the many flashes of lightning, slanting rain was seen bashing down on the windshield. Strong wind gusts preceding the approaching thunderstorm strove to buffet the aircraft sideways as we hurtled down the blacked out runway.

On hindsight the take-off should never have been attempted. With my hands and feet fully occupied in basic control, there'd been no time to set the flaps. The take-off roll would be longer and faster over the ground than normal. By the control pressures required to keep straight on to the runway and the delay in elevator feel, the wind was judged to be coming from behind my right shoulder. The artificial horizon, no doubt well over its allotted overhaul time, was not fully erected. Nothing for it, but to hope and pray that from where the take-off began there would be enough distance left for a safe lift-off.

Comparing one instrument with another was vital, but with so little time to become familiar with the instrument panel layout since starting engines, my eye wasn't able to locate any of the necessary 'clocks' without a hesitant search. Little outside light now came into the cockpit, my eyes were riveted to the flying panel. The blind flying instruments would be required in seconds as I plunged along the runway into total blackout except for the reflection of a lightning flash or two. My mind raced to make sense of the messages that the instruments were sending, speed, direction, attitude, balance. The indicated speed on the dial was by now close to lift-off, the directional gyro steady enough to be called reasonably reliable, the artificial horizon showing a left-hand bank with the wheels firmly on the ground. My right hand flew to the panel to re-set the instrument, in went the knob, out it came, while I prayed that the baby 'plane on the dial would be sitting on the horizon bar before we became airborne. I was in a dilemma, a Catch 22 situation rather like riding a horse, dangerous at both ends, uncomfortable in the middle, to stop then would mean over-running the strip on to ground rough enough to wreck both 'plane and pilot, should it overturn and catch fire. To continue with taking off on primary instruments only, into a wild night sky, risked a stall or some other sort of loss of control.

Things were happening fast, there was no time for a leisurely debate, decision time allowed only a split second. My right hand flashed back to the throttle levers to hold them fully forward just as a brilliant, blinding flash of forked lightning suddenly lit up the sky directly ahead of the aircraft. Night became day, without a doubt the metal bird was heading straight into the path of the airman's worst enemy, a cumulo nimbus storm-cloud which would be full of violent, saturated swirling air. The turbulence inside a 'cu nimb' has brought many a 'plane down both large and small. That was certainly no place for a hastily prepared pilot in a poorly equipped aircraft in the dark of night.

My heart pounded, sweaty salt ran into my mouth to sting my tongue. Eerie blue light, mixed with the white of the landing lights to show up the 'piano keys' rushing towards me, together with the oversized white numerals painted on the runway near the western threshold. The cloud, brought closer by a vivid imagination was probably a kilometre away. The spunky little machine then had the speed but with a roaring tailwind and without take-off flap set, was going to need more distance to gather take-off speed. A decision was made to remain firmly on the tarseal until she was more than ready to go, to haul off into the air when at the numerals. A more convincing speed was needed but the tail wind was holding her down.

She crept into the air when the column was eased back, not leapt, sagging' while I fought to hold her up. The wheels couldn't have been more than a foot or two from the ground when the 'piano keys' slid below. The landing lights picked out scrub long grass and the rotting stumps of fallen trees that too must have been perilously close to the still dangling wheels. Without looking down, by memory I felt for the knob on the undercarriage retract lever, pressed the release clip and moved it up.

While the hairiest take-off I'd ever made seemed to have taken ages, in reality only fifteen seconds or so had elapsed since I'd first shoved on the throttles to rid me of the mystery vehicle that seemed to be hell bent on ramming some part of the aircraft. That however, wasn't the time for self-adulation or even a breath of relief. With some unexpected complications, the flight from the 'Friendlies' had commenced but the battle wasn't yet over.

The down-flow of extremely turbulent air in advance of the cloud could already be felt as the Aztec was 'nursed' up to 100 feet, clawing for height enough to clear the palms in the flight path. Blinding rain completely shut out the sound of the engines, the landing lights glared back through a wall of water. For many a heart-stopping moment, there was no way of telling when the struggle to fly might end in failure atop a Pacific palm taller than the rest.

In increasing turbulence we must have skimmed over the palms for a quarter of a mile before the rate of climb needle began to show a more positive ascent. The fierce wind laid the palm fronds over horizontally like wet mops in a gale. The little Piper was turning on a supreme effort in conditions that the frame had never been designed for with the fall-out from the storm holding her down. All I could do was ride along with her, easing off, flattening for speed before lifting her up with the elevator each time the speed dial showed an increase.

Operating in another consciousness all my focus was on the flying panel with my eyes darting from one instrument to the next, checking, cross-referring, unsure which might be the best to trust. As much as possible the gyro heading that had been plugged in before leaving the ground was maintained. Another flash lit up the massive cloud with its bulging walls. Fighting to stay level, we plunged into the seething mass of typhoon in miniature.

Savage, frenzied gusts then tore at the light frame, the bumps so hard that I believed a wing or wings could fold or an engine break away from its mounts. Tail and wings waved about like a bucking bronco, while I laid into ailerons, elevator and rudder, albeit as gently as could be, to keep the aircraft in a flying attitude. There were frightening times when our flight was expected to be short, when the application of full aileron failed to bring a wing up until we were well laid over on one side almost out of control. Sickening physiological sensations and doubts stirred my mind, as I waited for the controls to take over and return us to an even keel, only to fall away on the opposite side. We were flying in Hell.

Suddenly both engines chopped when in a sudden drop and fuel in the partially filled tanks was suspended weightless, exposing the tank outlets. Although my seat-belt was firm my head hit the ceiling with a wallop, as I rode suspended in space as an astronaut, my hands groping for the control column my feet for the pedals. As a sandstorm might engulf a 'plane over a desert, grit flew up from the floor as my flight bag which had been parked on the passenger seat, emptied its contents in mid air. As with most pilots my flight bag was about as tidy as a Russian horse-doctor's satchel, maps and charts, ancient papers, long forgotten bric a brac flew about the cockpit in all directions. A second later the engines came to life again. The sudden rise slammed me down hard in the seat with enough force to drag my jaw down and the flesh sag on my bones.

Panicky thoughts then went to the wings and engines. Would the attachments be able to take such a savage beating, something was bound to give. Would it be the wings that would crumple like cardboard to send the aircraft plummeting down in pieces into the earth or sea below.

Those first few seconds in that thundercloud as I fought for dear life will never be forgotten. For too long I lived in an exclusive world of dread in the dim fluorescence of a cockpit in turmoil. The instrumentation was not well lighted, my hands too busy on the controls to adjust the rheostats, even if they could be found. Continuous rain on the hull that sounded like a heavy canvas being ripped apart by a giant hand, drowned out all else except the too frequent cracks of lightning. Rough air, multiple stabs of turbulence, continually jerked at the frame the thought of the wings clapping hands was always before me. Erratically, the needle of the sensitive altimeter wound around the dial, first one way then the other as the cloud drew the Aztec up then suddenly dropped her down, sometimes in an eerie light or wrapped in the most terrible darkness. Rough air shouldn't be fought with the controls, instead the frail metal bird must be coaxed through by letting her ride the waves, without giving a thought to altitude or speed. Those instruments were both in a world of their own, dancing a light fantastic in time with the shaking and shuddering.

Everything was now happening in slow motion, all effort went into riding level with the bounces and surges that would leave a good deal of the control to the ship's inherent stability. That way the 'plane would not be over controlled, able to ride out the storm, much as a yacht would with sails reefed in a gale force wind and raging seas.

With my eyes smarting from the incessant jabs of brilliant lightning and no longer bothered by having to maintain a constant altitude or speed, power was reduced, not only to ride the turbulence better but with a mind set on conserving fuel. For the first time since starting the take-off I was able to sit back in the seat, consciously loosen my grip on the control wheel, tighten my seat harness, wiggle my toes and locate the switch to adjust the instrument panel lighting.

That terrible weather must have kept me immersed for twenty minutes or more, until when passing through a gap between fat, bulging walls, a star was seen flickering through a mist of rain before it was wiped out by the closed darkness of the cloud. Only for an instant was it seen, but it was enough for me to know there was a world outside the cockpit, enough to renew my hope and strength. While some of the early turbulence had abated we were still wading along in rain with invisible tentacles of updraft drawing the Aztec up rapidly with force enough to press me down in the seat.

For the first time since beginning the bumpy ride, most instruments except the altimeter, were steady. Several hard looks at the instrument were needed to convince me that I was reading aright. Altitude was rising through 13,000 feet at a rate around 1500 feet a minute while flying level in smooth, steady flight, with the power drawn back to less than fifty per cent of maximum.

As a glider might soar in a massive thermal, we were being drawn higher and higher into the atmosphere, although by the attitude and power setting, we should be descending quite rapidly. Worry was getting to me, until the ditty 'worry is like a rocking chair, it gives you something to do, but gets you nowhere,' came to me from out of the past. Something had to be done and quick. On a night of risks another had to be taken.

Following take-off, the heading of the runway which was almost the same as the air track for Nandi, had been maintained. Under the circumstances a decision was made to turn away from that course in a bid to fly out of the 'cu nim' zone and into better weather. There was a chance that the flight path first taken had been along the length of a storm line. Without radar to assist in finding better weather, turning right or left could only be a guess. Based on the fuel situation a right turn was decided on. Without a supply of oxygen a descent would be necessary to where the air was more breathable.

Over years of mountain flying in New Guinea my body had adjusted to being at higher altitudes without the use of oxygen, my tolerance then being about 15,000 feet for twenty minutes before taking a puff on the bottle. The poor light in the cabin was not enough for a check on my facial colour or the blueing of my fingertips, the first visible signs of oxygen starvation that I knew of (some aviation medicos will have varying opinions on that one).

Breathing slowly and deeply now I swung the Aztec 45 degrees to the right, pulled the power off and shoved her nose down sharply, only to find that she wouldn't go down but kept rising! 14,000 feet came and went, with still lots of pressure on my behind. Fascinated, I watched the airspeed increase while we rose at a considerable rate. There was nothing else that could be done but hold to the new heading and keep the nose down without building up excessive speed. My eyes wandered from the panel, the dreary fatigue of hopelessness that sometimes accompanies a tense air journey began to set in. With the increasing tension I was tiring faster in the thin air. The intense savagery of the storm, the meaning for the flight, had taken its toll on me physically and mentally. If that star had not been sighted, I could have given up and submitted to the storm's fury.

With a lurching, sagging bump suddenly we broke free of the cloud. Instantly stars were seen flickering above and ahead. For the first time since departure, the sky was relatively clear. I whooped with joy, expending more valuable oxygen. The rising continued albeit more slowly as if the updraft knew that further attempts would be futile, my control prompts were being accepted. My knuckles were seen to be white from gripping the wheel so tightly. Now was the time to wriggle fingers and toes, relax strained muscles and joints, suck in thicker air with some full, slow, deep breathing, exhaling by the mouth.

Down we went at 1000 feet a minute, if there were clouds below they must have been thin and stratified for with the landing lights on, what appeared to be a 'vapour trail' could be seen smoking from the wingtips and over the wing. There was only a brief respite before the cloud tops forced me to level out at 10,000 feet and restore the power to the engines as I headed away from the storm line, going like a rocket and grateful for the sweeter air being drawn into my lungs.

As minutes passed, I hated even the briefest period when not seeing the stars, the trembling in my knees and hands gradually subsided, my limbs came under control again as we drove through the blackest of nights at a right angle to the required track. That was a problem of major concern. After ten minutes there was nothing else for it but to swing back on to the course for Nandi and take stock, believing that the worst of the weather had been avoided.

First, the office tidy up. Papers, maps, charts, pencil-case and oxygen mask were strewn all over the cabin. Flying with one hand, after searching with the interior lights on high for the first time, I retrieved my plotting implements and computer, to start in to some desperate calculations.

My first blunder had been to fail to log the time of takeoff but I could remember setting the aircraft's clock against my watch at about the time the car arrived at the airport. Takeoff would have been no more than three minutes after that, about 0418 local time. As for an air plot, that would have to come from memory too. The runway heading, alias the track to Nandi, had been flown for about twenty minutes, tracking north to quit the storm area occupied about ten, fuel on departure was 65 gallons, fuel used to 10,000 feet with up-draft assistance, say ten gallons. Fuel remaining therefore should be about 55 gallons, although the gauges were reading lower. After recalculating a few times it was plain to see that the fuel on board at the time would not be enough for me to reach Nandi.

At that point another decision had to be made. Should a return be made to the 'Friendlies' and hover around until dawn to face the consequences, or proceed with the prospects of going belly up into the sea 'somewhere near the Fiji Islands'? All that went through my mind. The fuel remaining would make for a tight squeeze even for a landfall in the Fiji's. Continuing the flight to Nandi was now completely out of the question. I gave myself ten minutes to ponder the issue while remaining on course. In the meantime my headset lead was plugged in and the radios brought on line. All frequencies tuned were ominously quiet, not a sound of human voice was heard through the heaps of pre-morning static.

A listening watch only was thought to be best while 'surfing' the most likely channels, forewarned is forearmed, by that time the news of the disappearance of the Aztec could be all around the 'Friendlies' by courtesy of the domestic radio network. That there might be a chance to monitor some station and listen to their version of the event crossed my mind. The radio type fitted in the Aztec made that impossible with all frequencies pre-set and locked. Nevertheless I flipped from channel to channel on the high frequency band for a few minutes just on the chance of picking something up that might be useful, without success. For the first time my mind turned to some of the difficult questions that might be asked wherever I arrived. Questions linked to an unannounced departure from a controlled international airport without runway lighting, which was officially classified for daylight operations only, customs, health or immigration clearances coupled with insufficient fuel for the proposed flight. Those were just some of the infringements that might have to be faced with an Australian registered aircraft. There would be others regarding the state of serviceability of the aircraft for such a flight, the aircraft's maintenance release as yet had not been sighted. The list was endless. Either way, I was heading for a mountain of trouble.

Having checked the calculations over several times, both engines were leaned off to a minimum of fuel flow. Expecting at least another hour before any reasonable daylight, I pondered over the options at my disposal. If the fuel aboard allowed me to reach the southeast coast of Viti Levu, I knew that a landing on Naselai Beach would be possible. The beach was used by Kingsford-Smith for take-off to Brisbane in 'Southern Cross' on the first air crossing of the Pacific to Australia in 1928. In more recent years and in lighter 'planes than 'Southern Cross' I'd used the beach several times, carrying one muscled Fijian man under one large bag of copra, for sale in Suva, the copra that is. With the tide on the ebb at the time, I felt sure that an emergency landing could be pulled off there without damaging the aircraft. I was in a desperate situation and up to my ears in trouble. It was then I decided to hold 10,000 feet as a minimum altitude for extra time and gliding distance should both engines cut out further down the track. Naselai and its long sweep of hard sand beach, was tucked away in my mind as a last resort.

Scudding through the tops of the ever-diminishing cloud, more of a calm settled over me, gratitude for the successful repossession of Dee's aircraft, for the safe passage through the cu-nimbs, the security of the smoother morning air and for the aircraft humming along sweetly save for the whistle coming from the damaged prop. With the rain gone, the whistling sound was louder than before.

Tired eyes took in the rev counter to watch the fine tip of the needle vibrate on the tachometer dial. There'd been no change in that since take off. My hand felt for more solid parts of the aircraft's tubular structure around the door and windows, with my fingertips confirming a slight vibration running through the airframe, in rougher air the vibration would not have been felt but I knew it was there. The prop was definitely out of balance. From experience I knew that the slightest vibration in a prop at the beginning, could lead to a major mechanical breakdown with the shedding of a blade, which could cause the runaway engine to sever the engine mounts. .

My mind was made up as I fell back on my previous Fiji experience. I'd had trouble with props shedding parts of blades before. All my effort must go into reaching Nausori, 180 kilometres short of Nandi. Sadly there would be questions asked, Nausori was a terminal for regional flights. Itinerant aircraft passing through Fiji used the major international airport on the western side of the island.

I longed for daylight that would see me able to read maps, charts and flight guides without squinting in the poor light and to again see the aircraft's wings and engines, the cloud scene or the ocean below, anything apart from the flight panel which had held my attention under arduous conditions for too long. As the minutes passed I leaned out the engines even more, until they must have been running on only the smell of an oil rag

The Aztec wasn't fitted with an EGT gauge (exhaust gas temperature), which assists the pilot to fine tune the engines for the appropriate best fuel flow. My eyes were glued to the standard gauges as fitted. Both gauges were reading close to their upper limits indicating that both could do with a little more fuel. Promising myself to always keep a very close eye on those needles the mixture levers were moved up a notch.

The sense of loneliness that must come to all solo over-water pilots at some time began to creep into my thoughts. My head was filled with what a fool I'd been to accept Dee's offer, all because of a stranded suitcase, if only the pilot had been a little gracious and waited a minute or two I wouldn't be where I was. There would be hell to pay if every pilot left trolley loads of luggage behind so as to keep to his schedule.

Phone calls to my part of New Guinea weren't easy to make in the days before STD (subscriber trunk dialling). Since meeting with Dee there'd been no chance to call my wife to tell her of the loss of 'Samson' and how my plans had been forced to change. At that time, my family would have been snug in their warm beds in our New Guinea highland cottage in the most beautiful valley, at an elevation of 5000 feet, in the belief that I was safe in one of the biggest and best of airliners en route to the US. Unless Dee had managed a call at a time when the telephone exchange was operating that is. The terrifying thought of being lost somewhere over the Pacific in a little known Aztec, without anyone knowing of it's disappearance for a day, week or month in order to raise an alarm, gnawed at me for a long time.

Next I began thinking of the soft drizzly mist that came down on our home almost every night. . The fog that formed in the early morning hours would have started to creep up the valley at that time of night, where the small town nestled among tall casuarinas and leafy gums around a one-way sloping airport. In German days several prominent peaks of a mountain range in the long cordillera of New Guinea had been named after Chancellor Bismarck's several sons, Herbert, Wilhelm, Otto and Helwig. Later in Australia days, like Topsy our town had grown up at the foot of Mount Otto in the Asaro Valley, accessible to westerners only by the much used, over-worked aeroplane. Germany had once ruled over the northern portion of that part of one of the biggest islands in the world.

Night rains there could be likened to English or Irish summer rains warmed by the Gulf Stream. The drizzle came down silently, soft and dewy. So gentle was the rain it could not be heard on a tin roof, but only by the drops dripping on to the broad-leafed plants that bordered the house. Fog, thick enough to cut, would roll up from the swift flowing Asaro River that divided the valley floor. As would a tsunami, the fog would swirl across the cleared slope of airport to hide the entire valley under a wet, grey blanket until well after the break of dawn. Children might set off for school finding their way only by local knowledge. Vehicles with their lights on crept along the roads at a snail's pace. House and office lights were needed sometimes well into the morning, as aircraft circled to wait for the fog to lift, or get diverted to more kindly ports.

When the fog dispersed and the sun broke through, a glorious day of sunshine could follow, the airport would come to life to portray a scene of regulated activity as the several operators caught up with interrupted flight schedules. The handling of the many 'planes of all types by the controllers on a sloping one-way strip and foggy morning was something to watch.

Day rains were different. In the afternoon the awe-inspiring mountains would begin to thrust up extra heavy clouds. Rain, thunder and lightning would roll down the valley from Mount Otto to sweep across the town. For an hour after the rains, barats and culverts would be rushing with flash-flood waters that had passed through the 'hydro haus' driving the generator that supplied the town with electricity. After the storm passed, the air would be the sweetest on earth, crisp, pure, unadulterated. I dearly loved the excitement of that town and craved to be there again with my loved ones.

Getting ahead of myself as I often did on long ocean flights, I selected the Nausori homer frequency, a non-directional beacon (NDB), watching as the needle rotated slowly around the dial without stopping. That could mean that the Aztec's direction finder was either out of order or out of range of the transmitter. There was nothing else to do except check the frequency in the flight guide, stay tuned, watch and wait, for the coming of dawn always brought with it the possibility of spurious radio signals. The aircraft equipment might not receive a signal from the beacon until we were much closer.

By the readings on the fuel gauges I could only hope that soon the finder would lock on to the homer with the needle pointing positively in its direction, for that was the only worthwhile long-range aid the Aztec carried. A hunt through the flight guide, to ascertain whether Nausori's homer transmitted twenty-four hours a day was needed. Although hampered by poor light, the small print was well searched without success. The next twenty minutes were tense with apprehension as I waited for some reaction on the radio compass needle. At 10,000 feet altitude a promising signal could be expected from 120 miles, which would mean that Nausori was less than one hour away, come in spinner!

Quite suddenly, as if coming out of a long, black tunnel into pure light, the needle ceased to gyrate then groped about the head of the dial obviously on the scent of a signal. For minutes at a stretch I pressed the earphones to my ears until I could hear the faint identification signal hidden amongst an early morning cacophony of static and Martian-like ripping sounds, 'dah dit – dit dah', the Morse letters for NA, just what was wanted. Caught up with relief, I shouted for joy as the needle slowly began to stabilise. Contact with the outside world had been made. In due time as we drew closer, the pointer would steady even more, the wind drift could be assessed, the inbound track established, for I felt certain that course alterations coupled with upper winds had moved the Aztec to the north of the direct track.

At 10,000 feet altitude dawn comes earlier than on the surface. The first sign of daylight came in from the southeast, lighting up the tops of some faraway towering cumulus, with the stars beginning to fade out. In proper light for the first time since leaving the 'Friendlies', the engines showed up, whirling props, aluminium wings, radio aerials, while the sea below still lay hidden in darkness under a layer of cloud.

As night became day I let her go on towards Nausori scudding through fleecy cloud, engines throttled down. The distance measuring equipment fitted was not compatible with anything other than an Australian station. Without ground aids to assist, the distance to Nausori could only be guessed. A pessimistic summary of fuel remaining at that time was 20 gallons slightly less than an hour's flight time considering that some fuel would not be useable. It was there that I gave serious consideration to the shutting down of one engine to complete the flight, but gave up on the idea all things considered.

In that way, flight was continued for another thirty minutes until the temptation to get below the cloud could no longer be resisted. A glimpse of the sea was highly desirable to determine the lay of the wind and the state of the surface. Ditching had by now become a distinct possibility. For the first time thoughts of a life-raft entered my mind, there wasn't a sign of one in the cabin which was surprising considering the number and style of over-water flights the 'plane had been making.

A search of the pocket behind my seat brought out a flotation vest in a protective wrap of transparent plastic. The tag on the package showed the vest to be six months overdue for service, nevertheless the wrapping was torn off and the vest placed on the seat beside me. To be doubly sure, another vest was taken from the passenger seat pocket, unwrapped and set on top of the other. Now it was time to see what kind of surprise might lie below the clouds. A gentle pressure on the controls lowered the nose as for a rate of descent of 200 feet a minute, an angle that would not expose the outlets in the fuel tanks should the air get bumpy.

Moisture began to slide up the windshield as we slipped into cloud again with scarcely a shrug of the wings. Imagination brought the Fiji Islands closer as we began to descend through cloud, then lo, at eight thousand feet the layer cloud vanished to allow an unrestricted view of the Pacific Ocean. The sun had only just begun to reach a vast ocean of wind-tossed water. Even from that altitude the wind-streaks (or wind-lanes in airman's parlance) creating whitecaps on the crest of the waves, could be made out. Based on that observation the wind in the lower levels was estimated to be coming from the southeast at about 20 knots. My breath came easier, there was some hope after all. In the lower levels I would be racing along on a fast air current that would eat the miles off towards Nausori much quicker than could have been imagined. Renewed hope brought me to the edge of my seat as I peered ahead for the sight of land. The needle of the direction finder was firm and steady, 'dah dit – dit dah', loud and clear through the phones, the fuel gauges closing on their lower limit.

It was time to call someone and pass on my flight details. Nandi responded to my third call the voice a sleepy one.

"Where are you from? " came the operator's voice. "There's nothing here on your flight, where are you bound? "

"Well, er, Sydney eventually." I replied acting dumb. "But right now I'm going into Nausori, my flight plan probably went there."

"It should have come through Nandi." he answered. " but obviously it hasn't, what type of aircraft are you, what's your ETA Nausori, your POB, your departure point? "

"Zero six five six " I guessed, careful to give him only the information he'd asked for except the point of departure. "A PA23, Piper Aztec, one person."

The voice was light-hearted and cheerful. " You're almost there, you'd better call Nausori now, sort out the flight plan bit with them on arrival, good morning, oh, just as well you're going into Nausorii, as of yesterday there's no fuel here at Nandi for aircraft other than turbine fuel for the international RPT's. (regular public transports). Several aircraft are stranded here. You must have known a thing or two! Good morning again! "

Having anticipated being asked for the names of pilot and owners, registration details and probably a demand for the filing of an Incident Report I was nothing short of amazed at the casualness shown to my early morning intrusion into Fiji's airspace. A quarrel too about the lack of flight notification had been expected. Had Nandi just brushed that off to put me off guard, or passed the buck for a grilling at Nausori? Should that be the case all hell could break loose.

With all those thoughts running through my mind, Nandi's remarks regarding the fuel situation was forgotten. With one eye on the state of the sea and the other on the fuel gauges I was living inside myself with both engines about to stop beating at any moment.

Through the haze, a smudge on the horizon heralded contact with the coast of Viti Levu. Humming along at a good speed with what appeared to be a strong tail wind, at six thousand feet the engines were allowed a little more fuel via the mixture controls, while all the time a close watch was kept on the dangerously low fuel gauges and for other signs of the motors quitting.

I'd decided that two thousand feet would be the lowest I'd go until being assured of making a successful glide landing without power. Anxious to be over a portion of land or reef should that happen, every nerve in my body screamed for the 'plane to move at twice the speed.

"Nausori, this is Charlie Uniform Whisky." I yapped into the microphone in what was hoped to be a calm voice. "A PA23, thirty miles out by estimate, in-bound one zero five on your NDB, out of five thousand, estimate Nausori for landing at five five."

There was a sort of stunned silence, which was fully expected. The operator, who had probably only just arrived in the tower, would be feeling guilty at having missed something in his early morning's self briefing. He'd be searching through his traffic cards and logs for clues about the unannounced arrival of a mystery Charlie Uniform Whisky right on opening time. In case the mistake was his he would try to show me that he was alert to the traffic situation around his airport. His voice came through with a markedly British accent mixed with frothy lips and a generous moustache.

"Charlie Uniform Whisky, this is Nausori, have you been in contact with Nandi, we have no details of your arrival here? "

Thumb poised on the radio button I didn't consider my reply to be a lie.

"Affirmative, Nandi transferred me over to you, I have your field in sight, request a straight-in to runway two eight if available. "

There was another long pause before a response came. While awaiting a reply I travelled another two or three miles. I'd chosen the runway that was closest to the nose of the aircraft, runway 28. A precious two minutes of time would be lost circling the airport for an approach into the wind from the opposite side of the airport should the man in the tower decide so. Desperate to get her on to the ground before the motors cut, my thumb was ready to stab the transmitter button again before his more formal tones came through the phones.

"Charlie Uniform Whisky, this is Nausori, we got no advice on you, d'you have an agent we can call, there is no traffic, the wind is 120 degrees twelve knots gusting to fifteen, altimeter is one zero zero eight, you got a fresh tailwind on two eight, best you land on one zero, confirm you want two eight? "

While all that was going on we scorched across the coast and the delta of the Rewa River, spinnaker up and fully inflated as it were and with the airfield in sight. Off the left wingtip, the trade wind was stirring up Laucala Bay, an old haunt of mine, the heavy white line of the surf visibly pounding the outer reef. Down below 2000 feet then, my guts felt sick with anxiety, radio chatter needed to be done away with.

"Negative on the agent, runway two eight is acceptable, joining final now! " I snapped, my voice rising and anxious, fully expecting to be queried about my picking up more than 20 miles in less than three minutes! Without a doubt the man in the tower had been caught off guard.

My hand reached for the throttle levers and drew them back. As the power came off, the Aztec was set in a steep glide for the runway, an angle that could cause the engines to die. As the speed reduced, flaps were drooped in small instalments followed by the landing gear in one large deposit. Fully committed now to a steep glide landing, there could be no changes or turning back. At that point I dare not push the throttles forward again for a go-round, lest both the engines quit, things were that close.

The controller took an age to respond, could he be blamed, quite possibly he'd talked with his supervisor about my extra speedy arrival from thirty miles.

"Charlie Uniform Whisky, this is Nausori, at your own discretion you are cleared to land runway two eight."

That landing wasn't really professional. Although a flat approach had been planned for safety with near empty tanks, I had been much closer in to Nausori's runway than expected, which called for a dicey, steep approach.

At the threshold the Aztec was at least two hundred feet not twenty, in a strong following breeze with the windsock fully inflated, horizontal and flapping its tail. The Aztec floated a third the length of the runway, before the wheels with their worn tyres contacted the surface. Brakes were needed to pull her up in what would be an unacceptable distance for the type and size of 'plane. With the Aztec racing like fury past the tower and its pilot readying to stand on the brakes, the controller could almost be heard saying to himself.

"Serves you right, you were told about the wind, twice."

After stopping, with me shame-faced, breathing hard and exhaling an immense sigh of relief, the Aztec was backtracked almost the full length of a long runway to where a Hawker Siddeley turbo-prop was holding pending my clearing. On my passing the Hawker, no doubt the Captain would be remarking to his First Officer what an unconventional landing the 'lightie' had made. Sweat in profusion was running down my face and neck, my hands were shaking. How embarrassing it would be if both engines decided to stop right there before that 'lightie' could clear, were my tremulous thoughts at the time! Fortunately both kept going.

After turning off the runway, the Tower was called again for parking instructions. Words that I'd half expected, even dreaded, stung my ears.

"Charlie Uniform Whisky, this is tower, do not go into the main terminal area, take the next taxiway left and park between the two buildings. Wait in your aircraft, inspectors will meet you there."

As expected, I was going to be in for some special treatment. By that time the authorities in the 'Friendlies' would surely have advised Fiji of some of the details of my unorthodox departure from their territory, if so, I was about to face the music.

All the way in to the allotted parking area I dreamt up a story for the inspectors. Say not too much until they revealed just what they knew became my mind set and whether in their eyes, my legal 'prank' as it would be called, was considered to be a serious breach of their air regulations. Pacific islanders are known to have a different point of view way on events that are important to us but not so important to them, a lot would depend on just who would be the judge.

As instructed the Aztec was nosed into the space between what turned out to be a small hangar and some kind of an engineering workshop which was vaguely familiar. As a swing on the right wheel was made to align with the hangar, the left engine was powered up to assist with the sharp turn. The engine gurgled for a second, spluttered and died. No amount of pumping on throttle or mixture levers could induce the engine to fire up again. From its last few gasps it was easy to see that the engine had starved of fuel. The right engine ticked on merrily while set to idle, with the prop in an intermediate whistling mode the sound magnified in the secluded space and with the left motor stopped. Before anyone in the nearby buildings could hear the unusual sound and come to investigate I pulled both mixture levers back to idle cut off. The engine wound to a stop.

"Charlie Uniform Whisky this is tower. You are to remain in your aircraft until inspectors arrive. Acknowledge"

In a husky voice I answered. "Charlie Uniform Whisky wilco."

As expected, I'd only just made it, a circuit of the field to land into the wind or a 'go-round' would have seen the machine on her belly in a neighbouring cane-field or burrowed through an Indian cane-grower's dwelling, many of which were scattered through the cane outside the boundaries of the airport. There was no doubt that my flight had been blessed with good fortune throughout, but the drubbing was about to start.

Minutes dragged on while I just sat in the seat, eyes closed, letting the tension drain from my body while in my mind I prepared a case 'for the defence' and thanked my 'lucky stars'. I say 'lucky stars' for a good friend of mine, an Anglican minister-cum-mission pilot, had once told me in a jovial way that if one breaks the rules of the air, God gets out of the aircraft and leaves you to it!

Many long-standing aviation rules had been broken that dreadful night. During the hazardous trip I'd uttered many a prayer. Then and there those prayers were added to with lots of thanks as I sat waiting the arrival of officialdom. If Father Doug was right, then I'd been given another chance. Ten minutes went by before I opened my eyes and looked about.

The Aztec was hidden from the control tower, the doors of both buildings that sandwiched the metal bird were closed, there wasn't a soul in sight. My mind was working overtime, driven by fear, telling me that at any moment a squad car could be expected to arrive at the enclosure, dust flying, tyres screeching. There'd be police officers, customs, imigration and health officials aboard. Some would be armed and in smart uniforms, lots of questions would come my way before I was marched off to the nearest police station for something more serious.

Sun poured into the cabin through the windshield and side windows, the air inside was dangerously stuffy, those parts of the cockpit in direct sunlight became too hot to touch. Sweat dribbled down my face and off my chin. Stains began to appear on my shirt. When nobody had arrived in half an hour and I was gasping for breath, I clambered out of the cockpit and walked around to cool off and stretch my legs. A quick look at the right prop showed scratch marks and the tip of each blade grazed and slightly bent.

Being unsure how the authorities might react to a foreign pilot disobeying instructions, my exercising always kept me in sight of the aircraft except once when I sidled behind the hangar to answer a call of nature. After spending half an hour sheltering from the hot sun under the wing, I climbed back into the aircraft, switched the radio on and called the tower.

The voice was unfriendly, not at all sympathetic, curt in fact. He sounded as if I'd interrupted something more important to him. The tones told me that further calls would not be welcomed.

"You were told to wait until custom officer come, you must wait! "

"Charlie Uniform Whisky wilco." I replied a little more timidly.

Noon came and went. By that time the air in the enclosed space between the buildings with its heat-drawing sealed surface, was wickedly hot. Sheltering under the wing meant moving about constantly to catch any shade. At three o'clock, being dehydrated and suffering severe thirst and with anger increasing I threw caution to the winds.

The sounds of vehicular movement at the airline passenger terminal about 300 metres away along a gravel, rutted perimeter track could be heard. Being careful to remain clear of runways and taxiways, so as not to upset the airport authority I set out for the terminal building. A large drinking bottle on a stand in a corner of the reception hall caught my eye. Without further ado I set about gulping cup after cup of cool water down until the bottle ran dry.

An employee of the local airline called out to tell me that the terminal would close after the next arrival in half an hour.

"Can I call the Tower on your 'phone?" I asked.

"Well, yes, you can, that's it on the corner of the counter next to the scales, but you won't get them, the Tower staff left at one o'clock today, big football game in Suva, New Zealand Maoris play Fiji, everyone's going there! "

So that was it. For some inexplicable reason, but probably due to the football game the Aztec's unannounced arrival had been overlooked by the inspectors, conveniently or otherwise I was not to know. The announcement came as a complete surprise to me.

My felonies were compounding, the spectacular exodus from the 'Friendlies' had been made without a General Customs Declaration or other necessary paper-work being completed, resulting in an unplanned arrival 'out of the blue' in Fiji. My passport now was not only without a 'Friendlies'departure 'chop' but also a Fiji entry 'chop'. When word reached Fiji about the Aztec's movements, I'd be classified as an illegal immigrant or more likely, a criminal escapee on the run similar to Ronald Biggs the Great Train Robber. How the lack of paperwork could be explained away had been uppermost in my mind ever since arriving.

A fuel tanker vehicle arrived in front of the terminal to prepare for the refuelling of the incoming airliner. The driver left his truck and sauntered into the terminal. Judging by the number of exchanges of 'bulas' heard, he was obviously well known to the staff.

International fuel carnet in hand, I approached him, determined to be friendly with the traditional Fiji greeting.

"Bula vinaka, my 'plane is over there between those two buildings, could you fill it up for me please? It takes Avgas of course. Here's an international carnet for payment. I'll be leaving tomorrow at about eight o'clock. Could we refuel about seven in the morning? " I asked.

He replied with a smile. "Ah, bula vinaka, I heard you come in long time ago. I'm sorry sir, since two day now we're not to supply fuel to anyone except Fiji registered 'waqavuka'. There's some fuel crisis. There's a ban on through all islands. Before I can serve you, I must have permission from manager."

I stared at him dejectedly, frowned and rubbed my hands. "Oh I see, that's too bad, where can I find him? "

"The manager has gone to Australia for important meeting, he's not coming back for a week, you should go on to Nandi, there's more chance you will get fuel there."

"A fat chance of that." I thought, knowing that the fuel remaining in the aircraft wouldn't be enough to get me to the runway with one engine. The state of the fuel in the aircraft was not mentioned, now that the hop had been made successfully and all was quiet, there was no point in telling the world the tanks were empty.

For a small private 'fee' the airline bus-driver agreed to give me a lift to the city. The commuter 'plane was landing as, in a sweat, I ran back to the aircraft.

With or without customs clearance and/or the confession of my many other sins, my resolve now was to retrieve my over-nighter, secure the aircraft and take the last bus to Suva. My nerves were all on edge with me being so angry, dazed and extremely tired. Food, drink and rest were top of the priority list before the pickle before me could be tackled.

At the aircraft a note stating my whereabouts was tied on to the door handle, should any officials arrive on the scene. During the search for pencil and paper, the message slip from the Royal Sunrise that was placed in my shirt pocket in the early hours that morning had fallen out. The paper was soggy with sweat, the writing smudged and only readable with some difficulty.

"Eleven pm, man came to see you, I say you go fishing early not to be disturb. He will come back see you early morning. Goodnight Mr Bryan."

Guilt feelings stirred within me making me feel lousy. Unknowingly the receptionist had lied for me, only to be betrayed. The news of the missing 'plane would spread like wildfire through the 'Friendlies'. Somehow I felt sorry for the pilot too for the embarrassment he'd suffer when trying to explain away the disappearance of the 'plane to his homeward-bound islands clients. It was certain that someone in the 'Friendlies' had been tipped off about the real purpose of my visit. Or could it be that the mystery man had wanted to talk things over and make a deal of some kind. Had the decision to snatch the aircraft been made too hastily or worse still, was I the victim of some deliberate lies.

Dee's words were well remembered and came back to me as I pondered over the note. "He's a tough guy from the used motor trade." which made me feel a little better. The escape as it happened might have saved me from cracked ribs, black eyes, a broken arm or nose, or a day or two or more in a 'Friendlies' gaol.

My thoughts were interrupted by the blast of a horn from the direction of the terminal. Picking up my bags I moved off along the path to the roadway.

On other long distance ferry flights in an unfamiliar, well used aircraft with several apparent discrepancies in the maintenance logs, at first the machine would be treated with distrust. The ferry pilot can never be sure whether the specified maintenance checks have been complied with or why the aircraft was being traded. Damaged parts can be replaced with out of time look-alikes. Airframe and engine logbooks can always be falsified to allow a profitable sale to go through.

There were many other things too that could raise doubts about setting out on a long ocean crossing. Glazed windscreens, non standard switches in odd places, sloppy fuel cocks, leaky propellers, engine oil leaks, mixture controls or prop pitch control levers out of alignment were some of the hazards that had to be faced. The non-sked charter pilot has a lot to put up with. There was also the possibility that the aircraft wouldn't trim to fly 'hands off', or an auto pilot controller which when engaged, would send the 'plane into a slow roll, stall or power dive. Flaps that blew in at the slightest touch of the selector could be extremely dangerous, particularly after take-off at heavy weights. The incessant crackle and spit of radios from in-house electrical interference were also amongst my pet hates. Quite some time was needed in flying the aeroplane to get used to, or outwit, the machine's several idiosyncrasies.

However, once safely across the particular pond or parched land mass and at the destination, any dislike one had for the machine would gradually subside while turning more into one of affection that could be likened to." I'd like to do that again." sort of thing. 'Planes have a character all their own. On the short walk to the bus, with the events of the past night cluttering my mind, I decided that in future the Aztec would be known as 'Miss Strongwing'.

At a bend in the track, I looked back to see the assemblage of aluminium alloys standing quite alone on the small square of bitumen between the buildings. She looked forlorn, sad, downcast, with her three, small, well-worn tyres resting on a scorching hot surface. The afternoon sun glinted on her perspex windows and painted metal frame all of which were in need of a good wash. She looked to be as utterly dejected as an Egyptian donkey, much like the first glimpse I'd caught of her standing in the rain and long grass at the 'Friendlies' airport. In the short time we'd known each other we'd been through a lot. A distinct feeling came to me that she liked being free of the life of neglect she'd been suffering. She wanted to be on her way again to her adopted home, Australia, while her pilot was leaving her to stand in the hot sun. Once at her home she would be better cared for, cleaned, painted in brighter colours, her flight and power innards adjusted to perfection. I knew then that she liked me too, for the way I'd let her have her rein in the thunderhead before coaxing her down to safety.

As I looked at her from the bend in the track for the last time that day, the droop to her chin told me that she must feel that she was being deserted and wasn't pleased with my going. Our journey together had only just begun, she wasn't hated as some of the others had been, yet neither was she loved, my feelings were those of a great admirer. There was a bond between us because she'd seen me safely through a pilot's worst nightmare, a night of terror. By rights she should have split asunder to fling me with all her scattered parts thousands of feet down through the clouds into the black waters of the sea. A close relationship had now sprung up between us. We needed each other for there was a lot to do before we could move on together.

A good check over was needed for signs of excessive stresses and strains imposed on her by the horrific turbulence. Her prop demanded attention by someone who knew props well. A knowledgeable man with a file could smooth off the jagged metal to proper shape. Props could be repaired that way. The flight could not continue without the prop being attended to. Her tanks needed filling to the brim too, that was another major problem to be faced before we could set off for Port Vila in the New Hebrides group, our next planned port of call.

En route to the city on the airways bus, the Indian bus driver told me that an explosive situation had developed in the Middle East. The fuel crisis was world wide and serious. It's a wonder that Dee hadn't told me about that. Within a few days and without rationing, the islands would be out of fuel altogether. Coming as I had from the inner parts of New Guinea, there hadn't been time or opportunity to know, or find out, just what was happening in the real world.

It crossed my mind that the only thing left for me to do was to take a commercial flight to Sydney and leave 'Miss Strongwing' to be uplifted by someone else at a later date when the crisis was over. The thought of that was unbearable, leaving a job unfinished and in a mess. By then, bureaucrats, legal eagles and diplomats would have become involved. Onward flight arrangements for 'Miss Strongwing' could be stalled, there was always the possibility too that a replacement pilot might not like the look of that prop and insist that it be replaced. The muck up with arrival formalities, although not completely of my making could see me delayed for a considerable time. On the 25-kilometre journey into Suva on the bus, the thought of having to leave 'Miss Strongwing' with the assignment unfinished made me turn quite sour, that was something I'd never done before.

The last thing required from the bus driver was the chat he seemed intent on having with me. By my being last to board the bus he had kept the forward passenger seat behind him reserved, making it difficult for me to ignore him. After his first remarks on the fuel crisis he seemed intent on asking only where had I come from and where was I going, along 'haven't I seen you somewhere before' lines. Most of his direct questions were evaded, while I showed signs of not understanding too much by complaining of a blocked ear and the noise of the vehicle, or with a cross question about a suitable hotel, not a flash one and just for one night. He gave up on the questioning and offered to deliver me to an hotel when the other passengers disembarked at the depot, where he felt sure a bed for the night would be available. As soon as I could, I sat back shamming sleep, while my mind turned the past days' events over, again and again.

When the bus reached the city, my mind was made up. I could have driven to Nandi and slipped out of Fiji on a regular airline, but I knew that I was morally committed to Dee, 'Miss Strongwing' and the successful completion of the flight. By hook or by crook I would stay with her to see our insane adventure through together. Just how that closure could be achieved would somehow have to be worked out.

Moving On

The driver's choice of a hotel was in Toorak that was not the Toorak of Melbourne but a more squalid part of the city. All night, people moved along the corridors, several in high voice, doors slammed, walls thumped, toilets flushed. Numbed by the day's events, both my mind and body craved sleep that wouldn't come. No sooner had a drifting off to dreamland started than a harsher, different sound jerked me awake. The threat of a possible 'rap on the door' seemed to electrify the room. Even the enticing smell of Madras curry floating up the stairwell couldn't lure me to the dining room.

Walking the streets not too far from the hotel was tried for a while to release some of the tension. Stumbling through an Indian bazaar alive with window-shopping tourists, feeling every bit a zombie forced me to retrace my steps to the security of the room. After taking a shower I flopped down on top of the bed, it didn't help. Again sleep eluded me. With my ears pricked, all night I listened. Every creak of the floor, every whisper in the corridor, was imagined as a police or customs raid to take me into custody. A fitful sleep came only in the early hours.

With the coming of dawn after only two hours of peace, Suva began to come alive again. The harsh sounds of delivery trucks or buses drifted in the still air through the opened window. At seven o'clock my pillow was drenched in sweat with the room getting hotter by the minute. Sunshine, with a good kick to it was streaming in the window. My stomach was beginning to remind me that I'd had little to eat in the past 48 hours. After taking another lukewarm shower, breakfast in the hotel's coffee shop was decided on regardless of the consequences.

I chose to sit at a corner table within earshot of a radio that was giving out local news items. While the news was being reeled off time was taken to put away a delicious tropical breakfast. The news was mostly about the international football game, nothing was broadcast about my escapade. Some of my lost confidence returned, but not all. That the incident would pass un-noticed was beyond belief, nevertheless plans for the day had to be made, things could be different at the airport. It seemed to me that the acquisition of fuel, plus repairs to the prop would be a major hurdle in the path to Sydney. There could be no easy-fix for my predicament.

With breakfast over a decision was reached. After returning to 'Miss Strongwing' to discover whether my note had been acted on, I would report to the police or customs to clear the matter up. I felt sure that such a move would bring 'hell and high water' down on me if an unsympathetic local bureaucrat, brainwashed in local law did the dealing. To him the facts of my arrival would be unlawful, unforgivable. A foreigner could hardly expect a fair hearing under the circumstances. To 'give myself up' seemed to be the only way out. For a while consideration was given to contacting a friend, a solicitor, to get some advice. Mark was a good scout who had battled for me once before. His residential 'phone number was listed but I had no idea whether or not he was in town for I'd not been in touch with him for years. Finally that idea was given up unless the situation worsened. At 8.30, in 'Bruno's Taxi' I was burning up the miles to Nausori airport, the fare agreed to before departure.

The route to the airport's terminal from the main road beside the river, wound its way around several wartime aircraft revetments. The driver was surprised when, en route to the terminal, he was asked to put me down at the corner of the perimeter track, my first task that day being to check on the situation with 'Miss Strongwing', and whether she might be suffering some form of internment.

"I not wait for you sir?" he asked.

"No need thank you." I replied while paying him off. "I'll be here all day."

When the buildings that hid Miss Strongwing came into view it came as a surprise to see the aircraft standing exactly where parked the day before, alone and with that haunted look about her. Somehow a picture of a mob of officials swarming round the area had taken my mind over. On drawing closer, there seemed to be an air of depression about her, the in-built droop to her chin accusing. Her very look somehow told me that she was busting to be on her way again as if saying "I got you safely through that terrible night remember, now you do your bit and fly me to Australia, the sun-burnt country I love, where I belong."

The note was still on the door handle, untouched it seemed. Should an official have paid a visit, surely the note would have been removed.

The Aztec would also be sealed and draped with NO ENTRY stickers. Red barricade tape would encircle her. Security men, full of importance would bar the way. The revelation took some time to register with me as I came to realize that the dangerous getaway-flight, followed by an unauthorized entry to the Fiji's had been overlooked by the local authorities.

For a moment a fierce anger surged up inside me. I'd been through a gut wrenching hell, while no one really cared where I came from or where I was going. It could only happen in the Pacific islands, laid back as they were. When the full realization hit me that I had over reacted, for the first time in more than 48 hours I relaxed completely. Half a minute later I was leaning on the wing, head down, chuckling to myself, letting the tension drain from my system.

Certain priorities were in need of some re-adjustment, positive decisions made. First of all 'Miss Strongwing' and her mechanicals needed attending to, but how? A complete list of those items should be drawn up, together with a what and where list of how some assistance might be found.

With sleeves rolled up I removed the engine cowls and started with a close inspection of the engine attachments for any cracks or other damage. I was aware that the inspection, done without a super powered magnifying glass that would pick up a hairline crack in the mounts if there were any, would not meet aviation engineering standards but the effort lifted my spirits tremendously when, with the naked eye, none were found. While the engine oil levels were in process of being checked, a man who somehow looked familiar emerged from the nearby engineering shop. As we shook hands I recognized him as a former member of the Catalina servicing crew at Lauthala Bay almost twenty years before and who was remembered as a really good conscientious technician, quiet and unassuming, who really knew his job. At that time I must admit I was a bit of an aircrew 'larrikin' most probably with a swelled head.

Born a 'kai viti' (a European born in Fiji), after discharge he'd joined the local airline as an aircraft maintenance engineer, obviously by his appearance climbing the ladder of success and no longer working with screwdrivers, spanners, lock-wire and pliers. A feeling that my 'good fortune' was gaining momentum welled up inside me, never having done him a bad turn. Weeks seemed to have passed since I'd talked to one of my own kind, so much had happened in the 55 hours since leaving Sydney. I was still trying to fit him into the picture when he spoke.

"Is that you Bryan, long time no see, where've you been hiding. I noticed the aircraft when I came to work this morning, it's a size or two too small for you isn't it, you must have arrived yesterday, we were closed, you know how mad they are on 'footy' here. We don't have many foreign aircraft coming through this airport nowadays. Why were you parked over here it's most unusual? "

My reply had to be guarded. It was far too early for my story to be told until I learned a bit more about the goings on in a Fiji that was in the first year of it's independence from Great Britain, no more a ceded colony but a nation.

"Nice to meet you again, Chris isn't it? I have no idea why I was sent over here and merely followed instructions, New Guinea is my place now and has been for some years since I left here, I'm ferrying this little beastic back to Sydney, she's not a beast really. I've named her 'Miss Strongwing', she did one heck of a good job in turbulence the night before last. Had to call in here for some fuel, that wasn't a really good idea for there's none here or at Nandi for itinerants like me that is. There's a world wide fuel crisis on of some sort, I'm down to bare metal and can't go anywhere until I get some. Have you by any chance got any avgas hidden away somewhere? "

His voice was genuinely sympathetic. "You must be exaggerating, are you? That's too bad, no, sorry, we don't hold any avgas, we've got an all-turbine fleet now. Even if we did we couldn't let you have any. Have you forgotten, only the oil-company sells fuel here, we're about their only customers, they don't get a lot of other clients. You shouldn't worry, you won't be going anywhere for a while, just enjoy Fiji until the crisis is over, why not, you must know your way around" We talked as we did a 'walk around' while he ran a professional eye over 'Miss Strongwing'.

"You know you've got a bent prop don't you, the right leg is down too, how did it get like that, the prop I mean? "

"Oh that's a long story, as you can see she's not in really good shape, have you got anyone who could help me with a prop fix, an oleo top-up, or anything else an engineer's more expert eye might see, a check of her structure for stresses and strains for instance. Since I arrived here this morning I've done some of that already, I just want to be sure."

He frowned as he thought for a while. "Sorry, we can't touch an Australian registered aircraft as you probably know. There's nobody here who's even got a license for an Aztec anyway, my company would sack me if we even take a look. It's a question of insurance. My advice is, get another prop sent up. When were you expecting to leave anyway? "

"Yesterday I had hoped. How about that - getting a prop over here could take weeks." I replied moodily as he continued to examine the aircraft. "I don't think the prop's that bad really, it gives a bit of a whine or whistle, the needle of the tachometer vibrates a tickle. I've been comfortable with it like that. What's needed is a good man with a file, that's all. My own opinion of course Chris."

When he spoke again it was in 'prophet of doom' tones. My heart dropped.

"If it was ours we'd chuck it away and get a new one. It looks as if its bent beyond a repairable limit. It's quite amazing that you came this far with a prop like that, I'd lose my license if I touched it." As he walked off he gave me a wink. In ten minutes he was back with good news.

"Some of the Fijians in the shop remember you from the Air Force or Fiji Airways. You may remember Leoni as one of the beaching-crew at Lauthala Bay. He's a master craftsman here. He's learnt a lot about props from old Charlie Ogilvie, he'll have a go at your prop but only after working hours today if it's not going to be a stormy night that is. Nothing official though, no signatures or anything, just slip him a few bucks which will go to his village, he doesn't want any strangers hanging around though while he's working on it, or you, only some men from his village plus a bowl or two of kava. Its nothing to do with us remember, no guarantees you understand? "

"Gee thanks." I crowed with a sigh of relief. I'd bet my bottom dollar that Leoni's work could be trusted. "I get the message. Don't worry, he won't be embarrassed by me talking to him during working hours. Say many 'bulas' to him for me please. Thanks Chris I owe you one. After cleaning up a bit here I'll shoot off back into town. I need to make a few 'phone calls about how I might get some fuel. I'll fix everything up tomorrow."

Chris's voice was cautious. "Don't let anyone see you give him anything will you? "

"I'll be discreet, you can be sure." I muttered under my breath as he walked off to the shop.

The biggest obstacles to onward flight had been taken care of but the fuel problem was still there sticking as mud to a blanket. I hung around for an hour or two waiting for a bus to go into the city. With things by now looking much brighter and my confidence restored I decided against contacting the customs authorities. "Let sleeping dogs lie." became the order of the rest of the day.

Every time the complementary 'airline passengers only' bus was taken the previously arranged fare increased somewhat. "This is because the risk I take to carry you. You are not proper passenger. " Muna the driver explained.

With things now moving in the right direction, the matter of the rapid increase in bus fares was put on the back burner.

Back at the pub, I checked in again but decided to have dinner at a resort around the harbour in the Bay of Islands. Again sleep came only fitfully. Fuel, or the lack of it, still curdled my mind. One more day would see me contacting Dee to tell him there was no way out, I'd have to use his return ticket or await the return of the fuel company manager, whenever that might be. With the extra expenses incurred by way of a pick up of 'Miss Strongwing' by another pilot some time in the future, I knew that Dee would be as 'mad as a meat axe'. Also another problem could arise if pilots were switched and the relief pilot failed to accept the repair to the prop. My fees would be adjusted by negotiation leaving me the loser, which meant a waste of time on my part for the great personal risk taken to life, limb and reputation.

"The boss is still away. We need his authority to supply any fuel to others than our regular clients. Yes, we still have some supplies of avgas. Sorry, we can't help you. Boss not here yet." The deputy-manager of the oil company's fuel depot advised me next morning. " I think he will not come for two or three days yet at the earliest."

Frustrated, I slammed the receiver down, then hurried out into the street to 'cool off'', as if that was possible in Suva. Outside a thought hit me that a walk into the nearby hillside suburbs would help to relax me and clear my mind. There I might try to locate the home that was our first after being married and posted to Fiji, a quarter of a century before. My Yashica camera went along after I'd purchased new film at Boots the Chemist, on the off chance that the place could be easily found.

Time, suburban development, plus luscious tropical growth, had dramatically changed the scene as remembered. While walking and searching the now unfamiliar streets, my shirt was saturated, my face burning, until finally the house was spied peeping through some leafy shrubs and trees in a well-kept tropical garden, a car parked in the driveway.

Drying my sweaty hands as best I could with an already sodden handkerchief, I took out my camera while moving up and down the road for a better aspect of the place in the view finder. Memories of life there flooded back, while I took a few shots, the last one near the entrance to the driveway. As I turned to leave, a woman's voice came to me from the garden. Why the person behind that well modulated voice was not over-friendly was soon learned.

"Might I ask why you're taking photos of my house? " she asked rather haughtily as she extricated herself from the shade between a row of super bright red and yellow cannas. "You can't do that sort of thing here you know, whoever you are."

Taken by surprise, I felt guilty. "Oh I'm sorry, I didn't see you there. Well, er, what can I say. This house was the first my wife and I occupied after we married and came to live in Suva twenty-five years ago. I was in the Air Force then, on the Catalina squadron at Laucala Bay over the hill there. I'm just passing through Suva, just thought I'd take a shot of the old place. It still looks brand new. I had a lot of trouble finding my way here. It had only just been built when we arrived. There has been a lot of growth and street changes since then too, sorry if I've done the wrong thing."

The woman had by then moved to the driveway where I could see her better. She certainly was a good looker about forty and with a slim figure, she spoke with what could be called a well-bred, Australian private school accent.

"Well how very interesting. " she said. "For a while I thought you must be James Bond, or some damned criminal planning further wicked activities. Well fancy that, twenty-five years ago, hmm, how interesting, we've lived here for only three years. From the Air Force you say, what are you doing now? "

As we chatted I told her the reason for my visit to Suva and the ensuing delay to my flight, making no mention of the perilous flight from the 'Friendlies'. For the second time that day my good guardian angel paid me a visit.

"Would you like to come and take a look inside. My marama, er, maid, will make you a 'cuppa' or maybe you'd prefer a cold drink, my husband's there. I'm sure he'd like to meet you, that is if he's not asleep. He's been to a crisis meeting of oil companies at Sydney, he only arrived back very early this morning, came by road from Nandi. "

"A business trip? " I inquired casually after the first excitement on hearing the words 'oil companies'. " I'd better not disturb him? "

She spoke lightly, cheerily. " Not at all, he'll be disappointed if he doesn't get to see you, he should be awake by now, ready for his afternoon heart-starter as he calls it. Everyone drinks too much around here, you can tell us what it was like here in the old days we hear so much about. "

"Don't worry about that. I can assure you we drank too much in the old days too."

"Oh really." she answered. "That is disappointing. Well I think you are very brave flying those little 'planes all over the Pacific. Come on in please, I'm sorry if I sounded like a shrew before."

Speaking from a deck chair in the shade on the patio, while swirling an ice-filled glass around in his hand, the Manager was most affable.

"I've been told that the crisis will soon be over" he announced. "The price of avgas will soar to unknown heights after this is over you can be sure. Yours is quite a story, what a remarkable coincidence you having lived here. I'll 'phone the crew at the airport with permission to fill you up, how can you pay. Do you have an international carnet? That's fine, the tanker driver knows all about those, just show it to him, he'll take down all the particulars, quite good for us really, some of our avgas is getting close to it's 'use by' date anyway. You have a safe trip now. You'll be leaving tomorrow, you'd better call the airport yourself to set a time for your re-fuelling. You want a lift back to town? Oh, one last thing, mum's the word about the avgas if you don't mind. "

Being tongue-tied all I could say was. "That is unbelievable, thank you very, very much, I'll always remember this return visit to our first home. Thanks too for the offer of a lift, but I'll walk down, can't get lost, it'll give me time to reflect on my good fortune, I thought I'd be stuck here for weeks, goodbye, thanks again."

Feeling like a million dollars by my change of fortune, at five pm I paid a visit to the Defence Club that claimed to never having had the doors closed since The Great War. The Club's building was well designed for the tropics, open, airy and with highly polished hardwood floors. The billiards room sported three tables. For country members requiring accommodation short or long term, ten single rooms were provided. A long, shiny, well-polished bar with 24/7 service, took up most of the wall of one large room, with a comfortable lounge and library adjoining. The more than ample staff comprised both Fijians and Indians in smart, white, high-collared military jackets, with either a 'sulu' for the Fijians, or long white trousers trimmed with green stripes for the Indians. All were proud of their long and loyal service to the Club.

Not long after I arrived, club members began to drift in from their work places. In half an hour I had met many old acquaintances including Mark my solicitor friend now looking his tropically influenced, sixty plus years, with still very much the look of a WW2 retired British Commando officer. At that time there was no point in telling him of my entry problems, with exit problems looming on the horizon.

With quite a number of members gathered around me, drinks began to fly about thick and fast. I felt so good as I shot a line or two about flying in New Guinea and flying an assortment of aircraft around that part of the world. On a high with my good fortune, I shouted drinks a couple of times for 'old time's sake'.

During that time an official of the Australian Trade Commission asked if he could accompany me on the trip to Sydney. A non-flyer, 'free loading' or sightseeing on a ferry flight, can be nothing more than a nuisance. Some ferry jobs mean the fitting of a tank in the cabin, limiting space, although not so in this case. I warned him of the possibility of being stranded along the route for some time for fuel or mechanical reasons. He assured me that he was going on a holiday and wasn't short of time.

My plan was to proceed via Port Vila in the New Hebrides, thence Noumea the capital of New Caledonia and on to Brisbane the first Australian landfall. With unfavourable weather conditions existing between Noumea and Brisbane, an extra fuel tank would have to be fitted which could cause considerable delay. Trying not to show any reluctance as to having him along, his proposal was OK'd when he offered to provide transport to the airport early the following day. Fares on the airport bus were rising dramatically to almost equal the price of a taxi.

Sleep came easier that night although I was still turning over thoughts of having to face Customs and Immigration officials without an appropriate 'chop' to my passport.

With a companion who would return his car to town, Dave picked me up at the hotel at sunrise. Jokingly, I told him that he'd better get used to fasting on the flight, breakfast on the Aztec was not on the program.

The fuel tanker was standing alongside 'Miss Strongwing' when we arrived. In the fashion of all Fijians the crew was cheerful as they went about their tasks. Avgas began gurgling into her tanks until each was topped to capacity. While 'buzzing' about the pre-flight checks and flight planning my frame of mind was happy, in contrast to the previous day when everything had been doom and gloom.

Leoni was hovering about not far from the aircraft, with a grin as wide as a barn door on his face. Choosing a time when we were both screened from the others by the tanker, I slipped him an envelope containing what I thought was a generous donation to his village, hoping that Dee would agree when he sighted my expenses claim, I could hardly ask for a receipt! The propeller looked to be straight as a die. The filing had stripped some of the paint off leaving the tip conspicuous with a shiny new look.

All he said was. "The propeller could not be balanced properly without taking it off. But it will get you home alright 'turaga'."

At the main terminal the local airline was receiving passengers for an International departure that for me was most fortunate as the several officers were working hurriedly to reduce the numbers waiting to receive their passport inspection. The whole affair though was much more relaxed than in most international terminals.

Posing innocently as international passengers, with Dave behind me, we joined the long line to the counter. With fingers flying the officer searched my passport for the entry chop, without success of course for none existed. He was softened up a little with praise for his beautiful country, as he kept on flipping the pages over. My heart thumped as I watched, while chatting ninety to the dozen, thinking of the embarrassment that would be mine if he started to ask questions.

"Your passport is very full, you must get another soon" he said as he raised the stamp and slammed it down hard on a vacant corner of a well-used page. "Next please." He called, looking at Dave.

I grinned with relief, picked up my small bag and headed off for 'Miss Strongwing' by sidling around the side of the building. Again nobody took any notice of the 'out of phase' direction I was taking. Dave followed knowing nothing of my entry problems, accepting our 'private aircraft' exit procedure from the terminal without question.

There were few to bid us farewell as we taxied from our parking lot and out to the runway in 'Miss Strongwing'. Standing outside their hangar, Chris and Leoni gave a friendly wave and watched us go.

As seen from the cockpit, the morning was quite beautiful but very hot. A cloudless, azure sky greeted us warmly. From their poles the windsocks drooped like wet stockings on a clothesline. For the first time since knowing 'Miss Strongwing', I was able to run through the pre-start and run-up checklists in a more professional manner. Ages seemed to have passed since my panic-driven start-up in the dark and rain at the 'Friendlies' airport. Now both engines had fired up on the first few rotations, engine temperatures and pressures were already in operating range, run-ups couldn't be faulted. Leoni had done a great job. There was only a slight quiver on the right engine's tachometer at full power.

With no other traffic about we were cleared to depart to the west from the intersection of taxiway and runway. There was no doubt that 'Miss Strongwing' had received more than a prop check during the night. The oil stains were all gone, her oleo legs were tight and rode smoothly, not a whine or a whistle came from the damaged prop. I could feel she was keen to go with renewed energy and even more sure that Chris knew something of that, bless his heart.

As we rolled to the take-off point Dave was treated to a pre-flight briefing as to where to find things and how to behave in an emergency.

"As you know our several flights are all over water. In a small 'plane like this it's best to wear your life vest all the time, that's why I've asked you to wear it now, you'll cool off at altitude. In the event of a ditching don't inflate until you're out of the cabin. First undo your seat belt, the only way out is through the door next to you, you'll be first out, you can guarantee I won't be far behind you." I explained. "Or maybe, depending on the urgency of the situation, you will have to follow me. There are plenty of vests aboard, keep an extra one in reach for safety's sake."

Panicky congestion in doorways or aboard small dinghies coupled with the bungling that might go on, were some of the other reasons for my not always agreeing to have passengers along on a small-'plane over-water ferry.

"The door latch is simple. Just turn the handle down until it unlocks then push the door out. If that doesn't work, kick a window out. Let's hope you had a good pee or whatever at the terminal to last the trip through to Port Vila, as you can see there are no toilet facilities aboard. A pee bottle is usually carried but not this time I'm afraid. There's no operative autopilot, or dual controls for you to worry about on your side. I'll be busy with the flying. In flight you'll probably be asked to hold or search the nav. bag for a Flight Guide or radio chart to keep you occupied, that's about it. We'll work things out as we go. We have no rations, we eat and drink after arrival at Port Vila, that's a much better method than crossing your legs for the last two hours, are you sure you can hold on, it's not too late to return yet, sure now? "

"Yeah, I feel I can last the distance OK." Dave replied nervously.

The tower cleared us to the intersection of the runway for take-off to the west and followed up with a clearance to Port Vila that I'd planned on. Unlike my arrival a few mornings before, the air was still, without a trace of any breeze.

"Charlie Uniform Whisky you are cleared to Port Vila. Track to join Bravo Five Niner Eight, on climb to 8000 feet, call Nandi thirty miles out, good morning sir, thanks for visiting the Fiji Islands. You are clear for take-off."

The sincerity in his voice gave me some guilt feelings my voice was calm as I replied. "It's been my pleasure I assure you, entirely my pleasure, good day to you sir."

With a thumbs-up to David, I poured on the power to the two 'flat-six' Lycomings. Both seemed eager to go and loaded up perfectly. In a manner quite different from the take-off of a few nights before, they both hummed smoothly at full power, as if asking for more. With lots of runway and the windless conditions, take-off speed built up rapidly.

Abeam the Tower I felt, rather than saw through the instruments, that she wanted to go aloft where she belonged. A gentle back pressure on the column and she was floating in smooth air, clawing for height. The altimeter read three hundred feet as we crossed the western threshold with the flaps in and the gear on the way up. If I hadn't seen the re-fuelling going on in front of me, I would have sworn that the tanks were empty, the flying controls felt so light to the touch.

With a slight jolt the gear locked up, the lights flicked to red. A slow, easy turn to the left began to where the best view of the bridge that spanned the Rewa and the township of Nausori would be possible. Now I began to remember some of the pranks of the US Air Force's P39 'Aircobra' pilots and their daring flights under the bridge during World War 2. In later years I'd considered performing the same feat myself in a De Havilland Rapide passenger bi-plane, just to be one up on Chief Pilot Fred who I knew was contemplating such a daring deed. I gave up the idea on realizing that civil aviation was beginning to get serious, what would be called 'such a reckless act' might lead to a permanent loss of license.

What had been for me an anxious, gut-wrenching ordeal over the past two days was suddenly and inexplicably over. The control tower operator wasn't to know what I'd been through. Forgetting for a moment that Dave occupied the seat beside me I gave a whoop of delight, filled with the joy of being up and away again. As Dave was without a headset and with the interference from engines and wind whistling over the airframe, he wouldn't hear any radio talk. To him the whoop I gave was passed off as an acknowledgment of a mischievous remark coming from the Tower. The gorgeous view of the topography below called for my attention. Already the Aztec was eating into the climb like a pigeon suddenly released from its loft.

"Miss Strongwing" was flattened down a little as we slid over Lauthala Bay. The sight of the stone breakwater, although now devoid of tethered Catalinas or Sunderlands, or a TEAL Solent or QANTAS Sandringham in the Braby pontoon, gave me an empty feeling in the stomach. All that remained of the once huge hangar, which with two Catalinas inside had somehow survived the 1952, 150 knot hurricane, minus only a small part of its roof. The concrete block on which it once stood was all that remained. The tram lines of several tennis or basketball courts could be seen etched on the surface. Engineering shops, pontoons, jetties, security gates each with a Grenadier Guard type guardhouse, a control tower poking up through a side roof of the hangar, had all disappeared, but not the memories of the good and bad times experienced there. The concrete slipway that so many flying boats on their beaching gear had used to roll to or from the clear, tropical water of the Bay, remained intact and by the looks was probably in use as a small boat ramp. The famous flying-boat station had all but vanished, taken over as part of a University campus.

Looking down, still vivid in my memory was the morning the famous world air navigator Captain P G Taylor, en route to Chile from Australia, almost came to grief there in the Catalina 'Frigate Bird', that is now in a Sydney harbour side museum. The towline connecting 'Frigate Bird' to the tractor was stretched to breaking point by 'PG's' excessive use of power on 'Frigate Bird's' engines on the run down the sloping ramp. This led to the tractor being almost in the water before the cable could be released.

Engines were meant to be at idle while the tractor let the flying-boat, on it's beaching gear, roll gently down the ramp and into the water while being steered by a man on the tail gear. The tractor followed with the cable fairly slack on the ground. However, so tight was the towline on 'Frigate Bird' caused by excessive use of power, that it couldn't be released in time with the main beaching gear, when 'Frigate Bird' became afloat. Still with the cable taut and the tractor driver readying to 'abandon ship' 'Frigate Bird' began to swing to starboard towards a submerged reef marked with bright red danger-buoys. The Cat draws about a meter of water when fully laden, as 'Pee Gees' ship was. The reef was known by us to be only a meter or so below the surface at high tide, hence the laying of danger buoys. With bated breath, from the veranda of the control 'tower' we watched the 'schimozzle' on the slipway, 'Frigate Bird' afloat and swinging to starboard, versus tractor striving to slacken the cable enough to allow the beaching gear to be dropped and the hook released from its attachment ring at the rear of the hull before the tractor was in the water. In short a 'tug-o-war' was going on.

For the all-Fijian crew clinging to each beaching gear leg, the situation was quite dangerous, particularly for the man trying valiantly to trip the release arm on the tail gear while clinging to the cable. Word somehow got through to the Captain per the radio in 'English as she should not be spoke', to bring the power back to idle while the beaching gear came off. Now freed of taking tractor, cable, beaching gear and ramp crew on a flight to Samoa, 'Frigate Bird' jumped ahead to cross the reef between two danger buoys, somehow (except for a miracle) without a scratch. The famous flight across the South Pacific Ocean to Valparaiso, Chile was saved from disaster and nearly ended there at the ramp at Laucala Bay, as the thin under surface of the hull crossed the reef with only an inch or two to spare.

As the Flight Commander (Training) for the squadron at the time I had briefed the famous navigator and his crew on the procedure to be used for slipping 'Frigate Bird' that morning and was very sure that all the points mentioned here were high-lighted before the crew were aboard. I had the impression that such famous flying-boat men didn't take 'the young Kiwi bloke' too seriously.

Nervously we watched 'Frigate Bird' bounce her way out of the Bay that was wind blown and running a heavy chop at the time to commence the flight to Samoa, Aitutaki, Tahiti, thence eventually on-to South America via Easter Island. We were left to wonder, whether flying boat and crew would ever be seen again. 'Pee Gee' made no reference to this incident in his book 'Frigate Bird', we wonder why, the Fijians involved who had risked life and limb were certainly deserving of an apology.

There were other incidents on the slipway too that are not mentioned here. Many stories have been told of the inherent skill of the muscled Fijian crew, beaching crippled Cats just minutes before they would have sunk. The skill of the Fijian barge-master with a sinking Cat under tow, the slick handling of the heavy main gear legs and the fitting of the tail wheel assembly, had been a joy to watch.

'Black Cat' pilots from the US naval base at Pago Pago, who sometimes visited the station in their flash amphibians, always preferred to tackle the slipway on the beaching gear, than on their own landing gear, for there were none in the world as quick and as efficient as the Fijians at that work. On all their visits the 'Black Cats' would reach the hardstand riding on the RNZAF's beaching gear, with their own landing gear unused and in their house in the wheel wells.

Grinning, fully relaxed then that the heat was off, I leant across to shout into Dave's ear. "We'll fly over Suva before setting course, it's a beautiful sight on a morning like this, the peninsula itself, the reef, the harbour and the mountains, enjoy it, take it all in. In the early days of Fiji Airways, on 'Flight One O One', we always flew over the city as the clock on Government Buildings that you can see down there, struck eight. We seldom missed in weather foul or fine, hail, rain or brilliant sunshine. The morning flight to Nandi was so regular that word got around that you could set your clock on the Fiji Airways string-bags. I'm not sure whether the clock still works. If it does then it will be chiming eight right now according to my watch. So eight o'clock is our set course time for Port Vila, I wonder if there's anyone down there who remembers?"

While Dave stared out on the magical scene as we crossed the outer reef of Viti Levu, I muttered under my breath.

"Isa lei dear Suva, this is one visit that I will never forget, thank-you for your act of kindness in forgetting about me the way you did."

Before setting course on the airway I decided to take a wide swing over the island of Mbenga (in Fijian the b is preceded by m when written) where in Catalina days, following a big blow, the crew of 'Four O Four Niner' uplifted four castaways from a battered canoe and flew them to safety. Who knows, this could be my last chance to see the island again. I think it was Gunner Eric Leech who, after the '52 big blow, had his dentures returned from Mbenga, along with a heap of Air Force material.

The thick wing of the low-wing Aztec tends to restrict a pilot's forward and downward view. A steep angle of bank was required to allow me to gaze down at the Pacific rollers pounding the several bombolas of coral reef offshore of the exposed bay. The anxious alighting, the pick-up and the rough water take-off there, was re-ignited in my memory as if it had occurred only yesterday. Memories, memories, the Fiji islands were full of memories for me. All around were stories of the great flying-boat days and the courageous men who crewed the Cats and Sunderlands around the Pacific islands, creating their own alighting areas, using their own initiative as they went (that Dee was then getting the benefit of), boys we were really, we were all very young. Looking back over fifty years, with the experience we had at the time, the tasks allotted us and their mostly successful conclusions were nothing short of remarkable in the light of present day aeronautics.

After circling once and pointing things out to Dave, the bay passed from sight as I levelled the wings, heading 'Miss Strongwing' out to the open waters of the Pacific Ocean towards Port Vila and the Coral Sea. My guess was that I would never see that place of adventure again. Soon there was nothing to see except sea or sky. At eight thousand feet the visibility was unlimited although some anvil-shaped tops could be seen probably seventy to one hundred kilometers away to the right of track.

The plan after re-fuelling at Port Vila on Efate Island, was to fly on to Tontouta, the international airport for French Caledonia, there to 'get set' for the longest haul to Brisbane, Queensland. Under favourable conditions we would reach Tontouta at nightfall. If Dee had kept his word an agent would meet the aircraft there. Accommodation and transport would be arranged and if required, some sort of a long-range tank would be available for installation should the onward weather situation demand.

She was swinging along smoothly now, with the power 'easy-easy'. Dave dozed while I navigated, radioed, all the time fiddling with the receivers to find a frequency that through a fault might bring in Radio Australia. Although only five days had elapsed since leaving Sydney, it seemed like an age. I was hungering for some news, particularly any with reference to my hurried flight from 'the Friendlies'. Even at that early stage I began to dread what the Australian Department of Civil Aviation might have in store for me. I couldn't imagine the stealthy uplift of the Aztec passing unnoticed. With 'Miss Strongwing' being registered in Australia, I was assuming that the officials in the 'Friendlies' were duty bound to notify the appropriate Australian authorities of the incident.

"Well, so far so good" I thought. "Worrying is like a rocking-chair that gives you something to do, but gets you nowhere. I probably won't hear anything until entering the Brisbane Flight Information Region late tomorrow, weather permitting, or maybe not until after landing at Brisbane's Eagle Farm."

Two hours into the flight we were really in the soup as the valiant little machine again began to take a hiding from the giant bubbles of purple-black cloud. Except for static, the airwaves were quiet as I sought clearance from Nandi for a higher level. For half an hour 'Miss Strongwing' suffered the heavy bumps at ten thousand feet. The turbulence there was worse, with the aircraft bucking about like a plastic play-toy in a gale. With low power and a good pressure on the column, we were soaring upwards quite rapidly, with the rate of climb indicator at times jumping to over a thousand feet a minute before dropping to hundreds in the opposite direction. The sudden rises, violent drops and flat skids brought Dave to life. He tightened his harness while I motioned him to place his hand on a solid part of the lining above his head, to save his skull from damage.

Some of the experience gained during my 'hurricane search' days nagged at me. From the squadron's experience, plus feedback from Pacific hurricane watch centres, six thousand feet altitude had proved to be the best for penetrating cu nimbs preceding a tropical cyclone. That theory was adopted as ten thousand feet was vacated in favour of six, not without some resistance to descend coming from 'Miss Strongwing.'

The 'best turbulence penetration speed' for the particular series of Aztec had been forgotten. The 'not too fast, not too slow, don't over control' technique was chosen as we sank lower into the murk with sheets of heavy rain then lashing the windshield. Oh for the comfort of some radar, I'd flown into a really big one. Lightning lit up the interior of the cloud as I reached for the cabin lights and instrument rheostats to wind them full up.

Without radar for guidance through the less turbulent areas, again I was forced into flying a constant heading, staying level without too much input on the controls. The lightning persisted, crackling and ripping all around us, while my eyes stayed pinned to the black panel and the instruments that were always jiggling about.

Dave was then on full alert, sitting up straight with wild, panic-stricken eyes, one hand clutching the roof, the other the front of his chair between his legs. I wondered whether he was having second thoughts about coming along.

We bumped, yawed and rolled in that fashion for twenty minutes or more with the airspeed fluctuating through thirty knots, the altimeter through five hundred feet. I needed to convince myself that the best altitude for less turbulence had been chosen, or whether by mistake the altitude for the best turbulence.

Thoughts of the previous strains put on the wing during that dreadful departure from the 'Friendlies', sapped the early confidence I'd started out with, believing that the worst part of the flight was over. Following my lucky escape, would fate rule that we would suffer a broken wing to tumble in pieces thousands of feet into the Pacific in broad daylight? The thought certainly crossed my mind. Glancing at Dave I could see he had turned a ghostly white with tinges of pale green. He caught my eye to give me a weak smile. A fine spray jetted through the door seals. The ear- piercing shriek of rain on the structure made talking impossible. I returned to the task of keeping 'Miss Strongwing' the right way up.

With an hour to go for Bauerfield, Port Vila, we were still in the soup. What was most needed was a terminal weather report but the airwaves were choked with static of the rushing water kind. Some thought was given to turning the radios off as their being of no use at the time, a thought that was put into action too late as a flash of lightning accompanied by a loud 'crack' almost blinded me. The absence of smoke coming from the radio box was a most welcome feature of the lightning strike that brought about the rapid turning off of that department.

An up to date route forecast had not been available at Nausori due to my flight plan not having been filed in time for the weather forecasters at Nandi to catch up.

Some of the islands of Vanuatu, the ex New Hebrides, are active volcanoes. Those islands can be tall and hard, almost always emitting smoke and ash, which when mixed with rain, reduces visibility to zero. Having been shut out of Port Vila before with a dramatic weather change that necessitated a diversion to Noumea's Ile Nou harbour in darkness, I began to sit up and take notice. Now I had to work hard on the controls of my bucking bronco, sometimes letting her have her head, sometimes helping her upright, always careful with the use of elevator and aileron, just letting her ride along with minimal pressure on the controls. In that kind of weather a pilot tends to get ahead of his aircraft, which was happening to me as I mulled it over. "With an hour to go, a hundred and fifty miles or so, there's time for me to fly out of this, but my big worry is the aircraft itself, can it take much more? "

On a hunch I turned to the sou' west only to run into a brilliant flash of lightning with a thunderclap that drowned out all other noise. So much for hunches! The lightning struck 'Miss Strongwing' on the nose with a horrible crackling, ripping sound. St.Elmo's fire danced along her long snout towards me for a second or two, my ears rang from the shock of the explosion in the earphones, which were ripped off as I rubbed my ears.

"That will put finish to the radios even if they were off" were my thoughts as the 'phones were cautiously replaced on my still smarting ears as realization came to me that the radio master switch should have been off before entering the storm. A lightning strike can pierce the skin of an aircraft, harm the electrical circuits, blow fuses or circuit breakers or as sometimes happens, melt parts of the radios causing a fire with a nasty putrid smell.

With some trepidation I began to hunt over the route's two high-frequency channels. Although bereft of any human voice both channels were clogged with static. Notification of my enforced adjustment to track would have to wait until communications were restored. To make matters worse the steering gyro then began to precess rapidly, requiring some attention from me every few minutes in the way of a re-set to 'slave' it to the magnetic compass that was also swishing about aimlessly at times.

Again I was getting ahead of myself, overcome with the feeling that we could over-run the island group whilst firmly embedded in the murk as there was still no sign of Bauerfield's non-directional beacon on the direction finder. Excited by the lightning no doubt, the finder's needle was rotating around the dial without stopping. With the direction finder, the compass and the steering gyro all going mad, doubts as to whether or not we were flying in the right direction started to creep into my mind. For all I knew we could be flying in circles, or away from Port Vila. There was nothing else for it but to keep the wings level and continually jab and re-set the steering gyro when the compass was temporarily stable. The rain, the lightning, the turbulence, seemed to get worse. Albeit slowly, time went by as 'Miss Strongwing' ploughed on bravely through the elements.

Suddenly, with a feeling that must be something like paddling a kayak over Victoria Falls, we emerged from the cloud into bright sunlight. 'Spat out' would be a better term. One minute our speed was evident by the fog and rain whipping over fuselage and wings, the next we hung motionless in space in clear air. It's an odd feeling and takes a second or two to readjust to the smoother air and the open sky. In a flash the pounding of the rain ceased, the windshield cleared, relatively smooth air replaced the heavy bumping and bouncing that had been ours for the past hour and a half. Dave's eyes stared ahead in disbelief while I unashamedly gave a hearty whoop of joy.

Five minutes out of the cloud and communications were restored. I cleared back to eight thousand and returned to track heading. With the instruments settling to a tolerable level of displacement, flying became much easier. Dave began to dry out some of the maps and charts that had spilled from the navigation bag when turbulence had again caused the contents to be strewn about the cockpit. Exhibiting the skills acquired in his office-based vocation no doubt, he had the maps folded and the bag neat and tidy in no time.

Free of the cloud and with no significant weather ahead except for a scattered layer at about six thousand feet, we both peered ahead for the first sign of the island group. In smooth flight now, inwardly I felt drained from the bashing we'd received, but tried not to show my feelings. Colour was beginning to return to Dave's cheeks and the knuckles of his hands. He seemed relaxed and could smile again without cracks forming on his face. The turbulence in the zone of 'cu-nimbs' we'd passed through was equally as vicious as that on the night of the flight from the Friendlies. For the second time, my hope was that we were now out of the worst and the remainder of the trip to Brisbane would be blessed with good flying weather. Getting ahead of myself again I began to imagine the first sight I'd get of the Queensland coast. By pressing the 'phones close to my ears, the faint identification letters of the Port Vila non-directional beacon could be heard, 'dit dah dah dit - dit dit dit dah – PV in Morse code.

"Any time now " I told myself " the needle will be on the nose. At eight thousand feet, we're about 75 to 80 miles out."

At 50 miles on my 'guess meter', voice contact with Bauerfield had been established. A ground visibility distance of three kilometers in smoke haze was reported. I began a power on descent with 'Miss Strongwing' again showing signs of eagerness. My estimate for the direction finder to lock on was premature for the needle continued to swing back and forth with the identification signal getting stronger as we sank into a thick, smoky haze with a slightly putrid smell about it. Without a reliable bearing from the finder I couldn't be too sure of our track. Had we strayed to the north, an ugly volcanic island, dark in shadow like a mountain on the moon, could bar our path, too far to the south and we could miss the island group altogether.

Now there were a number of small atolls that were visible only vertically beginning to slip past below. None of the rings of surf-lashed coral were conspicuous enough for a fix of our position. I could only hold on to the heading and navigate by deduced reckoning. A third eye would really be handy to watch for the rugged island of Efate while keeping visual slant-wise with the ocean.

Things were getting tense as things went on without making contact with other islands of the group too.

"This is known as stuffed haze y' know, haze with a solid centre." I called to Dave.

As my voice trailed off he waved an arm. Following his finger point, I could see a dark green blob of island, with breakers forming a white line of surf along its base. The radio compass needle now came up with some positive action. I stabbed the 'press to test', sending the pointer on to a reciprocal. On release, straightaway the needle flew to waver around the top of the dial. Port Vila was now proven to be directly ahead, the island of Efate hidden behind a curtain of thick, volcanic smoke.

As we descended visibility improved with the help of a slash of sunlight piercing the haze, outlining the rugged bush clad hills. With Dave's help the over-large map of the islands was folded to a workable size. While circling a prominent headland, we both studied the map from all angles. Finally we agreed as to our position being on the southeast coast of Efate about twenty miles from Port Vila. One didn't need to be a body language expert to read the look of relief on my face. My 'joyometer' was 'full on as I turned to Dave. .

"We're home and hosed." I called, while picking up the mike to call the tower. "We'll get a snack here, some gas, a leg stretch and take a pee, that should take around about an hour then on to Tontouta we'll go. A Beaujolais with dinner there tonight will be had by all."

With no other traffic about, the Aztec was taken in a lazy sweep over Port Vila's harbour before joining the pattern for landing. 'Miss Strongwing' was laid over quite steep above Iririki, a lush, green, partly forested island that split the harbour in front of the town. The reef jutting out from the island that we'd struck in a Catalina early one morning while manoeuvring for a glassy water take off away from the town, was clearly visible. Twenty-four years had passed since I'd heard the sickening crunch of the bombola tearing a hole in 4047's hull and the gurgling rush of pleasantly warm water, which filled the cockpit and my flying suit in seconds as the nose turret went under. Skipper, Pilot Officer Derek's angry voice filled the entire cabin in seconds too, his words unprintable.

Iririki had then been the governmental island home of the British Resident Commissioner in the days of the French/British/Australian administration of the condominium, jocularly called the 'pandemonium' government. Since that time it was easy too see that the pretty tropical island had undergone some major changes in the way of development. There was no sign of the Commissioner's mansion or were those buildings the remains after it having been turned into a fashionable resort I wondered. Many other grass-roofed structures, each with a sizeable jetty, had sprung up around the island. Several of those well remembered bombolas in the harbour seemed to have disappeared completely.

With our poor Cat half submerged on the edge of the reef in full view of the town, crew and passengers waited for several hours for help to arrive from shore. The passengers, senior members of the Western Pacific High Commission in Suva on a visit to Port Vila and the British Solomons, were not shown the respect due to them. A French ship was loading copra down harbour, boats could not be spared to take anyone off immediately was their story. A couple of hours later a Qantas Sandringham alighted in the harbour and glided easily on to the mooring buoy two hundred meters from our stranded Cat, the same mooring we had vacated that morning. The bowman and pilots waved at us in a fashion that looked to be sympathetic, we were feeling really deflated, ashamed almost, like raw amateurs alongside real professionals.

In a daring move by the crew after beaching gear had been flown in and utilizing a high tide, empty fuel drums and inflatable dinghies 4047 was eventually towed off the bombola, salvaged and returned to our station at Laucala Bay, Suva. Sad to say, not long after our mishap the regular Qantas Sandringham struck the same reef and sank to the bottom, fortunately without any casualties or loss of life. Some of the remains of that grand old flying boat were probably still there as I looked down on the scene years later. No one could ever feel good about that.

My reverie over I called to Dave. "Get yourself ready for landing, as you can see, the airport is very handy to town."

Port Vila was remembered as a quaint sort of place with a lot of French charm about it. The wartime airstrip had been closed after the war and re-planted in coconuts. While our Cat lay half submerged on the reef I was ordered to assess the old strip for emergency use by a

RNZAF Douglas C47 (Dakota) that was to bring in beaching gear and repair equipment for the attempt to salvage the boat. In the heat of a tropical morning I walked the full length of the ex-wartime strip by pushing my way through lots of small coconut palms, about five to six feet high by that time and other general undergrowth. Some of the bigger palms would need to be cut off short and the scrub cleared, apart from that the strip would be firm enough for the C47 was my assessment. The local government of the time OK'd the proposal only after some further persuasion from higher authority on 'our side'. In due time the C47 arrived with the gear, 4047 was salvaged. The repairs done would only allow for a flight to Lauthala Bay for major overhaul. With that over 4047 returned to New Zealand to end up on Rotten Row at Hobsonville flying Boat Station, the scrap heap. In the more than twenty years since I'd stalked along the length of that site, feeling most important, a major airport with a sealed runway, passenger terminal, hangars and control tower had sprouted up.

Straightening up after circling Iririki 'Miss Strongwing' was brought around in a steady approach to the long runway.

"Please ask the fuel tanker to meet us, we're going on to Tontouta, merci." went my call to the tower not knowing whether the man in the tower was French or not. .

The reply came in Anzac tones. " Wilco, the tanker's not been seen today. There's some sort of a fuel shortage on here. 'Phone me when you're down, there's a direct phone at the airline counter in the terminal."

"Dammit" I thought as 'Miss Strongwing's' worn tires kissed the runway. "That doesn't sound good. Leaving Fiji the way I did, I forgot a fuel crisis existed."

"You should have been warned in Fiji not to come here. There's no fuel available." Came the voice of the fuel depot's manager fifteen minutes later. "Nandi has known about the crisis for at least a week like all of us. Tontouta's the same, several aircraft requiring fuel have been sitting there for days."

"I left from Nausori not Nandi." I replied. "No mention was made of it there. I must go on, it's important for me to be in Tontouta to-night."

"Oh they all say that." he replied, throwing in a fair bit of sarcasm. "Our instructions are that no foreign aircraft are to have fuel. You can 'phone the boss in town if you like, here's the number, but it won't do you any good."

He called the number out so rapidly, I was still trying to get it into my memory box when he hung up.

The 'boss in town' was a nasty piece of work with a sharp tongue that would have won any telephone company's 'Insulting Tones' contest. I started to sweat, as he gave it to me for not accepting the depot manager's word, things got heated. I thought he might slam the 'phone down until I dropped what I thought were a few big names about, while at the same time exaggerating the importance of my mission.

From him I learned that selling aviation fuel was only a small part of his business as an indent agent. He claimed that he was only following instructions and was getting fed up with people like me pestering him. I hung in there, until finally he gave up.

His voice was triumphant. "You can have some of the 'bleeding' avgas I've got here which is not much. That will clean me right out and I won't have any more trouble from 'fellas' like you, but I know for a fact you won't get past Tontouta, you'll be there for weeks you'll see."

"How much have you got? " I asked politely while gritting my teeth.

"Not much. I'll give you enough to get you to Tontouta and out of my hair. I'll take a check on just how much we've got here. Call me back in ten minutes."

Depressed by the turn of events I walked over to 'Miss Strong-wing'. A flicker of an idea was creeping into my mind. While waiting to make the 'phone call I dipped the tanks. After waiting ten minutes, it was back to 'old grumpy' on the 'phone.

"There's a drum here with a 'use by' date the day after tomorrow, you can have that. If that don't get you to Tontouta we can't help you any more. If you want it say so now, it'll take some time to get it out to you."

That didn't leave me with much of a choice. All I wanted then was to be rid of the place. I gave him a really awkward serve. My voice began nervously, then meekly and finally apprehensively.

"One drum's not quite enough but I guess it will have to do if it's all you've got, I might have to glide the last few kilometers to Tontouta with the engines shut down. If I come down in the sea I could paddle or swim, the owners will be real mad if they lose their aircraft. Anyway I'll call my company in Sydney about it, it's a pity you couldn't give me a break and let me have more, you'll hear from them I'm sure if anything like that happens. Send a hand pump out with the fuel too will you? "

The line was ominously quiet, which made me think I'd gone too far. There was a trace of panic in the sound of his voice when he replied.

"For God's sake, don't do that. Look I don't want to be any part of your running out of b'....dy fuel, how much do you need, to get you right out of my hair, but I know you won't get past Tontouta for sure. The French won't give an Australian aircraft of your kind any preference like I'm doing, you'll see. We heard on the news just now that there's a tropical cyclone building up in the Coral Sea somewhere, you could be in for a rough trip."

"Really, that's the first I've heard of it. I haven't seen a recent forecast. Two drums will fill me up with some left over." I replied, throwing in my own brand of sarcasm for good measure. "I hope that doesn't run you short?"

I could hear him muttering at the other end as I put the 'phone down.

Time ticked by as we waited for the fuel to arrive. It came in the form of a mobile tanker with one thousand gallons aboard, which was great news, I could purchase by the gallon instead of by the drum!

The time spent waiting had been used to re-plan the flight, check the aircraft over, talk to the forecaster in New Caledonia and generally tidy things up. I was then convinced that a flight via Tontouta would end in a long delay. My mind change was to set out for Honiara in the Solomons, an area I was very familiar with and where people were friendly. A British Protectorate soon to set out on its own, the Solomons offered well-ordered administration through a properly trained public service that flowed on into all avenues of business. The peace and harmony of the place had been enjoyed many times before.

A further hitch occurred, when re-fuelling couldn't start until the 'boss' checked the international carnet. In a smaller vehicle the driver set out for town. He was away for over an hour, during which time I filed the change in flight plan. When re-fuelling was finished and I'd recovered from the shock of the price of the fuel however, there was no time left for an arrival at Henderson Field, Guadalcanal, before the airport closed for the night. Dee was going to have a fit when he received the fuel invoice with the summary of my expenses. Dave was finding my mood changes hard to follow, so I gave him some explanation.

"Tontouta's out, we'll not get past there for some time. We're going via Honiara, thanks to old 'belly-ache'. Even that's a border line case. There's hardly time to reach there before the airport closes, there are no night facilities. We'd have to be in the air in the next five minutes and have a more than perfect trip to make it before dark, that's far too risky, we'll have to stay the night here, sorry about Tontouta and Noumea, but at least you'll see a bit of Port Vila."

"Where are we going to after Honiara? " Dave asked.

"I'm planning on going the long way round, Port Moresby, Cairns, Brisbane, Sydney, you're going to get to see quite a bit of the seas around Melanesia at extremely low cost."

As we left the airport in a taxi, we passed from that transitory world of arrival by air to the island of Efate itself, seated comfortably taking in the scenery, while enjoying the unexpected luxury of motorized transportation without driver's responsibilities.

Port Vila had changed dramatically since my last visit. Hotels with more modern sewerage and drainage had popped up, bars, boutiques, flashing coloured lights, had also arrived. A fairyland at least by night, replaced the plain, French-colonial, jerry-built structures of yesterday.

My eyes looked about in vain for the Port Vila Hotel as last remembered. The verandah overlooked the harbour from where the Catalina mooring could be seen. Countless military and civil flying-boat aircrew had sat at the tables on that wide verandah while savouring the delights of some Pacific style French cuisine. For those brought up on bacon and eggs, toast, tea, roast beef and Yorkshire pudding, the 'croissants', 'poisson cru', 'les crepes', 'les fromages' with 'les fruit frais', café' and many more hard to pronounce delicacies, were to some an exciting view of another world, an uplifting new experience.

Others had a different viewpoint. A Catalina crewman who was a 'bacon, steak and eggs for breakfast' devotee and noted for his skill with conversational expletives, had once complained to me. "Skipper this is a ….. starvation diet for ….. airmen about to embark on a ….. ten to ……twelve…… hour….. flight."

He had been refused a second croissant by the waiter on the grounds that the management had decreed that at breakfast only one pastry per person was permitted.

After finding a cheap hotel to suit our pockets, checking in, cleaning up, we explored the streets of Port Vila looking for a typical French restaurant, to no avail. An Aussie style bar and restaurant was settled for with a 'happy hour' about to begin. Before long a couple of ex New Guinea 'fly-boys' I knew arrived on the scene. After swapping yarns for a couple of hours, we ate a seafood fare Aussie style.

For me the day had been a long one, the anxiety of departure, the extreme turbulence coupled with the unexpected thick smoke haze, the bickering over fuel, the difficulty with making international 'phone calls, the unscheduled night stop, had worn me out. At the table my head began to droop, the oblivion of sleep was needed. Choosing a quiet moment in the talk about a possible revolutionary uprising in the country, I took my leave, leaving Dave and the others free to talk about me.

Always with the ferrying of aircraft, there's the getting out of bed in the middle of the night. My tiny, battery powered alarm clock woke me at five am, after the best sleep I'd had in what seemed like weeks. 'Samson' was sorely missed at that point as soiled clothing was again dragged from the soft bag to be worn for the second time around. A good chance of re-uniting with Samson lay with me at Port Moresby the following day, which cheered me up no end and to a degree, calmed the agonies of early morning..

A fresh breeze had sprung up overnight, rustling the palms outside the opened shutters, broken clouds drifted across the stars. The cool touch of the shower made me aware again of the reality of the day ahead.

Breakfast, the ride to the airport, planning, pre-flight checks, Customs and Immigration formalities over, we roared off the runway at eight o'clock with 'Miss Strongwing' as eager as ever to be on her way home. Was it my imagination or did she actually tend to resist passing through the Tontouta heading as I turned her away low for Honiara instead. While taking a last look at the coral reef of the harbour island that had snared both NZ4047 and the four-engine Sandringham so long ago Port Vila was seen in the process of waking up.

Everywhere, people on the streets, at the wharves, or on small harbour craft gaped up at us as we swung past and straightened up for the climb to eight thousand feet. Not so evident on the surface was the thick smoke haze of the day before. Passing through two thousand feet the grand view of Efate that was expected didn't materialise, the coastline with its romantic looking inlets and islets was hidden in smoke haze. We now strode upward into a dirty-looking, grey, sooty mass, with the acrid smell of sulphur pervading the cockpit. At three thousand feet all traces of the surface and Efate had vanished below the thick, grimy veil of what was known as volcanic smog.

"Sorry Dave," I shouted. "That's as much as you'll see for a while, we'll be well to the west of Espiritu Santo before the surface shows up again. After that the next bit of land we'll see will be Guadalcanal, in about four hours."

Dave, who was showing signs of a 'night on the tiles' began to settle down for a nap. The side radio bearing taken from Espiritu Santo's homer came and went as he slept on. He wasn't missing anything. The sky belonged to us with nary a sight of any other aircraft or warnings of them on the radio. Outside, the sky was turning a delicate light blue with clear forward visibility. Gradually the thick smoke haze had all but gone, scattered clouds drifted below. The ocean glared back before starting to take on a deeper, heavier blue colour. The jumbled waves made for an exciting seascape of white horses prancing over the sea, bucking while frothing at the mouth.

Sleeping or even dozing on a long ferry flight in a one pilot aircraft is out of the question even though the desire to do both is sometimes hard to shake off. The pilot must keep pace with the swings or whims of the metal bird, where it's going and what time it is expected to arrive at the destination or any waypoint along the track. Log keeping is of prime importance, or a mental air plot of movement through an air mass that is also moving. The modern pilot in a modern 'plane, flying well above the weather, at altitudes that can be gauged in miles not feet and with so many accurate navigation aids at his disposal, doesn't have the same concerns.

On the first flight I made across the Pacific in a Beechcraft Baron the only long range aid at my disposal was a tiny T12C, automatic direction finder. Shortly before leaving San Francisco I was fortunate enough to learn accidentally through a friend, that the wartime Consulad's San Francisco transmitter was still available for use on the North Pacific. With only five minutes instruction on the use of the chart from the man who sold it to me, that valuable very low frequency aid, found on the lowest band of an automatic direction finder, was used with quite some success. 2000 kilometers from San Francisco the 24 hours a day signal was audible and useable, I had a 'pretty good idea' where we were. Counting and separating the mixture of 22 dots and dashes each hour though, nearly drove me 'dotty'. Consulad was used in the main by mariners in their ships at sea. I'd been told that every month a light 'plane ditched, or went missing between California and Hawaii due to navigational problems. I'm left to wonder how many of those pilots knew of the Consulad and the best method of navigating on it.

The sight of a line of tall, anvil topped storm weather clouds, directly across track about sixty or seventy kilometers away brought me back to reality. Even from the distance and in bright sunshine the lightning could be seen ripping from top to bottom of the cloud. For a time consideration was given to returning to either Luganville on Espiritu Santos or Port Vila, but the thought of sitting at either place while the powers-that-be debated the worth of selling me more of their precious fuel, drove me on.

The two violently rough segments of the flight endured since leaving the 'Friendlies', had rattled me. Surely another battle with the elements wasn't about to begin were my 'doom and gloom' thoughts. By the look of things, there was little chance of making a diversion around the storm cells. Without radar to assist in guiding 'Miss

Strongwing' through the worst lumps they'd have to be taken head on again using only guesswork.

Reaching over to touch Dave while pointing over the instrument panel to the mass of cloud ahead, he came awake as I yelled at his ear.

"Pull your seat belt up real tight, watch your head, put the latches on the flight bag. By the look of it we could soon be in for another bumpy ride."

My imagination kept bringing the giant wall of storm clouds closer as we bored our way towards them, although they were more than ten minutes away, which left time for me to set 'Miss Strongwing' up for her next ordeal.

While in the process of descending to 'six thousand feet' the power of the engines was reduced until the sound reached the nice, steady 'easy easy' note I liked best in turbulence. Tightening the throttle levers' tension nut, ensuring the pitot heat was on, the fuller tanks selected to the engines, preparations were made for the expected rough, wet ride, where all my attention would be fixed on the instruments and flying controls. (Engines starving of fuel in a bouncing aircraft while flying blind in turbulent cloud can and will divert the pilot's attention away from control of the aircraft, with sometimes disastrous results). My eyes took in the most important instruments of the flying and engine panels as hands, feet and belly were transferred to a 'relax mode' while at the same time pinning my backside well down into the seat.

Like a man adrift and out of his depth, Dave was smiling a sickly smile as if his face might crack as we approached the wall of bubbling cloud towering high above the fragile 'plane, directly in the flight path. In seconds thick, wet, purple clouds closed in all around us, rain ripped the metal frame with the noise of a chainsaw.

Inside, the swirling air of the' cu nimb' thrust the first stab, a stab that rolled 'Miss Strongwing' almost on to her side. Resisting the temptation to wind in excessive amounts of aileron she was left to ride back on her own in-built stability. Be prepared, 'do not over control' is a good motto in turbulent weather in such a light aircraft, do not try to beat the aircraft to do what it could probably do without your help.

No sooner had an even keel been reached when a mighty gust picked her up and shook her as a dog might shake a fluffy toy in its jaws. First, my body seemed to weigh a ton, as pushed hard down in the seat, we soared heavenwards. Next, both Dave and I were suspended as a couple of astronauts might be, weightless in the sudden drop, my empty hands groping for the control wheel, my feet for the rudder pedals. When all was re-united the wheel was gripped a little tighter. A quick sideways glance assured me that the wings were still with us but left me wondering whether the forecasting of weather in such isolated zones was of any use at all, as we rolled and pitched, yawed, thumped and bumped along. A red blob over the weather-man's map of the Coral Sea, a no-go sign, might have been a good idea that day. Ten minutes later Dave made the first use of a 'chunder' bag, more as a result of his late night he told me later. After that was over he perked up as we cleared the air by opening a vent that admit-ted a fine spray with the air that prickled the skin. Up to that time the trip over such an idyllic part of the Pacific must have been a bitter dis-appointment for him.

After being tossed about in a series of storms, a short period of rel-ative calm was granted us, although heavy rain still made tearing sounds as it lashed the windshield. Lightning flashed everywhere, St.Elmo's fire danced along 'Miss Strongwing's' long snout again.

After two hours of such very rough treatment fatigue began to set in. The directional gyro demanded so much attention, to a point where it was unable to maintain a constant heading for more than a minute before 'precessing' rapidly again. Whether some of the other vacuum driven gyro instruments would also fail to put me on a limited flying panel became another worry that was not pleasant.

Rather like Fiji, the Solomons had a 'big blow' season. My thoughts turned to arrival at Henderson Field. All the weather reports we possessed had originated in Nandi and were now well out of their valid time frame. The 'fair weather' forecast for our arrival on Guadalcanal (attached to the clipboard in Dave's care), was now soaking wet, smudged, unreadable and now committed to memory.

Somewhere ahead in the flight path the massive island of Guadalcanal reared as a wall of jagged crests of mountains to what was thought to be six thousand feet. In the wet season the summits of the island were often hidden in sullen, towering clouds. Imagination kept bringing the big island closer. Intense concentration was needed to overcome the dread feeling that when through a sudden break in the clouds an ugly, jagged tooth of granite might spring up from nowhere, rushing towards the aircraft at the rate of knots. That sort of a situation can put a pilot on edge. So there we sat in turbulent cloud with pelting rain lashing the windshield with some of the water forcing its way through tired seals to form a cloud of fine spray in the cockpit, or drip unremittingly cold and wet, onto our legs or into our shoes.

The radio continued to spew out ear-piercing shrieks of static while firm, but not too firm, handling of the controls was taken up. The whole effort was tiring me more than it should. With Dave watching me like a hawk, my hands and fingers on the wheel were purposely relaxed to let the tension drain from my shoulders as my toes 'wiggled' in wet socks.

Passing some kind of a joke or even miming some silly thing in those situations can sometimes do the relaxing trick. There was no chance of that at this time because of the ripping, tearing sounds of rain on the hull drowning out most of the engine noise. Just how those engines could absorb so much water and still run perfectly I'll never know. My praises and thanks went to the Lord at that time for aviation's dedicated designers and technicians.

My mental air plot placed me twenty minutes south of the big island before the weather began to improve. First the heavy rain eased perceptibly. Through the screens of rain, gaps of light began to appear. Minutes later the outlines of the separated shapes of towering cumulus appeared as the cloud thinned out. Breathing became a little easier. In only a few minutes I was able to give what was becoming the standard whoop of delight as we flew out of the storm clouds into smoother, clearer air. All that was needed was a lazy zig-zag or two to keep 'Miss Strongwing' clear of the remainder of the 'tall boys'.

For a while and with a dry windshield, we cruised steadily over a layer of low cloud, clinging as a verandah to the bottom of the storm area. Soon even that finished. Below us were the sparkling blue waters of the Pacific's Solomon Sea, ruffled in whitecaps from the 'south-east trades'. To me, exhausted by the battle, it was the most beautiful sight. For Dave's benefit I slumped in the seat while exhaling a great sigh of relief.

Although we were less than 150 kilometers from Henderson Field by estimate, there was still no sign of the beacon on the radio direction finder, meaning that we were in the 'shadow' of the very tall island, the waves from the beacon's transmitter being blocked by the island's mountains.

In clear weather now and with the southern coast of Guadalcanal in sight we surged on to cross the island with little of the messing about that is sometimes needed to dodge ominous mountain peaks.

Suddenly, definitely, the radio compass became alive, the needle pointing firmly to the beacon.

With Savo Island and Ironbottom Sound clearly in sight, the Tower at Henderson came in loud and clear. Down went 'Miss Strongwings' nose as we started into a fast descent for Henderson, on the plains near the sea on the northern side of the historic island. We came in high, aiming to level off at two thousand feet for a look over the Sound, Savo Island, Point Cruz and the town of Honiara, before taking up a wide circuit to land.

For me a visit to Guadalcanal by air could not be complete without thoughts of the naval and land battles that took place there in '42-43'.dominating the mind. The Sound was so still, sun drenched, peaceful and perfect, it was hard to see why it was named Ironbottom.

Under those deep and dreadful but tranquil-looking waters, lie the battered remains of more than a dozen warships of USA, Australia and Japan. There's no other place in the world where so many fighting ships of war lie in such close proximity one to the other, after having been sunk in battle, some with each other. One can't help but think of the dozens, or hundreds, of the sailors and soldiers that went down with them. Any time I see the Sound I am taken up with the futility of war.

The battle of Savo Island was explained to Dave as we circled the Sound. He sat back in the seat, quiet and thoughtful, as I joined for a very long final approach to the 'new' Henderson. The runway was now long, hard and free of any shell or bomb craters, only a third of the length was used up before I swung 'Miss Strongwing' on to a taxiway to the terminal area. Immediately I felt more at home now, in the more than four hours elapsed since leaving Port Vila, not a thought had been given to the fuel crisis.

Well-known as I am here with friends who can be relied on, we will be on our way in thirty minutes with fuel tanks full to the brim. A quick turn-around would mean an arrival in Port Moresby by late afternoon, with a strong possibility of Samson being retrieved. Those positive thoughts were mine as I chopped the engines at the bowser. It turned out that stupidly, like Goebbels, I believed my own propaganda.

Moresby was a 24-hour airport. There were no concerns about an after dark arrival. Linking up with Samson again was foremost in my mind. Years before a major aviation journal reported the story of the British Overseas Airways (BOAC) pilots who were changing over to British Airways, (BA) and who declared they were 'sticking to their uniforms'. I felt the same way.

How often are the best laid plans of mice and men thwarted? Most times it seems. The bowser at Henderson was in the hands of the regional islands airline. The attendant politely, but firmly, informed me that fuel would not be available, even after he was shown the International fuel carnet, which, thanks to Dee's foresight, included Honiara as a possible delivery point. He suggested that the company Manager should be contacted at his office in Honiara from the 'phone in a small office in the hangar. A feeling of frustration rose within me. Before ringing the numbers I sat to think things over. Something told me I was approaching a very high hurdle, to get set for the jump.

Some seven years before, my company in New Guinea had bought the only air company then operating in the Solomons, from its New Guinea based owner. The deal had included two obsolete, outdated aircraft, a regular service operating license, three dwellings, a leased hangar and town office along with a vehicle or two. The owner and I were good friends and on good terms. He confided in me that his Solomons venture had not gone at all well, mainly he thought, because his staff had not promoted the fledgling company for the Solomons indigenous population in the right way. In return for new airfields the government of the Protectorate was demanding regular services to islands with little in the way of an established economy. Twin engine 'planes were flying long distances with few passengers, mainly government servants. The Solomon Islanders were not being encouraged to fly. Worst of all, the Manager was not doing anything about the situation, with constant operating losses, very little profit and lots of requests for operating funds from the New Guinea owner. My friend just wanted out, while he concentrated on his business in New Guinea aviation and shipping, which was doing extremely well. From my view the Solomons were in need of amphibious services using modern twin engine US built machines of the Grumman make. In a British administered Protectorate that idea was not well received and tantamount to a bomb going off in government buildings!

After many trips to the Solomons, accounting and auditing appraisals and a hundred and one other things, with the complete approval of my Board of Directors, the sale was pledged. In discussions prior to the sale, we were told that staffing of the enterprise would be in our hands, we could 'hire or fire' as we thought fit but the regular services as standing must always be maintained. We all knew that when taking another business over, it's best to start out with a clean sheet, with people of your own choice and so it was with us. Members of our New Guinea staff would be transferred to the key positions in Honiara as the situation demanded. The Solomon's staff would be subject to re-appraisal except for one senior member however, who would be retained as Manager. That was the Board's decision where I had been out-voted.

From that time, in connivance with a friend or two on the Board, the man was a thorn in my side. In New Guinea I was into a heavy flying program. For him it was easy to know my whereabouts. Faced with any problem and he had lots, he would choose a time when I was absent from my office and confide with the company secretary or other Board members over the matter or send them personal letters that by-passed me. That particular trick is known as 'passing notes down the chimney' and is in no way related to 'whistle blowing'.

His worst 'sin' was to terminate Fred Ladd a person I had employed specifically to build up the Solomon Islander's confidence in their embryo airline. With thoughts to the future Fred was employed for his experience with amphibians and as one who through his personality alone could return a profit to the fledgling airline.

Fred's letter had left me disgusted, to quote "From the time I arrived it has been an unhappy event…he has not fitted me in socially nor endeavoured to harmonize…I very much wanted to stay and flying is my great love… takes no interest in 'first flighters' and couldn't care less whether the eyes of a Solomon Islander roll in fright on take-off or help them solve the mysteries of the seat belt…he seems to hold my 16,000 hours against me, I was quite prepared to '2'ic' here, enjoy flying and learn to love the people…has lectured me on airmanship and islands weather, that's funny, I thought I'd picked up a lot of that during my Rabaul and Solomons experience in Grumman 'Avengers' during WW2."

The effect of the rudeness, the arrogance behind Fred's termination that had caused him to write to me in such a manner stayed with me for a long time. When eventually I 'sold out' and left, the company the manager and I were not the best of friends. Now I was certain that when I picked up the 'phone and called the number, he would be the man at the other end, or it might be his wife who then worked in the office, another situation I had been unhappy with 'in the good old days'.

Things went much as expected with his voice sounding somewhat triumphant, not at all sympathetic. No, I couldn't have any fuel, stocks were low, it had been decided not to sell to an 'outsider'. I didn't feel like 'crawling' or pleading, that wasn't my style.

After he'd hung up I hitched a ride on a work-truck into Honiara, the intention being to make a call from the Post Office to Dee in Sydney, to give him an update on progress. I was also aware that Dee's company had a major share in the Solomons venture.

Time ticked by before the call came through, Australia and the Solomons suffered frequent breakdowns in telephonic communications. Dee was absent from his office on business. A message was left with his secretary covering all the details of my plight, plus a request for an urgent return call. Dee would have all the numbers. Still fuming, in a sweat but trying to remain calm, I sought out a taxi and returned to Henderson Field.

At the airport I stayed within earshot of the 'phone, killing time by going over the navigation charts and drafting a flight plan for Port Moresby. Only then did it come to my notice that 'Miss Strongwing's' high frequency radio wasn't fitted with the frequencies that were mandatory for the route Honiara/Moresby. Up to that time Miss Strongwing's set had served adequately, but I knew that an ongoing flight to Moresby without the frequencies specified for the route could only end in trouble. I was in despair while searching for an answer.

Then it came to me. The radio sets in the Solomons several 'planes I knew were of the same make and type as that fitted to 'Miss Strongwing'. The crystals for the various frequencies would therefore be interchangeable. Why not borrow an appropriate crystal and install it in the Aztec? The crystal required would not be needed in the Solomons region, as flights in the direction of Port Moresby for them were rare indeed. If borrowed, the crystal could be returned from Sydney within a few days.

Full of faith, hope, but not much confidence, I pranced off to the hangar office and 'phoned the Manager, although deep in my heart I knew pretty well what to expect. No, a crystal could not be bought, borrowed, or even temporarily stolen, they would be needed if a sudden call came in for a flight into that area.

"It's most unlikely that four 'planes would be hired at the one time would it not? " I queried in a cold calculating voice.

"That would depend on which type of aircraft got hired wouldn't it? I definitely can't let you have a crystal from any of our aircraft."

So the day ended, we were in for another overnight stay sorting out fuel and radio problems.

'Miss Strongwing' was moved from the 'bowser with no juice' to make her comfortable for the night, while Dave raced to the terminal to get a taxi on hold. Just in time too, no sooner had I re-parked the Aztec than a 'crop duster' rolled up to take on some fuel. The 'plane, New Zealand registered, was on permanent hire to spray Guadalcanal Plains Coy's extensive rice-paddies nearby. The pilot was affable and friendly, although obviously in a hurry, as he started into re-fuelling his spray-spattered metal bird.

How come I am so clever? His high frequency radio, providentially of the same make as mine, was only used when ferrying between New Zealand and the Solomons and the frequency I needed was never used anyway. Yes, most certainly I could have the appropriate crystal I needed, on a loan basis, but I would have to wait to make the change-over after his spraying task was finished. My 'good guardian angel' theory had been confirmed.

The sun had set when, with the crystal installed in 'Miss Strong-wings' radio set, Dave and I checked into the town's best and only seaside hotel, with a magnificent view across to Ironbottom Sound and Savo Island the centre piece of the Sound. We'd not eaten all day, or had anything to drink except water in sparse quantities out of recycled plastic cups.

In my room, the day's sweaty grime was washed away with a long, long, shower. After drying off I changed my clothes, the cotton pants, shirt and socks worn that day, for the cotton pants, shirt and socks worn the day before, while I thought of the joy fresh clothes would bring when I met up with 'Samson' again. With the radio fixed, fuel was then the last obstacle to be hurdled. To that end, everything now depended on Dee returning my call.

Half way through dinner I was called to the 'phone. The air service Manager had received a telex he explained in patronizing, reconciliatory tones, which had 'cleared the way' for him to allow me the fuel and the crystal I needed! A radio technician, borrowed from the government, would be on hand next morning to install the crystal. The unnecessary petty drama was over. I didn't say much, I'm sure my gloated feelings were flowing through the 'phone line with strength enough to be felt at the other end.

Long before the technician would have been on the scene the following morning to install the crystal, 'Miss Strongwing' soared into the drizzly air and set course for Port Moresby via the beacon at Munda on New Georgia. From there, the Solomon and Coral Sea presented the greatest distance yet attempted on our journey. The route wasn't a popular one, the fuel margins for 'Miss Strongwing' were slim, strict monitoring of fuel consumption over the route would be required.

Over Munda we piled into thick cloud with moderate turbulence again and remained there for more than three hours. Not as rough as on previous days, but enough to demand one's attention with a tight seat belt and a wary eye on the clocks, which was hardly pleasure flying to say the least.

Time came to test the crystal and call Port Moresby. The possible results of that call had hung over me like a pall as we crept up to the transfer point. Wonder of wonders, the reply to my first call came through loud and clear. Except for Dave getting tired of my yelling intermittently, I could have sung for joy. Of the several Port Moresby frequencies that could be required on the route the crystal chosen by me on a guess would serve for the remainder of the flight. Do y' hear what I keep saying about 'guardian angels'? My thoughts and thanks went to the 'crop duster' on Guadalcanal, zipping over the paddy fields at 'nought feet', spray off, pulling up for a tight tear-drop turn then down to the crop, spray on, lucky beggar, his own boss. If the drizzle we'd run into had reached Honiara well maybe he could have a day off.

Hours passed when through a break in the clouds, Dave was able to sight militarily historic Milne Bay at the eastern tip of mainland Papua New Guinea as we flew over, its' normally calm waters charged with masses of whitecaps. It was there that the Japanese had received their first real military defeat in WW2. Dave had read the history books of the action and was thrilled to see the two airfields that were so important to the Australian victory. Up to that time of day he hadn't seen much, he then took a much more keen interest in proceedings. We were scooting along now, ahead of time. From Milne Bay a heading was taken up that would take us away from the tall, spinal central mountains, to a less clouded area along the coast of Papua.

The final hour was uneventful, slipping over the blue, blue sea along the reef enclosed coastline (an extension of the Great Barrier Reef), with an eye always on the fuel gauges but knowing there were several coastal airstrips that could be used in any emergency. At last there was visibility and time to point out a few more of Papua's famous landmarks to Dave who hadn't seen a lot of terra firma since leaving Fiji, the route of the Kokoda Track for one. In bright, sticky sunshine we landed at Port Moresby after more than five hours of airtime.

Weeks seemed to have passed since setting out on the trip to the Friendlies. I had to force myself to believe that it was only seven days, so much had happened. My plan had been to proceed on to Cairns for an over-night stay, but the strain of the trip overall, with its weather and fuel uncertainties, had caught up with me. I needed a worry-free sleep for a change, plus some clean clothes, although I felt that there wasn't much chance of 'Samson' being around by that time through having been air freighted to Sydney to catch me up!

Knowing some of the vagaries of the airlines of the day however, I thought it was worth an enquiry at least. Miracles happen as I've mentioned before, my valued port might still be close by. After clearing Customs, I rushed to the airline's traffic counter, only to be told that Samson, the hard case, had left for Sydney two days before. The truth of that left me completely deflated!

There was nothing else for it but to take a twin- cab taxi to the shopping complex in the suburbs at Boroko, purchase a new set of under and over clothes, then go to an hotel for a good clean up. It was there that I had a vision of Dee's 'bean counter' complaining to him of the cost of a further set of under clothing on my expenses claim. Were they disposables, or did I use them only once might well be one of his suspicious, accountancy based complaints when auditing the cost of repossessing the Aztec. High on the priority list also was a call to Dee to tell him that I would be in Sydney very late the next day, to have him or someone with 'Samson', meet me on arrival at Bankstown if that airport was open, or if not then the Kingsford-Smith International. Again he was absent from his office 'on business' his secretary assuring me he would get the message. A call to wife Betty in the New Guinea highlands failed through the system 'being down'.

Faced with flights of a total of twelve hours I was at the Briefing Office very early the following morning. The 'weather-man' came up with a doom and gloom forecast. A massive tropical cyclone code-named Wanda, was on a rampage down the east coast of Queensland.

"You didn't know? " he questioned. "I'm surprised you didn't, coming from Port Vila and the Solomons you've been flying through some of Wanda's lesser cousins, the Coral Sea and the Gulf is full of 'em, Cairns itself will be OK, tho' I'd advise you to check on the southern weather before proceeding on to Sydney from there, you'll have some favourable tailwinds for part of the route too."

As my thoughts turned to the unread scrap of what looked like blotting paper on the clipboard in the aircraft, I didn't have the heart to tell him that most of our flight had been made without a valid route forecast.

Cairns was partly covered in low cloud and drizzle drifting in from the sea as we scudded across the islands of the Great Barrier Reef on the way in for landing. Meticulous in their search of 'Miss Strongwing's' interior parts for contraband, the customs officers took more than half an hour to check us over while we were asked to remain near the aircraft, each of us holding an opened umbrella, unable to get re-fuelled because of the rain.

"The Import Licence Number for the aircraft, can we have it now please? " the senior man asked, after our passports and luggage had been dealt with. Baffled by his question I got down to explaining the 'importation situation' dropping in Dee's 'phone numbers for good measure. After jotting down some of the information he hurried off, leaving Dave and I up in the air as to our fate. After nearly an hour, when he returned, it was to say we were satisfactorily cleared. Another personally stressful trauma was over.

We'd spent two hours on the ground before 'Miss Strongwing' lifted off the rain-soaked runway to join the southbound track to Brisbane. For almost two hours we flew above scattered clouds with the high overcast gradually creeping down on us. Nearing Rockhampton at 7000 feet, the two cloud layers joined company. We plugged on, in wet pea soup.

An unprecedented amount of chatter was then jamming the airwaves. 'Planes, airline and other, were coming from all directions.

'Rocky' Tower was sounding more like LA International on a busy morning. All I had to do was listen out to get the picture. The Brisbane area had been declared closed to all air traffic, by flight conditions and severe flooding of both Eagle Farm and Archerfield airports and the river city itself. Aviation communication channels were out of order. Fifteen minutes later a clearance to join the stream of diverted aircraft saw us on return to 'Rocky' and another night of separation from Samson.

With passengers stranded from the many airline aircraft, central city accommodation was at a premium. It was early evening before we were confirmed into a small private hotel on the outskirts of the cattle town, on a room-share basis, where my Boroko purchased clothing, was again put to use.

The room was without an STD 'phone, calls from the hotel weren't easy to make. To wait in line at the shabby phone box in the reception area for a call to Dee to advise him of the delay didn't appeal to me. He had the resources (and the 'fullness' to tack on to the end) to trace my whereabouts if he so desired, 'tomorrow' would have to be the day of arrival at Bankstown.

With the skies clearing, communications restored and a diversion around Brisbane possible, a 'non-stopper' to Sydney was planned the next day, a flight of about five hours. Reports of the flood carnage at Brisbane and environs were coming in. The deluge and consequent flood had destroyed thousands of homes, rail, air and road transport was at a standstill. When abeam Brisbane itself, we could see the rain pelting down and the lakes forming on the thousands of square kilometres of cropping, pastureland, highways and railways in the Brisbane and Lockyer Valleys.

Across the New South Wales border a tail wind helped to shove us along. As if knowing she'd soon be home 'Miss Strongwing' took the bit and with little guidance from me, sped on towards the Singleton homer with renewed zest flowing through her every rivet.

Bankstown was having a perfect day with a warm sun, a light breeze and little traffic as we joined for landing. The 'Flight from the Friendlies' was almost over with the aircraft showing signs of a hard fought battle. Miss Strongwing' was about to be returned safely to her rightful owners, my assignment completed. Dave was happy to have experienced a side of life he never knew existed. In the years to come he would be able to tell his children and/or grandchildren, of how he with a maverick pilot in a frail 'plane, had survived some of the worst 'storms of the air' 'somewhere over the South Pacific that included the Solomon and Coral Sea during hurricane 'Wanda'.

There wasn't a soul in sight as we came to a stop in front of Dee's hangar. For the first time I remembered that the day was Saturday. The hangar doors were closed, the tarmac a tomb. After all the trouble experienced en route to Sydney somehow Dee had been expected to welcome the arrival of his charge. The emptiness of what should have been a triumphant arrival for 'Miss Strongwing' left me completely deflated. There must be, there had to be, a message for me somewhere about the hangar were my thoughts as we clambered out on to a clean but only moderately warm tarmac.

For an hour we waited without a sign of anyone coming to receive and hangar the precious Aztec. The time was used to scribble a note to leave in the aircraft, which included the flying times for the maintenance people, the damage to the prop, the method suggested for the return of the crystal to the 'croppie' at Honiara by the first available flight and the payment of my fees.

With Dave becoming anxious to meet up with friends, 'Miss Strongwing' was closed up for the last time, covers, chocks at the wheels, controls locked, cockpit tidied up, props 'dressed' to the horizontal. As the door was closed for the last time the feeling was that her every rivet and rib was personally known to me. Soon she would undergo a full inspection in an attempt to discover if any part of the frame was bent or rivets popped, should the note left with her be taken seriously. Following that, a paint job would be needed on the leading edge of her wings, particularly where the paint had been stripped off by the force of the rain that worst of all nights. I told her that she would soon look and feel a lot better, as I ran a hand over her long, drooping snout and quietly said goodbye. At my suggestion Dave followed up with a little peck to her rain-chipped beak, before we gathered our bags and walked off to the Aero Club.

Before turning the corner of the hangar, I looked back to see her for the last time, alone and mute, on the wide concrete apron, the breeze gently stirring her pitot cover drapes, her engines as eyes, staring back at me solemnly. Somehow that last look told me that she was happy for I never saw her again.

At the Club we said our goodbyes. Dave caught a taxi to the city while I checked in to the accommodation. There was a message from Dee giving me his home number to call. He was at golf his wife declared, before she read out a message for me.

"So sorry I couldn't attend your arrival. Thanks for a safe delivery. The bad news is that your suitcase is not at 'Air-Freight' and if it was it couldn't be picked up by anyone except yourself, a necessary customs formality. It is believed to be at Brisbane. Call me on Monday at the office if you want any more help."

Any more help? There it ran through my mind that I would never see Samson again, ever. Obviously Saturday wasn't the best day for an 'off sked' arrival, weekends in Australia being what they were, with everybody heading for beaches, golf courses, tennis clubs, race tracks, TAB's and every other type of venue for all sorts of sports and pastimes. After such a hectic trip my feelings had been flattened by the style of our reception. The day I had expected to be full of triumph, cheer and goodwill had turned sour. Feelings of elation had turned to anger.

My clothes were scruffy. At the laundry the rather sticky contents of my bag were emptied into two machines. After setting them going with the machines doing the beating and tossing about there was time enough for a cool drink at the bar. When the machines stopped the clothes went into the dryer before some were ironed before being stashed into the bag again. Two hours later with the washing chores finished not only did I feel better but an important decision had also been made.

The return of the unused traveller's cheques, the receipts and settlement of the imprest account could be done by mail, the excess cash by telegraph, my fees finalized the same way. The apparent loss of Samson, wherever he was, in due time would have to be handled by the airline. There was no point in me hanging around. The following day would see me on a flight to New Guinea, for my dear highland home and family.

A fierce sun beat down on the tarmac as I came down the steps from the Boeing 727 at Jackson's, Port Moresby, exactly on time, leaving an hour for a transfer to a Fokker Friendship for the flight to the highlands and home. I raced along the covered walkway to be amongst the first into the arrival hall. With only carry-on luggage to hinder me, customs and immigration formalities would only take a few minutes. My turn soon came for a passport chop. The moustache of the New Guinean official was seen to quiver as he brought the stamp down with a great whack' on a half-filled page, with precision born of long practice. I sidled past his desk and headed for the luggage check table on the far side of the baggage carousel that was just beginning to rotate.

First class baggage began to pierce the split rubber curtain of the hole in the wall. Something there, not on the carousel but standing against the wall, then caught my eye. I'd know it anywhere. A black suitcase covered in stickers, unmistakably Samson, how, why, I didn't care.

The hall was filling up with arriving passengers elbowing their way up to the carousel to collect their luggage for inspection. No one seemed to take notice as I walked to the wall, took hold of Samson and proceeded to an inspection outlet. After reading my declaration the official waved me on. In a minute I was out on the pavement and heading for the domestic check-in counter, my long-lost traveling companion firmly in hand.

In the long check-in queue at domestic I kept him moving forward with my foot, watched closely as the traffic officer tied a GKA label to the handle and from a viewing window, watched as he was towed aboard a trolley to the Fokker then loaded into the forward locker. Very useful those stickers, they really stood out. This time there could be no mistake, as seasoned travellers we were about to travel home together.

Samson always liked going home. The kids would gather round him, giggling and jostling for positions on a bed as I opened him up to display the gifts for them that he'd sometimes carried over lands or oceans, while cast behind a ferry fuel tank, jammed between removed seats or specially adapted fuel hoses, or standing upright in the cargo hold of an airliner. Not to be left out of the fun, Jeffrey the cat would jump in, to take up an observer's position on top of rumpled clothes, watched jealously by our Corgis, Buddy, Brecon and Goldie, sniffing and snuffling around the 'hard case'.

An arrival home from the USA was special when Samson disgorged unusual metal toys, small and light, a play 'phone, a voice recorder, air guns for the boys, a pretty doll for Dianne, a furry toy-dog named Mikie for Kath, a music album for a loving mother, he'd carried them all home, safe and sound. Things wouldn't be so happy today. Not so much as a grass skirt, a lei or a straw hat from the 'Friendlies', a record of the Methodist choir in Suva of that soul-rending 'Isa Lei', a super smooth, carved ebony dolphin from the New Hebs or Solomons, a Koala or Kangaroo from Australia. Nothing! Not even a pay cheque!

When emptied of the unworn clothing inside him, Samson would be closed like an oyster and parked in his usual spot on top of the wardrobe in the main bedroom.

A little dust might gather on him there, but not much, regular dusting was a well-known feature of his house. There he'd wait patiently until taken down, wiped clean and packed for travel again. He might even depart with an extra sticker or two on his sides next time, telling the world he'd also been to those exotic Pacific Island places when really he hadn't.

I'd been flying the mountains again for almost a month when a cheque for $800 from Dee's 'bean counter' arrived in the mail. The attached note stated that $200 had been deducted from my fees for the repair required to one of the aircraft's propellers after return to Sydney. It was pleasing to learn that 'Miss Strongwing's' vitals had been attended to at such reasonable cost. If there were any repercussions over 'Miss Strongwing's' uplift none were mentioned. Any form of a receipt on my part was not asked for, nor was one given.

ANTILLES AIR BOATS

Some of the big news in Australian aviation in the early seventies of the 20th century was the purchase by Captain (General to some) Charles Blair, of the two Sandringham flying-boats of Ansett Airlines of Australia that plied the route Sydney to Lord Howe Island. The news of their withdrawal from that service had brought an angry response from the residents of Lord Howe and other aviation buffs who loved 'ye olde boats', all to no avail. Ansett claimed that they were just too expensive to operate from their base at Sydney's Rose Bay.

Charles Blair was a well-known US aviation personality, married to the famous movie star Maureen O'Hara. Charles (Charlie to Maureen, his friends and employees) was a pioneer in trans-Atlantic flying with American Export Airlines using Sikorsky VF44 flying boats. Also included in his long and distinguished flying career was inter-continental Air Mail flying and solo flights across the Arctic and the North Pole in a single-engine P51 Mustang, named by him as Excalibur III. Charlie was one of America's great pioneer pilots. After retiring as Pan American's senior pilot, he opened up Antilles Air Boats in the US Virgin Islands, headquartered at Christiansted, St. Croix, the new 'promised land' for the Sandringham and 'Sunderingham'.

Charlie had been awarded the Harmon Trophy for his flight across the North Pole, the Thurlow Award for his outstanding contribution to the science of navigation and the Distinguished Flying Cross for leading the first flight of jet fighters over the North Pole from Maguire Air

Force Base in New Jersey to Wethersfield RAF Station in England, without the use of any ground aids. The F84-F Thunderstreak 'Excalibur 1V' that Charlie flew, its guns stripped and replaced with electronic hardware, was amongst the first of the 'electrically gadgeted' metal birds.

Under Charlie's expert guidance, Antilles Air Boats had become one of the leading commuter airlines in the US if not in the world, by numbers of passengers carried and frequency of flights. Antilles Air Boats used Grumman G21 (Goose) ten passenger amphibians on shuttle services between St. Croix, St Thomas, St John, Tortola in the British Virgin Islands, San Juan and Fajardo in Puerto Rico.

In purchasing the two big flying-boats from Ansett, Charlie's plans were to expand his Virgin Islands network of air services further 'down island ' to Antigua, Martinique, Grenada, St. Maarten, Guadelope and Trinidad Tobago with upgraded tourist services. He had spotted the big 'boats' while on a visit to Australia with Maureen and asked to be on the mailing list if ever they were to be sold.

In due time both boats were flown to the US by Charlie and an Ansett pilot, where they met up with certification problems. As there were no identical types already on the US register, a full certification program was called for, carrying with it an expensive price tag.

Charlie was not a man to be put off by a few rules or regulations. He proceeded with his application for services in the Caribbean using the big metal water birds' from Australia after a modified certification process was completed. In the meantime the big boats were placed on the British Colonial register at Antigua, which raised another problem for him, that of operations from the US Virgins with a British registered aircraft! How complicated is the aviation world!

Charlie had a powerful string to his bow. He was an aeronautical engineer with access to influential offices in high places in the various ruling government agencies, so continued with his dream.

At about that time having heard of the happenings in the Virgin Islands, from New Guinea I submitted an application for employment with AAB. I had previously flown the Short Solent, Short Sunderland and Catalina and thought that I would stand a good chance of gaining a place in AAB's new enterprise. I had been in New Guinea for many years and things were changing there fast. I wasn't quite sure whether I was working for Air New Guinea (Air Niugini) or the Australian Air Pilot's Federation. The good days were over, heavy, politicised unionism had arrived and I just longed to be flying a 'water-bird' again, where a pilot was judged on merit and not on his particular robotic political leanings.

With the Sandringhams, Charlie had recruited from Ansett a very experienced ex-wartime Sunderland pilot, Captain Ron Gillies and licensed Sandringham Engineer Noel Holle, who with their families were enjoying the good life in the Virgin Islands.

My application went with a picture of me standing in front of a Dornier 27 at a New Guinea mountain airstrip, Wonenara by name, with a bunch of Kukukuku warriors who were each complete with bow and arrow and with pigs' tusks through the septum of their noses. In my letter, as a bit of a joke, I described myself as, 'I am the guy on the left'.

Within ten days of my application being mailed a telex arrived requesting I attend an interview at Christiansted St Croix, USVI. I reached Christiansted at a time when Charlie was away in New York on Sandringham business.

I liked what I saw of AAB, the ramp and hangar right in the middle of town. Every minute of the day it seemed a Grumman Goose was alighting in, or leaving the sunny, wind-tossed harbour, or powering up the ramp to the open-sided terminal and the locally famous 'Goose Grill'. All day long, seven days a week, the old world town suffered the roar of the 'Gooses' (note not Geese) engines blasting loud, spray flying as one would skim down, across, or up the harbour on take-off, or ramping after alighting on a harbour loaded with cruising yachts and power boats of all classes and descriptions.

As with St Thomas, the ramp was in the centre of the 18th century ex-Danish town, with its' colourful and quaint 'ginger-bread' architecture all guarded by a 17th century walled fort bristling with shiny, black cannons.

Noel's wife Margaret, an ex Ansett Sandringham air hostess, took me on a very instructive drive around the island of St. Croix (pronounced 'Saint Croy' in USA), taking in the many historic places of interest, where the names of Christopher Columbus or Sir Francis Drake were by-words. Margaret assured me that St. Dunstan's school, where her three boys attended, was a great school and would suit any youngsters we might bring with us too. I'd been wondering about that and was relieved to know that the schooling problem had been solved. It was easy to see that AAB was a family friendly organisation with the accent on friendly.

Left hand drive autos' drove on the left in the US Virgin Islands, tricky stuff, the moral of the story being that if you are stuck behind a slow-moving bus, stay there.

Most of all I was thrilled to see a Sandringham tied up to the jetty that adjoined the ramp. With Noel I was able to inspect the expansive flight deck, take the Captains seat and place my hand on the four throttle levers again, while my spittle flew around the instruments glare shield. That metal water bird was for me.

The interviews with Captain Bob Scott, Chief Pilot of AAB (when Charlie was 'off island') and others must have gone OK. A week after returning to Port Moresby I received an appointment by telex and a month later, with all household effects in the hands of shippers, with my wife Betty and youngest son Scott (16), we were on our way to a new life on the other side of the world, the exciting, steeped in history, US Virgin Islands.

We flew by Pan Am from Sydney through Auckland, Honolulu and Los Angeles to New York, where after a day's rest we switched to American Airlines for the final flight down to Christiansted on the island of St Croix. An AAB staffer showed us to our fully furnished apartment at 'Questa Verde' condominium, on a height that over-looked the town, harbour, Caribbean Sea, AAB's ramp and hangar, for us an exciting but rather different layout than Port Moresby.

While still in extra-long air-travel stupor, we'd only begun to un-pack when a knock came on the door. I couldn't believe my eyes at first for the caller was that great lady Maureen O'Hara herself, in her hands a teapot and a packet of tea.

"Coming from where you have, a tea drinking area, I thought you would like a nice cup of tea to settle you in" were her first words after introducing herself (which hardly needed doing). "I'm sure you must know how to make tea from a packet, not many people do from around here. Charlie is sorry he'll not be able to meet up with you yet. He'll see you in the next few days. We live just up the road a little" she announced in soft, lilting Irish tones. Being part Irish myself I just love to hear that accent. I was tongue-tied, nothing short of flabber-gasted as she went on.

"Charlie was very taken with that picture you sent, it tickled his fancy, mine too, he'll be happy to know you have discarded the bone through your nose and are wearing a 'shirrt' and trousers and your wife a very nice frock and shoes. Oh yes I have already received a report from the girls at the ramp."

Only then was I able to laugh at my impertinence. After posting the letter I had often wondered how it would be received, or whether I might have gone too far. Those questions had then been answered. There's always a build up in tension on taking up a new appointment, on just how things are going to work out, with all your eggs in one basket as ours were at that time.

Maureen's visit was short. After she'd gone, Betty and I were both very much more relaxed and happy with the decision that had been made. We were both taken up with the old world charm of what we'd seen of Christiansted and looked forward to the days ahead.

A few days later came my first meeting with Captain Charles Blair. Tall (very), slim, not carrying an ounce of fat, dark, handsome and a perfect gentleman, is how he's best described, with very little of the 'twang' of what is called an 'American accent' but more with the tones and sounds of a Bostonian to his voice, a conjecture on my part that was later proved to be correct.

In an office in the hangar at the Christiansted ramp he laid out the training program for me. The first and only 'real Sandringham', to which I had been assigned, was still being surveyed for certification. The other ship, a Royal New Zealand Air Force Sunderland (NZ4108) converted by Ansett Airlines to what was considered to be Sandring-ham status, would be cannibalised for spares at the Coastguard hangar and seaplane ramp at San Juan, Puerto Rico. Until the Sandringham was ready, I would begin my training on the Goose, take a written test and complete 200 sectors and 'alightings' under supervision, before being cleared to the line. To begin, I would be route and port familiar-ised from the right-hand seat of the Grumman Mallard, a fifteen place twin engine amphibian.

He was very friendly as he too joked about the picture I'd sent and was most interested to hear about New Guinea. He had flown around the jungles of South America. Through all that, I could see that he would be a strict disciplinarian, running a 'tight ship' as it were.

Training would commence at 7 am the following morning on shut-tles between Christiansted and St Thomas. I left his office with a Goose and Mallard manual under my arm, and a request from him to ask Betty if she would take up a job in the office as the Chief Pilot's secretary. As a cost-cutting exercise Charlie liked to employ husband and wife. When I announced that to Betty, at first she was reluctant claiming that she needed more time to settle in before starting work, however finally she accepted and went to work making a great success of the job in a very short time. At the rate of up to 20 flights each day that I was rostered on the flight schedule, the training moved on fairly rapidly.

Charlie flew with me on a final check the day the required 200 'splashdowns' in the Goose were reached. It was almost dark when as the last flight of the day I brought the Goose in to roost, making a straight-in approach to Christiansted's harbour from St.Thomas, with Charlie relaxed but watchful in the right hand seat. Air Traffic Control did not exist, AAB managed all flight following through a very busy radio network. On the harbour it was every man for himself, a system that seemed to work very well. Charlie didn't like his pilots spending too much time taxying to the ramp after 'splashdown'. The pilot must plan to finish with the alighting seaward of the ramp, always using good seamanship with time and space enough to allow the landing gear to be cranked down and locked, before the wheels reached the concrete upslope. Ramping was certainly not a job for a one-armed paperhanger! I was working 'like a drover's dog' on the crank while doing everything as per Charlie's book and making appropriate allowances for a brisk crosswind on the ramp.

After alighting and retracting the flaps, about 40 turns of the operating handle using the right hand was required to extend the landing gear, while leaning inwards and operating the throttle levers that drooped from the ceiling, with the left hand in order to line up with the ramp before the wheels found solid concrete. Always the third and fourth eye was needed to keep watch on the many small boats scurrying about the harbour and whose masters thought nothing of 'cutting' across the bows or racing alongside a float. AAB's Gooses were not fitted with water rudders or an electric gear-extension system which was considered to be a lot of trouble for the maintenance men, an extra cost for the owners and a bit too 'cissy' for their water flying men.

At first I had been quite amazed by the apparent ease with which the pilots executed that difficult manoeuvre up to twenty times per day at the various ports, in choppy out of wind conditions and on questionable ramps.

With the weather always hot, sticky and very often murky, an Antilles Air Boat Goose or Mallard pilot needed to be something of a contortionist, (never let the right hand or foot know what the other is doing). There were no over-weight pilots in Antilles Air Boats, due to them spending a good part of each flying day in a sweat. Charlie was very lean with a waistline to match his more than six and a half foot height (five foot eighteen). My eyes had been opened as to what I didn't know about scheduled, high frequency amphibious operations.

As I swung the Goose towards the ramp, having completed all the necessary drills under his expert eye, we could now see AAB's recently acquired Mallard, the pride and joy of the fleet, blocking our path on its belly just above the waterline half way up the ramp, laid over with the left float resting on the cement!

Charlie winced, although he gave no other sign of annoyance at what must have been the shocking sight of his most recent and expensive acquisition ever, lying as if mortally wounded on the cement. At the time AAB were operating 22 Gooses (note not Geese).

"Bryan " he said, as I turned away from the ramp and made a circle on the water, "that guy, 'Blazing Throttle's' has done it again, he's either forgotten about the gear or had a malfunction. Mark my words, no matter what the cause we'll learn that it could have been prevented had the pilot used both sides of his brain! That will take some time for the mechanics to jack the Mallard up, drop the gear out and tow it clear. We'll use the mooring to disembark our passengers. I'll go with them. You bring the Goose up when the ramp is available. You are now checked to the line, to fly between US Virgin ports only, until we get your work visa organised. You've done very well, congratulations, I can see that you're a real flying-boat man, we're pleased to have you aboard. I'll get on to your work-visa as soon as I can next week. With that you'll be able to extend your flights to the British Virgins and Puerto Rico. It will also lead to a Green Card for you."

Half an hour later, with the Mallard removed, the Goose was motored up the ramp and parked amongst a gaggle of others receiving their nightly clean-up with a fresh-water wash.

At the 'Goose Grill', the story was that 'Blazing Throttle's' Mallard had struck a floating object while alighting, which developed a serious leak in the hull after touching the water. 'Blazing throttles' had decided to head for the ramp without delay, making a fast approach 'on the step'. Through the small hole in the under surface made by what was most probably a floating bottle, the jet of water created by the excessive speed had lifted the floorboards, hit the ceiling and filled the cabin with a fine, misty spray, blinding, drenching and no doubt terrifying all the fourteen passengers.

With no time left to extend the gear he had bellied the Mallard on to the beaching ramp. Charlie's words came back to me, 'use both sides of your brain'. Would it not have been better to make a slower approach, was the debate going on around the bar of the 'Goose Grill' between the pilots, drop the gear out and get the wheels firmly on terra concrete? Who knows, Charlie thought so, 'Blazing Throttles' didn't. Charlie had known Harold Gatty but didn't act the same way. 'Blazing Throttles' wasn't fired on the spot. The damage to the Mallard was minimal and late the following day started on the usual round of the ports with a couple of new skins on the aquaplaning surface.

AAB paid a bonus to pilots of $6.00 for junior pilots and $7.50 to senior pilots, for every alighting over 200 per month. Merrily, I set out to achieve that target plus. A lot would depend on how the Chief Pilot 'dished out' the pilots' flying schedules. Bob, a Korean and Vietnam jet fighter veteran was a keen Goose flyer himself.

By then I was getting concerned about my USVI residential status, the visa issued at Port Moresby before my selection interview was a visitor's visa for a six months stay. I was told not to worry, the Virgin

Islands being a Territory of the US, had their own system of Work Permits and held AAB, Maureen and Charlie in high regard.

The week following the Mallard incident, Charlie left a message for me advising that a meeting with the Naturalisation Office had been arranged for the following week. He would take me there himself to discuss my work permit requirements that would lead eventually to my becoming a 'Green Card' holder. Next, another message came from him, stating that the meeting with Naturalisation would be delayed by a week due to him having to be absent from the island on business. Letting the visa matter rest with the people who knew best, I got down to the business of flying, at first receiving a good number of heavy flying days to hone up my skills and get me closer to the magical 200 plus per month.

AAB's alighting area in the harbour of St Thomas, the US Virgin Islands capital and centre of government, was close to an area known as 'the Cut', a narrow passage between Water Island and St Thomas through which privately owned power-boats or chartered small sailboats and yachts, exited or entered the harbour in seemingly endless opposing streams. Much of the Virgin Islands economy was based on cruise liner tourism and boat charters.

Where the two currents met, the water could be extremely rough. 'The Cut' could be a hair-raising sight through daylight hours where there always seemed to be a Goose step-taxying at high speed through the Cut, dodging the sea craft.

My first view of 'the Cut' had made me shudder, I couldn't believe such a congested area could be used as a high density flying-boat alighting area, for alighting must always be made one way, towards the ramp, regardless of wind and with the major airport of St Thomas less than a kilometre away handling lots of heavy jet aircraft movements simultaneously.

Of necessity, I soon adjusted to the 'get up and go fighter boy' policy of both Chief Pilot and AAB, with turn-round times of ten minutes from 'up the ramp then back to the damp' and where every minute counted, for there was always an abundance of passengers queued up at the ends of the several tentacles of the AAB network.

At St. John the flying boats of AAB arrived and departed from the open water outside a small bay that was chockers with anchored yachts. When taxying to the ramp that was situated in the bay itself, the space between the yachts from their swinging on the anchor, could change in the twinkling of an eye, the Goose or Mallard might be left with only a few feet to manoeuvre. A last minute ninety-degree turn was required to line up with a cement ramp only slightly wider than the Goose's main wheels! It was good to be in the air and away from that scene, where a tide or wind change would swing the yachts around to further narrow the available seaway. Their anchor cables had to be watched very carefully for fear of fouling a float, things were that close. Two hours could see the tides come and go or the wind gather or drop, the scene could be quite different for the next arrival but so far as ramping went St John was always hazardous.

When the appropriate wind and water conditions were met, take-off at St John could be commenced facing out to sea before exiting the yacht crammed harbour. As soon as the wheels were wound up, the engines roared at full blast, the yachties suffered a shower of wind and spray as a pay back. Everyone has 'their rights' in the USA and almost all take them up. Much care had to be taken too over the bow waves that extra large, high-speed motor cruisers filled with tourists created inbound or outbound from the harbour, leaving a hole in their wake deep enough to swallow a Goose or Mallard. All those factors kept a pilot wary and on his toes.

By and large I was very happy with the progress made, my first month on the line returned 143 'landings', my FAA (Federal Aviation Agency) flight check yielded an 'Above Average' assessment. In subsequent months the figure grew but never exceeded 200, while many senior pilots lodged claims for 300.

Then disaster struck at AAB and Maureen. Flying between Christiansted and St Thomas early one Saturday morning, Goose N7777V piloted by Charlie suffered a calamitous engine failure, catastrophic if you like, that blew the engine cowling away, sending shrapnel through parts of the hull. With a cabin full of passengers, the propeller feathered and all the power that could be squeezed out of the good engine, Charlie made an attempt to reach 'the Cut' at St Thomas, radioing that base to send a boat out as he expected a problem taxying on one engine when down on the water.

The US Coastguard was alerted, AAB marine staff on the St Thomas ramp set out in a boat immediately. A minute or two later another radio call was received from Charlie, requesting the boats to 'come well out' as he was finding it hard to keep the Goose in the air and make way towards St Thomas. N7777V would probably have to come down in the open sea short of the harbour near Water Island. That was the last message received from Charlie in his stricken aircraft.

An eyewitness later reported that there was a long and deep swell running off the island at the time, a brisk wind was blowing, the sea producing lots of waves with whitecaps. Another AAB pilot who was overhead but going in the opposite direction at the time confirmed the open-sea surface conditions at the crash site as being very rough, too rough for a Goose. When last seen N7777V was very low and would have had no other choice but to alight downwind.

The Goose seemed to smack the surface at high speed then rise into the air again, before crashing while catapulting on its left wing, to sink shortly afterwards. Some survivors, who were seen clinging to a wing panel floating on the surface, were soon rescued. Charlie and three passengers were found dead in the main body of the Goose, which was lying on the bottom in 20 metres of water so clear that the wreckage could be seen from the surface. In less than an hour their bodies had been recovered.

The Virgin Islands seemed to come to a halt that morning as news of the tragedy spread for Charlie was a celebrity figure, an icon in the Virgins, US airline and military aviation. For myself I was fraught with anxiety when the sad news first broke, for my work permit was still unattended to, my visa almost expired, and that was a job Charlie liked doing himself.

Maureen who was 'off island' at the time of the accident, returned a day or two later and immediately took over as President of AAB. Of her own volition she told me not to worry about the visa, she knew about it and would attend to it. At the time of his death Charlie was 68 years of age, having accumulated more than 40,000 hours since first going solo in 1928. I believe that figure to be correct, in the time that I knew him he always seemed to be flying long days on the various routes when on island and not away on business. He was a very 'hands on' President/pilot. The many long Atlantic flying-boat flights he made too would have contributed heavily to the grand total of airborne hours. All men think all men mortal, except themselves. Being a virtual newcomer to the company I was merely an observer of the events that followed in the next few weeks.

Betty, who was very popular with the staff, had settled into working in Flight Operations as Chief Pilot's secretary. As a real stenographer, a rare item in those parts, she found herself in demand by Maureen, sometimes transcribing and typing far into the night, the many lengthy, legal documents needed by company, FAA and National Transport Safety Board officials.

At first hand we were able to see the American system of air accident claims or counter claims in action as on the second day of the week following the accident, AAB was hounded by demands for compensation, amounting to some $US20 million, with more reported to be on the way. We were amazed at how calm our new President was over the assault that was mounting on her and Charlie's pride and joy.

Officers of the FAA were very quick to move. On the Monday following Charlie's demise, inspectors were at the St Thomas and St.
Croix terminals. As each Goose loaded up and taxied to the head of
the ramp preparing to go into the water, an inspector would first flash
his badge then signal the pilot to shut down. The aircraft's maintenance log, loading manifests and the figures thereon would be called
for and closely inspected, together with the pilot's licence and physical examination certificate. The reason for the aircraft being halted
when all was ready to go down 'into the damp', fully documented,
engines running, passengers seated and briefed was to ensure that the
pilot was fully intending to fly the aircraft. Fortunately the unwelcome
charade that was embarrassing not only for the inspector, the pilot,
passengers and for all the staff of AAB did not include me as I was on
a day off. Many of AAB's personnel had been with the company since
it's inception and were deeply affected by the tough on the spot audit.

The pilots of AAB all came through with a 'clean bill of health',
while most of the aircraft were pushed back and out of the flight line.
The passengers were instructed to rejoin the queue for another try on a
completely legal Goose if one could be found.

By noon, out of a total of fifteen aircraft on the line that morning,
twelve had been ordered out of the air for one discrepancy or another
in their technical records. That could be a minor repair not signed off
as having been attended to, or an overrun on a compulsory maintenance inspection of airframe, engines, propellers, or most serious of
all, a suspected gross take-off weight miscalculation. Each Goose also
underwent an extensive, external and internal inspection. The whole
operation on the part of the FAA was clinical and sickening to watch,
most inspections taking an hour of the inspector's time.

Slowly, the long line of passengers waiting to board flights dwin-
dled as those nervous of the situation before their eyes set off to the
airport to try their luck with one of the seven other airlines that plied
the route St Croix - St Thomas, until only a few 'loyals' remained on
the chance of taking a fully approved flight. The 'Gooses' that did fly

were sometimes only half filled. The Traffic Manager and staff were completely demoralised. Somehow, the Mallard that had been bellied up the ramp, passed the inspections and then became the mainstay of the company, flying from daylight to dark and foolishly sometimes after.

Charlie's funeral service was held at Christiansted, the burial at Arlington National War Memorial Cemetery, after Maureen's appeal for his interment there received the approval of President Jimmy Carter.

With that ordeal and a month's period of mourning over, Maureen got down to re-organize the company. First the Sandringham project was 'grounded' with the two aircraft to be stored at San Juan, Puerto Rico, pending their sale. To build up business again AAB would re-equip with Grumman Mallards although that type was in scant supply since less than 70 had been built during the 1950's. The long-term plan was to invest in the Grumman G111 (one eleven) Albatross when the military version was awarded the civil Supplemental Type Certificate (STC) then under due process.

AAB owned four ex-military low-time Albatross. With an eye to the future Charlie had three stored in the open in Arizona, the fourth had been flown to Christiansted and was in flyable condition at the international airport as a training aircraft. To retain its airworthy status that machine must be flown for two hours each month. The four would be the first to be upgraded to G111 status when the STC was finally approved. That forward step seemed to be not too far into the future.

Those too were Maureen's plans, but we all knew it was going to take a heap of money to see the plan through to fruition. Ramps and hardstands would need to be up-graded at substantial cost, environmental and noise pollution complaints from some of the citizens of Christiansted and St Thomas would have to be dealt with. At first AAB had to be trimmed down until reaching a safe, profitable operation again. From being the fifth busiest commuter operation in the world in passenger numbers, AAB had slipped down more than thirty places overnight.

Except for a few cases that were similar to mine, in general the pilots of AAB were retired US Navy, Air Force or Coastguard officers. Some were on 'standby' and were around for only a month or two during peak periods of the year, while others including several ex USAF colonels, were employed on a permanent basis.

All had one thing in common, a generous pension from the US government for their military service, in many cases over or near to $US2500 per month, a pension that was evergreen. Charlie was well aware of this and offered quite low salaries in addition. For those pilots, AAB's terms were accepted mainly for the pleasure derived from living the good life in the Virgin Islands, devoid of snow and with an all year round holiday air similar to Hawaii. AAB was a retiring job for them.

The Chief Pilot being an ex-US fighter jockey in Vietnam with the rank of Colonel, seemed to favour those ex-military pilots when setting the schedules, their rostered flying days always led to them achieving more then 200 'landings' per month. On passing 200 they were earning pension + salary + bonus while I earned only the salary part of the equation. Whenever I got close to 185 'landings', which was about one day short of hitting 200, I was taken off the schedule for the remainder of the month, while some senior pilots headed for the 300 figure. AAB was scheduling 120 flights a day around the network at that time, all in daylight hours. When the Chief Pilot was approached about the matter I was told "that's what seniority in Antilles Air Boats is all about. If they want to and I assure you they do, senior pilots get the bonus's, end of story."

But for Betty's contributing salary as his assistant, we would have found the going very hard. My Virgin Islands Work Permit had finally come through, that limited my flights to that territory only. Under the circumstances with dwindling Goose numbers, the magical figure of 200 was very hard to achieve, let alone exceed.

The Goose fleet had been whittled down to three aircraft and those were being flight-tested by the FAA as opportunity permitted for their future use in the US as legal, regular carrier equipment. During the testing program, with two FAA test crew and an AAB pilot aboard, a Goose in pristine condition after a major overhaul was lost at sea. After a blunder in the cockpit that caused both propellers to feather simultaneously, the pilot put down in the open sea a mile or two off Christiansted harbour. Having solved the feathering problem, both engines were started and the pilot prepared to take to the air again, no doubt feeling rather foolish for the Goose was outside the reef in full view of the town. Alas, slowly one wing float sank into and then below the surface, as the one-sided Goose began to roll and sink beneath the waves to the bottom 6000 feet below, never to be seen again. In their life vests, the crew abandoned ship to await rescue by AAB's Boston whaler.

Those of us who knew the Goose knew what happened. The drain plugs in the floats had not been replaced after the floats had been drained, a task that was performed by the ramp crew at each stop when the Goose was in normal service on the line and always checked by the pilot on his 'walk round' inspection before flight. Following the forced alighting, whilst afloat on the sea, the right float had filled with water with weight enough to drag that wing under in a short space of time. Under the circumstances with three pilots aboard it seemed to be a case of, 'I thought you dunnit?' The loss of the aircraft under those circumstances came as a shock to all of AAB's staff, particularly to Maureen. The very slim chance that the type then had of being retained as a public carrier appeared to be doomed.

A day or two later I was called to a meeting in the Chief Pilot's office with the two FAA testing pilots who were aboard the lost Goose. The Goose manual that Charlie had presented to me had been the master-copy. I was asked to hand the manual over as there was some difference of opinion on the propeller feathering procedure, a procedure that could be different from one Goose to another. Before doing so, together we went over the feathering method as laid down. It was soon clear that the manual was correct and that the pilot flying the Goose at the time had 'goofed'. AAB's aircraft had been purchased piecemeal after having various other owners, not all were standardised as to the manual. A grave error had been made that shifted the blame for the two props feathering simultaneously clearly on the side of the FAA inspectors. They left with the manual and a promise that it would be returned to me within a day or two. That was the last I saw of Charlie's master copy. Insurance for the 'two day old' Goose was paid in full, much to everyone's relief.

Resorts International of Atlantic City then began to invest in AAB by providing three Mallards and some executive staff. After a period of 'in command under supervision' with crack pilot Don McDermott, I was converted to type and returned to flying a two pilot aircraft interspersed with Goose flying on alternate days.

Don was teaching me more about rough water operating than I had ever dreamed of. He was one of AAB's non ex-military pilots, having been with AAB since graduating as a youngster from his first flight school and was known to have more than 12,000 hours on the Goose alone and could handle both amphibians with a flare and a confidence on water rough, very rough and extremely rough, as if each one was a tailor-made suit. Difficult alighting areas were just 'a piece of cake' to Don, once behind the controls he could make the amphibian talk, in the air or on the water, upwind, downwind or crosswind made no difference.

In a Mallard with Bill Mable, I flew down to Miami via Providenciales in the Turks and Caicos, to make an exchange of aircraft, thus making my first flight through the mostly defamed 'Bermuda Triangle'. I must admit a 'creepy' feeling took over me as I looked down on those mysterious waters that looked to be quite shallow far from land and where many ships and 'planes had mysteriously disappeared. I'm not sure whether or not I was having my leg pulled but I was told that sand blown on the wind from the Sahara Desert over the thousands of miles and hundreds of years, was thought to be the cause of the 'sandy bottom' shallowness of parts of the Triangle. Come to think of it Christopher Columbus did cross the Atlantic in those parts in record time for a ship that size and shape. All the time I kept a close watch on the magnetic compass for a sudden, confusing gyration that I had heard so much about, but nothing of the like happened while that so–called sinister area was transited.

At Providenciales, in low sandhills peppered with scrub on the landward side of the airstrip, I saw one of my old friends, a Catalina with a neglected, abandoned look about it. On making inquiries as to the history of the famous airboat to some of the airport officials, it was learned that the old Cat had simply come from nowhere one night to be abandoned by the crew after landing on the strip then driven into the rough under engine power where it was then lying. The crew were never seen then, or again for that matter. A drug smuggler who had either lost his way and made a forced landing being low on fuel, or had used Providenciales as a transfer point for his drugs was thought to be the culprit. What an inglorious end for such an historic aircraft were my thoughts, if only the means could be found to retrieve the old boat and put it into service again.

Four days later on the return flight from Miami to Christiansted in an exchange aircraft, the Catalina was nowhere to be seen having been 'mysteriously' uplifted two nights before. Another unfathomable mystery of a ghost aircraft and ghost crew had been created, that could be further built on by those many writers of Bermuda Triangle tragedies.

NTSB Report on N7777V. The National Transport and Safety Board's accident report for N7777V and Charlie was out and it wasn't good for Antilles Air Boats. Business dropped off dramatically. The engine that failed on Charlie's Goose on that very grim day had been crated from Europe with probably what were 'cooked up' documents of its history and state of readiness for installation. The NTSB, who judged the case and who traced the history, estimated the engine to be some hundreds of hours overdue for a complete overhaul at the time of the crash.

That really sent a shockwave through the company. Charlie, through being an aeronautical engineer, had been authorised to have sole charge of all mechanical and maintenance procedures within AAB. He was declared to be responsible in some ways for the accident, having written both the company's Maintenance and Operations Manuals himself in the early days, to gain the appropriate approvals for operations.

The in-flight emergency procedures section of the Operations Manual warned pilots of the poor single engine capability of the Goose. The manual stated that should a complete engine failure occur over water, the pilot should turn the Goose into the wind and carry out an emergency alighting on the sea, using the going engine and maximum flaps for a full stall touchdown, or 'pancake landing' as that is sometimes known as. For some reason Charlie had not carried out his own set of procedures, touching down on rough water very fast with a following wind. The report was also very critical of all facets of the operations of AAB, which had been leaked to the media, the company looked to be doomed.

Through all that, Maureen kept her cool and her faith in Charlie, getting on with trying to improve the chances of AAB's survival for his and their many employees sake. The Sandringham and 'Sunderingham' were advertised for sale. Before long a British millionaire, Edward Hulton, a man with a passion for 'ye olde British flying-boat', offered to purchase and restore the ex-RNZAF, ex-Ansett Airlines, converted Sunderland and return with it to the UK. Edward needed help, a lot of help, as he had no experience at all of aircraft. He was quick to learn and would not buy (Maureen was desperate to sell) until being assured of some technical assistance from within AAB, preferably someone who could also ferry the aircraft to the UK after its refurbishment.

Maureen asked if Edward could be told that I would assist, which would mean a move to San Juan, Puerto Rico for us. If the purchase went through, the Sunderland would be restored in the US Coastguard hangar at Isla Grande, San Juan.

For more than one reason an agreement with Edward was soon reached, for my part the main one being the salary. Edward's offer more than doubled both Betty's and my own put together. At the end of my stint with Edward, I was promised a happy return to AAB, which was a generous offer and pleasing to know, for my US Green Card was by that time well in process. With the purchase deal agreed to and signed, at the end of that month I moved to San Juan loaded with Sunderland and Sandringham technical and operations manuals.

Since arriving from Australia, the big 'metal water-bird' had been stored on beaching gear in a leaky old hangar near the waters of San Juan's inner harbour. At first estimate we thought that the repairs required to reach certification to a flying status would take at least six months. Over the years, water had dripped from holes in the roof of the hangar on to the left wing, causing corrosion in some upper wing panelling that had infected the rear spar. If someone, noticing the leaky roof in the early days of storage, had taken the trouble to have the 'Sunderingham' moved back about six feet on the beaching gear, there was ample room in the hangar, the corrosion could have been prevented. Qualified engineers with appropriate drawings would be required to devise an expensive repair scheme.

One of the first jobs undertaken after starting with Edward was to move the big water bird away from under the leak in the roof with the help of a tractor, a task that took about twenty minutes. The engines were intact with available hours, but for safety's sake after long storage, all would undergo an overhaul in the UK along with the propellers. Some parts were missing, having already been cannibalised for use on the Sandringham.

The last week in St Croix was spent at Maureen's house going through and separating papers and documents that applied to each boat, with Maureen supplying me with refreshments and lots of tuna sandwiches at lunch times. I was surprised by her knowledge of things 'flying-boat' and felt honoured.

Our family was given a farewell at the 'Goose Grill' one evening when Maureen presented us with a wooden replica of a Goose, the machine that had taken AAB from a two plane small beginning to a 22 plane operation, a standard farewell gift for AAB flying staff. During the presentation we were both commended for always using the correct pronunciation of her name Maureen, the accent being on the first syllable and not the second, MauREEN, as pronounced by most Americans.

The proposed changes to our location again, meant son Scott leaving St Dunstan's at Christiansted where he was then firmly established and making good progress, to attend school in Australia. That was a very hard decision for us all to make, one of the hardest we'd ever faced. With the selling up, the Chevy Zee 28 included and the packing up finished, with the long school summer vacation period coming up, Betty flew off to Sydney with him, leaving Jack and I to make the move to San Juan and Ed's Sunderland.

By that time Jack had gained his US commercial pilot's licence, multi-engine land and instrument rating at an approved school in Texas. He was down to act as co-pilot on the ferry flight to the UK with the Sunderingham when that became a reality, in the meantime he would learn all about the big flying-boat during phases of it's repair to flying status which would be a great rivet by rivet introduction to the type for him.

Before I arrived on the scene, Edward had already chosen a piece-meal group of mechanics from Florida for the restoration work. Although there were a few exceptions, their individual repair skills left much to be desired, such as the discovery of the mooring post in the bow being riveted only to the sheet-metal flooring and not on to the manufacturer's heavy, stainless steel plate on the keelson, and all for a wage bill of $US20, 000 per week. It was plain to see that Ed's inexperience in aircraft repair and maintenance had allowed the mechanics to take him for a ride.

Two months went by with little progress being made on the repair. Ed hired a Beech 18 to fly us to Miami to arrange secretly for a more professional crew to take over the work, purchase the specified aluminium sheeting and seek legal advice on how to break the agreement with the first group. The advice we got from our highly qualified attorney was simple enough.

"Get the police you speak of, to stand by. Spare no-one, kick 'em out from their boss down next payday, the good with the bad, ensuring that half your machine and machinery doesn't go with 'em. This is what you should do about their padlock on your container where your parts are stored in the hangar. San Juan police will guard the hangar for you over-night, I've been in touch with 'em."

The hangar at Isla Grande was shared with the Puerto Rican Police Drugs Squad Air Unit with whom we had a first class relationship. The Chief of the unit had warned us that whenever Edward or I left the hangar, the work slacked off, the riveting stopped, with some of the men having a sleep on the job in an attempt to recover from an all-night session of grog and gambling and then qualify for overtime rates at the end of the day. At 5pm, heading in to the overtime zone, they would all be as busy as bees on jobs that 'gotta be finished before we leave tonight'.

The lawyer's advice was accepted and put into practice without too much of a backlash, except for a threat or two from the Chief Mechanic making mention of our 'limey or convict ancestors'. Thanks to the presence of uniformed Drug Squad officers in our section of the hangar and the 'locking up' precautions taken as advised by our attorney, when Friday payday came around there was little other trouble to contend with.

During the period of the refurbishing of the 'Sunderingham', the Puerto Rican anti-Drug Unit 'captured' several aircraft actively moving drugs about the Caribbean - a DC3 with Wright 1820 engines, a STOL Maule and a badly damaged Cessna 337. These were parked outside the hangar for six months without any claimants coming forward and were eventually sold at auction. As told to us by the Chief, behind each of the aircraft lay an interesting, though dark story of intrigue 007 style, whether daring or stupid was hard to define.

Lost while caught above cloud in the San Juan area the pilot of the Cessna 337 threw his cargo out before finding a place to land, probably expecting to be over the sea. Some but not all of his cargo was mulched by the rear propeller that in turn was bent by the several cartons of his illicit cargo. Unfortunately for him, some packages that were intact landed in the centre of San Juan's international airport that had been the pilot's original destination, while he crash landed the 337 with it's buckled propeller in the shallows of a nearby beach. Needless to say he was apprehended and his aircraft confiscated. Smuggling drugs was a dangerous game with no quarters asked for or given. Night and day the Caribbean was plagued with aircraft of all types and sizes engaged in the illicit trade. Those pilots are not entitled to the title 'Flying Men' as depicted here.

Whilst we were in Miami, a contract was signed with Air Tech, a highly recommended, professional, airplane repair organization, to complete the work on the Sunderland. Some of their crew and all the specialist machinery required arrived in San Juan at the Isla Grande airport by chartered Curtis Commando (C46), a few days after the first group had departed the scene. In a generous gesture, the airport authority allowed the fence between the runway and the Coastguard hangar to be taken down to allow the C46 to taxy direct to the hangar for unloading.

Air Tech was horrified at the standard of work already completed and made apologies for their fellow countrymen, almost all the repairs fell below standard. For reputation's sake they would need to start all over again. The estimated time for the repair to be completed was again six months away, with the several months already paid for a write-off. Edward left for the UK and a visit to the money tree.

Betty had returned after settling Scott in with his sister Dianne near Sydney, to learn that her services were again required, this time as a seamstress, to stitch the new Irish linen fabric on to the ailerons and elevators of the 'Sunderingham', to the manufacturer's specifications. When finished, the stitching was examined and approved by British Quality Control Inspector George Alcock before being passed as fit for service. Now moving from secretary to fabric worker, Betty sat on a stool in the extremely hot hangar for hours each day doing the intricate work demanded and which George reported was of a very high standard. The 'Sunderingham's' ailerons were each the size of a light aircraft's wing, the stitching, X numbers to the inch with approved materials, must all be done by hand!

After being on the 'Sunderingham' repair scheme by that time for ten months and with still a long way to go, I began to get restless, having been grounded for too long. Edward was having his problems regarding his 'Sunderingham' as he was working towards obtaining a British registration for the metal water bird. The UK's Air Registration Board however thought otherwise, that auspicious body was not so keen for the 'ex this and ex that' Sunderland to return to its country of birth. ARB registration to Edward's liking was beginning to look unobtainable. I began to wonder why I had joined up with him.

Then came an answer to prayer from Maureen in St Croix. A US oil company was canvassing AAB for an experienced flying-boat pilot for an operation in South East Asia, namely Singapore, using Grumman Albatross SA16's and UF2's (USAF, USN designations). Would I be interested? I had made a test flight or two in the AAB Albatross at Christiansted that left me highly impressed, so I jumped at the opportunity.

A week later, the Chief of Air Operations of the oil company in Houston, had arranged for an interview in San Juan. There he laid out the details of the South-east Asia operation that would be based at Singapore, flying to their oilfield in the South China Sea. That wasn't really a 'hush hush' operation but a certain amount of confidentiality was required for political and commercial reasons and for the military sensitivity of the area of operations.

At the end of our two-hour meeting in a city hotel on San Juan's famous Condado, I was told that if I agreed to those certain conditions the job was mine. Full details would be available after arrival in Singapore. The pay, travel and other expenses that were offered, almost blew my mind.

Work on Edward's 'Sunderingham' had not only been hard, long, varied and flavoured with considerable drama, but also over-extended through the trouble with the initial repair team. The flying of the big water bird was still a long way off. I felt sure that he and Air Tech could carry on without me. An English University graduate, Ed had thrown himself into gaining a full technical knowledge of his boat and what was required from Air Tech for a successful restoration. For a ferry pilot he could use Ron Gillies, who at that time was refurbishing 'his baby' the purebred Sandringham in the same hangar alongside Ed's, for it's eventual return to a British museum. That was going to be a long job too, as funds for the project only came in dribbles. Ron was only too keen to make the flight to the 'promised land' in the Sunderingham and take on some of the overseeing of Ed's, while his own plans progressed. Edward agreed to my going and graciously accepted a month's notice.

In Singapore a year or so later it was learned that for some unknown reason, the 'Sunderingham' had actually been flown to England by well-known Australian flying boat pilot Brian Moncton.

We left our lofty apartment and 'amigos' at the Condado Del Mar condominium with lots of regrets. Our stay in Puerto Rico had been rich, educational, rewarding and highly enjoyable. We loved the people, the narrow streets of the Old City with their blue cobblestone surface. The stones, which are highly valued, had arrived as ballast in some of the thousands of Spanish galleons that plied the Oceano Atlantico from the Old World, to plunder the New, from the 15th century.

The Spanish colonial architecture in abundance around San Juan was a joy to see. The ancient fortress, San Felipe Del Morro, guarding the harbour entrance with its tiered batteries of cannon 40-50 metres above the sea had repulsed an attack by Sir Francis Drake. A shot from Del Morro killed Drake's Lieutenant and turned the British attack away from the plundering of San Juan. All that history before our very eyes had more than thrilled us.

The complex of buildings of San Juan's Old City takes the form of a giant amphitheatre framed by a formidable ring of walls, garitas and castle-like bastions. We had spent many happy hours strolling about while exploring the Old City and San Felipe Del Morro, enjoying social times with friends who in turn enjoyed their 'pina colada' at one of the city's many kerbside refreshment haunts. Pina Colada, a refreshing, rum based drink, mixed with cream of coconut, crushed ice and pineapple juice is reputed to have been created in San Juan. Tradition had it that every loyal Puerto Rican is obliged to visit the Old City and partake of a pina colada every week! The climate could only be called hot, with sticky, humid evenings and nights. Iced drinks long and sweet went well with the sounds of Spanish guitars, sometimes violins, from roving musicians entertaining the diners in every respectable restaurant.

The purpose of Sir Francis Drake's and the Duke of Cumberland's several attempts to breach Del Morro were to seize cargoes of gold and silver, stored while awaiting shipment to Spain in the many galleons that plied the Oceano Atlantico. Puerto Rico stands for 'rich port' in English. Drake retired with heavy casualties, the Duke of Cumberland's plans to attack from landside were foiled by an epidemic of dysentery within his soldiery. The Dutch also laid siege to the city, but couldn't take El Morro. However, before leaving they plundered the adjoining city, which was completely destroyed by fire.

Indeed, there was so much history to take in around the Caribbean, history being my best-loved school subject. The Spanish colonial era, the Antilles and Puerto Rico now had more meaning for an adopted New Guinea boy like me, although after two years in the area I'd only just scraped the surface while loving every moment.

SOUTH EAST ASIA

Another flight halfway around the world on Pan Am, took us to Singapore, one of the smallest but probably the most progressive independent nations in South East Asia. An island at the tip of the Malaysian peninsula, Singapore began its modern history in the early 1800's when an agent of the East India Company, Stamford Raffles (later Sir Stamford), saw the need for a new trading port to secure Britain's trade route to China via the Malacca Straits (the strait between Sumatra and Malaya). Singapore began as a 'free port' that in Englishmen's eyes anyway, would become 'the pride of the East'.

When I first laid eyes on that great island city from the Jumbo jet at 4 am one morning, after a delayed arrival from the US caused by Hong Kong's inclement weather, my view of Singapore was somewhat different to that of its founder.

As there are stars in the heavens, the sea of lights from hundreds of ships parked in and around the harbour, was reflected in the black water as the Jumbo approached for landing. Paya Lebar airport had been a Japanese fighter airstrip during the occupation of the island in WW2. Singapore ranks as one of the busiest shipping ports in the world with international air movements mounting each year also to equal those of some of the worlds' busiest.

We were both very tired, having not rested much on the flight San Juan, Houston, San Francisco, diversion to Taipei, then Hong Kong, Singapore with just one short night in San Francisco. Even at that early hour there was a surprising amount of international aircraft movement going on. Before we left the airport we said goodbye to our sweet little Corgi, Goldie and puss-cat Blackie, who were taken away for a month's sojourn in Singapore's quarantine station.

From the very first moment we were so impressed with the efficiency of the airport's passenger arrivals system as compared to others we knew, the incredibly long terminal building with a constant stream of arriving passengers bursting out into the warm air. In no time we were checked through customs and immigration and heading for a man near the hallway exit, who was seen to be holding a placard up on which my name was printed in large letters.

We discovered that he was the company driver, Mahmoud by name, a Singaporean of Malaysian extraction and a Muslim by religion. As he packed our bags on a trolley before leading us to the car park, he told us that he had been waiting for hours for the flight. Our apologies for the delay were met with an 'all in a day's work' nonchalant shrug of the shoulders. Inbound to the city he told us with some pride, that being so devout, he had spent much of his waiting time in a corner of the terminal, in prayer to Allah. Nevertheless, he still had four more sessions in the mosque to go before day was ended. (During our stay in Singapore, Paya Lebar airport was reverted to military use. Changi became the international airport as it is today).

Both city and environs were brightly lit as we drove into the city on smooth, well-designed roads to the Holiday Inn on Scott's Road near downtown Singapore, so well lit that traffic was not obliged to use headlights. Most surprising to me was the ultra-modern style of the ever so clean city, with its wide footpaths, broad, tree-lined roads and avenues. Even so early in the morning there was no doubt that Singapore was a disciplined, 24-hour city, so different from San Juan, which by that time seemed unreal to us and so far away. We were to remain at the hotel for several weeks, until suitable accommodation was found closer to where the two Albatross were based at Seletar on the Straits of Johore.

After being familiarised with the airport and staff, each week I travelled to Jakarta to undertake the tests for an Indonesian Air Transport Pilot Licence, a necessary requirement, for the aircraft although US chartered were on the Indonesian register. My studies were done at the Borobudur Hotel under the guidance of two ground instructors of Garuda Airlines. We shared breakfast, lunch and dinner together, while class was held in my room. I suspected that one of the men was more of a government intelligence agent than an aviation classroom instructor. When alone in my room I couldn't help but feel that I was being watched, there were few other guests to be seen on that floor. With nothing to hide I didn't search for hidden bugs or miniature cameras. Both men stuck to me like glue from 9am to 6pm each day going over the several subjects required for a pass in the licence.

Each Friday I rejoined Betty in Singapore, who was quickly becoming well acquainted with the island city's history and geography, through having made several trips by road to visit our two pets at the quarantine station at Jurong.

With the examinations successfully completed, we moved from the city hotel to a housing estate near Jalan Kayu, the British built village at the entrance to Seletar Air Base.

Prior to WW2 Seletar was the largest Royal Air Force base in the world outside Britain, accommodating both flying boats and many types of land 'planes.

Seletar had also experienced many exciting moments in history as a stop-over point to some of the great pioneering flights of the 20's and 30's, Kingsford Smith and Ulm, Bert Hinkler, Amy Johnson, Jean Batten, C.J.Butler, the first Air Mail flight from London to Australia and the not so joyous bombardment by the Japan Navy and Air Force and the capture and occupation of the station at the beginning of 1942.

In the 1920's Seletar had been a rubber plantation and at the time of our arrival was then a joint civil/military airport, some 600 acres of prime land, under the strict security of the Singapore armed forces. The original RAF guardhouse at the gates was still in everyday use.

The layout of the base, the flying boat slipways leading to the Straits of Johore, the hangars, the 'all-over' aerodrome itself and the barracks claimed to be the very best the RAF could offer prior to WW2. The senior officers and the non-commissioned married quarters, the roadways, lawns and gardens for the day were outstanding and well ahead of their time.

At the time of my arrival the once beautiful air base was still showing the after effects of the war. The three-year occupation by Japan forces and the post-war political changes had left Seletar with a rather tired look about it, but considering the dramatic changes suffered, the base was remarkably intact.

In the pre-war 'hey day', a posting from the UK to Seletar was highly sought after by Royal Air Force personnel. After visiting Seletar for the first time I knew that we would be very happy there. Until a house could be arranged for us on the base we would live in Seletar Hills a pleasant area close to the airport, I could then get on with applying myself to the task.

The airport offices of the Albatross flight were inside a giant ex Royal Air Force hangar at 'East Camp', still with large bullet holes in the huge, steel, sliding doors, from air attacks whether Japanese or Allied there was no way of knowing. The holes spoke well of the armaments used, for the doors were half-inch solid steel, the holes neat and only curled on the exit point of the bullet on the inside of the door. After Singapore fell, the Japanese had dismantled several hangars at West Camp then taken the steel girders off to Japan for either scrapping or further use. At war's end, the British insisted that the girders and other major parts were returned and the hangars reconstructed to exact specification on the original sites, which is how they stand today, or so the story went, or goes.

Conoco Seaplane Operations was allotted half the floor-space of the hangar for the two big amphibians in service at that time, one being an SA16B model the other a UF-2 tri phibian. The designations given to the Albatross series applied to either US Air Force or US Navy models, a tri-phibian being the description given to an aircraft capable of operating on snow or ice, water or land. Both aircraft were leased from the Indonesian Air Force, together with their co-pilots and flight engineers.

Captain Dick Ragan an ex Commander in the US Coastguard with hundreds of hours on the Albatross was Chief Pilot and the backbone of all operations, who immediately had my respect when I learned that he had acquired flying time on the giant Martin Mars flying-boat between California and Hawaii, near the end of WW2.

I was to be the sole non-American Captain in Conoco's 'Seaplane Operations' so miscalled. (whoever named the operation evidently didn't know the difference between a 'seaplane' and a 'flying-boat'). When I first met Dick, after showing me around he took me on a drive to the Changi Sailing Club where he was a member, being the owner of a gaff-rigged, engineless, 'Maine class' yacht or so he claimed, for Maine was his home state. His version of the type had been built locally. I liked Dick from the moment I first set eyes on him. He was an extremely casual person, with a 'gravelly' Humphrey Bogart voice, a cigar or some other 'fag' almost always between his teeth or lips and a penchant for 'chilli crab' at waterfront hawker stalls. He had lived in Guam and South East Asia for more than 20 years, having served also in Vietnam with Air America. What he didn't know about sailing and the Albatross wasn't worth knowing.

Having successfully passed the required tests for licensing I had been issued with a Temporary Certificate to see me through the Albatross Type Rating Sea and Land period. With me in the left hand seat Dick supervised me for two hours in the air, doing all those exercises that need to be done for a type rating. After shooting some ILS approaches (Instrument Landing System) at Paya Lebar airport, we finished off with several wheel landings on Seletar. Training areas solely for the air work that was required was internationally complicated and hard to get with all the conflicting States each with a share of the air space, Malaysia, Singapore and Indonesia, but somehow

Dick managed to come up with all the necessary approvals. Having previously had a little time on Maureen's Albatross at Christiansted, the exercises were all completed to a satisfactory standard, which cleared me for duty as a co-pilot under command training.

A few days later, in the right hand seat that time, at 0700 hours we lifted off on my first run to the oilfield that was off the Anambas Islands, South China Sea. Thus began the first of eight glorious years, flying one of the world's best amphibians out of 'the jewel of the East'. What more could one ask for. The Albatross had been credited with a record number of successful aircrew and other rescues from the open sea during the war in Vietnam. With jet assisted take-off (JATO) rough water take-off was a piece of cake.

After taking off from Seletar, we tracked across the Straits of Johore to the non-directional beacon at Johore Bahru, then turned to cross Singapore Island en route to Tanjung Pinang in the Riau Islands and part of the Indonesia archipelago. My time was taken up reading charts, which were new to me, watching and helping Dick handle the big 'metal water bird'.

American style radio procedures seemed to be favoured in SE Asia and were a good deal more informal than the standard phrases used in Australia or New Guinea. I'd already been broken in to the response 'Charlie' (for 'copied') and 'got the numbers' for the more formal 'received information Alpha, foxtrot etc' during my sojourn in the Virgin Islands and Puerto Rico.

Thirty minutes later at Tanjung Pinang, a wheels landing was made on the airport for customs entry into Indonesia and to load additional passengers and freights for the oil field, all scheduled to arrive from Jakarta by Fokker Friendship. With our visas and onward flight permits being checked while awaiting the arrival of the Fokker, the Albatross was fuelled from 50-gallon drums, in preparation for the flight to our water destination at Matak Island in the Anambas. Fuel in Indonesia was considerably cheaper than in Singapore, it came as a surprise to know that oil companies watched the fuel dollars carefully too and would always look for a bargain.

Leaving Tanjung Pinang we passed over only one small rocky island, whose name has never been found on any map of mine, but which looked to be a perfect haven for China Sea pirates. The weather was clear. One and a half hours after leaving Tanjung Pinang we were on descent to the alighting area, which was in a harbour, a deep bite in a ragged stretch of island coastline. The harbour was sheltered from the north but exposed to the weather from the south. Twenty miles out we had communication with the base that gave us an Indonesian style description of the wind and weather around the harbour. For my benefit, Dick took the Albatross around in a wide sweep of the island before setting up for an approach into the harbour from the south.

The alighting area was marked by orange coloured steel buoys, spaced about 200 metres apart, with the wharf area on the right side of us as we alighted. At first sight I could only conclude that the whole layout had not just happened, but had been carefully planned and so different from the areas used in the Virgin Islands. Any boats crossing the alighting area during an aircraft's approach at Matak were guaranteed apprehension and their boat confiscated by the company's harbour security force, which was not the case in the democratic US Virgin Islands (USVI) where everybody has their rights.

Dick took Victor Alpha Alpha in low through the narrow entrance, touching the water smoothly off the second buoy, his cheroot waggling up and down, his nose twitching. So well judged, the Albatross was finished with the air just off the beaching ramp. Up came the flaps, down went the wheels as we turned in to taxy between the large, red plastic marker buoys leading to the ramp and hardstand, the engines ticking over quietly with Engineer Supardi checking lights and locks on the gear.

There was nothing in the way of wind, Dick lined up to the ramp without any noticeable gunning of the engines. Seconds later the main-wheels contacted the ramp. Using only the inertia at first until

the nose-wheel also made contact, he then applied power to both engines as with a heave we came out of the water and closed with the
steeper slope that led to the parking bay and helicopter pads. At the
top of the incline a sharp 'one-eighty' to the right brought us around to
face the harbour down the ramp. Attendants moved in with the chocks
as the propellers came to a stop.

"Nice work Cap'n." I remarked, being quite impressed with the
performance as I sat taking in the scene, which was a bustling hive of
activity.

"That's nice of you to say so. We'll get the passengers off and let
the choppers get clear, then we'll do some water-work. Coffee will be
on in the pilot's room in the hangar. It'll take the choppers at least two
hours to bring the exchange crew in, they can't leave the rig until their
replacements arrive which will give us time for lunch before we go.
That's on in the hotel barge you can see there at the wharf. They put
on pretty good grub here. Meantime, I'm gonna have another smoke."
Dick drawled from the corner of his mouth, as he slid from his seat
and ducked out through the door to the passenger cabin.

Although it was almost a year since I'd flown off water, I was soon
familiarised as we flew out of the harbour for some practice in the
open sea. After an hour of 'circuits and splashes' near an adjoining
island, Dick asked me to move the alighting area further out to where
a whitecap or two could be seen.

In a flat-bottomed Catalina, the type of 'wavy' water before us
would call for a full-stall 'splashdown', with the bow cocked high in
the air to allow the first contact with water to be at the rear step of the
hydro-planing surface. There'd bound to be a solid bump and lots of
spray flying through the props, engines and over the windshield as the
flat bottom caught another wave or swell before losing way. A full
stall touchdown in a heavy sea with a 'Cat' could be very exciting,
even dangerous.

With the Albatross things were different. After taking off into wind and climbing to 500 feet Dick asked for a touchdown straight ahead where the sea looked to be quite rough. A little apprehensive, I was hoping that he fully understood what he'd asked for, as he talked me down to my first 'open sea' in the Albatross with few instructions on how to go about it, except for some on the use of the reversible propellers. As we got lower, although the sea was confused I could see that we were probably going to be cross-sea, time to kick in some left rudder to induce a swerve, to allow her to touch more along the swell than into it.

"Full flaps?" I called across to Dick with time running out. He was chewing on a fresh cheroot.

"Yeah" came the reply, the cigar waggling from the corner of his mouth. "Just flare normal. When she touches, go for reverse with a fair bit o' power, she loves this 'kinda' water. She'll stick on nicely, hold the pole hard back so as you won't get too much spray through the engines or on the windshield. That way she'll stop sudden too. When she's finished take the props out of reverse, give 'em time to cycle then go for another take-off. I'll set the props for you and the flaps. Try another this way, then we'll go about and try a couple more in the opposite direction downwind. After that we'll go in for some grub."

The training session finished with me in a sweat. On the short trip back to Matak base I knew I had started a new relationship and fallen in love again, this time with Victor Alpha Alpha the Albatross, or any other of the same type that might follow. The whole exercise had been a delight with Dick's laconic instructions turning the day into play. The aircraft's performance on water was unbelievable, when compared to other flying boats of comparable size. The rear step was vented through the wheel wells, a feature which assisted to 'jet' her into the air after only a very short run, on rough or smooth water. Loaded or unloaded, the take-off time in nil wind conditions was about the same, with the deep 'vee' of the front step allowing the Albatross to cut through the waves rather than bounce over them. The drooped leading edges of the wings too gave an additional boost to the take-off. Powerful Wright 1820 nine-cylinder radial engines of 1525-horse-power made for a magnificent amphibian (tri in that case). Need I mention the reversible propellers with electric heads, the hydraulically boosted rudder and the electric trims?

At the end of the seventh day of such training, when I'd flown the aircraft from the left hand seat from land and water for more than 25 hours, we had returned to Seletar late one afternoon when between puffs on his cigar, Dick drawled from the corner of his mouth as usual and pointed.

"That new white 'ess zee' registered rental car there in the parking lot is yours, gas supplied on your expense account. It's yours for as long as you're here, you'll get a new replacement every Christmas. Your flyin's okay, I can see that you're very familiar with the water-side of things which is the main reason we gotcha here, I'll send off your type rating details tonight. Next week you'll fly as Captain with the Indonesian crew, we'll have a talk about that before you go. Say, how about tonight we eat at that same seafood stall with the chilli crab at Ponggul in the way of a celebration. Shari can come along too, you bring Betty I'll bring Ruba. If you can find your way there, let's meet at eight o'clock?"

Shari was our office manager, a small, wiry Singaporean of Malaysian extraction, a man of many skills, languages and trades. In my 52nd year, some of the best years of my life had begun.

With me there were now three Captains in the unit, Dick and John McDonald a younger retiree of the US Coastguard whose Albatross experience had been accrued mainly on the wheels. The company required at least one Albatross to be available 24 hours a day, seven days a week 365 days a year for flights to the oilfield.

On 4-5 days of the week, regular flights were made for crew change of the oilrig and storage tanker. In addition to company personnel, Indonesian customs officers, sub-contractors, police, army and helicopter crews were also carried back and forth. The aircraft was licensed for 32 passengers, for our needs that had been cut down to 28 to allow weight and space for urgent cargo. The choppers carried 14 passengers, 28 from us filled two trips for them for flights to the platform and storage tanker in the South China Sea, 70-80 kilometres from Matak.

As time went on and more of the operation was learnt, the smooth organization that went on left me quite astounded. In addition to the regular schedule many emergency flights were required calling for transhipment of parts urgently required at the oil platform or the permanently moored 180,000 ton storage tanker 'Natuna'. Breakdowns on the rig often occurred when the failure of some small but necessary part held up production. Not all those parts flown to the field were small by any means, the rule was, if it wouldn't fit into the cabin with the seats removed, it soon would with everybody assisting with the loading thereof. Air freighted from the US or Europe to Singapore, the freight, whatever it was, would be taken to Seletar for onward shipment by the Albatross to the field, with the minimum of delay. This usually meant a special flight being made. Medical emergencies were high on the priority list too. Divers with 'the bends' or a rigger mangled by machinery or having inhaled toxic fumes. Always the exchange of oil rig crew to a regular schedule, continued unabated.

For the first time in my life in aviation, I was working with a company where operating funds were in never-ending supply. Our parts store at Seletar was packed with a million dollars worth of Albatross spares, the Chief of Maintenance gloated over his four spare engines in the system, one being overhauled in the US, one at Seletar, another in the shipping network somewhere on the Pacific, one in a crate at Matak. In the event of an engine change being necessary along the route, all bases were covered with an engine close at hand and another not far away.

With me on my first flight in command were First Officer 'Budi' Budiyono and Flight Engineer 'Sunny' Sonohardi. Both men were extremely polite and courteous and of very neat appearance. They had already made many trips to the oilfield, knew their jobs and went about them with a diligence that for me, the new boy on the block, was certainly confidence building.

The crews seconded to us were all members of the Indonesian Air Force, of officer rank from 5 Albatross Squadron at Semarang on Java, a good omen for me having once served with No 5 Catalina Squadron RNZAF in Fiji. For some reason that obscure connection although nonsensical, seemed to impress them and made us good friends. Their training on the Albatross had not included much in the way of water handling, almost all had flown as crew only from the land and so they were keen to learn the ways of the water, which for some were quite difficult. The Indonesian flight crews were exchanged every three months.

Captain Budiyono (IAF) came to us for a three-month stint many times and was a capable pilot with a command on the Air Force Albatross in his own service and one who really enjoyed flying and was always willing to learn more about water handling.

In the air, the Flight Engineer at his station behind the pilots, kept an eye on the engines, the fuel flows and looked after the passenger cabin prior to take-off, during flight, alighting and landing. On the ground he supervised the re-fuelling and did part of the 'walk around' pre-flight checks. On water the Flight Engineer would act as bowman in the event of a mooring being required while awaiting use of the ramp, which sometimes happened when two 'Albatri' were in operation. Surprisingly, none of the Indonesians could swim. Socially, by their own wish, they kept much to themselves in company provided quarters nearer to the city, although there were times when all staff joined together at company celebratory functions.

All enjoyed the shopping in Singapore and always left for home with loads of 'goodies' for their families. Altogether, the satellite 'seaplane' operation' was one happy family of expatriate Americans, Swedes, Brits and a lone 'New Guinlander', Singaporeans of different ethnic backgrounds, Indonesians, Chinese and Thais.

After a period of about nine months with the unit running smoothly, we moved to a hangar of our own on Seletar, an ex RAF WW2 fighter hangar in preparation for the arrival of a new, completely civilianised G111 (one eleven) Albatross that the company had ordered to replace the SA16B. It was known that Grumman Corporation was about to withdraw the certification of certain serial numbered military Albatross that were being used in unscheduled air transport, which included our operation. With the G111 becoming available, our company would either have to make a purchase or close shop so far as 'water-birds' went, a consideration that was out of the question. Wisely the former option was accepted and a firm order placed.

Certain Albatross aircraft with less than 6000 hours on the airframe, (spar caps), that were stored in the desert in Arizona would be converted by Flying Boat Inc. of Miami, Florida to G111.status. At the time I thought of Antilles Air Boats and wondered whether some of Maureen's aircraft would be the ones chosen for our use in SE Asia. Charlie had planned to make the G111 Albatross the prime mover for AAB.years before. Since leaving the Virgins and Puerto Rico, I'd heard on the grapevine that things weren't going so well with AAB and the Mallards, due to lack of finance caused by a major hurricane that destroyed several aircraft.

New, more powerful engines with auto feather, titanium spar caps, a drooped leading edge to the wing, airliner interior, were just some of the improvements that would give the old 'war bird' improved performance for its' civil role, plus indefinite life subject to it being maintained to Flying Boat Inc's specifications. At Seletar we all looked forward to the arrival of the G111.

Sadly the unit's pilots could not be spared for the uplift of the air-craft when it was ready. Professional ferry pilots were granted the privilege of delivering our new toy across the Pacific to Seletar early the following year. The night before Papa Alpha Mike, the first G111 off the production line and the first to be sold outside the US, was due to arrive at Seletar, a telex was received stating that as from midnight, the SA16B and UF2 could no longer be used in unscheduled air transport operations. The UF2 however, could be kept in minimal ser-vice as a back up aircraft to the G111 pending some other major decisions being made.

Following in PAM's footsteps came a team from Grumman to take us through a ground school before undertaking the type rating. We all thought this a little unnecessary, as there was not a lot of difference between the two types so far as pilots were concerned. Nevertheless, with the maintenance mechanics, we all sat through several days of lectures, listening attentively and passing the test successfully. Un-flappable Dick then flew to the US to qualify as a G111 training captain. When he returned he put John and I through our paces. Yet another type was 'chopped' into my licence.

The cockpit of the G111 was brand new with a Collins 101 pilot navigation system and colour radar. Full flap was reduced from 45 degrees to 30 degrees, which was going to make an open-sea emer-gency alighting a little harder and less safe. Operation of the devices that were new to us was soon learned. The flight engineer as such was then redundant and replaced with a male cabin attendant cum bow-man. In fact in our case, that meant the flight engineer merely changing his seat on the flight deck (that had been done away with), to one at the rear of the passenger cabin. A fancy toilet, a carpeted floor with airline type seating, sound proofing, air venting and easy to look at wall décor, brought PAM up to an interior standard any airline would be proud of. Our oilrig men would then travel to and from their job like guests to a Kings banquet!

The fully approved FAA performance charts were now of a regular public transport standard, which brought the G111's maximum allowable weight down slightly from the SA16B's although 28 passengers could still be accommodated with less margin available for cargo, that was of no great concern. The cruising speed of the two types was approximately the same at normal operating levels, 170 knots at 65% power at 10,000 feet. We were happy, the insurance company was happy. All agreed that Flying Boat Inc. had made a sound job of the conversion.

Although it couldn't be seen the titanium in the spar caps alone, wingtip to wingtip, cost more than a million dollars per aircraft, which meant an indefinite life for the G111, a privilege not awarded any other flying-boat in the world today to the best of my knowledge.

Two weeks after arrival PAM was in service to the oilfield and proving to be very popular with the travellers. There was talk about that the company was considering a second aircraft. That of course, would depend on the projected output of the oilfield. Pilot flying hours increased as huge overseas tankers came and went, their tanks (late holds) 'chockers' with crude oil pumped from the storage tanker.

Without too much warning, the South China Sea was suddenly swarming with Vietnamese boat people packed on to their ageing boats, heading for any oil platform or tanker they could find. In addition to our normal flights, we were now called upon to search for, or guide, those that were known to be in trouble in the vicinity of the Anambas, either mechanically, overloaded, or with sickness aboard. Several small craft that would be crowded with 15 persons on board were intercepted carrying 2-3 times that number, men women and children. Those were guided to the harbour at Matak, where the Indonesian police and army took over.

The Viet boats were not welcome on the oil-producing scene. After being watered, fed and vetted, the entire complement of each boat was taken by sea to an island for refugees somewhere near the Riaus, their boat seized and I suspect, in most cases, put to good use by the fishermen of the Anambas. Dozens of similar craft sailed through the area without being apprehended, bound for where, Java, the Indonesian archipelago or Australia, or did they themselves know?

Matak base once advised that somewhere southeast of the island a refugee boat had been set upon by a band of pirates, which were common to the area. The report had been received a week or more before we were called in. An intensive search by me with the G111 failed to find any sign of the 'boaties' or any of the vessels suspected of taking part in the raid. We could only hope that the report was untrue, having heard many stories of the callousness of China Sea and Malacca Straits pirates.

When a Super Puma helicopter with 12 persons aboard went missing between Natuna Island and a distant oil platform, in PAM again we searched for three days without result. The chopper was never found. Again we had been called in two or three days after the chopper had gone missing in extremely poor weather. Second or third hand information only was available to us, the flight following of the helicopter company concerned was of a very poor standard, worthwhile clues were unobtainable. Whether the chopper went astray before or after leaving the platform concerned was never determined, nor was there anyone who seemed to be in complete charge of the search operation with too many aircraft searching the one location on a 'choose yourself' basis.

Without a real leader the briefings were a mockery, chopper or fixed wing pilots were able to make their own choices of heights to be flown and areas to be searched. The weather was perfect with a glassy sea and only a light swell, cloudless skies with the radar returning a good picture of the surface. There were a number of false alarms as we radar-homed on to flotsam and jetsam, an overturned wooden dinghy, a half submerged, tumbled over cargo container. The amount of rubbish floating through the China Sea on its way to either some foreign shore or the bottom of the sea was remarkable, but unfortunately, yielding no clues as to the fate of the Puma. Had anyone or anything of significant value been found, a 'pick-up' by the Albatross would certainly have been possible, although the non swimmers in my crew were a bit of a worry.

Also discovered by an easy calculation, was the information that the Puma would have been on the extreme limit of fuel endurance. For the distance and time flown and the chopper's fuel capacity, the operating company and the pilot had left a lot to chance. In that particular case I was very disappointed at not coming up with a worthwhile find, a dinghy, life jackets or wreckage of some kind.

On searches in Catalinas during Air Force days, my crew's diligence had always been rewarded with good results. It was with a sad heart, when the search was finally called off and PAM and crew returned to the orderliness of Seletar and Singapore via Tanjung Pinang, empty-handed as it were. A feeling of guilt was mine for days at being so restricted in giving the search my best shot through being called in too late.

The following few days were spent in playing 'catch up' on the flights delayed through the absence of the Albatross on the search mission. A week or so later the 'Straits Times' reported that there were several Singaporeans aboard the helicopter when it went missing, which added to my disappointment. .

Another time, half an hour out from Matak on return to Tanjung Pinang, I watched as the hydraulics gauge slowly dumped all of its pressure. The manual wobble pump was tried by me for several minutes without a sign of a build up. The Flight Engineer then 'wobbled' for a while followed by the First Officer without any result. Somehow the hydraulic fluid had all been lost after retracting the flaps out of Matak. Both the landing gear and the flaps were hydraulically operated. I was faced with a decision as to what road to take. A return to Matak where there were no qualified technical assistants available to extend the landing gear for beaching on the ramp was ruled out, along with a belly landing at Tanjung Pinang Airport our planned destination.

A decision to bypass Tanjung Pinang and proceed to Singapore to alight in the Straits of Johore off Seletar for a fix by company mechanics was then made. A wheels up belly landing on ground anywhere was of course, out of the question. Overflying Tanjung Pinang for Singapore would present customs and immigration difficulties that would have to be dealt with somehow, as the 25 passengers were all Indonesians bound for Jakarta and to a man, without passports.

An hour and a half before arrival I called Singapore Control to advise them of my problem and the plan I had in mind, which was quite simple. To alight in Johore Straits off Seletar would not be anything new, as an ex-flying-boat station Seletar possessed a wide beaching ramp, although unused by water-borne metal birds for many years. Once there on the water, our mechanics could come alongside in a small boat, pull the gear out from the wells by the use of muscle power, lock the gear down, when I would taxi up the ramp to the hardstand for an appraisal by our chief engineer. With that over and the problem solved and repaired, PAM would go down the ramp, take off from the water then land on Seletar's long runway. On solving the customs and immigration problem the aircraft would go to our hangar for a permanent fix.

Simple was it not? A high security fence separating military from civil would prevent the Albatross from taxying direct to our maintenance base from the ramp. Everything was as 'clear as mud' in my head.

The next flight hour was spent almost totally in contact with Singapore, while I was passed from one official to the other to be interrogated to the 'enth' degree, until I thought I would explode by having to repeat over and over again the same details to different controllers! With all the repetitive talk going on a feeling crept over me that not something but everything had gone radically wrong.

On approaching overhead Seletar, dozens of small boats were seen 'put-putting' about in the selected alighting area in the Straits seaward of the ramp and runway, with a Singapore Water Police launch herding them like sheep. The instructions radioed to me forbade entry into any part of Malaysian waters, an imaginary line running down the centre of the Straits, so I brought PAM around to alight close in and parallel to the shores of Singapore Island. With the flaps unavailable, a soft but fast touchdown was made that ended abeam the old Sunderland beaching ramp, where the engines were stopped while the Albatross drifted.

Having been busy in the cockpit I wasn't sure just how the flight engineer cum cabin attendant had explained our predicament to the passengers whose first and only tongue was Indonesian. On stopping the engines it was obvious by the bow rising sharply that any pre-alighting briefing from the Cabin Attendant had been mis-interpreted for all the passengers had made a rush for the rear door wearing their flotation vests. With all the weight heading rearwards PAM was in danger of slipping, tail first, down to Davy Jones locker should sea water rush in through the open doorway where there wasn't a lot of freeboard when afloat and properly balanced.

Feeling the aircraft pitching made me scramble from my seat, jerk the door to the passenger compartment open to find a mass of humanity in the aisle shoving, pushing and jostling each other with the cabin attendant unable to retain any form of control, in fact it looked to me as if he had set his sights on being first out himself. The scene was one of panic at its worst. It took some prodding, shouting, elbowing and the ripping of several shirts on my part to restore some sort of order and have everyone return to their seats.

Outside the aircraft we were suddenly surrounded by what must have been forty, two-man rubber dinghies crewed by Singapore army personnel with a big police launch reversing up to PAM's bow. A man who looked to be one with authority, stood near the transom. In only a few seconds I unlatched the hatch in the roof above my seat, scrambled through and out on to the bow forward of the windshield.

"Captain, how long do you expect to stay afloat? " he called through a battery-powered megaphone for all to hear. "The boats will take you to shore, hurry, hurry."

I couldn't believe what he'd said. At that instant I realized that after all the explaining done on the radio en route to Seletar, for some reason the authorities hadn't realised PAM was an amphibious 'water-bird', we were expected to go to the bottom of the Straits at any moment! Explaining the true situation to him, that there was no need for anyone to panic for we weren't in any danger of sinking, took some time. Some of our passengers saw the opportunity to take to the boats lining up at the door. Orderly evacuation was then impossible with the flight engineer appearing to have lost all control in the cabin. Fortunately, there wasn't a sign of any current that would drift the Albatross away from where we first drew up and the boat with our work–force could be seen setting out from the slipway.

With all the shouting and revving of outboards going on, even my crew were getting nervous and wanting to leave for the shore on the dinghies, I was forced to adopt an attitude that could be taken for Captain Bligh of 'Bounty' fame when faced with a mutiny on his hands.

With the passengers gone and the workboat alongside under the wing, our mechanics began to force the gear to the 'down and locked' position. That wasn't as easy as stated in the 'Emergencies Manual' with the inflated tyres strongly resisting their immersion in the Straits murky water. When the gear locks were in place the police launch was waved away. Thanks to the officer in charge who was to me the only person there with practical sense and knew what was going on, the big launch backed off. I cupped my hands and shouted across to him that the engines would have to be re-started to allow the Albatross to move to the ramp, he must warn the dinghies to keep well away from the propellers. That he understood what was being said was clear to see as the launch made a clearway by herding several of the two-manners to one side.

The slipway probably hadn't been used by an aircraft for twenty years or more. Much to the amazement of all my marine audience, PAM heaved herself out of the water as I gunned her up the slope swivelled around on the hardstand and faced the Straits again, one propeller in reverse to allow for the absence of brakes.

Army and police officials galore swarmed around after the engines were shut down. Leaning from the cockpit window I signalled 'the helpers' to shove some kind of a chock in front of the wheels, a signal that took some time for them to understand and more time to do. No hydraulics, no brakes, simple.

Now for me it was question and answer time, responding to all the questions from all of them, all the time. Through all that, with my patience stretched to the limits, I discovered that the word 'Albatross' had been mistaken for 'Airbus' which had resulted in an 'overkill' of the rescue operation! Kind of weak but that's how it was.

While the mechanics worked at repairing a faulty cable to the hydraulic pump, I went over the whole affair with the Chief of Marine Police who could then see the funny side of the incident.

Chief Mechanic Hokan Geijer soon reported that a temporary repair could be made, in 15-20 minutes PAM would be able to go down into the water. The Chief of Marine Police caught on very quickly and immediately went out to his launch to begin clearing the boats from what would then be the take-off area. Soon we were 'down into the sea' again, pressure fully restored, landing gear jerking into place in the wells, flaps set for take off, taxying to an area that would ensure that the run into the air wouldn't in any way penetrate Malaysia's boundaries. Once airborne PAM joined downwind for runway 03 and was soon clearing with Customs at the terminal minus the passengers, who having arrived by rubber dinghy, would be in quarantine until a Fokker F27 came in to pick them up for Jakarta.

Even the Seletar tower operator on his high perch was fooled by the incident judging by the remarks he passed as I taxied past the tower en route to the hangar.

"That was very clever of you Captain, to come down and take off from the water again like that, very clever indeed! "

Coming from a man who must have seen the Albatross on the taxiway almost under his nose several times a week left me speechless. That he didn't understand that the Albatross was amphibious and had the inbuilt capability of using both sea and land as a surface is hard to believe. There are a lot of people in the aviation industry today who know so little about aeroplanes. In this case the controller's course should have included 'Aircraft Recognition'. Lots of unnecessary reports were completed in the next few days before the incident drew to a close.

It was always good to be home again in Singapore after being in the less developed areas of South East Asia. The population comprised people of many different nationalities, cultures and religions. As an ethnic group the Chinese predominated. The entire population were hard working, adaptive and innovative, taking great pride in their Singaporean identity. Many were English speaking and bilingual. Their technical skills, together with their law and order policies were of the highest order. Singaporeans lived and worked in the safest and cleanest city in South-east Asia. Hooliganism, graffiti 'art', thuggery, street violence, armed robbery, burglary and car theft were all comparatively rare, punishable by long terms of imprisonment and in some cases several 'strokes' of the cane. Those found guilty of rape, murder, or in the possession of dangerous drugs, faced execution by hanging.

Every citizen is expected to make a contribution, either as a member of the citizen's army or civil defence force, or by helping to keep the economy and social services going. Although they do exist, trade unions are moderate in their demands and don't have a lot to do in the running of the country, work stoppages or strikes were things of the

past. To an expatriate, it seems all Singaporeans work for the better-
ment of their island city. Although coined in the different times of the
nineteenth century, the term 'jewel of the east' certainly still has the
same depth of meaning for Singapore, it really is that jewel.

After living 'off camp' for two years, we were offered the use of a
fine pre-war, three bedroom, ex RAF bungalow, adjacent to our hangar on Seletar Air Base. Set in more than half an acre of lawn and with
tall casuarinas for a boundary, wooden shutters for windows, high,
fan-equipped ceilings and rooms of a generous size, the bungalow was
delightfully cool as compared to our more modern house 'off camp'.

18 Hyde Park Gate had been built as a senior officers dwelling, the
British certainly knew how to build tropical homes that unfortunately
never flowed on to Queensland Australia. When the property was offered us, being snobs at heart, we were only too pleased to move to a
place of such 'good address', which we knew would please some of
our 'rellies'.

After independence, much to their credit Singapore government
never did change the ever so British names of streets and districts. It
was told to me that the names were retained as an important part of
their colourful history, Brompton Road, The Oval, Orchard Road,
Scott's Road, Brighton, Newton Circus, Clifton and hundreds of others, to drop those names could mean the loss of their identity! Of
course there are many places named after Singaporeans or Malaysians,
pre-war and post-war too.

Ever since we'd been in Singapore our whole out-look on living
had changed. Betty was particularly impressed by the service provided
by the local merchants, when the grocer not only delivered the grocer-
ies ordered by 'phone, but placed the articles appropriately in the
pantry or refrigerator should we be absent from the house, the invoice
on the kitchen bench. Our house doors were never locked.

Well remembered is the day when with our 'phone out of order, I
walked across the road to our friendly Canadian neighbours, about a
hundred metres away to borrow their phone to advise the national tel-

ephone company of the problem. Returning down our driveway five minutes later, a repairman on a motorbike swept past me. Believe it or not, he had come to fix the phone. I could only scratch my head and look at him in disbelief, if that's not good service, what is?

Singapore was full of those sorts of surprises, from the rambling 'satay man' with a hot-plate on the luggage rack of his bike, to the junior constables whose job it was to check for any damage to the trees that lined every road and street and which were all catalogued. Power failures and our old enemy graffiti, were conspicuous by their absence.

Singapore was a gourmet's delight with streets of eating houses such as 'Food Alley and was a great place to live. Long lasting friends from all races and nations were made. Differing appetites were developed. Relatives and friends from around the world paid us numerous visits, my job, my life, could not have been happier.

When Dick's retirement at age 60 came about I was appointed Chief Pilot of Seaplane Operations (there's that word Seaplane again when it should be Flying-boat). At first he returned to the US but soon found he couldn't settle there. Having other members of his family already in Australia, he decided on a quiet life in Cooktown, North Queensland, where he built a house beside the river. Finally he returned to his first great love, Guam, where he'd spent many years in the Coastguard. He died there of the smoker's great enemy, emphysema, seven years later. Dick just wouldn't listen. Should the same ever happen to me, I'm sure it would have been passed on to me by him during those early flights while he puffed away merrily on his cheroot or cigarette.

The Malacca Straits area was the breeding ground of severe electrical storms known locally as Sumatras. Some days the weather could be hellish with lines of cumulo nimbus (cu nims), shoulder to shoulder, rising to 50,000 feet or more. Not all our trips to the field were trouble-free, far from it. On many a day, heavy rain, lightning and severe turbulence was encountered. Wide diversions from track were needed to avoid the worst, or so it was hoped. There the colour radar came into its own playing a major role in finding gaps or 'holes' that offered a safer passage through the towering masses of storm cloud.

When inadvertently I found myself in such a frothing mass with screeching static in the 'phones piercing my ear drums I'd pull the phones away from my ears and turn the radios off. Too late one day, the radome in the bow (nose to land lubbers) was suddenly hit by a bolt of lightning charged enough to crack the composite skin and burn the radios out, leaving acrid smoke coming out from under the radio console. That was frightening stuff.

The mostly Asian passengers would sometimes panic and become very hard to control, the engineer in the cabin found it difficult to maintain any semblance of order through hitting the panic button himself.

There were periods during the monsoon when Matak Island was obliterated by extremely low cloud and rain, with strong winds from the south stirring up huge waves ruling out a downwind alighting from seaward into the long, narrow harbour. On those occasions a curved approach from over part of the island would enable a touch down in a more sheltered corner of the harbour. While still planing, a swing through thirty degrees to the left brought the aircraft into the centre of the marked seaway. The whole process meant the aircraft was descending in a steep bank over the rain forest until reaching the sheltered waters of the upper harbour. I was about half way through that particular manoeuvre one day when an unknown 'something' impacted the aircraft followed by a sharp judder as the airspeed indicator needle began to perform rapid gyrations around the dial. A violent flutter in the ailerons could be felt through the control wheel. All that happened in what were microseconds, as the co-pilot also let out a frightened yell that sounded like "You hit a tree Captain, you hit a tree."

I was sure that some sort of a missile had hit the aircraft, tho' I knew that it wasn't a tree unless they grew to 250 feet or more. My thoughts ran to rebels or pirates, the area was home to them, could someone be using a low flying aircraft for anti-aircraft practice?

Somehow by instinct the Albatross reached the water safely with its aileron judder gradually dying out and the co-pilot still looking frozen and pop-eyed. Even after we were safely down and taxiing for the ramp, he kept muttering about hitting a tree. As I glanced along the left wing I knew we hadn't for I could see a gaping hole, close to half a metre wide, in the leading edge of the left wing immediately in front of the pitot tube (pee toe) that leads to the airspeed indicator.

Once on the ramp, the mystery was solved. A sea eagle with a large fish in its beak had broached the leading edge of the left wing to come to rest in a heap of feathers and blood-red flesh, against the forward spar. Little but 'splatter' was left of the bird but the fish was almost intact, although no doubt the whole two feet of it had suffered severe bruising! The crew were then smiling and laughing as if they'd known that all the time. The UF2 was called in to complete the flight and bring qualified sheet metal workers in to make a temporary repair, enough for PAM to return to Singapore for a complete fix.

Singapore received a fair share of the Sumatras that came from the island of the same name, vicious winds, terrific cracks of lightning, deafening thunder, sheets of rain. Horrifying, terrifying, are words not strong enough to describe a Sumatra. There were close to 80 fatalities one year during our stay in Singapore, attributed to people being struck by lightning during the dreaded Sumatras, mainly through them taking shelter under tall trees while bare-footed.

The stately casuarinas surrounding our house attracted many a lightning bolt with force and power enough to rip them open and litter the ground with their branches and needles. Singapore's storm-drains although wide and deep overflowed with flood water that would cascade madly over the roads. With so many houses on Seletar being set upon, the houses there were all fitted with lightning arrestors, which seemed to lessen the number of damaging strikes, leaving the casuarinas to bear the brunt of the fierce sumatras alone.

On the positive side you can get some lovely days in Singapore, with gentle breezes, sunny skies and glassy water around the whole island. Balmy nights too can be enjoyed, in a city where hardly anything happens before midnight in the way of night life.

A good deal of my leisure and recreation time was spent at the Changi Sailing Club, not far from the Changi Gaol of WW2 infamy. The gaol was much as it had been during the Japan invasion, the sight of it always brought back to me some of the horrific stories of prison life there during those times. Visits to the chapel deep in the gaol could be arranged for foreigners on application. Having taken relatives and friends on the chapel tour several times, I realise how the term 'in the clanger' came about.

The Changi Sailing Club held races for keelboats or catamarans almost every weekend, 'Round the Island' annually, that being a handicap event attracting many entries from various classes of yachts. The Club also possessed good eating and swimming facilities, the curry dishes there were judged to be amongst the best in Singapore.

With racing finished for the day, the boats washed and stowed, sailors could take their drinks to the jetty and watch glorious sunsets across the Straits of Johore towards mainland Malaysia. None were the spectacular bright red of the deserts as seen in Australia, but softer pinks, whites, yellows and blues, with moored yachts their halyards tinkling like chimes, lying to the tide in the shimmering waters of the Straits of Johore. There's always boat traffic there, huge tankers on their way to the dry dock at Sembawang, down to small ferries, the tankers seeming to be far too big to fit into the narrow straits. A yachtsman sleeping aboard might very well be rocked to sleep or suffer from 'mal de mer' caused by the wash from those huge vessels.

My contract, an evergreen, had originally been for five years. I had served eight years when age 60 loomed on the horizon. In that year, oil production had declined. The island base at Matak was losing some of its pristine rain forest, as it was turned rapidly into an airport. It was plain to see that the days of the Grumman amphibians were numbered.

I began to search the many good quality aviation journals for fly-ing-boat opportunities that ended in me being invited to the Claudius Dornier Seastar's factory at Oberpfaffenhofen in Bavaria, West Ger-many and from there on to the Paris Air Show. There I met up with Professor Claudius Dornier himself and two of his sons, Conrado and Camillo, who were to show their new design off that year. The 'Clau-dius Dornier Seastar, a turbine powered, centre-line thrust, ten place amphibian was one of the first to be made and certified using mostly composite materials. The 'Seastar' project was a private venture fi-nanced entirely by Professor Claudius and family, the factory was set apart from that of the Dornier Werke. At that time a prototype had been built in form enough for a flying display. The design followed much along the lines of earlier Dornier flying-boats from the 20's and 30's era, the main improvements being that Seastar was an amphibian with turbine engines and the still as yet unproved construction materi-als.

'Seastar's' wings, empennage, sponsons and hull, were made of composite material. The first time I set eyes on that unique design with it's extremely smooth as silk, glossy surfaces that would pass through the air or water without leaving a ripple, I felt that 'Seastar' was a winner.

Professor Claudius passed away suddenly at a time when I was vis-iting Oberpfaffenhoven as a consultant, which was the time of the Chernobyl disaster. His two sons carried on with the project until the re-unification of Germany drained the funds allotted to Seastar devel-opment by the German government. There was a lot of sadness about when the project dragged to a halt, for the Seastar marketing team had arranged many sales for the 'plastic bird (note not metal, times are changing), in SE Asia, many of which came from my efforts in the marketing field.

Matak Island was destined to become an airfield, in went the bull-dozers, down came the pristine jungle and up went the control and terminal buildings. For eight years we had operated from Singapore with the Albatross through weather thick and thin, accident-free and without major delays of any kind, carrying thousands and thousands of passengers safely. Why an expensive airport employing 120 staff was needed at that time I failed to understand. Following some negotiations, my serving time and retirement date was extended by six months, at which time the company wound up the sea operation. It was a very sad time for all concerned as each aircraft was flown out of Seletar to Jakarta, PAM to be parked in the open, to rot along with a lot of other types on an out-of-the-way airfield and the UF2 returned to the Indon Air Force, looking very smart in military colours.

Not long before the sea operation closed Captain Hank Hancock a retired ex TWA pilot from St Louis, Missouri paid me a visit at Seletar. Hank was about to head up Tropical Sea Airlines in Thailand utilising six Model 28-5-ACF Catalinas. He had heard of my impending retirement and at the time was canvassing the aviation world for suitable stock and staff. He left me with an assurance of a job in the TSA enterprise in the months to come.

As an aside, almost two years passed before I visited PAM on another project where both pilot and metal water bird were assigned a most urgent covert rescue mission in the Mediterranean. Now that's a long way from Jakarta. Departure for the scene was scheduled for 24 hours from the time of receipt of the request. The most modern amphibian in the world was found parked exactly where it had been left after being ferried from Singapore, in the open in front of a huge hangar devoid of any other aircraft. Batteries, radios, the most sensitive items when storing an aircraft for a long period, were still connected and in place as per operations, although they should have been removed and placed in an air-conditioned area soon after arrival. When the aircraft's doors were first opened and we entered the cabin the temperature inside must have been more than 60 degrees Celsius! The engines had not been turned in all that time either or been inhibited. At the very least I estimated that it would take seven days to prepare aircraft and crew for such a venture. Our mission was called off due to the time factor involved. The persons responsible for her welfare can only be described as negligent and unworthy of any title they might have held in their profession.

Having received a generous 'golden handshake' I decided to remain in Seletar while deciding the best thing to do with the rest of my life. In many ways I felt that I was at peak performance insofar as flying from water went anyway, so I searched around for opportunities as a free-lance pilot. The first came up quite quickly, hardly a 'water-bird' job but a ferry of a Beech Bonanza from Seletar to Madang in New Guinea.

The flight was made in three stages, Seletar/Bali (Den Pasar), Bali/Darwin, Darwin/Port Moresby, as permission for a direct flight to Madang was not forthcoming. The long-range tank was removed at Port Moresby after which the Bonanza was delivered, with seats re-fitted, to its new owner Mr Peter Barter of the Melanesian Explorer at Madang (later Sir Peter and a Minister in the government of Papua New Guinea).

That done a short-term contract came up with the Flying Ambulance in the 'Maldives', an independent island state in the Indian Ocean 500 miles to the southwest of Colombo, flying a midget, single engine 'Renegade' Lakes amphibian. The Maldives was a popular destination for the European tourist trade. My job included flying the resident doctor to medical cases in the outlying resort islands, or flying the patients in to the hospital at Male, the capital. Many of those using the service were suffering from 'the bends' after diving around the coral reefs with, I suspected, too little instruction in the art, judging by the numbers afflicted.

I'd only been there a short time when a late call came to fly a patient with the doctor off to Colombo, that would mean an over-water night flight of four and a half hours in the single engine 'Renegade' that was fitted with a 250hp engine, extra fuel tanks and provision for one stretcher in the extended cabin, plus a doctor or nurse. Although I'd left that type of aviation years before with the patient's life in the balance and the doctor ready, willing and waiting, there was no other choice. Fortunately the weather was perfect all the way, the patient surviving the ordeal.

A North American aviation group had only recently been granted an operating licence throughout the Maldives with a Twin Otter on floats. This group complained to the authorities that they should have been the first to be offered the flight for reasons of two-engine safety. They were quite outspoken about the apparent 'recklessness' of the 'Renegades' proposed flight to Colombo. It looked as if the complaint would be taken to a higher authority, the future of the flying doctor program looked grim.

All was resolved a week or so later, when an emergency call came for the doctor to attend a crashed Twin Otter in a lagoon 150 miles to the north of Male, the island capital of the Maldives. The 'Twotter' floatplane had been carrying 13 passengers including the Swedish ambassador to Sri Lanka to a special function at the resort island, when during alighting the right main float strut somehow buckled and the 'Twotter' capsized on to it's right side and sank. All the occupants had escaped through the main cabin door that luckily for a short period was uppermost, suffering only bruising and shock. The Swiss Doctor attended to them immediately. Nothing more was heard of the 'recklessness' of our flight to Colombo, as the operators of the Twin Otter were facing gaol terms following serious charges of their falsifying previous water operating experience in their application for an air service licence.

Nearing the end of my sojourn the Flying Ambulance had by that time engaged a younger, permanent pilot who was willing to live the life in the Maldives. After almost six months I was tired of sun, sand and sun-tanned, sometimes topless tourists and so returned to Seletar, six months of my retirement completed.

Next came an offer to relieve a Goose pilot at Alotau, Milne Bay, Papua New Guinea. Mr John Wilde and son John junior were opening up Milne Bay Air using a Grumman Goose and a Lake amphibian.

Against great odds, young 'John junior' had been battling along bravely to get a service started, with little experience in the field and needed a rest.

A land-based operation had been decided on at first, the two aircraft flew from the historic Gurney airfield scene of Japans first defeat in WW2. There was no water, electricity or telephone laid on to the field, which was quite a long way out of the town of Alotau by a gravel road. Servicing of both aircraft was performed at Port Moresby by an independent contractor, a system that caused many frustrating delays in getting small but important repairs done, costly too. If the aircraft couldn't be flown to Port Moresby, the engineer would need to fly to Gurney by charter or commercial airline to carry out the required repairs, he couldn't always down tools in his own shop and attend to us. Either way it cost a lot of money. Of all the frustrations experienced at the time, this was the worst.

In an endeavour to build up business, John senior offered many complementary flights to officials engaged in governmental business without any appreciable improvement in trade, his generosity was never rewarded. MBA was also meeting some local resistance to their 'invasion' of the area, as one local businessman put it, which culminated in the burning down of the small terminal that John had designed and built at Gurney, telephone and water included.

At that time John junior had returned from his vacation, thanks to my guardian angel I was in Port Moresby the night of the fire, making preparations to return to Singapore. The fire was blamed on a careless (or purposeful) tossing of a cigarette butt into a dustbin after the staff had departed the airport for the night, whether intentional or not was never discovered. John senior was mortified of course, but ready to try again.

With professional marketing and maintenance facilities I'm sure Milne Bay Air could have achieved success, but it was not to be. John senior decided on a landplane operation, which having had a name change or two, or three, operates very successfully today from a Port

Moresby base. The Goose, sold to an Australian buyer resident in the Philippines at first, is now registered in Fiji. The commission promised me by both parties for arranging the sale of the Goose has never been paid. The Lake lies at the bottom of the sea off Ferguson Island after an alighting mishap with a comparatively inexperienced floating hull pilot. Open water is not the best of habitats for the small 'water-bird' designed for operations from calm, inland lakes. It's the swell that gets 'em.

Leaving Seletar at last, I settled in Brisbane but my thoughts were always in the mountains, islands, rivers, lakes and lagoons of faraway places.

A close American friend, Hank Hancock of St Louis, Missouri, USA, an ex TWA Captain, was about to open Tropical Sea Airlines out of Bangkok at first using five re-conditioned Model 28-5ACF Catalina amphibians in a tourist network that was expected to be very promising.

Years before, whilst I was at Seletar with Conoco, Hank had told me of his dreams. He was married to a Thai lady, his dreams were about to come true, or so he thought. Bank finance had all been arranged through some influential members of his Board. Things were about to get underway with a job in the organization for both Betty and myself.

The rest is a long story of more shattered dreams, for the finances went in all directions except for the proper preparation of the flying equipment. Instead, super-modern class offices, dark-suited executives, loads of staff without a clue as to what their duties should be, received the 'bread' in big slices, until it was all used up without an aircraft ever turning a prop. Tropical Sea Airlines was obviously a front for the laundering of money or some other devious purpose unknown to Hank while he stood holding the baby. All ended with Hank and I walking around a half rejuvenated Catalina at St Louis, wondering what to do with the poor metal water bird. The Catalina, a Model 28-5ACF was the only one of its type in the world registered in the

Transport Category. Overhauled to a very high standard by the Central Intelligence Agency (CIA) the Cat had been used in the 'Bay of Pigs' operation in Cuba as an airborne communications platform. We had acquired the amphibian from Guatemala and flown it to St Louis at first, for interior improvements that included airline type seating and sound proofing. After some test flying it was taken to Mena in Arkansas for engine overhaul or replacement and finishing off work to be completed by a professional organization. Many towns in the US specialise in one particular industry, Mena was wholly devoted to aircraft repair and refurbishment that was another eye-opener for me.

Back in Brisbane I learned from a message coming 'down the chimney' that plans had changed. Tropical Sea Airlines were buying a Goose in Australia for $A400, 000, to commence their flight training program for national pilots. Neither of us knew who was making those major but mysterious decisions, for Hank had been appointed as President of the company and knew nothing about it. I was actually the first to solve the mystery after receiving a call from the Australian Department of Civil Aviation in Melbourne, who advised me that the Australian owner of the Goose afore-mentioned was seeking a pilot to ferry the machine from Melbourne to Thailand! A search of their records confirmed that I was the only qualified Goose pilot in Australia, would I undertake the flight, the pilot who had been assigned the task originally was not qualified on the Goose and had been withdrawn.

After a good number of sneaky inquiries, fuss and bother, I ferried that machine to the Thai Navy airfield at U-Tapao, Thailand, via Mildura, Leigh Creek, Oodnadatta, Alice Springs, Tennant Creek, Tindal, Darwin, Kupang, Den Pasar (Bali), Jakarta, Singapore (Seletar) and Penang. All was done as a landplane on the wheels and with standard fuel tanks, not a pint of water was seen over Central Australia.

From the beginning, the flight was shrouded in so much mystery I'd never experienced before and I hope, never to again. Accompanying me was the owner of the Goose and a licensed engineer on his way to marry his Thai sweetheart. He had helped to re-build the Goose that had been stored for a very long time since arriving from New Zealand.

We were held up at Darwin for a few days pending the arrival of some overdue funds at Melbourne from Bangkok. That was an uncertain period for me as the days dragged on and we lazed away the time, sightseeing around Darwin or swimming in the hotel pool. Suddenly those uncertain days of waiting were over when a 'phone call from the lawyers in Melbourne cleared us to move on. That Goose was by far the cleanest, best looking, best behaved of any I'd flown and a pleasure to fly although operations off water were not to be.

Strange things happened. While over-night in Singapore I received a message stating that for military purposes, arrival at U-Tapao, Thailand, must be exactly 4 pm on Saturday afternoon, which was the following day.

The clock was striking four as I brought the Goose in on a long final from the waters of the Gulf of Thailand for a smooth wheels touchdown and was ushered by the tower operator to the apron of a very large hangar. U-Tapao had been a huge US air base during the war in Vietnam. There were no other aircraft moving at the time, we had the airbase to ourselves it seemed.

Immediately on my stopping the engines, a gang of workmen mostly in Navy type dark blue overalls began unloading the equipment we'd brought, including my personal headset, which I had to retrieve after some argument about its ownership. With that invasion over, we stood around the aircraft with our personal gear, maps and charts, to await a clearance by Customs and Immigration. One hour, two hours went by then darkness fell, three hours, without any sign of the customs or any other vehicle. The workmen had trundled the Goose into the hangar, the doors were rolled closed, I never saw them again, or the Goose either. Without any lighting coming from the hangar where the Goose was parked, it was very dark and I was worried. A feeling came over me that all was not well, as if being set up for assassination. We were certainly extremely vulnerable on the unlighted apron. It seemed like hours before a mini-bus appeared on the scene to take us to a police post an hour's drive away.

After many delays and some confusing dialogue in the Thai language with immigration officials, our passports were 'chopped' and we continued driving on into Bangkok accompanied by the same two 'officials', where we arrived at two o'clock in the morning. Below the 'chop' in my passport was a neat, hand-written entry statement in Thai, that I presumed to be the explicit conditions of entry, but of course without an interpreter I had no idea what those conditions were. Mine was the only passport to receive special treatment, my so-called 'companions' receiving but one hard 'chop' only. During all that time I noted that my two shall we say 'crewmen' weren't the slightest bit concerned, as if they fully understood the goings on. I like to think that it was my long experience in SE Asia that told me that things were going awry, to be alert, observant and careful. On the long trip by road in the mini-bus to Bangkok, they had dozed and spoken little.

The journey for me ended at the International airport, where my 'watchman', who had stuck to me like mud to a blanket since leaving the customs depot, checked me into a transit hotel fifty metres from the terminal and then told me that I would leave by Qantas at 7 am, where to he didn't say, he would accompany me to check in at six. Not a really warm welcome. By then I knew of course that there was something rotten in the state of Denmark. In the meantime, the bus had departed with my two travelling 'companions' to an undisclosed destination. I've not heard of them or seen them since that night, but of course I'm old enough to know the smell of a rat when I smell one, as the saying goes.

I felt a lot like James Bond must have done at times, when after leaving the elevator the selector lights blinked and a hesitant touch of the button drew no response from the elevator. In my room I found the 'phone disconnected except for an automatic line to reception, that is pick up the receiver and the call is answered immediately. The operator acted dumb and advised me in absurd broken English that a light meal would be served in my room 'shortly' .I was virtually a prisoner, a dog-tired prisoner, spending a very restless night wondering what that was all about?

Sharp at six am, my 'watchman' was at the door of my room. We moved out to the elevator that was now working exactly as one should. At the check-in he stood talking to a female police officer, complete with revolver and motioned me to join the queue. She then directed me to the front of the queue and spoke in rapid Thai to the check-in clerk, who quickly came up with a ticket, a first class ticket and boarding pass. I was then escorted to the First Class Lounge where although still sleepy-eyed, I enjoyed a delightful breakfast before boarding for where? Singapore I discovered. I can only say that whoever organised my arrival and departure had a lot of influence and can only conclude that the whole 'schimozzle' had something to do with Hank and me and Tropical Sea Airlines. Months later, I heard that the Goose had been waiting for a qualified pilot and had not moved from the U Tapao hangar.

Back at St Louis, mystery unsolved, we decided to complete the refurbishment of the Catalina N5404J and endeavour to find a place for it in commercial aviation for so far as was known, it was the only Catalina in the world certified in the Transport Category.

On the Missouri River, the Mississippi and Lake of the Ozarks, with an approved FAA designee Ronnie Gardner, I underwent the civil type rating for CV-PBY5, sea and land. Several avenues for useful employment of the amphibian, such as marine salvage, fish hauling and tourist safaris were explored without success, no-one with the means could be found willing enough to take the big bite.

Wearying of all the associated problems, I advised Hank to sell. The Cat went on the market without having done much in the way of commercial flying.

Eventually N5404J was purchased by a group of enthusiasts from New Zealand, who I believe had illegally intercepted some correspondence between myself and the RNZAF and who at first I'd introduced to Hank and the Catalina. Two attempts to set out from Los Angeles to Honolulu ended with a return to LA having to be made with engine trouble. On the third attempt the Catalina somehow made Honolulu but on the next leg to Tahiti the pilot was forced to alight on the sea at night having again experienced an engine failure, this time off Christmas Island. Later, the one and only Transport Category registered Catalina left in the world, sank into the depths of the Pacific due to a leaking hull caused by the heavy contact with the sea. All those aboard were safe after having spent ten or more hours in a rubber dinghy, to be part of a dramatic rescue by a container vessel.

Before leaving Mena my recommendation to Hank had been that a double engine change would be necessary before I set out on the Pacific. The aircraft had been purchased from Guatemala without up-to-date records of mandatory maintenance of engines and airframe. That advice was ignored. Thus closed the heartbreak chapter of Tropical Sea Airlines.

When four years into so-called retirement, by chance I met Dennis Buchanan in the Brisbane International Terminal, the then owner of Talair in Papua New Guinea and an old friend and employer, as he was about to board a flight to Port Moresby. Typical of the man was an invitation for me to join up with his company Talair again. There was an acute pilot shortage in those parts, my age should not be detrimental to an appointment.

Acceptance of his proposal was easy but the requisite Work Permits difficult. For more than two years I struggled with 'dodgy' visas never really having a straight run with a Work Permit that wasn't restricted in some way. The PNG Consulate in Brisbane were showing signs of reverse discrimination, with never a thought given as to how their country could operate efficiently with insufficient pilots to man the 'planes to cover their huge, road-less nation. After taking leave for an urgent operation in Brisbane and the appropriate convalescence time, I waited for two months for my Work Permit to be approved to allow my return. Finally Dennis had to take my case to a very high PNG authority after which the consulate rang my home to tell me the Work Permit 'had mysteriously arrived'. I could depart the following day! Those were just some of the frustrations of working in a foreign land, one needs a lot of patience to cope with the paper work of bureaucratic officialdom.

Flying a Twin Otter again over what must be one of the most beautiful countries on earth was really enjoyable but any time I needed or was due for a break, or urgent medical treatment, I experienced problems with returning to PNG. The problem wasn't my own as employers all over PNG were facing similar situations where expatriate staff were concerned.

Eventually I worked my way into becoming a privileged 'tours pilot', four weeks on a heavy flying schedule (up to 120 flying hours), then three weeks off at home in Brisbane. In many ways though I felt that I was a slave, my future wasn't that bright that I needed sunglasses when looking at it.

One morning while I was in the process of starting up the 'Twotter' for a regular run down Gulf of Papua ports, I was radioed on Talair's discrete frequency by Guy Buchanan, Dennis's son. Guy had taken over a good part of the management of Talair's operations and asked me to take a call from Victoria Falls, Zimbabwe. The caller was Pierre Jaunet, owner of Catalina Safaris in Africa.

Ronnie Gardiner, the FAA designee in the USA who had given me the type rating tests on Tropical Sea Airlines Catalina on the Mississippi and Lake of the Ozarks, had given my name to Pierre who wanted to know whether I could come to Africa for a season of safaris with his Zimbabwean registered Catalina Z-CAT. I jumped at the chance, called Dennis, who having heard of my offer already from Guy gave me his blessings in the Australian language. At the end of my tour, about a week away, I returned to Brisbane for permission from Betty before taking off for Harare, time since 'retirement' six years.

Three seasons were spent in Africa with Pierre and Catalina Z-CAT on safari tours, visiting Tanzania, Kenya, Rwanda, Zambia, Zanzibar, Kilimanjaro, Lake Manyara, Mwanza, Lake Kivu, Birundi, Lake Tanganyika and on the Nile, Abu Simbel, Aswan, Luxor and Maadi at Cairo.

For most of the trips, that were tours of between eight and twenty-one days centred on Nairobi, I was assisted by co-pilot Dave Evans a citizen of Zimbabwe. Dave said that he knew Africa like the back of his hand while looking at the palm. Being new to the great continent, I couldn't have managed without him so far as finding unfamiliar places went, he having done many of the tours before. Dave's flying ability too was well above average and his attitude helpful, kind and considerate of my age. Sometimes he and Pierre didn't get on too well though and would 'barney' Irish/African style. Dave told me that he'd been fired a few times but re-instated an hour or two later when Pierre had cooled down. "That sounds a bit like Dennis and Papua New Guinea." I told him.

Many of our touring passengers were wealthy notables from USA, the UK, Italy, Switzerland and Germany even some from Australia. Pierre was a wonderful organiser, a hard worker in all fields, making every tour a memorable one for our guests. His 'carry on' office was a very large leather shoulder bag. When away from the aircraft he was never seen without that bag over his shoulder. The highlight of those tours for me came when I was told that 1992, when I first joined up with him, making sixteen journeys without a hitch, was his most successful year ever.

Pierre wasn't all goodness however, there were times when we disagreed, living and working close together for two weeks or six weeks at a time can cause friction in the ranks. I can say that those years were, after Singapore, amongst the best in my flying career.

I was resting in Australia from a four-month stint in Africa, when Pierre asked me to Captain his Catalina again on a charter around parts of Europe, South America and the USA. The proposed flight would mean the crossing of the South and North Atlantic, parts of the world that I was not so familiar with.

My previous tour in Africa had not been a happy one. Pierre was beginning to exercise his ownership authority, to cut corners as regards to safety. I was seriously considering taking a 'rain check' about returning to Africa to spend more time at home. The proposed expedition into foreign parts though, was hard to resist. That great adventure began seven years after retiring in Singapore! Indeed, with the promise of such a fantastic journey with one of my favourite aircraft, I had 'fallen on my floats' again.

ATLANTIC ODYSSEY

Winds blow to waft me, suns to light me rise;

My footstool earth, my canopy the skies'

Atlantic Odyssey really began for me when the 'phone rang in the middle of the night while I was at my son Jack's home in Sydney. Pierre was calling from Victoria Falls in Zimbabwe as he usually did, 'phone services from Harare where he lived were as to time and quality most unreliable. The connection was scratchy and echoed a lot.

"Bryan I want you to fly my Catalina again. This time it will be a six-week charter flight that will take us across parts of Europe, South America, the South and North Atlantic, the USA, Greenland, even Iceland. I want you in Harare next Thursday, for a test-flight and pre-flight planning, what a great trip that will be for us, the longest I've ever been offered. You will accept, you will be able to come yes?"

Requests from Pierre for his tourist safaris were always loaded with a lot of youthful, sometimes dangerous exuberance and at that time of night I was taken aback. Since leaving Talair in Papua New Guinea I had been flying his amphibious Catalina (CV PBY5A registered as Z-CAT) on safaris throughout Africa as far as the Nile and Cairo in Egypt, visiting 12 or more countries en route from Victoria Falls, both north and south-bound.

The apparent urgency of his request surprised me. Out of the blue as it came, I was taken completely by surprise, at that time a recall to

Africa had not been expected. For a trans-Africa safari he usually gave me a month's advice as to when I should be at the starting point, that had always been Harare in Zimbabwe, the hub of his safari ground tours and where his Catalina was based.

"Pierre, you've caught me in the middle of the night, quite unexpected. As a guess here and now I definitely can't make it by Thursday, I have family things to attend to. Your call has been diverted from Brisbane, I'm in Sydney five hundred miles away. There are a few things I must do before leaving, a return to Brisbane for one to get packed. Six weeks you say, that's a long time. I'll need to take a fair bit of gear with me, even mention of the North Atlantic makes me feel cold, as you know I'm mostly a hot-country man."

"I will get warm clothing for you, we'll be going to Holland first from where the charter will start. There the Catalina will be painted in the colours that the charterer has requested, they want us there two weeks from now."

"Pierre, organise the tickets from Brisbane via Sydney for South Africa's Saturday flight via Jo'burg, that's the best I can do. Fax me the details to Brisbane, I mean ALL the details so I can get the planning started while I'm on the way and get focused a bit. From what you've told me though, it sounds great. Will Dave be coming along?"

At that point the call faded out and couldn't be re-connected. An hour later the 'phone rang again. From Amsterdam the Tour Director for the proposed charter revealed the plans for his forthcoming 'Atlantic Odyssey' as he called it, pleading with me to accept Pierre's offer, a plea that was hard to refuse.

Between then and the time I was seated on the Jumbo out of Sydney, several long and detailed faxes had been dealt with, the globe of the planet in the office had been revolved a number of times, suitable winter gear packed into soft travelling bags and home arrangements completed with an ever-loving, ever-understanding wife. That is how one of the most thrilling, one of the most adventurous, one of the most stressful flights began in the twilight of my career.

When I arrived at Harare, the Zimbabwean registered Catalina Z-CAT was not quite ready, with an engine remaining to be re-installed in the left nacelle. The first working day was spent in getting briefed and having my licence renewed for the test flying to the satisfaction of the Zimbabwean air regulator's standards. To my dismay I discovered that the test flight could only take place after a statutory fine had been paid for a fifty-hour maintenance inspection that was not completed at Cairo on a previous voyage.

The responsibility really belonged to Pierre, the owner, for not advising his maintenance contractors of Z-CAT's movements but in my absence he had declared me, as Captain, to be responsible. The fine imposed was now more than three months overdue. We both attended the regulator's office and the matter was sorted out when Pierre under my cold, steady gaze, forked out $Zim1200 in cash, not a very big sum when converted to US, and a promise that there would not be any recurrence of the 'oversight' by us taking a licensed maintenance man along on similar journeys in the future. Pierre left the building looking rather shamefaced. From my point of view it wasn't a very good start to 'Atlantic Odyssey'.

With that nasty episode over, which had taken most of the day, only then was I able to hear more of the forthcoming air journey.

The charterers, Peter Stuyvesant Travel, were playing Z-CAT off against a British registered Catalina that was experiencing hold-ups in meeting certain British airworthiness requirements. It was doubtful whether or not their machine could reach the starting line at Amsterdam in time. Boiled down, the first machine to reach Holland would win the charter, which to me sounded rather like a rather shallow arrangement. Z-CAT was faced with thousands of miles to go to reach Holland in comparison to the short distance England/Holland for the British aircraft. However Pierre had accepted the challenge, now it was up to us to see it through. The deadline for departure of the charter from Amsterdam was in ten days time. Pierre was anxious for Z-

CAT to depart for Eindhoven in Holland, the collection point, as soon as air-tested and ready.

Late that afternoon the test flight was completed. It was dark before Z-CAT was fuelled to the maximum for the first leg of our ferry flight to Nairobi in Kenya, where fuel was more expensive. African fuel prices varied from the sublime to the ridiculous, one day, one place, one price, the next day another.

Departing Harare early the following morning from the longest runway in Africa, we reached Wilson airport, Nairobi, after a nine and a half hour flight with Z-CAT performing satisfactorily. There I was in familiar territory once more, many of Pierre's trans-Africa safaris began and finished at Nairobi.

Pierre owned a fine country residence at Karen on the outskirts of Nairobi where we stayed the night. A full day was needed to sort and load spares and victuals on to Z-CAT. The contents of a US 50 gallon drum of oil, was broken down into four-gallon jerry cans that were stowed out of sight along and between the catwalk floor and bilges. The fuel tanks were filled to maximum for the next leg, a fourteen-hour flight to Luxor, one of several points on the Nile familiar through me having already completed several journeys in Z-CAT across the African continent.

Excerpt from my diary on safari 18th October 1992

'At 31,000lb all-up-weight, the take-off at Loyangalani was OK but left no room for error and certainly needed the steady headwind coming off the lake. Flew north up Lake Turkana, which is sinister and murky. Circled island in centre of lake for sight of 'the biggest crocs in the world '(according to Pierre) but saw none then set course for Khartoum at 8,500 feet. Sighted White Nile about one and a half hours from Khartoum where the White' marries' the Blue, after flying over part of Ethiopia. The tracts of land adjoining the Nile that are irrigated seem to extend up to ten miles from the river, after which all is desert. Six hours fifty-five minutes Loyangalani-Khartoum. Arrival

very disorganised over visas etc. Waited in terminal two hours before being cleared. To Hilton Hotel on Blue Nile for accommodation. No alcohol, the passengers are quiet and look so genteel sipping soft drinks. Dinner at the Ivory Club.'

19th October 1992 Khartoum

'To aircraft to refuel which was a relatively simple operation for a change then a late afternoon river cruise, scenery as in the Bible. Saw Kitchener's frigate hard and fast on the left bank of the White Nile and building where General Gordon was slain. Bought antique Wilkinson Sword in souk in Khartoum in excellent condition.'

20th October 1992

'Up and away, out of Khartoum at nine-thirty for Aswan, temperature in 'the hots'. Horrible looking desert all the way to Abu Simbel before following the Nile which is actually all lake at that point. Radios busy at Aswan. Approach clearance not available until 10 miles out at 10,000 feet. Driven to Pullman Cataract Hotel after customs and immigration clearance. Met by the always smiling, genial General Noor, Egyptian Air Force Z-CAT's Egypt agent. Agatha Christie wrote 'Death on the Nile ' at this place. Nice dinner, belly dancer as entertainment. '

Mike Terrell, an American was acting as co-pilot and assistant mechanic on 'Atlantic Odyssey'. Mike had no previous experience with Catalinas. Harry Holdcroft, a Zimbabwean citizen originally from 'Cockneyland', was a qualified aircraft engineer of many years experience who joined Z-CAT to carry out the various inspections and routine maintenance that would be required en route. Last but not least, Frenchman Pierre Jaunet aircraft owner had the biggest job of all, that of cabin attendant, chef, chief purser and general organiser.

Pierre knew every nut, bolt and Philips screw in his amphibian, to use nautical terms, from bow to stern, beam to beam and could act in his own way in almost any crew capacity although not holding an appropriate licence. He was a truly remarkable man, with an outstanding knowledge of the mechanical side of things aeronautical and the African continent, geographically, historically and the mysterious ways of the many peoples and cultures of those ancient lands.

The last three hours of the fifteen-hour flight to Luxor were flown in darkness. In the latter stages we had been warned to give a wide berth to the wall of the Aswan dam where the anti-aircraft guns lining the wall were always loaded and ready to fire. Built by the Russians the dam is guarded zealously, any breaching of the wall could cause most of Egypt to be seriously flooded as far as the Mediterranean with thousands of casualties. Touch down on Luxor's airport was made as the last flight in of the night.

When on safaris, the Nile in front of the Winter Palace Hotel at Luxor was used for alighting, as a treat for our tourists. A launch and pinnace of the Egyptian Navy always met us there, with their sailors in impeccable white uniforms going through their 'coming alongside' drills every bit as well as the Royal Navy or Royal Australian Navy. Without any tourists to contend with while ferrying and for re-fuelling purposes, this time we came in on the airport.

Pierre's agent General Noor, Egyptian Air Force, who always handled Z-CAT's journeys in Egypt, met us at the airport with all arrangements in hand for a morning departure to Corfu, Greece. Z-CAT would be re-fuelled the following morning, a process that we knew from experience even with General Noor's powerful presence, was going to take some time and more than a little 'baksheesh'.

At the Winter Palace a late supper awaited us, with the strongest coffee I've ever tasted in the smallest cup I've ever seen. Pierre rushed off to 'phone Amsterdam to see if we were still in the race. Should the British Cat have arrived or was on the way to Eindhoven, we would return to Harare. Knowing all I did about Catalinas and the registration of non-standard models of the type, I was always confident that our flight would end in Eindhoven as planned. The British Cat was fitted with more powerful engines than those of the original design and had not been certificated for commercial passengers. Pierre returned to tell us that the green light was still ours, we would move on another stage.

En route from Nairobi our High Frequency radio had failed. On the ball as usual Pierre had ordered his British agents to have a manual awaiting us at Corfu to enable repairs to be done.

The late departure from Luxor necessitated the final three hours of the ten-hour flight to Corfu also being flown in darkness. There we came in to land from a right hand base leg. Seated in the left hand seat as I was, in the latter stages of the approach before turning on to final, the runway lights were obscured by the instrument panel's coaming. Mike failed to give me any prompts or cues as to when I should make the turn to final as a good co-pilot should. I was left to guess, we were still getting things worked out between us. The night landing at Luxor had been a straight in approach with the runway lights in view from about 50 kilometres out. The result was that I flew through the extended centre-line and was forced to drop a wing to sight the runway then swerve back to a straight approach when the runway lights came into view. We ended up too high and had to take power off to regain the glide slope. After landing I resolved to have a good talk with him when opportunity arose to get some cockpit procedures sorted out.

The hotel manager presented us with the pages of a radio type manual that had been faxed from the UK and had used up a complete roll of the hotel's fax paper. He was tight-lipped while he demonstrated the fax machine's depositing of yards of paper over the floor, but seemingly good-natured about the weird looking hieroglyphics of the circuit boards in the manual. I had a suspicion that we might be reported to the Grecian Intelligence Bureau as possible evildoers.

The daily 'phone call to Amsterdam indicated that we were to continue on to Eindhoven, the British still hadn't got their act together. Pierre seemed happier and proposed flying to Eindhoven the following day. On top of that he learned that the military airfield at Eindhoven closed at 5 pm local Netherlands time. With a late start expected because of re-fuelling, an arrival before that time would not be possible, instead a night stop at Cannes was planned, much to everyone's delight. .

After a five and a half hour flight we reached Cannes to be met with a snag so far as I was concerned. Australian passport holders must have a visa for France. For once, Pierre's usually immaculate arrangements had failed. We must either fly out, or I would be interned, the actual period not disclosed.

Pierre argued, all in French of course. "M'sieur, but this is my Capitan, I am a French citizen, I own the 'plane."

That was all to no avail as the law must be obeyed. The arrival of a more benevolent senior immigration official from the city, after much discussion saw us cleared to Avignon for the night, an 'out of sight out of mind' sort of decision. An hour's flight and we were in that beautiful ancient city with its Roman wall and Papal Palace. There was time for some sightseeing and relaxation, the first since leaving Harare, while Pierre spent 'oodles' of francs on 'phone calls.

After a four and a half hour flight the next day, over what must be one of the prettiest parts of the world, green fields, forests and picturesque French and Belgian villages, Z-CAT was at the airfield at Eindhoven, a joint, civil/military facility. The Eindhoven tower asked for a low fly-past before we landed for the benefit of the photographers already in position on the ground.

In a shallow dive we zipped past the large crowd gathered in front of the hangar that was to be our destination, pulled up into a steep banked turn, circled the hangar low, then glided down to a soft landing in their full view. Our positioning flight was over in 46 hours 50 minutes flying time, with four re-fuelling stops.

On the ramp, before we could stop engines a Netherlands Air Force airman with marshalling batons directed Z-CAT into the hangar. Where I came from we didn't do that sort of thing, which was taboo, there were rules against taxying an aircraft engines going, props whirling, inside a hangar. Very cautiously I followed his signals, until Z-CAT's high tail and wide span of wing was well inside. Only then did I get the signal to cut engines.

Mike and I ran over the shut down checklist and began to clamber down the ladder from the forward passenger compartment. Before we reached the ground, scaffolding on wheels was being positioned around wings, fuselage and tail plane. Z-CAT was to begin her transformation. The British Catalina could not be in position on time and so the race was won.

In an office adjoining the hangar the Director of the tour, Hans Weisman, gave out all the details while we listened avidly to his every word, the flight was going to be one long, big adventure.

The next three days were hectic. In one day Pierre drove me around Holland at a very fast pace, he is fierce in a motor-car, in a bid to obtain a French visa for me as a further two or three overnight stops in France were planned on. At high speed we drove to The Hague, Rotterdam, and Amsterdam in search of an appropriate French consular office without success, at times going the wrong way in one-way streets, How we missed being pulled over by the police or very angry citizens I'll never know. Not until late in the afternoon in Amsterdam, right on closing time, did Pierre draw up outside a consulate that would be his last hope. Together we waited in a long queue for fifteen minutes or more. Just as Pierre got to one of the three service windows, down came the grille, the consulate was closing for the night. Seething, almost weeping with rage, Pierre banged on the wall, shouting for a supervisor at the top of his voice, while waving my Australian passport about furiously in the air.

A fierce argument started between him and a senior official, while I bowed out to wait in an adjoining room, talking to a young New Zealander who was there on some other business. During our discussion he revealed that New Zealanders had not been required to have a visa for France since the mining of the 'Rainbow Warrior' in the Auckland harbour by French Intelligence, you could have knocked me over with a feather! I reached into my valise and came out with my still valid New Zealand Passport, reaching Pierre only just in time before he and the consul began a wrestling match. By the look Pierre gave me when I showed him my New Zealand Passport, I knew that he could have killed me. He took time to wave the passport under the consul's nose as we moved out, I'm not quite sure why, the consul wasn't to know that both passports were mine. The large doors slammed shut behind us. A whole day's motoring wasted, not to mention the fuel and stress. The Cannes incident was also unnecessary had we known about the New Zealand visa situation. C'est la vie.

In the car he never spoke a word, he was so full of fury. As he had business to do in Amsterdam that evening or so he said, he dropped me at the railway station, as I suspected, a form of punishment.

My return to Eindhoven and Z-CAT was by train, which for me was a very pleasant experience with a fun time thrown in with some fellow passengers in the crowded carriage. Next day the whole fiasco had been turned into a great joke to all and sundry, with Pierre in a jovial mood accepting some of the blame. That was such a relief.

By the afternoon of the third day the re-painting of Z-CAT was finished. The time taken for a partial strip and re-paint was hard to believe, work had gone on around the clock. In shiny new colours Z-CAT was pushed out of the hangar on to the ramp for a photograph shoot, while Harry checked her over and we stowed all the gear aboard again. The workers had done a really good job, Z-CAT looked as if she had just come out from the factory as a new machine with the sun's rays glinting on her shiny blue, white and red paint-scheme.

Late that evening our goodbye was said in the form of a low fly-past for the photographers as we headed off for Schiphol airport at Amsterdam. 'Atlantic Odyssey' would commence the following morning, a journey that was going to take us to, or through, four continents, across the North and South Atlantic and on the day planned for the start months before, although the pilot had been arranged only 14 days previously! That was quite an achievement. You can be sure that Hans looked very happy, truly his travel extravaganza, his dream for a long time, was about to get away to a good start.

There was a big crowd of well wishers, families, friends and dignitaries at Schiphol the next morning. Hans asked for a special flight to be made before we left, for those who had helped the project behind the scenes. I wasn't to know it then but even before he'd boarded, Hans had started in to his 'impulse flight changes'.

During that flight, Schiphol Tower asked for a low turn over their tower which stood isolated between the several well-separated runways. We were only too happy to oblige and scooted around with our left float tucked up to the wingtip almost poking in the top windows of the gigantic structure. Schiphol airport covers an immense area, several huge runways separated by what must be hundreds of hectares of well-mown lawn without a blade of grass out of place! There were no complaints coming from the tower staff, instead they thanked us for a job well done.

The take-off had been planned for ten o'clock. With all the speeches going on in Dutch it was easy to see that there would be a delay. Our first passengers would be journalists, well-known photographers and personalities from Holland Broadcasting and Veronica Broadcasting, the Producer Yvonne Belonje, plus three winners of the various competitions held for a prize of a once in a lifetime trip on a Catalina.

At 1215 hours Pierre had everyone comfortably seated. Z-CAT's two big Pratt and Whitney radials burst into life. Minutes later we roared along the gigantic runway, floated off as only a Catalina can and set course for Le Bourget airport in Paris. Three additional competition winners would be uplifted there, together with more engine oil, spares and stores. All arrangements at Paris were in the hands of Pierre's daughter Sandrine.

Flying low across Holland, Belgium and France is hard to describe for it was breathtaking at least for Harry and me. Mike and Pierre knew that part of Europe quite well and were able to point out to us all the places of interest on the way, particularly the First World War battlefields. The route was dotted with picturesque villages, fairylike Alice in Wonderland chateaus set in expansive grounds, mansions and chalets, all with circular driveways lined with wide-spreading trees. From above it was easy to imagine that we were looking down on the 16th century. Then came the military cemeteries near almost every village, with their row upon row of white crosses or headstones. Even in the aircraft with its noisy engines those were sobering moments, there seemed to be a hush over the area as we winged past. The local time was easy to find, every village seemed to have a large clock in a high tower, which was readable from 1000 feet. A big question troubled me at that time, a question that for me is still unanswered. What happened to the Germans who were killed in France by the thousands also, are any of their graves in France, or should I not ask?

Every airport we came upon and tried to avoid for reasons of good airmanship, begged us not to stray so far away but give them a closer look at the old war-bird. We were only too willing to oblige, which almost always ended in taking Z-CAT on a low pass over their airport. Time passed all too quickly, soon we were landing at Le Bourget.

I'd been to the famous Paris Air Show a couple of times before when consulting for Claudius Dornier Seastar, when Le Bourget was decked out in all it's finery, with huge crowds, exciting, spectacular air displays going on all day, pennants, flags and banners flying from every building and chalet. At Paris Air Show time, for the air-minded Le Bourget was the place to be.

Things were not the same there that day. The airfield was hardly recognizable minus the huge crowds, flags, banners and the rows of portable sales chalets alongside the busy runway, Le Bourget to me looked sad and drab. Even the airwaves were quiet, Z-CAT it seemed, was the only aircraft on approach at that time.

Pierre, Harry and other helpers took some time to decant a 50-gallon drum of oil into jerry cans that Sandrine brought out to the airfield in a very small vehicle. After a check with customs (no trouble with my NZ passport that day) we were moving out on to the historic runway again, with Lake Biscarosse, near the Atlantic coast to the west of Bordeaux in our sights as the destination. The alighting on the water there would be the first of many we were scheduled to make en route on the voyage. A map of the alighting area in Lake Biscarosse was not available, which left me wondering what I'd let myself in for.

The passengers were really taken with the expansive viewing area from the blisters as we journeyed towards southern France. Mike and I were constantly on the trims as they moved forward or backwards swapping positions. That's the name of the game in the Catalina, viewing the passing scenery from the 'blisters'. For scenic viewing, no better 'plane has ever been built.

The lake to my amazement was gigantic, almost an inland sea. I made a very smooth touch down on the step and with a 'follow me' launch leading, water taxied for a beaching ramp in a cove at the head of the lake. The passengers were delighted and treated me as if I was P. G. Taylor coming into Valparaiso from Easter Island! Due to some permanent obstructions being added since it was last used, the ramp wasn't available for Z-CAT's beaching. There, a reception, the first of many, awaited us.

After tethering Z-CAT's tail on to the ramp, we all went to a lakeshore building that originally had formed part of the factory where the giant four-engine Latecoere 300 flying boats were built prior to and during WW2. The Latecoeres flew regular services across the Atlantic to South America during wartime and for a short period post-war. In Z-CAT we would be tracing parts of the routes they pioneered. The more one travels the more one learns of the world. As a surprise I came to learn that certain areas of the south of France were unoccupied by the Nazis during WW2. The big flying boats remained in production. Was it my imagination that no one seemed to want to talk too much about that and were not so interested in the Catalina? Maybe it was because my French was only good enough to cause misunderstanding.

The following morning was joyride time. A number of flights were made while a local man followed Z-CAT in a Cessna 172 floatplane to take photographs. The young fellow chose a very difficult method. I can only hope that he was successful for he didn't ask for any sort of a briefing before we started. His chosen method, to follow Z-CAT throughout the take-off from the water was dangerous, for him particularly and worrying for me. He would be in turbulence enough to flip the Cessna and unable to keep pace with his low powered floatplane. Lake Biscarosse was a very popular place, attracting many tourists and campers with their tents and caravans. Plenty of interest was shown in the Catalina and its running mate's antics from the camping public. I never did get a photograph of that event or ever meet the pilot.

Before take off for Biarritz, where we would refuel and clear French customs, three more competition winners joined us. Take off from the lake was made on sparkling clear water with a slight ripple on the surface. Z-CAT just loved those conditions. Under full power she lifted off smoothly and cleanly with our 18 passengers, four of a crew and what seemed to be tons of luggage and photographic gear, after a modest run across the lake into a light breeze. With the Atlantic always in mind, I put our visit to Lake Biscarosse down as the real start to our journey, while taking a sweep over the Latecoere factory then setting course for the 'whistle-stop' port of Biarritz where a fuel tanker would be waiting for us.

Customs, immigration and health formalities went without a hitch, soon we bade farewell to France with Z-CAT's bow pointing towards the Pyrenees, Spain and hopefully Gibraltar at the end of the day, thanks to the long days in that part of the world at that time of year.

I hadn't looked forward to passing through the Pyrenees with tourists aboard who wanted to see things other than clouds. A heavily laden Catalina is short on quick climbs and tight turns and it was my first experience in shall I say, those historic European mountains. In studying the route I had pictured myself in a similar situation in tropical New Guinea in the same type aircraft. The difference was in the weather.

As we approached the forbidding looking mountain shapes, I could see that we were going to be blessed with perfect weather for the passage through. The peaks all etched the horizon in clear weather, the many valleys either side of our route also looked to be clear of low cloud or fog. In any sort of a wind, I knew there had to be some turbulence in that area that would need watching, but fortunately only light breezes prevailed. Some weaving was necessary at times when approaching a rise, to ensure sufficient terrain clearance the slight to moderate turbulence was not worth worrying about. As quoted previously, worrying is like a rocking chair that gives you something to do but gets you nowhere.

From the large viewing windows and the blisters, the passengers were rewarded with the most glorious, spectacular views of mountain and valley while chugging along happily in the cool mountain atmosphere. From where I sat at the sharp end, I was wondering where Z-CAT could be taken should an engine fail or some other emergency arise, without a stretch of water or any flat ground in sight. My heartbeat settled down again only when after bursting out from the mountains we were flying over sun-baked Spain. That country looked so hot and dry in comparison to France. The song with the words 'the rain in Spain falls mainly on the plain' had no meaning that day, when the plains looked as if they'd never ever had a single drop of rain. One could almost feel the ancientness of the land and the age-old farming methods, with lots of horses in evidence on the roads and by-ways.

In all we made an excellent north-south crossing of Spain with plenty to interest our passengers, as Pierre, with the aplomb of a Parisian restaurateur, plied all aboard with the wines suited to the occasion and finger food aplenty, though omitting to serve his flight crew with any wine of course. Eating the same fare as our guests while in flight was a no-no for me regardless of the temptation.

We came to the shores of the Mediterranean some distance to the east of Gibraltar, there was no mistaking 'the Rock' when it came into view. A runway landing only had been authorised there, we were to land to the east. I was warned not to stray to the right on the final approach, not even by a whisker, or Z-CAT would be in Spanish airspace that would constitute an infringement of international air law. How ridiculous was that when we'd already spent most of the afternoon in Spain's airspace! Half way down the runway there was a busy pedestrian crossing. At 1700 hours workers were heading off for their homes across the runway in Spain or vice versa. As we ran over the crossing at speed, our wheels firmly on the ground, hundreds of people were seen backed up at the traffic lights on each side of the runway, waiting to cross when the lights were changed by, I presume and hope, an Air Traffic Controller.

Air control was in the hands of the Royal Air Force, who directed me to a secluded parking area adjacent to the tower and alongside a Nimrod maritime reconnaissance jet, a Comet converted for a maritime role. As everyone disembarked, all necks were craned for their first look up at the Rock that towered over the airport like a giant sentinel. It's not possible to be within sight of the Rock and not be taken back three, four or five hundred years to the days of pirates, brigands, buccaneers and the King's Navy with its man 'o wars. The dispute between Britain and Spain over sovereignty of the 'Rock' still goes on.

A reception on the airport was not permitted. We adjourned to our hotel to meet the local journalists and media. There was a good deal of interest in the Catalina, for Gibraltar had been amongst other things, a flying-boat base during WW2. Several men came forward with memories of how the Sunderlands and Catalinas too came and went from the Rock in those days on missions to and from the Bay of Biscay, the Mediterranean and the seas off West Africa.

Gibraltar has many tunnels dating back 200 years, since the days when Sir Charles Brook and the British Navy ruled the Mediterranean waves. Some of the tunnels were used mainly for storage (we weren't told what) and were at the time of our visit off limits to the tourist. The Rock's harbour-front area was a very colourful place, so interesting with narrow, steep, winding roads, trading and eating shops, bars or taverns, some carved into 'the Rock' itself.

Next day, our photographers climbed high on 'the Rock' to secure pictures of Z-CAT alighting on the water far below. First though, permission for the flights had to come from the RAF who thankfully were extremely co-operative but issued a warning that breaching Spanish water-space in any way could cause a major high-level diplomatic row too, that could mean a delay to our departure. The harbour itself was impossible for what was planned by the Director, by being congested with anchored ships and boats.

After lifting off along the runway past the traffic lights, I flew Z-CAT very low down the remainder of the runway with her wheels elbowing up, while gradually edging her over to the narrow strip of what was judged to be the only space available in British waters for touch down. Many small yachts were moored very close to the sealed runway, there wasn't enough space left for any water taxying. After first touching the water she was kept going in a curving left turn, banked and with floats and wheels up, to ensure we didn't infringe Spanish waters. After planning on the step for half a mile or so, I lifted her off and came around the Rock again for another run.

After three such touchdowns and curving getaways, the photographers had what they wanted and sent a message for me to alight near an extra large luxury yacht with vertical aerofoils for sails, that was coming in from the Straits. That couldn't be done of course, for the yacht was in Spanish water and would remain so. Instead, several low passes were made around the yacht, that seemed to please the photographers on the rocky heights, but I've never heard whether or not it pleased those aboard the yacht or the Spanish authorities, our Director did things like that.

At the hotel that night the demonstration was hailed as 'dramatic', 'superb', 'unreal' by the local observers. The RAF Commanding Officer told me that at one point in the curve Z-CAT had been about half a wingspan in Spanish territory, but at that time no complaints had been received! Hurrah, hasta la vista!

Those sorts of manoeuvres are speedily written about but in fact occupy most of the day waiting for official clearances to arrive and favourable reports from the photo men. I'm sure the pedestrians got their money's worth with the wide-spanned Catalina, engines roaring, skimming over the pedestrian crossing at ten feet, then slicing into the British waters of the harbour in a controlled curve.

On the way back to the hotel lots of the famous baboons that have lived on the Rock for many generations were seen sitting outside their air-conned lairs taking in the glorious views of the Med. The baboons of Gibraltar must not be fed or molested in any way, being a protected species by law. Bravo Gibraltar!

The following day we set off from Gibraltar for Lanzarote, Canary Islands, via Tangier and the Moroccan coastline. As we progressed to the south the temperature began to rise until inside the heavily laden Z-CAT the air was really hot. The climb to 8000 feet took a long time with Hans the Director all the time calling for a lower level to allow the passengers to see a little more of West Africa. Like him we too would have liked to fly lower, but clearance to do so was not available. When finally we reached our allotted altitude, due to the heat Z-

CAT was not flying but only 'staggering along', my pleas to Air Control for a lower altitude were all turned down.

To make things worse, while en route the Director in another impulsive change of mind, asked for a diversion to Agadir, Morocco. The country over which we were 'staggering' at that point, looked to be surprisingly fertile with brilliant green cropping on a large scale, there was plenty for all to see.

After four hours and forty minutes we landed on the runway at Agadir to be met with a hostile reception. The authorities had not been advised of our arrival, which was not surprising for application to do so was never made. Hans and Pierre bore the brunt of their complaints for all the time we were there, which was spent mainly in paying exorbitant landing fees and making arrangements to leave. There were no refreshments on offer at the terminal, nearly two hours passed before we lifted off the runway for Lanzarote with everyone hoping that Hans wouldn't change his mind again. Contestants and organisers were both beginning to see that movement by air through certain parts of West Africa could have its problems, argument, arrogance, had no part to play, only coinage. However, all were cheerful about the experience as we soared out over the blue Atlantic for the Canaries. Hans promised not to change his mind in the air again on the spur of the moment and stick to the flight plan for the day, but with all respect, he found it hard to keep his promise.

In some ways the welcome at Lanzarote was not as warm as expected either. The customs officials griped over the 'importation' of the photographic and television gear. All passengers and crew were obliged to cool their heels in the customs hall for two hours before Hans and Pierre were able to console them and the equipment could leave in the hands of the film crew.

A pleasant night was spent in the charming old world city with its many 15th and 16th century forts, with their well-preserved, shiny black cannons guarding the city from headlands and islands in the harbour. I just love old cannons, they take me back to the time when men were men and women were glad of it.

The following day we did a 'jolly' to Gran Canaris, a flight of about 2.7 hours in our metal water-bird, spending the day sight-seeing there and returning to Lanzarote at nightfall. I was surprised by the barrenness and bleakness of the islands of the Atlantic we'd seen up to that point. Volcanic in nature, ugly in appearance, with little or no greenery on the slopes, they were quite unlike most islands of Polynesia, the Pacific, New Guinea and parts of South East Asia that I knew. Both places were popular destinations from Europe, mostly Portugal, for tourists who evidently came to see steep, grim-looking scoria slopes. My feeling was that something really big in the way of an earthquake and its follow up tsunami was going to happen in those parts one day. Should the scoria on the steep, bare slopes, through earthquake, movement of the plates, rain or all three, decide to slip into the sea, the world could be in for that 'big one'. Although enjoying the experience, I was glad when we said goodbye to those islands.

In the nine days since leaving Eindhoven, Z-CAT had been flown every day and thanks to Harry, Mike and Pierre, was running like a charm. Hans seemed to think that if we didn't fly point to point on any day, but instead did demonstration and sightseeing flights, that, in his view, was a day off for the flight crew! The most important thing was that the passengers seemed to be enjoying themselves immensely, but it was hard for me to catch up on enough sleep.

The next leg took us to the Cape Verde Islands (Cabo Verde). En route we pulled in to Nounandhibu in Mauretania. It wouldn't surprise me to know that the name meant sand, for the Sahara runs its' big dunes right down to the waters' edge of the Atlantic Ocean. I'll wager that there's not been a blade of grass seen there in many a decade.

Fishing seems to be the biggest industry with dozens of boats working off the immediate shore. The coastline for miles is littered with the skeletons of hulks that have either run aground or been abandoned. The airport's terminal was in a sad state of disrepair, the toilets disgusting and indescribably filthy. To prove that the runway was indeed sealed as in the flight guide meant choosing roughly where it might be found, then scraping through a foot of sand until some bitumen showed up.

There was not enough space in the vehicles for everybody to go to town. Harry and I volunteered to watch Z-CAT while the rest of the team took the short trip. A lone cameleer was the only person we saw while we waited in the aircraft. We had strict instructions that we were not to take any photographs. Tough luck Mr. Cameleer. Our guess was that our tourists would soon return when they first saw the town. In half an hour they were back and eager to be on the way again. We were only too willing to oblige and soon left lost and lonely Nouandhibou behind, under a cloud of sandy dust. Later I learned that Mauretania had been Saddam Hussein's only ally in the Gulf War. Quote "A joke went around stating M's contribution to the war being the provision of sand that was bagged for the protection of buildings and gun-sites in Kuwait and Baghdad. By it's still being on the top-secret list, that information has never been confirmed unquote. "

Three hours and fifty minutes later we were landing at the airport at Sal in the Cape Verde Islands, a little more sophisticated than Mauretania and again a popular tourist destination of the modern kind.

Each day saw us getting closer to making the South Atlantic hop to Natal in Brazil. Our flight there was to retrace the steps of Jean Mermoz, pioneer Portuguese airman. I was trying to focus on that flight and beginning to get a little nervous, having not seen or heard anything in the way of Search and Rescue facilities on that part of the African side of the Atlantic. I'd never flown anywhere before where the radios were so quiet. The big worry being faced was that the high frequency radio was still not working in any sort of a reliable fashion, either that, or some of the stations called were simply not listening out or not answering. The manual faxed to us at Corfu was far too technical for our needs and proved to be of little help.

After a night's stay at Sal we flew Z-CAT down island to Praia, where I made an open sea alighting for the benefit of cameramen perched on high rocky cliffs overlooking the chosen area.

The word 'chosen' is used lightly, the area was certainly not chosen by me, but by Hans and Pierre, who had made promises from thousands of miles away, weeks before, that I knew nothing about, but with all bases loaded for the 'open sea' segments, I was expected to meet the challenge.

A big oily Atlantic swell was running, that was hard to define exactly, but roughly at an angle of 40 degrees to the shoreline. The approach was made with Z-CAT pointed obliquely at the rock-lined cliffs. At 100 feet off the sea Mike called that he couldn't see any swell, while I looked towards where surf in big quantities was breaking on the rocky shoreline that told me to be watchful. Mike was signalled to bring the revs up.

I watched the clocks as he increased the rpm to 2300. The engines' voices lifted to a more urgent note with power now in stand-by mode for a possible unexpected bounce or missed touchdown. Down lower to the water the swell was seen to be more pronounced. For a while I thought I would get away with a step landing that always looks better on film and so made plans for that to happen, but the keel clipped the top of a swell which threw me into the air, a full stall landing was necessary as the cliffs came in fast and my gasps for breath too. Probably believing that the bounce had been arranged for their benefit, the cameramen thought the 'demo' great, the shots would serve to be a valuable part in the documentary!

Taxying as close to shore as I thought safe under the circumstances in a very deep swell, Z-CAT was motored up into the wind, while the bowman, Pierre, was signalled to sling out the spare anchor and pay out lots of line when both engines stopped. Z-CAT drifted back quickly, the rope straightened as the anchor dug its flukes in, waves began to smack under her bow, a sure sign that the anchor was holding. The plan was to ride on the anchor while the participants were filmed going to and from the shore in small boats, which even then were pitching fast and furious in trying to get alongside the port blister for the pick-ups. I was beginning to miss the disciplines of trained flying boat airmen and the marine craft crews of our Air Force.

Suddenly an onshore wind sprang up as the black underbelly of a cloud came in from the sea, 'white horses' galloped across the surface, big spots of rain drummed solos on the hull and wings. Z-CAT began pulling on the anchor rope while pitching high then sinking away as the swell raced through. After hearing a few solid sounding 'smacks' under the bow followed by an ominous silence from that direction, I knew that the anchor wasn't holding and had started to drag. The mast of a big yacht anchored nearby began to swing back and forth like a pendulum, halyards tinkling madly, their crew like ours busy at the bow with their anchor chain. Gone was the slap of the waves under her bow forever, a glance at the shore told me that we were drifting backwards and fast with Z-CAT's tail then less than 70 metres from the rocks.

From my overhead hatch I yelled to Pierre to haul in the anchor rope. That exercise alone would be tough going for him, the engines were needed and quick. Only just in time the boats were waved aside, Pierre heaved the anchor up and over on to the wet heap of rope he'd already fed into the anchor compartment, followed them in, then slammed the bow hatch closed, while Mike and I went into starting both engines, with the rocks now very much closer to Z-CAT's not so pretty stern. A failed start in that situation would be disastrous, fortunately both engines started up without a quaver.

With the bow then trying to duck under each crest as it raced in and with Z-CAT now moving forward, the swell had grown into waves almost at their breaking point. We were rising sharply then sinking in a cloud of spray. My mind was made up. If Z-CAT was to survive she needed to be out of there before the squall reached its peak, as if by magic the sea had turned into a mass of creamy foam.

To be along the swell on take-off, meant being crosswind. With my heart in my mouth I wound on full right aileron, gave her maximum rudder with my left foot and powered up fully on the right engine to get her into what I shall call the crosswind state of readiness. Like the grand old girl she was she responded to the urgency in my hands and feet, holding her bow across the wind with the seas waiting to swallow the left float. Waiting for the bow to rise I reached for the 'floats' switch flipped it up then went for full power on both engines with the column fully back on my guts, the right aileron wound fully up, my left leg fully forward locking the rudder. When the windshield cleared of the spray as she climbed to top her bow wave, the bow was eased down a little by my releasing some of the back pressure, not much lest she punch into the swells too hard and damage the more fragile centre portion of the bow that had once been the bomb-aimer's window. Out of the corner of my eye I could see the lee float, then in retraction, skipping the waves only by inches. With every metre gained the ailerons were having more effect, the wings were able to be levelled by my winding some aileron off but she still needed lots of rudder to keep her sluicing along the aft side of the swells.

Then came a loud thump as she took a cross sea under the belly and leapt into the air, although sagging. We were far too slow for pure unadulterated flight but I knew she must stay there so locked my arms to hold the attitude so freely given, with our keel just brushing the waters. With engines screaming, props racing at full speed and a slight turn into the wind, gradually she worked herself out of the near-stalled condition with the airspeed then on the increase. At my signal Mike reduced power for the climb as I turned for the nearby airport my heart thumping like a steam engine with the wheels spinning on wet rails. As we turned, the cliffs with the photographers were hidden in the rain. We had escaped only just in time.

I have always had a great confidence in Catalinas. At that moment I could have kissed her. I shall always remember Praia and those seconds in the cockpit of the fifty-year old 'P-boat', only feet above the swirling sea, hanging on the props. That sealed my faith in them for all time. Harry, Pierre and Mike were shaken up by their experience, which had been part of a learning curve for them. Sudden changes in weather that wouldn't trouble a landplane can wreck an anchored flying boat being only the first part of the lesson that must be learnt.

From Praia we flew back to Sal to prepare for the crossing of the South Atlantic, Sal to Natal in Brazil. That day's 'rest' was taken up with fuelling to maximum, re-packing loads and trying to get the HF transceiver on line without success. From Sal we would carry only the camera crews and their equipment, replacement participants were to take a commercial flight to Natal to join up with us again.

We were off before dawn on a cloudy, drizzly day, with everyone believing or pretending that he was Jean Mermoz, the famous French seaplane pilot who in the 1930's flew the Atlantic several times and on one flight, through an engine malfunction, had been forced to make an emergency alighting alongside a ship in mid-ocean. With all due respect to Jean Mermoz most of my thoughts were on another Jean, Miss Jean Batten, a young New Zealand girl who soloed over the same route in a single-engine Percival Vega Gull in 1937 to break the record for a South Atlantic crossing. To most young men and boys of the time including me, Jean was the most gorgeous looking heroine, mostly photographed in her white flying suit and helmet with her goggles parked on her forehead. Prior to WW2 Jean held a good number of world records, all without the help of 'Woman's Lib'. She was the sort of lady any man would throw his best overcoat down into the muck for her to walk on.

The low clouds and drizzle kept us flying low and on 'doglegs' that kept us clear of all the lesser islands of Cabo Verde, after which a climb to 6000 feet was commenced. As the first grey light of morning crept into the cockpit, gradually the cloud cleared enough for me to be able to spot the whitecaps that were being stirred up by a strong surface wind. With brooding storm clouds directly ahead, a turbulent sea below with wave crests that frothed and gurgled, we set off for Brazil.

Very little in the way of groundspeed was being gained from the wind with the GPS (global positioning system) calculating 105 knots. Altogether it was a dull start for a dull day. A deep blue ocean, flecked occasionally with the dots of lazy whitecaps, scattered fleecy clouds overhead, had been expected. Instead, sinister-looking, grey-black clouds blocked the horizon, merging with the grey of the sea.

Soon those same clouds opened up and poured their innards down from a mid-high, black belly. There wasn't a lot of turbulence as the rain drummed on to the hull, with visibility down to zero. Without radar I had no way of telling whether or not the storms could be avoided and gave up the thought of even trying when our groundspeed began to creep up, 120,130 knots.

For a fully laden Catalina early in a long flight, we were by then doing better than average. A decision was made to hold to our track and ride it out. The wind, from the northeast, was drifting us to the left of track, which proved the weather forecaster to be right on the button, we were going to cross in less than fifteen hours.

With nothing of interest to be seen outside, we settled down into the routine running of the aircraft, sea and sky hidden from view. For short periods only the rain lessened as we entered a clearer patch, only to return to the same old drumming sounds again in a few short minutes. Mike was busy on the HF every half hour or so but with little or no success. We tried contacting any high-flying commercial jets on the international distress frequency, to pass our position reports on to the authorities, again with no result. Unlike the Pacific, there seemed to be little or no air traffic in that area at that time. With the air waves so quiet our world was only us, as if the Big Bomb had gone off and we were the only survivors left on the planet.

Four hours had passed since the last communication we'd had with the Sal control tower, I was beginning to feel exactly like Jean Mermoz or Jean Batten must have felt more than fifty years before, alone over the South Atlantic in miserable weather, eyes glued to the compass, with no-one to talk to. By then I imagined, alarm bells would have sounded in some air control centre, on the fate of the aged amphibian.

There was one advantage we had over the early aviators of course, the GPS that kept us exactly on track and with an accurate ground-speed available at a glance. Thoughts of the two Jeans, who would have been equipped with only a basic magnetic compass, left me feeling a little guilty, a 'sissie' even.

Five hours must have passed, when much to my relief we entered a fine weather zone with slivers of sunlight beginning to slant down on to the blue of the sea, which was capped with myriads of white-topped waves. For the first time that morning everyone aboard seemed to relax, as sandwiches and coffee was served by that man of all trades, the ubiquitous Pierre.

A full time listening watch on the emergency VHF frequency was decided on, to simply forget about the HF ever working again. As we pressed on, the overcast dissipated and we were flying in an almost cloudless sky.

Gradually, under Harry's watchful eye, I whittled the mixture levers back, while keeping the cylinder temperatures stabilised, until by experience we knew that the fuel consumption had fallen to less than 70 gallons an hour with even more reductions possible as Z-CAT became lighter. At that stage there was fuel galore to get us to Brazil.

The hours slipped by with everybody getting sleepy, nine, ten, eleven, twelve, when faintly the identification signal of the beacon at Fernando de Noronha, an island off the coast of Brazil was heard. It wasn't long before that extremely rugged island with its one sharp 'sugarloaf' of a mountain came into view to the left of our track. The sun was getting low.

Some time was lost in taking a swing over the island for the benefit of the film crew and for me too, for I knew that during our stay in Natal, Z-CAT was scheduled to visit de Noronha for an alighting on the water.

I didn't like at all what I first saw. The island had no protecting reef. There were steep cliffs around the entire perimeter all pounded by Atlantic rollers everywhere on every coast. Most islands have a lee or more sheltered side to them, not this one. The small boat harbour that was protected by a short stone breakwater on the south western side of the island left no room for a flying-boat to anchor, let alone alight. There was however, a good-looking runway that had been built and used by the Americans during WW2, on a flat near the 'sugar loaf' about the middle of the island. The dusk of approaching night only allowed a minute or two to take all that in as we passed, while swinging on to the final course for Natal.

Thirty minutes later we were in contact with Natal tower, our first communication with any station since leaving Sal thirteen hours before. I half expected a reprimand of some kind, even a semi jocular 'where've you been all day, we've been getting worried' to prepare me for a report over the crossing of the South Atlantic in radio silence. Thankfully nothing was heard on that score.

Natal was experiencing heavy showers that necessitated an instrument approach to the rain-drenched runway. Flight time from Sal had been exactly fourteen and a half hours. Another notch could be carved on my belt to mark the crossing of one of the world's great oceans. I summed it up as a wet departure and a wet arrival with some clear weather in between.

Brazilian television waited to greet us as we disembarked from Z-CAT, the reception took hours, followed by a very long bus ride to our hotel. We reached there in the early hours of the morning heads drooping on to chests and too tired to eat or drink. How I looked forward to 'dreamtime'.

Our iron-man Director Hans however, had different ideas. I met him in the corridor on the way to my room to be informed that I would be picked up at seven am to go to the Natal Yacht Club on the Potengi River to assess the river's suitability for an alighting by Z-CAT. Following that I would continue on to the airport and fly Z-CAT in to the

Potengi for several 'joy' flights from the river with local dignitaries. There was little 'dreamtime' for me, I'd hardly closed my eyes before a rap on the door warned me that it was time for clean up and breakfast, both to be quick.

After a meeting at the Port Authority the Harbour-Master himself took me out on the river in the Port's launch, while through bleary eyes I made the necessary inspection. With little ceremony the area was declared suitable for Z-CAT's operations and a mooring site was also chosen for the laying of the mooring buoy offered by the Yacht Club. The Harbour-Master, a very friendly soul with good manners, presented me with a flight cap with leafy gold 'wiggles' on the peak and inscribed also in gold letters: " CAPITANIA DOS PORTOS DO RIO GRANDE DO NORTE ". As a memento of the occasion and a fabulous trip, although it doesn't fit, the cap will long be treasured.

A drive to the airport followed to discover that overnight as a tribute, a B25 (Mitchell bomber) and an A20 (Boston) had been parked either side of Z-CAT, making for a worthy picture of three of the best WW2 war birds, that was a great thrill for me and a great sight for any air enthusiast to say the least. .

During the afternoon three flights were made from the river without incident although Z-CAT scraped across a shallow shoal at least once while taxying up-river for take-off. The Port Authority's launch, with my newfound friend the Harbour Master in control, did a great job in clearing the alighting area of light boat traffic then guiding me through the shallows. For the first time on the journey I was in the hands of someone who knew what they were doing in guiding a flying-boat with a large wingspan and limited turning ability on a swift flowing river, his launch was always in the right place at the right time.

With a swift current running, turning Z-CAT around for the downstream take-off was very demanding, but was somehow managed without any damage to launch or metal air machine. While going upstream, the trick was to initiate a turn to the right, the opposite direction to that desired, using the left engine, then quickly reverse the controls and apply full power to the right engine, using the inertia to break through the wind until she could be straightened up facing down the river flow. That was tricky stuff that sapped a lot of energy from a very tired pilot. There I would hold her straight with asymmetric use of the engines while the gear retracted, then get into the take-off without delay to get an effective rudder control by the slipstream, before wind or current could take over again. Gear retracted did you say? Yes, the gear is extended when on the water to provide stability in the absence of drogues and to protect the hull when in shallow water. On this occasion the Harbour Master was always in the right place with his launch, seeming able to anticipate Z-CAT's every move, holding position always in view and well clear of us during those wide left turns.

Mooring Z-CAT off the clubhouse each time between trips was tricky too, with yachts at their permanent moorings, the ever-present swift current and many skiffs and other small boats scuttling about, all vying for a closer look at the unusual scene in the boat 'harbour'.

After the third trip Hans signalled enough was enough, to tie up and come in to the banquet in the clubhouse. By that time I was dog tired, my ears were still ringing from the previous day's long flight. While the official speakers were still going through their paces extreme tiredness took over causing me to nod off with my head drooped over the table.

Several ex Brazil Airlines Catalina pilots who had really enjoyed the ride in Z-CAT were present at the banquet. When one of them heard that we were going to Fernando de Noronha the following day, he warned me against alighting on water there. Brazilair had preferred to use the runway on their many flights to the island, a warning that put me on the alert for trouble. The banquet for the flight crew, excluding Pierre, was over early due to Z-CAT having to be returned to the airport after which a long bus trip to the hotel awaited us which meant missing out on the champagne and any other frivolities that seemed to be in plenty and laid on for our group.

On that last take-off from the river, pungent smelling smoke from the radio console poured through the cockpit. Our DME (distance measuring equipment) had burnt itself out, the cause probably being that water from rain and spray had penetrated the circuit boards wiring in the set and shorted into a fire. Without a spare we were gradually getting down to the basics so far as radios and aids went. 'Atlantic Odyssey' was becoming more like a game of strip poker, we would just have to manage without the DME until a replacement was found. VHF radio alone would get us through to the United States where repairs could be arranged more easily.

After arriving at the hotel at a very late hour, Hans asked me how my day off had gone! The sad part is, he actually meant what he said. Having had but three and a half hours sleep in the past 48 my answer is unprintable. Such is the life of a free-lance Catalina pilot. C'est la guerre.

The two and one quarter hour flight to Fernando de Noronha was short and pleasant. First we landed on the airfield to give the television crew time to get into position with their equipment on the cliffs overlooking the planned area, which was Praia all over again but with higher, steeper cliffs. Because of the cauldron of heavy water visible from the cliffs in and around that part of the island a conference was called for. After a great deal of negotiation with all those concerned, the site for the cameramen was changed to another further along the forbidding coastline towards the boat harbour. The change in plans meant the shifting of their heavy gear and didn't bring smiles to their faces. Hans looked grim and unsmiling but reluctantly accepted the need for re-siting his photo crew in the cause of safety.

Owing to the big Atlantic swell an approach from seaward along the swell toward the island was made followed by a 'stall landing' close in to the cliffs. There's nothing like being prepared for anything when alighting on open water. Unlike Praia, that time the stall went perfectly, touching on the rear step and only once, before pan-caking in. I taxied up as close as possible to the seaward side of the small breakwater, switched off, while Pierre tossed the anchor out again with loads of heavy manila rope attached. The breeze took her rearwards away from the breakwater until she brought up on the anchor. Soon waves were smacking under her bow as she pitched up and down on the swell. Z-CAT was safe so long as her crew were aboard to handle any emergency, such as a broken anchor line, springing a leak, or suffering a swing of the wind that might see the tail colliding with the breakwater. If the anchor should drag or the line break Z-CAT would be taken away from the shore and not on to the rocks.

For two hours the participants and television crew played at movie stars, boarding and leaving Z-CAT from rubber dinghies then paddling to shore. Mike, Harry and I, kept a good watch on the weather and the anchoring scene, relaxing on couches in the blister when it was not taken over by the 'stars' in their bikinis, always watchful lest the wind and weather scene should change. A wind reversal would have to be acted on very quickly.

Finally, all filming was finished and the wind hadn't changed. When all were aboard engines were started, we moved up slowly on the anchor, while Pierre hauled in and stowed the rope. With that over Z-CAT was too close to shore to risk a power turn. The engines were 'blipped' down to a couple of hundred revs per minute on the magneto switches, the wind was strong enough to overcome the thrust from the slow whirling props and carry Z-CAT backwards. When well clear a reverse turn was made between puffs of wind. Battling with the throttles during a two-engine magneto check we moved downwind and well out to sea. The take-off would have to be directly at the cliffs, followed by a smart left turn to avoid some of the higher ones, that was all in a day's work.

As we went further out, the swell increased, Z-CAT began pitching higher, spray was flying until throttles were chopped and she swung up into the wind. Mike called the water take-off check-list, Pierre confirmed through the peep-hole that the gear was up and locked firm and snug, without seaweed or flotsam trailing from the wells.

Looking at the island from seaward, I began to fit the conditions in for the take-off. Was Z-CAT far enough out for the distance required for take-off? The swell was running across the wind again, the best of friends that would help to lift us off. Far from the shore we were in a whitecap zone that eased off in the shadow of the island. Closer in during take off, we'd be planing into smoother water. The conditions were acceptable for the tanks held only a minimum amount of fuel.

With the countdown started, I sat and waited for a swell to pass under her, then as she began to rise on the next I called to Mike for full power while I held the column firmly on my 'tummy' that time, my feet firmly on the rudder pedals not the brakes. Spray lashed at the props and windshield as at first she bucked and bumped through the roughness with her engines singing while I held her on a gyro heading, easing off on the column as she rode up. The windshield cleared as 'floats up' was selected to ensure that neither float dragged through a wave. The cliffs were then looking awfully close and stared back unchanging, stark, dark, ominously still in the evening air.

The bow rose up as we met more bumps, the airspeed indicator began to register as the first cross-sea came at her, there's always one of those to contend with, while the speed built up and the cliffs raced in. Another cross-sea threw her into the air while with my hands and feet she was kept from sagging on to the water again. Then she held to the air only inches from the water and the floats almost home at the wing-tips. It was as if she was asking for a lean to the left so as to pass over the boat harbour, where the cliffs were lowest and where quite a large crowd had gathered. Only then could another successful 'open sea' take-off be recorded, although unlike 'Pee Gee's departure from Easter Island, without the assistance of two JATO bottles (Jet assisted take off). There was a lot of similarity between Easter Island and Isla de Noronha in shape and size but Z-CAT was much lighter than 'Frigate Bird'.

Mike flew us back to the airport and greased us on in inimitable fashion. The day that had been rather dreaded was over. Some of my thanks went to the ex Brazilair Catalina pilot for his timely warning.

While we put the covers over the cockpit and engines that Pierre was always fussy about when Z-CAT was parked in wet weather, from on top of the wing I could see out over the cliffs to where we had sat out the afternoon guarding Z-CAT. In the failing light, the waters although still tossing had changed colour, heaving up those long and fast swells from a black and forbidding looking sea. The day, the exercise, had lasted several hours it was so good to be re-united with terra firma again. The photographers were happy, Hans was happy, that made everyone happy. The uncertainty of Isla de Noronha, which had been troubling me had been dealt with. The only way out of a fear problem sometimes is to go through it, find a break-thru, there are no drive thru's.

Returning to Natal the following day, at the airport we were united with some new participants who had flown across on an Aeroflot service. With everyone and everything ship-shape we set off for Belem, arriving there after dark after a relatively easy flight along the coast, logging seven and a half hours for the day.

Catalinas had operated from Belem from 1943 to 1983. A memorial stands there for the thirty-one machines involved over the years. What better place for the operation of metal water birds than around the mighty Amazon basin! Another eye-opener for me too, having always thought that Cats belonged only in the South Pacific, Fiji, Polynesia, New Guinea, New Britain, New Zealand, Australia and the ex Dutch East Indies! There is always something to learn.

At Belem, our beloved Z-CAT was purposefully parked near a working DC3 and a Curtis C46 Commando as a tribute to all three ageing machines. After two days of being entertained handsomely, we set course along the Amazon on a flight to the Acatjuba Lodge on the Rio Negro, not far from Manaus. There we spent the night in cabins

on stilts beside the river, or more correctly above the river and probably only a few feet from any Cainan alligator that might be searching
for food scraps. We awoke to the sights and sounds of those beautifully coloured Macaw parrots flitting through the trees.

Curious Indians in canoes had paddled about Z-CAT as she lay
safely at anchor near the Lodge that night, with Pierre's generator
running to service the refrigerators and bilge pumps. After dark, all
the lighting on and around the lodge came from coloured oil lamps set
high and low in the trees, making for a spectacular night scene in such
an environment. We would have liked to have spent another day there,
the river and jungle was so peaceful and quiet, the ringing in my ears
had almost stopped, but all good things must come to an end.

After a brief stop at Manaus for fuel and customs the next day, we
flew northward over Venezuela aiming for a sight of the famous Angel Falls. Surprisingly to me, Manaus so far up the Amazon was a
very large city with a skyscraper or two and a population between half
and one million souls.

Unfortunately the weather prevented us from seeing the world's
highest water drop. The very high country that fed the falls was covered in rain, cloud and mist, an extremely dangerous environment for
a heavily laden Catalina. After a slow climb to 9000 feet, staggering
along over high terrain searching for breaks in the cloud that might
lead to the Falls, Mike came to realize that navigating solely on a Radio Navigation Chart in such terrain wasn't easy, while at the controls
I was fully committed to keeping us all alive as I fought to dodge the
many 'stuffed clouds'!

Before my arrival in Harare, acting on Mike's advice, Pierre had
decided against bringing along the box that contained the World Aeronautical Charts, part of Z-CAT's normal equipment, to save weight,
a decision made without my knowledge or informing me in any shape
or form. That was not really good airmanship on their part, or mine for
that matter, for I should have checked that the WAC's were aboard
and if they weren't put them aboard myself. After some very tense

moments, thousands of feet above Z-CAT's single engine capability, staggering along close above high, rocky, mountainous terrain in poor visibility, without being able to sight the 'Falls', all the time knowing that the slightest cough from an engine could bring disaster upon us, a halt was called to the search, further efforts to find 'Angel Falls' were abandoned. Z-CAT was turned on to a course for Trinidad Tobago in the Caribbean.

For a good part of the way it teamed, there was little to see except rain and through that occasionally the rain forest below. In semi darkness we left the coast of South America to fly across the Caribbean Sea past Trinidad and on to Tobago.

Some years previously I had been flying for Antilles Air Boats out of St. Croix, US Virgin Islands. The next few days for me would be quite exciting, flying along the Lesser Antilles through more familiar places. Since my being in St Croix, Antilles Air Boats had been wiped out in a typhoon. The owner Maureen O'Hara Blair had decided to shut up shop.

After the untimely death of her husband, flying boat pioneer Charles Blair, Maureen had carried on bravely as President of the volatile amphibian airline that at one time was one of the busiest commuter airlines in the world. The closing down of the company must have been a bitter blow to Maureen, the shuttle air services between islands, city centre to city centre, would be sadly missed.

A late arrival at Tobago saw us being bullied by customs officials again, over the import of photographic and television equipment. Somehow Hans managed to get us through to our hotel and with all the equipment, but slightly late for dinner. Filming went on that night with the participants seen to be enjoying the steel bands and the calypso tunes that went with nightlife in the tropical Caribbean.

A slight hitch to our otherwise mechanically trouble-free flight occurred next morning. On the engine run-up a magneto drop was detected on one engine, probably an after-effect of the heavy rain we'd flown through the previous day across Venezuela and an all night drenching while parked. Back on the ramp Harry and Mike worked fast to fix the problem, when a plug change did the trick. An hour and a half later we set off for Beef Island in the British Virgin Islands arriving there after five and a half hours. En route the photographers were rewarded with spectacular moving and still shots of St. Lucia, Martinique, Dominica, Guadeloupe, Antigua, St. Kitts and St Marten, from the blisters and other windows.

Our visit to the British Virgins had been planned to coincide with a Peter Stuyvesant sponsored yachting and wind surfing regatta that had attracted sailors from all over the world. The seas were alive with literally hundreds of yachts heeled over in racing mode, scurrying around the many courses set between the islands.

Z-CAT became the guest of honour, receiving a lot of attention as I set her down in the open water of the Sir Francis Drake channel the following day. I had been to Peta Island before in Goose and Mallard 'boats of AAB and felt completely at home in the big waves, although the photographic helicopter hovering over Z-CAT on take-off often had me worried. He was very close, too close at times, the blast of air coming down on Z-CAT didn't make take-off that easy. That was another case of the organisers not keeping their pilot very well informed of the plot and the chopper pilot being a little careless in choosing an 'every man for himself' attitude in picture taking.

The next sector was to take us to the Cayman Islands. I had asked Hans for permission to fly over St Croix for a look at Christiansted and Questa Verda, the condominium where Betty and I had lived, but the weather was foul, a very dismal day in fact, the permitted diversion was abandoned.

In driving rain we flew past San Juan in Puerto Rico without seeing anything of the massive and of course famous El Morro, the massive Spanish fort on a point at the harbour entrance where for the benefit of the passengers, the Gooses or Mallards of AAB made their low turn for the alighting area near the Isla Grande airport. We flew on to Mayaguez on the western side of Puerto Rico for customs and fuel. Another hitch to proceedings, Mayaguez could provide us with a customs clearance but there were no fuel services. So it was back to Boraquin (Ramey Air Base) to fuel up in those wet conditions, before setting out for the Cayman Islands. Out of Puerto Rico, much to my relief we began to see where we were going and where we'd come from, the seven and a half hour flight past Jamaica was completed in beautiful weather, the day ending with the sun going down and a nice dry runway to land on.

George Town, the Caymans main centre was found to be a spic and span place with not a speck of rubbish anywhere, neatly painted buildings, excellent roads and smart looking transport, a very 'glitzy' place indeed for that part of the world. The main tourist attractions were boating, diving, snorkelling, swimming, sailing, glass bottom boat cruises, deep diving along the Cayman Wall in a submersible with large viewing ports, viewing a turtle farm and watching the huge stingrays at play in Stingray Bay.

We flew there on my 'day off' to alight amongst scores of yachts and sailboats, which were no doubt, the play toys of their prosperous owners.

Without giving me his exact location on the radio, that was understood to be on a certain conspicuously coloured yacht with pennants flying, our official photographer asked for a take-off towards the yacht as described. The take-off was started with me believing he was stationed aboard that vessel. Z-CAT was aimed to pass close by the port side. The direction indicated held a number of anchored yachts that needed dodging. Z-CAT was planing and fast, my eyes were darting hither and yon when I was shocked to see a head popping up out of the water some thirty metres ahead of the speeding Z-CAT and only a few metres to the left of the bow. Guess who it was? With yachts either side there was little I could do but continue with the take-off and watch his head pass about midway between the hull and the left float that was in process of retracting! Paparazzi bah! Some people will do anything for THAT picture. In the case I write of, the picture turned out to be very good so all was forgiven.

From the Caymans we crossed to the Yucatan Peninsula, to the town of Chetumal in Mexico, to alight on Lake Bacalar. From there, our participants, Pierre and TV crew made an expedition to the Mayan temples hidden in the rain-forest, while the flight crew ferried Z-CAT to the airport and took up residence in a city hotel for two nights. There was a chance for a real day off at last, in a town where a siesta was observed alas there wasn't a sombrero or poncho in sight. Normal activity in the town started up about 5pm. I liked that aspect, if only some of the northern towns and cities in Australia that suffer from searing heat at mid-day would do the same.

On leaving Mexico we flew across the Gulf of Mexico and the Mississippi Delta from Chetumal to New Orleans. En route early into the flight we circled several Mayan temples, amazing, mysterious, age-old structures, that could be likened to the Pyramids of Egypt although they were not surrounded by sand, but hidden in the most inaccessible places in the rain forest.

What a change to be at New Orleans with hordes of happy tourists taking in the French quarter. On arrival at Lakefront Airport the US customs gave Z-CAT and us all a real going over, but it was so good to be in the States again and not have a language problem. Necessarily efficient but very courteous is how I would describe the reception there. From New Orleans we routed to Toccoa in Georgia where our party did some white-water rafting. It was nice to be flying through and over Georgia not marching, as some of my ancestral namesakes had done.

The highlight of the trip to New York was the flight over Washington DC where we received a clearance to fly along the Potomac, to within a mile or so of the Washington Monument, The Pentagon and Capitol Building. "No closer please sir." came the controller's voice as the TV cameras aboard whirled and cameras clicked. That was one of the greatest privileges accorded us on the flight, but there was more to come. With the Twin Towers in sight we made for Teterboro Air-port via the East River. All that in one day, as Michael Caton did in 'The Castle' an Australian movie production, I thought I 'must be dreamin'.

The following day, with a clearance from the US Coast Guard we made a short flight to alight at a pre-arranged point on the Hudson River at the Statue of Liberty. Rain squalls were drifting about, shutting out parts of the river at the time, which required a circle or two being made before heading in to alight beside the Coast Guard cutter. We were not really close to the Statue, for President Bill Clinton was at a meeting nearby the monument and security forbade us going any closer. The Coast Guard informed us that we were the first to obtain an approval to alight there in 35 years due to the commemorative flight of Z-CAT honouring Peter Stuyvesant, first governor of New York.

The instructions from the Coast Guard ordered us not to shut down engines, circles were made on the water while the photo men aboard kept busy. Other photographers were at the Statue of Liberty filming us on the water. They would need those big, zoom lenses. Before very long, the cutter indicated that we had almost overstayed our welcome and signalled us to be on our way. I opened the taps and after only a short skid across the waters of the Hudson we were airborne and heading back to Teterboro.

The weather cleared up in the afternoon, another photo trip down river was called for, this time taking in Manhattan, the Statue again without alighting and the liner Queen Elizabeth 2 departing New York. The squalls had gone, the sun was out, the scene was stupendous with the numerous aircraft and blimps along the river doing what we were doing, taking pictures. From there we headed up the Hudson River passing over West Point Military Academy, to Lebanon in Vermont taking in a real change of scenery, green pastureland, rolling hills, forests and valleys. Vermont lived up to its reputation as the most beautiful place.

At Lebanon the party were taken on balloon rides, which I thought would give me a day free for some relaxation. The following day however, with crew only aboard, we were obliged to take Z-CAT down to Albany to get our radios attended to. Most of that rest day was spent hanging about the airport while the technicians worked hard on the repairs. Arriving back at Lebanon in light rain late that night I was faced with making a difficult instrument approach using two Visual Omni Ranges, the second an ILS with a glide-slope that guided us between the rugged hills surrounding the airport. The balloonists had met with a mishap and one or two of them were slightly injured but not enough to prevent them staying with the tour. Another very tiring 'day off' was over.

Presque Isle, Maine, was the next fuelling stop en route to Deer Lake, Newfoundland. The chill of the northern regions was now beginning to be felt. More than fascinated, I watched the State of Maine slip by underneath us with its many lakes forests and wetlands. Betty's grandfather had come from Maine to New Zealand as a young man, some time late in the 19th century, believed to be about the time of the American Civil War. Somehow that made Maine a special state for me to cross one hundred and twenty years later. The family had originated in France, as Huguenots, they'd sailed off to settle in Maine during a period of religious persecution in Europe.

We hurried through the US Customs formalities and the refuelling, setting off for Deer Lake, Newfoundland after only about an hour's stay. The days were getting longer with little fear of running out of daylight. Through drizzle and rain we touched down after a total of six and a half flying hours from Lebanon.

The weather was cold and miserable to say the least, with rain continuing through the night. My free day while the participants toured, was marred by having to shift accommodation from our lakeside hotel due to some of our personnel smoking in the dining-room during meals and refusing to 'butt out' when asked. That took up a good part of the day for me with no luck coming my way for a so-called 'free day'. Stately pine forests, old buildings that were very warm inside and a Hudson bomber mounted on a stand to commemorate Atlantic Ferry Command during WW2 comprise most of my memories of Deer Lake.

At the airport Z-CAT was parked alongside a Canso water bomber of the Province of Newfoundland. Maintained in a pristine condition, the Canso was in the charge of a pilot who to me was the very picture of a lumberjack, heavy check shirt, his pants held up with braces, and of course his chin sporting a beard. By the state of the weather at the time, firebombing would be 'sometime in the future'.

The next leg to Greenland was dreaded somehow, with fears of icing up in an aircraft with thick, wide wings that were not fitted with any sort of anti-icing devices. The ground temperature at take-off time was a mid-summer 9 degrees Celsius. Wet soggy clouds hung about the airport and were forecast for part of the way. Altogether that was a gloomy outlook that matched my feelings. The climb out was made through cloud, the temperature gauge then being my best danger-warning instrument. When the gauge read 1 degree and Z-CAT was at a safe altitude the climb was discontinued while awaiting the break in the clouds that was forecast.

In an Air Force Cat I'd been iced up before. Wings, turrets, struts, blisters and empennage, all gathered a thick coat of ice in seconds. That occurred half way between Fiji and New Zealand. The only way the coating of ice could be shaken off was by descending into warmer air. Should that have happened over land and not sea, the flight might have ended in a collision with 'mother earth'.

We were now leaving the coast of Newfoundland when suddenly as if by magic the clouds disappeared. The calm and very blue North Atlantic appeared, a picture of polar serenity that went on forever and ever. Our second ocean crossing had begun. Half an hour later, the first iceberg I'd ever seen showed up, a pure white pyramid in a deep blue sea as smooth as a glacial lake. As time went on more and more appeared. My friend Hank had told me that once when he was ferrying a Cessna float job across North Atlantic, he had put down beside an iceberg for self-relief, a short rest and a dip of the fuel! At the time I really didn't believe him, now as I looked down I knew that he hadn't been pulling my leg, the water was as calm as a mill pond.

We began steering on the GPS and gyro alone as more than 30 degrees of magnetic variation crept in. Looking to the south, I couldn't help but dwell on the 'Titanic' disaster and the huge new ship lying for so long thousands of feet below the surface of the seemingly peaceful and tranquil ocean, which was not the North Atlantic I had expected.

More than two hours before we were due on the Greenland coast, the snow-capped mountains of that great island stood out in relief. The air was so clear with not an ounce of cloud between us, which must have been a distance of more then 400 kilometres. Slowly we drew up to that grim land of granite and ice and made radio contact with the station at Qarqotoq in the Julianehabs Fjord where Z-CAT was to alight. We were expected, the weather was clear with a fog bank to the west. The operator suggested we get a move on as the fog in summer had the habit of moving in to smother the fjord and harbour by late afternoon. I signalled Mike to move the power up, our ETA (expected time of arrival) picked up by only a few minutes. Catalinas are not renowned for their rapid acceleration. From then on the operator gave a fog report every ten minutes. When we were thirty kilometres out from the fjord by guesswork, he called to say that both the fjord's harbour and town was completely covered in fog. My heart pounded a little more on hearing that, I was out of my comfort zone.

From on top the fog wasn't very thick. Looking down as I brought Z-CAT over the town I was able to catch sight of several buildings and part of the boat anchorage as well as several large icebergs just off what appeared to be a breakwater. I needed to be quick. The broad front of fog was moving quite rapidly up the fjord, I'd never seen fog move so quickly before, while at the time I was sitting and watching it happen from on top.

Chasing the front end of the fog up-fjord until I was able to see the surface clearly, took a minute, when I leant Z-CAT over in a steep, descending banked turn until facing down towards where the settlement should be. Gliding her down close to the water, the tiny gap between surface and fog could be seen along with the bases of several 'bergs'. The water underneath was flat calm. I flew her down to a smooth alighting, coming off the step to finish the run in thick fog. On the surface there was visibility enough to creep on idling engines towards the town that was estimated to be some 2 kilometres ahead and keep well clear of the 'bergs' and ice floes on the way. Soon a heavy launch appeared out of the gloom, it was time to switch off and take a tow by a pilot who knew the icebergs by name and would know every inch of the way. There was little in the way of wind, we were towed quite close to the breakwater and the biggest 'berg' in the area.

Being a little cautious about the possibility of the launch's superstructure crunching parts of Z-CAT's empennage or wings in coming alongside the blister, I had the passengers disembark from the bow as we drifted. With Pierre we worked out a mooring plan, the fjord was far too deep for our anchor. The boat-master was highly skilled, during all the activity with boats moving about her, Z-CAT suffered not a scratch. On going ashore the cold began to be felt that made me thankful for the Arctic mid-summer use of the heavy clothing brought with me. Those aboard who were short on winter clothing, ran off to a store to purchase more suitable wear. We left Z-CAT with the ship's temperature gauge reading 1 degree Celsius. The flight from Deer Lake had taken eight hours and thirty minutes.

Sometime during the first night in the fjord a runaway ice floe dented the left side of Z-CAT's hull, but not with force enough to puncture the metal or pull a rivet. During the two days spent at Qarqotoq, we checked her over many times. My thoughts then went as to how the engines were going to start after sitting close to an iceberg for so long with her oil almost at freezing point. That was another new experience for me, a mostly tropical man.

While waiting for our tourists to complete their Greenland experience, Harry and I worked out a plan for starting. Everything would depend on a sound battery which was one of our better achievements, for Pierre had equipped Z-CAT with a portable generator which was run at nights to serve the bilge pumps, or the refrigerators in the warmer climes and charge up the batteries too. The generator had been running continuously since we'd arrived, mainly for the bilge pumps.

Tours at Qarqotoq consisted of boat rides through the floes and on sledges on the ice pack. At least one of the boats became jammed in the ice that caused a rescue team to be called out. Such journeys are not for the faint-hearted.

On the morning of departure with the temperature steady at 1 degree, a tow for Z-CAT to an area well clear of the largest iceberg was requested, where there would be room to circle while warming up the engines. Harry had pulled the props through twenty or more blades to prevent a hydraulic lock with the thick, cold oil, which was no mean feat for a sixty-years and over man under the prevailing conditions. All that to prevent over-use of the battery. Extreme temperatures can suck the life out of a battery very quickly. A failed start could see us in Greenland until the following summer.

After casting off from the big tow launch I wound the engine on the starter for another twenty blades before flipping the mags on. When it fired up the engine was kept on idle for a considerable time while the oil circulated through the system and second time around, began to warm up, which must have taken at least ten minutes while Z-CAT went 'round and round' in a tight left circle. With the right engine running satisfactorily and enough temperature showing on the gauge for it to keep going, the left engine was cranked up and a similar warm-up procedure followed before being able to steer a straight course on two engines, keeping well clear of other 'bergs' as we went.

A double engine run while taxying up the fjord, put Z-CAT in position for take-off between the 'bergs. After 'goodbye-ing' Qarqotoq with the customary overhead buzz, a track was taken up through an adjoining fjord for Narsasarnak, where Z-CAT was due to be refuelled for the flight to Hofn in Iceland.

The flight up that fjord took me back to mountain valley flights in New Guinea and Milford Sound in New Zealand, wet clouds pressing down, fog smirched granite walls off each wingtip.

With Mike directing I climbed, descended, turned this way and that, seeking gaps in the thick clouds that persisted in the fjord. With the ice floes occupying most of the surface, there was absolutely no way a precautionary alighting could be made in the fjord. Finally there was a pass to get over that led to Narsasarnak, with only 100 feet of clearance between crest and cloud base. With my heart in my mouth, for I wasn't really sure what lay on the other side, I edged Z-CAT across the granite saddle to burst out into sunshine and find myself on a convenient right base leg for landing on the more than ample runway. We were there but I didn't quite know how. Although at times he had spoken and looked as being anxious, Mike had been a tower of strength during that short but exciting flight. That was another time when a World Aeronautical Chart would have made navigation easier and safer. By then Mike would have been fully aware of the blunder made in not bringing the charts along, which also brought to my mind that as regards the use of a WAC in a Greenland fjord in marginal weather conditions, it would be best to let a sleeping dog lie.

Aviation fuel at Narsasarnak is reputed to be amongst the most expensive in the world, calculations are made in dollars per litre. Pierre was wincing as he dished out the dollars there. In less than an hour we were on take off for Hofn on the eastern coast of Iceland.

The morning's fog had cleared enough for a circling climb to be made to the 9000 feet required to pass over that part of Greenland, which was by then sunglass country. The sun glared back from icy, snow clad granite peaks that soared to the left and right of us, Greenland's beauty at its best, although packed with danger. The many fjords were smothered with floes, my eyes were always on the search for an emergency landing or alighting place but without success. Had an engine or engines packed up, I'm sure all would be over for 'Atlantic Odyssey'. Relief came only when we crossed Greenland's eastern shoreline and soared out over the pack ice that persisted for miles from the coast, to commence the crossing of Denmark Strait. Nothing green was to be seen during our short stay in Greenland, for me it was a most forbidding place.

As we flew across the Strait I couldn't help but think of HMS Hood lying in shattered pieces on the ocean floor. A salvo from Hitler's battleship Bismarck blew Hood apart and sent her to a cold, watery grave more than three miles down, with almost all her crew. Only three men survived. Bismarck also went down in the same area with few survivors.

The flight time to Iceland was a shade over eight hours. What a difference between the two arctic island countries! There are plenty of green areas in Iceland that resembled to me anyway, parts of the South Island of New Zealand. Immense glaciers, several kilometres in width flow down from the central mountains, miles and miles of them and most appear to be quite accessible by foot. Surprisingly, nearer the coast, in contrast to Greenland there are many large areas of green pastureland, where cattle, horses and deer roam. The people, English speaking, blond and blue-eyed Caucasians, were most friendly, intelligent and looked to be extremely healthy. One mustn't ask whether they are of Danish, Norwegian or Swedish descent, oh no, they are 'Icelanders' through and through, with their own language and must be known and respected as such. Again my eyes were opened. Buildings, roads and airports were all very well maintained. The locals seem to have a distinct feeling of pride in their country. Everybody aboard seemed to enjoy their stay there with those lovely people.

While in Iceland my main task was to take Z-CAT into the Jokul Sarlon glacial lake, which was spattered with icebergs, again for the benefit of the photographers and the participants. With our passengers we waited at Hornafjordur's airport until receiving a radio call telling us all was ready with the photo men at the glacial site.

After a 30-minute flight the Vatnajokull glacier was intercepted a mile or two above where it spilled into the lake. From there Z-CAT glided down the immense glacier very low over the jagged ice, so as to be in position to alight on reaching the lake. The foot of the glacier however, ended abruptly more than 300 feet above the surface of the lake, making a touchdown impossible in that direction without running out of lake. Whoever it was who chose that direction for alighting and positioned the boats accordingly, must have thought Z-CAT a 'chopper' not a flying boat that's not able to make a vertical descent.

After first passing over the lake we radioed the TV crew several times about the problem without receiving a reply. I switched the program into making three curving 'touch and goes' along and across the widest part of the lake. Z-CAT was then on a path that was at right angles to that originally chosen by the boat party, who could be seen in a dinghy half a mile away at the foot of the glacier. The lake was slightly sunken and congested with tall 'bergs' and a bit too small for an 'off the step' finish then having to backtrack for further take-off. Having completed our task, or so we thought, we returned to the airport at Hornafjordur.

Ten minutes after landing there came another request from the photo party for Z-CAT to return to the lake, they'd missed their photographs through being in the wrong position. The boat had been moved to a point that would be more suited to the photographers, alongside the path we'd used on the first attempts.

Z-CAT hadn't been re-fuelled since arriving from Greenland, the tanks were dipped, there was enough fuel remaining for another try. Of course we were only too happy to oblige, the result being one of the most beautiful pictures taken by Frans Lemmens, of Z-CAT plan-ing past a giant 'berg' in the lake. Another happy 'day off ' was over. The whole exercise took up most of the day and a good part of what little night there was left. At that time, Iceland was experiencing more then 20 hours of daylight, the remaining four being semi-daylight. It's uncanny how your body, not the light or a time clock, tells you when it's time for bed.

Before taking off from Hornafjordur for the Shetlands, we were warned by the control tower operator not to fly near the deer farms situated off what I shall call the 'top end' of the runway. The prevail-ing wind favoured that direction. The deer could easily be frightened by such a big 'plane flying low. To comply with the tower's request, Z-CAT went off the small runway, downwind, out and over the town's glacial lake. And so we left our arctic hides in clear sunny weather, on a bearing that would take us over the Faroe Islands, (a possession of Denmark) and on to Sumburgh at the southern end of the main island of the Shetland Islands.

Before we reached the Faroes, quite unexpectedly the weather clamped down, we were forced to fly low, through and under, grey, wet clouds in heavy rain conditions that lasted all the way to our des-tination. The only view our passengers were able to get of the Faroes through the rain was the lower one hundred feet of the cliffs on the islands' southern side, as I hugged the coastline around to rejoin the track.

Sumburgh's airport was extremely busy with many giant helicopter movements to and from the various oil platforms in the adjoining North Sea, plus what is now normal everyday air traffic. The weather for us remained bitterly cold and wet. There we had accommodation close to the airport in a fabulous, castle-like hotel that from outside looked uninviting, cold and bleak, but was in fact most welcoming, warm and snug inside.

RAF Catalinas had been based in the Shetlands during WW2. A great deal of interest was shown in our grand old lady. A non-flying day off at last, we were taken on a drizzly drive past the ruins of castles to nearby villages and towns all set in the numerous sheltered bays around the island. That was real picture post-card country, but what happened to the sun and the trees?

An hour was spent inspecting the long abandoned WW2 flying-boat base at Sullum Voe before returning to the warmth of our hotel in a castle. The off-shore open water alighting that had been planned was cancelled, when with me, Hans from the cliffs saw the size of the waves that only a short time before had caused a huge oil tanker to founder causing one of the world's major environmental disasters. At last on our long journey my advice was heeded, when I explained that five metre waves weren't in the best interest of Z-CAT or those on board, or the successful continuation of 'Atlantic Odyssey'.

The Shetlands have much wildlife, otters, seals, a wealth of birds that at the time of our visit had not fully recovered from the losses caused by the oil spillage. Now of course the small Shetland 'ponies' by the dozen, grazing in the shelter of thick stone fences, also need a mention.

That night, our last night before returning to Amsterdam, was spent in the bars and lounges of the hotel, while our fanatical photographers, in complete disregard, contempt almost, of the many other patrons engaged in their own sociable world around tables and on chairs and sofas, moved people and furniture about to set up shots of our participants in festive mood. Why some of the hotel's patrons did not ask our team outside for a duel of sorts I'll never know. Or could it be the thought of being 'in the movies' helped to smooth things out. To me that kind of behaviour seems to belong to a lot of media people. Blame their 'mums' is the trend these days. Maybe they didn't teach their kids basic manners. With the lounge almost in chaos I decided to take a 'rain-check'.

ODYSSEY

The Final Sector

My alarm sounded at 6 am next morning. Driven by what must have been a gale, rain spattered on the casement window of my room, wind whistled through the many gaps in the ages old window frame. Checking my watch while making a few mental calculations on time changes over the past six weeks, I knew that there was still an hour to go before the hotel's early morning call would arrive by 'phone. I'd learned over the years to set my own alarm an hour ahead just in case that call never came. Rolling over, pulling the blankets up over my ears I decided to hibernate while running the coming day's events past my mind.

Breakfast for crew and passengers had been arranged for any time after seven-thirty. Following that, two mini buses would take us all to the terminal on the airport that was only a mile away. There'd be a flight plan to submit, a job that Mike loved doing, heaps of gear to load aboard, an all over check of Z-CAT for Harry and myself.

With all necessary formalities completed we'd board Z-CAT for a leisurely flight to Schiphol Airport, Amsterdam, a flight that would, sadly, end 'Atlantic Odyssey'. The great air journey that had started for me in Zimbabwe was almost over. From Amsterdam then Paris, we would ferry Z-CAT back to Harare, her African home.

My thoughts switched to some of the highlights of the trip. The 46 hours in the air called a race to Eindhoven, over the African deserts, lakes, valleys and the River Nile of the Bible. The sadness of heart I'd felt when passing over El Alamein, for those young, southern hemisphere men, some known to me when still a boy, who lay there so far from their homelands. The waste of war, the puddle of the Mediterranean after the vastness of the Pacific, the old world architecture, the massive populations of Europe and the apparent barrenness of some of the lands, until France began to appear under the bow that is.

For my part 'Atlantic Odyssey' had been arranged hurriedly, leaving no time for crew co-ordination training or bonding the four of us for such a big enterprise, or rest, or sight-seeing in those parts of the world one might never see again.

The visa incident at Nice brought a chuckle from me and the race around Holland too with Pierre driving for a full day to find a consulate that could issue me with a French visa, when all the time a visa wasn't required for me as a New Zealand citizen with a dual passport. The answer to that had been in my valise and close to me for all that long, fast, frustrating day's drive, as also on arrival at Nice.

The amazing transformation of Z-CAT's paint scheme in only three days and the start of the air journey that was then coming to an end, all came back to me that early morning. Except for me, none of the crew had much to do with Catalinas before and were not highly familiar with the old water-bird, first designed in the mid 30's. An autopilot as in the military versions wasn't fitted to Z-CAT, the heavy, cumbersome aircraft must always be flown by hand. The fifty-year old civilian 'boat' was extra heavy on the controls when compared to a modern medium to heavy aircraft and other types of similar age. Firm and long inputs of the controls were required from the pilot to achieve the desired result.

Pierre had promised all the participants some time in the cockpit to try their hand at flying the old war-bird. No 'natural pilots' with sensitive buttocks, fingertips, toes and the soles of their feet had by then been found, most of those who tried their hand at the controls were quite confused after only a very short time.

Snuggled up in bed, trying not to doze off, my thoughts were drawn to some of the darker events that had dogged the flight after the first group of our passengers joined us in Holland and Biscarrosse. There had been several confrontations with the Tour Director, about his bad habit of interfering in air and sea safety matters including changes to the planned route and the many promises made without consultation, many of which had been broken on accommodations, adequate rest times, winter clothing, alighting areas, loading control and common-sense air discipline.

For six weeks we had been in close contact with each other, only then with the flight almost over had some of those problems been dealt with. The ones that hadn't were in my opinion best left alone, now that we were in 'the straight'. For me who had often been affronted, it would be best to keep my mouth shut and look a fool, than to open it and let everyone know that I was.

The antiquated high-frequency radio Pierre had installed hadn't worked since our departure. A repair manual had been faxed to us at Corfu but proved to be of little help in solving the problem, for not one of us was an experienced radio repairman. The complicated diagrams and the nomenclature of the manual to us meant nothing. I shuddered at the thought of the fifteen or so hours spent in radio silence on the South Atlantic crossing from Cabo Verde to Natal. So much for standard flight following, with no-one in Air Control seeming to be concerned over the absence of our position reports or the long silence on our part. What was the purpose of a flight plan? Did those in Brazil believe that we were communicating with Africa or Europe in all that time, had those in Cabo Verde or West Africa assumed we were in touch with Brazil over the period? To me it was surprising that no questions had ever been asked about that long and arduous day over the grey, storm-wracked South Atlantic, as a covert wartime mission might be made, in radio silence.

Demonstration flights had been requested at each place, without prior advice as to when, where and for whom. Compulsory attendance at all receptions, servicing of Z-CAT, re-fuelling situations, plus always the hunt for oil to top up the 54 gallons carried to feed the two oil hungry Pratt and Whitney radials had never been taken into consideration in the original planning.

The row I'd had with the Director over the choosing of the open Atlantic off Praia and Fernando de Noronha for an alighting by Z-CAT for the benefit of the participants and photographers, without asking the pilot for an input, stuck in my mind. 'No' had been my answer to the request for the full load of passengers he'd promised, much to his disappointment.

The spray scudding off the tops of a heaving Atlantic swell in the Sir Francis Drake channel off Peta Island in the British Virgins which was most unsuitable for Z-CAT by its being filled with charter sailboats and wind-surfers to create other hazards. That day would long be remembered. Especially when the Director dived from a yacht anchored nearby in an endeavour to regain Z-CAT, not realising that we were drifting downwind at quite a fast rate much faster than he could swim, to water that would provide turning room. Had the engines not been started and Z-CAT moved up into the wind to intercept him he might well have drowned, judged by the struggle he was making to keep his head above water. We had no idea that he was taking a swim away from the aircraft when the anchor was about to be weighed, he'd not told anybody of his intentions. That was a very close call not only for him but for me too, nobody likes to lose a man overboard under those conditions.

I guess it was nerves, in all ways the flight had been memorable, although the Tour Director's bad habit of intercepting those calls that were meant for me, added a sour note. It could be a Meteorological telephone briefing, a pilot who was about to fly close in to us for photographs and who I most certainly wanted to discuss procedures with or an alighting area report from someone who knew the scene. Whatever it was I had been bypassed with a lot of information vital to successful, safe operations. On several occasions I'd only learned about a change to our flight plan after becoming airborne and setting course for the planned destination.

Flight controllers, along with me, had become terse when asked for a last minute change to the approved clearance. A heap of international complaints were bound to be in the hands of the Zimbabwean air authorities when we returned to base. So be it, the flight was nearly over, relax and enjoy became my resolve, although the weight of the problems I'd had with the Director still lay heavy upon me.

The obviously gloomy weather then had to be faced, after a restless night and not sleeping well. A lot of concentration was needed to heed my wife's words when last we spoke to each other and mention was made of some of the problems that had come my way. 'Always keep smiling' was her advice.

At the end of the day, the passengers would leave us in Amsterdam. I looked forward to a few days break in Paris, Pierre's hometown. There too, my wife Betty would meet us for the return ferry flight to Zimbabwe.

Suddenly I was jolted out of my reverie by a tired-sounding tinkle from the telephone on the bedside table. The Director must have missed that one, could it be that a hotel patron had clouted him after being pushed into a corner of the lounge to make room for the cameramen the night before. No, he'd still be asleep, fond of late nights as he was. A sleepy voice with the formal rounded tones of an Englishman, read out the weather forecast for the route to Schiphol. Low clouds, scattered rain, favourable winds smack bang on the tail (my words not his), a fast crossing of the North Sea was to be ours, relatively speaking of course.

Sleep was over for me. From my flight bag I took out a chart, my thirty-year old computer, to prepare the flight plan and calculate the flight time to Amsterdam. Focused on the practicalities of the last sector of the charter as I was, the Director and his habit of interfering were forgotten. I vowed the flight would be well ordered, harmonious, punctual, if arrangements were changed at the last minute I would greet the change cordially and without complaint, Atlantic Odyssey's long flight must end with everybody on good terms.

At breakfast all the team were noticeably jolly, except the Director who was last to arrive, red-eyed and only just able to raise a smile. The young European passengers, all of whom had won the trip through winning one of the various competitions, were eager to return home and no doubt recount their adventures to their friends and relatives. The very professional film-crew who had laboured tirelessly over six weeks for a successful documentary record of the flight were, like others of their kind, intent only on getting their film developed and edited.

With everyone hoeing into their bacon, sausages and eggs, I announced the delayed departure time for Amsterdam as 11 am local time because of the favourable winds. The announced delay certainly seemed to please the film crew as more shots of the islands were required, the others I think were a little disappointed. We were to arrive on the dot of five pm Dutch time at Schiphol where a civic reception was planned.

At Sumburgh's airport, a small crowd of well wishers and aircraft enthusiasts had gathered on the chance of being able to inspect the only Catalina they'd ever laid eyes on before it departed their shores. During the early part of World War 2, Catalinas had been based in the north of the Shetlands to patrol North Sea areas. Now more than fifty years later some folk had travelled considerable distance by sea and road from the northern isles to witness what might very well be the last veteran PBY ever to visit those wet and windy isles. They were all given time to clamber through and over the aircraft. Finally it was time for us to leave, we shook hands all round, then climbed aboard. Most of our passengers preferred to board by the short ladder to the forward compartment than the taller ladder to the left blister.

Engine run-ups were slow in coming, in colder climes the oil for the air-cooled engines took more time to circulate and warm up. "Zulu Charlie Alpha Tango you are cleared for take-off " came the voice from the Tower. "If it's OK with you sir, would you please make a fly-over before departing, there are many here who are very interested in your aircraft."

I'd been getting that sort of request all along the route, particularly in Europe where Catalinas are rare metal birds. It's always a good excuse for a bit of daring-do or mild 'beat-up' in aviation parlance. The feeling is, well, sort of special.

"Wilco" I replied. "And thank you for a pleasant stay in the Shetlands from all aboard our most venerable Catalina". Releasing the brakes while pushing the throttles up I signalled Mike to take them over and set maximum take-off power. Soon we were hurtling through the drizzle down the puddle-soaked runway.

The Tower's request for an 'overfly' before departing was answered with a low turn over his glasshouse before turning away to climb over a grey, white-capped North Sea for Schiphol.

Amongst his many other achievements Pierre was also a great host aboard his Cat. He soon had the passengers sampling some of his choice French wines and scoffing delicate hors-d'oeuvres whilst he prepared a sumptuous lunch. Not for the flight crew of course although I suspected that Harry was joining the bun-fight. Our servicing engineer was not too slow in taking a quaff from a flask of whisky at times. For that I forgave him, his job was to service the aircraft when on the ground, an 'off-beat' task that sometimes took him well into the night on a lonely tarmac and off to sleep whilst in flight.

On a flight such as 'Atlantic Odyssey' the passengers like to feel they are participating, most enjoy assisting the crew with some of the on board duties. Through the bulkhead doorway, a lady's hand that belonged to Yvonne Belonje the Producer, reached up to me with a thick, tasty, tuna sandwich and a mug of Pierre's special coffee.

There's no joy in flying in cloud on a touring flight. The passengers like to see things, anything. Over land it's animals, rivers, lakes, coastlines, cities and towns. Over sea, oilrigs, boats, ships, yachts, icebergs and islands. There's lots of debris in the ocean that can't be seen from a high-flying jet, flotsam and jetsam of all kinds. To provide the passengers with at least some viewing below the murky, grey clouds, 3000 feet was chosen as the cruising height where at least something of interest might be seen. The PBY Catalina is a flying-boat amphibian designed over fifty years before and is not noted for its flying performance with an engine failed. While 3000 feet was not my preferred height, it would at least give me some time to meet any emergency that might arise. With all the gear accumulated on our great air voyage, plus the fuel load, a quick mental calculation and a glance at the rate of climb, told me that Z-CAT was near to the maximum civil gross-weight limit.

In the post-war civilianising of certain Catalinas, the wartime gross weight had been reduced considerably to meet single engine performance specifications for Transport Category aeroplanes as required by International Civil Aviation rules.

Catering and photographic gear, servicing tool boxes, spares, refuelling hoses, manuals, a petrol driven pump, an outboard motor, small drums of oil, not to mention the many souvenirs collected, were added to considerable personal baggage. During periods when the aircraft was idle, both Pierre and the Director stowed items on the aircraft that were neither weighed nor manifested. These were stowed in cavities under or behind seats, or in cupboards that melded with the curve of the keelson, exactly what could be tucked away out of sight was quite surprising. That day 'ye olde boat' felt sluggish. Considering the heavy, cold air over the North Sea we were encountering, the climb rate should have been higher. The weatherman had been right on the button. By the lay of the whitecaps and wind streaks we were flying directly downwind.

Twenty minutes after departure we were tucked up close to the base of the clouds. With Z-CAT flying level and the speed building up I waited for the cylinder temperatures to stabilise before setting the cruising manifold pressures and reducing the rpm. The temperature gauge of the left engine took slightly longer to drift back than the right, which was not unusual. Gradually the needle fell to the desired temp. Mike was called to set 60% cruise power, while I was thinking how good it was for Pierre's fuel bill to be reduced for the day by the increase in groundspeed by us cruising directly down the wind streaks. Unless circumstances decided otherwise, Mike and I usually shared the flying, two hours on, two hours off. The first two hours that day were mine.

Pierre had promised the passengers to have at least some time sitting in one of the pilot's seats on their long journey. Although I preferred the aircraft to be well settled down into a steady cruise before any changes were made, Mike, without a word slipped out of his seat down on to the catwalk and signalled a pretty female competition winner to climb up to the second pilot seat. The sudden unauthorised changeover annoyed me and would not be tolerated in most two-pilot aircraft operations. Complaints to Pierre on Mike's several breaches of good air discipline had been met with indifference.

"He is a big help to Harry, that's important, don't upset him." was his answer.

The worst aspect was that the passenger was never advised as to HOW to climb into the seat and what not to touch or grab in so doing. The young lady hauled herself up on the vacant control wheel, the left sleeve of her heavy jacket flipped a couple of switches on which weren't needed, while I cursed under my breath and strove to keep the aircraft's nose down by pushing hard against her tight grip on the control column. Remembering my vow of the morning, for the enjoying of a harmonious trip at all costs, I somehow managed a smile as she wriggled herself in to a comfortable position and struggled with the seat harness, after all it wasn't her fault. That man of mine sure needed some instruction in that department, but then he didn't think so, nor was then the time or place to start a training program. Nothing could be gained by making a big deal of the incident I'd just have to live with it until opportunity arose further down the track.

As crew we'd rubbed shoulders with one another for weeks, pre and during flight, in buses, in hotels and on excursions. The small insignificant habits of anyone that would normally be overlooked, were beginning to irritate each of us, we were all looking forward to the final sector being over and the reception that we knew was awaiting us in a few hours time. For me the promised five-day rest period in Paris with Betty for company, where Pierre wanted to shop for equipment for his tour business in Africa, was the icing on the cake. The matter of air discipline and manners, slipped from my mind as I gave the lady in the right hand seat, my full attention, explaining some of the mysteries of the controls and flight panel.

Half an hour later the drizzle stopped, the clouds lifted slightly, the ocean below was a cauldron of white foam. In the first hour our tireless 100-knot Catalina was more than 130 nautical miles out from Sumburgh, VHF communications had been established with London Centre. I felt re-assured, knowing that the Brits wouldn't overlook a venerable flying-boat amphibian tracking across the icy wilderness of the North Sea, as happened on the South Atlantic crossing. If the favourable wind continued we were going to be early for the reception despite the delayed take-off. Closer in to the Dutch coast, time could be lost by dragging the power back to wartime patrol-search settings. With the big Pratt and Whitney's ticking over quietly on only the smell of 100octane, the old girl would muddle along at 90 knots or less if need be, determined as I was to hit Schiphol as the clock struck five. A circle or two might even be necessary to waste time. To return to the point of departure 'as the clock strikes five' after a six-week journey around the Atlantic with a fifty year-old Cat, in my view was quite an achievement.

The time soon came for the lady passenger to give up her perch for another participant, a young Dutch policeman. By that time she'd learned not to let herself down on the control wheel as she vacated the seat. By then a veteran with common sense, she was able to explain to her replacement, the correct manner in which to gain the seat and apply the harness.

It was during their changeover that an insidious pressure on my right foot was felt. A quick glance at the co-pilot's rudder pedals gave no evidence of the policeman's 'number tens' resting on the pedals as often happened when passengers mistook the pedals for footrests. At first my eyes flicked to the turn and slip needle to find an out of balance situation with the ball out of centre and then became riveted on the manifold pressure and rev counter gauges.

"Ah " I mulled hopefully, noting that the left engine's manifold pressure was subsiding steadily and the weight on my foot increasing. "That's strange, the engine seems to have picked up some carburettor icing, tho' the carb temp gauge says it hasn't? " An attempt to arrest the drop in pressure by moving the throttle lever up failed to change a thing, the manifold pressure continued to slide down as the throttle lever was advanced.

The right engine was behaving normally. Both carburettor air temps remained normal and correct. No doubt about it, I was in for something quite serious as the power in the left engine dissipated, the oil pressure dropped sharply and the cylinder temperature raced upwards. In a lifetime of flying all sorts of airplanes I'd met with engine failures before. All worthwhile multi-engine flight training includes a lot of emphasis on engines failing in all stages of flight and the actions necessary by the pilot. A certain gut feeling told me that a really bad one was on the way for me and what a place for it to happen over the North Sea in a well laden Catalina.

I yelled across to the policeman who had hardly settled in for his half hour of viewing from 'the bridge'. "I'm sorry son you'll have to leave there, there's a serious engine problem coming up, move quickly

and get Harry the servicing engineer up here, tell him it's urgent."
Harry was well known to and always very popular with the passengers
for his off-duty antics as a comedian.

The man's understanding of English wasn't that good. He must
have detected the urgency of the situation by the look in my eyes or by
my pulling the emergency release of his harness. In seconds he had
clambered out of his seat and disappeared like a scared rabbit through
the bulkhead door, into the passenger compartment.

After he'd gone, things in the cockpit went from bad to worse.
Harry had just got to his station behind me and was looking over my
shoulder through the small port, as I closed the throttle and mixture
down then punched the appropriate feather button in the ceiling. The
propeller jerked to a stop, not wound as in most novels, the three
blades mute, standing stock still in an inverted 'Y', as idle as a painted
ship upon a painted sea. Oil was beginning to ooze through the joins
in the panels of the engine nacelle to slide underneath the wing. By
that time my right hand was on the engine fire extinguisher, thank
God it wasn't required. Winding the rudder trim knob in the ceiling, to
take the weight off my right foot kept me busy.

"I've just feathered the left Harry." I blurted. " the one above your
head. Take a look. No oil pressure, cylinder off the clock, no manifold
pressure, revs on the blink, you haven't got a cure for that have you
now? " Without waiting for his reply I went on. "You stay where you
are, call calmly for Mike to come up here and quick, I need some help
from that side of the cockpit, he'll be down there chatting, some big
decisions have to be made." As Harry glanced up over his shoulder at
the frozen prop, his normally ruddy complexion turned a deathly
white.

The failed engine had only recently been partially overhauled before being re-fitted in Africa. All the work had been done in a hurry to
meet our deadline in Holland. I knew that Harry had some fanciful
idea that carburettor heat was not needed in Africa, where Z-CAT
normally flew on safari tours. Africa's a big place, there's no telling

where or how high the aircraft might have to be taken. Did he have other such ideas I asked myself? In our discussions mention had been made of the DC3's in New Guinea picking up carburettor icing in the higher altitudes and that was a very hot country. The engine had been given a cursory service at Sumburgh by Harry after arriving from Iceland. He was an independent character who worked without any other senior supervision and who sometimes 'tinkered' with improvisations that were not in the book. Suddenly I remembered that in the early days of our association, I'd once heard him say he lock-wired the carburettor air shutters off on his engines. I began to wonder. No, it couldn't be that, there would have been more warning, the failure had been too sudden, the right engine would have suffered the same complaint that would have shown up on the gauges.

By the time Mike was seated I had Z-CAT in a gentle banked turn, returning to Sumburgh being foremost on my mind. The right engine was racing on METO power (maximum except take off) with a rate of descent of about 200 feet a minute showing on the vertical speed indicator gauge.

"Put out a Pan call." I yelled across at him. "Our best chance is Aberdeen, get me the bearing and distance, we'll never make it back to Sumburgh against this wind on one engine, we'll be down to less than 75 knots groundspeed, it'd take us more than two hours, we'll have to flog the right engine if we can stay in the air that is, it won't take that kind of treatment for long, we could be in the drink. Take a look at the water down there, there's not much chance of surviving in that for more than a minute or two."

Looking down at the froth on the sea, one didn't need to be a marine biologist to see that any surface vessel would have a difficult time riding the seas, a Catalina, thin skinned and clumsy in wingspan would have no hope at all. Alighting on such rough water could be fatal. Rivets on the planing surface were bound to loosen to separate the thin aluminium sheeting and let water in, or possibly a wing-tip float could be torn off by severe side-loading. Icy water would flood and swamp the hull in no time.

It was re-assuring to know that Pierre had hired a 20-man rubber dinghy for the journey. The dinghy was stowed against a bulkhead in the rear passenger compartment. Modern safety equipment is expensive. That dinghy was on hire, subject to purchase at about $US15,000 if the seals were broken and the raft used. In addition we carried a 'five-manner' with a small outboard motor for ship to shore jobs. Under the circumstances, the small dinghy couldn't be depended upon, for it was inflated with a foot pump that took a lot of time and a lot of energy. During our normal safaris in Africa, after any use it was rolled into a bundle and stowed in a corner of the 'tower' amidships. Inflatable vests there were in plenty, in pockets throughout the aircraft. At that time my hands were fully occupied in controlling the machine. Half way through the turn I knew our only hope for survival lay in a diversion to the northern Scottish coast and Aberdeen.

"We're not going to be able to maintain height at this weight " went my shout across to Mike. "You keep the right engine on METO power, put out a Mayday, tell London we're going to try for Aberdeen, yes Aberdeen, we need every assistance, I'll take up a rough heading until you can get me the track and distance which will be dead across the wind." Mike worked like a drover's dog for a few minutes. The 'Mayday' distress call went out American style, not copybook perfect but I knew London got the message. Right engine screaming, we'd slipped down to almost 2500 feet during a gentle 90-degree turn.

Pierre, sucking on an unlit pipe, stood on the catwalk beside me looking tense and worried. "It's going to be touch and go." I told him. " We can't maintain altitude, get the passengers into their vests, you too, everyone."

"But they'll get frightened." he blurted.

"And they'll be more frightened in the North Sea without a vest, just do it boss. Another thing, that hired dinghy is very heavy, get Harry to help you, get it ready for launching at the port, that is the left blister, there's every chance we'll be needing it if we can't stay up." Now 'the boss' was one who valued a dollar. He could see part of his projected profit for the trip disappearing in salt water and rubberised plastic. He glared at me before disappearing back to the cabin.

The wings were level, Z-CAT was pointing in the right direction, the right engine roaring away on METO power as I sought to find an airspeed that would slow the rate of descent with the aircraft still controllable, a minimum control speed or Vmc. I settled for 80 knots on the indicator. At 79 the elevator began to judder. At 81 the rate of descent further increased. So 80 it was, though still with a rate of descent bordering on 200 feet a minute.

We were now down to 2000 feet in clear weather beneath the clouds. A 30-knot wind howled from right to left directly across our track. If the rate of sink couldn't be eased we'd be ditching in a little over ten minutes. Very close down to the water, a cushion of air compressed between our huge wings and the sea, might keep us airborne a little longer. Our situation could only be classified as desperate.

1500 feet came and went, nothing was surer, unless we could get rid of some weight, we were doomed for the North Sea. London Centre came on to instruct us to call Aberdeen, frequencies provided. My heart was pounding as I passed our situation as calmly as I could. Then came the day's first miracle.

"A chopper will be alongside you in a few minutes." came the voice of the Aberdeen Controller. "He has you in sight and will approach on your left side, he's a civilian chopper from an oil platform, he has no suitable rescue gear for your situation but will monitor your progress until a properly equipped rescue craft intercepts you in about twenty minutes. You can arrange a chat frequency with him if you like on 'india delta foxtrot' frequency (International Distress Frequency). Go ahead with your persons on board again please sir?"

"Eighteen." I responded. "That is one eight."

With that went a sigh of relief, we were in good hands, although I knew that we weren't yet out of the woods.

"Thank you Aberdeen, knowing there's a chopper escort is a great comfort, thank you again."

I called Pierre up, told him about the chopper, there wasn't time and I didn't have the heart to tell him that rescue services might cost him a considerable amount of 'dosh' some time in the future. Yelling in his ear was the only way to make myself heard above the high-pitched scream of the over-worked engine.

"The only way we're going to stay airborne long enough Pierre and reach the Scottish coast or Aberdeen is to lose some weight. "

The power had then been advanced to take off (TO), a setting to which a two minute limit applied under normal circumstances, such as on an actual take-off. These were not 'normal circumstances' the engine would have to be used 'through the gate' unsparingly. Rate of descent had decreased to 150-feet a minute we were down to 1000 feet. My voice was firmer when I continued.

"The spares and all baggage must be jettisoned, it's a matter of life and death, photographic gear, everything, can you manage that through the blister, throw out everything you can find, it's our only chance."

I was getting ahead of myself. Only then did I remember that our civil Catalina had outward opening blister windows or 'boobles' as Antoinette, Pierre's wife called them, unlike the ones on our Air Force craft that opened inwards to allow a 'point-five' machine-gun to be poked out over the side. Heaving gear from our blister during flight would not be possible and there wasn't much time left.

"Forget I said that boss, the only other thing that we can get rid of is fuel, if we don't lighten up somehow we're in to the drink for sure."

Pierre was highly knowledgeable in anything mechanical but specialising in motor vehicles, the road tour business in Africa with a fleet of Land Rovers demanded much from him in that field. He also knew his Catalina very well. Catalinas when refurbished to civilian status, had the military fuel dump valves with their connecting tubes removed, jettisoning fuel from Z-CAT wasn't possible. The fuel tanks were an integral part of the wing, the nuts for the draining of the two tanks were situated underneath and almost flush with the wing, a four-foot stretch either side from the ex flight-engineer's station in the 'tower'.

Wild, desperate thoughts then ran through my mind, as I shouted into Pierre's ear again.

"Would you have a go at opening the left fuel tank drain, from the sliding window in the tower, you might be able to reach it from there, the nut for the drain is lock-wired securely, you'll need to cut that, you should get someone to hold you by the ankles in case you fall out. Do you feel like trying, there's no one else, that's all that's left for us, the left side plug when looking forward remember. "

"I think I can do it" he replied eagerly, fear showing in his face "Before I have opened them when servicing on the ground, from a platform on scaffolding."

"It'll all be different in an 80 knot cold wind, half of you will be out the window, be careful, will you try?"

"Yes I will do it."

" OK, just unscrew it enough for the fuel to start draining, don't try to shut it off, let all the fuel drain out."

 "All of it, there should be more than three hundred gallons in there? " he questioned.

"That's about eighteen hundred pounds of weight we could well do without, it may save our lives, sorry, all of it. Before you do, make sure your European mates who smoke stop smoking altogether now and I mean now. Stop means stop completely. Have Harry check all ashtrays for smouldering butts and ash. I'm going to turn all radios and electrics off. You get Harry to disconnect the battery in the rear passenger compartment too and stow the leads safely and separated.

Any sparks and we'll go down in history as the last of the flying bombs that ceased to fly. Hurry there's not much time."

The effect of the slipstream would be enough to turn the fuel into a fine, misty spray as it left the tank through the drain, that would swirl about in all directions, inducing a highly volatile explosive risk situation in the cabin should it be ignited by a spark from an ash tray, radio box or a loose battery terminal. The tank drain was directly behind the lower nacelle of the engine. Another worry was whether the fuel in the right tank would be enough to get us to Aberdeen. Z-CAT was not fitted with fuel gauges. At normal cruise on two engines at gross weight, Z-CAT's fuel consumption was 70- 75 gallons an hour. Flogging one engine at more than TO power, fuel consumption would jump to 120 gallons an hour.

The GPS then warned me that the wind had backed and was now more on the nose. Groundspeed towards Aberdeen was down to little more than 80 knots.

With Pierre gone about his most important and no doubt unsavoury task of trying to dump more than $US2000 worth of profit into the North Sea, our chase chopper was advised to keep well clear while that was going on, we'd be off the air until finished and then some. By then we were through 700 feet, frightfully close to the water. I'd had a good look at the sea, which was very confused, making it doubly hard to judge the best ditching direction. About forty-five degrees to the wind would see Z-CAT ditching along the line of swell so far as I could make out, should our good engine give up, as seemed more than likely, or the sink rate continue to the very surface of the sea.

The right propeller screamed so much I felt sure that the heavy blades must surely fly off the hub and the engine off its mounts as we sank closer to the frothing water. Pierre would take some time to climb into position in the 'tower', break the lock-wire and unscrew the drain plug. It might be that the plug would be too tight and hard to move. With the outside air temperature at four degrees Celsius, he would be hampered by a blast of very cold air as he leaned out the small sliding window. One thing that I could be assured of was that Harry would give him the right sized spanner to take with him for the job.

While waiting for a progress report and between monitoring instruments, my eyes continually searched the surface for the state of the sea. A gliding turn to the right with a full stall into the water had been planned should the engine blow itself apart. That the engine was being tortured and couldn't be expected to operate at extreme power for very much longer was easy to see, something had to break. For more than half an hour it'd been on more than maximum permitted power, the cylinder temperature was hovering near maximum. Unashamedly I closed my eyes and prayed and I mean prayed, real hard, to the one true God, for the deliverance of all crew and passengers. Later Mike told me that at that time he thought I'd gone to sleep but was amazed that the aircraft flew on most accurately without help from anyone it seemed. I've been wondering about that ever since too, but really I know the answer.

I called the chase chopper. The big 'fella' was keeping close watch on us about thirty metres to port. "We're about to start to try to dump some fuel and shut down the radios. If that doesn't work there's a good chance that we'll have to ditch. If the spray's sucked into your turbines it won't do you any good. I'd advise you to keep well clear."

The reply came quick and sure. "Good luck, we'll be here."

I yelled to Harry. "In the absence of our flight attendant on more important business, will you check that the passengers are fastened in securely and have their life-vests on correctly. Shoes off everybody, no moving about by anyone except yourself and Pierre, the forward facing passengers should lean forward on a cushion or some heavy clothing when we hit the water, be prepared for a quick exit into the dinghy via the port blister. Tell them not to scramble, shove or push, evacuate in an orderly fashion, let me know when you've completed."

Minutes that seemed like hours, dragged by without me knowing how Pierre was faring, while the altimeter slipped below 500 feet, the right prop screaming constantly and mercilessly. I felt sure that my flying days were coming to an end and we were going to ditch into a merciless sea, to drown or freeze to death.

"Pierre hasn't been able to lighten us up." I shouted to Harry when he re-appeared.

"That would be a difficult job under more favourable circumstances. Better get him in and seated in a safe place for ditching. He's not going to like it, but that's the way it's got to be."

The altimeter had just reached 400 feet when suddenly Harry bellowed at me through the doorway.

"The fuel's started draining skipper, he's done it, I can see it, the tank drain has been opened OK, he has done it."

"That's great is he still with us? "

"Yeah, he's coming down from the tower now, golly you want to see the cloud we're leaving behind, you'd swear that it's smoke and we're on fire. "

I wished Harry hadn't said that last word fire, my eyes clung to the altimeter. My prayer had been answered. Through the controls I could feel Z-CAT getting lighter every second. It must have taken six or seven minutes for all the fuel to be sucked from that tank while the altimeter sat on 400 feet. For the first time since the failure we were holding an altitude, not much of one, but holding.

The fuel vapour streaming from the opened drain then began to permeate the interior of Z-CAT. No one, no thing was spared the acrid smell, taste or fine coating of 100 octane as it was sucked into the cabin via window seals and ventilating shutters then circulated to all and every corner until breathing became difficult. Opening a sliding window for fresh air drew in a mist of high-octane fuel. Some of the passengers began coughing and spluttering. My prayer now was that none of the smokers, nerves getting the better of them, would accidentally light up a smoke as I waited for the big bang.

Pierre was standing beside me with a triumphant grin on his face. He'd done a great job but congratulations would have to wait.

"Thanks Pierre" I yelled. "We seem to be able to hold height although we haven't got much. We're still on a knifeedge with the one engine, one cough and we'll be in the drink. I'm going to bring power back to METO, just to see if she'll stay here on that. The fumes will take a while to disperse smoking is forbidden, can you get me a wet towel to breathe through until they do, I'm feeling a bit squeamish. We're eighty miles from Aberdeen, about an hour to go, and please, no-one except yourself and Harry to move about the cabin, everyone sit tight and alert to the situation."

Ten minutes later, on METO power, eighty knots indicated speed, I watched as the altimeter began to edge up very slowly at about 50 feet a minute.

A rescue chopper with the distinctive colours of RAF Search and Rescue suddenly appeared off the left wing tip, close enough for me to see the crew waving. The first chopper peeled off, to return to his interrupted schedule. Feeling bad about not being able to give him a word of thanks a nasty temptation ate at me, to turn the radios on and transmit, but with the smell of 100 octane still very strong, the 'Tempter' lost control of me while all my focus transferred to the tortured engine. My ears were bursting from the continual high-pitched scream coming from above and behind me, a distance of only a few feet. I knew that if the engine seized due to its right hand rotation, the prop would fly forward, then away to the right, probably taking part of the cockpit and possibly the wing with it. I shut my mind to that thought.

Without a stammer, the engine ran like a well-oiled sewing machine while gradually Z-CAT was eased higher, 500 feet, 550 feet, 600 feet, while I watched the altimeter in a trance. Every foot up was precious then, allowing more time to set up a ditching if things got worse, while below, the wind still swirled across the wild, white-washed North Sea.

When assured that the fumes had completely dissipated, after getting Harry to connect the battery and generators again, I called the chopper.

"You will see that we've managed to gain a little altitude, have we got enough to clear any hills between us and Aberdeen or should we follow the coast around? Time is precious. That's about all the height we can expect, all now depends on our engine holding up, we're still on extremely high power, stay close please, a ditching or precautionary landing is still a possibility."

"Fear not, 800 feet will get you direct easily, we'll be with you all the way in. " came the calm reply. "On reaching the coast you can call Aberdeen Approach, he'll give you radar vectors for the airport from there, through us he's got you on his monitor now."

The coast of Scotland was in sight through misty rain at about 10 miles. A formidable barrier of granite cliffs had been expected, but instead, lush green meadows ran almost to the sea. At only what seemed to be a snail's pace, we crept towards the shoreline until in a magical transformation we were soon flying over manicured fields dotted with sheep and cattle. Then came rolling hills, warm looking country with cottages, fences, hedges, lanes, a tiny village or two. A wonderful feeling of relief came over me, although our plight was still serious.

Our sudden low approach over the paddocks, with the engine roaring it's heart out, startled many of the horses and other livestock caught grazing. They scattered in panic as we thundered overhead. On roadways, pathways and fields all faces were upturned to make out the unusual sight. The clouds were down low, the tops of most hills were visible although some weaving was necessary to stay in the clear. Great care had to be taken, each weave cost a little in altitude.

The larger paddocks on either side then took over from the North Sea as a site for a crash landing, until replaced by another further ahead. Our Cat had a sturdy keel, there was more chance of survival in a Scottish paddock than in the wild sea we'd only just left behind.

"Zulu Charlie Alpha Tango this is Aberdeen Approach, you are 20 miles from touchdown, request your fuel remaining please? "

"Aberdeen Approach this is Zulu CAT, critical on fuel, estimate one five minutes."

"Zulu CAT, Aberdeen, understood, we'll bring you in off a right turn on to runway two seven. The weather's deteriorating here, runway visibility less than one kilometre in drizzle, traffic is about to depart runway zero 'niner', runway two seven will be clear for your arrival."

The last 20 miles were a nightmare as the clouds again forced me below 500 feet while scudding in and out of the foggy mist, the windshield a butcher shop window of the older kind. Each second I expected the engine to quit, if not through bursting at the seams then through lack of fuel. My pulse raced, my hands sweated, my thick leather gloves were sopping wet from inside. At five miles out the Controller manoeuvred Z-CAT to line up with a runway that couldn't be seen, as connection was made with the instrument landing system but well below the certified approach slope. With Mike we went through the landing checks but left the landing gear up until the runway appeared. The extra drag caused by dangling the big wheels in the airflow would require the extra power I didn't have. Should the runway not be spotted in the next mile or so there would be no chance of an overshoot being made. When 'gear down' was selected the wheels of the heavy, clumsy gear, extended outwards from the hull at first then dropped into position to be locked, followed by the smaller single nose-wheel from under the bow. With the gear extended it became imperative for Z-CAT to make the runway, there was no spare power if we were falling short, nor did I feel like overshooting past the field into unknown country, with such poor visibility.

Three miles, two miles came, still without sight of the runway, both windshield wipers in high-speed mode slashed through the stream of piled up water, rows of tiered grey stone houses began to slide below. With less than a mile to go there was nothing left but to chance it and select the landing gear down. The wheels normally took about 15 seconds to lock into place, sometimes longer, the left wheel first followed by the right and the nose-wheel last. On occasions, particularly after being immersed in water for a period, the gear needed to be re-cycled to get a positive lock. Should that happen I would probably reach the runway with the gear half out, half in, the gear would collapse, Z-CAT would be wrecked along with my reputation.

Listening intently for the whirring sound of the hydraulic pump after the gear was selected down took up the next 15 seconds while I clung to the localiser. Then the 'thunk' and slight shudder was heard and felt as the locks went home. Three green lights lit the panel. Harry reported he'd checked the down-locks through the peephole. All was well in that department, but the runway was still hidden behind a curtain of rain while I held 150-feet altitude.

The approach needed to be flat and certainly was, lest the tank outlet starve and the engine quit with so little fuel remaining in the tank. At about half a mile, the runway lights appeared, blurred through the rain. For the first time since the left engine failed, the throttle lever was brought back below METO as a powered glide was taken up for the threshold.

Not wishing to stop on the runway after touchdown and be unable to taxy in the required direction, I let her roll to a taxi-way that would allow for a left turn to the parking bay utilising the inertia, as the passengers clapped and let out a loud cheer. Mike reckoned I'd turned from the runway too fast. He was forgiven for he hadn't ever tried to taxi a Cat on land on one engine when a turn towards the live engine can be nigh on impossible in limited space without burning out the brakes.

The marshaller, in his wet weather gear and waving orange batons disregarded my gesticulations from the window for a left turn for final parking. Making a right turn under his directions we ended up doing the very thing I was trying to avoid, that was a sharp turn towards the going engine. Had Z-CAT been marshalled to park from a left hand swerve that job would have been quite easy. Our Cat with it's huge wing-span ended up a bit 'skew-whiff' to the bay, with half a wing suspended over a taxiway and an exasperated marshaller striking his head with a baton and no doubt any watchers thinking that the Catalina's pilot was very casual about the parking of his charge. I never did get a chance to explain to the man with the bats the reason for my seemingly un-professional parking, while he obviously was unaware of my predicament and must be forgiven. After signalling 'cut engines' with his bats he stalked off. Such is life. Old Lizzie would need to be straightened up by a tractor, which would be a job for Harry. When Pierre heard of that he could be quite annoyed, a towing tractor would cost and I would be blamed.

I sat in my seat and let the tension drain from me while ambulances, fire trucks, police and rescue vehicles teemed into the parking bay. The rescue chopper with bone-domed crew waving, air-taxied to a position beside the grateful Catalina they'd escorted safely home. I was forgotten, as Customs, Immigration and dozens of other airport officials gathered around to welcome our exhausted but jubilant passengers as they climbed down the ladder at the blister, led by the Director himself.

With his camera clicking and flashing, our still photographer kept a picture record of our unrehearsed single engine arrival. Because of his impetuous, irresponsible running around the parking bay, Z-CAT, the chopper with it's blades whirling and other rescue vehicles, he was rounded up by an irate official, who, with a wave of an arm and a stab at the air with a finger, indicated that the terminal enclosure was the best and only place for him. Top marks for Scotland. Let orderliness prevail were my thoughts on knowing that at last our on-board 'papa-

razzo' had been brought to heel. On the entire journey he had taken
many a foolhardy risk not mentioned here. I couldn't help but smile as
I bobbed down through the roof hatch and clambered down from my
seat.

As chief spokesman, the Director would be in his element, it would
be nice to have heard his version of the engine stoppage incident as
told to the officials. Before departing Holland, I had urged him to treat
the fifty-year old amphibian flying boat with respect and not overload
her. He'd chosen to listen more to Pierre, who knew little about basic
aircraft performance. So be it. We'd had a remarkable run of good
fortune, which I hoped everyone concerned would learn from.

There was no doubt that the passenger compartments had been
abandoned in haste, without so much as a backward glance. Flotation
vests, blankets, pillows, food and drink containers, personal clothing
was strewn throughout, on the chairs, some dropped carelessly along
the catwalk.

From a canvas holster on the bulkhead below 'the tower', I drew
out the fuel dipstick, climbed up on to my chair, slid the ceiling hatch
open again and exited from the cockpit past the feathered prop on to
the wing. From there I had a bird's eye view of the excitement going
on below. Backslapping, embracing, excited talking and hand shaking
was still going on, I'd been forgotten. The Director, Pierre, Harry and
Mike were fully occupied with the officials and didn't look up. Kneeling while unscrewing the fuel cap, I dropped the long stick into the
right tank, with my left hand over the opening to prevent any rain getting in. The stick hit bottom with a hollow sounding 'ding'. When I
withdrew the stick not a millimetre of fuel showed, the end of the stick
was as dry as the Simpson Desert. The tank, for all practical purposes,
was completely empty. The landing must have been made with only
the fuel remaining in the lines and carburettor. For a fleeting moment
only I considered re-starting the engine to see just how much running
was possible with the remaining fuel, but with everybody milling
about I gave up the idea. My guess was that if the engine started at all

it wouldn't run for very long. Instead, while kneeling to replace the cap I gave my heartfelt thanks to God for our deliverance.

From atop the wing I stared across the open turf towards our landing runway, the runway that had so graciously received the stricken Cat. Five minutes after switching off, pelting rain ahead of a thick, swirling blanket of fog had enveloped the runway and was on course for the parking bay and the adjacent buildings. In seconds the cold blast shook the aircraft as I made for the security of the cabin via the cockpit roof. Those below made for the shelter of any vehicle parked close by Z-CAT, some boarded mini buses or scrambled up the ladders into the cabin again.

As I made my way to the rear or 'blister' compartment via the cabin, high-stepping over the bulkheads as I went, I could hardly believe my eyes. Parked in it's usual stowage place, in a gap between two forward facing seats and a bulkhead stood the 20-man dinghy in its heavy plastic protector with the seals intact. To say that I was surprised would be putting it mildly.

My instructions to Pierre, who claimed Flight Attendant qualification from Air France, had been to prepare the dinghy for launching through the port blister. Right on cue my Celtic anger began to well up inside me. How anyone could be so mean, callous and irresponsible about other people's lives was beyond comprehension. The dinghy was heavy and awkward to lift and carry. Two strong persons were needed to move it. Time taken for launching from the blister would be at least five minutes. There would be no time to remove the heavy package from its stowage and prepare it for launching in the panic that would follow a ditching, always with the added possibility of a damaged aircraft tossing about on a wild sea. That was not an easy job, it had been tried before but with personnel who knew what they were doing. Straps in place, thick plastic cover intact, it was obvious to anyone that the dinghy had not been touched since passing pre-flight inspection at Sumburgh that morning, an inspection that entailed only a peep at the dinghy 'twixt bulkhead and seats.

A fury welled within me as I climbed down from Z-CAT. The short walk to the terminal through the rain, carrying my bags, helped me to calm down a little. By the time a trolley had been found and Pierre was in sight, I had cooled off some more. There he was, facing the press with their photographers, trying to make little of the incident. Of more importance to the Director and rightly so, was the arranging of tickets for the passengers to catch a commercial flight to Amsterdam that would depart Aberdeen about thirty minutes later. From that view, things couldn't have been better. They would arrive at Amsterdam in time for the reception but without the legendary Catalina that had served them so well. I took pity on both of them on seeing their peaked faces, tight lips, nervous hands that were shaking uncontrollably.

Remembering Pierre's valiant efforts of draining the fuel from the tank that probably saved everyone's lives I decided that the matter of the untouched dinghy could wait for a more opportune time. My gut was still in a knot although some of the tension was slowly draining away.

As I said farewell to our passengers as they left to board the jet to Amsterdam, the Director who was at the end of the line, hissed in my ear. "Don't speak to the press about this."

Before I could utter a word or shake my head he had gone. My throat was parched. I needed some sort of a drink. With the trolley and Harry we went to the bar where I settled for a glass of their warm beer. Half way through, Pierre arrived with our accommodation details, a nearby transit hotel. He sat beside me and pushed a brown envelope my way along the table as he said.

"It will take several days to change the engine over, there's enough US in there to get you to Paris for a few days rest with Betty, keep in touch about coming back here for the test flight, then we'll go on to Amsterdam for our final farewell."

My heart was truly warm and grateful as he paused before going on. "There's a flight leaving here at seven in the morning. You are booked. The ticket's are in there, keep in touch in Paris through Antoinette, and thank you once again Bryan for a truly great effort today."

I was humbled and couldn't speak for a while, having entered the terminal with many dark thoughts about the day, Pierre and the Director. Finally I managed to get something out.

"And thank-you Pierre for your Herculean effort in dumping the fuel, without that we were lost, you are the real hero. I've heard of people receiving high awards for that sort of thing, I hope the Director understands what you did for us all and makes things good for you with a nice big bonus, thank-you again." That's all I could manage, there were tears in my eyes as he left.

What I needed most of all now was the seclusion of a hotel room to rest and contact those I loved on the other side of the world. Harry and I sat in the warm comfort of the crowded lounge bar for some time, waiting for the courtesy bus, while I let the tension drain from my body down to fingertips and toes. Outside it was teeming with rain. By that time, in typical fashion, Pierre would be 'yacking' on the 'phone about his replacement engine. A spare was always crated and ready in Harare for shipment by air to any point on the globe, which this time was London, then by truck through to Aberdeen.

"Harry." I said when Pierre had gone. "As an engineer you well know that the right engine has been overworked today. That it's still bolted in the mounts is unbelievable after the workout we gave it. The two minute take off maximum has been exceeded many times over. You will have to tell Pierre that it will need a strip at the very least, if not changed altogether, before we go on. That's tough on Pierre I know, but it's something that has to be faced. As the engineer with the responsibility in these matters I'll leave that with you, I'm not going to see much of Pierre before I depart in the morning by the looks."

Harry was an employee of the company in Harare which over-hauled Z-CAT's engines. While he didn't sound too enthusiastic about calling his company, as maintenance engineer for the trip, the ball had been tossed back into his court and was out of mine. The call for us to take the bus to the hotel came over the PA. I grabbed my well-used soft bag from the trolley and made off for the door. Besides thoughts of my family, my mind drifted back to Z-CAT, standing in freezing rain on a storm swept hardstand. The men who'd flown long, danger-ous missions in Catalinas in similar climes during the war were now remembered. Many of them would have arrived back at their base in far worse condition than us that day. My rage was over then, my heart thankful and quiet.

The five days spent in Paris with Betty were wonderful, after which I returned to Aberdeen, test flew Z-CAT with a new engine fit-ted and a good report received from Harry. After the test flight he had signed the engineering log clearing both engines for normal use. "It'll get us home the way it is where it will be taken out for a complete overhaul." he said when asked about it.

We then flew on to Amsterdam for a final farewell with our pas-sengers at their yacht club at Lelystad on the Zuider Zee, with Z-CAT anchored near the boat harbour.

After Amsterdam, Hans came along with us to Paris, claiming that he had permission for Z-CAT to fly over the city past the Eiffel Tower en route to the Le Bourget airport. When over the heart of Paris there was a lot of jabber on the radio that I didn't understand but I suspected that we were in trouble. On landing at that famous airport I was or-dered to stop, shut down engines and remain on the runway. In minutes the gendarmerie arrived in two cars to place all those aboard Z-CAT under summary arrest, the charge being that flights over cen-tral Paris past the Eiffel Tower were not permitted other than by French military aircraft on Bastille Day. Things looked very danger-ous for a while as the senior officer and Pierre talked things out. The chief of the 'cops' of course would only be carrying out the orders of the air authorities. I couldn't help feeling that if Pierre flew into one of his rages we would all be taken into custody and interned, but he remained calm throughout. To me the officials were most courteous.

After half an hour or so, I was given permission to taxi Z-CAT off the runway to a quarantine parking area where Pierre and the Director, who was waving a typed letter which he claimed was the permit, were marched off for interviewing. When Pierre returned an hour later it was to tell us that he was in deep trouble but we were all cleared to leave the airport at that stage. He seemed confident of handling the problem successfully himself, although it would take several days to clear the matter up. As Capitan-pilot I had expected to end up in the 'bastille', but not so in France where the owner of the aircraft, in our case being French, would be the one responsible for any alleged breaches of local air regulations. I thought that was a great idea, but doubted whether the same scheme would work in Australia, New Guinea or the USA.

The extra few days in Paris were wonderful days that were spent at leisure with Betty taking in some culture as we were not allowed near our misguided Catalina, quarantined as it was.

Finally all was fixed and we were on our way to Zimbabwe loaded with spares and other goods. Pierre was reluctant to reveal the result of our unauthorized flight over the Tour Eiffel but he did say that Han's written permit was suspect. I in turn, suspected that 'someone' copped a heavy fine which I hoped would be refundable by Hans and Peter Stuyvesant's 'Atlantic Odyssey if that 'someone' was Pierre.

From Paris our first night was spent at a village near Pinerolo out of Turino in Northern Italy, which must be one of the most beautiful places in Europe. An ancient castle looked down on the village were we stayed which was reported to be the setting for Alexander Dumas' 'The Man In The Iron Mask' for it was the actual place where that event occurred under one of the 'Looey' Kings of France.

The day after arrival at Turino a courtesy flight was made for Pierre and Antoinette's relatives and friends before setting out. We reached Corfu in the late evening to find most restaurants closing, leaving us to settle for a dinner on a hastily prepared table in an alley-way.

Now came the long flight to Luxor over the Med again for another late arrival at the city on the Nile. With an early start the following day on the program no time was available for a Nile cruise or to take in some of the mysteries of Agatha Christie's novels. Pierre was anxious to be at his adopted home again where seasonal ground tours were about to get underway.

Leaving Luxor with full tanks necessitated departing at the coolest time, 4 am in the morning. On take-off there, the cockpit panel lighting failed half way down the long runway. Harry crouched on the catwalk under the flight panel and shone my small flashlight on to the instruments while we made a one-eighty and crept up the Nile with Mike map-reading for me without a map. On reaching an altitude where a safe turn could be made we left the Nile on a course that would take us over the Nubian Desert. That was another very hairy, scary time, the departure could be described as an IFR one, (I follow rivers), the upriver Nile in that case as it lay hidden below.

Hours later abeam Khartoum, we were engulfed in a severe dust storm, forging on for more than two hours before breaking clear. There was plenty of time to reflect on the effect of abrasion from sand going on in those poor engines, when we were able to sight them. The wing's leading edges were showing signs of being stripped of their comparatively new paint. Exactly 15 hours from take-off we were setting down between the runway lights on Wilson Airport, Nairobi and our comfort zone again.

The next day was spent there, while Pierre visited his home to pick up more effects for shipment to Harare. From Nairobi a flight of 9-10 hours would see us at Harare, again our most memorable journey would be over. From there, a night or two later Betty and I would return to Brisbane on a Qantas commercial flight via Perth and Sydney.

When I reached Wilson airport and Z-CAT on the morning of departure, I was surprised to find that Pierre and Harry had already finished re-fuelling.

"We came out early, fuel is much cheaper since we were last here and cheaper than Harare, we'll take a good load with us, we've topped up to 1400 gallons, seven hundred a side." Pierre declared authoritatively. Had the North Sea experience been forgotten already I wondered?

The 1400 gallon figure was far above that required for a flight to Harare with ample reserves. I was a bit put out by not being consulted but still being firmly committed to my resolve, tried not to show my true feelings. Some people just didn't seem to understand Africa and the effect of air density on aircraft performance, any type of aircraft, jet or piston, young or old. We would be flying for 1100 miles over terrain never much less than 5000 feet elevation and as hot as Hades, in an aircraft that could maintain only 4000 feet altitude at the authorized weight on a single engine. With 1400 Imperial gallons, six persons, luggage, spares and other equipment, for a good part of the flight to Harare we would be in a situation where height would have to be sacrificed should an engine malfunction.

Following the North Sea incident, I was a bit testy on the subject of single engine flight for any length of time in a Catalina. That was not such a worry en route Harare with crew only on board, as there were several large lakes almost on track where an emergency alighting could be made, but I resented not having been advised before the fuel was taken on. Once in the tanks there was no way that the fuel could be de-canted within the time and with the resources available. However, my resolve had been to keep things happy to the very last mile, so I muttered my acquiescence.

The same old routine at Wilson went on while receiving the customary customs and airways clearance before Z-CAT joined the long queue for the take-off runway. Wilson was an exceedingly busy airport at all times with aircraft of all sizes and shapes using the right angled landing and take-off runways.

The sun was hot, the temperature high, resulting in a density altitude of 6200 feet for take-off. At that elevation the maximum manifold pressure available from the engines would be reduced to 40 inches, not 48 as at sea level. I didn't hurry her off, the feeling in my hands was that I was flying an extra heavy stone pilfered from the Great Pyramid, every bit of the runway was used before we began to climb out over a wide flat plain with a giraffe or two and an elephant meandering out of our flight path.

It felt good to be on the last leg of our long journey. Although I loved flying Z-CAT I needed my familiar city, home, family, friends and rest. Passing 1000 feet above the terrain I began to relax while continuing with the climb as planned to 8000 feet altitude, which of course meant that we would only be 3000 feet above the hot and dusty landscape.

Z-CAT's altimeters read 8000 feet about 40 miles from Wilson, when Betty was heard calling me from her seat on the starboard side of the forward passenger compartment, that oil could be seen pouring from the right engine. When I looked around, her window was almost blotted out with streaks of black oil. The right engine was about to have a major breakdown, the engine that had been over-worked over the North Sea.

'Here we go again' I thought and immediately started to turn around for return to Wilson. Before the turn was completed there was a loud bang with more oil lashing at the window. Mike, who again had been in the cabin instead of the co-pilot seat, then came forward to where he should have been, to say that we had 'blown a pot' (cylinder) and should return to Wilson and that part of the cowling was hanging adrift! Did he think that I didn't know was my greatest concern?

"You're a bit late, can't you see by the compass that I'm already on the way there?" I replied rather tersely as he climbed up to his flying perch. .

Although leaking large amounts of oil we still had pressure, at least some power was available from the engine. A decision was made to keep the engine going before it gave up altogether. The sun above, the terrain below, were burning hot, there would be a battle ahead to reach Wilson still in one piece. My hands were full controlling an extra heavy Z-CAT, the radio console just out of my reach. Mike was instructed to get on with a 'Pan' call to Wilson to tell them we were returning with an engine falling apart.

With the left engine on METO power (maximum except take-off) and at least some power still available from the right engine, Z-CAT started to sink at a rapid rate. 20 miles out of Wilson we were down to 6000 feet altitude (1000 feet above terrain) Harry reported that the windows of the starboard blister were 'covered in oil'.

Would the oil in the engine last through to a landing now became my biggest concern, or would the propeller have to be feathered? My feeling was that without some power coming from the sick engine we would never make the airport.

Closer in, with all my attention going into keeping Z-CAT in the air I asked Mike for an estimated distance from Wilson, he had a better view from his seat, as I made for a right base leg along and below the level of the hills adjoining the field. From the air that part of Africa is all much the same colour, the skyline always shimmering and hazy, seldom clear-cut. Without local knowledge and experience airstrips are hard to spot from a distance. Seated on the left as I was I couldn't sight the runway, for it was hidden by the instrument panel's hood on the starboard side.

"Twelve miles." went Mike's reply, without a hint of any urgency in the tones. .

Believing that we were much closer in to Wilson than twelve miles my heartbeat went up a notch or two. With Z-CAT sinking at such a fast rate, twelve miles would see us at ground level before reaching the runway. Half a minute later Mike called again. "You are too high, we'll never make it from here."

Down went the right wing to give me a better look. Wilson's runway was seen as far too close for any sort of a successful approach. The direction being flown would take us over a built up area of Nairobi, a Wilson no-fly zone. There was nothing else for it but to make a 'two-seventy' and try again from a left hand approach if height and ground clearance could be maintained during the turn. That was a very dicey, heart-stopping situation. Both engines were tearing their hearts out, the tower controllers offering little assistance in keeping other aircraft clear until I got down, the air jammed with their useless jabber, how I wished that everybody would just shut up for a minute or two! At three hundred feet above the threshold of the runway, a wide left turn was made to final, not caring whether or not a landing clearance was available. In the last few seconds, the power came off as Z-CAT slid across the hills in a glide for the threshold. Some extra speed was carried for the flare, knowing that there'd not be much float left in her considering the extra load of fuel she was carrying. Thanks to the full tanks we were well above the authorised landing weight, having not burnt much fuel off during the short flight.

The touchdown was smooth enough but necessarily fast. At first aerodynamic braking was tried by holding the nose up. When she fell on to the nose-wheel I went for the brakes. All the brake power available was used to pull up almost at runway's end, with smoke pouring from both brakes and the tower, in a high pitched voice that smelt of panic, letting me know about it. That was another very close call notched in my career and with the overload of fuel, one that I would not like to repeat. Z-CAT was far too heavy for Wilson's short, hot and high, landing runway.

When in a fury I approached Mike about his 'twelve miles out' it was to discover he'd used the international airport DME (distance measuring equipment) for reference, thus giving me a distance from that airport, not Wilson. Was it any wonder I was so high and unable to see the runway because of the instrument panel hood. Oh for some crew co-ordination training.

When clear of the runway and parked, the brakes were still smoking like chimneys. With them fully released, Harry stood by with a fire extinguisher, warning those approaching not to stand at the side of any wheel in case a tyre begin to burn, or a wheel shatter by the heat.

The engine was sorely hurt with some of its cowling missing, some intestines hanging loose and oil still pouring down on to the tarmac. Betty was my first concern. That brave girl was flushed and excited about the experience but relatively calm. With the rush and tumble, the long flight Luxor/Nairobi, her first flight in the Catalina hadn't been all that enjoyable. Her first warning of the oil leak and the time it gave me to turn around in fact had saved the day.

Pierre soon had everything under his control again and didn't seem to want to listen to my 'told y' so'. He announced that on the following day we would all fly commercial on Air Zimbabwe to Harare. An engine would have to come from Harare which would take some days to arrange. Z-CAT would be towed out of the way to the maintenance terminal area, when a tow vehicle could be arranged.

As we carried our luggage across the tarmac to await transport I took a last fond look at Z-CAT, wounded but repairable, somehow sad-looking although standing proudly and looking at us from over the heads of a crowd of interested spectators. I knew somehow, that she was watching us leave her. She would be in despair at not being able to complete her long flight across three oceans and continents, to bring her crew home safely as a parting gesture, until we might join together again, sometime, somewhere.

If only a proper inspectional strip had been made of that engine after the flogging it received going into Aberdeen, instead of a paper inspection, she might well then be on her way there. Her place was not over the hot wastes of Africa, or standing wounded on a stinking hot tarmac at Wilson, she needed cool, sparkling water underneath her belly.

Goodbye dear Z-CAT and many thanks, you are a really good 'metal bird'. You have given of your best on two occasions where a more modern aircraft and crew might have failed the test. When we meet again, may you be fully repaired and well maintained, may your colours never fade or your aquaplaning surfaces 'rot, leak or soften', you are one of the best of man's metal water birds. Au revoir.

THE LAST HURRAH

Whilst I toured around Africa, Dennis Buchanan had fallen out with the PNG Government over fares and staffing matters. In a rage no doubt, he had withdrawn his fleet of almost fifty aircraft from regular airline and charter service throughout Papua New Guinea. Most of the machines had been flown to Australia for later sale as he started up Flight West Airlines out of Brisbane.

The last attack I made on New Guinea was to assist a national company commence charter operations with three Twin Otters of varying Series, two of which were already leased out to an operation out of Port Moresby. All three were of Dennis's ex Talair fleet.

In the years I'd been away, New Guinea had changed rapidly. There was now much more widespread evidence of drunkenness, theft and violence amongst the indigenous population, on the roads and in the towns, the expatriate population weren't setting such a good example either. The national Managing Director had pleaded for my help with one aircraft on charters from Goroka, the headquarters of his trade-store empire.

The Twin Otter had been bought months prior to my enlistment, with the buyer's not aware that the high-time turbine engines as fitted when on Talair's fleet strength, could not be part of the sale, unless the new owner had appropriate qualified staff and engineering facilities to be able to comply with the maintenance flow-on for the high-time turbine engines. In short a 'big boob' had been made, that aircraft could not be used in charter operations under the Goroka Air Services flag. My first job was to obtain insurance coverage and a ferry permit for the machine to return to Cairns in northern Queensland, where it came from, for the re-fitting of low-time engines, an extra high cost in itself which could have been avoided. Apart from that setback, the machine was in excellent condition.

As is common with national companies in New Guinea, all staff are 'wantoks' (same talk or tribe) or blood-related, which can be detrimental to overall performance, staff appointments by brotherhood just don't work, for it was the brother-in-law of the Managing Director who had advised him on the purchase and had made the mistake with the engines.

Each monthly director's meeting saw a new set of 'directors' around the table, while the extended family had a go at playing 'bisnis'. Bills weren't paid until after the service had been suspended such as telephone or electricity. Modern computers had been purchased without anyone trained properly in their mode of operation. It was their belief that the cabin attendant, (males preferred under the conditions that existed at the time), a mandatory crewmember at certain times on a Twotter, could be recruited from a family member who might be passing by and would feel like a trip through the skies. On one occasion I was ready to take off with the company's carpenter, sockless, bootlaces flapping about his ankles and with a grubby, 'holy' T-shirt somehow hanging on him, sitting in the seat allotted the cabin attendant making ready for take-off, with a grin on his face as wide as a door. The eighteen passengers did not receive any sort of a briefing on safety procedures including the function of lap-straps.

My objections to that sort of practice were always given in a nice, decent, encouraging way, but were enough to have me branded as a racist. If ever there were some questions to be asked of the 'director' responsible for staff recruitment, he could never be found having disappeared as if into thin air. The company logo on the hangar hung 'skew whiff', suspended only by untidy ropes markedly out of parallel with the facia of the building. Before I went mad, I needed a confidante, but alas, none could be found.

However, the Twin Otter had found a profitable niche for the owners. In the first nine months of operations, the earnings for the one aircraft totalled 1.3 million kina, several pre-independence airstrips had been re-opened, the managing Director's face was wreathed in smiles, leaving me with the feeling that he thought he had done all the 'hard yakka' himself.

For routine inspections or even minor fixing, the aircraft was flown to a fully approved maintenance facility at Madang. The directors of GAS were hard to convince that approved parts and places only were to be used with the aircraft, not trade-store kerosene, or nuts, bolts and screws from Mitre 10. My contract, that had not been sighted since it was signed on the day of arrival, was for one year. Toward the end of the year a Douglas DC4 was introduced under the company's licence for a six months trial to explore the possibilities of the basing of a free-lance heavy freighter in New Guinea. The DC4 had regular work to do transporting vegetables to Port Moresby at 15 tonnes per trip, with many other good prospects in the offing. The owners of the DC4 however, carried few spares for their aircraft, which was sometimes grounded for a week at a time awaiting parts. Worst of all, by written agreement and banker's approval, the earnings of the DC4 which were to be paid into 'number one' account surprisingly had ended up in another 'number two' trading account, intentionally or not who knows, leaving the DC4 owners bereft of local funds. Bad feelings were stirred up between parties at that time, when the family members responsible were not brought to account.

An experienced national pilot for the Twotter' had by then been engaged. Apart from myself, all staff were now of Papua New Guinea highlands origin. Somehow I knew it was far too early for me to leave. Although there were some exceptions, I gained the impression that the Managing Director felt that he had a full grip on the job and the staff would prefer the company to be totally nationalised.

For me, more than 20 years had been spent flitting through mountain passes, over the broad and lush valleys of the hinterland and out to the islands bordering that great country, that was itself running out of control. Scott, the youngest of our five children had been born there and was proud of the fact. Eldest son Roger had trained and qualified as a licensed Maintenance Engineer, middle son Jack had flown both charter and commuter in New Guinea before joining Qantas, to eventually fly worldwide as Captain of the Boeing 747-400. The two girls Kathryn and Dianne had both married pilots who were flying in New Guinea at the time. Our 'tribe' of 'wantoks' had certainly put a lot into aviation in New Guinea. In many ways our efforts had been rewarded although it was disappointing to see the country corrupted and broken almost beyond repair, politically and economically. As the saying goes 'you can't turn the clock back to the 'good old days' of Australian Administration in that case, how the people have suffered. Reluctantly, I thought it best to end my contract and leave PNG for the last time.

When aged three months over 70 years, my final flight in New Guinea was in Twin Otter, Mike Mike Uniform, with a maximum load of fresh vegetables from Kegl Sugl, 8000 feet up the southern slopes of Mt Wilhelm, to Goroka. As always happened, loading was slowed by bad ground organization and had taken far too long. A cabin attendant to assist with the loadings couldn't be found before departure from Goroka, mine was a solo effort that day.

Wet afternoon cloud was rolling down the mountainside as I wound up the two Pratt @ Whitney PT6 engines and whined down the sloping strip, tucking in under the clouds after lift-off while continuing to descend down the escape route, the narrow Chimbu valley. I hoped for a break in the clouds that would allow a climb to commence and a reverse course started for I was racing the clock as to last light and closing time at Goroka's airport. Another five minutes and the rising wind, clouds and rain on the mountain would have prevented any take-off being made that time of day.

Before the town of Kundiawa, where the Chimbu met the Wahgi, came into view, I was down to 6000 feet in the narrowest part of the valley. The late sun revealed some breaks in the cloud cover in the broader valley beyond the settlement. What the military would call a 'left wheel' was made there to pass over the southern slopes of Mt Kerigomna to the Mai River which would take me northwards to the Dalou Pass, the Watabung or Kaw Kaw Gap and the Goroka Valley.

My mind went back 34 years to Monono, Bob, Ruth and their kids, Joe Nitsche and his 'Vee Dub', that very dedicated lady, Myra Radke and the national tribesmen who had all played a part in my rescue from the Dornier. As I turned the Twotter' to follow the Mai, the sun glinted on the roof of the old Monono mission house but only for an instant. The building at the base of the Elimbari escarpment was almost hidden then by the trees that had grown much taller since being planted by Bob. When he had returned to the US with Ruth seriously ill and dying, the tiny hill-strip had been closed and reverted to cultivation. For me the area had an air of desolation about it. The winding white road with a crushed limestone surface susceptible to landslides, which Joe had driven on that wet afternoon, was then the only means of access to the mission property and was hard to see. I wondered how the wallpaper that we'd gifted Bob with and helped him apply, was being treated by its new owners. My guess was that the road hadn't been maintained much, or at all, in the almost thirty-four years that had passed.

Clouds were down on the Kaw Kaw range, the last hurdle before Goroka. The Dalou Pass was completely obliterated with cloud and rain, the Watabung Gap shrouded in clouds and drizzle too. A turn to the south was made for the Kaw Kaw Gap where late rays of sunshine could be seen piercing the cloud screen. By twisting my head around as I approached the gap at right angles, I began to see into the Asaro valley. That was one of those times in New Guinea when a pilot needs a backbone not a wishbone. In a diving turn, less than 100 feet over a dip in the range, the Twotter' flashed between the two peaks that guarded the huts of the small village on the summit, clouds smoking over the wings, rain spattering the windshield. In seconds ground clearance had increased by 2000 feet as I pushed the nose down and dipped into the valley. So much like falling over a cliff, suddenly I was over the green, treeless, flatness of the valley, three sides of which were bordered by very high mountains, the torrent of the mountain sourced Asaro River with its cataracts and rocks, clearly visible below. Then it was safe to take up a heading for a daub of late sunlight acting as a beacon in the mountain shadow that concealed Goroka's airport. The man in the Tower cleared me to land while I was still a long way out from the field, probably because he could then close the Tower's ageing equipment down and go home.

During my absence at Kegl Sugl, the afternoon rains had come and gone. I motored halfway up the long, sloping runway that was glistening with wetness, before touching down. Taking care not to wear the brakes out, the Twotter' was left to coast along the curving taxiway leading to the terminal, with both props feathering, while letting her glide to a stop in front of the terminal as the fuel was shut off.

That the Twotter' was the last movement for the day was obvious, forgotten by the 'so called' traffic supervisor, there were no loyal subjects about to assist with the unloading, the terminal closed. It was one of those days too when a volunteer to act as cabin attendant to assist with loading had been hard to find, the weekly 'vegetable job' to Kegl Sugl was not a popular one, for it meant work in loading, unloading and manifesting heavy sacks of 'vegies', a task not suited to 'company director's', I worked alone.

The sacks containing perishable items were pulled out, packed on a trolley and parked under a wing. The heavier bags would be left inside the aircraft with the doors left open for better ventilation throughout the night. Cabbage and cauliflower sweated profusely while packed tight together and would soon sweat, smell and rot. I went through the cabin and relieved the pressure on those bags that were accessible. After putting the covers on the appropriate parts, locking the controls, chocking the wheels, it was almost dark. In a sweat I tossed the Manifest Book with the details of the flight dutifully completed, on to the seat in the cockpit, retrieved my flight bag and stalked off to where my 4WD was parked only to find the security gate padlocked on the opposite side. To exit the apron, a climb over a six-foot wire fence was the only way out before first heaving my flight bag over on to the other side. The night security man with his bow and arrows was nowhere in sight, my 4WD the only vehicle remaining in the parking lot.

In the short twilight, from behind the wheel of the 4WD beside the terminal, I caught my last glimpse of Mike Mike Uniform, standing proudly on the shiny tarmac, with 12,000 foot Mount Michael standing out as clear as a bell as a backdrop, to the south of the lush valley.

For almost a year her journeys had been my journeys, through good days and wet cloud-soaked days, past cloud hidden mountains stark and ugly, over river plains, across beautiful though treacherous seas, loaded with vegetables, mining tools and their handlers, cigarette cartons, fuel drums, helicopter wreckage, cadavers, mourners, revellers, passengers bent on urgent business or weekend hideaways. She was still in very good shape, her paint scheme still as bright as when delivered from Talair. Her inner linings though were then more than a little torn and frayed by the careless handling of baggage by the cargo crew.

I'd left New Guinea before, for more glamorous places around the world, always knowing that I'd be back one day. The changes to the town in the few short years I'd been away were remarkable, with Dennis, one of the town's biggest ever employers, shutting up shop. An ominous, dark, almost hostile air then lay about the once flourishing, pretty town. The hangar with the drooping, crooked sign, the deserted terminal, somehow took on my mood and appeared to be sad, depressed, unwanted.

For minutes I sat behind the wheel taking in the scene, ghosts from the past bringing to my mind some of the more pleasant memories of 'taim bipoa' (time before). Dennis the Menace, his ' pogo stick and tantrums', 'Poppa' Raasch and 'Cranky' Frankie the engineering bosses, Rob'ought'er Shaw, d'ye ken John Flynn, 'Waddles' Wardill, Laurie 'McCatch', Knight and Daley known as John, Deevers known as 'Keef', Geoff More or Less, the Latin dancer man 'Pax Marka', 'Rocky' Riebeldt, the always Frank King and hosts of others. My tears had to be choked back at the thought of some of those times. There had been some real characters through that place over the years.

Most of all, those pilots who had lost their lives in the furtherance of the development of air transport around the Shangri La of a valley came back to memory. Why, why, was the so-called 'advancement' the country had made worth the cost, or had all been a waste of time, and life? Except for the gloom, some of the sites of their passing from this life might be seen from where I sat. Low in spirit I engaged second, the only gear to which the company 4WD responded and chugged off to 'my little stone-house in the north', a sad reminder of the Bobby Gibbs days, flying in New Guinea finished with me forever.

Two days later, Christmas Eve, a year to the day since first arriving, I flew home to Brisbane. A late afternoon departure evidently prevented any of the extended 'family' being there to see me off, in fact I'd not seen any of the staff or the family's many co-directors since my late arrival from Kegl Sugl. They must have learned by jungle telegraph that I'd returned safely with the vegetables or, if it would occur to them, they would be able to see whether or not Mike Mike Uniform was parked in the usual place at the terminal the next day and not on the missing list.

My last sight of the magnificent, never to be forgotten valley of 'shangri la', from the 'jump-seat' between the pilots of the DC4, was a tearful one, as Gordon weaved the big metal bird up to a safe height and out of the valley.

Alas, due to the Customs and Immigration at Jackson's Airport, Port Moresby shutting down without notice early on the afternoon of Christmas Eve, the DC4 could not be cleared for Cairns although abundant advance notice had been given. The pre-Silent Night, Holy Night, Blessed Evening, was spent in an airport hotel wondering whether or not the appropriate officials would be well enough to attend the airport with a clearance for the DC4 on Christmas Day the following morning!

Well they were, but arrived late, the planned for seven am departure didn't happen until nine am. We reached Archerfield, Brisbane, via Cairns and Eagle Farm late in the day, my home in Chelmer only after most of the Christmas pudding had been scoffed. That's the story of an airman's life, my life, always missing out on the good things that go with family and friends.

Sadly, six months later Twin Otter 'Mike Mike Uniform' crashed at Mount Otto, 5 kilometres from Goroka, killing the pilot and a company director, seriously injuring a senior family member, injuring the company's legal representative and destroying the daily newspapers meant for Goroka. The new Managing Director who was appointed after the accident as Directors changed seats, found he was in the hot one and decided to wind up his then fully nationalised company.

From our quiet home at Lowood west of Brisbane, Queensland, I would often see the RAAF fly over our hilltop property near 'Nobby's', on their way into or out of Amberley Air Base. There are Caribou's that sound like real aeroplanes, F18 Hornets, and those 'Pigs' of Eff-one-elevens' (F111's) that don't. Often the sweet country air is shattered, not polluted, by those angry sounding 'metal birds', although today 'polluted' is a more 'politically correct' term. As yet the Eff-one-elevens have not been told of the change and so sound exactly the same.

At 'Nobby's', day or night we love to hear the brisk movement of aircraft over the house, which takes me back to the good old days, salad days and the 'thoughts and talks' of flying men in their metal birds.

Times have moved on, they'd be young 'fella's' flying 'em these days, good fella's mind you, just what I was like once, but young 'fellas' who wouldn't know what a 'Tiger' was if one flitted past 'em upside down (briefly you understand, for the engine won't run for long when inverted), or whether it was a Harvard, Oxford, 'Chippie' or Magister goin' roun' and roun'.

Been there, done that. I've been licensed to fly all of these, some you fly not so much with your brains, but more with your hands, feet and knees.

The Catalina flying boat, known by Americans as the PBY, (slanged to 'Pee Boat', 'tis their right), is a very tricky 'metal water bird' to taxy whilst afloat or to alight at night. (Those without wheels do never 'land' on water but more correctly do 'alight'. Now I ask you, can a bird 'land' in a tree, or a parachutist in the sea?

Then from the four engine 'heavies' I've flown, comes the Short Solent and Sunderland, real big 'metal water birds' that came from what 'New Ozzies' knew as Motherland and were certainly not short. Short in that case being the manufacturer's name, not the dimensions of the hull.

The DC3 and C47 are as to flying much the same, some were named Dakota, late in '45 'tho, one became a 'floater'.

Fokker's Friendship with turbines, Dart and Rotol props, which go on whirling when the turbine stops, were in their time state of the art.

From the Percival stable here's a few more too, Vega Gull, Proctor One, Five and EP9, are amongst those that I once flew.

With de Havilland's famous label, there's the Tiger, Fox Moth, Rapide and Drover. You fly 'em on your own those ones, should you be considered able. Their cockpits have room only for you, not two, the Chief can't say, let go the stick sprog while I take over.

Mustn't forget 'Ozzies' Avro Cadet that will roll and loop more like a jet and one of the best I've come across yet.

The Ceres, fixed gear, 'thirteen forty' radial and geared prop, with the hopper filled to top, lifts a super ton on every hop.

Cessnas by the dozen (well almost) have also been flown, on none of them has the engine been blown, the handbook 'how' never was I shown. The 170, 180, 182, 185, 205, 206, 207, Four Eleven, Three Three Six and 'Four- 0-Two' are some of the Cessnas that I once flew.

From Beechcraft comes the Queen Air, Bonanza, Twin Bonanza and their speedy Baron brother, they are the most well built 'planes, better than most other.

We're not finished yet by any means, please do not close the door, there's the Dornier 27, the pride and joy of Dornierwerke, designed for peace not war.

The Auster? Yes and one with floats (that from me just got no votes). Hang on a shake, while I run through logbook five and give you some of other make.

An Aztec (or two) and PA30 will see me through the Piper craft.

Phil Bennett's tiny home-built Thorpe was quite a craft, tho' waiting for it's flying permit almost drove me daft.

De Hav Canada's Twin Otter (Twotter), a turbine-powered machine, on arriving in New Guinea was the best we'd ever seen. With power so smooth and plentiful there's nought it could not do, nowhere it could not go, of course in Canada they're used on ice as well as snow.

Now let's move on to amphibs, the Lake Two Hundred and its' Renegade son, the Widgeon, Goose and Mallard of the Grumman run, leading to the Albatross, the Gee One Eleven (note not Eff) and easily the greatest one. That's some of mine that I best remember and of each of whose club, I am actually a member.

ODE TO THE CATALINA

Catalinas known as PBY's, are here mentioned last, not just because they're not so fast, but 'cos they're metal birds with war acclaim, that are dying fast, without a name.

There's not much writ of what the 'Cat-boats' did, while the Imperial Japan Navy around the Coral Sea hid. Like me, a Cat's not seen in the sky these days, again like me, they're out to graze.

To Rabaul, New Britain, in the dark of night they went, from Bowen or from Cairns, to bomb, harass, or rescue, (not on pleasure bent), the airmen crewing them like you and me, some doting mothers bairns.

A speed of a hundred knots down low, meant a trip of twenty hours or so, while you young 'fella', in those 'Eff One Elevens', with thunderous roar and much 'gung ho', do soar so high, to join your bowser in the sky! That in our day was not quite so.

From Perth to Ceylon, thirty hours from shore to shore and sometimes more, the Catalina flew. Across the Indian Ocean in just one hop, all the while fearing the engines would stop, before at Ceylon they were due.

A trip done without using a homing device that saw the sun rise twice the steering done by moon, sun and stars, with the Navigator sometimes sighting Mars. Always nice it was and always meant to alight before the fuel was spent.

Duty done and tethered up without a chafe, a barge 'longside to take the crew ashore, only then was their Cat safe. Their ears for several hours would ring, while they ate and slept as would a King.

Top Secret dispatches or microfilm mail, is what they took and a 'Vee Eye Pee' with a four-fifty page book. As the miles to Ceylon so slowly diminished, he would get there with his book just finished.

From Darwin too, have you heard of this, Cats from there not a night would miss.

To Java, the Celebes, Luzon, even China they would go, in harbours there, their mines to sow or pick up from the land or sea, the wounded or the worried who from the strife of war, their rescue must be hurried.

So you young pilot 'fellas', who fly your 'planes thru' skies so high, give thought to those who dream below and sigh, who too have done the daring things you do, and who so much want to fly again like you, but in the main with brains now slow, not quite so fast, nor so high, and with a little less 'gung ho'.

Remember too, when everything's a kilter and time seems out of phase, stop and think that, like most of us, you will know them as the good old days, tho' some say that the only thing you get from looking backwards is a sore neck. What a joy it is to find the right words for the right occasion.

We moved to Tasmania not to escape the Caribous, Hercules, Eff One Elevens, Eff Eighteens or the huge C-Seventeens for we loved them, it was the drought and heat of sou' east Queensland that influenced our decision. There's no sign, sound or smell of the 'Spirit of the Air' down here as in Queensland or many 'Flying Men' or Metal Birds except when the Roulettes are around. Instead we have the much loved 'Spirit of Tasmania' on its daily sailings across Bass Strait, a stirring sight as she enters or exits the Mersey which is smirched by the controversial, insignificant and rather sinister 'Spirit of the Sea' statue she passes near the entrance to Devonport's harbour. There's no mention made here of 'Ye olde flying-boat' or the men that flew them on the 'Tassie' scene. More's the pity.

As it is written, 'words fitly writ, are like apples of gold and pictures of silver.

May your flying days be as happy as mine were.

EPILOGUE

FINAL FLIGHT
by Kathryn McCook

In honour and remembrance of one so proud
Best remembered for his flying career, overseas and around
Instead of using a car … my Dad used a plane
He flew us over the mountains to visit friends, again and again
Omkolai, Banz, Dumpu and Goroka
All of these places and even Asaloka!

Monono, Madang, Hagen and Lae
They too heard the sound of Dad's aeroplane buzzing away
Search and Rescue, Medical Emergencies
Cargo pods packed with kaukau, rice and bush pigs
Flying his passengers or injured men – these were Dad's daily gigs

His role was important in PNG aviation
He contributed to the development of a brand new nation
His adventures were extraordinary and took us far and wide
His aircraft were diverse – all were flown with pride

My Dad was a true champion of the air
A pilot extraordinaire
His wings were tuned for perfect flight
Flying with Dad and his aeroplane was sheer delight

Last week his runway lit up one last time
I heard his engines rev so I turned around …

Hatches, Harness, Trim
Mixture, Pitch, Fuel
Flaps … 10 degrees
And we're off !

All of a sudden … he was gone

BOOK REFERENCES

Wings of Gold. James Sinclair
Frigate Bird. Captain P G Taylor
First and Furthest. Jack Riddell
Red Ball in the Sky. Captain Charles Blair
Gatty - Prince of Navigators. Bruce Brown
A History of Civil Aviation in New Zealand.
Capt. Maurice McGreal
Flying Logbooks. The Author
Letter No. 37, 2-4-65. Fred Ladd

PHOTO CREDITS

RNZAF
Betty McCook
Scott McCook
Rob Wright
Martin Skeates
Franz Lemmens
TALCO
James Sinclair

www.ingramcontent.com/pod-product-compliance
Ingram Content Group UK Ltd.
Pitfield, Milton Keynes, MK11 3LW, UK
UKHW051648140525
5920UKWH00020B/96